THE GUINNESS BOOK OF MUSIC

SECOND EDITION

Robert and Celia Dearling
with Brian Rust

Guinness Superlatives Limited
2 Cecil Court, London Road, Enfield, Middlesex

Editor: Beatrice Frei
Typography: Jean Whitcombe
Layout: David Roberts
Artwork: Don Roberts and Herb Barrett
First published in 1976
Second edition 1981

Published in Great Britain by
Guinness Superlatives Ltd,
2 Cecil Court, London Road, Enfield,
Middlesex

Set in Ehrhardt
Printed and bound in Great Britain by
Butler & Tanner Ltd, Frome and London

British Library Cataloguing in Publication Data

Dearling, Robert
Guinness book of music.—2nd ed.
1. Music—History and criticism
I. Title II. Dearling, Celia III. Rust, Brian
780'.9 ML160

ISBN 0-85112-212-4

Illustration on title page:
Street Music 1789. (Mary Evans Picture Library)

Contents

Preface 5

I SETTING THE SCENE 6

II MUSICAL INSTRUMENTS (See also Index) 12

1. **Primitive, ancient and obsolete** 12
   - Idiophones 14
   - Aerophones 15
   - Membranophones 16
   - Chordophones 20
   - Aquaphone 25
2. **Orchestral instruments today** 26
   - Woodwind 26
   - Brass 30
   - Strings 32
   - Percussion 34
   - Occasional visitors to the orchestra 35
   - Unconventional playing methods 38
3. **Instruments of unusual interest** 40
   - A collection of unique instruments 44
   - Submerged instruments 52

III COMPOSERS 53

The first composer 53

Royal composers 54

Masters of the King's/Queen's Musick 55

Nonagenarian composers 56

Centenarian composers 58

The longest-lived composer 58

Unfortunate composers 59
- Blind 59
- Deaf 60
- Insane 60
- Murdered 60
- Suicides 61
- War deaths 61
- Unusual deaths 62
- Unlucky 62

Women composers 62

Groups of composers 64
- The Five 64
- The Mannheim School 65
- Viennese School (18th century) 65
- Second Viennese School 65
- North German School 66
- Les Six 66
- Camerata 66
- La Jeune France 66
- Bolognese School 66
- English Lutenists 67
- Synthétistes 67

Families of composers (see Index) 67

Nicknames 70

Pseudonyms 71

Facts and feats 74

Spare-time composers 77

Honoured composers 78

Musical forgeries 80

IV ORCHESTRAL AND INSTRUMENTAL REPERTOIRE 81

The concept of tonality 81

List of keys 83

Degrees of the scale 88

Orchestral music 88
- Symphony 88
- Overture 93
- Symphonic poem and tone poem 94
- Suite, divertimento, serenade, etc 94
- Concerto 95
- Variations 107
- Other forms 108

Chamber music 109

Solo instrumental music 111

Some instrumental music facts 112

Nicknames and subtitles 113

Familiar titles to unfamiliar music 136

Air and music 137

Animals and music 137

The Devil and music 144

Geography and music 144

Medicine and music 147

Months and seasons and music 148

Politics and music 149

Wars and music 149

V OPERA, CHORAL AND VOCAL 153

Opera 153
- A chronological introduction 153
- Operatic proliferation 157
- Unusual or exotic settings 157
- Gilbert and Sullivan 160
- The libretto 162

Harlequin operas 167
Unusual names 168
Operas about composers 168
Numbers 169
Unusual effects/props 170

Non-operatic vocal music 172
A chronological survey 172
Mass 173
Missa Brevis 174
Requiem 174
Oratorio 175
Passions 176
Te Deum 176
Cantatas 177
Sacred concerto/symphony 177
Conductus, motet, madrigal 178
Hymns 179
Song 180
Lieder 182
Works of massive proportions 182

National anthems 184

VI ORCHESTRAS AND CONCERTS 197
Definitions 197
Modern orchestras 197
Concerts 199
Music for the masses 206
Gigantic gatherings 207

VII MUSIC LITERATURE 209
Oldest notation 209
Modern notation 209
Note lengths 210
Time signatures 210
Bar lines 210
Music in print 211
Musical dictionaries 211
Encyclopaedias 211
Journals 212
Musical criticism 212
Programme notes 212
The composer as author 213
Musicology 214
Italian musical indications 214
Opus 226
Thematic catalogues 226
Music appreciation 230

VIII THE TWENTIETH CENTURY SCENE 231
Notable firsts 231
Greatest jazz influences 232
Hard times 232
Jazz/dance instruments 234
Partnerships 238
Unusual deaths 241
Women jazz musicians 242
Early starters/long-lived jazz musicians 243
Versatile musicians 244
The golden age of big bands 246
Country Music 249
The 1950s: Rock 'n' Roll 250
The 1960s 250
The 1970s 252
Facts and feats 253
Pop songs from serious music 254
Modern 'serious' developments 255

IX MECHANICAL MUSIC MAKING 259
Composers who wrote for mechanical instruments 264
Recorded sounds 265
Radio 271
Television 273
Electronic music/musique concrète 273
Computer music 276
Live electronics 277
Synthesisers 277
Bibliography 278
Index of names 279
Index of instruments 287

Preface

This second edition expands, updates, modifies and improves upon the first by making very substantial alterations to the text. These alterations have been generated in many ways, one of which was the result of the authors' decision to change the emphasis in some fields of music, include new items to replace old ones which have served their purpose, and to increase the interest value of the book for both specialist and non-specialist readers.

The need to update some facts and feats with new information has resulted in many minor and some major changes. The biggest alterations are the result of facts and opinions supplied with astonishing generosity by countless kind correspondents from all parts of the world.

In the Preface to the first edition we lamented the fact that a book of such wide scope cannot be issued first in a 'revised' edition. By taking note of the large number of suggestions that have come in from readers and by correcting the errors that inevitably slipped through the net last time, we have improved this revised edition, but the invitation to readers still stands: corrections, suggestions and amendments will be received gratefully.

Acknowledgement is made, in addition to those mentioned in the Preface of the first edition, to correspondents too numerous to list, but especially to the following for their particularly interesting and helpful suggestions: Roger Bennett, London; Paul Bulatoff of Paganini Documentation, Groningen, Holland; Philip Catelinet, Kent; Charles Cleall of the Scottish Education Department; the well-known British composer John Dankworth; Hugh Davies, London; Michael Finkelman, Pennsylvania; Eric Hancock, Bristol; Lillian James, Wisconsin; Philip Lane, Cheltenham; F P Lynch ALCM, Prestwich; Romano Rossini, Italian Ambassador in Cyprus; Louis Siegel, Florida; Ivor Solomons, Norwich, and J F Wilson, Port Chalmers, New Zealand.

Our greatest debts are to the well-known broadcaster and author Paul Gambaccini, co-author of *The Guinness Book of Hit Singles*, whose assistance in checking facts concerning the complexities of recent pop music has been invaluable; to W A Chislett, a long-established contributor to the British record magazine *Gramophone*, whose encyclopaedic knowledge was generously placed at our disposal; and to Aaron I Cohen, compiler of the *International Encyclopaedia of Women Composers (Classical and Serious Music)*, to be published in 1980 by R R Bowker of New York, for his full and prompt response to queries concerning his special fields of musical research.

It has been realised from comments in many letters that we failed to make clear the non-encyclopaedic approach to the first edition of *The Guinness Book of Music Facts and Feats.* Our lists of animals, or geography (or whatever) and music, were never meant to be exhaustive; to be so, the book would have had to run to many volumes. For this new edition we have tended in such sections to replace some titles with new ones in order to give a wider coverage, but, as will be seen in our piece on the most frequently used nicknames and subtitles of works, it is simply impossible to give full and definitive lists even of material already collected. Nonetheless, additional items for this and for any other section of the book will be welcomed with the same warmth as other constructive suggestions.

In addition to the Contents list at the beginning of this book, the Second Edition carries a new index of Instruments together with an index of names and dates which, in order to save space, have been generally omitted from the main text.

Throughout this book musical works are identified according to established thematic catalogues. See Section VII: Music Literature.

Section 1
SETTING THE SCENE

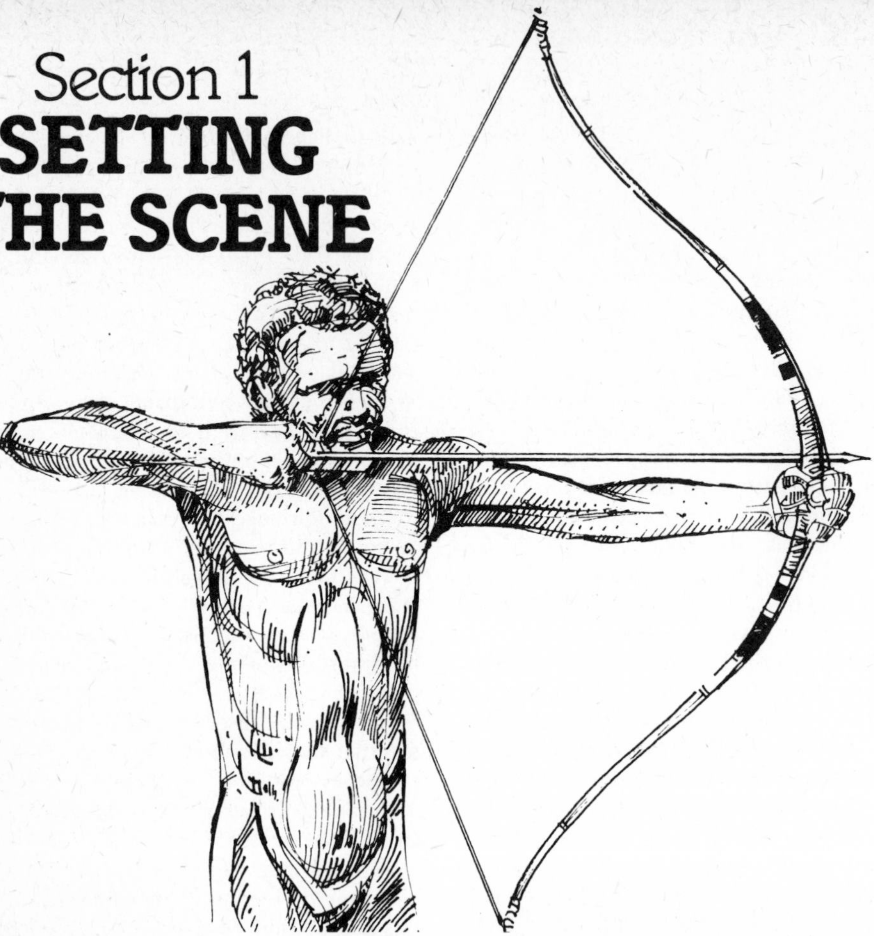

Intelligent man has existed on this planet for nearly 2 000 000 years. At the very core of man's nature is an urge to produce music, either of the rhythmic, percussive variety, or of the sort to awaken echoes in his surroundings by raising his voice in joyful cries. As far as we can guess, primitive man was as fascinated by these sounds as is man of the 20th century, and we may, therefore, take a bold step and assert, with only instinct and common sense to back us up, that music, too, has existed on this planet for nearly 2 000 000 years. Plenty of time for the art form to have reached a degree of complexity and perfection, perhaps; yet we must point out parenthetically that the greater part of music performed today is organised according to rules and principles laid down in an extremely short period by a handful of composers between 250 and 300 years ago. Before that, different rules applied, and if we look back far enough we come to the days before there were any rules, to the days when music was merely a spontaneous expression of uncivilised man. As this Section unfolds it will be seen that the word 'merely' in the previous sentence is out of place; uncivilised man's musical expressions were among the most important of his activities—there was nothing inconsequential or simple in them.

The first musician ever was a member of a nomadic tribe who unexpectedly lifted his voice in a canyon between high, smooth rocky walls. Through the combination of the vibrations he produced and the echo thrown back at him, he discovered the mysterious pleasure of sound which had abruptly taken a first step along the path towards organised music. Vaguely perceiving the possibilities he had unleashed, he spent a few minutes experimenting with shouts and calls of various pitches until other members of the tribe, fearful of the invisible spirits he had aroused in the cliffs, called him away. The game was abandoned until another day–or another generation.

In time, groups of these primitive cave-dwellers would be found experimenting vocally among the cliffs and among themselves; and we may be sure that the experiments became more complex, necessitating some kind of code of discipline, since spontaneous music quickly becomes boring, and unruly extemporisation by several voices soon turns into a competition to see who can shout the loudest. Clearly rules had to be made, and we may visualise one of these savages taking it upon himself to attempt to control and regulate his companions' enthusiasm, indicating with threatening gestures his displeasure at some sounds and his boredom with others. An image is emerging of the **first chorus master** encouraging his performers with a bovine femur in his hand.

Gradually it was realised that high notes travelled farther and were more penetrating than low ones, and they were thus suitable for long-distance communication. Deep notes, on the other hand, were lost in open spaces, but in confined areas such as caves they set up a powerful resonance which excited the performers, at the same time frightening the listeners. For these superstitious peoples, who trembled as the echoes of the caves reverberated round them, certain sounds came to possess certain magical significances, and those with the loudest and most powerful voices gradually found that they had a power over the rest with which they could control and influence. **The first enchanting** had come into being. Through a series of lucky coincidences it was found that certain incantations augured well for a successful hunt or ensured a plentiful supply of drinking water from the skies.

We shall have occasion to return to the influence which these chanters wielded among their tribes.

About the same time, plus or minus a few thousand years, **the first instrumentalist** lived. Swinging his club at a potential meal, he missed and accidentally struck a rock. The resulting sound terrified him, for the rock rang like a gong. Emerging from his hiding-place later with a curiosity stronger than his fear, he tentatively hit the rock again, revelling in the deep, resonant sound which, as he struck harder and harder, rolled round the area, attracting other tribe members who had travelled some distance to discover what strange phenomenon was disturbing for the first time a world of natural animal and elemental noises. The carrying properties of the sound having thus been proved, the rock was thereafter used as a signal to tribe members who were out of shouting range. It signalled to them of danger or of success in the hunt; the first utility music had been created, simultaneously with the first musical instrument.

If such spectacular results were obtainable from a piece of rock and a club, perhaps other materials would also yield results. Experiments were made in tapping and hitting a variety of substances, and it was merely a question of time before a number of different types of non-membrane drum were evolved. It was discovered that thigh-slapping and hand-clapping produced a sharp rhythmic sound, and that an animal skin, when pegged tightly over

Illustration from a Grecian vase depicting a group of female figures playing harp, kithara and lyra. (Staatliche Antikensammlungen und Glyptothek München)

a shallow pit, would resonate the air inside the pit and produce an eerie, penetrating noise when hit with a stick. A covering of bark made a stronger membrane which would withstand the impact of dancers' heels; it was found also that the charm bracelets worn on wrist and ankle by these dancers made a pleasing jingling sound in time to the rhythm of the dance. Therefore, open rattles were soon cultivated and, alongside them, enclosed rattles in which seeds or pebbles were put into a gourd to be shaken at the end of a short handle.

The first wind instruments were also invented in a haphazard manner. An old straw or hollow reed was found to produce a note when blown in a particular way, and modifications to the length of the tube produced alterations in the note. A major discovery was made by a native with a sharp stone and the time to experiment; by cutting holes in the length of the tube and then 'stopping-up' the holes successively with the fingertips, a whole range of notes could be produced. The increase in variety of the first flutes over the first drums inevitably led to further experiments, and a wedding of instrumental and vocal techniques brought about the voice-flute (a simple flute through which the player hums or sings) which is still in use even today in some areas of Europe and Asia.

A thin sliver of wood or grass in the airway was found to change the sound of the instrument into something more piercing (children still stretch a blade of grass between thumbs for the same purpose), and the foundation was laid for the invention of single- and double-reed instruments.

A curious kind of 'wind-percussion' instrument developed from the stamping-pit principle. The sticks which were used to strike the skin or bark were sometimes hollow, and it was found that the column of air within the stick resonated with the vibration of the concussion. With a shaped top, these 'stamping-sticks' were promoted from their role of producing the sound in the pit-drum to having independent status.

An animal horn, truncated and hollowed out, was found to possess a strange new character which, when blown from the narrow end, thrilled the blood of the hunter. Consequently, animal horns came to typify the sound of the hunt for food on the hoof, and **the first hunting-horns** had arrived, ripe for development through incredible sophistications over the ages until their modern perfection, which has removed from them all traces of their savage origins. A whole family of instruments grew from these early experiments with animal horns, a family ranging in size from the massive Wagner tuba to the tiny Baroque trumpet; and in shape from the slender simplicity of the herald trumpet and post-horn to the intestinal complexities of some specimens in the history of the development of the modern orchestral horn. The finger-holes bored in the early cow-horn represent the first step in the attempts to wrest more than the basic notes from the instrument; and modern machinery appended to the cow-horn's descendants range from the subtle perfection of the horn's rotary valves to the spectacular sliding action of the trombone.

Primitive flute made from a reindeer bone.

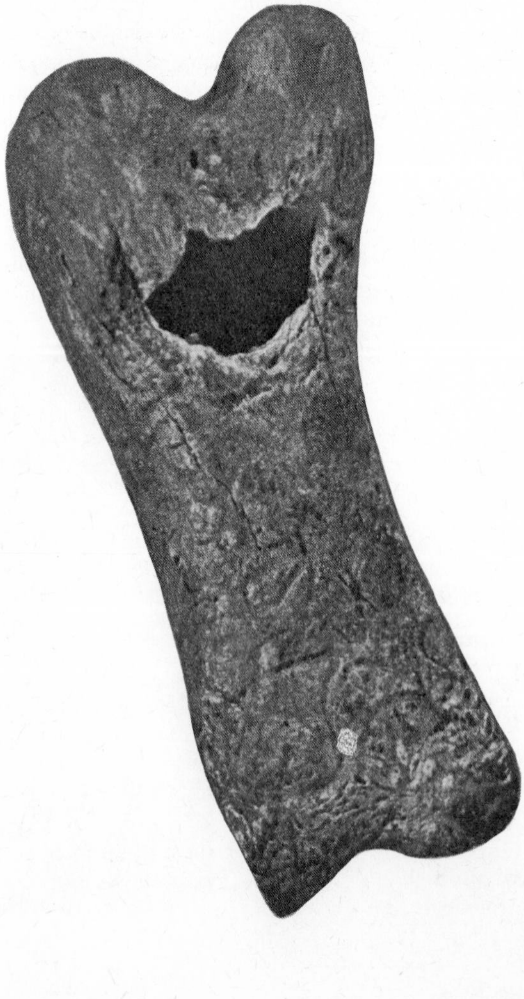

A Greek hero shown blowing a conch-shell trumpet, the sound of which is said to have conquered giants. This is one of the most primitive of all instruments.

The humblest of all wind instruments, the zampogna, made of oat straws, are still in use today in the Mediterranean and Balkan areas.

Animals provided the material also for two other early instruments: the scraper, made from a notched bone which might be pressed against a resonator of some kind, and the conch-shell trumpet.

Non-instrumental music, too, was developing. Experimenters were discovering that the human voice is capable of a wide range of pitch, volume, and quality, and that the blending of some tones pleased more readily than others. Gradually, through aeons of trial and error, experience produced results which led ultimately to the great traditions of unison choral singing, and to polyphony. Doubtless many of these early experiments included both vocalists and instrumentalists. The imagination reels at the sound which must have been produced by a handful of players on crudely fashioned instruments, blowing and banging with abandon, accompanying (or, more accurately perhaps, vying with) vocalists giving forth in the coarse, throaty, tortured voices, often modified by hand-to-windpipe or fist-to-chest rhythmic embellishments, which they had cultivated for carrying power and penetration, rather than artistic, purposes. The phases of self-control, discipline, experiment, and sophistication undergone between such occasions and a modern performance of, for example, Handel's *Messiah*, are too numerous to imagine.

It is probable that stringed instruments were the last of the main groups to appear on that prehistoric scene. A hunting-bow, when not being used for its meat-winning purpose, might have indicated to some idle cave-man that the taut string, when plucked, would resound, and that by altering its tension or length a different note would result. Two bows, if treated with powdered rock or animal fat to encourage abrasive action, and then rubbed together crosswise, may have set off a developing stream of ideas which led to the violin family, a group which has evolved alongside the plucked lute family (but often merging with it, see Part 1 of Section 11) until the development of the wide differences between the stringed instruments which we encounter today. It should be pointed out in the interest of accuracy that the first representation of a bowed instrument shows a player holding a bow some 10 ft (3 m) long, much longer than the Danish Bronze Age hunter's bow and the military long-bow of the Middle Ages, and unwieldy in the extreme for both musical and aggressive purposes. This enormous bow may have been constructed for a specific purpose which is now obscure, but it hardly affects the image of the archer experimenting with two crossed bows.

It will be seen that, in the everyday accoutrements of a cave-man's life, all the ingredients existed for the development of the instruments and the vocal techniques of today. Even the ultra-sophisticated grand piano has developed from a simple frame of strings which were struck with a little hammer (see Dulcimer and Psaltery, Part 1 of Section II), while the Stradivarius violin is basically a wooden box and strings developed to a point of loving perfection by skills and techniques which have evolved over centuries of gradual advancement and improvement.

The reader may be forgiven for feeling cheated by the above. He is presumably reading this book in search of facts, several of which have been enumerated, but not a single one has been, or can be, substantiated in detail or even placed in its correct chronology. However, it is hoped that the foregoing will illustrate the extreme antiquity of the origins of music, and that these origins were certainly, and in every case, the results of chance or coincidence.

From the quicksands of conjecture we move to the slightly less hazy area of educated guesses.

The concept of form was a late factor in the history of music. The performances given by the artists discussed above would have had little or no over-all design from the constructional viewpoint, apart perhaps from rudimentary devices such as a recurring motif, but there is likely to have been one exception. Of all the forms and styles of music with which the 20th century listener is familiar, one, and one only, was known to music's earliest performers: **descriptive music**.

One of the most natural things for a performer to attempt, once he has become familiar with his instrument's characteristics, is to try to imitate the sounds he hears round him. Thus the player of a primitive reed-pipe might try to reproduce on his instrument the vocalisations made by birds and singers; the horn-player might imitate the bellowing of a bull; and our primitive violinist, with bow and box and strings, might try to reproduce all the natural sounds of a thunderstorm. Folk-musicians of this century still tell stories on their instruments, as A L Lloyd has illustrated so clearly in his broadcast talks. Single performers will recount long and involved folk-tales entirely in music, reproducing dances, dramatic happenings, the calls of animals, and even the emotions of the narrator; it is difficult to imagine that our proto-musicians did not indulge their feelings also. What more natural than for the player of a reed-pipe to convey his moods of depression or elation through music? The 'Age of Sensibility' was merely reawakened by the mid-18th-century Germans!

These musical tales might have been aided by a vocalist to tell the story. Perhaps he would act a part in order to clarify and enhance the narrative, the logical step then being for another 'character' to join in. Thus commenced the long line of development which led, through an infinite variety of plays, masques, passion dramas, entertainments, dramatic madrigals, cantatas, etc, to the most sophisticated and artificial of all musical activites: **opera**.

Early singers would certainly have praised their deities in song, at the same time asking a few meteorological or hunting favours in return, and even if the music bounded with enthusiasm, it was still technically a **hymn**.

In prehistoric times, therefore, the foundations were laid for tone poem, opera, and hymn, forms which were still to take countless thousands of years to become the stylised works we know today, but which nevertheless cannot be called by other names.

These are essentially benign forms. They were joined by something less innocuous; the combination of music and magic was to produce an altogether more sinister concept.

We know that a deep male voice, used with imagination in the right surroundings, could strike dread into primitive souls. There can be no doubt that this knowledge was exploited by some singers to gain power within the community, and this strange connection between music and what has become known as 'the black arts' has persisted in greater or lesser intensity to the present day. In the days of the primitives, life, music, superstition, and religion were, as it were, one entity. Once a certain stage had been reached in civilisation, a stage at which man realised that there existed greater things than his imagination could grasp, the unknown powers of the spirits began to be equated with the mysterious power of music. A force which possessed the power to stir and move the soul and yet was intangible and invisible must have been sent by the spirits, and, therefore, the spirits must be rewarded or placated. Early civilisations frequently buried their dead with provisions for the journey to, and residence in, the next world; and among these provisions often were to be found musical instruments, whether or not the deceased had had musical connections. Mythologies of all countries and all periods are awash with references to music and musicians. Musical instruments figure in early rock-carvings and cave-paintings. Everywhere music existed to assist in work, sleep, combat and relaxation, but most potently of all in magic.

In some primitive communities the individuals who sang or played upon instruments were so feared that they took on a position only slightly less exalted than gods. Theirs was the power to control the elements. It was they who officiated at spring fertility rites, at circumcisions, at harvest gatherings, at solstices and equinoxes, and at all the other important functions and festivals of those superstition-ridden years. They were held in equal, if not greater, awe than priests and medicine-men. So great was their influence, and so jealously did they guard their power, that countless cruel activities grew up round the mystique of music. For instance, only men were allowed to operate the bull-roarer (see Part I of Section II), women had to be rounded up and put out of sight before that piece of wood might be lifted aloft to sound its strange message. If by chance a feminine eye fell on a bull-roarer, the possessor of that prying eye would summarily be put to death. And if a man had been responsible for the forbidden feminine viewing, he too would be executed. A similar mystique surrounded certain kinds of trumpet. Very often the death would be hideously slow and excruciating in an effort to appease the offended invisible spirit residing within the instrument. Similar taboos and penalties exist even today in certain backward countries, females being forbidden to touch, or even to see, certain 'sacred' instruments. Little wonder that the mythologies of the world became saturated with stories of musicians with their magic powers, of men and gods dwelling in instruments or adopting each other's identities.

The 'power' of music, then, to regulate the lives of men and women is as old as music itself. We may wonder at the gullibility of the ancients in allowing sounds to so influence and control their emotions, working, eating, sleeping, and battle activities—yet are things so different today? The first few notes of a familiar entertainer's signature tune are enough to trigger the modern brain to signal the appropriate action of the body—to listen or to switch off; advertisers realise the potent subliminal power of music in TV and radio commercials. In factories and hospitals, and even in farming, music is used to obtain better results, relaxed patients, or more milk! The last ten years or so have witnessed the realisation that carefully chosen music is of use in the relief and perhaps the cure of some nervous disorders, but before we enter ultra-technical areas let us remember the simple and basic use made of music in impelling large groups of individuals to rise, to eat, to do battle, or to sleep.

The army bugle is still fulfilling these functions.

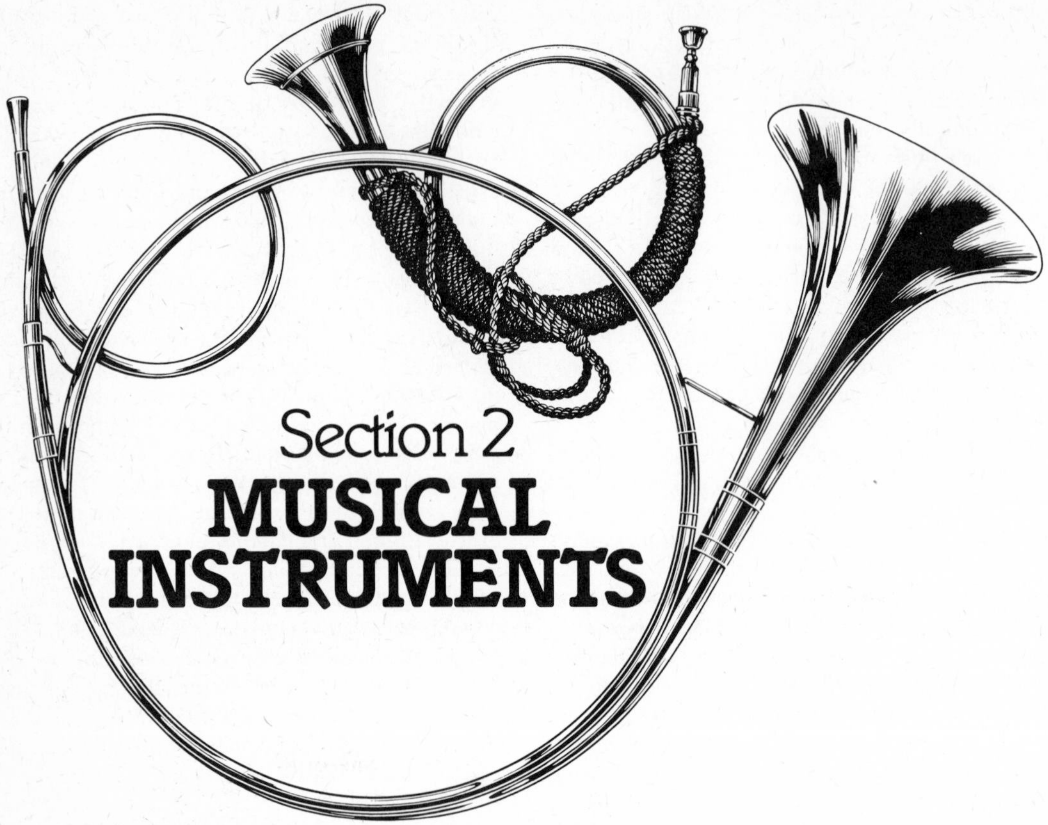

Section 2
MUSICAL INSTRUMENTS

1. Primitive, ancient and obsolete

Possibly the earliest known indication that man played musical instruments in prehistoric times comes from an engraving in the Cave Des Trois-Frères (named after the three sons of Count Bégouen, one of whom discovered the cave on 20 July 1914) in the Pyrenees of the extreme south-west of France. The engraving is of a dancing figure, wearing a stag's head, horns, coat, and tail. In, or near, his mouth is what appears to be a flute (or perhaps a bow), and it is possible that he is dancing to his own music. Before him prance two oxen, one with its head turned towards him as if listening. This cave-drawing dates from some 20 000 years ago.

No other representation which might be construed as human musical activity is known between this date and the 7th century BC. A drummer, in a mural in Anatolia (Turkey) discovered in 1961, plays for a group of twelve dancers dressed in leopard skins.

Thereafter, musical representations are common in the cultures of Egypt, Greece, and Rome, as the following instrumental details show. It has been considered most useful to group together under one heading primitive, ancient, and obsolete instruments since they do not easily separate from each other. Some primitive and ancient instruments, for instance, are still in use in virtually unaltered form while many obsolete instruments are of no great antiquity.

The generally adopted divisions of woodwind, brass, strings, and percussion which are adhered to in Part 2 of this Section despite the occasional inadequacy of the system, collapses completely when primitive and ancient instruments are considered, the categories being stretched to their

Roman Lituus, developed from a cane to which was attached an animal horn. This metal—often bronze—instrument was in use throughout the Roman Empire and as far north-west as Ireland.

Roman Cornu, a military and ceremonial instrument whose voice was described by Horace as a menacing murmur. This example was some 11 feet (3·75 m) long; its weight was taken on the player's shoulder by a wooden crossbar.

utmost until their edges merge imperceptibly. For this reason the alternative grouping originated by Curt Sachs in his *The History of Musical Instruments* is used. Brief explanations of the contents and boundaries of each group are followed by discussion of the most prominent instruments therein. The actual number of different instruments known from the earliest times is truly vast and it is, of course, not possible to give details of each and every one, nor the alternative names by which many of them are known. This may be the place, however, to mention what is undoubtedly the **world's oldest instrument**: the Stalacpipe Organ in Luray, Virginia, USA, in which stalactites millions of years old have been tuned by grinding. They are struck by rubber mallets fired by electronic impulses, controlled from a keyboard.

It will be seen that many primitive and ancient instruments developed into designs which are still in use, and the reader is therefore advised to use Parts 1 and 2 of this Section in conjunction so that a true historical picture may emerge.

The basic principle by which instruments work is very simple: they set up vibrations in the air with which they are in contact. These vibrations may be brought about in four[1] different ways and instruments, therefore, divide into the following categories, which were worked out by Curt Sachs:

Idiophones
Aerophones
Membranophones
Chordophones

Idiophones

This group comprises instruments made of materials which produce a sound when scraped, rubbed, or hit, without further modification having been made to that material, and without the intervention of other materials. Modern instruments in this group include the xylophone, cymbals, gongs, and castanets; less common are the following examples:

BULL-ROARER

One of the simplest of all instruments, the bull-roarer consists of a flat piece of wood to be whirled round the player's head on the end of a piece of string. Its passage through the air produces a frightening sound, often of elemental proportions, and primitive peoples considered that this 'sound from nothing' represented the voices of dead ancestors. It was also believed to have magical, medical, and meteorological powers. Although of world-wide distribution, its best-known association today is with the Aboriginal tribes of Australia, and it has been used in the Suite from the ballet *Corroboree* (1946) by the Australian composer John Antill. Three 'thundersticks' (another name for bull-roarers) are required in Henry Cowell's *Ensemble* (1924) together with two violins, viola, and two cellos.

HORSESHOES

By suspending old horseshoes which he found in his uncle's village smithy, John Davy, the 18th-century opera composer (see Section V), constructed an instrument upon which he could play simple tunes. This principle is applied also to the **stone star**, a horizontal instrument in the centre of which sits the player with striking stones in each hand. The stone star is still used in Africa.

SANSA

Thus named after the Congolese tribe among whom the instrument was first discovered, it is also known by the following names: Kaffir piano; likembe; marimba (but not to be confused with the instrument described on page 36); mbira; thumb piano; toum; zeze.

Its metal plates were fastened at one end to the sounding-board, the free ends being sprung down and released by the fingers and thumbs. It is this principle of vibrating metal which led to the construction of the first musical-boxes (see Section IX). George Crumb included a sansa in his *Night of the Four Moons* (1966).

SISTRUM

Latin, from Greek *seistron* (*seio* = shake).

An extremely early and simple coloristic instrument, widely distributed throughout the world at the dawn of history. The instrument could be used as a rattle or struck with a stick.

TRINIDAD STEEL DRUM

The West Indian steel drum consists of an oil-drum the head of which has been divided into a number of sections, each of which produces a different note when hit with a rubber beater. Although essentially a percussion instrument, the steel drum is well suited to the production of melodies, and 'steel bands' possess a remarkably sophisticated repertoire in which melody, harmony, and rhythm all play a vital part. The writer has heard a thoroughly acceptable performance of Mozart's *Eine Kleine Nachtmusik* played by a West Indian steel band.

YAMSTICK

An Australian Aboriginal instrument of the most basic kind: a simple stick used to beat out the rhythm on trees, shields, the ground, or anyone

[1] Or five, see page 25.

or anything which happens to be near by, to heighten the excitement at the wild ceremonial totemic dances known as 'corroborees'.

Aerophones

Instruments which contain a column of air within a cylinder or cone. A sound is produced when this air is vibrated by the player's lips or by a single or double reed, or (most primitive of all) by air passing across the top of a tube, as in the flute and the recorder. Modern instruments in this group include the flute, oboe, trumpet, horn, and saxophone families. These were preceded, or are supplemented, by more primitive instruments.

ALPHORN OR ALPENHORN

A long, wooden horn used for signalling in the Alps. Its first references date from the 15th century although it is undoubtedly of prehistoric origin. Best known for its use in Alpine districts, it is nevertheless widespread in Europe.

The alphorn has attracted the attention of classical composers on rare occasions: Rossini imitated its call in his *William Tell* Overture (1829), but Leopold Mozart actually wrote a *Sinfonia Pastorale* in G (alternatively attributed to Hofstetter) for *corno pastoriccio*, ie: alphorn, with strings. At a Hoffnung Music Festival Concert at London's Royal Festival Hall (13 November 1956) Dennis Brain played the finale of the symphony, using an ordinary garden hosepipe fitted with a horn mouthpiece. Jean Daetwyler has also written a concerto for alphorn and orchestra.

AULOS

In ancient Greek music, the word for pipe, corresponding to the Roman *tibia*.

The aulos is the ultimate origin of all double-reed wind instruments. The strident tones of the aulos were produced by a double reed which was actually inserted into the mouth-cavity. The pressure required to vibrate this reed was so great that players had to wear bandages to prevent their cheeks from bursting. Due to its flexibility—its range was two and a half octaves—the aulos was a widespread and highly popular instrument in antiquity, and it survives in double-pipe, and even triple-pipe, form in Mediterranean areas today.

BASSET-HORN

The origin of the basset-horn is attributed to the instrument-making firm of A and M Mayerhofer of Passau, in Bavaria, about 1770, and was designed to extend the lower range of the clarinet. The name possibly derives from a German diminutive of 'bass', and the name—'Horn'—of the actual inventor. The first composer to use the instrument extensively was Mozart who, from about 1781, wrote a series of chamber, choral, and orchestral works exploiting its subtly different qualities. The first concerto for the instrument is now thought to be Mozart's A major work, K 622, written for the 'basset clarinet' which extends four semitones below the standard clarinet, thus equating with the lower part of the basset-horn range. Isolated works for the instrument exist by Beethoven and Mendelssohn, and a basset-horn concerto in F by Alessandro Rolla in manuscript at Einsiedeln, Switzerland, bears the date 24 April 1829, although the work itself carries internal evidence of considerably earlier composition.

BASS HORN

A Frenchman named André Frichot developed the bass horn from the serpent at the beginning of the 19th century (it was also known as the 'English horn'–not to be confused with the cor anglais–since Frichot lived in London) but it survived barely 40 years, and then only in military bands, before being superseded by the ophicleide and the tuba.

CORNET AND CORNETT

The name *cornetto* is a diminutive of Italian *corno*: literally 'a small horn', but the word has stood for two entirely different instruments in musical history which have alternated in prominence. In English the method of differentiation is simple: 'cornett', with double 't', was a medieval wooden or ivory instrument with finger-holes which operated like a brass instrument. It was used mainly for the upper melody in open-air bands and in church music, usually in association with trombones (earlier, sackbuts). The instrument might be straight (muto) or gracefully curved (ronto). It was incorporated in the orchestra from the inception of such organisations, but its last appear-

A wooden Cornett of the 15th century.

ance seems to have been in the Viennese production of Gluck's *Orfeo* in 1762, although it continued in use in churches until the next century.

'Cornet', with one 't', is a species of piston-valved bugle which was developed (in France?) in the mid-1820s. It appeared in Parisian opera in 1830 and in Berlioz's *Symphonie Fantastique* the same year; it also found a place as the upper melody instrument in brass/wind bands in England, and during the present century this has been its main role, its orchestral use fading out apart from exceptional instances. A performance of Berlioz's symphony with the authentic cornet parts is today, despite the modern taste for faithfulness in performance and instrumentation, still a rarity.

With this interest in authentic performances of old music, however, has come a revival in popularity of old instruments, among them the cornett, which is no longer a rarity.

While English terminology allows no confusion between cornet and cornett, when other languages, particularly German, are considered, room for error is introduced. The following list of names may be of assistance:

	CORNETT (wood or ivory; medieval)	CORNET (brass; 19th century)
Ger:	*Zinke; Zink; Kornett*	*Piston; Pistonkornett; Kornett; Ventilkornett*
Fr:	*cornet à bouquin*= 'goat cornett'	*cornet à pistons; pistons*
It:	*cornetto*	*pistone sopranino; cornetta; cornettino pistone*

The earliest cornetts were of animal horn: the German word *Zink* means the smallest branch of a stag's antlers. Finger-holes were first bored in the instrument in the 11th century, and with the use of wood and ivory allowing greater possibilities in construction, a family developed ranging from the tiny cornettino to the S-shaped bass member, the serpent.

CRUMHORN

The Old English word 'crump', meaning crooked, led to the name 'crumhorn' for a wooden instrument, with finger-holes, which curved upwards at the end like a hockey-stick. Its names, in various countries, were subject to a certain overlapping:

Eng/Ger: crumhorn/*Krummhorn*
Fr/Eng: *cromorne*
It: *schryari*
Fr: *tournebout; cornemusa* (not to be confused with *cornemuse* and *cornamusa*, both of which mean 'bagpipe', qv)
Ger: *Schreierpfeife*

The crumhorn was a double-reed instrument which was popular from the Middle Ages, but which died out during the 17th century.

DIDGERIDOO OR ILPIRRA

An Australian Aboriginal instrument consisting of a hollowed-out tree branch into which the player hums or whistles. Its origin is probably prehistoric.

Killer used didgeridoo

DARWIN: A row between two Aborigines over maintaining tribal tradition was ended with a didgeridoo.

Long Harry took the long, wooden, pipe-like instrument and beat fellow-elder Kevin Frog to death with it.

A court cleared Long Harry of murder but remanded him for sentence for manslaughter.

(Daily Express, 17.3.1979)

LUR

Constructed of bronze in the shape of mammoth tusks, these early trumpets were widespread in northern Europe in the Bronze Age. They are relatives of the Roman *lituus* and the Irish *karnyx*, and examples have been found with remarkably sophisticated mouthpieces. The main use for such instruments was in religious festivals, where they were employed in pairs.

PANPIPES OR SYRINX

Said to have been played by the god Pan to the water-nymph Syrinx, the simple panpipes are of extreme antiquity. Each pipe produces only one

Contrasts. David Bulanatji wearing a British greatcoat and native headgear, competes with the noise of London Airport with his didjeridoo, an aboriginal instrument made from a log hollowed out by termites. (Popperfoto)

note (in this respect the panpipes are in fact the simplest form of organ): a collection of pipes is bound together in order of size, the lower ends being blocked. The instrument has played very little part in concert music through the ages, being regarded mainly as a pastoral instrument, although Telemann included a tiny *Flauto Pastorale* for syrinx and continuo in his *Der Getreuen Music-Meister* (1728). Romanian folk-orchestras still make extremely effective use of the panpipes.

RECORDER

It: *flauto a becco; flauto d'eco*
Fr: *flûte-à-bec; flûte douce*
Ger: *Blockflöte; Schnabelflöte* = 'beak-flute'

The earliest recorders were made from the bones of animals and have been discovered in Upper Palaeolithic ('Late Dawn Stone') sites of the Aurignacian period (*c* 25 000–22 000 BC). The instrument seems to have entered Europe from the East via the Slav countries, and its popularity outshone that of the shawms during the Middle Ages. The name 'recorder' comes from the Old Anglo-French *recordour*, which meant an imitation of the song of a bird.

In 1510 King Henry VIII kept a large collection of instruments at Westminster, including 76 recorders and a similar number of side-blown flutes. A quarter of a century later, by which time there were four distinct sizes of the instrument, the first recorder manual was written by Sylvestro Ganassi dal Fontego, 'Musician to the illustrious authorities of Venice'. By the beginning of the 17th century there were as many as nine sizes of the basically unaltered design, but thereafter a decline set in. Only three sizes were in general use at the start of the 18th century (descant, alto, bass) but the instrument was well established in serious music circles, both Bach and Handel writing extensively for it. During the 18th century the superior power of the flute, together with some prominent propaganda on the latter instrument's behalf by King Frederick the Great, contributed to the eclipse of the recorder. It was revived in about 1912 by Arnold Dolmetsch, who also encouraged interest in old music for the instrument. Among modern composers to have written for the recorder are Hindemith (Sonata for recorder and piano, 1932) and Luciano Berio (*Gesti*, for recorder alone).

During the 19th century the English flageolet, derived from the higher members of the recorder family, held a certain popularity among amateurs, leading to the construction of double and even triple flageolets, after the double recorders and double shawms of earlier times.

EARLY TRUMPETS (see also Lur)

The trumpet had wide distribution throughout the East and Africa in the days before the Romans. Its earliest examples were straight, without modification of any kind to the simple tube, and, therefore, severely limited in melodic possibilities. The dividing-line between horns and trumpets is, to say the least, hazy until modern times, the two types developing along much the same lines and being used for similar purposes: mainly signalling on the hunting and battlefields. However, the true trumpet first appeared in Sicily in the 11th century; called *busine*, it evolved from the Roman *buccina*. The trumpet also held ceremonial responsibilities until its decline during the 18th century, before which, in the Late Baroque era, it enjoyed a spectacular development. At the time, trumpeters were regarded as among the most important personages at royal courts, occupying, with their drumming colleagues, a position physically above the rest of the orchestra.

The loss of high trumpet (clarino) technique led to interest being shown in extending the number of notes available in the lower register; the invention of keyed trumpets, and subsequently of valve trumpets during the early 19th century leading to the perfect instrument we know today.

Membranophones

These are instruments in which a membrane is stretched across a hollow body (the resonator) and then made to vibrate by rubbing or hitting. Modern membranophone instruments include the drums and tambourine; only a selection of the huge number of more primitive instruments may be mentioned.

BONGOS

Small, high-pitched, basin-shaped drums, joined together in pairs and held between the knees. They are struck by the fingers and thumbs which set up a sharp resonance from the vellum heads. Although of great antiquity, they are only occasionally found in the modern orchestra; they have spread, instead, from their Cuban surroundings, via Latin American dance bands, into many areas of popular music.

FRAME DRUM

A membrane is stretched over a simple round or square frame and is struck by a beater or by the fingers, depending upon the size of the instrument. Early examples date from Asian prehistory, but they are still in use in the East, and a sophisticated form has entered the orchestra as the tambourine.

FRICTION DRUM

This describes the method of playing rather than the instruments themselves, which may be of widely varying types. In some friction drums the fingers or hands are rubbed over the membrane (as is the case in the modern orchestral tambourine for sustained notes), but in the majority of instances the skin is pierced by a stick or a chord, which is rubbed or revolved to produce a vibration at the membrane. Once again the principle is extremely old but still survives in primitive cultures. For example, the Romanian *bohaiu* (=bullock) has a single head through which emerge strands of horsehair. When the hair is pulled with fingers treated with rosin, the *bohaiu* emits a cattle-like sound.

HOURGLASS DRUMS

These are double-headed drums with narrow waists, almost like two flattened, tumbler-shaped basins joined at their pointed ends. Chords run outside the instrument between the two heads, and pressure on these chords produces increased tension at the skins. The notes obtainable, therefore, are infinitely variable, and a proficient drummer will cause the drums to 'speak' in an eloquent and excitable manner. These hourglass drums, which might be struck by fingers and thumbs or by a wooden beater, originated in India at least 2000 years ago and have spread into Africa and as far east as Japan. The capacity to 'speak' in an almost human way has led to the hourglass drum being employed in Africa as one of the 'talking' or 'message' drums.

MIRLITON

Mirlitons of great variety are found throughout the last few thousand years. Today the best-known example, and an ideal illustration of the principle, is the simple comb-and-paper. The voice is projected against a membrane, which resonates in sympathy, producing a rasping sound. The toy kazoo is another example, as are the Chinese flute in which one hole is covered by a membrane, and the African mirliton, in which one end of a horn is covered by a type of tough spider-web. At a Round House Concert in London on 31 January 1972, the audience and BBC Symphony Orchestra were to have played *With 100 Kazoos*, specially written by David Bedford, but the conductor Pierre Boulez refused to include it.

SLIT-DRUM

Often of enormous length, the slit-drum consists of a hollowed-out tree-trunk in the upper face of which is a slit of varying width and shape. When hit with heavy beaters, these drums can be heard over great distances and are used for signalling in the African jungles in which they originated. Virtually every village, no matter how small, possesses a slit-drum, as much as a status symbol as a musical necessity.

TABOR

This old word for 'drum' (compare Fr: *tambour*) might refer to almost any type of ancient drum. More specifically, it is used for the tiny drum that formed half of the equipment of the pipe-and-tabor artist, who marched along with a pipe in one hand and a beater in the other with which he played upon a drum suspended from a strap round his neck. Recently, tabor has come to mean a species of narrow, long drum with a single snare. This latter was the instrument called for by Bizet in his Suite from *L'Arlesienne*, and by Copland in *El Salon Mexico* and *Appalachian Spring*.

Chordophones

The two basic parts of these instruments are a chord and a resonator, the two joined together. The chord might be scraped by a bow or plucked with a finger, and when the chord vibrates the resonator amplifies the sound. Modern instruments in this group include the violin, guitar, harp, and piano families, in the last of which, of course, the strings are hit by hammers; less well-known examples of chordophones cover an extremely wide field.

BALALAIKA AND DOMRA

An early stringed instrument allied to the lute and the guitar which was widespread as a folk-instrument in Europe from about the 17th century. The balalaika, together with its larger relative the domra, were modernised towards the end of the 19th century, and the improved form is now considered to be the national instrument of Russia. It is made in six sizes: piccolo, primo, secunda, viola, bass, and contrabass; the domra family is similarly constituted. Concertos for balalaika and domra have been written by respectively Shushakov and Budashkin.

CLAVICHORD

The principle behind the operation of the clavichord dates from the late Middles Ages; the oldest dated example was built by Domenico da Pesaro in 1543 and is preserved in Leipzig University. Like the virginals, the strings run parallel to the keyboard, but the method of sound reproduction is totally different from the harpsichord group: metal blades, called 'tangents', strike the strings from below, and the note produced is dependent upon the length of string left to vibrate. With this principle of not more than one note obtainable per string, some chords become impossible to produce, but this is no disadvantage since the instrument was basically melodic and was the most essentially intimate of all keyboard instruments, its sound being barely loud enough to be heard through a closed door.

CRWTH

This is the Welsh name for an instrument also known as the 'crowth' or 'crowd' (Eng), *cruit* or *crot* (Celt) which was last used in Wales at the beginning of the last century. It originated in the 1st century BC and was developed from the lyre. Later versions (*c* 1300) were equipped with a fingerboard and played with a bow. This modification made the instrument into an ancestor of the violin family. Alternative names from the Middle Ages stress this connection:
Ger: *Fiedel*='fiddle', Fr: *vielle*='viol'.

DULCIMER

Fr: *tympanon*
It: *salterio tedesca*='German psaltery'
Ger: *Hackbrett*
(See also Psaltery, below)

One of the instruments which contributed to the invention of the pianoforte, the dulcimer consists of a rectangular box across which strings are stretched; the strings are hit with little mallets. The dulcimer was introduced into Europe from Persia during the 15th century and has survived well into the modern age, even though it has only rarely found a place in serious music.

The 'zither', a fretted, plucked relative of the dulcimer, was used occasionally in the serious music of the 19th century, notably by Johann Strauss II, but it is as a café instrument that it achieved fame for its prominent part in the film music for Carol Reed's *The Third Man* (1949), the 'Harry Lime Theme' played by Anton Karas becoming immensely popular. The American 'Appalachian dulcimer' is in fact a true zither.

The German composer and dulcimer player, Pantaleon Hebenstreit constructed a large and complicated dulcimer early in the 18th century and this had a hundred years or so of currency as the 'pantaleon'. The composer Christian Siegmund Binder was said to have been an excellent pantaleonist.

A local variety of dulcimer is the east European 'cymbalom'. Zoltan Kodály incorporated the instrument in his Suite from the opera *Háry János*

(1926), and the Byelorussian composer Valter Kaminsky has composed a concerto for cymbalom and folk-orchestra. The instrument is also used, often with incredible virtuosity, in Romanian folk-bands.

FIEDEL OR FIDEL OR FIDULA

Introduced into Europe from the East in about the 9th century, and played vertically in front of the player supported on his knee, the fiedel developed into the chin-held design during the Renaissance. It gave rise to the whole family of viols and violins, and the type cross-fertilised with the lute-type to such an extent that there may be found, scattered about the history of music, a confusing array of allied instruments, including bowed lutes and plucked viols. In short, it is true to say that this family of instruments has undergone continuous modifications right up to the peak of perfection in Italy early in the 18th century.

GUSLI

This is not to be confused with the Yugoslavian bowed lute, *gusla*. The gusli is a Russian folk instrument related to the psaltery and the zither and is called for by Rimsky-Korsakov in his opera *Sadko* (1898). The instrument had its virtuoso in the person of Vasilii Fiodorovich Trutovski, who played a variety of gusli, probably fitted with a keyboard.

HARPSICHORD

Fr: *clavecin*
It: *clavicembalo; cembalo; gravicembalo*
Ger: *Kielflügel; Cembalo*

The earliest origins of the harpsichord can be traced to the 14th century. In the Victoria and Albert Museum, London, there is preserved a harpsichord built by Hieronymus of Bologna: it is dated 1521 and is the oldest harpsichord to which a date can be ascribed with certainty.

King David is seen playing an instrument in some early representations; it is plucked, has a sounding-board behind the strings, and resembles the psaltery which was brought to Europe by the Saracens and Moors in the early Middle Ages. The psaltery, branching off on its way to the dulcimer which led ultimately to the development of the pianoforte, eventually evolved into the harpsichord family, which reached its greatest popularity during the first half of the 18th century. Literally thousands of harpsichord sonatas appeared in print (see, for example, Domenico Scarlatti in Section IV). Perhaps because of the limited carrying power of the instrument when in the company of even a small string orchestra, the harpsichord was slow to achieve solo status in a concerto. It is thought that the Brandenburg Concerto No 5, BWV 1050 (before 1721) of J S Bach was the first to include a solo harpsichord part, and even then it is merely an episode, although one of great length, in the first movement; for the rest of the work it 'concertises' with the other soloists, a violin and a flute. Bach's own harpsichord is still to be seen in the Museum of the Music Highschool in Charlottenburg. His seven solo harpsichord concertos all appear to be arrangements of concertos for other instruments.

From the earliest symphonies the harpsichord was, or could have been on an ad lib basis, included in the bass line as part of the continuo. The first symphonic part specifically designed for the instrument (although, ironically, evidence suggests that it may have been played after all on a fortepiano since that instrument was popular at the time in England) is a series of arpeggios introduced for performance by the composer towards the end of Haydn's Symphony No 98 in B flat. This was first performed in March 1792 in the Hanover Square Rooms in London.

From the fourth quarter of the 18th century the harpsichord began to give way to the more flexible, wider-ranging, powerful pianoforte until it became completely eclipsed in the 19th century, but during the past few decades composers have come to recognise its value again as a soloist, and concertos have been written for it by Manuel de Falla (1926), Frank Martin (1952), and others.

LUTE

The earliest forms of lute were already widespread at the beginning of recorded history. Illustrations exist of lute-players from Mesopotamia of 3000 BC, and tomb-paintings prove that lute-like instruments were well known to the Egyptians of the

18th Dynasty (1567–1320 BC). Similar evidence shows that the lute was played in ancient Greece and Rome: Nero, it is said, fiddled while Rome burned. In fact, he played the lute.

From its possible origins in the Near and Middle East, the lute spread in most directions, as the name chart which follows demonstrates, changing its form and name, but still remaining basically the same in over-all principle and design. It was introduced into Europe by the Moors and Saracens in the 8th century who brought also its Arabic name *al'ud* or *el'ud*, from which the word 'lute' is derived. The meaning of *al'ud* is 'flexible stick'; however, the translation adopted in some reference books, 'the wood', appears to be incorrect.

The first published music for lute was a set of dances by Francesco Spinaccino, printed by Petrucci in Venice in 1507.

It is pointless to discuss the matter of the instrument's first orchestral appearance since the lute has always been one of the stand-bys of art, as well as folk, bands since the beginning of organised music. It was still being employed in the orchestra at the beginning of the 18th century (J S Bach wrote for it in his *St John's Passion*, BWV 245, of 1723) and possibly its last orchestral appearance was in Handel's opera *Deidamia* in 1741.

Vivaldi wrote a concerto for the lute (RV 93), the lightly scored orchestra of two violins and bass balancing the delicate tone of the soloist. He also wrote a concerto in D minor (RV 540, of 1740) for lute and viola d'amor, accompanied by muted strings and muted harpsichord, and there exists also a large concerto (RV 558, also of 1740) which includes in its scoring parts for two *theorbos*, or large lutes.

Although it is not possible to give here a list of the names by which many of the obsolete instruments were known, an exception is made in the case of the lute (and of the bagpipe, see 3. Instruments of Unusual Interest). From its beginnings the lute had a wide influence on instrumental design, its successful construction being taken by following makers as a pattern for a vast variety of instruments which are widely spread throughout the ancient and modern world. Whether the lute is the true ultimate ancestor of the violin is an arguable point; what is plain is that the clear divisions which developed later between lute, lyre, guitar, and viol families become increasingly fuzzy the further one looks back into history.

VARIETIES AND DESCENDANTS OF THE LUTE

This list is not complete (and it would be neither useful nor possible to make it so), but it will serve to illustrate the wide range of the lute, geographically and constructionally.

Name	*Remarks*
al'ud	Arabian term, 'flexible stick'; also used in Persia
angelica	English, with at least 16 strings
angélique	French, = angelica
archicistre	French; a large cittern
archlute	English, = theorbo
arcicetera	large Italian cittern
arciluta	Italian, = theorbo
balalaika	Russian, with triangular body
bandola	small Italian variety of lute
banlira	Ukrainian, 5-stringed plus drone
barbat	Persian; the name indicates its shape: 'the breast of a duck'
biwa	Japanese, a large version of the Chinese p'ip'a. Other Japanese varieties are: bugaku biwa, chicuzen, gekkin (4-stringed), genkwan, jamisen (or shamisen, 3-stringed and spade-shaped, unfretted and played with a plectrum), ku, and satsuma
cai dan nguyet	Vietnamese
cartar	Persian, = '4-stringed'
chitarra battente	Italian, small chitarrone
chitarrone	Roman theorbo with a very long neck
cithare	English, = cittern
cither	English, = cittern
citole	English, = cittern
cittern	European flat-backed wire-stringed lute, played with a plectrum
cobza	Romanian variety of cittern
colascione	17th-century Italian long lute
dital-harp	a harp-lute combination with finger key, invented in England in 1798
domra	Central Russian large balalaika
dutar	Persian, = '2-stringed'
el'ud	Arabian, = al'ud
erh hu	Chinese bowed lute with 2 strings and a hexagonal body
Erzcister	large German cittern

esrar or esraj	local varieties of Indian sitar
fandur	3-stringed Caucasian straight-bodied bowed lute
gadulka	Bulgarian rebab
gambus	widespread throughout North Africa and Asia
guitar	European (especially Spanish) fretted lute with a flat or slightly convex back
guitar-fiddle	small European bowed guitar
gunbri	Sudanese long lute
gunibri	North African and Arabian long lute without tuning pegs
gusle	Yugoslavian, single-stringed
harp-guitar	English, = dital-harp
harp-lute	English, = dital-harp
hu' ch'in	small Chinese 2-stringed bamboo-bodied lute ('ch'in' = 'to forbid', ie: to exclude evil spirits)
hu hu	Chinese 3-stringed coconut-shell-bodied lute
kabosa	North African and Asian varieties (cf: kobus)
kamanga a'guz	Egyptian spiked viol-lute
kemanje	Persian, 3-stringed sometimes with drones
kobus	Arabian, a variety of mizhar (qv)
kobuz	a variety of qupuz, found from Greece to Central Asia
la ch'in	a North Chinese tapering bowed zither with 20 strings
laghouto	large Greek lute, played with a plectrum
laud	Spanish, = 'lute'
Laute	German, = 'lute'
lira	Greek variety of rebab
liuto	Italian, = 'lute'
lute guitar	Hybrid English instrument
luth	French, = 'lute'
lutina	Italian, 'small lute'
machete	Portuguese, small fish-shaped lute
mandola	Italian, a large mandolin
mandolin(e)	Italian 8–10 strings tuned in pairs and played with a plectrum
mandora/ mandore	small Italian lute, between $\frac{1}{2}$ and $\frac{3}{4}$ size. The name may come from *mandorla* = 'almond (-shaped)'
mandorin	Italian small mandora
Mandürchen	German, = mandurina
mandurina	Italian, very small mandora
masenqo	Ethiopian single-stringed bowed lute
mizhar	small Arabian lute with tapering neck
ourumi	Nigerian lute
outi	Greek fretless lute
paduan	very large variety of theorbo from Padua, Italy
panctar	Persian, = '5-stringed'
pandora	Ethiopian, with indented body
pandurina	Italian, very small mandora (= mandurina)
pandurion	Greek (= Italian pandurina)
panturi	Georgian pandora
p'ip'a	Chinese short lute, pear-shaped and with 4 silk strings. It is at least 1800 years old
qabus	Arabian variety of qupuz
qitara	North African short lute
qupuz	Eastern European small pandora originally from Turkey
rabab	Arabian. The earliest-known bowed lute, a boat-shaped instrument with one or two strings, developed during the 18th century
rabob	Tajikistan and Afghanistan, similar to the sarod
rabob assa'ir	Egyptian plucked rabab
rebab	a European/North African rabab with a pear-shaped soundbox
rebec	European pear-shaped bowed viol
san hsien	Chinese, short lute similar to the Japanese shamisen. The name means '3-stringed'
sarangi	Indian, short 3-stringed bowed lute
sarinda	very short Indian bowed lute with multiple strings
sarod	Indian short lute
saz	Turkish, very small with gut frets
shuang ch'in	Chinese, 4-stringed with octagonal body
sitar	Indian long, sophisticated lute with 4–7 strings plus a sympathetic range. The word is from the Persian meaning '3-stringed'
su hu	Chinese, 4-stringed with hexagonal wooden body
ta hu ch'in	Chinese bowed lute with a pear-shaped body
tambura (tanpura, etc)	Indian long lute with 4 metal strings, not fingered, and usually played as an accompanying drone

Ravi Shankar with sitar, an Indian development of the Persian three-stringed lute. (Popperfoto)

tanbur or tanpur	widely distributed from West Pakistan to Turkey; very large body with gut frets
tan ch'in	Chinese cylindrical bamboo body with 2 strings
tar	Armenian long gut-fretted lute. The name means simply 'stringed'
theorbo	European, a large lute dating from the second half of the 16th century
theorbo-lute	European, double-necked with paired strings
ti ch'in	Chinese. The body consists of half a coconut shell; 4-stringed
tiorbo	Italian, = theorbo
trichordon	Greek, = 'three-stringed'
troubadour-fiddle	= guitar-fiddle
vihuela de mano	Spanish, = 'hand lute' (*vihuela* derives from the same root as 'viol')
vina	long Indian twin-gourd fretted lute played horizontally. Other Indian varieties include: kaccapi vina, kinnari vina, koca vina (all bowed), mayuri (Sanscrit: 'peacock'), prasarini vina, sanktika vina (bowed), and tayus or taus (Hindustani: 'peacock')
wol kum	Korean
ya cheng	Chinese horizontal bowed zither of about 14 strings
yueh ch'in	Chinese, = 'moon lute', with a round body and 4 strings

An Egyptian pictograph representing a non-vowelled sound 'n-f-r'. One may assume from this that the instrument was known to the ancient Egyptians by a name somewhere between *nafor*, *nofer*, and *nefur*, but not *nafír*, which was the name of the antique Arabian long trumpet.

LYRA; LYRE

A prehistoric instrument which has had enormous influence on the construction and development of stringed instruments through the ages. It was originally made from the horns of an antelope, across the top of which was attached a yoke from which a maximum of seven strings ran to the body of a tortoise-shell with a membrane stretched across the top. The lyra was probably the root of instruments such as the harp, and indeed of many instruments from all over the world which incorporated strings fixed directly on to an amplifying membrane. In Roman times orchestras consisting of many hundreds of lyra-players were assembled.

PSALTERY (see also Dulcimer)

Early Biblical references to the psaltery seem to be confused with a species of harp, an instrument with which its development was approximately contemporary. In its early forms the psaltery consisted of a shallow rectangular box across which usually about a dozen strings were stretched. These were plucked with a plectrum or the fingertips, the instrument being stood or held vertically. As it developed, the instrument acquired more strings and a triangular shape and came to be laid flat. Some species were played with hammers; this led to the invention of the pianoforte, on the way branching off into local varieties of psaltery such as the east European cymbalom. The plucked psaltery, on the other hand, led, with the development of mechanical plucking agents operated from a keyboard, to the harpsichord family. The Russian composer Barchunov has recently written a concerto for two psalteries and orchestra.

SPINET

Fr: *épinette*
It: *spinetta*
Ger: *Spinett*

The spinet, originally called 'clavicymbalum', dates from the start of the 15th century, but did not become widespread until the 17th; thereafter it co-existed with the harpsichord and clavichord until all three instruments gave way to the forte-piano towards the end of the 18th century. Opinions vary as to the origin of the name. It may be from the Lat: *spina*='spines'='quills', with which the strings were plucked, or from an Italian instrument-maker Giovanno Spinetti. It was an even more domestic instrument than the harpsichord and its comparatively simple construction encouraged amateur makers to design and build their own, often widely differing, models. The 'clavicytherium', also known as 'couched harp', was a type of upright spinet.

VIRGINALS

The name does not derive from the fact that the instrument was played by Queen Elizabeth I since it was known as that before her birth. It comes instead from the Lat: *virga*='rod'='jack', the rod which carried the quill past the string. Popular in England from the time of the first printed music for the instrument (*Parthenia*, 1611), its use paralleled that of the harpsichord and spinet and like the latter it possessed only one string to each note. Although exceptions existed, the easiest way to remember the basic difference in playing position relative to the instruments is to imagine the strings as viewed from the player running across from right to left in the viRginaLs, but away, or from south to north, in the SpiNet.

Aquaphone

This category does not appear in Curt Sachs's study; it has been found necessary here to institute it to accommodate just one instrument, the 'glass harmonica'; this, by its very oddness, refuses to fit into any of the other four categories. Considerable modification has taken place to the materials used in its construction, so it cannot be classed as an idiophone; there are no strings or air columns to vibrate, thus ruling out chordophone and aerophone classes; and there are no membranes.

The 20th-century virtuoso of the glass harmonica, Bruno Hoffmann, shown here playing a collection of rum glasses. (Popperfoto)

GLASS HARMONICA

Also known as the 'euphon' and 'clavicylindre', the glass harmonica was a product of the imagination and sensitivity of the 18th century. Basically, the principle stems from the idea of producing notes from glasses or tumblers which are tuned by being filled to different levels with water. 'Musical glasses' were performed by the Irishman Richard Pockrich in London in 1743 (in 1759 he was burned to death in a fire which also engulfed his glass-and-water instrument). In 1746 Gluck played 'a concerto on 26 drinking glasses tuned with spring water' at the Haymarket Theatre in London, although it is not recorded whether the work was adapted or specifically written for the new instrument, nor by whom.

Benjamin Franklin, often given the credit for inventing the glass harmonica, merely adapted existing principles when he completed his instrument in 1763. The glasses, fitted one in another, were half submerged in water and were rotated by a treadle, the edges being activated by wetted fingertips.

Much value was put on the ethereal sound thus produced. It was said to have magical soothing qualities, and the Swiss composer Franz Xaver Joseph Peter Schnyder von Wartensee wrote a descriptive piece entitled *Der durch Musik überwundene Wüterich* ('The Angry Man Calmed by Music') in about 1830, in which the volatile temper of the pianoforte is gradually calmed by the soothing ministrations of the glass harmonica. Saint-Saëns included the 'harmonica' in the 'Aquarium' movement of his *Carnival of the Animals*, Op 22 (1886): probably the glass harmonica was the instrument he required.

This century has seen the occasional use of water with conventional instruments. John Cage has modified the tone of gongs, for instance, by lowering them into a tub of water.

2. Orchestral instruments today

No attempt is made here to describe the construction or working of the instruments of the modern orchestra, apart from a table of the extreme upper and lower notes obtainable from each, since technical and constructional details may be obtained from numerous reference books.

What *is* attempted for each instrument is a brief note concerning its origin and, in order to pinpoint its 'acceptance' into so-called 'serious' music, the dates of its first use in the orchestra (concert or opera), its first true concerto, and its first use in the symphony. Usually, these appearances were preceded by the instrument's use in chamber or solo works, but as this field of intimate music-making is the proving ground for most instruments, the earliest uses often being undocumented and lost in antiquity, these particular origins have not been followed up, especially as the resulting details would be of little interest and no help in the understanding of the history of the instrument.

The grouping employed here is that of the modern orchestra: woodwind, brass, strings, percussion. Also included are the concert keyboard instruments (piano and organ) which lead a separate activity as well as being featured from time to time in the orchestra.

Woodwind

PICCOLO

It: *flauto piccolo; ottavino*
Fr: *petite flûte* Ger: *Kleine Flöte*

1. Prehistoric; via flute and sopranino recorder. The name is an abbreviation of It: *flauto piccolo*='little flute'.
2. Handel's *Water Music* (1717).
3. Vivaldi's three concertos, RV 443, RV 444, RV 445 (all before 1741)
4. Beethoven's Symphony No 5 in C minor, Op 67 (1805), last movement.
5. Arcady Dubensky, the Russian violinist and composer, wrote a capriccio for solo piccolo in 1948.

FLUTE

It: *flauto* Fr: *flûte* Ger: *Flöte*

1. Prehistoric; via recorder. Lat: *flatus*='breath' or 'blowing'. Alternative names, referring to the angle at which the instrument is played, are 'cross flute' and 'transverse flute':

   It: *flauto traverso* Fr: *flûte traversière* Ger: *Traversflöte; Querflöte*

2. Lully was the first specifically to call for the flute in 1672 in his operatic scores. All earlier, and many later, requests for 'flute' meant the then more usual recorder.
3. Vivaldi's *VI Concerti à Flauto Traverso* Op 10, printed by Le Cene, Amsterdam, in *c* 1729/30.
4. Alessandro Scarlatti's twelve symphonies (after 1715). These include one or two flutes in a

semi-soloistic capacity and, therefore, antedate Vivaldi's Op 10 (see above) by a decade or so. By 1750 the flute was being used coloristically, rather than as a solo instrument, in the symphonies of the Mannheim School (Fils, Jan Stamic, etc).
5. Henry Brant may be said to have composed the first 'exclusive' flute concerto: his *Angels and Devils* (1931) is for solo flute with an orchestra consisting of three piccolos, five flutes, and two alto flutes. In 1970 Zsolt Durkó (Hungarian) wrote a Concerto for twelve flutes and orchestra.

Modern oboe (right).

Modern clarinet (left).

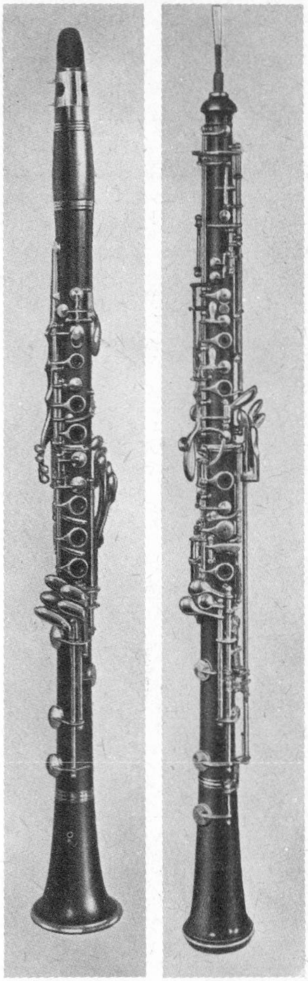

OBOE

It: *oboe* Fr: *hautbois* Ger: *Hoboe* or *Oboe*

1. Middle Ages; via the schalmey family. The name comes from Fr: *hautbois*='loud wood'.
2. Lully's ballet *L'amour malade* (1657)
3. Marcheselli (1708), but the instrument was used in solo and duet in the symphonies of Torelli before the end of the 17th century.
4. Torelli: several symphonies, eg: G 31.

CLARINET

It: *clarinetto* Fr: *clarinette* Ger: *Klarinette*

1. Invented by J C Denner (1655–1707) during the last decade of the 17th century; via the recorder and schalmey families. The name means literally 'little clarino', since early examples had a tone similar to that of a trumpet.
2. Vivaldi's oratorio *Juditha Triumphans*, RV 644 (1716). Handel's *Riccardo Primo* of 1726–27 contains two clarinet parts written for August Freudenfeld and Franz Rosenberg.
3. Vivaldi's RV 559 and 560 (before 1741). In 1742 in Dublin, a Mr Charles played a (solo?) clarinet concerto which is unidentified and may have been an arrangement from a work for a different instrument.
4. In 1753 the Concerts Spirituel in Paris included symphonies by Jan Stamic with clarinets replacing the oboe parts; three such works were published by Bayard in Paris in 1755–60.
5. The principal differences between clarinet and oboe, both of which occupied much the same range in the early years of the former's development, are that the oboe is of the double-reed family of conical bore, while the clarinet family possess a single reed and are cylindrical in bore.

Key
1. Origin (with name derivation if known).
2. First use in the orchestra.
3. First true concerto.
4. First use in the symphony.
5. Additional facts.

NAMES AND FREQUENCIES OF NOTES

The system used is the standard one based on the piano keyboard for easy reference, taking the note C at 261·6 cps as 'middle C'. In this system, the octave middle C to the B above serves as a reference upon which the upper and lower octaves depend. The C above middle C is noted as C′ (ie the first C above middle C), the next as C″, and so on. Octaves below middle C are noted as C, to B, and C,, to B,, and so on.

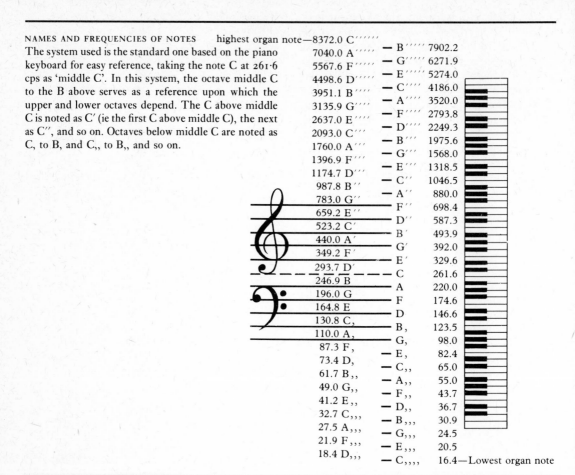

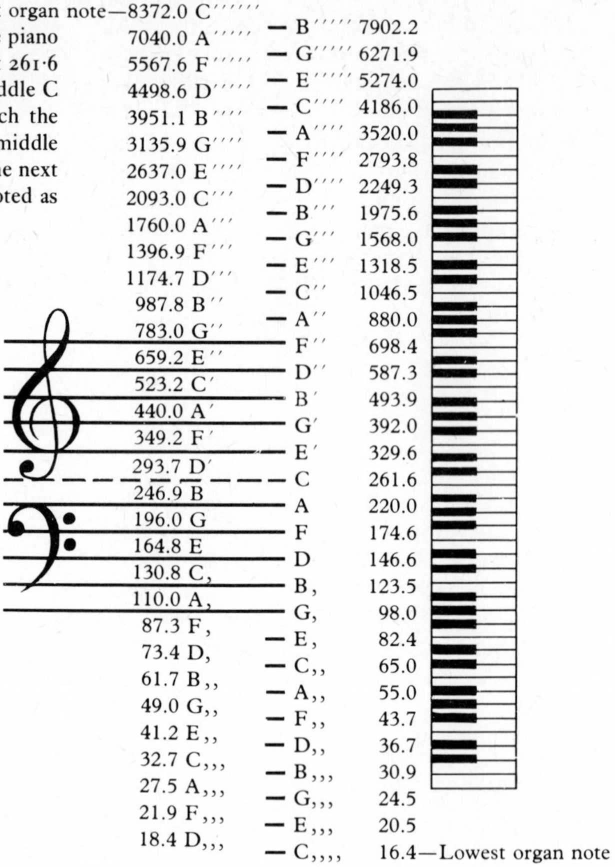

Highest and lowest notes of familiar modern instruments.

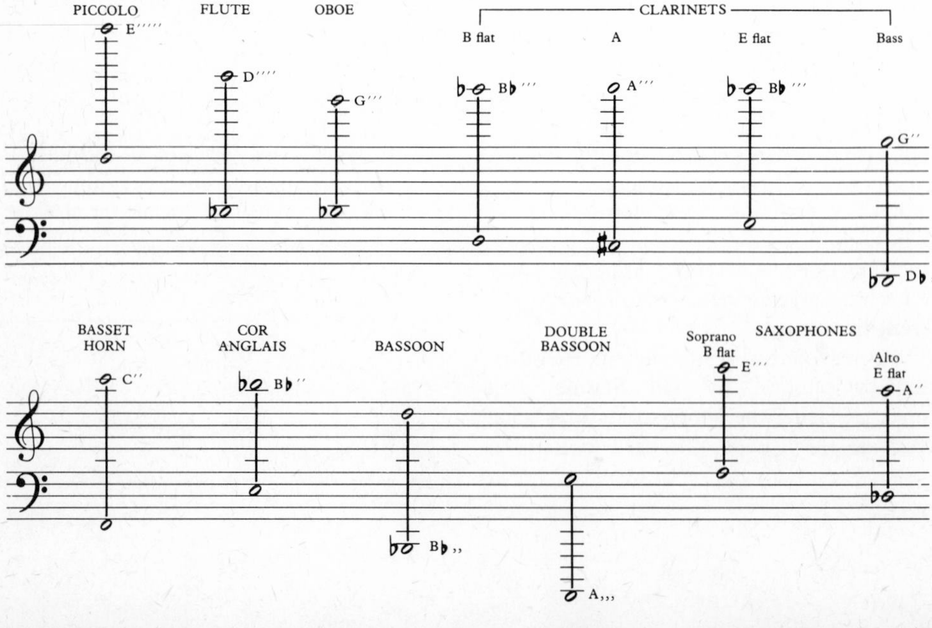

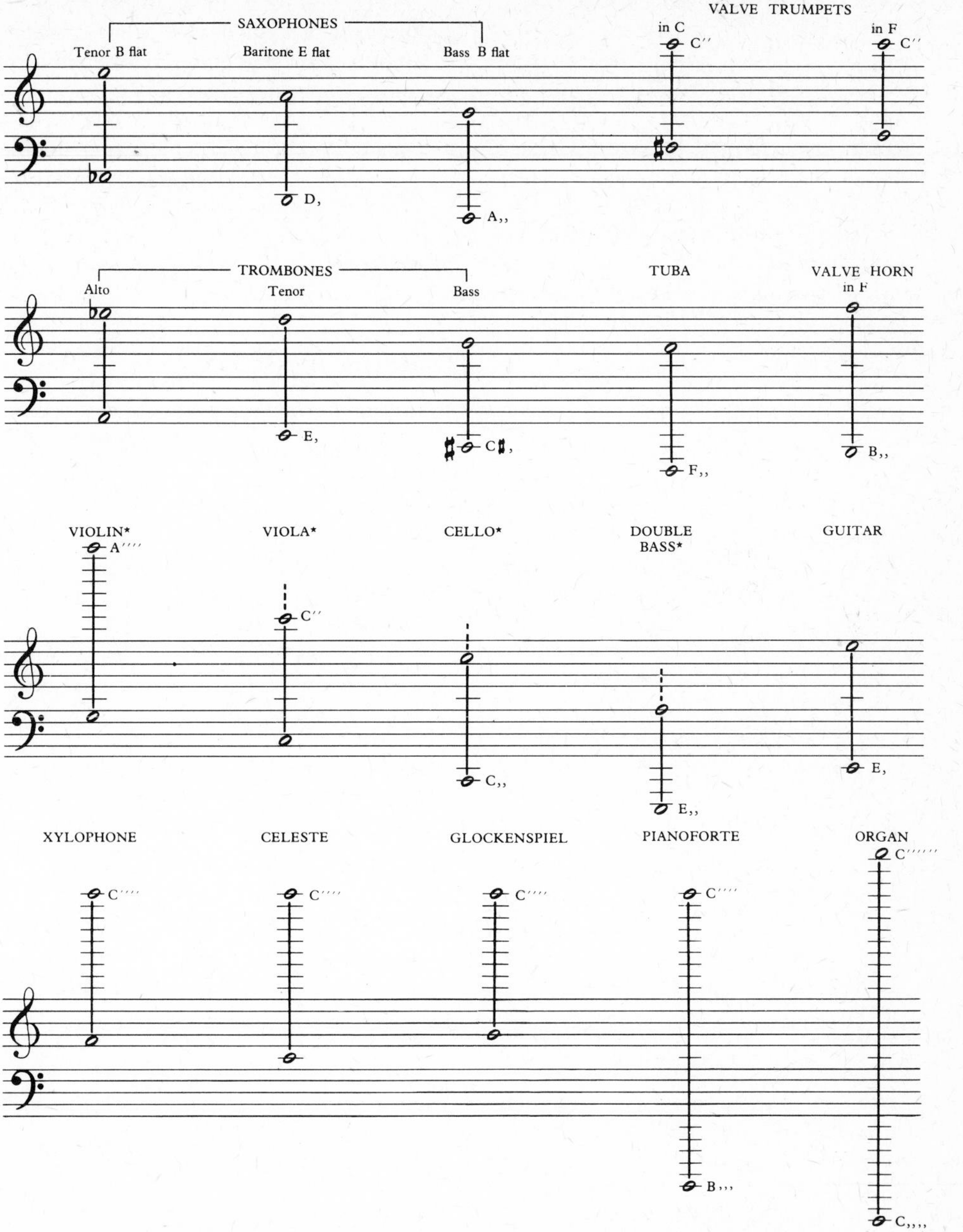

TIMPANI are notated in the bass clef at actual pitch, the tuning being indicated at the start of the piece; changes of tuning during a work are indicated by a direction in the score: for example, *change C to C♯*, or *muta C in C♯*.

The normal extremes of range are

*The purity and quality of extreme upper notes on bowed stringed instruments depends upon the skill of the players, and may be several tones higher than those shown for viola, cello, and double bass. The usual upper extreme of the violin is given as B''' (1975·6), but an extension up to F'''' (2793·8) is not unusual today. Tchaikovsky's Violin Concerto requires the soloist to reach A'''' (3520·0), but in bar 6 of the Finale (*Passacaglia*) of his Violin Concerto Op 15 of 1939, Benjamin Britten calls for B'''' (3951·1) from the soloist.

The first clarinet virtuoso was Joseph A Beer (1744–1811), whose two clarinet concertos were written *c*1780, at about the time he became a member of the Berlin Hofkapelle. He was an associate of Carl Stamitz, who also composed a number of clarinet concertos. The development of the clarinet family had reached such perfection by the beginning of the 20th century that a performance of Mozart's Symphony No 40 in G Minor, K 550, could be given at the Brussels Conservatory in which all parts, in their correct registers, were taken by varieties of clarinet.

ENGLISH HORN

It: *corno inglese* Fr: *cor anglais* Ger: *Englisches Horn*

1. Purcell wrote for a 'tenor oboe', but the first reference to a cor anglais is in Vienna in the 1760s. The origin of the name is obscure, but it may refer to the instrument's bent shape: 'angled horn'.
2. As 1, above.
3. J M Haydn: lost. Paganini: *c* 1805: lost. The earliest extant concertante work is Donizetti's Concertino in G (*c* 1820).
4. Haydn's Symphony No 22 in E flat, 'Philosopher' (1764).

BASSOON

It: *fagotto* Fr: *basson* Ger: *Fagott*

1. Italy, about 1540, introduced as the lowest of the double-reed group and known as the *dulzian*. The name 'bassoon' comes from It: *bassone*='big bass'.
2. Early 17th century.
3. Vivaldi wrote some 38 bassoon concertos, none of which is easy to date. All were composed before 1741 (Vivaldi's death date), but it is not possible to state whether any antedate Boismortier's Op 26 (1730) which includes a bassoon concerto.
4. End of the 17th century. Although not usually specified at this time, the bassoon was employed as a part of the continuo in orchestral music from early days.
5. Johann Ernst Galliard wrote a so-called 'sonata' for 24 bassoons and four double bassoons. It was performed at Lincoln's Inn Fields Theatre, London, in 1745. Concertos for the instrument are still being written, as the recent examples by Peter Hodgson and by Helmut Eder (1968) illustrate.

Key
1. Origin (with name derivation if known).
2. First use in the orchestra.
3. First true concerto.
4. First use in the symphony.
5. Additional facts.

DOUBLE BASSOON

It: *contrafagotto* Fr: *contre basson* Ger: *Kontrafagott*

1. Its development and use followed closely after those of the bassoon. It appeared in Berlin in 1620.
2. Handel introduced it to England from the Continent for special effects in opera and oratorio.
3. Henk Badings produced a concerto for bassoon and double bassoon with wind orchestra, and Ruth Gipps's *Leviathan* is scored for double bassoon and orchestra.
4. Beethoven's Symphony No 5 in C minor, Op 67 (1805).
5. Haydn used the instrument to good effect in his oratorio *The Creation* (1797/98).

SAXOPHONE

It: *sassofono* Fr: *saxophone* Ger: *Saxophon*

1. Invented by Adolphe Sax (hence the name) in about 1840, and patented in Paris six years later.
2. J G Kastner's oratorio *The Last King of Judah* (1844).
3. Debussy's *Rhapsody* (1903); Holbrooke's Concerto (1928).
4. R Strauss's *Domestic Symphony* (1904).

Brass

TRUMPET

It: *tromba* Fr: *trompette* Ger: *Trompete*

1. Prehistoric; used as a signalling and warlike instrument from the beginnings of human aware-

ness when wooden or animal horns were blown to attract attention. Our name for the instrument has considerable antiquity; it may be of onomatopoeic origin.

2. Trumpets were a part of the very earliest orchestras and, until the 18th century, they virtually dictated the development of orchestral groups and the music played on religious and ceremonial occasions.
3. Cazzati, in 1665. Although his works were called 'sonatas', they are in fact concertos for solo trumpet and orchestra.
4. Torelli, before 1700. Many of the works written for the San Petronio Cathedral in Bologna by Torelli and his associates were entitled 'sinfonia', 'sonata', or 'concerto' virtually indiscriminately. Therein, the trumpets were used soloistically. Non-solo parts appeared in symphonies at Mannheim and elsewhere in the 1740s.
5. The keyed trumpet dates from 1796, and Haydn's famous Trumpet Concerto of that year was written for it; the valve trumpet appeared in 1835 and was first used in Halévy's opera *La Juive* in the same year. The first sonatas for trumpet and continuo were published by Fantini, together with his trumpet instruction book, in 1638. The earliest work for clarino trumpet was a 'method' by Cesare Bendinelli, published in 1614 with his *Tutta l'arte delle Trombetta.* Modern trumpet concertos have been composed by Arutyunyan (1950) and Raymond Hanson (1952), and there is one for two trumpets by Desmond Macmahon.

HORN

It: *corno* Fr: *cor* Ger: *Horn*

1. Prehistoric. The development of the horn is so inextricably bound up with that of the trumpet that names, uses, and shapes have been frequently confused and were often indistinguishable. The word 'horn' may be onomatopoeic in origin, but the instrument's origin as the prepared horn from the head of an animal must not be overlooked.
2. Cavalli's opera *Le Nozze di Teti e di Peleo* (1639).
3. Vivaldi: there are two concertos for two horns, RV 538 and RV 539, but as their dates are not known they may have been antedated by J S Bach's Brandenburg Concerto No 1 in F, BWV 1046 (between 1717 and 1721), which also employed a pair of horns. The first concertos for a solo horn were probably the five of Op 4, published in London in 1742, by Hasse, and played in Dublin that year (but see 5, below).
4. Torelli, before 1700: G 37. The two horns in this work are used for orchestral colour, without solo parts.
5. Mattheson reports that there was a blind travelling horn-player in Hamburg in 1713 and that he 'produced more tones than an organ but with less mathematical precision'. This report indicates the possibility of hand-stopping as early as 1713, and hints that there may have been solo horn concertos for this player to perform at this date. Perhaps Telemann's D major Horn Concerto was composed as early as this. A pair of silver, valveless hunting-horns made by Johannes Leicham Schneider in Vienna in 1775 was sold at Christie's in Geneva in 1976 for £9500.

TROMBONE

It: *trombone* Fr: *trombone* Ger: *Posaune*

1. In 14th-century Spain and England, developed from the Roman *buccina* (a trumpet with a slide). The word 'trombone' is an augmentation of the name *tromba* (Italian for 'trumpet'). The Old English word 'sackbut' for trombone comes from the 15th-century French *sacqueboute*='pull-push'.
2. Used in 17th century as part of the bass line, especially in church music.
3. Wagenseil's Concerto in E flat (*c* 1760?).
4. The symphonies of Torelli come into the category as described in 2, above. Beethoven's famous use of the trombone in the finale of his Fifth Symphony (1805) is antedated by the Symphony in D (*c* 1773) by Joseph Starzer, the scoring of which includes alto, tenor, and bass trombones.
5. Anton Adam Bachschmidt (1705/9–*c* 1780) was a trombone virtuoso who lived in Eichstädt. He may have been the earliest instrumentalist to

specialise in the trombone. The instrument is still receiving attention as a solo instrument, as a recent concerto by Ian Parrott testifies. Nielsen's Flute Concerto (1926) has an important part for bass trombone.

TUBA

It: *tuba* Fr: *tuba* Ger: *Tuba* or *Basstuba*

1. Developed about 1829 and patented in 1835 in Berlin. The word comes from the Roman name for the long, straight trumpet.
2. Berlioz's *Symphonie Fantastique* (1830), in which it takes the part of the obsolescent ophicleide.
3. Vaughan Williams' concerto, written for a London Symphony Orchestra Jubilee Concert at London's Royal Festival Hall on 13 June 1954. Philip Catelinet was the soloist and Sir John Barbirolli the conductor. Derek Bourgeois: Bass-tuba Concerto.
4. As 2, above.
5. The English composer John White has written a symphony for organ and six tubas, and a work lasting three and a half hours entitled *Cello and Tuba Machine* (1968), and in 1967 Walter Hartley wrote a Tuba Sonata, Op 76. In the Hoffnung Music Festival Concert held in the Royal Festival Hall, London, on 13 November 1956, Chopin's A minor Mazurka Op 68/2 was played by Gerard Hoffnung himself and members of the Morley College Symphony Orchestra in an arrangement by Daniel Abrams for four tubas.

Strings

VIOLIN

It: *violino* Fr: *violon* Ger: *Violine; Geige* (the old German name for 'rebec')

1. The Welsh *crwth* developed from the lyre in the 1st century BC, and in turn evolved gradually into the viol family. Successive modifications, through the *lyra da braccio*, brought the violin to its modern form in northern Italy around 1505. The word 'violin' comes ultimately from Lat: *vitulari* ('to be joyful', 'to skip like a calf'), through Lat: *vitula* (the root of 'fiddle'), Middle English 'viel', and 'viol', thence 'viola', the diminutive of which is 'violin'=a small viola.
2. Since its introduction in the early 16th century, the violin, after an uncertain half-century of competition with the older viols, has been the stand-by of the orchestra.
3. Torelli: Op 8, Nos 7–12, published in Bologna in 1709, but written perhaps a few years earlier. Torelli's Op 8 also contains the earliest concertos for two violins (Nos 1–6).
4. See 2, above.
5. The best-known violin-maker was Antonio Stradivari (*c* 1644–1737), pupil of Amati and teacher of Bergonzi, Guarneri, and others. The first great composer/virtuoso of the violin was Arcangelo Corelli (1653–1713).

VIOLA

It: *viola* Fr: *alto* Ger: *Bratsche*

1. Similar to the development of the violin.
2. As for violin.
3. Telemann (probably before 1721).
4. As for violin, but solo parts were included in Mozart's Sinfonia Concertante in E flat, K 364 (1779), and in Berlioz' symphony *Harold in Italy*, Op 16 (1834).
5. Benjamin James Dale wrote an Introduction and Andante for six viole in 1911.

CELLO (This is the accepted English abbreviation for 'violoncello')

It: *violoncello* Fr: *violoncelle* Ger: *Violoncello*

1. Developed alongside the other members of the violin group. The name 'violoncello' means literally 'small violone': see Double bass, below.
2. As for violin.
3. Corelli: in his concerti grossi, Op 6, published in 1715 but written many years earlier, the solo cello supports two solo violins. Jacchini wrote the first solo cello concerti in 1701.
4. As for violin.
5. Helmut Eder wrote *Melodia-Ritmica* in 1974 for twelve cellists of the Berlin Philharmonic Orchestra.

The New String Family. A full-size standard lamp on the right gives an idea of scale. Under a portrait of Geminiani the new instruments are ranged as follows: on the table from *l* to *r*: treble, descant, sopranino; on the floor from *l* to *r*: tenor, alto, baritone, contrabass and bass. (Godfrey New Photographics Ltd)

DOUBLE BASS

It: *contrabasso* Fr: *contre basse* Ger: *Kontrabass*

1. The development of the double bass followed the rest of the violin family, but stopped short, failing to oust the slope-shouldered configuration of the bass viol, known as the 'violone'. The name 'double bass' is functional: the instrument is designed to 'double' the 'bass' (ie cello) line.
2. As for violin.
3. Vaňhal's Concerto in E (*c* 1770?).
4. As for violin, but note also Dittersdorf's Sinfonia Concertante in D for viola and double bass, Kr 127 (*c* 1775), in reality a four-movement symphony with prominent solo parts for the string instruments.
5. Probably the earliest double bass virtuoso was Caspar Bohrer (1744–1809) who was also a trumpeter, but the most famous was undoubtedly Domenico Dragonetti (1763–1846), the Venetian-born player and composer for the instrument. The most spectacular works for the instrument are a fugue for four double basses (1939) by Dubensky, and *Quadrat* (1969) for the same group by Apergis. Franz Anton Hoffmeister wrote a quartet for double bass with string trio early in the 19th century, while the present century has seen the appearance of several works for the instrument, including sonatas by Ferenc Farkas and István Kardos, and a duo for two double basses by William Sydeman. Rodney Slatford, the English virtuoso bassist, knows of more than 200 concertos for double bass.

Key
1. Origin (with name derivation if known).
2. First use in the orchestra.
3. First true concerto.
4. First use in the symphony.
5. Additional facts.

THE NEW STRING FAMILY

The Catgut Acoustical Society of America, dissatisfied with the limitations of the string family listed above, proposed in 1958 a new family of eight instruments. They are treble, soprano, mezzo (=the standard violin), alto (a very large viola), tenor (slightly smaller than the standard cello), baritone, bass (approximately the same size as the standard double bass but without that instrument's sloping, 'viol', shoulders), and contrabass. The new family was shown in England in 1974, and a set is kept at the Royal College of Music, London. Frank Lewin and Henry Brant have composed music for the new octet.

HARP

It: *arpa* Fr: *harpe* Ger: *Harfe*

1. Possibly prehistoric and certainly pre-Egyptian in origin, it was well established in the Middle East by about 1200 BC and reached its present form by 1792. The word 'harp' probably derives from the plucking action of the fingers; compare Lat: *carpere* which is connected with harvest-time, the 'picking season'.
2. Incorporated from the earliest times in instrumental groups.
3. Handel's Organ Concerto in B flat, Op 4/6 (published in 1738), originally for the harp.
4. Berlioz' *Symphonie Fantastique*, Op 14 (1830).
5. Czerny wrote a *Konzertstück* for eight pianos and twelve harps.

Percussion

TRIANGLE

It: *triangolo* Fr: *triangle* Ger: *Triangel*

1. From Turkish military bands of antiquity. The name of the instrument, of course, describes the shape.
2. M Haydn's incidental music to *Zaire*, Per 13 (1777). However, orchestral inventories list the instrument in Hamburg in 1710 and in Dresden in 1717.
3. Mention should be made, in the absence of a concerto designed specifically for the triangle, of the use made by Paganini of the triangle in the third movement *La Campanella* of the Violin Concerto No 2 in B minor, Op 7 (1826), and in the corresponding movement of his Violin Concerto No 4 in D minor (1830).
4. Georg Glantz's 'Turkish' Symphony (1774).

CYMBALS

It: *piatti; cinelli* Fr: *cymbales* Ger: *Becken*

1. As for triangle. The name is derived possibly from the Gk: *kumbe*=cup.
2. Nicolaus Adam Strungk's opera *Esther* (1680).
4. Georg Glantz's 'Turkish' Symphony (1774).

SIDE DRUM OR SNARE DRUM

It: *tamburo militare*
Fr: *tambour militaire; caisse claire*
Ger: *kleine Trommel*

1. Descended from the earliest small drums of prehistory, via the military tabor of the Middle Ages. 'Side' refers to the fact that the drum is slung round the neck of the player on a strap and hangs against the hip; 'snares' are the wires running across the lower head of the drum.
2. Handel's *Musick for the Royal Fireworks* (1749). Marais is said to have used it in 1706.
3. Nielsen, in his Clarinet Concerto (1928) makes extensive use of a side drum as a solo instrument, as does Lopatnikov, the Estonian composer and pianist resident in the USA since 1939, in his Piano Sonata.
4. Grétry, in his multi-movement 'symphony' which acts as the overture to his opera *Le Magnifique* (1773).

KETTLE-DRUMS

It: *timpani* Fr: *timbales* Ger: *Pauken*

1. Originated in the ancient Orient. Originally the size of kettles, the instruments should nowadays perhaps be renamed 'cauldron drums'.

Key
1. Origin (with name derivation if known).
2. First use in the orchestra.
3. First true concerto.
4. First use in the symphony.
5. Additional facts.

2. Monteverdi's *Orpheo* (1607).
3. The 19th century saw many works (by Berlioz, Lesueur, etc) in which timpani are given important and prominent parts to play, but the first true concerto for timpani is that by Julius Tausch (*c* 1870). There is a report—so far unconfirmed—that a Timpani Concerto by Jiří Družecký (1745–1819) has been found recently in an East European archive.
4. Torelli's Symphony in C, G 33 (before 1700).
5. The earliest timpani parts which have survived outside the opera house are the two pairs in an anonymous Mass of 1682(?), formerly attributed to Orazio Benevoli. Berlioz used 16 kettle-drums in his *Requiem* (1837).

BASS DRUM

It: *gran casa* Fr: *grosse caisse* Ger: *grosse Trommel*

1. From Turkish military instrumental groups of antiquity.
2. Rameau's ballet héroïque *Zaïs* (1748).
4. Georg Glantz's *Turkish* Symphony (1774).

Occasional visitors to the orchestra

Where known, the origin or date of invention is given, together with the instrument's first, or earliest important, use.

WOODWIND

ALTO FLUTE This appeared in the 18th century as an extension of the flute family. Paul Felix von Weingartner used it in his opera *Die Gefilde der Seligen* (1915), as did Hans Pfitzner in *Palestrina* (1917).

BASS CLARINET First made in Paris in 1772; Meyerbeer's *Les Huguenots* (1838).

HECKELPHONE, a baritone oboe invented in 1903 by Wilhelm Heckel (after whom it is named) of Bierbach-am-Rhein; Richard Strauss' *Salome* (1905).

BRASS

EUPHONIUM is a tenor tuba in B flat, invented about 1840, possibly by Sommer of Weimar. Used mainly in brass bands. Joseph Horowitz has written a concerto for it.

FLÜGELHORNS, a group of instruments of varying sizes which appeared early in the 19th century. They feature extremely rarely in serious music, but Vaughan Williams employed one in his Symphony No 9 in E minor (1958).

POST-HORN, a simple straight trumpet-horn which announced the arrival of the mail-coach in the 16th to 18th centuries. Johann Beer wrote a concerto for post-horn in B flat, hunting-horn in F, and orchestra (*c* 1695).

WAGNER TUBA, first built in 1870 to specifications laid down by Richard Wagner and employed in that composer's *Ring* cycle of music dramas (1869–76). Bruckner and Richard Strauss have also used the instrument, as has Felix Draeseke in his *Symphonica Tragica*.

STRINGS

GUITAR, the national instrument of Spain, evolved in that country from the lute in the 16th-century and has been used in serious music and folk-music from that time. In addition to Rodrigo's popular *Concierto de Aranjuez* (1939), guitar concertos have been written by Henri Tomasi (1966), Castelnuovo Tedesco (1939), Stephen Dodgson (1956), and many others. The diminutive ukulele, which never appears in the orchestra, is of Portuguese origin.

MANDOLIN, a variety of lute which diverged substantially by the 18th century, when it became associated particularly with Naples. Vivaldi wrote a concerto for one mandolin (RV 425) and another for two (RV 532). Verdi used a mandolin in *Otello* (1887), and both Mahler and Schoenberg have scored for the instrument.

PERCUSSION

BELLS are more suited to the church belfry but have on occasion been used in the orchestra, eg: Dalayrac's opera *Camille* (1791), but their place is more commonly taken by **tubular bells,** which were first used by Sullivan and Stanford towards the end of the 19th century. The unforgettable bells in Tchaikovsky's *1812* Overture were originally intended to be those of the city of Moscow.

CASTANETS, from Sp: *castaña*='chestnut', the shells of which the instrument resembles in shape. Of Oriental origin, they came to Spain via Africa in the Middle Ages; there they settled as an instrument with which to accompany the dance; Bizet's *Carmen* (1875).

CELESTA, invented in Paris about 1880 by August Mustel. Widor, in his ballet *Der Korrigane* (1880), was the first to employ the celesta, but by far the best-known use is in the 'Dance of the Sugar Plum Fairy' in Tchaikovsky's ballet *The Nutcracker* (1882).

GLOCKENSPIEL (Ger: meaning 'bell-play') in the 18th century meant a structure of real bells struck by hammers operated from a keyboard, a development of a Roman instrument of the 4th century. Handel used such a device in his oratorio *Saul* (1739). A later version of the glockenspiel emerged in the 19th century, minus the keyboard, in which metal plates were struck by hand-held hammers; the name is now given to an instrument with a keyboard, but the metal plates are replaced by tubes, giving rise to the alternative name 'tubophone'. Wagner and others have scored for the glockenspiel.

GONG (TAM-TAM) Originating in the Far East, the gong attained popularity in France at the time of the Revolution; Gossec's *Funeral March on the Death of Mirabeau* (1791).

RATTLE. Rattles and scrapers had magical significance in primitive times and they remain standard equipment of tribal witch-doctors. Lepers were compelled to sound rattles as a warning of approach, and rattles warned of gas attack in wartime. Their use in the orchestra dates from Beethoven's 'Battle of Vittoria' Symphony, Op 91 (1812), where they imitate musket-fire.

Melior est MORS, quam VITA.
ECCLE. XXX.

'Dance of Death' by Hans Holbein—the earliest known picture of a xylophone. (Mary Evans Picture Library)

TAMBOURINE, of extreme antiquity, used in the time of the Romans at festivities. Clementi's Twelve Waltzes for piano and tambourine, Op 38 (1798).

TEMPLE BLOCKS, a wooden instrument in the shape of a skull, hit with a stick; Walton's *Façade* (1923).

XYLOPHONE (Gr: *xylon* = 'wood'; *phone* = 'sound'), developed from the simple two-slab signalling instrument of primitive peoples. The earliest known picture of the instrument is in *Dance of Death* (1523–25) by Hans Holbein, in which one skeleton plays while another dances. The Japanese composer Toshiro Mayuzumi has recently written a Xylophone Concertino.

Lumbye was the first to use it in his *Traumbilder* (1873), but the best-known use dates from the following year: Saint-Saëns' *Danse Macabre*.

MARIMBA, a species of xylophone which developed in Africa, in which gourds act as resonators.

A sophisticated development of the marimba is the **vibraphone**, invented in America (as vibra-harp) about 1910, but called by today's name only since 1927. Marimba concertos have been written by Akira Miyoshi (1969), Paul Creston (1940), and Mario Kuri Aldana (with wind orchestra); Oliver Nelson contributed a concerto for xylophone, marimba, vibraphone, and wind orchestra, and Vagn Holmboe wrote one for recorder, strings, vibraphone, and celesta.

WIND MACHINE, an invention of the early 20th century consisting of a rotating silk-covered cylinder rubbed by a pasteboard tongue; Richard Strauss' *Don Quixote* (1897).

WOOD (OR CHINESE) BLOCKS, a series of hollow wooden blocks similar to temple blocks, above, struck with a stick; Gershwin's Piano Concerto in F (1925).

Keyboard

ORGAN

The principle of the organ—one pipe to each note—extends back to the panpipes of antiquity. In the pre-Christian era the instrument had divided into a series of portative (ie portable, to be played on the march) and positive (ie also portable up to a point, but much heavier and played in a stationary position). Experiments were made with different methods of note production (eg the Roman water-organ, or *hydraulis*), but the organ did not achieve multiple keyboards or pedals until its integration into church services in the Middle Ages. The first full-time organ-builder was Albert van Os, who worked in the Netherlands during the 12th century, and the earliest music to be written specifically for the organ dates from two centuries later. The peak of organ composition came with the music of J S Bach early in the 18th century. Apart from oratorio and other liturgical works, the organ is rarely heard in the orchestra today; when it is, as in Saint-Saëns' Third Symphony (1886), it makes an unforgettable impact.

Handel produced a number of organ concertos, including one for two of the instruments, and the organ is still featured occasionally, as for instance in the Concerto (1938) by Poulenc and the three concertos (1947–8) by Siegfried Reda.

PIANOFORTE

The familiar pianoforte is a recent invention, reaching its modern perfection with the introduction of the iron frame in about 1859. Its origin, however, is found in the dulcimer of the Middle Ages, a levered mechanism replacing the dulcimer's manual hammers during the 14th century. Bartolomeo Christofori of Padua constructed **the first true pianoforte** in 1709. **The first printed music for the instrument**, 'Sonate da Cimbalo di piano, e forte dello volgarmente di martelletti' by Lodovico Giustini, appeared in Florence in 1732. However, the instrument first achieved popularity in London. On 16 May 1767 at Covent Garden Theatre in London, Charles Dibdin accompanied Miss Bickler in 'a favourite song' from T A Arne's oratorio *Judith* (1764) on the pianoforte: this is the **earliest known appearance of the instrument in public**. The first public piano solo was played in Dublin the following year by Henry Walsh, and a fortnight later in London—on 2 June 1768—J C Bach performed on the instrument. This composer's *Sei Concerti per il Cembalo o Piano e Forte* . . ., Op VII, dating from about 1776, are the first piano concertos.

This 18th-century dulcimer is an ancestor of today's pianoforte.

The first English works written specifically for pianoforte (without the expected 'or harpsichord or organ' alternatives) were the ten sonatas of John Burton, composed in 1766.

The first works in which harpsichord and fortepiano are set against each other, thus stressing the difference in tonal qualities, were composed in about 1780 by Heinrich Joseph Riegel. In 1740, C P E Bach had composed his Concerto in F, W 46, for two keyboard instruments and orchestra, often played today as a concerto for fortepiano and harpsichord, but in fact written for two harpsichords and orchestra. The same composer's Concerto in E flat, W 47, actually written for fortepiano and harpsichord, appeared in 1788.

The first upright pianos were manufactured

at Gera, Germany, by Christian Ernst Friederici in *c* 1770.

Attempts to sustain the tone of a struck piano string may be said to predate the invention of the instrument itself. The theory was put forward by Leonardo da Vinci in the 15th century that a 'mill' system would produce a sustained tone from any stringed instrument; this device is found in the hurdy-gurdy. In 1789, Schnell's 'Anemo-corde' vibrated the strings by a jet of air, and Hawkins produced an instrument employing rapidly repeating hammers in 1800.

Miscellaneous

ACCORDION AND CONCERTINA The accordion was invented in 1822 by Friedrich Buschmann of Berlin, who called it 'Handäoline'. Larger instruments are equipped with a keyboard and are called 'piano accordions'. Pietro Deiro and Roy Harris have produced concertos for the accordion; Roberto Gerhard included it in his Concerto for Eight Instruments without orchestra; there are concertos by Jindrich Feld (1975) and Paul Creston (Op 75, 1958); and it appears in Joseph Schillinger's *North Russian Symphony* (1931).

The main difference between the accordion and the concertina, which was invented in 1829 by Sir Charles Wheatstone, is that, on the depression of one key, the accordion will produce two different notes as the instrument is drawn, then pressed, while the concertina produces only one note for both actions. Further, the concertina is never equipped with a keyboard. Serious compositions have been written for the concertina, including concertos by Giulio Regondi, its first virtuoso, and Wilhelm Bernard Molique; and Tchaikovsky's Suite No 2, Op 53, of 1884, includes parts for four concertinas. Matyás Seiber wrote a work entitled *Spring* for accordion orchestra.

ONDES MARTENOT Invented in 1928 by Maurice Martenot and originally known as 'ondes musicales'. The sound is produced by the movement of the hand in relation to a vibration-sensitive metal rod attached to amplifying equipment: the nearer the hand, the higher the note. The first work to incorporate the instrument was Dimitri Levidi's *Poème Symphonique* (1928). Concerts with as many as eight of the instruments have been given, and a Concerto for ondes Martenot was composed by Jolivet in 1934; it is also given a part in Messiaen's *Turangalîla-Symphonie* of 1948.

HARMONIUM The cheap and simple development of the organ has drawn only slight attention from serious composers, among them César Franck, Karg-Elert, and Lefébre-Wély. Dvořák included it in a handful of chamber works, and Mahler incorporated it in his Eighth Symphony (1907). It was invented in Paris by G J Grenié in the 1830s, when it was called 'orgue expressif'. Alexandre François Debain developed it into the harmonium we recognise today. Iain Stinson and John Whiteley set up a harmonium-playing marathon record of 72 hours on 6–9 January 1970 in Surrey, England.

UNCONVENTIONAL PLAYING METHODS

There has always been an element of experimentation in instrumental techniques: the virtuoso violinist, for instance, might force an increase in the range of tone and effect available from his violin, creating new virtuoso boundaries and adding to the store of playing techniques for the benefit of future virtuosi. Not so legitimate, perhaps, are the weird uses to which some instruments have been put in order to create certain effects, uses which sometimes verge on abuses.

The violin has been subjected to much attention by experimenters. *Scordatura*, ie the deliberate mistuning of one or more of the strings, seems to have been specifically called for first by Biber about 1674 in his so-called 'Rosary Sonatas'. The effect has also been used by Vivaldi, Haydn, Paganini, Mahler, and has been extended to other members of the string group by Schumann and Kodály (cello), Wagner (double bass), and many others. *Col legno*, literally 'with the wood', directs that the bow should be played upside-down, with the wood in contact with the strings. Biber was the first to employ this effect also, in the first movement of his *Battalia*, a descriptive sonata (1673); Haydn also used it in the slow movement of his Symphony No 67 in F (*c* 1778), but the best-known example occurs in 'Mars', the first movement of Holst's *The Planets*, Op 32 (1914–16).

Among other unusual playing techniques is the strong pizzicato, in which the strings are plucked so violently that they rebound against the belly of the instrument with a snap. Once again Biber was responsible for inventing the effect to imitate musket-shot in *Battalia*; Bartók used the device tellingly in his String Quartet No 3 (1927), and other composers (eg Shostakovich) have followed.

In Rossini's Overture *Il Signor Bruschino* (1813) the violinists are instructed to tap their lampshades or music stands with their bows, and in George Crumb's *Songs, Drones and Refrains of Death* (1968) the violinist is required to slacken the hairs of the bow to produce a weak, disembodied sound.

Yet again it is Biber who has the distinction of introducing another string effect, this time for the bass viol: he placed sheets of thick paper between the strings so that, when they were bowed normally, the instrument produced a dry, crackling sound, as of boots marching to a military drum, in *Battalia*. Much later, Richard Strauss directed that the double bass, the bass viol's successor, should be bowed *below* the bridge in *Salome* (1905) to represent the death-rattle of Jokanaan.

The 'slap-bass' technique of rhythmic playing is well known in jazz circles and has been used by Charles Ives (who described the effect with vivid humour as 'con fistiswatto'). In *Labyrinth 3*, Lou Harrison asks for the strings of the double bass to be hit with mallets.

Rodion Shchedrin, the modern Russian composer, has brought a lively imagination to bear on orchestral technique: in his Concerto for Orchestra (1959) he requires the horn-players to 'pop' their instrument by slapping the mouth of the bell with the flat of the hand. The same work calls for a piano in which paper is placed under the dampers to produce a nasal sound in imitation of a balalaika.

Chords from a solo horn have been asked for by a number of composers, the earliest possibly being Weber in his Horn Concertino in E minor, J 188 (1806). Four-part chords are produced in the following manner: the player blows one note conventionally but simultaneously hums another, usually lower, note, thus producing two tones. From the difference between these notes another tone emerges (the 'difference tone'), and a sum of the two basic frequencies produces a fourth tone at the top (the 'resultant tone').

Robert Watts's *Duet for Tuba* requires that coffee and cream be served from two of the instrument's spit-valves.

Percussion has always been a favourite area for experimentation, the imaginations of Beethoven, Lesueur, Berlioz, Nielsen, and Stravinsky among many others bestowing upon the 'kitchen department' a rich supply of invention. Berlioz, for instance, required that the bass drum be laid flat so that percussionists might play it in the manner of timpani, and Nielsen called for the timpani to be struck with birch twigs in the slow movement of his Symphony No 2, *The Four Temperaments* (1902), a usage which calls to mind the effect produced by birch rods on the bass drum in the 'Janissary [Turkish] Music' in Mozart's *Il Seraglio* (1782). Other effects too numerous to detail in a general book of this nature include the placing of objects such as coins and chains on timpani heads and striking suspended cymbals with items as diverse as sponges and spanners.

Probably the most serious abuse has been reserved for the noble pianoforte. An interesting early example occurs in Bernard Vignerie's *Battle of Maringo* in 1802. At points indicated in the score the player is requested to represent cannon-shots by stretching both hands flat over the lower three octaves of the keyboard and banging down to sound every note simultaneously. Many modern composers have directed that the strings should be played directly (first, perhaps, in 1923, in Henry Cowell's *Aeolian Harp*), bypassing the keyboard, by such objects as finger-nails, nail files, combs, carpenters' hammers, spoons, brushes, etc, and by 'preparing' the piano in various ways in order to modify the tone. Mauricio Kagel, in *Transition II* (1959), requires two pianists to play entirely upon the inside of the instrument with drumsticks and other weapons, and in *Und so weiter* ... (1975) Luc Ferrari, in addition to amplifying the tones electronically and mixing them with quadraphonic tape sounds, instructs that billiard balls and other objects be placed on the strings and soundboard; and the soprano in David Bedford's *Music for Albion Moonlight* (1965) screams the word 'Hell' into the interior of a piano to make the strings resonate, while milk bottles are applied direct to the strings in the same composer's *Come In Here Child* (1968).

Among *avant-garde* composers these excesses are by now so common that they have moved out of the category of 'unusual use'. John Cage has written a full-scale concerto for prepared piano; and to prove that other keyboard instruments are not immune from such treatment, Hermann Rechberger includes ten prepared glockenspiels in his children's piece *Mobile 4* (1977).

Unusual treatment of instruments does not always result in abuse, but at the opposite extreme consideration may sometimes be said to go too far. LaMonte Young, for instance, wrote his *Piano Piece for David Tudor No 1* in 1960, the instructions for a performance of which are as follows:

'Bring a bale of hay and a bucket of water onto the stage for the piano to eat and drink. The performer may then feed the piano or leave it to eat by itself. If the former, the piece is over after the piano has been fed. If the latter, it is over after the piano eats or decides not to.'

Finally, note should be made of a piece of experimental music in which the performers have to operate their 'instruments' by remote control from a distance of at least 9 ft 9 in (3 m). It is *Distance* (1962) by Ichiyanagi. Michael Nyman reports a performance in which the object was to produce the sound of fizzing liver-salts. A lighted cigarette was fitted in the end of a long tube and was then brought into contact with a row of matches lined up on a long board. When the player inhaled, the first match flared and the fire ran along the matches until meeting a balloon at the end of the board. The balloon was filled with water which, when the balloon burst, fell into a bucket in which the liver-salts waited. The resulting fizz was collected by contact microphones attached to the bucket and relayed to the audience.

3. Instruments of unusual interest

At the end of the previous subsection (2. Orchestral Instruments Today) we discussed some of the many odd actions which players are directed to carry out in order to produce unusual effects from their instruments. Instrument-builders, too, have frequently allowed free rein to their imaginations. Results have been varied: to the inventors have been brought sometimes the unique effects they sought, sometimes merely a certain notoriety, and frequently a few polite smiles.

Firstly in this subsection are discussed the freak designs which often were built in quantity to satisfy some fashion or fad, and the closing part describes some of the unique instruments which have graced—and sometimes embarrassed—musical history. The order of each part is alphabetical since a grouping together of types would serve little purpose.

AEOLIAN HARP

Imagine a rectangular frame across which are stretched a number of strings all tuned to the same note. This device is then stood in a breeze and the strings vibrate in the passage of air. As the strength of the wind increases, overtones emerge from some of the strings to combine with the basic notes, producing a weird, unearthly, disembodied sound. This type of instrument, a mongrel somewhere between aerophones and chordophones, existed at the dawn of history: King David is said to have owned one. During the 19th century the instrument was fitted with a keyboard which controlled shutters to direct the wind on to certain strings at will, the strings by now being tuned to various notes, but the indefinite attack of the notes made the aeolian harp, the name of which commemorates Aeolus, the wind god, unsuitable for serious music, and it remains a curiosity but one of considerable charm.

BAGPIPE

The bagpipe originated in prehistoric times, possibly in the Middle East or China as an 'external' version of the multiple-pipe aulos. The player's cheeks of the latter were replaced by a bag of air squeezed under the arm and the chanter and drone pipes equated with those of the aulos. The bag was originally made of the skin of a lamb or goat, minus the hindquarters; air is introduced into the bag via a pipe, either from the player's mouth or from bellows operated under the player's other arm. By the 13th century bagpipes of many different varieties were widespread in Europe and Asia, and soon they began to be made in different sizes.

The 'elbow pipes' (Ir: *uilleann*, later corrupted to 'union pipes') appeared in Ireland in the 16th century, and it is this type which found favour with the French in the *cornemuse* of that period.

The main modern difference between Irish and Scottish pipes is that the former has three drones, the latter two, in addition to chanter and 'breather'.

Although considered primarily as a pastoral instrument and as such often imitated in musical works dealing with the birth of Christ, the bagpipe also has connections with military endeavours in conjunction with drums; this use dates only from the 18th century. The Gurkha pipe bands of Nepal to this day strike terror into the hearts of friend and foe alike.

A representation by Albert Dürer of a bagpipe, one of the most widespread of primitive instruments. (Victoria and Albert Museum)

ALTERNATIVE NAMES FOR THE BAGPIPE

askaulos	Ancient Greek
biniou	French; mouth-filled and operated by two players
Blâterpfîfe	Ancient German, = 'bladder-pipe'
cabrette	French; bellows-filled
chorus	Early English name also sometimes applied to the crwth
cornamúsa	Italian; mouth-filled
cornemuse	French; mouth-filled
Dudelsack	German: to play an instrument badly (from 17th century) and also from the onomatopoeic word dudel(dum)dei; perhaps from the Polish name *dudy* + sack
dudy	Polish and Czech, with a single chanter
dutka	Romanian; mouth-filled
elbow-pipes	Irish. See *uilleann*
gaida or gayda	Bulgarian; primitive mouth-filled
gaita gallega	North-west Spanish; bellows-filled
koza	Polish; bellows-filled
loure	From the Normandy region of France
masak	Hindustani
moshug	North Indian
musette	French; bellows-filled
piffero or piffaro	Italian; bellows-filled and with a single chanter (cf *zampogna*). The name is also sometimes given to the Italian rustic oboe which often accompanies the *zampogna*
piva	North Italian; mouth-filled
Platterspiel	German, = 'bladder-play' (cf *Blâterpfîfe*)
Sackpfeife	German, = 'bagpipe'
Sachphîfe	Ancient German
s'ruti	Southern Indian
tibia utricularis	Ancient Roman, = 'skin-flute'
uilleann pipe	Irish, bellows-filled, and fitted under the arm, to be squeezed by the elbow (uilleann)
union pipe	Irish; corruption of 'uilleann pipe'
zampogna	Italian; mouth-filled, with two chanters
zampoña	Spanish, bellows-filled
zampouna	Modern Greek

Uses were made of the musette by Lully in some of his opera scores in the late 17th century, and Leopold Mozart wrote a concerto (1755) for bagpipe and hurdy-gurdy, with string orchestra. In

1773 Michael Haydn wrote a symphony in C, the scoring of which includes two 'pifferi' whose parts may be taken by two cors anglais or two bassoons (Per 10). Vlastimir Nikolovski has written a symphony (1970) in which a bagpipe is heard.

BARYTON

Now obsolescent, this six-stringed bass gamba, sometimes with as many as 40 sympathetic strings which could be plucked with the left thumb, came into prominence in the mid-18th century when it was adopted by Prince Nicolaus Esterházy, the employer of Joseph Haydn. The composer produced numerous works for the instrument, including twelve divertimenti, 126 trios, 24 duos, and two concertos. However, Haydn was not the first composer to write for the instrument: Johann Georg Krause composed baryton music as early as 1704, and there is evidence that the instrument existed for a century or so before that.

CHROMOMELODEON

An instrument invented by Harry Partch in Chicago in 1942. In appearance it is like a harmonium, but it produces a 43-tone scale also invented by Partch.

DACTYLOMONOCORDO

A single-stringed instrument to be played by one finger, invented by one Guida of Naples in about 1877.

HARDANGER FIDDLE

A Norwegian folk-instrument named after the district from which it originated in the 16th century. The earliest surviving example (dated 1651) is preserved in the Bergen Museum. The instrument developed from early Norwegian fiddles such as the *gigja* and *fidla*, and from the viola d'amor.

Its four strings cross a bridge which is less arched than that of a normal violin, making the production of multiple stopping an easy task for the players who make a speciality of highly embellished and harmonised variants to the basic dances for which the instrument is mainly used. Among these dances are the *halling*, *springar*, and *gangar*. Four or five sympathetic strings of wire lie below the played strings.

There exists a concerto for the instrument and several concert works by Geirr Tveitt and Eivind Groven.

HURDY-GURDY

The 10th century saw the introduction of the coarse and complicated hurdy-gurdy, also known as *symphonia* and *organistrum*. The strings were set in vibration from below by a resined wheel which was cranked by hand, and the strings were stopped by tangents operated through a keyboard. Of course, all the strings were sounded together by this mechanism (*Symphonia*='sounding together'; this is also the Greek root of the musical form 'symphony': see Section IV) and no variation could be produced in the quality or amplitude of the sound. These limitations eventually outweighed the advantages of sheer volume which the hurdy-gurdy possessed at country-dance festivals, and during the Middle Ages the instrument, originally regarded as of high class, sank to the level of the street musician and the beggar. In the 18th century the tendency was for the instrument to improve its social standing since it had become associated with pastoral happenings, these being back in fashion among the aristocracy.

Leopold Mozart composed a concerto for the bagpipe and hurdy-gurdy (see also 'Bagpipe'), written in such a way that the player, by changing instruments during pauses, could play both parts. The French composer Charles Baton was a virtuoso on the instrument, for which he also wrote chamber and concerted works; and as recently as 1972 Sven-Eric Johanson wrote a Hurdy-gurdy Concerto.

A later development of the hurdy-gurdy was the Italian *lyra-organizzata*, which incorporated a simple organ into the mechanism. Joseph Haydn wrote five concertos for two of these instruments, dedicated to King Ferdinand II of Naples, in 1790.

NAIL VIOLIN

The name refers to the method of discovery (rather than invention) of the instrument. Hanging his bow on a nail in a ceiling beam at his home in St Petersburg, the 18th-century German violinist Johann Wilde accidentally scraped the nail and was attracted by the resulting resonance. Subsequent experiment produced a cylinder of thick wood, the 'nails' or staples of which were driven in to different depths. The outermost bars of these staples are played with one or two violin bows.

OLIPHANT

This was a crescent-shaped horn originally made from the tusk of an elephant and imported into Europe from Byzantium during the 10th century. Also called the *huchet* or, in a tiny version only a few millimetres long, the *Hifthorn* (Ger: *Hief*= 'the sound of a hunting-horn or bugle'), it was used for hunting in England and was often made of solid gold, so highly did the Middle Ages regard their ceremonial and sporting instruments.

OPHICLEIDE

By about 1850 the ophicleide, a brass instrument, had replaced the serpent as the bass instrument of the cornett family in French church music and in military bands elsewhere. The name comes from Gk: *ophis*='snake'; *kleides*='keys', therefore 'a keyed serpent'. It achieved success during the mid-19th century, but gradually fell from use as its range became covered by the bass tuba. A wooden ophicleide, the serpentcleide, bastardising the name as well as the instrument, was invented about 1850 by Thomas Macbean Glen of Edinburgh.

SERPENT

Developed as a bass cornett during the 16th century and made of two shaped pieces of wood bound together, the serpent was able to produce a wide range of volume throughout its two and a half octaves, but its tortuous shape may have combined with its unreliable tone production to put it out of fashion during the 19th century. Its use in France was primarily in the church, but Handel discovered the instrument in London and employed it in his *Water Music* (1717) and the *Musick for the Royal Fireworks* (1749). Mendelssohn, Berlioz, Rossini, and Wagner all utilised it.

Above: A street hurdy-gurdy of about 1850. (Mary Evans Picture Library)

Below: Serpent, made by Millhouse, London, *c* 1800.

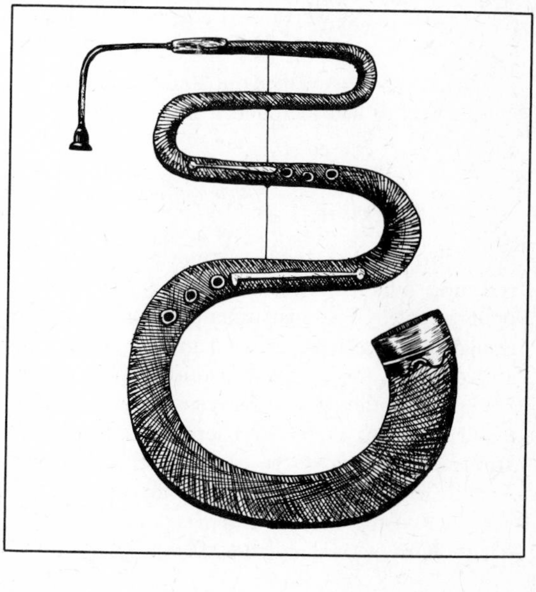

It was called *Schlangenrohr*='snake tube' in Germany, and the 'black pudding' in the north of England.

TROMBA MARINA

The marine trumpet possibly originated in the Slav countries during the Middle Ages. It was known by the Greek term 'monochord', referring to its one main string, but the strange name 'marine trumpet' has a less obvious derivation. The instrument is long and slender, reaching a maximum of 7 ft 3 in (2·2 m) and tapering from 7 in (17·8 cm) to 2 in (5·1 cm); it was roughly triangular in cross-section.

In its early days the thin end was placed against the chest while the other was held aloft at an angle away from the player. The outline of player and instrument from a distance might have resembled that of a herald trumpeter. Alternatively, or in addition, the sound may have suggested that of a trumpet: a single bowed string, lightly stopped to produce harmonics, passed over a bridge which was partly free to vibrate against the table thus producing a harsh, grating sound. Two other eventualities may account in turn for the components of the name: 'marine', by the resemblance to the naval megaphone ('speaking-trumpet') of the time; and 'trumpet' from the fact that the instrument was used in nunneries in place of the real trumpet (hence the German name *Nonnengeige*='nun's violin'). Another German name for the instrument was the *Trummscheidt*='drum-log'.

The tromba marina died out about 1750, but not before Vivaldi had included it in a concerto, RV 558.

VIOLA D'AMOR

Frequently called 'viola d'amore', supposedly referring to its seductive tone, the correct spelling omits the 'e'. The instrument, for many years thought to have been evolved in England in the 17th century, was in fact introduced into Europe, via Spain, by the Moors. Its resonant and characterful tone is produced by a series of sympathetic strings lying below the seven bowed strings. Vivaldi wrote a concerto for this instrument and the lute, accompanied by muted strings and muted harpsichord (a rare coloristic effect), RV 540 in D minor, as well as several solo concertos, and J S Bach used it, for instance, in several cantatas. More recently, Meyerbeer included it in *Les Huguenots* (1836), Wilhelm Kienzl in *Der Kuhreigen* (1911), and Hindemith's Sonata for the Viola d'amor, Op 25, No 2, dates from 1929.

VIOLA POMPOSA

Said, without evidence, to have been invented by Johann Sebastian Bach. It is a five-stringed cross between the viola and violin; a concerto for the instrument was composed by Karl Heinrich Graun in about 1750, and another by Giovanni Battista Sammartini a few years later.

A collection of unique instruments

The highest price attained in auction for a violoncello is £145 000, at Sotheby's, London, on 8 November 1978. The instrument was made by Stradivarius in Cremona in 1710.

The greatest number of musicians required to operate a single instrument was the six needed to play the gigantic orchestrion (or apollonicon) built in 1816. The orchestrion was one of the many types of harmonium built experimentally in the 19th century.

The largest stringed instrument ever constructed was a pantaleon 11 ft (3·4 m) long with 276 strings, invented by the German Pantaleon Hebenstreit and operated by George Noel in 1767.

The longest single-word name of any musical instrument is 'hydrodaktulopsychicharmonica', which is a variety of musical glasses.

CLAVICHORD

The oldest surviving clavichord was built in 1543 by Domenico da Pesaro. It is to be seen in the Leipzig University.

DOUBLE BASS

The world's largest double bass stood 14 ft (4·26 m) high, built in 1924 by Arthur K Ferris in Irona, New Jersey, USA. Its soundbox was 8 ft (2·43 m) across and it weighed 11·6 cwt (590 kg).

The Stradivarius cello (1719) which attained an auction price of £145 000 at Sotheby's on 8 November 1978. (Courtesy Sotheby Parke Bernet & Co)

The world's largest playable guitar. See below. (Photo: Gordon Counsell, Ontario)

DRUM

The largest drum ever constructed was built in 1961 by Remo Inc of North Hollywood, California, for Disneyland. In early days the size of drums was limited by the area of intact animal skin from which the heads were made, but with modern materials such as sheet plastic the size of a drum is theoretically unlimited: the Disneyland big bass drum has a diameter of 10 ft 6 in (3·2 m) and a weight of 450 lb (204 kg). There is a real danger with large drums that the concussion of beater on head could set up internal resonances which could cause the instrument to explode.

GUITAR

The world's largest playable guitar is 9 ft 10 in (3 m) tall and weighs 380 lb (172 kg). It was built by the Odessey Guitar Company, of Vancouver, Canada.

The most expensive normal-sized guitar is the German *chittara battente*, built by Jacob Stadler in 1624 which sold for £10 500 at Christie's, London, on 12 June 1974.

The oldest datable harpsichord. The inscription translates as: 'Behold how everything contained in air, heaven, earth, and sea is moved by the sweet sound of melody.' (Victoria and Albert Museum)

HARMONICA

The world's largest harmonica is 8 ft 2 in (2·5 m) in length and requires the combined efforts of six players at a time. It incorporates one bass, one polyphonic, and eleven chromatic mouth-organs, and was reported in 1963 by the Society for the Preservation and Advancement of the Harmonica.

The harmonica is the most popular of all musical instruments, at least among players: in 1965 an estimated 28 million harmonicas were sold in the USA alone.

The decorated and inscribed bell of a silver valveless hunting horn sold at Christie's (International) SA, Geneva, in November 1976 for SFr 38 000. (Courtesy Christie's (International) SA)

The first Harmonica (mouthorgan) **Concerto** was composed by Michael Spivakovsky in 1951 for Tommy Reilly; and others appeared in 1954 (by Malcolm Arnold) and 1955 (by Arthur Benjamin). Darius Milhaud wrote a Suite for harmonica and orchestra in 1943.

HARPSICHORD

The oldest harpsichord to which a date can be assigned with certainty is preserved in the Victoria and Albert Museum in London. It was built by Hieronymus of Bologna in 1521.

A construction plan for a harpsichord by Henricus Arnault of Zwolle is dated 1435 and is **the oldest known reference to the instrument.** It shows five sound-holes, and the instrument was built in the shape of a wing.

The most expensive harpsichord is a Flemish instrument of 1642, for which £9600 was paid by a private buyer at Sotheby's, London, on 27 November 1969.

The harpsichord with the most manuals was the *Archicembalo*, invented in the mid-16th century by Nicola Vicentino to overcome the limitations imposed by unequal temperament. Its six keyboards offered the opportunity of playing with perfect tuning in any key. Vicentino's *Archiorgano* of 1561 applied the same principles to the **organ.**

HORN

The earliest surviving horn is a hartshorn in the Bernoulli Collection, Switzerland, dating from 1455.

The longest wooden horn is one constructed from a branch of a cypress tree with the 'knee' gouged out. It is 26 ft 5 in (8·1 m) long and is owned by Horace Allison of the USA who made it. He uses no reeds or valves, but can produce numerous well-known airs by lip tension and air pressure.

An alphorn built by Herr Stocker of Switzerland in 1976 measures 43 ft $11\frac{1}{2}$ in (13·4 m) and weighs $70\frac{1}{2}$ lb (32 kg).

KAZOO

The kazoo is described in detail in Section VIII: The 20th Century Scene, where it takes its rightful place among the informal instruments which have been employed in jazz and popular music. Here it is necessary only to detail **the world's largest kazoo.** It is a monster instrument weighing 43 lb (19·5 kg) and measuring 7 ft (2·1 m) high by 4 ft 5 in (1·3 m) wide, and was reported by Barbara D Stewart, 'Manager and Kazoo Keeper' of the Kazoophony, Rochester, New York, in July 1975. The instrument is operated by four players simultaneously.

OCARINA

A bass ocarina measuring 28 in (71 cm) by 10 in (25 cm) and weighing 11 lb (5 kg) was constructed by Charles MacHenry Lindsay in the 1940s. After his death the instrument passed to Louis Seigel of Dunedin, Florida, who claims that it provides a superior alternative to the bass viol and the tuba for dance work, being more easily portable, tunable, and easier to play. In addition, it has built-in facilities for electronic amplification.

OCTOBASS

A monster bass viol, 13 ft (4 m) high, invented in 1849 by J B Vuillaume of Paris. Its three strings were tuned from the lower end of the instrument, and stopping was effected either by hand (if the player had sufficient reach) or by pedals. Berlioz was said to have been enthusiastic, possibly more with the idea than with the instrument itself, and Karl Geiringer who heard it in the 1940s reports that the tone was unexpectedly weak.

In 1889, a John Goyers constructed his 'Grand Bass' which stood 15 ft (4·6 m) high.

Numerous reports of outsize double basses have appeared during the last two and a half centuries. The earliest is possibly that surrounding Joseph Kaempfer, a member of Haydn's orchestra at Esterháza. His instrument, known as 'Goliath', was 'unusually large'. For travelling (Kaempfer visited London) the instrument was dismantled by the unfastening of 25 screws.

PIANO

Two of the earliest of Christofori's instruments are still in existence. One, made in 1720 and heavily restored, is to be seen in the Metropolitan Museum in New York; another dated 1726, is preserved at Florence, in the Kraus Museum. This latter piano still possesses the original leather hammer-heads.

The world's ugliest piano was the one presented to Napoleon III by Queen Victoria on the occasion of his marriage. It is constructed in the shape of Napoleon's hat and, when it was sold in December 1971 for £220 to Tokyo University, a representative said that the instrument is 'unbelievably grotesque'.

The lightest baby grand piano weighed only 379 lb (172 kg). It was made by the Blüthner Piano Company, utilising aluminium for many of the parts, for use in the German Zeppelin *Hindenburg.*

The highest price commanded by a piano or by any musical instrument is $390 000 (£177 273), paid in auction by an American banker at Sotheby's, New York, in March 1980 for the Steinway Alma-Tadema pianoforte. Built in the mid-1880s, it is decorated with designs by Sir Lawrence Alma-Tadema, the Dutch-born English artist noted for his Greek and Roman classical scenes.

The Siena Piano, the history of which is filled with adventure. See text. (Popperfoto)

The heaviest grand piano was made by Chas H Challen & Son Ltd, London, in 1935. It weighs $1\frac{1}{2}$ tons/tonnes and has a length of 11 ft 8 in (3·55 m). The longest bass string measures 9 ft 11 in (3·02 m).

The most adventurous history of any musical instrument was experienced by the so-called 'Siena piano'. It was built in about 1798 by Marchesio of Turin and became a wedding-present to Rebecca Marchesio and Antonio Ferri upon the occasion of their wedding in about 1820, and was taken to the Ferri farmstead in Siena. Antonio Ferri, a grandson of this union, built the cabinet which survives today from wood reputed to be from the pillars of Solomon's Temple. The panels are some 5 in (12·7 cm) thick in places, and are carved to saturation-point with cherubs, drinking scenes, etc. In 1867 the instrument was shown at the Paris Exposition as the piano of which Liszt said that the tone was 'divine'. The following year it was made another wedding-gift, this time to Crown Prince Umberto from the city of Siena, and was taken to Rome by the Prince. Its following years were obscure and probably peaceful, but apparently the instrument was looted by the Germans during the Second World War and taken to North Africa to entertain the Nazi troops. Left behind during their retreat after the Battle of El Alamein, it was discovered by a salvage party and nearly blown up when suspected of being a booby trap. Somehow it had acquired a thick coating of plaster which hid its true identity even from specialists, and this and the sand-filled interior rendered the instrument useless for playing until repairs were carried out by the British Army. For the rest of the war it accompanied an English troup of forces entertainers, but on VE day it was in Tel Aviv, where it was left in the care of a scrap-dealer.

Its most ignominious period had arrived, during which it served as anything but a musical instrument: a meat-storage cabinet, a beehive, and a chicken incubator, among other things. It was at last rescued by Avner Carmi, the piano-tuner and grandson of the piano virtuoso Mathis Yarmovsky. Carmi removed the plaster with the aid of 24 gal (109 l) of acetone and rebuilt the action and stringing. The only part of the workings to remain in original condition was the miraculously preserved sounding-board. Carmi worked from 1950 to 1953 before the instrument was brought back to playing condition, after which it was shipped to New York where a series of recordings of its 'period' but unremarkable sounds were made. Once back in Israel with Carmi, the Siena Piano became of political interest. Following President Sadat's historic peace-making speech in December 1977, Carmi offered the instrument to the Rommel Museum in Mersa Matruh, Western Egypt, as a contribution to 'the Israeli-Egyptian honeymoon'.

TRUMPET

The earliest dated trumpet to survive was made in 1523 by Ubaldo Martini of Siena. It is preserved in the Berlin Musical Instrument Collection. The ceremonial trumpet discovered in the tomb of Tuth-ankh-Amon may be dated to before *c* 1340 BC.

The smallest trumpet in the world was made in Berne, Switzerland, by Karl Burri. It has three valves, and measures 5 in (12·7 cm) in length.

An 18th-century Italian trumpet whose fearsome appearance is matched by the harsh sound produced by the serpent's vibrating tongue. (Popperfoto)

TUBA

The world's largest tuba is still in use in a South African circus. It stands 7 ft 6 in (2·3 m) high and measures 3 ft 4 in (1 m) across the bell. John Philip Sousa (1854–1932), the American 'March King', commissioned the instrument in 1896: it took two years to build and contains 39 ft (12 m) of piping.

The largest tuba in England is another which Sousa commissioned at the same time. Its weight is 100 lb (45·4 kg), and it measures 6 ft (1·8 m) high and 3 ft (0·9 m) across the bell. It is at present owned by a former member of the Johnny Dankworth Band in London, having been reputedly left behind by Sousa after an English tour, when it came into the category of excess baggage. Both Gerard Hoffnung, the musician, comedian, and cartoonist, and 'Professor' Jimmy Edwards, the comedian, have played the instrument in public.

Albert Denkert of Karlshafen, West Germany (here shown with his son) made this collection of instruments from one million matchsticks. (Popperfoto)

Leatherworker Fritz Meng of Bad Homburg, Germany, with a playable violin made of leather. Its tone is said to resemble that of an oboe. Herr Meng is responsible also for the leather 'painting'. (Popperfoto)

VIOLIN

The most valuable violin in the world is a Guarneri del Gesù which sold for £180 000 at the London dealers J & A Beare in August 1979.

Antonio Stradivari (*c* 1644–1737), a pupil, along with Andrea Guarneri, of Nicolò Amati (1596–1684), was **the most famous violin-maker of all time.** Working all his life in Cremona, he produced violins, violas, and cellos, 712 examples of which are known to survive. His best instruments were produced during his so-called 'golden period' from 1700 to 1720.

Bells

These instruments are often imitated in music, either by non-bell-like instruments playing carillon-like music (as for instance in Bizet's incidental music to *L'Arlesienne* of 1872) or by voices singing bell-like motifs (Carl Orff's *Carmina Burana* of

1937). Alternatively, the actual sounds are reproduced by instruments such as the tubular bells or the glockenspiel. These latter uses are discussed above (see 'Percussion'). Here we are concerned with non-musical bells, mainly in places of worship.

The earliest known bell dates back to about 3000 BC; it was the 'Huang Chung' ('Yellow Bell') which established a standard musical tone for performances of Chinese temple music.

The earliest surviving bell dates from about 1000 BC. It is a handbell which may have been used for religious purposes, and was recovered from an archaeological site at the Babylonian Palace of Nimrod in 1849 by Mr (later Sir) Austen Henry Layard.

A 37-bell carillon played from a keyboard and pedals. Instruments of this kind were well known in the Netherlands by about 1600.

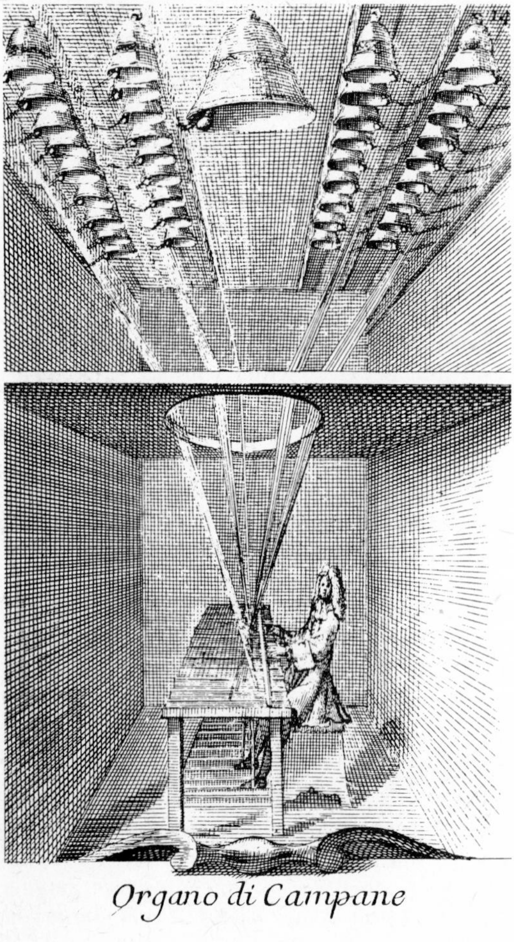

Organo di Campane

The oldest dated bell in England is to be found in Lissett Church, near Bridlington, Humberside, England. In October 1972 it was discovered to bear the date MCCLIIII (1254).

The world's largest bell was cast in Russia in 1733. Known as 'Tsar Kolokol' ('King of Bells'), it was designed to be hung in the Kremlin (completed in 1510), Moscow, but by mischance it was cracked in a fire in 1737 before it had been sounded. It rests today on a platform in the Kremlin, and stands 19 ft (5·8 m) high, measures 22 ft 6 in (6·9 m) in diameter, and weighs 193 tons (196·1 tonnes). In addition to this silent monument, Moscow holds the record for **the largest sounding bell** at a weight of 128 tons (130 tonnes).

The world's most famous bell is 'Big Ben', the hour bell in the Clock Tower of the House of Commons, London. It was cast in 1858, weighs 13·575 tons (13·8 tonnes), and has been broadcast daily by the British Broadcasting Corporation for many years.

The world's largest carillon is that of the 72-bell Laura Spelman Rockefeller Memorial Carillon in Riverside Drive Church, New York City, of which the 18·25 ton (18·54 tonnes) bell mentioned below is a part. The whole carillon was built by Gillet and Johnston, Croydon, a well-known and long-established firm of potters.

The heaviest carillon in the United Kingdom is in St Nicholas Church, Aberdeen, Scotland. Its 48 bells weigh a total of 25·4 tons (25·8 tonnes) and the range of the notes is nearly four octaves.

The world's highest belfry, in terms of distance from ground-level, is located 700 ft (213·4 m) up in Metropolitan Life Insurance Tower, New York City. The bells therein can be heard at a distance of 28 miles (45 km).

NOTABLE BELLS OF THE WORLD, BY COUNTRIES

Country	*Location*	*Date cast*	*Weight in tons/(tonnes)*
Russia	Kremlin, Moscow	1733	193 (196·1)

Burma	Mandalay ('Mingun Bell')	*c* 1815	90 (91·4)
Japan	Honshu ('Choin-in')	?	74 (75·2)
China	Peking	?	53 (53·9)
Germany	Cologne Cathedral ('Petersglock')[1]	1923	25 (25·4)
Portugal	Lisbon Cathedral	14th century	24 (24·4)
Austria	St Stephen's Cathedral, Vienna ('Pummerin')	1957	23·6 (23·9)
France	Montmartre, Paris	1898	19·4 (19·7)
America	Riverside Drive Church, New York City[2]	1931	18·25 (18·5)
Czecho-slovakia	Olmutz, Moravia	1931	17·9 (18·2)
Spain	Toledo Cathedral ('Campaña gorda')	1753	17 (17·3)
Great Britain	St Paul's Cathedral, London ('Great Paul')[3]	1881	16·76 (17)
Canada	Montreal Cathedral ('Bourdon')	1847	11·075 (11·2)
Belgium	St Ramoldus Cathedral, Mechlin	*c* 1600	9 (9·1)
Poland	Danzig	1453	6·05 (6·2)
New Zealand	Wellington War Memorial	1929	5 (5·1)
Switzerland	Schaffhausen ('Schillerglock')	1486	4·42 (4·5)

[1] The world's **heaviest** swinging bell.
[2] This bell was cast by the firm of Gillet and Johnston of Croydon, Surrey, England, and is the **heaviest tuned bell** in the world.
[3] This E flat bell in the south tower of the Cathedral is inscribed 'Vae mihi si non evangelizavere' ('Woe is unto me, if I preach not the gospel'), Corinthians 9:16.

An Indian floral ornament with a cobra from which hangs a small bell. (Popperfoto)

Organs

The largest and loudest musical instrument ever made is the Auditorium Organ, Atlantic City, New Jersey, USA. Built in 1930, the instrument has two consoles with a total of twelve manuals, 1477 stops, and 33 112 pipes (from $\frac{3}{16}$ in (0·5 cm) to 64 ft (19·5 m) in length). Its 'flat-out' volume generated by blower motors of 365 hp (370 cv) equalled that of 25 brass bands, but the instrument is today only partly functional. The ophicleide stop of the Grand Great is **the world's loudest organ stop.** Operated by a pressure of 100 in (254 cm) of water, its pure trumpet tone is six times greater than the loudest of locomotive whistles.

The first cinema organ in the UK was installed in the Palace, Accrington, Yorks (now Lancs.), in 1913.

The world's largest church organ is in Passau

The first Japanese underwater string quartet who appeared on Fuji TV on 2 October 1979. (Courtesy: Fuji Telecasting Company Ltd)

Cathedral, Germany. Built in 1928 by D F Steinmeyer and Co, it has 16 000 pipes and five manuals.

The largest cathedral organ in Britain is that completed in Liverpool Anglican Cathedral on 18 October 1926, with two five-manual consoles of which only one is now in use. The 9704 sounding pipes range from 32 ft (9·75 m) to $\frac{3}{4}$ in (1·9 cm).

Europe's largest theatre organ is the Mighty Wurlitzer previously in the Odeon, Manchester, but now sited in that city's Free Trade Hall.

The 'highest' organ. In September 1971 an organ 'of considerable weight' was pushed to the top of Ben Nevis, 4406 ft (1343 m) high, by Kenneth Campbell of Sutherland. It is not recorded whether the instrument, once there, was actually played.

The biggest travelling organ is 26 ft (8 m) in length and 9 ft 9 in (3 m) high. It was built in the Black Forest, Bavaria, Germany, and its range is vaguely reported to be 'from super bass to super soprano'.

Submerged instruments

In 1947 an Irish harp fitted with water-resistant nylon strings was played under water. Unfortunately, history has not recorded where, by whom, or why this exercise was carried out.

In March 1975 an underwater performance of Handel's *Water Music* (arranged by ?) was given on solo violin by Mark Gottlieb in the Evergreen State College swimming-pool in Olympia, Washington, USA. Mr Gottlieb reports that he is still perfecting his sub-aqua technique, concentrating especially on his bow speed and his detaché. Is it to be predicted that similarly appropriate venues may be chosen for future performances of Vaughan Williams' *Sinfonia Antartica*, Holst's *The Planets*, Haydn's 'Sun' Quartets, and Offenbach's *Orpheus in the Underworld*?

Section 3
COMPOSERS

The first composer

Consideration of this question brings the realisation that the description 'composer' is a relatively modern one. Firstly, it means one who composes, or orders, sounds, which he or she takes from a hypothetical chaos of an infinite number and type of sounds, into an intelligible sequence. Secondly, it has to be established that the composer has existed since the beginnings of music, but most of the time he was synonymous with the performer who composed the music spontaneously during performance, no attempt being made to write it down. When methods were eventually evolved for representing the played tone by the written character (see Section VII) it was done at first by composers whose names have not survived.

In the 12th century Richard Cœur de Lion (1157–99) composed simple ballads; no earlier personage who wrote down the music he composed can be established, so it seems that **the first composer** was a royal one. However, His Highness's ballads were by way of being folk-music—little more than popular songs of the time—and for so-called 'art music' we must turn to the composer Pérotin, known as 'Pérotin-Le-Grand' and 'Perotinus Magnus' (*c* 1160–*c* 1220) of Paris, who composed from 1180. Among his works are the first in the emerging art of polyphonic singing.

King Richard I, first Royal composer. (Mary Evans Picture Library)

Royal composers

The following list of reigning monarchs and their relatives who composed music should, perhaps, more correctly be added to the list of part-time composers (see below). Many royal personages attempted composing music during their leisure hours, often with only an elementary knowledge of the art, and even some whose output of music was tiny have been included.

Others met with fair success. Probably **the most musical of all monarchs** was Frederick the Great, whose four concertos for flute and 120 flute sonatas (*not* 121 as is usually given: Nos 8 and 60 in Spitta's list are identical) still receive occasional performances and recordings. In addition, his Symphony in D for two flutes, two horns, and strings stands beside similar works of the time (1742) as of at least equal quality.

The first royal composer was the well-known ballad-writer Richard Cœur de Lion. However, royalty of extreme antiquity (eg: in China up to 3000 BC) composed and performed their own music.

A composer of the more modern style of ballad is **the most recent royal composer**: King Phumiphon Adunet of Thailand (b. 1927) who wrote 'His Majesty's Blues', a tame and traditional 'pop' number. Between these extremes lies much regal talent. The list which follows is in chronological order within nations.

The British Isles

Richard Cœur de Lion (1157–99) (see above).

Henry V (1387–1422). He (or Henry IV?) is mentioned (as 'Roy Henry') as a composer of church music in the Old Hall Manuscript.

Henry VIII (1491–1547), writer of some popular court pieces.

Anne Boleyn (Bullen) (*c* 1507–36): her ballads included one entitled 'O Death Rocke Me On Slepe', which is said to have moved her husband.

Wilhelmina Caroline of Ansbach (1683–1737; wife of George II) wrote 'Church Call' which is still played before church parade in some army units.

Albert of Saxe-Coburg-Gotha, christened Francis Charles Augustus Albert Emmanuel (1819–61; consort of Queen Victoria), composer of the first work to be played in public in the Royal Albert Hall (see Section VI).

Austria/Hungary

Ferdinand III (1608–57), Emperor of Austria and the composer of songs.

Paul Esterházy (1635–1713), Prince of the famous family later associated with Haydn, his compositions include music for the Church.

Leopold I (1640–1705), Emperor of Austria and the composer of instrumental pieces.

Joseph I (1678–1711), Emperor of Austria; he composed a number of vocal and instrumental works.

Rudolf (1788–1831), Archduke; later Archbishop of Olmütz. He was a pupil of Beethoven and the dedicatee of the 'Archduke' Trio, Op 97. As well as being a performer, Archduke Rudolf composed a number of works.

Belgium

Josephine Clementine, Princess (1764–1820).

Denmark

Caroline Amelia of Augustenberg (1792–1866), wife of King Christian VIII, and a composer of salon pieces.

Maria Theresa Ahlefeldt, Princess (1755–1823).

France

Marie-Antoinette (1755–93), a musical and cultured queen who regularly attended society concerts in Paris, and who composed light salon pieces.

Germany

Ernst Ludwig (1667–1739), Landgraf von Hessen, composer of instrumental music.

Wilhelmina (1709–58), Markgräfin von Bayreuth, and a favourite sister of Frederick the Great, wrote a harpsichord concerto in G minor which has achieved two recordings.

Frederick the Great (Friedrich der Grosse; Friedrich II, 1712–86), see above.

Anna Amelia (1723–87), Princess of Prussia, another sister of Frederick the Great and a pupil of Kirnberger. She wrote marches, chorales, etc.

Friedrich Wilhelm II (1744–97), composer of occasional court pieces and songs.

Friedrich Wilhelm III (1770–1840), composer of occasional court pieces and songs.

Louis Ferdinand (1772–1806), Prince of Hohenzollern and a nephew of Frederick the Great. Referred to by audiences who appreciated his joyful works as 'Beethoven with sunshine', he was respected by that composer and received the dedication of the Piano Concerto No 3 in C minor, Op 37.

Poland

Prince Joseph Michael Xaver Francis John Poniatowski (1816–73) was the grand nephew of the last King of Poland. He composed a dozen operas, salon pieces and songs, etc.

Helene Paulowna, Princess (1824–73).

Portugal

John IV (1604–56), King of Portugal and a motet-composer.

Pedro IV (d. 1831), King of Portugal and a former King of Brazil. He wrote the Portuguese National Anthem.

King Oscar I (1799–1859).

Princess Eugenie (1830–89).

Princess Therese (1836–1914).

The last three were composers of salon music and ballads.

Spain

Thibault IV (1201–53), King of Navarre and a composer of songs.

Alfonso X (1221–84), King of Castile and a song-writer.

Thailand

Phumiphon Adunet, King of Thailand (see above).

Masters of the King's/Queen's Musick

While composers in some countries are chosen to perform certain 'official' tasks in providing music for royal or State occasions, England is the only country to maintain an official court composer. He is known as 'The Master of the Queen's Musick', the archaic spelling of the last word indicating the antiquity of the post.

Today, the appointment is made by the ruling monarch in consultation with advisers, and the duties are nominal. The composer thus chosen is likely to provide music for the most important of State occasions such as investitures, coronations, royal births, but there is no binding compulsion to do so, and the Master of the Queen's Musick accepts the honour (always well deserved) without the drudgery which attended the post in its earlier history.

Evidence exists that James I employed a specific court composer, but the post was not officially recognised until 13 June 1626, when Charles I made provision for the position as part of the royal household. He awarded the title to the composer who had faithfully served his predecessor, and on 11 July 1626, Nicholas Lanier was appointed **the first Master of the King's Musick.** Lanier served that monarch until the latter's execution in 1649, and was reinstated to the post by Charles II after the Restoration.

The duties of the King's composer in the early days ranged from obtaining parts and copying them for performance, rehearsing and conducting, to being responsible for the behaviour of the court musicians both inside and outside the concert-room.

Sir Edward Elgar, Master of the King's Musick 1924–34, on the steps of the Abbey Road Recording Studios, London, with Yehudi Menuhin in 1932. (EMI Records Ltd)

Of the 19 Masters of the King's/Queen's Musick to date, only three (Nos 2, 6, and 12 in the list below) have retired from the post. In all other cases the composers were serving at the time of death.

Nonagenarian composers

Considerable sympathy and publicity are given to artists, especially composers, who retain their powers well into their old age. It is well known that Verdi wrote *Otello* during his 74th year and *Falstaff* six years later, and that Vaughan Williams continued composing until shortly before his death at the age of 86; Stravinsky, too, remained remarkably active until the last of his 89 years, and Sibelius lived until 92, but apparently ceased composing at the early age of 60, living out the rest of his life in well-deserved retirement and comfortable semi-isolation in his beloved Finland.

90 years old

Adam, Johann Ludwig (or Jean-Louis) (1758–1848), Alsatian pianist and composer.

Alcock, John (1715–1806), Doctor of Music (Oxon), organist in London, Plymouth, Reading, Lichfield; composition pupil of John Stanley. As a novelist he wrote under the pseudonym 'Piper' (=organist).

Carrillo, Julián (1875–1965), Mexican microtonalist.

Esplá, Oscar (1886–1976), Spanish, but lived mainly in Belgium.

Gui, Vittorio (1885–1975), Italian composer and conductor.

Harris, Sir William (1883–1973), English organist and composer, mainly for his instrument.

Hill, Alfred (1870–1960), Australian composer who wrote *Overture of Welcome* in which the instrumentalists enter one after another, thereby reversing the procedure adopted in the last movement of Haydn's 'Farewell' Symphony.

Huë, Georges Adolph (1858–1948), French opera-composer.

Huygens, Sir Constantijn (1596–1687), Dutch musician, poet, politician, diplomatist, gymnast, artist, and playwright.

Ropartz (1864–1955), whose name is given as Joseph Guy-Ropartz and as Guy Marie Ropartz. He was a French composer and pupil of Massenet.

Spengel, Heinrich Ritter von (*c* 1775–1865), German.

91 years old

Bertini, Giuseppe (*c* 1756–1847+), Italian musician and church composer at Palermo, at least 91 when he died.

Foerster, Joseph Bohuslav (1859–1951), Czech nationalist composer of many types of music.

Gretchaninov, Alexander Tikhonovich (1864–1956), Russian composer of songs, piano music, and the once-popular 'Credo' from his Liturgy No 2, Op 29 (1908).

Heger, Robert (1886–1978), German conductor and composer.

Huss, Henry Holden (1862–1953), American composer of many types of music and a teacher; he was a descendant of the Czech national hero John Huss.

Jiránek, Alois (1858–1950), Czech pupil of Fibich.

Malipiero, Gian Francesco (1882–1973), one of the most prominent of modern Italian composers, he was also a writer and musical editor concerned with ancient Italian music.

Rieger, Gottfried (1764–1855), German, worked at Brünn.

Scott, Cyril (1879–1970), English symphonist, pianist, poet, and writer.

Siret, Nicholas (1663–1754), French composer and wind-player.

Tritto, Giacomo (1733–1824), Neapolitan opera-composer.

92 years old

Boulanger, Nadia (1887–1979), French composer and renowned teacher.

Friml, Rudolf (1880–1972), Czech, naturalised American, composer of light operettas, for example *Rose Marie* (1924) and *The Vagabond King* (1925).

MASTERS OF MONARCHS' MUSICK

Composer	*Born*	*Appointed*	*Died*	*Served*
1. Nicholas Lanier	1588	1626	1666	James I; Charles I; Charles II
2. Louis Grabu	*c* 1638?	1666	1694? (ret 1674)	Charles II
3. Nicholas Staggins	?	1674	1700	Charles II; James II; William and Mary; William III
4. John Eccles	1668	1700	1735	Anne; George I; George II
5. Maurice Greene	1695	1735	1755	George II
6. William Boyce*	1710	1757	1779	George II; George III
7. John Stanley	1713	1772	1786	George III
8. Sir William Parsons	1746	1786	1817	George III
9. William Shield	1748	1817	1829	George III; George IV
10. Christian Kramer	*c* 1788	1829	1834	George IV; William IV; Victoria
11. François Cramer	1772	1834	1848	Victoria
12. George Frederick Anderson	*c* 1801	1848	1876 (ret 1870)	Victoria
13. Sir William George Cusins	1833	1870	1893	Victoria
14. Sir Walter Parratt	1841	1893	1924	Victoria; Edward VII; George V
15. Sir Edward Elgar	1857	1924	1934	George V
16. Sir Henry Walford Davies	1869	1934	1941	George V; Edward VIII; George VI
17. Sir Arnold Bax	1883	1941	1953	George VI; Elizabeth II
18. Sir Arthur Bliss	1891	1953	1975	Elizabeth II
19. Malcolm Williamson	1931	1975		Elizabeth II

*Boyce took over duties unofficially in 1755 on the death of Greene; he retired on account of deafness in 1772.

The Finnish composer Sibelius, who lived to the age of 92, photographed in 1923. (Royal College of Music)

Marin, Marie-Martin Marcel de, Vicomte (1769–1861+), French composer, violinist and harpist, at least 92 at death.

Seeger, Charles (1887–1979), American conductor and composer. He and his composer wife Ruth Crawford brought into the world three children who have made their marks in folk-music: Pete, Peggy, and Michael.

Sibelius, Jan Julian Christian (1865–1957), symphonist, one of the greatest of 20th-century composers and the greatest to emerge from Finland.

Strong, George Templeton (1856–1948), American friend of Liszt.

Zavertal, Ladislas Joseph Philip Paul (1849–1942), conductor and composer of Polish descent who worked in Italy and in the British Isles.

93 years old

Widor, Charles (1844–1937), Parisian writer, organist, and composer of the popular Toccata from the Organ Symphony No 5, Op 42/1. He was in fact active in orchestral and chamber music, and a song-writer.

94 years old

Mouton, Charles (1626–?), French lutenist, said to have been still alive in 1720.

Preyer, Gottfried (1807–1901), Austrian church composer and organist.

Stolz, Robert (1881–1975), Austrian, a pupil of Humperdinck and the composer of *The White Horse Inn*, *Wild Violets*, *Rainbow Square*, and other shows.

95 years old

Caffi, Francesco (1778–1874), Venetian composer, musicologist, and writer.

Charpentier, Gustave (1860–1956), French.

Ganz, Rudolf (1877–1972), Swiss conductor, pianist, and composer.

Gossec, François-Joseph (1734–1829), Belgian composer of operas and about 100 symphonies, one of which is now thought to be by another nonagenarian: Witzthumb (see below).

Perti, Giacomo Antonio (1661–1756), Bolognese opera-composer and writer of chamber works.

Ruggles, Carl (1876–1971), American painter and composer of deeply thought and uncompromising music.

96 years old

Araújo, João Gomes de (1846–1942). Brazilian.

Brian, Havergal (1876–1972), **the most prolific of all English symphonists,** having 32 to his credit.

Casals, Pablo (1876–1973), the world-famous Spanish expatriate cellist was also a skilful composer.

Maschitti, Michele (Michel, Miquel, or Michelly) (*c* 1664–1760), Neapolitan violinist and composer.

Witzthumb, Ignace (1720–1816), symphonist (see Gossec, above), probably of Bohemian origin, who settled in Paris.

97 years old

Floyd, Alfred Ernest (1877–1974), English organist, conductor, composer, and broadcaster who spent most of his life in Australia.

98 years old

Berger, Francesco (1834–1933), English song-writer, piano composer and teacher in London. Hon Sec of the Royal Philharmonic Society.

99 years old

Rein(c)ken, Johann (or Jan Adam) (1623–1722), German organist and composer. It is said that the great Bach walked many miles to hear his improvisations in Hamburg.

Weinert, Antoni (1751–1850), Polish opera-buffa composer.

Centenarian

Büsser, Paul Henri (1872–1973), French pupil of Gounod and composer primarily of dramatic works.

104 years old

Lang, Margaret Ruthven (1867–1972), American, pupil of, among others, Chadwick and MacDowell, began composing at the age of 12. Her works include over 100 songs, choral and other vocal music, piano and chamber works, and music for orchestra.

The longest-lived composer is said to be le Comte de Saint-Germain who, according to confused reports, was born about 1660 and is still alive. If this seems incredible, what are we to make of his own report that he had discovered a potion which would prolong life indefinitely, as it had already prolonged his own for more than 2000 years? Among his other extravagant claims are that he can make gold and diamonds, that he could speak virtually all the European languages of the 18th century and that he is the finest violinist and composer who ever lived. In respect of this last claim, examination of his 13 sonatas in the British Museum (published by Walsh, 1750, and by Johnson, 1758) show them to be average works for their period.

A sober estimate of his dates is *c* 1710–*c* 1780 (*Encyclopaedia Britannica*), but this fails to take into account his reported conversation with Rameau in Venice in 1710 and a Paris appearance in 1789. In addition to being an alchemist, scientist, composer, and violinist, he was a singer in those days and travelled widely through Europe and the Middle East, from London (where he met Horace Walpole in 1743) to Persia, from Tunisia to St Petersburg (Leningrad); and herein perhaps lies part of the answer to the mystery. We are dealing with two Saint-Germains, father and son, both gifted in deception and proficient in music and the sciences, each of whom had the knack of leaving deep and lasting impressions wherever they went. The various reports from widely separated centres (there is even one from India, dated 1756), and the claims of the discovery of the elixir of life, would lend credence to the longevity story in those superstitious days, and there would be no one with the fortune to be in more than one place to coincide with Saint-Germain's visits in order to spot the discrepancies in age.

The truth of the matter may be guessed at as

follows: a man born towards the end of the 17th century was self-assured and plausible enough to be taken at his word in the matter of his wild claims. He travelled all over Europe, making impressions and money, and was, for those days, exceptionally long-lived: perhaps a nonagenarian. Somewhere during his travels he sired a son who later saw the financial advantage of keeping the old man alive, but he was not so skilful in the deceptive arts, so the reports after the 1780s become fewer until a Viennese sighting in 1821. Thereafter the joke spent itself.

Until the sensation-seeking 1970s! As recently as 28 January 1972, a Richard Chamfrey appeared on French television claiming to be the real Comte de Saint-Germain. The audience witnessed him 'change lead into gold', which activity seems to have enabled him, during the last century and a half, to give up music as a means of making money. His trick, if it was one, was successful, but less credence is given to his latest claims: that he commutes between Earth and Mars, and that his age is now 17 000 years. It is surprising that his modesty during the 18th century was so well developed as to permit him to deny 14 800 years of his life; on the other hand it may be that for him Einstein's theory of time dilation works in reverse during his extra-terrestrial jaunts.

George Frideric Handel, who went blind towards the end of his life. Mezzotint by C Turner. (Royal College of Music)

*Unfortunate composers**

Musical history is dotted with the sad figures of composers who had to fight severe disabilities, or who met their ends in tragic or unusual circumstances. Of all the misery catalogued below, most poignant must be that suffered by deaf composers.

BLIND COMPOSERS

Bach, Johann Sebastian, went blind in later life.

Bériot, Charles Auguste de, the Belgian violin composer and virtuoso who also built violins and was an artist, poet, and sculptor. He suffered from paralysis towards the end of his life in addition to blindness.

Cabezón, Antonio de, Spanish keyboard composer, blind from birth.

Delius, Frederick Fritz Albert Theodor, English, ended his life blind and partially paralysed. He was enabled to continue composing through the patient and selfless assistance of his amanuensis, Eric William Fenby.

Handel, George Frideric, went blind in 1753, but continued composing with the assistance of John Christopher Smith, himself a noted London composer.

Helmbrecht, Christian Friedrich Franz, German; though blind from a very early age, he learned to play the organ, piano, harp, flute, clarinet; composed organ pieces and devised a musical notation for the blind.

Hollins, Alfred, Scottish composer, organist, and pianist who received an Honorary DMus at Edinburgh University, was blind from birth.

Labor, Josef, Austrian organist, composer, and teacher.

Linley, Francis, English, who, although blind from birth, composed for voice, piano, flute, and organ; became a successful music seller, taking over Bland's famous London publishing house in 1796.

MacFarren, George Alexander, an extremely successful 19th-century English composer, now hardly known, totally blind for the last years of his life.

*For information of composers' full names and dates please refer to index.

Paradis, Maria Theresia, a blind female Italian composer who worked in Germany.

Parry, John, blind Welsh harper, collector, and composer of harp and guitar music.

Purkis, John, English organ composer blind from childhood.

Rodrigo, Joaquin, Spanish composer of the world-famous *Concierto de Aranjuez*, blind from the age of three.

Smareglia, Antonio, Italian operatic composer, became blind in 1900 at the age of 46.

Smart, Henry Thomas, English composer of vocal and church music, blind for the last 15 years of his life.

Stanley, John, English, blinded at the age of two by an accident.

Suda, Stanislav, Czech, blinded when only a few days old.

Templeton, Alec Andrew, Welsh, famous for his *Bach Goes to Town*, was blind from birth.

Widor, Charles, long-lived French composer (1844–1937) of the popular *Toccata* from Organ Symphony No 5.

Xyndas, Spyridon, Greek guitarist and opera composer.

DEAF COMPOSERS

Beethoven, Ludwig van, started to notice symptoms of deafness before he was 30, and the malady grew progressively worse until, towards the end of his life, silence closed in completely. In spite of this he continued composing right up to the end: the Choral Symphony and many of his greatest piano sonatas and string quartets were composed during the last ten years of total silence.

Boyce, William, English author of 'Heart of Oak' and Master of the King's Musick (George III). He went deaf in later life, but put his silence to good use by collecting for posterity the works of earlier English church composers.

Dupin, Paul, French, known as 'Louis Lothar'. He lost his hearing while still a youth, but regained it about 1900.

Lambert, George Jackson, English composer whose increasing deafness forced him to retire from his post as organist in 1874. But for this misfortune, he and his father would successively have held the post of organist at Beverly Minster for a full century from 1778.

Lvov, Alexei Feodorovich, Russian violinist and composer of the first Russian national hymn.

May, Frederick, Irish, deaf from the age of 29.

Nazareth, Ernesto, Brazilian composer totally deaf towards the end of his life.

Smetana, Bedřich, one of the best known of Bohemian nationalist composers, went deaf in 1874, succumbing also to mental illness.

Zweers, Bernard, Dutch composer, deaf in old age.

COMPOSERS WHO WENT INSANE

Blodek, Vilém, Czech, whose last four years were blighted by mental disorder.

Chabrier, Alexis Emmanuel, French. Melancholia led to paralysis and death.

Donizetti, Gaetano, Italian operatic composer, died insane.

Fel, Antoine, French singer and vocal composer, died in Bicêtre asylum.

Frank, Ernst, German opera composer and conductor, died in a Viennese mental home.

Gurney, Ivor Bertie, English poet and song-writer, also a composer of orchestral music, etc, sustained injuries during the First World War which led to insanity and death.

Jullien, Louis Antoine . . ., French conductor and composer of light music, possessor of no fewer than 36 forenames, died insane at the age of 48.

Moorehead, John, Irish violinist and theatre composer, went insane in 1802 and was imprisoned in London. Upon his release he joined the navy, but hanged himself soon afterwards in Kent.

Roseingrave, Thomas, English composer and friend of Domenico Scarlatti, lost his reason in 1737.

Schumann, Robert Alexander, German, suffered from a mental disorder which led him to attempt suicide. He died in a mental home.

Scudo, Pierre, Franco-Italian song composer, died in an institution at Blois, France.

Smetana, Bedřich, Bohemian, whose deafness (see above) led to his mental collapse.

Wesley, Samuel, English composer of church and concert music, received a head injury when young which ultimately led to his insanity.

Willmers, Heinrich Rudolf, German pianist and conductor, died in an asylum at Vienna.

Wolf, Hugo, Austrian, one of the world's greatest song-writers, suffered for many years from depression before finally going insane in 1897. He died in a Viennese asylum in 1903.

COMPOSERS WHO WERE MURDERED

Cambert, Robert, the composer of the first French opera, was murdered by his servant.

Herschel, Jacob, German, brother of Sir William Herschel the astronomer and composer, was strangled in a field near Hanover.

Koczwara, František, Bohemian composer, violinist and double bass player, known in Germany as 'Franz Kotzwara', strangled in London by a Miss Susannah Hill, a prostitute at Vine Street, St Martin's.

Leclair, Jean-Marie, French violinist, dancer, composer, and one of the greatest violin virtuosi of his day, was murdered on the steps of his Paris home, perhaps by a jealous rival.

Mozart, Wolfgang Amadeus. The allegation, perpetrated in Rimsky-Korsakov's opera *Mozart and Salieri*, that Mozart was done to death by Salieri, has never been proved, although there is evidence to show that Mozart's demise was due not to natural causes but to some kind of poisoning.

Neruda, Josef, Czech. Both he and his wife were murdered.

Obousser, Robert, Swiss of Belgian origin, stabbed to death in his Zurich flat in 1957.

Stradella, Alessandro, Italian, one of the world's first symphonists, is said to have been assassinated by agents of the lover of a lady with whom Stradella had eloped. The story, whether true or not, has given rise to a novel by Marion Crawford and operas by Abraham Louis Niedermeyer (1846) and Flotow (1844), the composer of *Martha*.

Reversing the above, the tale goes that Carlo Gesualdo, the Italian Prince and composer, arranged for the murder of his wife and her lover.

COMPOSERS WHO COMMITTED SUICIDE

Carey, Henry, English song-writer, and the composer of 'Sally in our Alley'.

Clarke, Jeremiah, English composer and organist at St Paul's Cathedral, London. He was the true composer of *Trumpet Voluntary*, for long attributed to Purcell. Being unlucky in love, Clarke shot himself.

Distler, Hugo, German composer and organist who was unable to tolerate the terrors of wartime Germany.

Maxfield, Richard Vance, American modernist pupil of Roger Sessions.

Moorehead, John. (See Insane composers, above.)

Nedbal, Oscar, Bohemian operetta composer. Long-standing financial worries wore him down until he reached breaking point at Christmas 1930.

Pedrotti, Carlo, Italian, drowned himself in the River Adige at Verona.

Powell, Felix, Welsh composer of the popular World War I song 'Pack up your troubles in your old kit bag', was unable to take the advice of his brother (the lyric writer).

Warlock, Peter, composing name of Philip Heseltine, writer and editor of old English music. His best-known composition is probably the song cycle *The Curlew* (1922).

Zimmermann, Bernd Alois, German composer of, *inter alia*, the cantata *In Praise of Stupidity*, shot himself.

COMPOSERS WHO MET DEATH DUE TO WAR ACTION

Borde, Jean Benjamin de la (1734–94), French, guillotined.

Butterworth, George Sainton Kaye (1885–1916), English composer and collector of folk-music, killed at the battle of the Somme.

Dahmen, Wilhelm, Jr (1769–?), Dutch cornist and composer who joined the English Army and lost his life in Spain.

Farrar, Ernest Bristow (1885–1918), English, killed in action in France less than two months before the end of World War I.

Fleishman, Veniamin (1922–41), Russian, pupil of Shostakovich, died during the Siege of Leningrad. His unfinished opera *Rothschild's Violin* was completed by Shostakovich in 1968.

Gadomski, Henryk (1907–41), Polish composer, died in Auschwitz.

Granados, Enrique (1867–1916), Spanish. Travelling to England, he was drowned when HMS *Sussex* was torpedoed in the English Channel.

Haas, Pavel (1899–1944), Czech-Jewish, met death in a Nazi gas-chamber at Terezín.

Harris, Clement Hugh Gilbert (1871–97), English composer, fought with the Greeks in the Greco-Turkish War and was killed at Pentepagadia.

Izbicki-Maklakiewicz, Franciszek (1915–39), Polish, killed by the Nazis at Luków.

Jaubert, Maurice (1900–40), French, killed in action in France.

Laparra, Raoul (1876–1943), French, killed in a Paris air-raid.

Lawes, William (1602–45), musician to King Charles I, killed in battle during the Civil War in the Siege of Chester.

Leigh, Walter (1905–42), English pupil of Hindemith, killed in action in Libya.

Magnard, Lucien Denis Gabriel Albéric (1865–1914), French, killed (or took his own life?) during the German invasion of France.

Moczyński, Zygmunt (1871–1941), Polish organist and composer, died in a Nazi concentration camp.

Novotný, Jaroslav (1886–1918), Czech, killed while fighting Bolshevik revolutionaries in the Ural Mountains.

Padlewski, Roman (1915–44), violinist and composer, killed while a member of the Polish underground army during the Warsaw Uprising.

Stadler, Alfred (1889–1943), Polish, shot as a hostage by the Nazis.

Stephan, Rudi (1887–1915), German, killed in action in Galicia.

Svento, Truvor (1910–39), Finnish, killed in action at Summajoka.

Vièrne, René (1878–1918), French organist brother of Louis, killed in action in the last six months of World War I at Verdun.

Webern, Anton (1883–1945), Austrian disciple of Schoenberg, killed by an American sentry at

Mittersill, Upper Austria, at 9.45 pm on 15 September 1945, outside his son-in-law's house, in a tragic case of mistaken identity. The sentry, although not musically aware himself, is said to have suffered from acute guilt for the rest of his life, dying in the mid-1960s in a sanatorium.

COMPOSERS WHO MET DEATH IN UNUSUAL CIRCUMSTANCES

In this list, natural causes are ignored unless they were contributed to by the unusual circumstances.

Chausson, Ernst, French, **the only composer to have written a concerto for piano, violin, and string quartet,** died after crashing his bicycle at Linnay, France, on 10 June 1899.

Delvincourt, Claude, French, was badly wounded during the First World War in spite of which he led a youth orchestra during the Second World War as a cover for subversive activities during the Nazi occupation of France, but he met his death in a road accident.

Edelmann, Johann Friedrich, German composer, guillotined in Paris.

Gautier, Pierre, French, drowned, with his entire opera company in a sea disaster off Sète, France.

Goudimel, Claude, a French composer of Catholic music who made the mistake of turning Protestant. He was among the victims of the St Bartholomew's Day massacre of Protestants.

Hoesslin, Franz von, German, killed with his wife in an air crash in September 1946 during the return journey from a concert at Barcelona.

Linley, Thomas, English, promising son of his like-named father, drowned in a boating accident in a lake at Grimsthorpe, Lincolnshire.

Lully, Jean-Baptiste (originally Giovanni Battista Lulli), Italian, naturalised French in 1661. He was composer at the Court of Louis XIV and he kept his ensemble together by beating loudly on the floor with a heavy staff. Accidentally striking his foot one day, he developed a tumour which proved fatal.

Mercure, Pierre, Canadian composer, killed in a car accident in 1966 in Paris.

Nathan, Isaac, English composer of the opera *Merry Freaks in Troublous Time* (1851), died in Sydney, Australia, under the wheels of a tramcar.

Parsons, Robert, English, drowned in the River Trent at Newark.

Schobert, Johann, German composer of instrumental music who lived in Paris. He and his family were wiped out after mistaking toadstools for mushrooms.

Wise, Michael (*c* 1648–87), English, organist, composer, and Master of the Choristers at St Paul's Cathedral, London. Losing an argument with his wife one evening in Salisbury, his home town, Wise rushed out and attacked the first person he saw. Unfortunately for him it was the nightwatchman who was armed with a billhook which he used on Wise with lethal effect. The report of the death, from *Notes for biographies of English musicians* by Antony à Wood reads: 'He was knock'd on the head and kill'd downright by the Night-watch at Salisbury for giving stubborn and refractory language to them on S. Bartholmews day at night, an. 1687.'

Zoeller, Karl (Carli) (called Léon Marteau), German composer, prime-mover in the re-establishment of the viola d'amor and the compiler of a thematic catalogue of the works of J J Quantz (MS, 1883, in the British Library, London), died after a fall during the Military Tournament at Islington, London, on 3 July 1889.

UNLUCKY COMPOSERS

Alabiev, Alexander Alexandrovich, Russian, accused of murder after a card game in 1825, and exiled to Tobolsk, Siberia, his native town.

Arnić, Blaž, Yugoslav composer who fought with Tito's partisans, but was imprisoned at Dachau in 1944.

Bittner, Julius, Austrian (see Spare-time composers), suffered a severe illness as a result of which both legs were amputated.

Laks, Szymon, German, spent four years (1941–45) in Auschwitz, but survived.

Macmillan, Sir Ernest Campbell, Canadian, imprisoned as a PoW (1914–18).

Messiaen, Olivier Eugène Prosper Charles (b 1908), French composer and pianist, was held in a German PoW camp in Silesia in 1940–41. During this time he wrote his only major chamber work, *Quartet for the End of Time*, composed for himself and the only other proficient instrumentalists in the camp: a cellist, a clarinettist, and a violinist.

Pound, Ezra, American composer who was found guilty of Fascist sympathies in Italy (1945), was extradited to the USA and confined to a mental hospital (1946–58); upon release he returned to Italy.

Tregian, Francis, English amateur and compiler of the Fitzwilliam Virginal Book, was convicted of recusancy and thrown into Fleet Prison, London, in 1609.

Wesley, Samuel, English. In 1787 at the age of 21 he toppled into a road-mender's hole and spent the rest of his life struggling with the resultant mental disability.

Women composers

The present listing has been substantially revised from that in the first edition to include many new names whilst retaining female composers of fame and prominence.

The first festival of Women's Music, organised by the Women's Interest Center, took place in America in the Spring of 1978.

Aleotti sisters, Raffaela and Victoria, Italian madrigalists.
Archer, Violet (*née* Balestreri), American symphonist.
Bacewicz, Grazyna, Polish violinist and composer.
Badarzewska, Thekla, Polish, wrote *The Maiden's Prayer* at the age of 18 and died at 23.
Beach, Amy Marcy (*née* Chaney), **the first American female to write a symphony.**
Berberian, Kathy, American singer, composed *Stripsody* for her own performance. In it, she takes exclamations from strip cartoons and welds them into a unified whole. Her indignant vocalisation of 'Good Grief!' is one of the most memorable humorous moments in modern music.
Billington, Elizabeth, English soprano and pupil of J C Bach, wrote keyboard sonatas before the age of 12.
Boulanger sisters: Nadia (Juliette) and Lili (Juliette Marie Olga). These two French composers achieved their greatest fame for their teaching abilities.
Bourges, Clémentine de (?–1561), French, possibly **the earliest Western woman composer,** said to have died of a broken heart after her husband had been killed in battle against the Huguenots.
Bright, Dora (1863–1952), English composer of three operas, piano concertos, etc, and as a pianist she was **the first to give a recital of wholly English music.**
Britton, Dorothy Guyver, American composer with great interests in Orientalism.
Bronsart, Ingeborg von (*née* Starck), Swedish pianist and composer.
Caccini, Francesca, Italian composer at a Florentine court; daughter of the famous Giulio Caccini.
Calegori, Maria Caterina, Italian singer, organist, and composer of motets, madrigals, and masses. Known as Sister Cornelia when a nun in Milan.
Candeille, Amélie Julie, French singer, pianist, harpist, actress, and composer. She was composer, librettist, and principle singer in the opera *La Belle Fermière* (1792).
Chaminade, Cecile, French pupil of Godard.
Charrière, Isabelle de, Swiss of Dutch origin, an important letter writer, feminist, and novelist.
Cianchettini, Veronica Rosalie (*née* Dušek), Bohemian pianist and composer, daughter of J L Dušek.
Coleridge Taylor, Avril Gwendolen, American, daughter of the composer of *Hiawatha's Wedding Feast* and herself a composer of songs, a Piano Concerto, etc.
Crawford, Ruth (see Seeger).
Dale, Kathleen (*née* Richards), English author, pianist, musicologist, and composer who wrote under her maiden name.
Davies, Dotie, English, wife of André Messager, composed under the pseudonym Hope Temple.
Dianda, Hilda, Argentinian pupil of Malipiero.
Dlugoszewski, Lucia, American experimentalist.
Drinker, Sophie Hutchinson, American musicologist and amateur composer, who for years worked for the advancement of women composers and their music.
Dvorkin, Judith, American song-writer.
Fleites, Virginia, Cuban neo-classicist.
Flower, Eliza, English, remembered for her hymn *Nearer, My God, to Thee.*
Gabashvili, Nana, Russian, a student at Tbilisi Music School, she has to date written some 300 songs, sonatas, marches, and a children's operetta.
Gaigerova, Varvana, Russian symphonist.
Gipps, Ruth, English pianist, conductor, and composer; pupil of Vaughan Williams, she has composed vocal, chamber, and symphonic works.
Glanville-Hicks, Peggy, Australian, pupil of Vaughan Williams, now resident in America.
Grabowska, Countess Klementyna, Polish pianist and composer who lived in Paris for the last 18 years of her life.
Hamilton, Catherine (*née* Barlow), English (or Welsh?) harpsichordist; only one work, a Minuet, survives. She met Mozart in Naples in 1770.
Hernández, Gisela, Cuban impressionist.
Holst, Imogen, English composer, conductor, and promoter of the music of her father, Gustav Holst.
Hopekirk, Helen, Scottish/American pianist and songwriter.
Jacobina, Agnes Marie, German composer for the piano.

Imogen Holst, English woman composer, with Steuart Bedford, grandson of Liza Lehmann, a composer of songs. (Courtesy EMI/Anthony Lloyd-Parker)

Janotha, Marie Cecilia Natalia, Polish, pupil of Clara Schumann, and of Brahms. It is said that her dog never missed her recitals.

Kinscella, Hazel Gertrude, American writer, composer, and musicologist.

Lane, Elizabeth, English, began composing at the age of six and had completed over 70 works by the age of 14. Her *Sinfonietta for Strings* was premièred at Fairfield Hall, Croydon, London, on 29 December 1978.

Lang, Margaret Ruthven (1867–1972), American, **the world's longest-lived composer** (see above).

Lefanu, Nicola, English composer of vocal and instrumental music, started composing in 1969.

Lehmann, Elizabeth (Liza) Mary Frederika, famous English soprano, composer of songs including *In a Persian Garden*, and an opera *The Vicar of Wakefield*. Grandmother of Steuart Bedford.

Leiviskä, Helvi Lemmikki, Finnish symphonist.

Loder, Kate Fanny, English wife of Sir Henry Thompson the surgeon. She wrote, *inter alia*, an opera called *L'élisir d'amour*.

Lutyens, Agnes Elizabeth, English twelve-tone composer.

Maconchy, Elizabeth, English composer of a wide range of works; pupil of Vaughan Williams.

Makarova, Nina Vladimirovna, Russian, wife of Khachaturian and pupil of Mussorgsky.

Marić, Ljubica, Yugoslav microtonalist and disciple of Hába.

Mendelssohn-Bartholdy, Fanny Cacilie, German, sister of Felix and composer of songs and piano pieces, some of which were published under her brother's name.

Moberg, Ida Georgina, Finnish opera and symphony composer.

More, Margaret Elizabeth, English, pupil of Josef Holbrooke and daughter-in-law of Granville Bantock.

Musgrave, Thea, Scottish pupil of Nadia Boulanger.

Oliveros, Pauline, American *avant-gardiste* interested in mixed-media work, eg: *Night Jar* (1968) for viola d'amor, tape, film, and mime.

Pade, Else Marie, Danish electronic music composer.

Prieto, Maria Teresa, Spanish symphonist.

Rees, Cathrine Felicie van (of Dutch origin), operetta composer of the 19th century and **the only female composer to write a national anthem.** See Section V.

Reisserová, Julie, Czech pupil of Foerster.

Rennes, Catharina van, Dutch singer/composer.

Rodríguez, Esther, Cuban chamber and choral composer.

Rylek-Staňková Blažena, Czech microtonalist.

Sarnecka, Jadwiga, Polish composer for the piano.

Schumann, Clara Josephine (*née* Wieck), German composer/pianist and wife of Robert Schumann.

Scott, Lady John Douglas (*née* Alicia Ann Spottiswoode), Scottish nonagenarian composer of *Annie Laurie* and *Loch Lomond*.

Seeger, Ruth Crawford, American stepmother of Pete Seeger, the folk-singer.

Sepúlveda, Maria Luisa, Chilean violinist, pianist, singer, and composer.

Smyth, Dame Ethel Mary, English, studied in Germany. She became a suffragette and was jailed in 1911 for two years. She was made a Dame in 1922; wrote orchestral music and operas.

Sutherland, Margaret, Australian composer of operas, etc. Pupil of Sir Arnold Bax.

Tailleferre, Germaine, French composer/pianist and a member of Les Six (see below, 'Groups of Composers').

Tate, Phyllis Margaret Duncan, English opera composer; has also written orchestral music including a Saxophone Concerto.

Vorlová, Slávka, first Czech woman to take a degree in composition (1948).

Weir, Judith, English oboist and composer, a pupil of John Tavener and Robin Holloway, and of Gunther Schiller at Tanglewood, USA, with whom she has studied computer and *avant-garde* music.

Weissberg, Julia Lazarevna, Russian, pupil of Rimsky-Korsakov and Glazunov.

Weldon, Georgina (*née* Thomas, then Treherne), English, friend of Gounod. She spent six months in jail in the 1880s, having been found guilty of some musical irregularity.

Wennerberg-Reuter, Sara Margareta Eugenia Eufrosyne, Swedish organist and composer.

Williams, Grace, English, pupil (but not a relation) of Vaughan Williams, and of Wellesz in Vienna.

The only composer to have undergone a sex-change operation is the American Walter (now Wendy) Carlos, well known for her synthesizer creations of the music of Johann Sebastian Bach in the recording 'Switched-On Bach'.

Groups of composers

There have been several instances of composers grouping themselves together in order to concentrate their aims, or who were grouped together by circumstances in a certain locality. These so-called 'schools' often represent important centres of musical activity. Some of the most prominent are given here, together with their members.

THE FIVE (late 19th-century Russia)

A term invented by the writer and critic Stasov; this group of composers was also known as 'The Mighty Handful'. All, apart from Rimsky-Korsakov, were 'spare-time composers' (see below), and even he began his career as a naval officer.

Balakirev, Mily Alexeyevich
Borodin, Alexander Porphyrevich
Cui, César Antonovich
Mussorgsky, Modest Petrovich
Rimsky-Korsakov, Nikolai Andreyevich

MANNHEIM SCHOOL (mid-18th century Germany)

An influential group of composers centred upon the court of the friendly and approachable Karl Theodor, Elector of Mannheim. The Elector himself was a keen cellist and flautist, and he demanded from his players a concert or an opera every day. The founders of the 'School', whose aims were a previously unattained perfection of orchestral technique, the development of exciting orchestral effects, and the integration of wind instruments into the orchestral palette, were among the earliest composers of the homophonic symphony. (Where applicable, composers' names, mainly Bohemian, are given in the original after the better-known German forms.)

Holzbauer, Ignaz
Richter, Franz Xaver (... Frantísek ...)
Stamitz, Johann Wenzel Anton (Stamic, Jan Václav Antonín)

The three composers built the new orchestra in 1742 out of the court musicians who had played at Mannheim since 1724, and before that in about 1710 at Düsseldorf. After the consolidation of the new Mannheim orchestra, the musical establishment was expanded by the arrival of other composers, most of them from Bohemia, among them being:

Cannabich, Christian
Filtz, Anton (Fils, Antonín)
Toeschi, Carl Joseph (an Italian, originally Carlo Giuseppe Toesca della Castellamonte)
Tzarth or Zart(h), Georg (Čart, Jiří).

During the second half of the century a second generation of composers influenced by, or working at, Mannheim appeared, among them:

Beck, Franz (František)
Cannabich, Carl, son of Christian
Danzi, Franz
Eichner, Ernst
Erskine, Thomas Alexander, the Scottish Earl of Kelly, who brought back to the British Isles the principles of the Mannheim School
Fränzl, Ignaz
Stamitz, Anton, son of Johann
Stamitz, Carl (Karel), son of Johann

VIENNESE SCHOOL (mid-18th century)

In the middle of the 18th century Vienna was an extremely active musical centre. The composers listed below did not necessarily work together; rather they gravitated to the Austrian capital while maintaining their independence, and it is only during the present century that the composers have been thought of as forming a group. A representative selection is given:

Albrechtsberger, Johann Georg
Bonporti, Francesco Antonio
Cimarosa, Domenico
Dittersdorf, Carl Ditters von
Koželuh, Leopold Antonín
Monn, Georg Matthias (or M G)
Porpora, Nicolò Antonio
Salieri, Antonio
Vraničky, Pavel
Wagenseil, Georg Christoph

It is, of course, the first Viennese School to which Haydn (although he worked outside Vienna until towards the end of his life), Mozart, and later, Beethoven and Schubert belonged.

SECOND VIENNESE SCHOOL (early 20th century)

Led by Schoenberg, the Second Viennese School became the centre of experiments into twelve-tone music, and the three main names (below) are regarded as the founders of the new method of composing. However, it is only fair to point out that the Austrian composer Josef Matthias Hauer (1883–1959) was developing along similar lines slightly before Schoenberg, in 1912.

Schoenberg, Arnold
Berg, Alban
Webern, Anton von

NORTH GERMAN SCHOOL AT THE TIME OF FREDERICK THE GREAT (18th century)

A vital and prolific centre of music pivoted round the Potsdam court of the flute-playing King.

Bach, Carl Philipp Emanuel
Bach, Wilhelm Friedemann
Benda, Franz (František)
Benda, Georg (Jiří Antonín)
Graun, Johann Gottlieb
Graun, Karl Heinrich
Kirnberger, Johann Philipp
Marpurg, Friedrich Wilhelm
Nichelmann, Christoph
Rodenwald, Carl Joseph
Rolle, Johann Heinrich
Schaale, Christian Friedrich
Schaffrath, Christoph

LES SIX (early 20th-century France)

Music critic Henri Collet invented this name in 1920 for a group of five French and one Swiss (Honegger) composers:

Auric, Georges
Durey, Louis
Honegger, Arthur
Milhaud, Darius
Poulenc, Francis
Tailleferre, Germaine

CAMERATA (16th–17th-century Florence)

This was a group of Florentine dilettanti who met at the palace of Count Giovanni Bardi, himself a musician, scientist, and writer, from about 1580 to 1608. The prime interest of the group was a revival of Greek drama, which they thought had had the accompaniment of music for much of the time. In the group were several poets, and it is probably due to their influence that the composers of the group sought to break away from the polyphonic singing of the time in order that the words of the songs might be understood the better in a homophonic setting. In this way, the Camerata was **the first to produce homophonic songs** which, because of the clarity of the words, began to take on a narrative function, leading gradually to a dramatic aspect. The stage was thus set for the first operas, which were produced by the composing members of the group:

Composers
Caccini, Guilio, singer/composer
Cavaliero, Emilio de'
Malvezzi, Cristofano
Peri, Jacopo, singer/composer
Strozzi, P

Poets
Chiabrera, Gabriello
Marino, Giambattista
Rinuccini, Ottavio, the first librettist (see Section V)

LA JEUNE FRANCE (mid-20th century)

A group of French composers who formed an association after the Second World War under the guiding influence of Messiaen, a pupil of Dukas and Dupré:

Baudrier, Yves
Jolivet, André, a pupil of Varèse
Lesur, Daniel
Messiaen, Olivier

BOLOGNESE SCHOOL (late 17th century)

A group of composers based in and around the San Petronio Cathedral in Bologna towards the end of the 17th century. They included:

Alberti, Giuseppe Battista (or Matteo)
Aldrovandini, Giuseppe
Bononcini, Giovanni
Grossi, Andrea
Jaccini (or Iaccini), Giuseppe Maria
Pasquini, Bernardo
Perti, Giacomo (or Jacopo?) Antonio
Torelli, Giuseppe

The group, or 'school', was responsible for some of the first symphonies and instrumental concertos ever written (see Section IV).

THE ENGLISH SCHOOL OF LUTENIST SONG-WRITERS (16th–17th-century London)

This group of composers, all active in London at about the same time, forms a 'school' only in a loose sense. They were probably acquainted, and they all wrote songs or 'ayres' with lute accompaniment.

Attey, John, the first alphabetically, but the last to publish lute songs (in 1622)
Campian, Thomas
Cavendish, Michael
Corkine, William
Dowland, John, the most famous and successful composer of his time
Ford, Thomas
Hume, Tobias
Jones, Robert
Pilkington, Francis
Rosseter, Philip

SYNTHÉTISTES (1925– Belgium)

A group of Belgian composers who followed the teaching and principles of Paul Gilson, an influential critic and mentor. Among his disciples were:

Bernier, René
Bourguignon, Francis de
Brenta, Gaston
Dejancker, Théo
Otlet, Robert
Poot, Marcel
Schoemaker, Maurice

Families of composers

The largest family of composers possessed the name Bach. Altogether 64 members of the Bach family took up music as a profession in the two centuries between 1600 and 1800. Of those only a proportion were composers as distinct from performers: many of the earlier Bachs are described as simply 'town musician' or 'organist', which neither includes nor precludes the possibility that they wrote music which has not survived. Of the proved composers, the following is a list of the ten most important in chronological order of their birth dates. The nicknames attached to Johann Sebastian's four composing sons refer to the musical centres in which they mainly worked.

BACH

Johann Christoph (1642–1703), worked in Eisenach, brother of below.
Johann Michael (1648–94), worked in Gehren, brother of above.
Johann Bernard (1676–1749), worked in Eisenach; nephew of the brothers above.
Johann Ludwig (1677—1731), worked in Meiningen; distant cousin of Johann Sebastian.
Johann Sebastian (1685–1750), worked in Cöthen and Leipzig.
Wilhelm Friedemann (1710–84), the 'Halle' Bach; first son of J S.
Carl Philipp Emanuel (1714–88), the 'Berlin' or 'Hamburg' Bach; second child of J S.
Johann Christoph Friedrich (1732–93), the 'Bückeburg' Bach; sixth child of J S.
Johann Christian (1735–82), the 'Milan' or 'London' Bach; seventh child of J S; friend of Abel and Mozart.
Wilhelm Friedrich Ernst (1759–1845), worked in Berlin; the second child of J C F.

Other identification problems may occur in the following families:

BENDA

1. František (1709–86), worked in Dresden in 1733; later with Frederick the Great in Potsdam from 1736; known as 'Franz.'
2. Friedrich Lud(e)wig (1746/52–92/94); son of 4; worked in Schwerin and Königsburg.
3. Friedrich Wilhelm Heinrich (1742–1812/14), eldest son of 1; pupil of Kirnberger, worked in Potsdam and Berlin.
4. Jiří Antonín (1722–95), worked with Frederick the Great from 1742; succeeded Stölzel at Gotha in 1749; held positions in Hamburg (1778) and Vienna (1779) before returning to Gotha in 1780. Probably the most prolific of the Benda family, Jiří wrote many symphonies, operas, and other music of all kinds. Because of his extended career in German centres, he was known as 'Georg'; references to 'G Benda' or 'J Benda' usually refer to Jiří Antonín even though the initials serve equally for other members of the family.
5. Jan (Giovanni) (1715–52), violinist and composer; died in Berlin.
6. Jan Jiří (1685–1757), one of the original Czech composers of the family and father of 1 and 4.
7. Johann Georg (see No 6).

8. Joseph (*c* 1724–1804), worked in Berlin from 1740; promoted to Konzertmeister in 1786.
9. Karl Hermann Heinrich (1748–1836), son of 1.

Two female members of the Benda family who married composers and who themselves composed:

Juliane Reichardt (1752–83).
Maria Carolina Wolf(f), probably the wife of Adolph Friedrich Wolf(f) (?–1788), himself a pupil of one of the Bendas.

HAYDN

Brothers Franz Joseph (1732–1809), worked in Esterháza and London, returning towards the end of his life to Vienna; and Johann Michael (1737–1806), worked in Salzburg. Both associated with Mozart.

LOEILLET

One is likely to come across the following given names, suggesting that there were four separate composers:

1. Jacob-Jean-Baptiste
2. Jacques
3. Jean-Baptiste
4. John

Franz Joseph Haydn, at the age of 58, suffering his first sea crossing during the journey to England at the end of 1790. (Radio Times Hulton Picture Library)

There are only two brothers involved here, in fact, each of whom changed his name. Both were born at Ghent and their original names were:

2. Jacques (1685–1746)
3. Jean-Baptiste (1680–1730)

For the last 25 years of his life, 3 Jean-Baptiste worked in London where, presumably for ease of use, he Anglicised his name to 4 John. 2 Jacques worked in Brussels, Munich, and Versailles and sometimes called himself 1 Jacob-Jean-Baptiste. It will be seen, therefore, that 3 Jean-Baptiste is identical with 4 John, and 2 Jacques is identical with 1 Jacob-Jean-Baptiste. Matters are further complicated by two other factors: both brothers wrote music for flute which to outward appearances seems similar, and the similarity to the name Lully, when pronounced in the French manner, has confused some publishers into presenting music by Loeillet as music by Lully, disregarding the wide difference in dates: Jean-Baptiste Lully (1632–87).

MARTINI

The following names are likely to be met in any study of 18th-century music. Only two brothers appear to be involved (No 16) but the similarity of their name to that of many other composers should be borne in mind. It is hoped that the following list will assist in identification:

1. Martigni, Gianbattista. Possibly a distorted version of 12 or 16a.
2. Martin, François (1727–57).
3. Martin, Philipp, a lutenist active *c* 1730–33.
4. Martin y Soler, Vicente (or Vicenzo) (1754–1806), not to be further confused with Antonio Soler (1729–83).
5. Martinelli, Antonio, active in Paris *c* 1750.
6. Martines (or Martinez), Marianne von (*c* 1744–1812), female pupil of Haydn and Porpora; worked in Vienna.
7. Martinetti. Probably a distorted version of Martinelli.
8. Martinez de la Roca, Joaquín (16 ?–17 ?), Spanish operatic composer.
9. Martini, Abbate Giovanni (18th century), worked in Venice.
10. Martini, S L (?).
11. Martini, Giuseppe (1703–79).
12. Martini, Giovanni Battista (or Giambattista) (1706–84), known as 'Padré Martini'; worked in Bologna.

13. Martini, il Tedesco (1741–1816) (ie 'Martini the German', whose real name was Johann Paul Aegidius Schwarzendorf). Alternative versions of his given names are Jean and Giovanni Paolo.
14. Martino, Filippo (=3 ?).
15. Martino, Johann Baptiste =16a.
16. Sammartini. Two brothers:
(a) Giovanni Battista (1698 or 1701 to 1775); (b) Giuseppe (*c* 1693–*c* 1750/1).
Originally San Martini or San Martino, the names of these two composers have undergone considerable confusion and distortion. By convention rather than logic the names are given usually as follows in order to aid differentiation:
(a) Giovanni Battista Sammartini, worked in Milan.
(b) Giuseppe San Martini, worked in London.
There exist early editions of sonatas by 'Giuseppe San Martino di Milano' etc, the correct attributions of which may never be resolved.
17. San Martino—see 16.

MOZART

A clear father–son–grandson case. It is probably true to say that, had not the son been so overwhelmingly great, his father's and his son's music, attractive though it is, might never be heard today.

1. Johann Georg Leopold (1719–87).
2. Wolfgang Amadeus (christened Johannes Chrysostomus Wolfgangus Theophilus—both Amadeus and Theophilus mean 'loved by God') (1756–91).
3. Franz Xaver (later known as Wolgang Amadeus II) (1791–1844), a pupil of Albrechtsberger and Salieri, and the composer of over 50 works. Unfortunately his fate has been to fall too completely into the eclipsing shadow of his father.

SCHMIDT, SCHMITT, AND SMITH

A German case similar to the Italian Martini. Traces of the lives and works of the following musicians have been found in reference books:

1. Schmid, Fr X (=Franz Xaver?).
2. Schmidt, Antoni.
3. Schmid(t), Ferd(inand?).
4. Schmidt, Johann Christoph (1644–1720/28?), Kapellmeister in Dresden.
5. Schmidt or Schmitt, Joseph (or Giuseppe) (*c* 1750?–1808/15?), a prolific composer of symphonies and chamber works.
6. Schmidt, Leopold.
7. Schmiedt, Siegfried, a keyboard composer active *c* 1780–90.
8. Schmitt, F (=1?).
9. Schmitt, Johann Christian (1712–95)=John Christopher Smith, Handel's amanuensis.
10. Schmitt, Joseph (1734–91), like his near-namesake, 5, a composer of many symphonies and chamber works.
11. Schmitte, may refer to any of the above when given without further identification.
12. Smith, John Christopher, of German origin—see 9.
13. Smith, John Stafford (1750–1836), composer, conductor, and organist in London who collaborated with Sir John Hawkins in the preparation of the latter's *General History of the Science and Practice of Music* (1776).
14. Smith, Theodor, an English (?) composer of keyboard music, active *c* 1780.

STRAUSS AND STRAUS

Five distinct and unconnected families are involved:

A: Strauss, Johann (I) (1804–49), an Austrian populariser, if not the inventor, of the Viennese waltz which, together with other dances, swamped musical activities in that city in the 1830s. He sired three musical sons:

1. Johann (II) (1825–99), rival of, and later successor to, his father at the head of Viennese dance music. His output was immense and his popularity by far outshone that of his father.
2. Josef (1827–70), a reluctant musician at first, once he was caught in the swirl of family activities his talent flourished, and although he never attained his brother's popularity he was arguably a more profound composer.
3. Eduard (1835–1916), best remembered as a conductor, he nevertheless composed more than 250 works. He was the father of:
Johann (III) (1866–1939), primarily a conductor in the tradition of his uncle (Johann II) and grandfather (Johann I).

B: Strauss, Franz (1822–1905), no relation to the above. He was a horn-player in the Munich opera and the composer of an attractive Horn Concerto and other works. He was father of:
Richard (1864–1949), known chiefly for his operas, eg: *Salome* (1905), *Elektra* (1908), *Der Rosenkavalier* (1910), *Arabella* (1932), and *Daphne* (1937); also for tone poems, horn concertos, songs, etc.

C: Strauss, Christoph (*c* 1580–1631), Austrian composer of church music. No known connection with any later musical family.

D: Straus, Oscar (1870–1954), Austrian composer of operas and operettas, *The Chocolate Soldier* being among the best known of the latter. He was unrelated to Family B, but his *Three Waltzes* was based upon music of

Johann I and II; Oscar Straus himself contributed the final act.

E: Straus, Ludwig (1835–99), Austrian violinist (not a composer) who travelled widely before settling in England, where he led Manchester's Hallé Orchestra and was Queen Victoria's 'solo violinist'. There is no evidence of any relationship to any of the figures listed above.

Nicknames

Composers, as well as their works (see Section IV), have been given nicknames. They range from the flippant, through the physically descriptive, to attempts to identify the recipient's place in the history of music. In both this section and the following, Pseudonymous Composers, some names which appeared in the first edition of this book have been removed to make way for others.

COMPOSER NICKNAMES

Nickname	*Composer*	*Remarks*
Bassetto	Grassi, Francesco	Roman composer, *c* 1701
Belgian Orpheus, The	Lassus, Roland de	
Berlin Bach, The	Bach, C P E	
Bückeburg Bach, The	Bach, J C F	
Buranello Il	Galuppi, Baldassare	Born on the Venetian island Burano
Caro Sassone, il	Hasse, J A	Known thus in Italy
Clemens non Papa	Clemens, Jacob	Name given to prevent confusion with Clemens Papa, the Flemish poet
Divino Boemo, il	Mysliveček, Josef	Also known as Josef Venatorini—anything, it seems, to relieve the Austrians with whom he worked from wrestling with his real name
English Bach, The	Bach, J C	The only member of the illustrious family to make his living as a composer in England
Father of the Symphony	Haydn, F J	A misleading epithet since the symphony had reached an advanced form before Haydn entered the field. 'Godfather of the Symphony' would be more accurate
Father of Swedish Music	Roman, J H	
Hamburg Bach, The	Bach, C P E	
Hunchback of Arras, The	Hale, Adam de la	French trouvère
London Bach, The	Bach, J C	Worked in London from 1763
Longstrides	Bedyngham, J	Fifteenth-century sacred composer, presumably of ample gait
Milan Bach, The	Bach, J C	Worked in Milan before going to England
Music's Prophet	Monteverdi, Claudio	From him sprang the roots of opera and other vital forms
Napoleon of Music, The	Rossini, G A	He is said to have conquered Europe with his music
Old Nosey	Bas(s)evi, Giacomo (Cervetto)	Perhaps a reference to a physiognomical characteristic
Papa Haydn	Haydn, F J	Refers to his alleged paternity of the symphony; see Father of the Symphony, above
Prince of Music, The	Palestrina, G P de	This name was engraved upon the lid of his coffin
Red Priest, The	Vivaldi, A L	He is said to have had startling red hair
Signor Crescendo	Rossini, G A	Not the inventor of this device (see Section VII), but certainly one of the most demanding employers of it
Strauss of Italy, The	Respighi, O	So-called perhaps by jealous Italians

Nickname	*Composer*	*Remarks*
Sweetest Swan, The	Marenzio, L	An admired madrigalist also sometimes called 'The Divine Composer'
Wife of Haydn, The	Boccherini, L	An unkind name, given to indicate that, although of the same family as Haydn's, Boccherini's music has an effeminate weakness and insubstantiality (see p 74)
Wundermann, Der	Saint-Germain	See the Longest-lived Composer, above, for the alleged reasons for the name

Pseudonymous composers

Throughout musical history composers, for a variety of reasons, have chosen to write under pseudonyms. Southern Europe in the 18th century saw a rash of alternative Arcadian names, a few of which assumed the role of nicknames, and in the same century there was a craze for anagrams and back-spellings. Of more practical use are those names chosen to render their owners pronounceable and recognisable in the foreign countries in which they were working; sometimes these names are 'translations' of the meanings of the originals, while others are apparently arbitrarily adopted local names. In most cases simplification seems to have been the aim.

Pseudonym	*Real name*	*Remarks*
Adams, Stephen	Maybrick, Michael	Composer of *The Holy City*
Agricola, Alexander	Ackermann, Alexander	Dutch motet-writer who adopted the Latin name when working in Spain
Arcimelo	Corelli, Arcangelo	Italian composer; Arcadian form
Arma, Paul	Weisshans, I	Hungarian student of Bartók
Ben Haim, Paul	Frankenburger, P	Israeli conductor and composer
Berlijn, Anton	Wolf, A	Dutch composer and conductor
Berlin, Irving	Baline, Israel	American composer of Russian origin who wrote *I'm Dreaming of a White Christmas*, etc
Caesar	Smegergill, W	English lutenist and song-writer
Coperario, Giovanni	Cooper, John	English composer, dissatisfied with his mundane name
Copland, Aaron	Kaplan, A	American composer of East European origin
Duke, Vernon	Dukelsky, Vladimir	Russian composer resident in New York since 1929
Duncan, Trevor	Trebilco, Leonard	Scottish composer of the signature tune of the long-running BBC TV series *Dr Finlay's Casebook* ('March' from the *Little Suite*)
Dvorsky, Michael	Hofmann, Josef	Polish pianist and composer
Esipoff, Stepan	Burnand, A	English piano composer and friend of Liszt. See also Strelezki, A
Foss, Lukas	Fuchs, Lukas	German-born American pianist/composer
Fürstenberger, von	Gordigiani, Luigi	Italian pianist who composed under this pseudonym and under 'Zeuner'
German, Edward	Jones, Edward German	English composer of *Tom Jones*, *Merrie England*, etc
Gore, Gerald Wilfring	Riegger, Wallingford	American, one of eight pseudonyms, this one is strictly anagrammatic

Pseudonym	*Real name*	*Remarks*
Halévy, J F F E	Lévy, Jacques François Fromental Elie	French operatic composer whose daughter married his ex-pupil Bizet
Hammer, F X	Marteau, Franz Xaver	German cellist/composer at Pressburg in 1783
Hardelot, Guy d'	Rhodes, Helen	Female composer. 'Guy' from her maiden name; Hardelot from her French birthplace.
Hervé	Ronger, Florimond	French composer for the stage
Hopkins, Antony	Reynolds, Antony	English composer; also a well-known broadcaster
Imareta, Tirso	Yriarte, Tomás	Near-anagram used by a Spanish poet and symphonist
Ireland, Francis	Hutcheson, F	Irish doctor and composer of catches and glees
Irvid, Richard	Marquis Richard d'Ivry	French operatic composer
Joncières, Victorin de	Rossignol, F L	French composer. Also wrote as a critic under the name 'Jennius'
Keler-Béla	Keler, Adalbert von	Hungarian march- and dance-composer
Klenovsky, Paul	Wood, Sir Henry	English conductor who, when orchestrating Bach's famous organ Toccata and Fugue in D minor (BWV 565), decided to perform it under the name of a recently deceased Russian composer
Lara, Adelina de	Tilbury, A	English pianist and composer. De Lara was her mother's maiden name
Lara, Isidore de	Cohen, I	English opera composer
Linjauna, Jaakko Armas	Lindemann, J A	Finnish; changed his name in 1935
Linko, Ernst Frederik	Lindroth, E F	Finnish; changed his name in 1906
Linnala, Eino Mauno	Bergman, E M	Finnish; changed his name in 1906
Lothar, Louis	Dupin, Paul	French composer; see Deaf Composers, above
Mathis, G S	Seiber, Matyás	English; used the pseudonym when writing for the accordion
McColl	Dawson, Peter	Well-known Australian singer who composed *Boots*
Meyerbeer, Giacomo	Beer, Jakob Liebmann	German composer primarily of stage music
Mortimer, Philip	Knight, J P	English song composer
Nipredi	Pedrini, T	Anagrammatic name of ?Italian composer at the Chinese Emperor's court in the 18th century
Novello, Ivor	Davies, David Ivor	Welsh composer of musicals and of the song *Keep the Home Fires Burning*
O'Byrne, Dermot	Bax, Arnold Edward Trevor	English; used this pseudonym only for his literary works
Offenbach, Jacques	Wiener, Jakob	Born at Offenbach, Germany. Other references give Levy and Eberscht as his real name, but Wiener appears to be correct
Palestrina, Pierluigi	Pierluigi, Giovanni	Took his name from his birthplace in Italy
Pinto, George Frederick	Sanders, G F	English prodigy who died at the age of 20; took his maternal grandfather's surname. The elder Pinto is said to have been an extremely capable musician, able to sight-read with the music upside-down
Regnal, Frédéric	Erlanger, Frédéric d'	Composer of German/American parentage, naturalised English
Riadis, Emil	Khu, Emil	Greek; adapted his mother's maiden name: Eleftheriadis
Rudhyar, Dane	Chennevière, Daniel	French composer who lived in America from 1917

Pseudonym	*Real name*	*Remarks*
Senez, Camille de	Wayditch von Verhovac, Count Gabriel	German composer of 14 operas
Sharm	Marsh, John	Anagram; English composer
Siklós, Albert	Schönwald, A	Hungarian musicologist and composer, changed his name legally in 1910
Sommer, Hans	Zincken, H F A	German; also anagramised his name to Hans Neckniz
Strelezki, Anton	Burnand, A	See Esipoff
Strinfalico, Eterio	Marcello, Alessandro	Italian composer; Arcadian form
Stuart, Leslie	Barrett, Thomas A	English musical-comedy writer: *Floradora* (1899); also composed *Soldiers of the Queen*
Suppé, Franz von	Suppe-Demelli, Francesco Ermenegildo Ezechiele	Operetta-writer of Belgian origin
Thorn, Edgar	MacDowell, Edward	American; an occasionally used pseudonym
Venatorini, Josef	Mysliveček, Josef	See also il Divino Boemo under Nicknames, above
Vincent, Heinrich Joseph	Wunzenhörlein, H J	Viennese operatic composer
Warlock, Peter	Heseltine, Philip	English composer who committed suicide
Wynne, David	Thomas, D W	Welsh church composer
Zeuner		See Fürstenberger

The composer with the most pseudonyms was the Englishman Charles Arthur Rawlings (1857–1919). We are grateful to his grandson Henry Vauvelle-Wright of Surrey who has kindly supplied information about C A Rawlings and his brother Alfred William Rawlings (1860–1924), also the possessor of a number of pseudonyms. Both were pupils of Charles Gounod and were extremely prolific, composing for organ, piano, violin, mandolin, military band, and other groups including full orchestra, and their music was published in Europe (Czechoslovakia, Holland, Germany, Sweden, Denmark, France, and England) as well as in Canada and America.

It is not known whether the following lists of pseudonyms are complete since some works may have been published under different names in countries that failed to notify the fact to the English Performing Right Society.

Charles Arthur Rawlings
Jean Augarde
Haydn Auguarde
Jean Bartelet
Paul Blanc
Emile Bonheur
F Bonheur
Georges Bonheur
Isidore Bonheur
Otto Bonheur
Raymond Bonheur
Theo Bonheur
Emile Bonte
Faulkner Brandon
Louis Brandon
Emile Bronte
Paul Carolon
Henri Clermont
Auguste Cons
Eugene Delacassa
Paul Delaporte
Leo Delcasse
Eileen Dore
Jean Douste
Denis Dupré
Seymour Ellis
Paul Genèe
Robert Graham
John Gresham
Maxine Heller
Emerson James
Harrington Leigh
François Lemara
Gilbert Loewe
Angelo Martino
Alphonse Menier
Nita
Carolan Le Page
Paul Perrier
Maxine Pontin
Elsie Rawling
Abe Rawlings
Horatio E Rawlings
Wellington Rawlings
Carl Reubins
Carl Ritz
Carl Rubens
Edward Sachs
Emile Sachs
Hans Sachs
Ralph Seymour
Herman Straus
Maurice Telma
Gordon Temple
Leon du Terail
Paul Terrier
Thomas Thomé
Claude de Vere
H Verne
Oscar Verne
Beryl Vincent
Sidney West
Christine Williams

Alfred William Rawlings
Leslie Conyers
Max Dressler
Gustave Dumas
Pete Dwyer
Florence Fare
Edith Fortescue
Stanley Gordon
Hamilton Henry
Marcus Hope
Louis Jasper

Felix Lemoine	Ivan Stephanoff
Gladys Melrose	Ivan Tchakoff
Guy Morris	A de Tchatchkoff
Tito Natale	Horace Templeman
Paul Peronne	Jules Therese
Paul Perrion	John William Tomlinson
Edward St Quentin	Lionel Tree
G de St Quentin	Constance V White
Ch Stephano	Sydney Wyman

C A and A W Rawlings were the last of a family of musicians dating back to 1703. Their two brothers and sister were also active in the music world: Ernest Rawlings (1871–1919) as a traveller for a music publisher, Walter Rawlings (1865–88) as a bandsman in the Highland Light Infantry, and Emily Rawlings (1851–1940), a singer trained by Sir Julius Benedict, who became a teacher of music.

The American hymn-composer Philipp Paul Bliss is said to have disguised his works under more than 60 pseudonyms.

Composers: facts and feats

The most ingratiating composer could be said to be Luigi Boccherini (1743–1805). In a period of musical history, when the tendency was to think of music in black and white, with half-tones and subtle statements the exception rather than the rule, Boccherini went to considerable trouble to present the reverse image. The direction 'sotto voce' ('in an undertone') abounds in his music to such an extent as to become almost a mannerism, and mild-mannered rhythms and sweet, gently curling melodies put his style apart from the more conventional 18th-century composer.

Examination of his nearly 600 works, amounting to some 1400 movements, reveals that the following directions appear:

Affettuoso ('affectionately')	20 times
Grazioso ('gracefully') or con grazia ('with grace')	25 times
Amoroso ('lovingly')	37 times
Soave ('agreeably', 'sweetly', 'delicately', 'gently', 'caressingly', 'lightly'), also soave assai ('extremely ...') and soavita, and once even soave e con grazia	54 times
Dolce ('sweetly') or Dolcissimo ('very sweetly and gently')	148 times

Also to be found are Armonico ('harmoniously'), con innocenza ('with innocence'), piacere ('pleasingly'), and allegretto gentile ('not too fast, lightly and cheerfully', 'pleasingly', 'elegantly', 'gracefully'), together with hundreds of directions calling for very quiet playing (*pp* and *pp sempre*).

Contrast the above with his use of forceful indications, and his essentially gentle and pleasing nature becomes clear:

Appassionato ('passionately')	8 times
con brio ('with fire')	6 times
con forza ('with force')	once

The most tortuous distortion of a composer's name surrounds the Flute Concerto in D by Pokorný, which was attributed to, and has been recorded as by, Boccherini. This particular misattribution seems to have come about as a result of a misreading of the name on the autograph:

Other distortions occurred during the 18th century, which may be fairly termed 'the Age of Inaccuracy' where music is concerned: Schmidtbauer became Bauerschmitt or Baurschmidt, etc, Holzbauer became Olxburg, and Wagenseil became Vagausell. There are countless other examples.

The most arrogant composer was Richard Wagner (1813–83). Many stories circulate to illustrate his high-handed attitude with his associates; one which typifies his overt disdain of the Jewish race is the report of his habit of conducting the music of Mendelssohn only while wearing gloves. At the end of the performance he would remove the garments and throw them to the floor, to be removed by the cleaners.

It was due to this anti-Semitic attitude that the Third Reich 'adopted' the music of Wagner and the spirit of Wagnerism, at the same time banning the performance of Mendelssohn's, and all Jews', music.

Gloves were also worn by Louis Antoine Jullien (1812–60) when he conducted Beethoven in London, but the gloves were pure white, were brought to him on a silver tray, and were intended as a mark of deep respect.

Incidentally, Jullien, himself a composer, was

blessed with **the most forenames.** At his baptism at Sisteron, France, where his father played a Violin Concerto at the Philharmonic Society, each of the 36 members of the Society insisted that he should stand as godfather. Thus, the baby was named:

Louis Georges Maurice Adolf Roch Albert Abel Antonio Alexandre Noé Jean Lucien Daniel Eugène Joseph-le-brun Joseph Barème Thomas Thomas Thomas-Thomas Pierre-Cerbon Pierre-Maurel Barthelemi Artus Alphonse Bertrand Dieudonné Emanuel Josué Vincent Luc Michel Jules-de-la-plane Jules-Bazin Julio César Jullien. See Unfortunate composers, (**c**).

The fastest composer? This question has often been asked, but the answer cannot be clear since the question is imprecise. The *consistently* fastest composer must be Schubert who, as we see below, composed over 1000 works (each of his operas, cycles of songs numbering up to 24 individual items, suites of dances for piano or orchestra, and other groups of compositions counting as *one* each) in eighteen years, five months (May 1810 to October 1828). There are many instances in which Schubert would start and finish a work during the course of a single day.

Even this pace of composing may be surpassed by other men working *in spurts*. Vivaldi is said to have been able to compose a concerto in all its parts faster than his copyists could copy it; likewise Telemann (see below). Rossini is supposed to have been so laggardly for much of the time that he had to work fast on occasion to meet theatrical deadlines. A story, probably apocryphal, relates that an irate impresario, faced with an overtureless opera, locked Rossini in a room with manuscript paper and pen until he had written the overture. The composer is said to have passed the completed pages out through a window one by one to the waiting copyists. The story, attractive though it is, does not explain why that impresario found this course easier than the one usually adopted in such circumstances of borrowing an overture from another opera: the Overture to *The Barber of Seville* (1816) had already served for *Elisabetta, Regina d'Inghilterra* in 1815, and for *Aureliano in Palmira* two years earlier.

In modern times rapid composing is less common, due perhaps to the less demanding conditions in which present-day composers are required

Richard Wagner. (Radio Times Hulton Picture Library)

Paganini, Italian violinist and composer and the fastest violinist of all time. (Lithography by Begas/Popperfoto)

to conceive their music. Hindemith, however, on Tuesday, 20 January 1936, composed a *Meditation* for viola (his own instrument) and string orchestra in just over five hours in memory of the death of King George V which had occurred that day. The composer took the solo part at the rehearsals the following morning and the work was broadcast by the BBC that evening. *Meditation* is a work in four sections, lasting a total of 15 minutes.

It has been necessary to omit artistic feats in this book, but the following concerns an artist who was also a composer, and serves further to substantiate Paganini's reputation as one of the world's greatest virtuosi. He was the **fastest violinist,** playing his *Movimento perpetuo* ('Perpetuela') in three minutes, three seconds. With a note count of 2212, equating with 2228 semiquavers, his speed was faster than twelve notes per second.

The youngest composer of music which is still available for performance is Wolfgang Amadeus Mozart, whose earliest work was a Minuet and Trio in G, K 1, dated 1761, when the composer was four years old. Several more pieces appeared the following year, and thereafter his output accelerated until by the time he was 20 he had written his first 30 numbered symphonies (and several unnumbered ones) including the great Nos 25 in G minor and 29 in A, twelve Masses and numerous other church works, eight operas and other stage works, more than a dozen sonatas for various instruments, 13 string quartets, the B flat String Quintet, K 174, and countless divertimentos, cassations, serenades, dances, marches, keyboard pieces, vocal works, and concertos. In the last category are five for keyboard (mostly based on the sonata movements of acquaintances), five for violin, one for bassoon, and the Concertone (= 'large concerto') for two violins and orchestra.

At his death at the age of 35, Mozart's total of works stood at or about the 1000 mark.

Despite their extraordinary fecundity, both Franz Peter Schubert and Jakob Ludwig Felix Mendelssohn-Bartholdy were comparatively late starters. Mendelssohn's earliest works date from his early teens, and works of true genius from his 17th year (the Octet in E flat and the Overture to *A Midsummer Night's Dream*); Schubert's earliest work is a Fantasia in G for piano duet, completed on 1 May 1810, when he was 13. He went on to compose over 1000 works in all forms then current, many of them not performed until many years after his death at the age of 31. Schubert is unique among composers for his astonishing productivity, especially since every one of his works must be regarded as 'early'.

It should be mentioned that Camille Saint-Saëns is said to have composed music at the age of three years, but none has survived from this period.

The most promising composer may have been the Finnish youngster (1920–36) Heikki Theodor Suolahti who, at his death at the age of 16, left a complete *Agnus Dei* (1936), a Violin Concerto (1934), a *Sinfonia Piccola* (1935), and, in incomplete form, a Piano Concerto, an opera, a ballet and some tone poems. In quality, Professor Andrej Rudnev writing in *Grove V* described them as 'Amazingly mature works of romantic style'.

The most prolific composer of all time was Georg Philipp Telemann (1681–1767). His works are in process of being catalogued by a group of German scholars to be published as the *Telemann-Werke-Verzeichnis* by Bärenreiter in Kassel, Germany. This project was begun in 1950 and is still not complete; therefore it is too soon to attempt to give an accurate list of his compositions.

It is known, however, that he composed 40 operas, 40 passions, over 100 cantatas, and countless (as yet) orchestral suites and overtures (some estimates make it nearly 600, although a published thematic catalogue—see Hoffmann in Section VII—lists only 135, of which one is a doubtful attribution), concertos for virtually every melody instrument in existence at that time, hundreds of keyboard works and chamber pieces, etc. No other composer covered so wide a field so prolifically.

The composer who inspired most imitation and who provided the basis for most later works was Gioacchino Rossini, whose highly personal and spirited style serves as inspiration for many composers. Apart from the unacknowledged compositions which lie in the wake of Rossini's successful formulae, the following openly admit the Italian's influence:

Benjamin Britten: *Soirées Musicales* (1936); *Matinées Musicales* (1941)—based on themes by Rossini.

Eric William Fenby: *Rossini on Ilkla Moor* (1948), an overture in which the well-known Yorkshire song is subjected to Rossinian orchestration and development.

Fritz Geissler: *Italian Comedy Overture after Rossini* (1958). Rossini-like fragments are set into modern harmonic language and built into a work in buffo-overture form.

Mauro Giuliani: *Rossiniana*, Suites Opp 119 and 121.

Renato de Grandis: *La Rossiniana*, Divertimento (1968), also turned into a ballet.

François Hainl: *Fantasy on Themes of William Tell.*

Hans Ludwig Hirsch: *Homage to Rossini*, a twelve-minute work for full orchestra.

Gordon Jacob: Overture: *The Barber of Seville Goes to the Devil.* A mock Rossini work of great wit and charm.

Bohuslav Martinů: *Variations on a Theme of Rossini* (1959) for cello and piano.

Ottorino Respighi: *La Boutique Fantasque* (1919); *Rossiniana* (1925). In both these works Respighi, by adapting some of the lesser-known music of Rossini to ballet presentation, has popularised music which might otherwise have been known only to specialists.

Archduke Rudolf: *Variations on a Theme of Rossini.*

Franz Schoberlechner: *Fantasia and Variations on a Theme of Rossini*, Op 38 (1823). Schoberlechner was a pupil of Hummel.

Franz Peter Schubert: Overtures in the Italian Style: in C, D 591 (1817); in D, D 590 (1817). Written at the height of Rossini's popularity, Schubert is said to have set out to prove that writing a Rossini overture is a facile achievement.

Dmitri Shostakovich: Symphony No 15 in A, Op 141 (1971). The first movement contains several references to the famous 'galop' from Rossini's *William Tell* Overture.

Sigismond Thalberg: *Fantasy of Rossini's 'Moise'*, Op 33; *Fantasy on Rossini's 'Barbiere'*, Op 63.

Spare-time composers

There are many composers for whom the activity of composing occupied only a fraction of their time, part, or indeed the majority, of their energies being channelled elsewhere. The list below omits the many priests and cantors who also composed, since the dispensing of music was in many instances an integral part of their duties.

Additional names were given in the first edition.

Balakirev, Mily Alexeyevich (1837–1910), worked for five years (1871–76) as an official in the expanding Russian railway system.

Belcher, Supply (1751–1836), American innkeeper who wrote an opera titled *The Harmony of Maine*, produced in Boston in 1794.

Berners, Lord (Gerald Hugh Tyrwhitt-Wilson) (1883–1950), composer of the ballet *The Triumph of Neptune* (1926) and many parodistic and ironic works (eg: *Du bist wie eine Blume*, a song dedicated to a pig), was also diplomat, painter, novelist, and illustrator.

Billings, William (1746–1800), one of the earliest American composers; a song-writer and lyricist noted for his fuguing hymn tunes, he was by trade a tanner.

Bittner, Julius (1874–1939), Austrian, pupil of Bruno Walter and opera composer; a lawyer by profession.

Borodin, Alexander Porphyrevich (1883–97), world renowned because of his 'Polovtsian Dances' from the opera *Prince Igor* (1890) and other delightfully tuneful works, he was in fact an amateur musician, his time being absorbed largely by research into chemistry for a Russian university.

Bowles, Paul Frederick (b 1910), American composer, linguist, and author of novels and short stories.

Burghersh, Lord (John Fane) (1784–1859), English opera composer and prominent soldier.

Cage, John (b 1912), American *avant-garde* composer who has so many other activities that he may be regarded as an all-rounder: he is commercial artist, critic, teacher, poet, writer, lecturer, etc.

Campian, Thomas (1567–1620), English song-writer who was also poet, lawyer, and physician.

Cui, César Antonovich (1853–1918), a General in the Russian Army.

Dahl, Ingolf (1912–70), German-born American composer, writer, and teacher.

Dibdin, Charles (1745–1814), English composer of numerous operas, also a theatrical manager, publisher, and author.

Herschel, Wilhelm Friedrich (1738–1822), the famous German astronomer who discovered the Martian polar caps and the existence of the planet Uranus (which he called 'Georgium Sidus'), and who postulated the theory that some so-called 'variable' stars were in fact double stars with a common centre of gravity (a theory since proved to be correct), was also a talented composer and organist.

Hoffmann, Ernst Theodor Wilhelm (1776–1822), the German writer immortalised in Offenbach's opera *The Tales of Hoffman* (1881), was a theatrical manager, lawyer, artist, and municipal official. He revered Mozart, adopting the name Amadeus to replace Wilhelm, and he composed instrumental music, an opera, etc.

Ireland, Francis (real name: F Hutcheson) (1721–80), Irish doctor and glee composer.

Ives, Charles (1874–1953), American experimental composer who was a successful businessman until ill health in his late 40s dictated a less strenuous career.

Kryzhanovsky, Ivan Ivanovich (1867–1924), Russian army doctor and composer.

Lichtenthal, Peter (1780–1853), Austrian doctor and amateur composer.

Moore, Patrick (b 1923), English broadcaster and amateur astronomer, composer of two operas.

Morgan, Justin (1747–98), American full-time horse-breeder, also teacher, innkeeper, and composer.

Mussorgsky, Modest Petrovich (1839–81), Russian composer of *Boris Godounov* and *Pictures from an Exhibition* (both 1874), he was an army officer and later a civil servant.

Rimsky-Korsakov, Nikolay Andreyevich (1844–1908), Russian naval officer before turning to music full time.

Rousseau, Jean-Jacques (1712–78), the Swiss author, philosopher, religious and political thinker (he wrote *The Social Contract* in 1762), was an active composer in France.

Teplov, Grigorii Nikolayevich (1719–89), the composer of the first Russian 'art-songs', he was also a prominent politician.

Xenakis, Iannis, Romanian-born Greek composer (b 1922), assistant during the 1950s to Le Corbusier, the architect.

The most exclusively pianistic composers were both expatriate Poles. Fryderyk Franciszek Chopin (1810–49), a piano virtuoso himself, was born near Warsaw, but later settled in Paris and never returned to Poland despite widespread tours. Not a single work of his composition excludes the piano. His output of nocturnes, waltzes, mazurkas, polonaises, etc, is well known, as are his two piano concertos. In addition there are many songs, a cello sonata, all accompanied by piano, and a piano trio in G minor, Op 8. The purely orchestral ballet *Les Sylphides* is merely a selection of arrangements from his piano works orchestrated by various musicians, the most widely known being Roy Douglas. Various other orchestral pieces (under such titles as *Chopiniana*, *La Nuit ensorcelée*, *Chopinata*), come into the same category of arrangements from piano originals.

Leopold Godowski (1870–1938), another renowned Polish virtuoso, who adopted American citizenship, wrote a vast corpus of compositions almost (apart from a number of songs and violin pieces accompanied by piano) exclusively for his instrument.

By contrast, as the composer calling for **the most divers instrumentation,** we may cite the American pupil of Dallapiccola, Salvador Martirano (b 1927) who, in addition to conventional requirements for orchestra, wind sextet, string quartet and other chamber ensembles, choruses, piano and solo voices, has scored for marimba, celesta, amplified night-club singer, tape, three film projectors, gas-masked politico, and helium bomb.

Opposite top: The 'tallest' composer was Gian-Carlo Menotti (American, of Italian origin, born 1911) who, according to information he inserted on a US immigration document whilst thinking about his next libretto, stands '11 feet, 5 inches' tall.

Opposite bottom: Roy Harris, quintessential American symphonist. (Courtesy: International Communications Agency)

The most brittle (?) composer was the American, Roy Harris (1898–1979), who broke his left arm, his nose, and a finger on his right hand on the football field in 1913, fractured his spine in 1930, and broke his right knee into 20 pieces in a car accident in 1953.

An imaginary composer was Pierre Ducré, invented by Berlioz to account for the ancient style of the 'Shepherd's Farewell' in *L'Enfance du Christ*.

The most married composer was Eugene Frances Charles d'Albert (1864–1932), German (of French descent, born in Scotland) composer of the opera *Tiefland* (1903), who had six successive wives.

The only composer without a nose was Josef Mysliveček (1737–81), Bohemian, known as 'il Divino Boemo.' He was the victim of a quack surgeon who decided that the only way of curing 'the divine Bohemian's' veneral disease was to cut off his nose.

Honoured composers

Perhaps the greatest honour to be bestowed upon an English composer is to receive the appointment of Master of the Queen's (or King's) Musick, but other composers have received different honours:

The earliest composer to be awarded a Doctorate of Music at Cambridge was Robert Fayrfax (1464–1521), who was thus honoured in 1504.

The first composer to be knighted by an English monarch was Henry Rowley Bishop (1786–1855), honoured by Queen Victoria in 1842. Bishop wrote the timeless song 'Home Sweet Home'.

The youngest Oxford music graduate was John Stanley, blinded at the age of two, who graduated in July 1729 at the age of 16½ years.

The two most honoured composers were Alexander Campbell MacKenzie, Scottish violinist and composer. He received honorary music doctorates from St Andrews (1886), Cambridge (1888), Edinburgh (1890), and Oxford (1922) universities, LL.D from Glasgow (1901), M'Gill (1903), and Leeds (1904); he received the Gold Medal of the Royal Philharmonic Society (1923); he was knighted by Queen Victoria in 1895; and he was created Knight Commander of the Victoria Order in 1922.

Ignacy Jan Paderewski (1860–1941) the Polish pianist, composer, and the first Polish Prime Minister, received honorary MusD from Yale (1917), Cambridge (1926), New York (1933); LL.D from Oxford (1920), Columbia (1922), South California (1923), Glasgow (1925); PhD from Lwów (1912), Cracow (1919), Poznán (1924). His awards included the Great Cordon of the Order Polonia Restituta; the Great Cross of the Order of the British Empire; the Grand Cross of the Legion of Honour; the Great Cordon of the Order of Leopold; the Great Cordon of the Order of SS Maurice and Lazarus; the City of Warsaw Music Prize; and he received the freedom of the City of Lausanne. Poland acknowledged him posthumously with the Cross of 'Virtuti militari', and in 1978 a statue sculpted in 1939 by Michael Kamienski was at last unveiled in Warsaw after being preserved in the Polish National Museum since the end of World War Two. During the Nazi occupation it was kept hidden for fear of being destroyed by the Germans.

The composer of the noisiest symphonies was reputedly the Italian Abbé Giovanni Pietro Maria Crispi (1737–97), who wrote sixteen symphonies in the bright, martial key of D major (his two others are in G major). He was said by Sir Charles Burney to have composed symphonies 'too furious and noisy for a room or, indeed, for any other place'. It should be borne in mind that this opinion is based on 18th-century premises and does not take into account the symphonic extravagancies of the 19th and 20th centuries.

A most exciting life was led by Giovanni Giuseppe Cambini (1746–1825), an Italian composer of a vast amount of chamber and orchestral music. He is reputed to have abducted a young girl in Naples and, sailing with her to Leghorn, they were waylaid by pirates. Their future was to be a life of slavery. Romantic writers would have us believe that Cambini was bound and manacled by the pirates, who then set about violating his young companion, of whom nothing further is heard. Later, while in slavery, his master allowed him to practise the violin and, impressed by his playing, he allowed the musician his freedom.

Perhaps more reliance may be placed on the rest of the story: to Paris in 1779, subsequently to be involved musically and politically in the French Revolution, after which he is said to have forged (or 'ghosted'?) quartets for publication under the name of Boccherini. 'Riotous living' accounted for his poverty during the last years, and his life ended sadly in total obscurity.

José Marín (1619–99), Spanish composer of operas and zarzuelas, also experienced adventure: he was imprisoned as a highwayman and murderer, but escaped.

An expert composer, noted also for his proficiency in swordsmanship, was le Chevalier Joseph Boulogne Saint-George (1839–99), a French mulatto who held a prominent position at the court of Le Comte d'Ogny in Paris in the 1780s.

Musical forgeries

Henri Casadesus (1879–1947), the French composer of music in imitation of 18th-century style. Works said to be by Johann Christian Bach and Carl Philipp Emanuel Bach are still current. Unlike Kreisler (below), Casadesus never admitted his forgeries.

Fritz Kreisler (1875–1962), the world-renowned Austrian violinist and composer, frequently introduced into his programmes items by ancient composers, such as Vivaldi, Pugnani, and Dittersdorf. In 1935 he announced to the world that these items (which were henceforth titled '... in the style of ...') were of his own composition.

Charles Zulehner (1770–1830), German composer who worked in Mainz (where many of his compositions are still preserved in the Schott Archives). He passed off his music as by Mozart, evidently many years after the latter's death, since, if Mozart himself found difficulty in maintaining a financial balance with the real thing, what chance would a forger have?

Section 4
ORCHESTRAL & INSTRUMENTAL REPERTOIRE

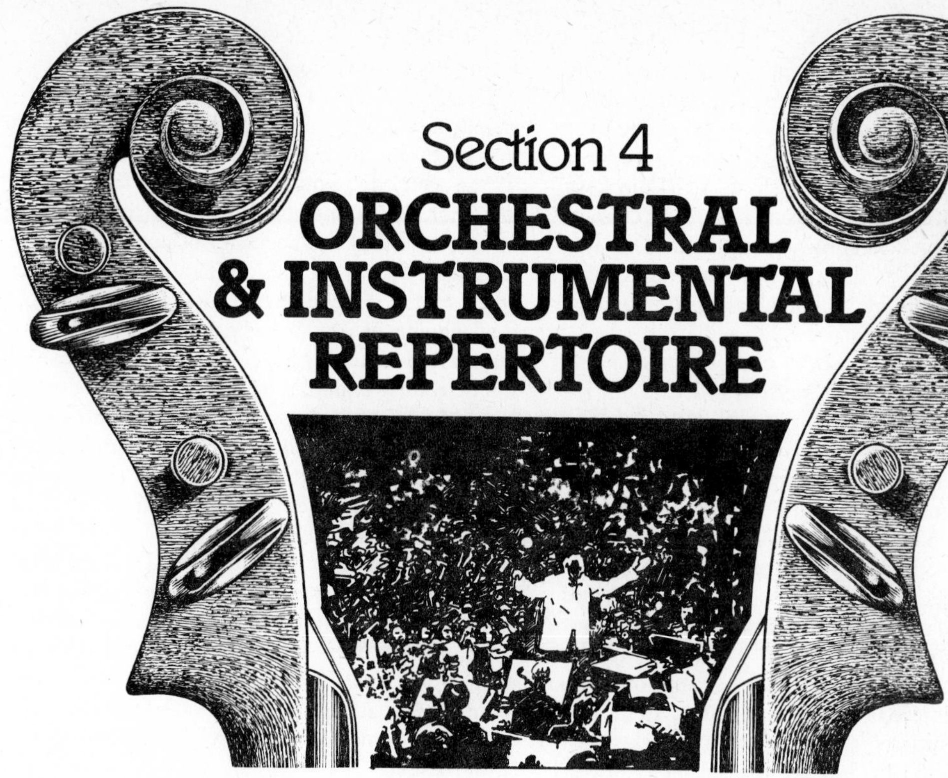

'There are three kinds of music: first, the music of the universe; second, human music; third, instrumental music.'

These words were written in the year AD 515 by the Roman philosopher Anicus Manlius Severinus Boëthius under the heading 'De Institutione Musica'. It is not clear precisely what he meant by 'music of the universe', unless he was referring in some vague way to a mysterious harmony of space and/or natural phenomena, but by 'human music' it is obvious that he meant music which is sung. Last, and by implication the least important in his list, comes 'instrumental music'. It is understandable that he should have thought little of music produced solely through instruments because the capabilities and variety of instruments available at that time were very much narrower than is the case today. In fact, the 'human music' of that time was produced by an instrument—the voice—which has remained unchanged during the intervening 1500 years, while instruments have changed, multiplied, and evolved to an extent which would have been beyond the craziest dreams of the later Romans.

This Section attempts to outline the basic forms of instrumental music, which composers have developed since it first began to have an identity of its own during the 17th century.

Firstly, let us look briefly at one of the foundations of the whole art of music: tonality.

The concept of tonality

For more than three centuries, from the latter half of the 16th to the beginning of the 20th, the concept of key or tonality ruled the composition of music. Developed out of the ancient 'modes', the key system we are familiar with today was well established by the Baroque period, at which time it was, however, a purely technical feature of composition. Early in the 18th century, with the development of music of strongly contrasting characters, and with the gradual increase in the size of performing groups, 'key' began to have some meaning to composers outside the purely technical necessity of having to write 'in' one in order to be harmonically grammatical. Minor keys indicated a strength and muscularity in the character of the music while music written in the major was of a 'positive', or optimistic, mood. Key in music, therefore, became analogous to colour in painting.

It was also found that certain instruments sounded better in certain keys. Woodwind, for instance, favoured the 'soft' keys with flat signatures: F major, B flat major, E flat major, and their relative minors: D minor, G minor, and C minor. Violins, on the other hand, sounded out well in the sharp keys: G major, D major, and A major, since these keys encouraged the use of 'open' strings. Further, some instruments could be played *only* in the keys in which they were constructed: trumpets were usually made in C or D, horns in D and F, etc, and in other keys only the occasional note was playable by them. Logically, then, if a composer wished to write a work which was to make a brilliant effect at a ceremony or festivity, he would choose a key in which the violins would be at their most brilliant and trumpets could be used, together with their ubiquitous companions the timpani: D major. Therein, also, the brazen sound of hunting-horns could be employed if required.

It is for that reason that at least half of the many thousands of concert symphonies, curtain-raising overtures, and ceremonial serenades written during the 18th century are in D major.

The Baroque strength of minor-keyed works changed to a feeling of pathos and tragedy during the central years of the 18th century. At this time the novelist Friedrich Maximillian von Klinger was a member of a literary movement in which deep passions and tragic drama were foremost. His novel *Sturm und Drang* (1776) ('Storm and Stress') supplied the term for the movement, and composers seized the style for their own ends. It became the fashion for composers to write serious, tragic, even belligerent, works in minor keys.

During the years surrounding the turn of the century (ie the years of Beethoven's ascendancy), another change came about in the use and choice of keys. For one thing, brass instruments were being evolved that could play chromatically and were thus no longer partly restricted to the keys of C, D, and F with which they were by now traditionally associated, and a similar change was coming about in respect of woodwind instruments. These were the years, too, during which the brilliance of the violins could be enhanced by sheer numbers so that the necessity of accommodating the music mainly, or predominantly, to their open strings for brilliance of effect was losing its force. The choice of key was becoming a subjective choice to be made by the composers, and they did not hesitate to exploit their new freedom of coloration. Major keys were in the main used for extrovert works in the 19th century while minor keys became the bringers of soft subtle shades and deeper emotions of a romantic nature.

Unless he has perfect pitch, the listener is unlikely to be able to recognise the key of a work simply by hearing it even if he might readily detect key changes within a piece, yet the characteristic aura of a key is a definite if mysterious phenomenon. In the list which follows many of the points raised above are illustrated: the prominence of festive and occasional works in C and D, and the Baroque strength, classical anger, and romantic fervour of the works in minor keys. But the reader may find, in going through the list, that a number of pieces in, for instance, G major, are among his particular favourites. No explanation is offered for this, but the reader is invited to draw his own conclusions about it after mentally comparing the works under each key heading.

Before we go on to the list, an explanation about the word 'in', in titles such as 'Concerto *in* A major'.

The convention of identifying musical works by keys grew out of practical considerations. Court orchestras of the 17th and 18th centuries, faced with a large and ever-growing library of music from their composers' production lines, might be asked to prepare, for instance, 'the A major Concerto' for performance, and the musicians would thus identify the required work simply by turning to the opening pages of their parts until arriving at a work with three sharps in the key signature. They were not concerned at that time that the work was not *wholly* in A major, the slow movement being in A minor, E major, or whatever. The work commenced in A major, and that, as far as identification problems were concerned, was the end of the matter.

This convention continues to this day. It encounters obstacles, however, where accuracy is concerned (see comments below, under 'D flat major'), and it should be realised that usage demands clarity: 'Brahms' Symphony No 1 in C minor', but pedantic punctiliousness demands accuracy: 'Brahms's Symphony No 1 commencing in C minor', since the work ends in a blaze of C major.

List of keys

The list is in chronological order within each key, and mainly only works of popular prominence and significance have been included. Also given are the key 'signature' (ie the clue given to the performer at the head of a piece to direct him to sharpen or flatten the right notes for the key), and the related key in the opposite mode.

Although the subject of key in relation to colour has been alluded to above, it is fruitless to draw the analogies further than personal impressions will take them, since there is no technical or scientific basis for the supposed connections. Nevertheless, two composers, Rimsky-Korsakov and Scriabin, both masters of orchestral 'colour', have given their opinions about some key and colour relationships. Their impressions are noted against the keys concerned merely so that the reader may compare them with each other and with his own. Also given for some of the keys are the impressions of the German composer Johann Mattheson and some other authorities. Mattheson's impressions were listed in his *Das neu eröffnete Orchester* (Hamburg, 1713) and show that his favourite keys were G minor, C major, F major, G major, and A minor, while he showed a positive antipathy towards E flat major, B major, E major, F minor, F sharp minor, and B minor.

C MAJOR 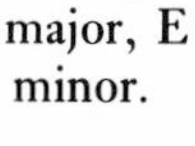

An 'open' key, ie no sharps or flats in the signature. Relative minor: A minor.
One of the 'trumpet and drum keys'. This is the key of optimistic obviousness which can also embrace deep feelings. Rimsky-Korsakov saw this key as white; Scriabin as red. Mattheson described it as rough, bold, suitable for joyful situations but also, in the right hands, for tenderness.

Vivaldi: Violin Concerto, Op 8/6, 'Pleasure' (*c* 1725).
Mozart: 'Coronation' Mass, K 317 (1779); Symphony No 36, K 425, 'Linz' (1783); String Quartet, K 465, 'Dissonant' (1785); Piano Concerto, K 503 (1786); Symphony No 41, K 551, 'Jupiter' (1788).
Beethoven: Piano Concerto No 1, Op 15 (1797).
Haydn: String Quartet Op 76/3, 'Emperor' (1799) (note however that the 'Emperor's Hymn' movement itself is in G major).
Beethoven: Symphony No 1, Op 21 (1800); Overture *Leonora* No 2 (1805); Overture *Leonora* No 3 (1806); String Quartet, Op 59/3 (1806).
Rossini: *La Scala di Seta* Overture (1812).
Schubert: Symphony No 6, D 589 (1818); 'Wanderer' Fantasy, D 790 (1822).
Weber: *Der Freischütz* Overture, J 277 (1822).
Schubert: *Rosamunde* Overture, D 797 (1823); Symphony No 9, D 944 (1825?); String Quintet, D 956 (1828).
Berlioz: *Symphonie Fantastique*, Op 14 (1830).
Schumann: Symphony No 2, Op 61 (1846).
Tchaikovsky: Serenade for Strings, Op 48 (1880).
Sibelius: Symphony No 3, Op 52 (1904–7).
Vaughan Williams: *A Sea Symphony* (No 1) (1912).
Sibelius: Symphony No 7, Op 105 (1925).
Shostakovich: Symphony No 7, Op 60, 'Leningrad' (1941).
Vaughan Williams: *Sinfonia Antartica* (No 7) (1953).

C MINOR 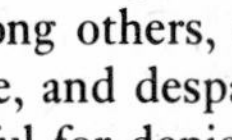

Three flats: b, e, a. Relative major: E flat.
Often chosen for its dark and dramatic quality (particularly in that, by modulating to its tonic major, C major, it brings a victorious brightening of the music in the peroration). Quantz regarded this key, among others, as suitable for music of audacity, rage, and despair, Mattheson as sweet, sad, and useful for depicting sleep.

Vivaldi: Concerto for Strings, RV 130, 'Al Santo Sepolcro'.
Haydn: Keyboard Sonata No 33, Hob XVI:20 (1771).
Mozart: Mass, K 427 (1782–83); Piano Concerto, K 491 (1786).
Beethoven: Piano Sonata, Op 13, 'Pathétique' (1798).
Beethoven: Piano Concerto No 3, Op 37 (1800); *Coriolan* Overture, Op 62 (1807); Symphony No 5, Op 67 (1807).
Weber: Concertino for clarinet and orchestra, J 109 (1811).
Schubert: Symphony No 4, D 417, 'Tragic' (1816); Quartet movement, D 803 (1820).
Beethoven: Piano Sonata, Op 111 (1822).

Brahms: Symphony No 1, Op 68 (1877).
Bruckner: Symphony No 8 (1885).
Saint-Saëns: Symphony No. 3, 'Organ Symphony' (1886).
Rakhmaninoff: Piano Concerto No 2 (1901).
Shostakovich: Symphony No 8 (1943).

C SHARP MINOR 

Four sharps: f, c, g, d. Relative major: E.

Haydn: Piano Sonata No 49, Hob XVI:36 (*c* 1777/79?).
Beethoven: Piano Sonata, Op 27/2, 'Moonlight' (1801); String Quartet, Op 131 (1826).

D FLAT MAJOR 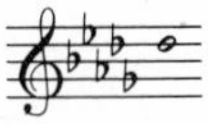

Five flats: b, e, a, d, g. Relative minor: B flat minor.
An extremely rare key for a major work. Rimsky-Korsakov saw it as dusky warm; Scriabin as violet. A number of short works employ the key, but the only major work known to the author to be listed as in D flat major is:
Robert Farnon: Symphony No 1 (1941).

It should be mentioned that Mahler's Symphony No 9, although usually listed as being in D major or D minor, is an example of this composer's 'progressive tonality' technique: it starts in D major, but the final Adagio is in D flat. Taking the precedents of Beethoven's Symphony No 5 in C minor, his Choral Symphony in D minor, and Mendelssohn's Symphony in A minor, 'Scots', all of which end in their respective tonic major keys, Mahler's Ninth Symphony should be listed as being in D major; however, its important use of D flat in the finale, tonally remote from the key of the opening, should lead us, perhaps, to describe the work as being 'in D major–D flat major'. This, unfortunately, then ignores the prominent use of E major, D minor, G minor, and other keys in the work.

D MAJOR 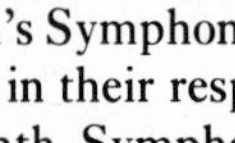

Two sharps: f, c. Relative minor: B minor.
A martial, military key suitable for festive occasions in which instrumental brilliance is required. This description is borne out by both Rimsky-Korsakov and Scriabin, who described the key as yellow, sunny; and as yellow, brilliant respectively. Mattheson saw it as forthright, arrogant, warlike, and animated.

Handel: *Water Music* (the section with trumpets) (1717).
Bach: Orchestral Suites Nos 3 and 4 (*c* 1720); *Magnificat*, BWV 243 (*c* 1723); Brandenburg Concerto No 5, BWV 1050 (*c* 1723).
Handel: *Musick for the Royal Fireworks* (1749).
Mozart: Violin Concerto, K 218 (1775); 'Haffner' Serenade, K 250 (1776); 'Post-horn' Serenade, K 320 (1778); Symphony No 31, K 297, 'Paris' (1778); Horn Concerto No 1, K 412 (1782); Symphony No 35, K 385 'Haffner' (1783); Symphony No 38, K 504, 'Prague' (1786); Piano Concerto, K 537, 'Coronation' (1788); String Quintet, K 593 (1790).
Haydn: Symphony No 101, 'Clock' (1794); Symphony No 104, 'London' (1795).
Beethoven: Symphony No 2, Op 36 (1802); Violin Concerto, Op 61 (1806).
Rossini: *Semiramide* Overture (1823).
Weber: *Oberon* Overture, J 306 (1826).
Mendelssohn: *Fingal's Cave* Overture, Op 26 (1830) (also partly in B minor, the relative minor key).
Brahms: Symphony No 2, Op 73 (1878); Violin Concerto, Op 77 (1878).
Sibelius: Symphony No 2, Op 42 (1901).
Shostakovich: Symphony No 5, Op 47 (1937/38).
Vaughan Williams: Symphony No 5 (1943).
Elgar: *Pomp and Circumstance March No 1* (1901) ('Land of Hope and Glory').

D MINOR 

One flat: b. Relative major: F.
A brooding and passionate key, sometimes chosen for its semi-religious feeling. It has the advantage that trumpets and drums may be used to give added emphasis at cardinal points. Mattheson: devotional, tranquil, but at the same time noble.

Vivaldi: Concerto Grosso, Op 3/11 (1712).
Marcello, A: Oboe Concerto (*c* 1716).
Bach: Harpsichord Concerto No 1 (1732?).
Haydn: Symphony No 26, 'Lamentatione' (*c* 1768).
Mozart: Piano Concerto, K 466 (1785); Requiem Mass, K 626 (1791).
Haydn: Mass No 9, 'Nelson' (1798); String Quartet Op 76/2, 'Fifths' (1799).
Beethoven: Piano Sonata, Op 31/2, 'Tempest' (1802); Symphony No 9, Op 125, Choral (1823).
Schubert: String Quartet, D 810, 'Death and the Maiden' (1826).
Schumann: Symphony No 4, Op 120 (1841, revised 1851).
Brahms: Piano Concerto No 1, Op 15 (1858).

Mussorgsky (arr Rimsky-Korsakov): *Night on a Bare Mountain* (1867) (ends in D major).
Brahms: *Tragic Overture*, Op 81 (1880).
Dvořák: Symphony No 7, Op 70 (1885).
Bruckner: Symphony No 9 (1894).
Sibelius: Violin Concerto, Op 47 (1903/5); Symphony No 6, Op 104 (1923).
Vaughan Williams: Violin Concerto (1925).

E FLAT MAJOR

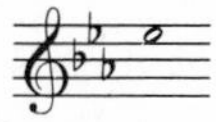

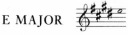

Three flats: b, e, a. Relative minor: C minor.
This is Beethoven's 'heroic' key, but it has not been seen in this light by many other composers. Usually it is adopted for music of a mellow beauty in which melodic grace plays a large part. Rimsky-Korsakov thought of the key as dark, gloomy, bluish grey, and Scriabin as steel colour with a metallic lustre. For Mattheson this key represented pathos, earnestness, and sorrow, and is absolutely devoid of sensuality.

Vivaldi: Violin Concerto, Op 8/5, 'Storm at Sea' (*c* 1725).
Mozart: Sinfonia Concertante, K 364 (1779); Horn Concertos Nos 2, 3, and 4, K 417, 447, and 495 (1783–86); Piano Concerto, K 482 (1786); Piano Quartet, K 493 (1786); Symphony No 39, K 543 (1788); String Quartet, K 614 (1791).
Haydn: Piano Sonata No 62, Hob XVI:52 (1794); Symphony No 103, 'Drum Roll' (1795); Trumpet Concerto (1796).
Beethoven: Symphony No 3, Op 55, 'Eroica' (1804); Piano Concerto No 5, Op 73, 'Emperor' (1809).
Weber: Clarinet Concerto No 2, J 118 (1811); *Euryanthe* Overture, J 291 (1823).
Schubert: Piano Trio, D 929 (1828).
Schumann: Piano Quintet, Op 44 (1842).
Liszt: Piano Concerto No 1 (1849).
Schumann: Symphony No 3, Op 97, 'Rhenish' (1850).
Bruckner: Symphony No 4, 'Romantic' (1874).
Tchaikovsky: *1812* Overture, Op 49 (1881).
Elgar: Symphony No 2 (1911).
Sibelius: Symphony No 5, Op 82 (1914/15).
Shostakovich: Cello Concerto No 1, Op 107 (1959).

E MAJOR

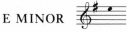

Four sharps: f, c, g, d. Relative minor: C sharp minor.
Despite the apparent brilliancy imparted to the key by the use of four sharps, this comparatively rare key seems, except for Mattheson, to attract friendly, self-confident music. Rimsky-Korsakov: blue, sapphire, sparkling; Scriabin: bluish white. Mattheson: fatal sadness and despair; pain akin to death.

Vivaldi: Violin Concerto, Op 8/1, 'Spring' (*c* 1725).
Bach: Violin Concerto No 2.
Scarlatti, D: Harpsichord Sonata, L 23, Kk 380, 'Cortège'.
Rossini: *Barber of Seville* Overture (1816).
Weber: *Jubel* Overture, J 245 (1818).
Rossini: *William Tell* Overture (1829) (the storm music, etc, is in E minor).
Dvořák: Serenade for Strings, Op 22 (1875).

E MINOR

One sharp: f. Relative major: G.
A certain exotic grandeur attaches to this key. It has its dark side but also a brilliant and full-blooded confidence. Quantz linked this key with C minor as suitable for music of audacity, rage, and despair; Mattheson heard it as thoughtful, profound, and sad: fast music in E minor will never be happy.

Haydn: Symphony No 44, 'Mourning' (1771).
Weber: Horn Concertino, J 188 (1806).
Rossini: *William Tell* Overture (1829) (see also E major).
Chopin: Piano Concerto No 1 (1830).
Mendelssohn: Violin Concerto No 2, Op 64 (1844).
Brahms: Symphony No 4, Op 98 (1884).
Tchaikovsky: Symphony No 5, Op 64 (1889).
Dvořák: Symphony No 9, Op 95, 'From the New World' (1898).
Sibelius: Symphony No 1, Op 39 (1899).
Vaughan Williams: Symphony No 6 (1947).

F MAJOR

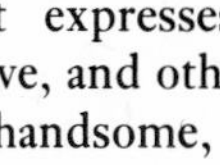

One flat: b. Relative minor: D minor.
The traditional 'pastoral' key, and the key of hunting-horns (as also is D major). Being a 'flat' key, it is particularly suitable for woodwind soloists. Rimsky-Korsakov: green; Scriabin: red. For Mattheson it expresses beautiful sentiments, generosity, love, and other virtuous feelings. It is like a proud, handsome, and wholly good person.

Handel: *Water Music* (the section with horns) (1717).
Bach: Brandenburg Concertos Nos 1 and 2 BWV 1046–7 (1723).
Vivaldi: Violin Concerto, Op 8/3, 'Autumn' (*c* 1725).
Bach: *Italian Concerto* for solo harpsichord, BWV 971 (1735).
Mozart: Oboe Quartet, K 370 (1781).

Beethoven: Violin Sonata, Op 24, 'Spring' (1801); Symphony No 6, Op 68, 'Pastoral' (1806); *Egmont* Overture, Op 84 (1810); Symphony No 8, Op 93 (1812).
Schubert: Octet, D 803 (1823).
Beethoven: String Quartet, Op 135 (1826).

F MINOR 

Four flats: b, e, a, d. Relative major: A flat.
One of the darkest of the commonly used keys, F minor has drawn from some composers their bitterest music. Mattheson regarded it as tranquil, tender, but with a depth and power close to anxiety and despair: black melancholy, provoking horror in the listener.

Vivaldi: Violin Concerto, Op 8/4, 'Winter' (*c* 1725).
Haydn: Symphony No 49, 'Passione' (1768).
Beethoven: Piano Sonata, Op 57, 'Appassionata' (1806); String Quartet, Op 95 (1810).
Weber: Clarinet Concerto No 1, J 114 (1811).
Chopin: Piano Concerto No 2 (1829).
Tchaikovsky: Symphony No 4, Op 36 (1878).
Shostakovich: Symphony No 1, Op 10 (1925).
Vaughan Williams: Symphony No 4 (1935).

F SHARP MINOR 

Three sharps: f, c, g. Relative major: A.
A rare and exotic key. Mattheson: 'here is the sadness of love, unrestrained and outlandish'.

Haydn: Symphony No 45, 'Farewell' (1772).

G MAJOR 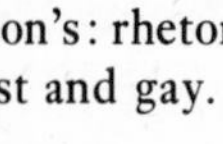

One sharp: f. Relative minor: E minor.
An open and optimistic key, in some ways more so even than C major, since G rarely embraces deeper music. Rimsky-Korsakov's impression was: brownish gold, bright; Scriabin's: orange-rose; Mattheson's: rhetorical—an all-purpose key at once earnest and gay.

Handel: *Water Music* (the sections without brass instruments) (1717).
Bach: Brandenburg Concertos Nos 3 and 4, BWV 1048–9 (1723).
Mozart: Violin Concerto, K 216 (1775); Serenade in G, K 525, *Eine Kleine Nachtmusik* (1787).
Haydn: Symphony No 92, 'Oxford' (1789); Symphony No 94, 'Surprise' (1791); Symphony No 100, 'Military' (1794).
Beethoven: Piano Concerto No 4, Op 58 (1805/6).
Dvořák: Symphony No 8, Op 88 (1889).
Vaughan Williams: *A London Symphony* (No 2) (1914).
Elgar: *Pomp and Circumstance March No 4* (1907) ('All men must be free').

G MINOR 

Two flats: b, e. Relative major: B flat.
Mozart's 'tragic' key, this has been used also by other composers to express deep emotion. Mattheson, as so often out of step with other authorities, described it as perhaps the most beautiful key, combining earnestness, sweetness, liveliness, grace, and tenderness.

Corelli: Concerto Grosso, Op 6/8, 'Christmas' (*c* 1700).
Vivaldi: Violin Concerto, Op 8/2, 'Summer' (*c* 1725).
'Albinoni' (actually by Giazotto): Adagio for strings and organ.
Haydn: Symphony No 39 (*c* 1768).
Mozart: Symphony No 25, K 183 (1773).
Haydn: Symphony No 83, 'Hen' (1785).
Mozart: Piano Quartet, K 478 (1785); String Quintet, K 516 (1787); Symphony No 40, K 550 (1788).
Haydn: String Quartet, Op 74/3, 'Horseman' (1793).
Brahms: Piano Quartet No 1, Op 25 (1861).
Bruckner: Overture (1863).
Moeran: Symphony (1937).

A FLAT MAJOR 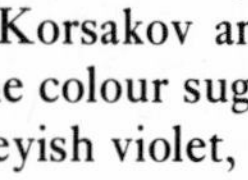

Four flats: b, e, a, d. Relative minor: F minor.
Another rarely used key. Elgar's symphony mentioned below, is not the only symphony to have been written in the key: there are several examples from the 18th century by Vaňhal and Gassmann. Rimsky-Korsakov and Scriabin very nearly agreed as to the colour suggested by A flat, the former giving greyish violet, the latter purple violet.

Haydn: Piano Sonata No 31, Hob XVI:46 (*c* 1767).
Sibelius: *Finlandia*, tone poem, Op 26 (1899).
Elgar: Symphony No 1 (1908).

A MAJOR 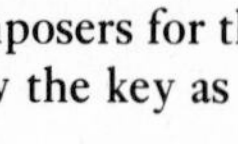

Three sharps: f, c, g. Relative minor: F sharp minor.
The brilliance associated with the early Romantic symphonies listed below is due partly to the fierce and raw tone of horns in A. The key has also attracted composers for the solo clarinet. Rimsky-Korsakov saw the key as rosy and clear; Scriabin

as green; Mattheson as affecting but brilliant; suited to sad feelings and violin music.

Mozart: Symphony No 29, K 201 (1774); Violin Concerto, K 219, 'Turkish' (1775); Piano Concerto, K 488 (1786); Clarinet Quintet, K 581 (1789); Clarinet Concerto, K 622 (1791).
Beethoven: Violin Sonata, Op 47, 'Kreutzer' (1803); Symphony No 7, Op 92 (1812).
Schubert: Piano Quintet, D 667, 'Trout' (1819).
Mendelssohn: Symphony No 4, Op 90, 'Italian' (1833).
Liszt: Piano Concerto No 2 (1839).
Bruckner: Symphony No 6 (1881).
Scriabin: Piano Sonata No 8, Op 66 (1913).

A MINOR 

'Open', ie no sharps or flats. Relative major: C. Music of strength and seriousness, with a misty, undefined sadness. Mattheson: somnolent, in a plaintive, refined way, and suitable for keyboard music.

Bach: Violin Concerto No 1, BWV 1041.
Weber: *Abu Hassan* Overture, J 106 (1810); *Preciosa* Overture, J 279 (1821).
Schubert: String Quartet, D 804 (1824).
Beethoven: String Quartet, Op 132 (1824–25).
Mendelssohn: Symphony No 3, Op 56, 'Scots' (1829).
Schumann: Piano Concerto (1845).
Grieg: Piano Concerto (1868).
Brahms: Concerto for violin and cello, Op 102 (1887).
Sibelius: Symphony No 4, Op 63 (1911).

B FLAT MAJOR 

Two flats: b, e. Relative minor: G minor.
A happy, self-confident key, to which composers often turned in later life as a vehicle for their most mature thoughts. Scriabin saw it as steely, with a metallic lustre, but Rimsky-Korsakov did not commit himself. Mattheson described the key as magnificent but also delicate.

Bach: Brandenburg Concerto No 6, BWV 1051 (1723).
Vivaldi: Violin Concerto, Op 8/10, 'Hunt' (*c* 1725).
Mozart: Bassoon Concerto, K 191 (1774); String Quartet, K 458, 'Hunt' (1784); Piano Concerto, K 595 (1791).
Haydn: Symphony No 98 (1792); Symphony No 102 (1794/95).
Beethoven: Piano Concerto No 2, Op 19 (1794/95).
Haydn: 'Heilig' Mass (1796); 'Theresia' Mass (1799).
Haydn: 'Creation' Mass (1801); 'Harmonie' Mass (1802); String Quartet, Op 103 (unfinished) (1803).
Beethoven: Symphony No 4, Op 60 (1805).
Schubert: Symphony No 5, D 485 (1816).
Beethoven: Piano Sonata, Op 106, 'Hammerklavier' (1818); String Quartet, Op 130 (1825).
Schubert: Piano Trio, D 898 (1827).
Schumann: Symphony No 1, 'Spring' (1841).
Brahms: Piano Concerto No 2, Op 83 (1881).

B FLAT MINOR 

Five flats: b, e, a, d, g. Relative major: D flat. An emotion-filled and sometimes angry key.

Chopin: Piano Sonata No 2 (1839).
Tchaikovsky: Piano Concerto No 1, Op 23 (1875).
Walton: Symphony No 1 (1935).
Shostakovich: Symphony No 13, 'Babi Yar' (1962).

B MAJOR 

Five sharps: f, c, g, d, a. Relative minor: G sharp minor.
Rimsky-Korsakov described this rarely-used key as sombre and dark blue, shot with steel, and Scriabin regarded it as bluish white. Very few major works have been centred in B, the large number of sharps in the signature presenting intonation difficulties. Mattheson heard the key as aggressive, hard, ill-mannered, and desperate.

Haydn: Symphony No 46 (1772).
Brahms: Piano Trio No 1, Op 8 (1854).

B MINOR 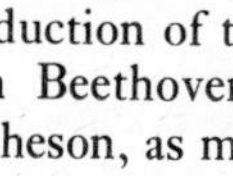

Two sharps: f, c. Relative major: D.
Tchaikovsky's 'black despair' key, and used also for music of religious strength and forceful tragic drama. Bach's use of it in the B minor Mass enabled him to brighten to the key's relative major for the introduction of trumpets and drums. On one occasion Beethoven described the key as 'black'; Mattheson, as moody, glum, and bizarre.

Bach: Suite No 2 for flute and strings, BWV 1067; High Mass, BWV 232 (1733).
Vivaldi: Symphony, RV 169, 'Al Santo Sepolcro'.
Schubert: Symphony No 8, D 759, 'Unfinished' (1822).
Chopin: Piano Sonata No 3, Op 58 (1844).
Liszt: Piano Sonata (1853).
Borodin: Symphony No 2 (1876).
Brahms: Clarinet Quintet, Op 115 (1891).
Tchaikovsky: Symphony No 6, Op 74, 'Pathétique' (1893).
Dvořák: Cello Concerto (1895).
Shostakovich: Symphony No 6, Op 54 (1939).

DEGREES OF THE SCALE
The ascending notes of a scale are named as follows:

8. Tonic
7. Leading note
6. Submediant
5. Dominant
4. Subdominant
3. Mediant
2. Supertonic
1. Tonic

Orchestral music

The orchestra evolved in the theatre in the role of accompanist to stage action, but as it developed it gradually took on a separate identity until it began to be listened to for its own sake. Once this step had been taken it became necessary for composers to write independent music for orchestra. The various types of composition which have appeared since that time are discussed here.

SYMPHONY

Probably the most 'important' form for a modern composer to approach, since a new symphony is expected to contain the greatest and most profound thoughts of the artist, presented skilfully and, so to speak, in evening dress.

The word 'symphony' has been used during the last 300 years for four different musical concepts:

1. A work for full orchestra usually in more than one movement, in which one or more of the movements is based on sonata form.
2. An orchestral work, in either one or three movements (occasionally more), used as an introduction to an opera. In this meaning, the words 'overture' and 'symphony' become identical.
3. A work for orchestra or small instrumental group which shows a marked tendency on the part of the composer towards what later came to be known as 'symphonic thought', but which was written before the development of sonata form (such works are often little more than extended fanfares). These early symphonies might be termed 'proto-symphonies'.
4. An instrumental introduction to a song or aria; sometimes also an instrumental interlude within an aria.

Today the word 'symphony' has come to mean almost exclusively the type of work described under 1, above. A short description of 'sonata form', therefore, becomes necessary, so that the principles and endeavours behind a composer's thought processes when producing such a major work may be appreciated. In its simplest layout, a movement in sonata form will fall into four sections:

(a) EXPOSITION: a presentation of a theme (A), a linking passage raising the basic key five full steps to the 'dominant key', wherein a second theme is presented (B). Another short linking passage called 'codetta'='little coda'.
(b) DEVELOPMENT: a discussion, sometimes blending the two themes (A) and (B) and sometimes exploiting their contrasts.
(c) RECAPITULATION: a re-presentation of (A) and (B), but both in the main (tonic) key, sometimes modified thematically and dramatically in the light of what has taken place in the Development.
(d) CODA: an 'ending' or 'tail-piece' to tie loose ends and to round off the movement.

The importance of sonata form cannot be overstressed, either in the discussion of how composers treat it, or in the necessity of the listener grasping its principles in order to appreciate what a composer is trying to do in his sonata-form movements. Therefore, at the risk of seeming to dwell unnecessarily on this basic and elementary subject, we shall discuss further the possibilities behind sonata form in the hope that the listener, coming fresh to a work using this form as its main foundation, will understand and enjoy the composer's thoughts the more completely.

But first a word of warning. Having read a programme note in which a movement is described as being in sonata form, the listener should not expect the first sound he hears to be the start of (A). It is true that it *might* be so, but it is more likely that the movement will commence with a slow introduction, or at least will have a few bars to prepare the way, analogous to an after-dinner speaker rising to his feet, clearing his throat, and saying: 'Well now, unaccustomed as I am . . .'. Let us take a few moments to examine the first movement openings of Beethoven's symphonies in this light.

SYMPHONY NO 1: a slow introduction which establishes the main key with apparent difficulty.

SYMPHONY NO 2: a long, slow introduction rich in thematic fragments.

SYMPHONY NO 3: two sharp chords, then immediately into the first theme (A) on cellos.

SYMPHONY NO 4: long, slow introduction in mysterious mood to heighten the bright optimism of the first theme (A) of the Allegro vivace. Note the method by which the introduction is linked to the first theme: a hard crescendo and a rushing upward figure repeated eight times, giving the effect of an accelerando. The Allegro vivace actually starts at the top of the second upward rush, but the first theme does not appear until the last of these preparatory flourishes. It is as if the first theme has been 'rescued' from the clouds of the introduction, an idea greatly extended at the start of the recapitulation.

SYMPHONY NO 5: no introduction whatever. The first theme (A) is flung at the audience immediately.

SYMPHONY NO 6: the first note to be heard is the start of a drone-like support on violas and cellos; the first theme (A) starts immediately on a weak beat in the first bar.

SYMPHONY NO 7: an enormous, slow, introduction of more than 60 bars. The lead into the Vivace again features a quasi accelerando on hopping woodwind.

SYMPHONY NO 8: no introduction. Theme (A) starts immediately.

SYMPHONY NO 9: an extremely quiet throb or murmur of strings and horns from which crystallises the titanic first theme (A).

With these many possible ways of launching a symphony, Beethoven gave to future composers ideas which have been copied, modified, extended—and even ignored in favour of completely new concepts.

With the introduction out of the way, the **Exposition** may start in earnest. The basic plan of two contrasting themes may be modifed in countless ways: one theme only may appear, perhaps in two guises, in which case the movement might be described as 'monothematic'. More likely in 19th- and 20th-century symphonies, however, is a profusion of themes or 'ideas' or 'motifs' which ideally should contrast each with the other. Often it is difficult on first hearing to sort out how many themes there are and where they begin and end.

In the **Development** these themes are discussed. It is up to the composer to decide whether both, or all, themes will appear for treatment, or whether he will extract from one of the themes as much mileage as possible. Alternatively, of course, he may decide to introduce an altogether new theme, either on its own or in conjunction with previously heard material. Beethoven, in the 'Eroica' Symphony (No 3), brings his development section to a huge climax, and then immediately introduces a completely new theme in a completely new key, thus leading to another area of development. Whichever subjects the composer chooses for his development section, this is usually the part of the movement in which most of the drama takes place, the opportunities for free-ranging thought being virtually limitless.

Recapitulation: After the drama of the **Development,** the themes heard in the exposition are played again, but their characters are often transformed in the light of what has happened to them in the **Development.** In some works, the **Recapitulation** will be 'regular', ie the themes will appear much as they did before, with the important exception that the second theme (B) is now in the main key of the piece. In other works the material of the **Exposition** may be so altered that it becomes only vaguely recognisable. The original order of the themes may be reversed; some of the material may be omitted entirely; new material may be added. Once again, the composer has the entire say as to what happens in the **Recapitulation** without a violation of the principles of sonata form taking place.

Coda: This is the tail-piece which brings the movement to an end. In earlier symphonies it was sometimes little more than a pair of 'that's that' chords (and occasionally not even that), but as the symphony as a form developed the **Coda** gained importance until, again in the case of Beethoven, it assumed the proportions of a 'second development'. The most extreme example is that of the finale of Beethoven's Symphony No 8 in F, the proportions of which are:

EXPOSITION: theme (A) starting at bar 1; theme (B) starting at bar 48; theme (C) starting at bar 68.

DEVELOPMENT: starting at bar 91.

RECAPITULATION: starting at bar 151 (A), with (B) at 224, and (C) at 243.

CODA: starting at bar 267 and lasting until bar 502 (with a new theme introduced at bar 286).

Therefore, the formally complete section of the movement lasts 266 bars, while the **Coda** takes 235 bars, almost as long again.

The above description of usual sonata form may be condensed to a diagram (1 p. 90), with which we may compare a diagram of the finale of Beethoven's Eighth Symphony (2 p. 90) to illustrate how far a composer may deviate from the plan while still producing a formally viable piece of music.

Diagram of 'textbook' classical Sonata form in comparison with sonata form as modified by Beethoven in the last movement of his Symphony No. 8 (see previous page)

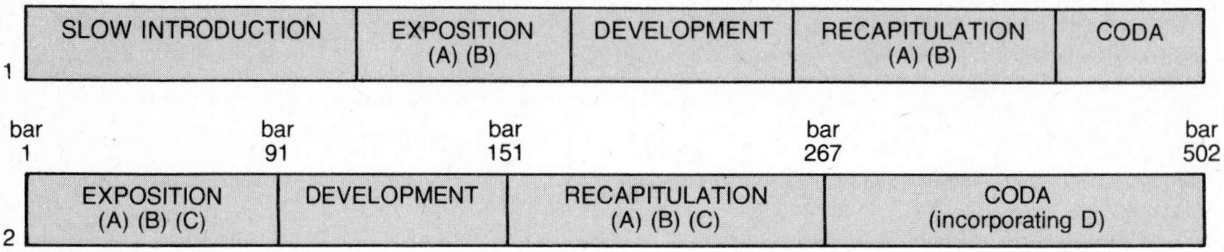

Sonata form is usually used for the first movement of a symphony; it may be used also for the slow movement and the finale, and it may even influence the construction of the Minuet or Scherzo which shares with the slow movement the central part of a standard symphony. However, a number of other forms are also commonly found in the symphony such as 'variation' and 'rondo' or derivations of them, and the Minuet or Scherzo movement is almost invariably in A–B–A form; ie the main movement leading into a contrasting central section (called by the old-fashioned term 'trio' since at this point the convention was to reduce the music to three voices or parts) and then a repeat of the main part. Beethoven instituted a modification of this plan: A–B–A–B–A, in which the trio appears twice, and a coda hinting at B closes the movement, and some composers have followed this idea with or without modifications.

The above outline of symphonic form, lengthy though it is, does not exhaust the possibilities open to composers, some of whom have created their own forms with greater or lesser success. Sonata form, which was developed gradually by a multitude of composers working together or separately, each one learning from his predecessors and including ideas which worked while rejecting others which did not, is not easily bettered by one composer working independently. There have been successful new forms created during the present century however, by such independently minded composers as Sibelius, Mahler, and Nielsen. Their handling of symphonic form requires patience and deep study on the part of the listener to reveal the composer's inner intentions.

Once the listener has mastered the basic outline of sonata form, he will find that many of the types of music he is likely to hear will conform in greater or lesser degree to its principles: the principles, that is, of contrast developing into conflict and thence into final resolution. Composers have employed sonata form for their overtures, sonatas (of course), string quartets, piano trios, and virtually every other field of music, including even opera and Mass. Almost it would be true to say that an understanding of sonata form leads to the understanding of most music which is written in what we have come to know as the standard tonal concept.

The first symphony, by which, of course, we mean a symphony in the third sense (see above), was written by Giuseppe Torelli (1658–1709) born at Verona. He worked in Bologna and was required to produce music for the festivals held in the San Petronio Cathedral in that city. By extending his fanfares and interspersing solos and string-band 'padding' between them, Torelli, certainly without realising it, was moving towards the kind of concerted instrumental work with contrasting timbres and thematic fragments which was later to play such an important part in symphonic evolution. Unfortunately, it is not possible precisely to say which of Torelli's works was composed first since, at the time, they were not considered historically important enough to date, or even to catalogue. Indeed, it is doubtful whether the composer would have expected his music to be remembered for longer than a week or so, by which time he would have produced more pieces to satisfy the demand for new ceremonial music. It was amid this atmosphere of rapid production, and the necessity for providing new music to be played by constantly altering groups of instrumentalists, that Torelli wrote many differently scored works within the same basic framework of the three-movement proto-symphony in fast-slow-fast design. In addition, the perennial problem of terminology enters into this discussion: there is no basic difference between a Torelli sonata for trumpet(s) and strings and a sinfonia or a concerto for the same forces, although, when the composer took advantage of the opposing galleries in the San Petronio Cathedral to write for two orchestras, one in each, answering and echoing phrases across the high-vaulted body of the building, he appears to have adhered to the descriptions 'sinfonia' and 'concerto' only, reserving 'sonata' for more modest works.

Before leaving the subject of the earliest symphony, let us examine one of Torelli's works, his Symphony in C, No 33 in Giegling's Catalogue. It is scored for an orchestra which, at the end of the 17th century, must have seemed excessively noisy, but which would have made a thrilling impression in the great cathedral hall:

Soloists	*Orchestra*
4 trumpets	2 oboes
2 oboes	bassoon
2 violins	violins 1 and 2
1 bassoon	violas
1 cello	cellos 1 and 2
	double basses 1 and 2
	timpani
	basso-continuo (comprising 2 organs and trombone)

Its three movements are in the form later used by Vivaldi for the majority of his concertos: first and third movements in ritornello-rondo form (ie a main idea repeated over and over again with modifications, separated by contrasting material), between which comes a slow contrasting section.

Torelli's first movement ritornello is a stunning rhythmic fanfare employing the full force of four trumpets and timpani. This is continued over violin figuration which is then extended alone. With the return of the fanfare, the trumpets imitate the violins' virtuoso passage-work, and then hand it over to the lower strings and the bassoon. More fanfares lead to a section for solo oboes, but these are brushed aside by yet more fanfares which close what in a later symphony we would call the 'exposition'. A new and quieter idea appears in which the figurations of the violins are extended (or developed), giving contrast to a trumpet-dominated movement, but once again the trumpets enter with their original idea (recapitulation), and a number of solo oboe and solo violin passages lead to a final fanfare, as heard at the very beginning, bringing the movement to a half-close.

The Adagio is merely a short linking passage for full string band without brass or wind. The gigue-like finale is less martial than the first movement, and in the middle of the movement the trumpets lead a new and more melodic idea which is taken up by the other instruments. Oboes, bassoon, cello, and violins all have their solo opportunities, before Torelli springs upon us perhaps his greatest surprise: a quiet ending.

This feast of jubilant trumpeting and drumming, even if it cannot be proved to occur in the *very* first symphony, at least shows that Torelli was a worthy composer to instigate one of the most influential and important musical forms of the last 300 years, a form in which the composer is expected to reveal his deepest thoughts.

A recording of this remarkable work was made by the Zagreb Soloists' Ensemble conducted by Antonio Janigro, although unfortunately, excellent though the performance is, the conductor has chosen to present the work with reduced forces. Did he feel, perhaps, that the world was not yet ready for the onslaught of sound which Torelli unleashed in one of the first symphonies ever written?

So-called 'sinfonias' by Alessandro Stradella (1642–82), written for string band for concert use at unspecified dates may also be considered to be among the earliest to contain the first vestiges of symphonic feeling.

The earliest four-movement symphony was long thought to have been by the Austrian composer Georg Matthias Monn (1717–50), whose Symphony in D, dated 24 May 1740, has the following movement order: 1. Allegro; 2. Aria: Andante un poco; 3. Menuetto; 4. Allegro. This symphony is scored for two flutes, two horns, bassoon, and strings, and is No 1 in Wilhelm Fischer's Thematic Catalogue.

However, a date of 1724 is given for a 'sinfonia' for two violins, cello, and violone by the Venetian composer Alberto Gallo, whose dates are unknown. His symphony is laid out on the following plan: 1. Allegro; 2. Menuet (:) Allegro; 3. Adagio; 4. Presto.

An even earlier possible contender was broadcast by the BBC in about 1952. It was announced as a Symphony in D minor by Gioseffo Placuzzi, for lute, two violins, and harpsichord, the lute taking a semi-solo part. Its movements were: 1. fast;

2. slow and aria-like; 3. of moderate speed, in 3/4 time; 4. fast. The announcer stated that 'this is probably the earliest work in this form to be called a symphony', and he gave its date as 1692.

The most prolific symphonist was Johann Melchior Molter (*c* 1695–1765) who worked as Kapellmeister in Karlsruhe from 1722 to 1733, and then again from 1743 until his death. The total usually given is 169 symphonies, but the thematic catalogue of his works in the Karlsruhe Landesbibliothek includes a number of duplicates, some chamber works and concertos and several fragments, thus reducing his total to 147, but even so Molter has a clear lead over his nearest rivals in symphonic proliferation: Johann Gottlieb Graun (1703–71) with 117; Johann Cristoph Graupner (1683–1760) with 113; and Karl Ditters von Dittersdorf (1739–99) with 107, of which several are lost, and Franz Joseph Haydn with 109, one of which (the unnumbered 'Symphony A' in B flat) is as likely to be by Wagenseil.

The composer of the greatest number of extant symphonies in the 20th century is Alan Hovhaness (b 1911), an American composer of Scottish/Armenian descent. He is enormously prolific, having written (April 1980) 43 symphonies, many of which are based on Armenian and other Eastern subjects. His First Symphony (ie that now known as Symphony No 1, 'Exile'), was first performed in Birmingham in 1938 under the baton of Leslie Heward; a version revised by the composer is published by Peters. However, owing to his change of creative direction in the 1930s, Hovhaness felt compelled to renounce his earlier music, and at the time he destroyed seven of his symphonies. If that total is added to the number of still-existing symphonies, we find a symphonic total of 50 to date.

Also worthy of mention are the English symphonist Havergal Brian with a total of 32; the Russian Nikolai Yakovlevich Miaskovsky who composed 27; and the Finn Erik Fordell with 26 up to 1970.

The first symphony to include parts for human voice was *Schlacht Sinfonie* in C minor (1814) by Peter von Winter, a Munich operatic composer who preceded Beethoven in this field (the *Choral* Symphony) by nine years.

The first Russian symphony is usually considered to be Rimsky-Korsakov's No 1 of 1865, written while the 21-year-old composer was serving as an officer in the Russian Navy. There is, however, an anonymous *Symphony on Ukranian Themes* which dates from about 1800, but strictly the earliest Russian symphonies were written by Maxim Sosonowisch Berezovsky (1745–77) who was sent to Bologna by Catherine the Great to study with Padré Martini in 1765. As yet, Berezovsky's, and possibly many other composers', symphonies lie unheard in Russian archives because that country is notably laggardly in excavating 18th-century musical treasures when compared with the oustanding work being done in Czechoslovakia, Hungary, and Poland.

The first Portuguese to write a symphony was João Domingos Bomtempo, whose E flat Symphony dates from *c* 1800.

The first Finn to write a symphony was Axel Gabriel Ingelius. It dates from 1847.

The first Mexican to write a symphony was Ricardo Castro, whose Symphony No 1 was composed in 1883.

The first Black to write a symphony was William Grant Still, whose *Afro-American Symphony* was composed in 1931. He was also **the first Black to conduct a major American orchestra** (1936) and **the first Black to have an opera given by a major company.** However, the French Mulatto Le Chevalier Joseph Boulogne de Saint-George composed both operas and symphonies in the last quarter of the 18th century. Louis Moreau Gottschalk, of Jewish/Creole parentage, also wrote symphonies and operas. His dates are 1829–69.

The first American woman composer to write a symphony was Mrs Amy Marcy Beach (1867–1944), whose *Gaelic Symphony* was written in 1895.

UNUSUAL SYMPHONIES

The longest concert symphony ever written is by the Englishman Norman Rutherlyn. It is entitled 'A Legend in Music of the Life and Times of Sir Winston Churchill' and its 18 movements would take approximately two and a half hours to play, but it has so far not reached performance.

The shortest symphonies of recent times are the six for small orchestra written between 1917 and 1923 by Darius Milhaud. Each takes four minutes or less to perform.

Robert J Farnon wrote his First Symphony in 1941 in the unusual key of D flat major.

Georg Glantz (active during 1763–75), a Kapellmeister in Pressburg, Germany, wrote a symphony in 1774 for Turkish instruments alone, without strings. The scoring was for flutes, oboes, clarinets, trumpets, horns, bassoons, cymbals, triangle, and bass drum.

Charles Koechlin wrote a symphony entitled *Seven Stars*, based on the characters of film stars. Thus treated are the actresses Clara Bow, Marlene Dietrich, Greta Garbo and Lillian Harvey, the tragedian Emil Jannings, the comedian Charlie Chaplin, and the actor Douglas Fairbanks.

Anton Reicha, French/Bohemian composer, wrote a four-movement symphony in D, the full title of which is *Musique pour célébrer des grandes hommes qui se sont illustres du service de la nation française*. This work was designed to be performed in the open air, the audience to be placed at a position 50 paces from the orchestras, behind which, at a distance of a further 100 paces, were the drums. Two orchestras were to take part, these being separated by at least 30 paces, and also included in the scoring were parts for cannon and infantry march past. Among Reicha's pupils were Berlioz, Franck, Gounod, and Liszt.

The Japanese composer Yasushi Akutagawa composed his *Erolla Symphony* in 1958. It comprises 20 movements, to be played in any order. This concept of formal indeterminacy may be traced back at least a quarter of a century to Henry Cowell's experiments (eg: String Quartet No 3, *Mosaic*, of 1934).

Pavel Vraničky's *Quodlibet Symphony* (1798) begins with the arrival of the orchestra one by one (the order *and* method—walking, running—precisely specified by the composer), who then commence to build up the first movement. The middle two movements consist of a collection of arrangements of popular folk and concert items of the day by Weigl, Paisiello, Salieri, Meyer, Haibl, and Mozart, including a complete performance of the *Magic Flute* Overture. The *Quodlibet Symphony* then closes with a movement based on a folk-tune also used by Leopold Mozart, in which the orchestra gradually disperses. The final trick recalls Haydn's tactful joke in the finale of his *Farewell* Symphony (1772).

The *St Vartan* Symphony (1950) by Alan Hovhaness contains, with 24 movements, probably the greatest number of separate sections of any symphony.

The *Wine* Symphony (No 4, 1979) by Derek Bourgeois is in nine movements, each representing the 'flavour' of a wine-growing area. The work opens with all the players inserting their fingers in their mouths and imitating the 'pop' as corks are drawn.

Albert Siklós (originally Schönwald) composed his Symphony No 3 in 1899. Its title is *Aethérique* and it is scored solely for twelve double basses.

Dai-Keong Lee, the Polynesian symphonist, composed what he called a 'Symphony with a Tahitian Happening', in which a Tahitian dancer appears. **This is the only symphony to include a part for dancer.**

OVERTURE

There are four distinct types of overture:

1. The single-movement, symphonic, sonata-form **Opera Overture** in which the development section is either abbreviated or omitted altogether. Mozart's *Marriage of Figaro* Overture is a good example; others will be found in the overtures of Beethoven, Mendelssohn, Weber, and Wagner.
2. As above, followed by a slow movement and a quick finale. The 18th century abounds with examples by Vivaldi, Galuppi, D and G Scarlatti, F J Haydn, and virtually every other operatic composer. Mozart provides perfect examples of this **Italian Overture** form in his so-called 'Symphonies' Nos 23 and 24 (K 181 and 182). In many cases the finale is constructed from greatly shortened material from the first movement. This form is also known as the 'Italian Overture', and Mozart's Symphony No 32 in G, K 319 (actually titled *Overture in the Italian Style*) illustrates the type precisely. A mongrel type is found in the same composer's *Magic Flute* Overture, in which a slow introduction leads to a rapid main movement. In central position is the 'slow movement'—merely three groups of developing chords—and this is followed by a development of the rapid material and a full recapitulation. The whole is capped by a short coda.

3. The so-called **French** ***Ouverture*** (note the spelling), **introduced by Lully about 1660,** consisted of a declamatory slow introduction, often in strongly dotted rhythm, followed by a fast movement, usually of fugal character. In some cases several French-style dances follow. Telemann wrote very many of this type of overture, as did Fasch and Hartwig and many other Germans, in whose country the French style in all forms of art was in vogue for much of the first half of the 18th century.
4. The **Concert Overture**: In form it may be similar to 1, often with a slow introduction, but it is not associated with a stage work and is often descriptive in character. Mendelssohn's *Fingal's Cave* Overture is the archetypal example; the two overtures of Brahms also fall into this category.

   Overture types 1, 2, and 3 are usually used as introductions to operas or other stage works, although type 3 merges imperceptibly with the multi-movement ouverture-suite for concert use, of which the best-known examples are the four by J S Bach. See Suite, below.

NOTABLE OVERTURES

The first overture in which the mood of the music was meant to prepare the audience for the drama to follow in the opera was that written by Gluck for *Alceste* in 1767. It is an overture of type 1, but it is unusual in maintaining a slow tempo throughout. The composer explained: 'I feel that the overture should acquaint the audience with the mood of the opera.'

The first overture designed to be played after the rise of the curtain on the First Act of the opera is Grétry's *Le Jugement de Midas* of 1778. It is a hybrid overture which refuses to fall into any of the above categories. Its descriptive programme dictates its form: a slow introduction depicting dawn, a gentle Andantino in which a shepherd's pipe is heard, storm, and a return to the shepherd music.

The first overture of type 2 preceded the opera *Olympiade* (1697) by Alessandro Scarlatti.

The first overture of type 2 to be written by an Englishman was that to the opera *Peleus and Thetis* (*c* 1738) by William Boyce.

The only overture to include a part for solo voice is that to the opera *Uthal* (1806) by Méhul: a soprano utters two declamatory notes at the climax. In addition, the unconventional scoring of the piece calls for the full orchestra including four horns and harp but *minus* trumpets and violins.

SYMPHONIC POEM AND TONE POEM

This is a large-scale orchestral work of descriptive character, the limits of which shade off into three other forms: (*a*) the concerto (Richard Strauss's *Don Quixote* is a symphonic poem for cello solo and orchestra, while Berlioz's *Harold in Italy* is a symphony for viola solo and orchestra of a strongly descriptive nature); (*b*) the symphony (Berlioz's *Symphonie Fantastique* is a descriptive symphony, and Debussy's *La Mer* is a tone poem in a form and layout close to the symphony); and (*c*) the overture (Beethoven's *Egmont* and *Coriolan* overtures, and Dvořák's *Hussites* Overture are concert overtures with symphonic poem intentions). The symphonic poem is a direct descendant of the mood-setting overtures of Gluck, Cherubini, Méhul, Weber, and Mendelssohn.

The first symphonic poem is César Franck's *Ce qu'on entend sur la montagne*, after Victor Hugo, completed about 1846.

The first British symphonic poem is *The Passing of Beatrice* (1892) by William Wallace.

SUITE, DIVERTIMENTO, SERENADE, ETC.

Of these, the **suite** is the oldest form, being a string of dance movements which gradually evolved into a cogent and contrasting order, often including bourrée, courante, sarabande, menuet, gigue, etc, but with endless variations in the sequence. J S Bach wrote four magnificent orchestral suites, still called **Ouvertüren** in Germany. (A fifth Suite, in G minor, for strings and continuo, has not been proved to be a work of this composer; it is nevertheless an excellent piece in late Baroque/early Classical style.)

Later in the 18th century, out of the suite and the lighter type of symphony, grew the **divertimento** and **serenade** (also cassation, *Finalmusiken*, etc), bright and entertaining pieces of many movements, liberally sprinkled with minuets (the one dance form which survived from the old suite) and usually ending with an extended rondo. The biggest compositions in this form were the serenades, and these often contained concerto-like elements in one or more movements. Taking Mozart again as an example, his output contains many such works, of which the Serenade in D, K 203, is an eight-movement work, buried in the midst of which is a three-movement violin concerto. The Divertimento in D, K 251, has six movements in which the solo oboe is given a part of concertante proportions.

CONCERTO

The word covers a multitude of forms which may be dealt with in four groups:

1. The **vocal concerto** of the 17th century, wherein the term is used in its purest meaning of a group of voices joining together in concerted effort.
2. In the early 18th century, Italian composers used the word for a string sonata when no one instrument was given soloistic importance. These works are in the direct line of musical evolution to the concert symphony.
3. A work in several (usually three or four) movements in which one instrument is given the position of highest prominence. In the 18th century the soloist was expected to contribute as much to the musical argument of the piece as to his or her own technical reputation, but as the century progressed the display aspect of the concerto became more and more important. This trend continued through the early 19th century, the orchestra taking a decreasingly important role, but the second half of the century saw the orchestra becoming a more active participant in the discussion. The present century has gone even further in this direction, some concertos being more in the nature of a duel between soloist and orchestra.
4. An early form of concerto, the **concerto grosso**='great concerto', is a work in which, at first, a string trio of two violins and cello, and later any number or description of instruments, were supported by a string band. The form was obsolete by the middle of the 18th century but was reborn a few years later in the **sinfonia concertante.** This was a two- or three-movement work in which a group of instruments was displayed against an orchestra. Gradually the rather meaningless word 'sinfonia' was dropped from the generic title, and the surviving component is still used to describe showy works for several instruments with orchestra, although the description 'concerto for orchestra' is also used.

Examples of the above groups were written by:

1. Adriano Banchieri; Andrae Gabrieli; Giovanni Gabrieli.
2. Torelli; Vivaldi; Albinoni; Manfredini.
3. Torelli; Vivaldi; Locatelli; Tartini; Mozart; Beethoven; Mendelssohn; Chopin; Brahms; Tchaikovsky; Dvořák; Grieg; Rakhmaninoff; Sibelius; Walton, etc.
4. Concerto grosso: Stradella; Corelli; Vivaldi; Albinoni; Bonporti; Leo; Avison; Stanley, etc. (Sinfonia) Concertante; Viotti; Pleyel; J C Bach; Sarti; Mozart; Haydn; Cambini; and in the present century: Bartók; Blacher; Martinů; Bloch; Hanuš; Ridout; Holmboe (eight of them); Frank Martin; Barraud; Lutosławsky, etc.

'Concerto' is not the only word used by composers to indicate a work for soloist(s) and orchestra. In the 18th century **Concertone** was occasionally employed, meaning a large concerto; Mozart's K 190 in C, basically for two violins with prominent parts also for cello and oboe, is the best-known example. Giuseppe Sarti also wrote a Concertone in E flat, in which the soloists are two clarinets, two horns, two violins, viola, and cello, supported by a string orchestra.

Konzertstücke='concert studies', have been written by Weber (for clarinet, and for horn), Busoni, and others; concert rondos (in effect or in fact these are isolated concerto movements) by Mozart; Beethoven, etc, and Rodrigo wrote a concert serenade for harp and orchestra. Khachaturian has written a concert rhapsody for cello and orchestra.

Also to be found are Elegie, Poeme, Romance (or Romanza), Lyric Movement, Fantasie, Theme and Variations (see also the purely orchestral species, below), Ballade, etc, and of course the Symphonic Variations by Franck, Bax, and Bentzon.

CONCERTOS FOR UNUSUAL INSTRUMENTS AND COMBINATIONS

By far the most usual instruments chosen for spotlighting in the concerto form are the piano, the violin, and the cello (see below for the first of each), but display works for other instruments are by no means uncommon. The reader is referred to the details given in Section II under specific instruments, to which may be added the following:

FLUTE WITH FEMALE CHORUS: John Fernstrøm (Op 52).

OBOE, OBOE D'AMORE, COR ANGLAIS, MUSETTE, AND ORCHESTRA: Edward Bogusławski (1971).

BASSET CLARINET: Concerto in A, K 622 (1791) by Mozart—the well-known Clarinet Concerto in its original form.

POST-HORN AND HUNTING-HORN: Johann Beer: Concerto in B flat.
In the 18th century the orchestral and solo horn was still referred to as a 'hunting-horn' (or 'cor de chasse' etc); therefore, solo concertos by Haydn, Mozart, Rosetti, etc, were in fact concertos for hunting-horn.

SOUSAPHONE (or tuba): Jurriaan Andriessen (1967).

CHINESE VIOLIN: Concertos by Chok Yin Tai and Liang San Po.

DOUBLE BASS AND SAXOPHONE: *Ka*, by H J Hespos.

ELECTRIC VIOLIN: Michael Sahl (1973).

PENTACHORD (a species of five-string viol): K F Abel.

BANDONION (or accordion): Robert Caamaño (Op 19, 1954).

QUARTER-TONE PIANO: Hans Barth: No 1, Op 11 (1928); No 2, Op 15 (1930).

SITAR: Ravi Shankar: Concerto for sitar and orchestra (1968).

STRING GROUPS: Following on from the early 18th-century concerto grosso for a group of (usually) three string soloists and string orchestra, **the ultimate in massed string soloists** comes with a work entitled *Constellations*, Op 22 (1958) for twelve string groups, composed by Per Nørgård.

PIANO TRIO. In addition to the well-known example by Beethoven, both Podešva and Bocaccini have tackled this combination.

ORGAN, HARP, AND TIMPANI: Jan Hanuš: Sinfonia Concertante, Op 31 (1954).

PERCUSSION: Darius Milhaud: Concerto for percussion and small orchestra (1930).
Leonard Salzedo: Percussion Concerto.
Many other works featuring percussion alone or with other instruments have been written by, for instance, Carlos Chavez, George Antheil, Roland LoPresti, Alan Hovhaness, David Bedford, Robert Moran, and Edwin Roxburgh.

SEVEN WIND INSTRUMENTS, TIMPANI, PERCUSSION, AND STRINGS: Frank Martin (1949).

HARP, HARPSICHORD, PIANO, AND DOUBLE STRING ORCHESTRA: Frank Martin: *Petite Symphonie Concertante* (1945).

VOICE: Glière: Concerto for coloratura voice (soprano), Op 82 (1943).
Zsolt Durkó: *Dartmouth Concerto* for mezzo and orchestra. This work is a setting of a Masefield poem about the death march of the lemmings.
Bliss: Concerto for piano, tenor, strings, and percussion (1921).
Paccagnini: Concerto for soprano and orchestra (1965).
See also Fernstrøm under Flute, above.

Benjamin Frankel's *Concerto for Youth, Audience, and Orchestra* was written in 1968 in response to a commission from the town of Unna in north Germany. For a successful performance, the audience should bring in any type of musical instrument which they happen to possess, failing which they should clap, whistle, stamp, etc.

The concerto for the most unusual instrument is probably that (or, rather, *those*, since there are several) written by the Viennese composer J G Albrechtsberger to include the trombula. The works involved are, according to the catalogue of Lászlo Somfai:

No 7: Concertino in D for trombula, mandora, and strings (1769).

No 8: Concerto in F, à 5, for mandora, crembalum, and strings (1770).

No 9: Concertino in E flat, à 5, for trombula, harpsichord, and strings (1771).

No 10: Concerto in E for crembalum, mandora, and strings (1771).

Of the three unfamiliar instruments named in this list, 'mandora' may be disposed of immediately: it is simply a species of lute as noted in the list in Section II. According to Somfai's catalogue, in a footnote on p 184, 'crembalum' is another name for 'trombula': 'Trombula, oder Crembalum: Maultrommel (guimbarde).' The only problem, then, is to identify the trombula.

The Concertino in E flat (No 9 in the list above) was identified by Albrechtsberger as 'Concertino in Eb. a cinque Stromenti (for) Tromb, Cemb Del Sig: G: A:', and the score gives the parts as for 'violins I and II, Bass, Tromb, and Cembalo'. The two references to 'Tromb' have led musicologists to believe that the solo instrument should be a trumpet ('tromba'), but examination reveals the solo part to be chromatic. Hitherto, music history has taught that the 18th-century trumpet, like the horn of the same period, was a non-chromatic instrument (ie the available notes were restricted to the harmonic series of the basic tone of the instrument), and that chromaticism did not become

King David playing the harp. (Scala/Vision International)

An example of an early 14th-century Italian harp and bellows organ. (Mary Evans Picture Library)

Above: German Musicians of 1520. (Mary Evans Picture Library)

Below: Harpsichord, built in Venice by Giovanni Baffo in 1574. (Angelo Hornak/Vision International)

'Hearing', P. P. Rubens Brueghel, 1395. (Museo del Prado, Madrid)

Above: The world's oldest working organ at the Eglise de Valère in Sion, Switzerland, built in 1390. (Musées Cantonaux du Vallais)

Left: Lira, made in Bologna in the 17th century. (Scala/Vision International)

Top right: Sculptures by Eila Hiltunen and unveiled in Sibelius Park, Helsinki, in 1967. A representation of the composer can be seen on the right. (Stan Greenberg)

Right: *l* to *r*: Cosima Wagner, Richard Wagner, Franz Liszt, and Baron Hans von Wolzogen, an important writer on Wagnerian subjects and the first editor of the Beyreuter Blätter. Painting by W Beckmann, 1880. (Wagner Museum, Lucerne)

Johann Sebastian Bach, the central figure of a most important family of composers. Portrait by Elias Gottlieb Haussmann. (Royal College of Music)

possible on the trumpet until the invention of the keyed trumpet by the Viennese trumpeter Anton Weidinger about 1796. It was for Weidinger's 'keyed trumpet', incidentally, that Joseph Haydn wrote his Trumpet Concerto in E flat, the first to be written for the keyed trumpet (1796), and the most famous of all trumpet concertos. To find a concertino in the same key dating from a quarter of a century earlier, and including a chromatic part for what was apparently a trumpet, makes nonsense of this particular piece of musical history, and has led some writers, among them the American musicologist Mary Rasmussen, to put forward the theory that an unidentified inventor known to Albrechtsberger, or perhaps that composer himself, developed a chromatic trumpet, later imparting the intelligence of its existence to Haydn (who knew Albrechtsberger in Vienna in the 1790s). Haydn then is thought to have brought this information to Weidinger, who developed the idea into the keyed trumpet for which Haydn wrote.

However, a further doubt is thrown on the credibility of the trumpet as the soloist in this particular work (Somfai No 9) by the composer's demand for only *five* instruments (ie the violin parts were not meant to be multiplied). The balance between two violins, a double bass, a keyboard instrument, and a trumpet, bearing in mind that the average volume of sound from one trumpet is approximately equal to the average volume from 14 unison violins, would be ludicrously weighted in favour of the brass instrument, and this has been proved by recordings of the work in which a trumpet does in fact take the solo part.

Clearly, the indication 'tromb' cannot mean trumpet. What, then, does it mean?

One possible, and perhaps the only possible, alternative is 'trombula'. Two other suggestions have been the slide-trumpet (like a small trombone), and the trombone itself, but both these instruments would lead us again into balancing problems. Furthermore, for his Trombone Concerto (Somfai No 6), Albrechtsberger took the trouble to spell out the word in its entirety on the title-page: 'trombone'.

The 'trombula' remains to be examined. The word is a diminutive of tromba, which in turn shows relationships with Scot: *trump* and *tromp*, the Fr: *trombe de béarn* and *trombe de laquais* (= 'servant's trumpet') and the Jew's trump of 16th-century England. The Ger: *Maultrommel* (literally 'mouth-drum') is possibly a distortion of an imported word in this family, although the 'drum' component is almost equally descriptive. All these terms point straight to one instrument: the Jew's harp.

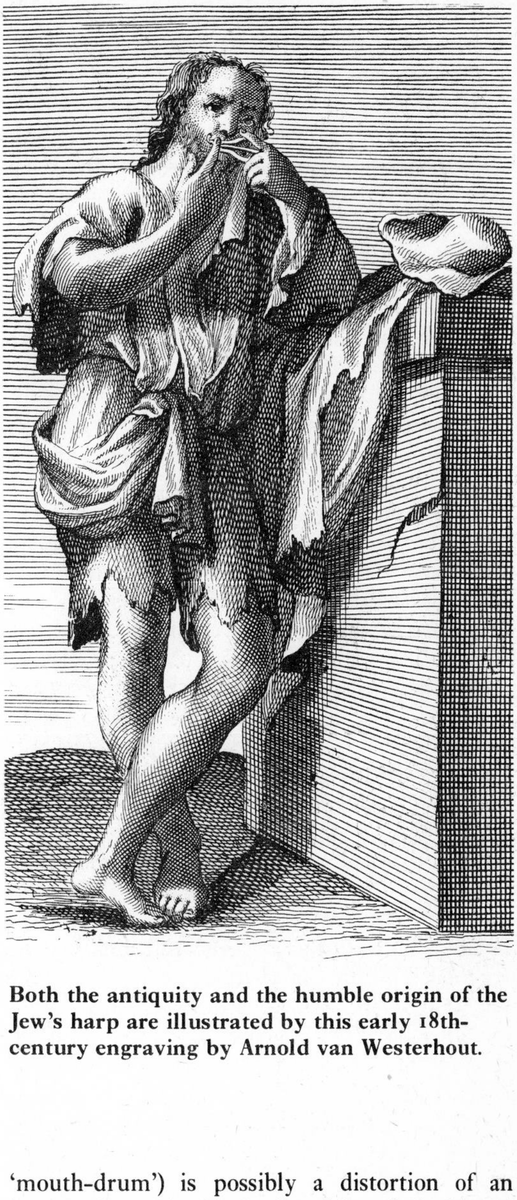

Both the antiquity and the humble origin of the Jew's harp are illustrated by this early 18th-century engraving by Arnold van Westerhout.

If we accept that Albrechtsberger's four works were in fact written for the Jew's harp, two questions remain to be examined. First, why did the composer use two distinct terms ('trombula'; 'crembalum') for the same instrument? Secondly, the Jew's harp is a harmonic (ie non-chromatic) instrument just as much as is the mid-18th-century trumpet, which would appear to put us back to the beginning again.

In answer to the first question, we may assume that two different types of instrument were known to Albrechtsberger, although both of the Jew's harp family. Amplification of this supposition will be found in the possible solution to the second puzzle.

It was by no means unknown for travelling Jew's harp virtuosi to tour Europe in the 18th century, and for them to specialise in playing more than one of these instruments simultaneously. For a player to accommodate two instruments in his mouth was common; more than that would have required a device in which several Jew's harps were attached to a framework of wood. With a series of instruments each tuned to a different pitch, chromatic melodies would have been playable by proficient virtuosi. It is to be noted that such frames existed until well into the 19th century, some having provision for up to sixteen Jew's harps. Is it out of the question that a trombula virtuoso visited Vienna and that his playing impelled Albrechtsberger to compose some works for him; and that the said virtuoso had with him also a differently constructed frame of instruments which he called by the name of 'crembalum'?

The composer of the most concertos is Antonio Vivaldi, who produced some 488 known examples (as listed by Pincherle, Kolneder, Fanna, Ryom, *et al*). However, this total may be regarded with suspicion for various reasons, some factors reducing, others expanding, the number.

Due to the lax terminology of the 18th century, the word 'concerto' was used indescriminately by Vivaldi and others so that works more accurately entitled 'sonata', or 'sinfonia', have been included, notwithstanding the fact that a separate section for sonatas exists in the various numbering systems. It has been found, also, that a number of works attributed to Vivaldi are alternatively ascribed in certain sources, and in many cases the correct author cannot yet be discovered.

Having reduced our total by the above means, we may now expand it by examination of external evidence. Vivaldi joined the Ospedale della Pietà di Venezia as composer in charge of musical activities in September 1703. In 1713 he was granted leave of absence for an unspecified period, which we may assume to have been about a year. From 1718 to 1722 he apparently commuted between his native Venice and Darmstadt, and in 1723, on his return to Venice, he was contracted to produce two concertos per month for the Ospedale. From 1725 to 1735 his movements are unknown in detail, but he evidently travelled in Europe for much of the time, putting in frequent appearances at Venice; he died in Vienna in 1741.

It is probable that the contract of 1723 for two concertos per month was based on his known capacity: by then he had had published several sets of concertos and sonatas and had been astonishingly busy in the opera-house, so it was known that he was no laggard. In addition, he had accumulated a certain amount of fame at home and abroad, so the contract was likely to have been drafted well within his capabilities rather than it running any risk of stretching them. We may assume, then, that his production *up to 1723* had been in the order of, at the very least, two concertos per month; due to his other responsibilities his concerto-writing may have been halved during his busy years from 1718 to 1722, giving us twelve per year. The same reduction may be assumed during the vague years 1725–35, and we shall leave entirely out of account his final year of 1741, which we know was spent at least partly in Vienna, where he died.

With these speculations in mind, together with the certain knowledge that they may be faulted in many particulars if the true facts of Vivaldi's life and travels are ever incontrovertibly revealed, we may draw up the following table of *possible* concerto production:

Date	*Known or surmised circumstances*	*No of concertos?*
Sept 1703	Joined Ospedale della Pietà	6
1704–12	Relatively uninterrupted work	216
1713	Vacation	–
1714–17	Resumption of uninterrupted work	96
1718–22	Darmstadt/Venice alternation	60
1723–24	Contracted to write two concertos per month	48
1725–35	European travelling/Venice	132
1736–40	Relatively uninterrupted work	120
	Conjectural total	670

As intimated, these figures must be underestimates. In his early days he is said to have composed a concerto faster than his copyists could render it into parts for the instrumentalists, and it is within possibility that for some of his visits he produced a fresh batch of works to impress his hosts, thus putting his average higher for that period. In addition, as has been said, his operas were many and varied and his production of sacred vocal works and instrumental sonatas was also immense. From these somewhat computerised figures, however, we may feel entitled to expect that more concertos by Vivaldi are awaiting discovery. Meanwhile, his total of existing works in this form must stand, at 488, as far and away in excess of that of any other composer.

The most versatile concerto composer is probably the Frenchman, Henri Tomasi (1901–71), who wrote for flute, oboe, clarinet, saxophone, horn, trumpet, trombone, violin, viola, cello, double bass, harp, and guitar.

The first cello concertos were written by Jacchini and published in 1701.

The first violin concertos appeared in 1709 in the set of twelve concertos by Giuseppe Torelli, Op 8, but they may have been composed several years earlier.

The first concertos for piano were written by J C Bach and appeared about 1776.
(See also Section II.)

The composer of the most violin concertos is Vivaldi, who wrote 238 known examples.

The composer of the most flute concertos was Johann Joachim Quantz (1697–1773), whose 300 such works were mainly written for, and while in the service of, the flute-playing King Frederick the Great (see Royal Composers in Section III).

The concerto with the most soloists is by Vivaldi. Two concertos, in fact, both in C major, RV 558 and RV 555 are scored for eleven soloists:

RV 555: violin, two violas, two flutes, oboe, cor anglais, two trumpets, two harpsichords, with strings.

RV 558: two flutes, two salmoè, two violins in tromba marina, two mandolins, two theorbos, cello, with strings.

John McCabe's 'Mini-Concerto' (1966) is for 485 penny-whistles, percussion, and organ.

The first concerto to specify parts for clarinets. At least two works by Vivaldi were written for two clarinets, which play very much in the style of trumpets and, therefore, differ from the Mozartean use as mellow, seductive instruments. Vivaldi's concertos including clarinets were probably written in the last year or so of his life, and each is scored for two oboes, and two clarinets, with string orchestra (RV 559 and RV 560). Another concerto, RV 556, with the subtitle 'Per la solennità di St Lorenzo', is scored for two flutes, two oboes, two clarinets, bassoon, two violins, and string orchestra.

The only piano concerto to include human voices is Busoni's Concerto No 2, Op 39 (1904), a massive five-movement composition, the finale of which includes a male choir singing a text by the Danish poet, A G Oehlenschläger.

'Concertos' for solo keyboard instrument without accompaniment:

Alkan: Concerto, Op 74, for piano.
Bach: *Italian* Concerto, BWV 971, for harpsichord.
Alkan: *Concerto Symphonique*, for piano.
Schumann: Concerto for Piano without orchestra (Sonata No 4 in F minor, Op 14, 1836).

Variations

Every one of the smaller forms has been transferred to the orchestra at one time or another, just as was the instrumental sonata, although unlike the sonata—which became the orchestral symphony—most of the other pieces retain their instrumental names. Possibly the most important and widest-used large orchestra form, apart from those mentioned in the foregoing sections, is the 'theme and variation' set. Important examples, among many others, of orchestral variations have been written by:

Bentzon: *Symphonic Variations*, Op 92 (1953).
Brahms: *Variations on St Anthony Chorale*, Op 56a (1873) (an arrangement for orchestra from a piece for two pianos).
Britten: *Variations on a Theme of Frank Bridge*, Op 10 (1938). *Variations and Fugue on a Theme by Purcell: The Young Person's Guide to the Orchestra*, Op 34 (1945).
Arensky: *Variations on a Theme by Tchaikovsky*, Op 35a.
Dvořák: *Symphonic Variations*, Op 78 (1877).
Elgar: *Enigma Variations*, Op 36 (1899).

Benjamin Britten, composer of one of the best-known sets of variations: The Young Person's Guide to the Orchestra, based on a theme by Purcell. (Popperfoto)

In respect of this last named, perhaps one of the most popular works by any English composer, it is well known that Elgar never gave the clue to his enigma. The theme is not heard during the work, only its bass counterpoint being played, and it is upon this bass that the variations are constructed. All that the composer would ever say on the subject was that the melody was extremely well known; but every suggestion put to him as to its identity was warded off impatiently.

Roger Fiske, in *The Musical Times* for November 1969, convincingly suggests on harmonic grounds that the tune is 'Auld Lang Syne'. It would be neat to consider the case closed at this point since the choice of that tune is most appropriate to the nature of the work, dedicated as it is to 'my friends pictured within'.

Returning to the subject of variations in general, it should be remembered that some of the greatest sets occur in symphonies. Those that conclude Dvořák's Symphony No 8 and Beethoven's Symphony No 3, 'Eroica' are universally known, and the chaconne which comprises the finale of Brahms's Symphony No 4 is a close-knit and masterly set. Less well known are the numerous examples in the symphonies of Joseph Haydn (Nos 31, 72, 42, 47, 53, 55, 63, 70, 82, 85, 91, and 103, etc).

An interesting hybrid lying somewhere between the variation form and the symphony is the awkwardly titled *Symphonic Metamorphosis on Themes of Carl Maria von Weber*, by Hindemith. It is indeed symphonic in that it is in four contrasted movements, and it is metamorphic in that it takes a series of (little-known) themes by Weber and uses them as material upon which the whole work is constructed. It should be pointed out, however, that the word 'metamorphosis' is not an alternative for 'variations' since the themes of the older composer are taken merely as starting-points and are not subjected to variations in the usual way.

Delius's Variations entitled *Appalachia* (1902) is unusual in that a chorus is used in the concluding section.

Other forms

Orchestral works have been written also with the following titles:

Ballade (Einem).
Canzona (G Gabrieli).
Capriccio(so) (Einem; Holst).
Dances: Bolero, Chaconne, Mazurka, Minuet, Polka, Waltz, etc.
Essay (Barber).
Étude (Martin).
Fanfare (Mouret).
Idyll (Janáček; Martinů; Wagner: *Siegfried Idyll*; Butterworth).
Legend (Dvořák; Svendsen-really a concerto movement).
March.
'Music' (Bartók; Jorgenssen).
Partita (Albrechtsberger; Walton).
Phantasy or Fantasy (Coates; Larsson).
Piece(s) (Schoenberg; Bartók).

Poème (Fibich).
Rhapsody (Alfvén; Bloch; Chabrier; Dvořák; Enescu; German; Liszt, Moeran).
Scherzo (Dukas; Dvořák).
Scherzo Capriccioso (Dvořák; Susskind).
Sinfonietta (Janáček; Martinů).

Chamber music

The dividing-line between orchestral and chamber music is not always clearly defined. Stravinsky wrote for a 'chamber group' of 13 players (*Dumbarton Oaks* Concerto in E flat, 1938) and works such as Mendelssohn's Octet for two string quartets, and Spohr's Double Quartets for the same groups, have orchestra-like textures. On the other hand, some composers of full-scale symphonies seem to have in mind chamber sonorities for much of the time: Sibelius, Mahler, Shostakovich, and Nielsen among them. The 18th- and early 19th-century octet for wind and strings is of approximately the same texture as the 18th-century symphony for two oboes, two horns, two violins, viola and cello/bass, but it is more correctly a chamber conception because each player has a semi-soloistic function in the octet, whereas in the similarly scored symphony the wind instruments often merely support the harmonies, with a harmonic and rhythmic foundation provided by the lower strings, the violins carrying most of the melodic argument. (This over-simplification will stagger and perhaps collapse under too close a scrutiny because of the wide differences between composers' practices, but it will hold good for early symphonies and will serve to illustrate the historical foundation upon which composers built.)

Most chamber forms have the numbers of players implied in their titles; nonet (for nine players), octet, septet, sextet, quintet, quartet, trio, and duo (or duet). Some quintets and quartets are for a soloist and four or three, respectively, supporting string instruments. These are called 'piano quintets', or 'flute quartets', etc (which does *not* mean compositions for five pianos or four flutes. A flute quartet is for flute, violin, viola and cello, whereas a work for four flutes is called specifically, 'quartet for four flutes'), and are in effect small-scale concertos: Mozart, J C Bach, and other composers of their time wrote works entitled 'concerto' in which the accompanying string 'orchestra' could consist of one instrument to each string part. Occasionally *ad lib* wind and horn parts would be made available, and when these were used the string parts might be strengthened accordingly, making the work into a 'concert concerto' rather than a 'chamber concerto'. This fluidity was very much a matter of convenience in the 18th century: what use was there in writing a work which could be played only by a large (for the time) orchestra of 20 or so players, thus excluding the many 'societies' which had at their disposal only a few players? The orchestral trio and orchestral quartet of the composers of the Mannheim School (see Section III) similarly took into account pliable groups of players.

When there is no soloist the quintet, or more usually the quartet, would consist of strings only and would then become a small-scale symphony. Haydn is said to be the 'Father of the String Quartet', although the foundations upon which he built his paternity were ancient and widespread, stretching back into the consorts of viols of the 16th and 17th centuries. An even smaller symphony is formed by the string trio which, in some of the works of the 18th-century Mannheim School, were written in such a way that the parts may be multiplied. These were known as 'orchestral trios'; in the next generation of composers of the Mannheim School the same principle was applied to 'orchestral quartets', the best-known examples of which were by Karl Stamitz.

Duets may be for a wide variety of instrumental combinations. The true duet is one in which both protagonists have an equal share of the argument, as in those by Boccherini for two violins (Gér 56–62), or the same composer's fugues for two cellos or two bassoons (Gér 73); the so-called 'Eyeglass' Duo by Beethoven is for viola and cello, and other works exist by Telemann (two violins), Pleyel and Michael Haydn (violin and viola) in their Op 44 and Perger 127–130, respectively. Telemann is guilty of a *Duett* in A for two bass gambas! Moving away from the string repertoire, we find sonatas for clarinet and bassoon by Beethoven, and for two keyboards by Mozart, Müthel etc, but in mentioning these examples we are merely taking arbitrarily from an enormous repertoire.

Still technically in the realm of the duo or duet, but thought of more as accompanied solos for melody instrument and bass or keyboard, are the even larger quantities of sonatas for violin, cello, flute, oboe, or indeed any instrument whatever, with piano or other keyboard instrument. Paul Hindemith has shown in his didactic works a wide variety of accompanied solos within the lists of a single composer: there exist sonatas for flute, oboe, clarinet, bassoon, trumpet, trombone, violin, viola, viola d'amor, and cello, all accompanied by piano. Two hundred years earlier Telemann, in addition to producing pieces for most of these instruments, also added to the repertoire solos (accompanied by basso continuo) for recorder, oboe d'amore, viola da gamba, descant gamba, and even for bass gamba. One of his prettiest little items is a piece in E for panpipes and harpsichord.

But by far the largest number of works in this group are for violin and piano. Starting during the time of Mozart, when the keyboard was the dominant partner with the violin merely accompanying, the latter instrument gradually became more important with Beethoven and his contemporaries, until, with Schumann, Brahms, and many other 19th-century composers, the violin was the soloist proper, the piano simply providing an accompaniment, although often an important one. By the end of that century the so-called 'violin sonata' had turned into what was a duo for violin and piano in all but name, both instruments having equal say. A most odd example was written in 1922 by Bartók. His first sonata for violin and piano is written in such a way that the two players seem to be completely at odds. It is as if one were listening to two sonatas, one for piano, the other for violin, being performed simultaneously. In fact, critic Ernest Newman, in his notice of the first performance, after registering his disgust with the music, said as much: 'It was as if two people were improvising against each other.'

SOME CHAMBER MUSIC FACTS

Vladimir Stcherbatchev wrote a nonet scored for string quartet, piano, harp, violin, dance, and light. Hardly less bizarre is Ives's *Scherzo: Over the Pavements* (1906–13), for piccolo, clarinet, bassoon, trumpet, three trombones, piano, cymbal, and drum.

The first wind quintets (ie symphonic works for flute, oboe, clarinet, bassoon, and horn) were written by Cambini. His first examples date from about 1795.

The composer of the most guitar quartets (violin, viola, cello, guitar) is Paganini, who composed 21, five of which are lost.

The composer of the most string quintets is Luigi Boccherini. The standard string quintet is scored for two violins, two violas, and cello, but Boccherini favoured the alternative setting of two violins, viola, and two cellos (the scoring chosen by Schubert for his C major String Quartet, D 956 of 1828). Boccherini's totals, written between 1771 and 1802, are:

Quintets for two violins, two violas and cello	24
Quintets for two violins, viola and two cellos	113
Total	137

Bernard van Dieren, Dutch composer, critic and author, wrote a string quartet (Op 22) for the unusual combination of two violins, viola, and double bass.

Milhaud's String Quartets Nos 14 (1948) and 15 (1949) are written in such a way that they may be played either separately or simultaneously. (See also Section V: Raimondi.)

The earliest published sonatas were those (now lost) for various string groups by A Gabrieli, which appeared in 1586.

The earliest keyboard quartets were by the Italian Carlo Boni, published in Paris in *c* 1770. They were for harpsichord, violin, viola, and bass, the scoring also used for a 'Symphony' (*c* 1772) by Kolb, and for three quartets by Pleyel, published by André, Offenbach, *c* 1785 (the first and last being arrangements of string quartets). Mozart's two 'Piano Quartets', K 478 and 493, written in October 1785 and June 1786 respectively, were published by the same firm in the latter year.

The first composer to introduce the minuet into sonatas was Benedetto Vinaccesi, whose *Suonate a tre* were published in 1687.

A String Quartet (No 6, 1963) by Jan Kapr includes a part for baritone solo.

The first inventions, in the sense of suites for violin and bass, were written by A F Bonporti about 1715. The same term was used later by J S Bach for solo harpsichord music.

The earliest sonatas for two violins date from 1613. They are by the Italian Salomone Rossi Ebreo.

The earliest sonatas for one violin are by the Italian Biagio Marini, composed in 1617.

The first violin sonatas by an English composer were by William Young, but were published at Innsbruck in 1653.

The composer of the most violin sonatas, with a total of 191, is Giuseppe Tartini, who wrote also at least 125 concertos for the instrument.

The composer of the most flute sonatas was King Frederick the Great (Friedrich II of Prussia) who wrote 120 for his own use.

Solo instrumental music

Although it might be thought of as being part of the chamber music repertoire since it is ideally performed in a smallish room or chamber, solo instrumental music usually falls into a different category. Once again any instrument may be involved, but by far the most widely known and accepted solo music is for piano or some other keyboard instrument such as the harpsichord or organ. Strictly speaking, however, such music is duple in effect since the player has two hands with which to produce two distinct registers, the 'melody' register (right hand) and the accompanying 'bass' (left hand). In theory, keyboard music for two hands can exist in as many as ten lines, one for each finger and thumb, but in practice even the most complex rarely goes above four parts except for chords.

The forms such music might take are multifarious: sonata, suite, concerto (in this case without a supporting orchestra—see above), variations, prelude and fugue, chaconne, passacaglia, and many other types of dance (Chopin's piano compositions show a tremendous variety of stylised dance forms, none of which could be danced to), ballads and other forms 'borrowed' from vocal music, and arrangements from works for other combinations of instruments or full orchestra. Liszt, for instance, produced piano arrangements of Beethoven symphonies which, as examples of the arranger's art, deserve consideration as masterpieces in themselves.

It is the sonata which has attracted the most serious attention from composers for the solo keyboard instrument, and large numbers of keyboard sonatas were written by Domenico Scarlatti, C P E Bach, Haydn, Mozart, Beethoven, Clementi, and Schubert, to mention only the best known, up to the early 19th century, since when important sonatas have been produced by Chopin, Schumann, Brahms, Liszt, Rakhmaninoff, Scriabin, and others.

The organ, the so-called 'King of Instruments', also has a large repertoire of solo music. The first composer to come to mind in this context is J S Bach, but his huge and inclusive output of music for the instrument was preceded by works by John Bull, Sweelinck, Frescobaldi, Buxtehude, Pachelbel, and Bruhns, all of whom contributed to the organ literature which Bach used as a foundation and so easily capped.

After Bach (and indeed well before him), the literature for organ and harpsichord overlapped: what could be played on the one was usually equally suitable for performance on the other. With the possible exception of a few works for the pedal harpsichord, it is inconceivable that Bach's organ works should be played on the harpsichord. The loss in original textures and grandeur of the over-all effect would damage the works too seriously. Later in the 18th century, however, the dividing-line was not so hard and the works written for organ by many English composers, and by Haydn, Mozart, and Beethoven, are not so seriously affected by performance on a different instrument, simply because the works themselves are usually not of such consequence as those by Bach.

The 19th century saw the production of a small but important organ literature by Mendelssohn, Brahms, Liszt, Franck, Saint-Saëns, Reger, Widor, and Vierne. Since this late romantic flowering, the organ repertoire has been in the hands of a few specialist composers, only the occasional important work being produced by musicians of wider interests, among them Nielsen and Messiaen.

Solo works for instruments other than the piano or organ are much less common and are, owing to the danger of a single sound colour boring the ear, usually of much shorter duration. Often it will be found that such works are composed for instructional or practice use and are, therefore, enjoyable almost exclusively for the player. An exception may be made in the case of the masterly works of J S Bach for solo violin, solo cello, and solo flute. His lute works, too, exist within the realm of music designed to be enjoyed by the listener as well as by the performer.

The guitar repertoire is large but it has been developed mainly, and with one or two surprising exceptions, by composers who concentrated on the instrument, almost to the exclusion of other types of music. The Spaniard Fernando Sor was known as the 'Beethoven of the guitar' in the sense of being foremost a virtuoso and only secondly a composer (thus paralleling Beethoven's role in earlier life). As the national instrument of Spain, the guitar has naturally attracted composers of that country or who had origins or affinities with Iberia: Ponce, Turina, Halffter, Falla, and Villa-Lobos have also written for the instrument. The 'surprising exceptions' mentioned above are Berlioz, Weber, and Paganini, all of whom showed an interest in it, but of these only Paganini left music for solo guitar. Weber used it occasionally to accompany songs, while Berlioz included it in his treatise on instrumentation.

The guitar, like the other stringed and keyboard instruments discussed above, is a chord-producing as well as a melody-playing instrument. This accounts for its relatively wide popularity among composers, a popularity which cannot extend to most other instruments. Unaccompanied solos for oboe, horn, trumpet, clarinet, bassoon, etc, exist but are rare and of minor importance; percussion solos are slightly more common especially with young composers, and a number of solely percussion marches exist, dating from the early 18th-century French courts.

Some instrumental music facts

The piano nocturne was invented by John Field, who published the first in 1814, but it is evident that he had merely transferred to the keyboard a chamber type (and at times a vocal type; for Mozart and other composers wrote 'notturni' for voices and instruments) which was well established as a mood piece during the latter half of the 18th century. In addition, both Mozart and Haydn wrote multi-movement works of divertimento type with this title. At the time of Field's first set, Chopin, who adopted the form and made it distinctly his own, was four years old.

The impromptu was invented concurrently but separately by Heinrich August Marschner and Jan Hugo Voříšek, both of whom published pieces with this title in 1822. The name was taken up later by Schubert (in 1827), Schumann (1833), and Chopin (1836).

The inventor of variations is thought to have been Hugh Aston, who died in 1522. He was an English composer mainly of church and keyboard music. An alternative English name for variations was 'divisions'.

The composer of the most keyboard passacaglias is the American Stephen Gersch, born 1948, who has written over 300.

The earliest keyboard solo sonatas date from *c* 1695. They were written by the German composer Johann Kuhnau.

The first sonatas specifically for pianoforte were by the Englishman John Burton, whose ten examples were written in 1766.

The composer of the most sonatas for keyboard was Domenico Scarlatti who wrote 555 (according to Kirkpatrick). Recent research has attempted to add a few more to this total, but the question of authenticity arises, particularly as some of the additions are supposedly early works, and Domenico's father Alessandro wrote pieces in a style similar to his son's earliest attempts. Even more amazing, when considering Domenico's output of harpsichord sonatas (the earliest works were called 'Essercisi'='exercises'), which were written mainly in Spain for the Royal Palace at Madrid, is that they come from the last 20 years or so of his long life.

Nearly all of his sonatas are single-movement works, although Kirkpatrick puts forward a strong case for many of them to be performed in pairs. A few early multi-movement sonatas exist for harpsichord and violin, but they are uncharacteristic and unremarkable. Many of the sonatas carry nicknames such as 'Pastorale', 'The Cat's Fugue' (the story being that the composer's cat suggested the theme while promenading on the keyboard), and 'Cortège'.

The 19th century saw a busy production of piano sonatas, among which Beethoven's 32 stand as a mighty testament to the range and subtlety obtainable from the newly established *Hammerklavier*, or true 'hammered' piano. In the present century the output to date of 93 piano sonatas by the English composer John White represents **the modern record.**

The composer of the most organ sonatas was Josef Gabriel Rheinberger, who wrote 20 between 1868 and 1901.

The longest instrumental work. This question raises the subject: When does music cease to be music?

A few years ago it was reported that a 26-minute work entitled *In C*, by the American Terry Riley, in which the solo pianist plays only the note C for the entire performance, was given by the Norwegian pianist Siri Nome. It is further reported that the lights in the recital room were switched off to add atmosphere, and that when they were turned up at the end of the performance, Siri Nome was alone.

The French composer Erik Satie's aptly titled *Vexations* must come into a similar category. It consists of a 52-beat unbarred idea, with the indication 'Très lent', played 840 times with as little variation as possible. The first performance, organised by John Cage at the Pocket Theatre, New York, in 1963, lasted 18 hours 12 minutes and was performed by a group of ten pianists in relay. Since then there have been many other performances: the second was in Berlin during August 1966, at which a relay of six pianists took part: for her second stint Charlotte Moorman introduced a novel way of breaking the monotony by appearing unclothed from the waist up. Her reasons were both musicological and financial: Satie, it is said, 'loved nudity', and John Cage bet her $100 she wouldn't do it. On this occasion the performance of the music took 18 hours 40 minutes.

The first *solo* performance of *Vexations* was given at the Arts Laboratory, Drury Lane, London, on 10–11 October 1967 by Richard Toop. According to reports he was sustained during the performance with cucumber sandwiches in black bread, and chocolate, but it is not recorded whether Satie's contribution to the proceedings also served to feed him up. Apparently not, since Mr Toop gave another performance, of a little over 24 hours duration in January 1968. The following year a performance was attempted in Australia, but was not finished because the soloist was rushed to hospital in a coma after only 17 hours.

Vexations was published for the first time in England in the periodical *Music Review* in 1967.

Of similar effect but with rather more variety is a method of composing minuets according to the bar order dictated by the throw of dice. It consists of 16 bars of 3/4 time attributed to F J Haydn. A performance utilising all 940 369 969 152 permutations would last in the region of 900 000 years without observing formal repeats. There has been no notice of a complete performance so far.

The longest non-repetitive work is a recent piece called *Sadist Factory* by Philip L Crevier of New York. It consists of all possible permutations of the scale of C major and occupies 1680 pages of computer print-out. Total playing time is calculated at 100 hours. If this piece were to prove successful there is nothing to prevent Mr Crevier from putting his computer to use in similar explorations of the other scales.

A work called *Solo for Double Bass*, written in 1969 by Malcolm Fox, is said to last, when played at the extremely fast tempo indicated, 73 000 000 000 years, but it may be assumed that a certain amount of repetition is involved.

Works with nicknames and subtitles

A large number of works in and out of the current repertoire are identified only by key and perhaps an opus number (eg Symphony No 4 in B flat, Op 60 by Beethoven). For many music-lovers who are exasperated or perplexed by references to 'the Beethoven B flat' or 'Mozart G minor' (as if these were the only works written in these keys by these composers), the addition of a nickname or subtitle to a work is a useful mnemonic, and a large number of works have been given such titles. It is not our task here to decide which of these names are appropriate (as indeed some are) and which downright silly (a larger category!); there can be no doubt that such names are useful in identifying and memorising the works which bear them.

In preparing this list, the aim has been to include all the well-known names in the hope that it will be useful for those who can remember the name only and who need to find out the full and correct title and composition date of the work. In the 'Remarks' column a brief note is given as to the origin or cause of the name (where known), but in the cases of the Mendelssohn *Songs Without Words*, the Chopin Études, and some other groups, the meanings of the names are self-evident and are easily guessed from their romantic connections.

Also given are a selection of lesser-known titles, supplementing those in the first edition. It is hoped that these titles, and the reasons for them will prove of intrinsic interest even though much of the music is unlikely to be heard in a lifetime of listening.

In the matter of identification, the reader is referred to the list of thematic catalogues in Section VII.

NICKNAMES AND SUBTITLES

Name or subtitle	*Work*	*Composer*	*Remarks*
'About our Beautiful Country'	Symphony No 3 (1954)	Ambros	
Accademico	Violin Concerto in D minor (1925)	Vaughan Williams	The composer later rejected the title.
'Adélaïde'	Violin Concerto in D, K A 294a (*c* 1775?)	Mozart	Supposedly dedicated to the eldest daughter of Louis XV, Mme Adélaïde de France. It is now thought that the dedication has strayed from another work, and that the concerto itself may not be genuine Mozart.
Adieu, L'	Song Without Words in A minor, Op 85/2 (1845)	Mendelssohn	
Adieux, Les	Piano Sonata in E flat, Op 81a (1809)	Beethoven	In full: *Les Adieux, l'Absence, et le Retour*. Dedicated to the Archduke Rudolf, who was about to leave Vienna for a time.
'Aeolian Harp'	Étude in A flat, Op 25/1 (1837)	Chopin	
'After the Heritage of My Dear Father'	Symphony No 5 in F, Op 39 (1948)	Moyzes	See *Podla Odkazu Drahého Otca*.
'Age of Anxiety, The'	Symphony No 2 for piano and orchestra (1949)	Bernstein	Based on a poem by W H Auden.
Alla Rustica	Concerto in G for strings, RV 151	Vivaldi	Written in 'rustic' style throughout.
'Amaryllis'	String Trio (1964)	Schuman	
'American, The'	String Quartet in F, Op 96 (1893)	Dvořák	Written at Spillville, Iowa, and based partly on American (Black) themes.
An das Vaterland	Symphony No 1, Op 96 (1863)	Raff	
An die Freunde	Symphony No 2 in C, Op 46 (1940)	Pfitzner	
'Antar'	Symphony No 2, Op 9 (1868)	Rimsky-Korsakov	Antar was a 7th-century Russian poet.
'Antartica'	Symphony No 7 (1953)	Vaughan Williams	Based on the film music written by Vaughan Williams for *Scott of the Antarctic* (1948).
Appassionata	Piano Sonata in F minor, Op 57 (1806)	Beethoven	A title invented by the publisher; it refers to the passionate nature of the music.
Appassionata	Song Without Words in A minor, Op 38/5 (1838)	Mendelssohn	

Name or subtitle	*Work*	*Composer*	*Remarks*
'Arabesque'	Piano Concerto (1930)	Becker	
'Archduke'	Piano Trio in B flat, Op 97 (1811)	Beethoven	Dedicated to the Archduke Rudolf.
Arevakal	Concerto for orchestra No 1, Op 88	Hovhaness	
Arjuna	Symphony No 8, Op 179	Hovhaness	
Arte del Violino, L'	12 Concerti and 24 Caprices for violin, Op 3 (1733)	Locatelli	A milestone in violin composition.
Assunzione di Maria Vergine	Concerto in C for violin and two string orchestras, RV 179	Vivaldi	Written for the Feast of the Assumption.
	Concerto in D for violin and two string orchestras, RV 582	Vivaldi	
'At Home'	Piano Trio, Op 38 (1924)	Křička	
Au Tombeau du Martyre Juif inconnu	Concerto for harp and strings (1976)	Williamson	Inspired by a visit to a memorial in Paris commemorating unknown victims of a Nazi concentration camp.
'Babi Yar'	Symphony No 13 in B minor, Op 113 (1962)	Shostakovich	Commemorates the Jewish cemetery at Babi Yar, Kiev.
'Battle of Vittoria, The'	Symphony (1813)	Beethoven	Also known as 'Wellington's Victory'.
'Bee's Wedding, The'	Song Without Words in C, Op 67/4 (1845)	Mendelssohn	Also known as 'Spinning Song'.
'Belief'	Song Without Words in C, Op 102/6 (1845)	Mendelssohn	
'Bell, The'	Symphony No 2 (1943)	Khachaturian	The opening of the work is said to be bell-like.
'Bells of Zlonice, The'	Symphony No 1 in C minor, Op 3 (1865)	Dvořák	The young composer lived at Zlonice and may have incorporated the motifs of the town's bells into the work.
'Beltane Rites, The'	Symphony (1978)	Pert	Old Scottish May Day festival rites.
Berceuse	Song Without Words in F, Op 53/4 (1841)	Mendelssohn	
'Big Mountain, The'	Symphony No 1 (1960)	Mills	
'Birthday, The'	String Quartet No 10 (1940)	Milhaud	Written to commemorate the 80th birthday of Mrs Elizabeth Sprague Coolidge (1864–1953), American music patroness who has financed many projects in Washington DC, Yale, Pittsfield, Massachusetts, and elsewhere.
'Black Keys'	Étude in G flat, Op 10/5 (1833)	Chopin	
'Black Mass'	Piano Sonata No 9 in F, Op 68 (1913)	Scriabin	

Name or subtitle	*Work*	*Composer*	*Remarks*
Boreale	Symphony No 8, Op 56 (1951–52)	Holmboe	Meant to indicate to the first audience, which was supposed to have been Viennese, the Nordic character of the work, the title proved useless since the first performance was after all given in Copenhagen.
'Brandenburg Concertos'	Six Concerti Grossi, BWV 1046–51 (1717–21)	Bach	Written for the Markgrave of Brandenburg.
'Bravo Mozart!'	Concerto for oboe, violin, horn, and orchestra (1969)	Argento	A work of the homage type.
Breuker	Concerto for clarinets, saxophones, and strings (1968)	du Bois	
'Butterfly's Wings'	Étude in G flat, Op 25/9 (1837)	Chopin	
'Byzantine'	Piano Concerto (1959)	Marić	
Caccia, La	Violin Concerto in B flat, Op 8/10 (*c* 1725)	Vivaldi	One of several Vivaldi concertos depicting a hunting scene.
'Cakewalk'	Symphony No 4 (1937)	McDonald	
Capricieuse	Symphony No 3 in D (1842)	Berwald	An imaginative but appropriate title.
'Cat's Fugue'	Sonata in G minor, L 499, Kk 30	Scarlatti, D	The theme is supposed to have been suggested by a cat walking along the keyboard of the composer's harpsichord.
'Cat Waltz'	Waltz in F, Op 34/3 (1838)	Chopin	The composer is supposed to have derived his inspiration in the same way as did Scarlatti (see above).
'Celestial Gate'	Symphony No 6, Op 173 (1959)	Hovhaness	
Cetra, La	Six Concerti for oboes, flutes, bassoon, and strings (1738)	Marcello, A	An imaginative title for a series of inventive concertos.
Cetra, La	Twelve Concerti for violin and strings, Op 9 (1728)	Vivaldi	
Champêtre	Concerto for harpsichord and orchestra (1929)	Poulenc	
Chasse, La—A frequently used title for a style of musical painting which was very popular during the 18th century and since (see also *Caccia*, above, and 'Hunt', below). This list is a selection only.	Sonata in D, Op 16(17) (*c* 1787)	Clementi	
	Trio in C, Op 22/3 (pub 1788)	Clementi	
	Sonata in B flat, for two oboi da caccia and bass	Fasch	
	Sonata No 12 for viola d'amor and guitar	Hrac(z)ek, A I	
	Symphony in G for four horns, shotgun, and strings, DTB 3:29	Mozart, L	
'Choral'	Symphony No 9 in D minor, Op 125	Beethoven	Continuations of a line begun in 1814 by Peter von Winter.

Name or subtitle	*Work*	*Composer*	*Remarks*
'Choral'	Symphony No 8 (1952)	Cowell	
'Choral'	Symphony No 8, Op 133 (1972)	Penberthy	
Cimento dell' Armonia e dell' Inventione	Twelve Concerti for violin and strings, Op 8 (*c* 1725)	Vivaldi	The title is an imaginative one which, translated, means 'The conflict between Harmony and Invention'.
Cinque Trombe	Concerto in D minor, for two violins, two oboes, two flutes, bassoon, and strings, RV 566	Vivaldi	A title given to several Vivaldi concertos (of which this is an example); it appears to mean merely that five blown instruments are included (two flutes, two oboes, and bassoon). No trumpets are involved.
'Classical'	Symphony No 1 in D, Op 25 (1917)	Prokofiev	Written 'in the style of' the classical composers.
Colloqui	String Quartet, Op 48 (1940)	Moeschinger	
'Colloredo'	Serenade in D, K 203 (1774)	Mozart	Used, but probably not written, for the name-day of Archbishop Colloredo.
'Concerto Royal'	Violin Concerto No 3 (1958)	Milhaud	
'Concord, Mass, 1840–60'	Piano Sonata No 2 with flute and viola (1909–15)	Ives	Honours personalities who were prominent in that town: Emerson, Hawthorne, the Alcotts, and Thoreau.
'Consecration of Sound'	Symphony No 4 in F, Op 86 (1832)	Spohr	
'Consolation'	Song Without Words in E, Op 30/3 (1834)	Mendelssohn	
Cornetto da Posta	Concerto in G for violin and strings, RV 327	Vivaldi	Doubtful authorship: attributed to G B Somis, in an alternative source.
	Concerto in B flat for violin and strings, RV 363	Vivaldi	
'Coronation'	Piano Concerto in D, K 537 (1788)	Mozart	Said to have been played during the festivities surrounding the coronation in Frankfurt of Leopold II.
Cortège	Sonata in E, L 23, Kk 380	Scarlatti, D	The music suggests a procession.
'Creation'	String Quartet No 2 (1962)	Ceremuga	
'Creation'	Symphony No 1 (1972)	Heiniö	
'Creation'	Symphony (1899)	Wallace	
'Czech Eroica'	Symphony in F, Op 47 (1945)	Vomáčka	
'Dalai Lama'	Cello Concerto (1966)	Marttinen	
'Dance'	Symphony (1929)	Copland	Adapted from the ballet *Grohg*.
'Death and the Maiden'	String Quartet in D minor, D 810 (1826)	Schubert	The second movement uses the theme of the song of that name, D 531.

Name or subtitle	*Work*	*Composer*	*Remarks*
Delle Macchine	Piano Concerto No 6 (1964)	Malipiero	
De Noël	String Quartet No 1 (1959)	Poniridy	
Didone Abbandonata	Piano Sonata in G minor, Op 50/3 (1821)	Clementi	
Didone Abbandonata	Violin Sonata in G minor, Op 6/10	Tartini	
'Dissonance'	String Quartet in C, K 465 (1785)	Mozart	Remarkable for the harsh dissonances in the first movement.
'The Distant Home'	Violin Sonata (1955)	Kučera	
Di Tre re	Symphony No 5 (1951)	Honegger	A soft D (re) on basses and timpani ends each of the three movements.
'Divine Poem'	Symphony No 3 in C, Op 43 (1903)	Scriabin	
'Dog Waltz'	Waltz in D flat, Op 64/1 (1847)	Chopin	In which a dog is depicted chasing its tail. The piece is also known as the 'Minute Waltz'.
Don Quichotte	Suite in G for strings (1761), Hoff G 10	Telemann	The work describes events in the story.
'Dramatic'	Symphony No 3 (1969)	Matej	
Dramatica	Symphony (1903)	Cassadó	
Dramatica	Symphony No 5 in B minor, Op 41, for soprano and orchestra (1960)	Kabeláč	
Drammatica	Symphony (1915)	Respighi	
'A Dream about the Violin'	Violin Sonata (1962)	Flosman	
Dumky	Piano Trio in E minor, Op 90 (1891)	Dvořák	Based on the Czech dance of that name.
'Easter'	Symphony No 4 in C minor (1905)	Foerster	The movement titles are I: 'The Road to Calvary'; II: 'A Child's Good Friday'; III: 'The Charm of Solitude'; IV: 'Holy Saturday Victorious'.
'Ebony'	Concerto for clarinet and orchestra (1945)	Stravinsky	Written for Woody Herman.
Eco in Lontano	Concerto in A for two violins and strings, RV 552 (1740)	Vivaldi	One of several 'Echo Concertos' by this composer.
'Edward'	Ballade in D minor, Op 10/1	Brahms	
Eine Kleine Nachtmusik	Serenade in G for strings, K 525 (1788)	Mozart	Mozart's own name for his most popular work.
Elegie	Song Without Words in D, Op 85/4 (1845)	Mendelssohn	
'Elegy'	Trio for flute, viola, and harp (1916)	Bax	
'Elegy'	Symphony No 1 (1965)	McCabe	
E Morta	String Quartet (1963)	Chlubna	

Name or subtitle	*Work*	*Composer*	*Remarks*
'Emperor'	Piano Concerto No 5 in E flat, Op 73 (1809)	Beethoven	A title used in English-speaking countries only. There is no authority for the name.
Eroica	Fifteen Variations and Fugue in E flat, Op 35 (1802)	Beethoven	The name was first attached to the symphony—'Written to the memory of a hero.' The contradanse theme in the finale was also used in the earlier Variations, leading to the name being inappropriately attached also to them.
Eroica	Symphony No 3 in E flat, Op 55 (1804)	Beethoven	
Espansiva	Symphony No 3 in F–A, Op 27 (1910–11)	Nielsen	Indicates the expansive mood of the work.
'Essay Sonatas and Sonatinas'	Six Sonatas (1753) and Six Sonatinas (1786) for keyboard instrument, W 63	Bach, C P E	Published as appendices to the composer's book *Essay on the True Art of Playing Keyboard Instruments*, which appeared in two editions, 1753; 1786.
'Estray, The'	Song Without Words in B minor, Op 30/4 (1834)	Mendelssohn	
Estro Armonico, L'	Twelve Concertos for string soloists and string orchestra, Op 3 (1712)	Vivaldi	The fanciful title means 'Harmonic Fantasy' or 'Whim'.
'Exile'	Symphony No 1, Op 17/2 (1936/70)	Hovhaness	
'Eyeglass'	Duo in E flat, for viola and cello	Beethoven	In full: 'with the obligato for two eyeglasses'. It was written for Nicolaus Zmeskall, cello, and Beethoven himself, both of whom wore eyeglasses.
'Fair is On!, The'	Symphony for Young People (1969)	Morrison	
'Faithful Shepherd, The'	Six Sonatas for musette, or viele, or flute, or oboe, or violin, with bass, Op 13 (*c* 1737)	Vivaldi	More usually known by the Italian original title: *Il Pastor Fido.* Musette and viele, and to a lesser extent the flute and oboe, were known as pastoral instruments in the 18th century.
'Fall of Warsaw'	Étude in C minor, Op 10/12 (1833)	Chopin	
Fantastique	Symphony, Op 14 (1830)	Berlioz	A descriptive and, in places, lurid, autobiographical fantasy.
Favorito, Il	Concerto in E minor for violin and strings, RV 277, Op 11/2 (*c* 1729–30)	Vivaldi	
'Feast of Saint Lawrence'	Concerto in C for two flutes, two oboes, two clarinets, bassoon, two violins, and strings, RV 556	Vivaldi	In full: *Per la solennità di S Lorenzo.*

Name or subtitle	*Work*	*Composer*	*Remarks*
	Concerto in F for violin and strings, RV 286	Vivaldi	
	Concerto in D, for violin, two oboes, two horns, timpani, and strings, RV 562	Vivaldi	RV 562 is the only known Vivaldi concerto in which timpani are required; the recent Ricordi publication, however, omits these instruments.
'Feast of the Assumption of the Virgin Mary'	See *Assunzione*, above		
'Festive'	Symphony in E (1854)	Smetana	Smetana's only symphony is also known as 'Triumphal Symphony'. The finale closes with an extended and grandiose presentation of Haydn's 'Emperor's Hymn'.
'Fiery Angel'	Symphony No 3 in C minor, Op 44 (1928)	Prokofiev	Based on material from the opera of that name.
Fileuse	See 'Spinning Song', below		
'Fleecy Cloud, The'	Song Without Words in E flat, Op 53/2 (1841)	Mendelssohn	
Fluido	Trio for clarinet, viola, and marimbaphone (1966)	Lachenmann	
'Folk Song'	Song Without Words in A minor, Op 53/5 (1841)	Mendelssohn	Also known as 'Song of Triumph'.
'Four Seasons, The'	See 'Seasons, The'		
'Four Temperaments'	Theme and Variations for piano and orchestra (1946)	Hindemith	Both take as their theme the medieval description of the humours or temperaments of man: 'Four Humours reign within our bodies wholly, And these compared to four elements, The Sanguine, Choler, Flegeme, and Melancholy.'
	Symphony No 2 in B minor–A, Op 16 (1902)	Nielsen	
Frei aber Einsam	Sonata for violin and piano (1855)	Brahms; Schumann; Dietrich	A 'joint' composition, each composer contributing one movement. The title translates as 'Free but lonely'.
'From my Life'	String Quartet No 1 in E minor (1876)	Smetana	An autobiographical work.
'From the New World'	Symphony No 9, in E minor, Op 95 (1893)	Dvořák	Written during the composer's visit to the American continent.
Funèbre	Symphony in F minor for strings (1725)	Locatelli	Written after the death of the composer's wife.
Funèbre	Concerto in B flat, for oboe, two salmoè, violin, two 'viole Inglese', and bass, RV 579	Vivaldi	No specific occasion has been recorded to account for the dark mood of this work.
Funèbre et Triomphale	Symphony, Op 15 (1840)	Berlioz	Commemorating the July Revolution of 1830.
Für Elise	Albumblatt in A minor (1810)	Beethoven	'Elise' has not been identified.

Name or subtitle	*Work*	*Composer*	*Remarks*
Für Kenner und Liebhaber	Sonatas, Rondos, and Fantasias for keyboard, W 55, 56, 57, 58, 59, and 61	Bach, C P E	'For Professionals and Amateurs', a group of eighteen Sonatas, thirteen Rondos, and six Fantasias which were meant to be relatively easy to play while at the same time appealing to the professional musician.
Galante	Cello Concerto (1949)	Rodrigo	
Gardellino	Concerto in D for flute, oboe, violin, bassoon, and bass, RV 90	Vivaldi	Features the then fashionable bird-song imitations. The work was later published (*c* 1729–30) for flute and strings as Op 10/3.
'Gastein'	Symphony (1824) (LOST?)	Schubert	A symphony was composed at Gastein but was lost; some musicians believe that the Grand Duo in C, D 812, for piano duet is a reduced version of the symphony; others, that the 'Great' Symphony in C, D 944, is the *Gastein* Symphony (see below).
Gesangszene	Violin Concerto No 8 in A minor, Op 47 (1816)	Spohr	In the style of a vocal scene.
'Ghost'	Piano Trio in D, Op 70/1 (1808)	Beethoven	From the eerie character of the second movement.
Giocosa	Piano Sonata No 2, Op 82 (1959)	Bartoš	
Giocosa	Sonata for clarinet and piano (1949)	Blažek	
Giocosa	Symphony (1951)	Mihalovici	
'Golden'	Sonata in G minor for violin and bass (No 9 of *Ten Sonatas*)	Purcell	
'Goldfinch'	See *Gardellino*		
'Gothic'	Symphony No 1 in D minor (1919–27)	Brian	The largest work ever written (see Section V).
Gothique	Symphony No 9 for organ solo, Op 70 (1935)	Widor	
Graziosa	Sonata for orchestra (1947)	Uhl	
'Great'	Symphony No 9 in C, D 944 (*c* 1825)	Schubert	So named, it seems, not for any intrinsic greatness, but merely to differentiate this work from the 'Little' (qv) Symphony in the same key. See also 'Heavenly Length'.
'Grief'	Étude in E major, Op 10/3 (1833)	Chopin	
'Gulliver, His Voyage to Lilliput'	Symphony No 2 (1914–35)	Kelley	

Name or subtitle	*Work*	*Composer*	*Remarks*
'Haffner'	Serenade in D, K 250 (1776)	Mozart	Both works written for the Salzburg Haffner family.
'Haffner'	Symphony No 35 in D, K 385 (1782)	Mozart	
Hainburger	String Quartet No 2 (1943)	Eckhardt-Gramatté	
'Hallelujah'	Concerto in B flat for organ and strings, Op 7/3 (pub 1760)	Handel	Incorporates a motif from the famous chorus in *Messiah.*
Hammerklavier	Piano Sonata in B flat, Op 106 (1818)	Beethoven	Written specifically to be played on the *Hammerklavier*, the forerunner of the modern piano. All of Beethoven's last sonatas were designed to be so played. Correctly, therefore, the title should be appended to them all. (A similar case occurs with Haydn's 'London' Symphony.)
'Harmonious Blacksmith'	Harpsichord Suite No 5 in E (Air and Variations)	Handel	The famous story surrounding the blacksmith at Stanmore who is supposed to have inspired Handel appears to have no foundation.
'Harold in Italy'	Symphony, Op 16 (1834)	Berlioz	Inspired by Byron's *Childe Harold.*
'Harp'	Étude in A flat, Op 25/1 (1837)	Chopin	
'Harp'	String Quartet in E flat, Op 74 (1809)	Beethoven	The pizzicato passages in the first movement have attracted this name.
'Hate and Love'	String Quartet, Op 11 (1937)	Holoubek	
'Heavenly Length'	Symphony No 9 in C, D 944 (1825?)	Schubert	Schumann's name for the work. See 'Great', above.
'Heaven-Tearing'	Symphony No 6 (1919)	Langgaard	
Heroico	Piano Concerto (1942)	Rodrigo	
'Highland Ballad'	Harp Concerto (1966)	Tomasini	
'Historical'	Symphony No 6 in G, Op 116 (1839)	Spohr	The history of orchestral writing is illustrated by the four movements: 1: 'Bach and Handel, *c* 1720'; 2: 'Haydn and Mozart, *c* 1780'; 3: 'Beethoven, *c* 1810'; 4: 'Today, *c* 1840'.
'Hoffmeister'	String Quartet in D, K 499 (1786)	Mozart	Published by the Viennese publisher Hoffmeister; therefore, a meaningless title.
'Homage to Haydn'	Soundpiece No 2 for string quartet or string orchestra (1936)	Becker	
'Homage to Mozart'	Symphony No 5 (1942)	Becker	
'Homage to Weill'	Concertino No 3 for chamber orchestra (1976)	Holloway	
Hommage à Falla	Symphony No 2 (1945)	Ardévol	
Hommage à Stravinsky	Chamber Concerto No 3 (1948)	Kalabis	

Name or subtitle	*Work*	*Composer*	*Remarks*
Hommaje a Pedrel	Symphony (1941)	Gerhard	
'Hornpipe'	Concerto Grosso in B minor, Op 6/12 (1739)	Handel	The finale has a dance-like rhythm.
'Hunt'	String Quartet in B flat, K 458 (1784)	Mozart	The finale suggests a hunting scene. See also *Chasse* and *Caccia*, above.
'Hunting Song'	Song Without Words in A, Op 19a/3 (1830)	Mendelssohn	
'Hymn of Praise'	Symphony No 2 in B flat, Op 52 (1840)	Mendelssohn	The choral finale is in the style of a hymn of praise. This is, incidentally, Mendelssohn's 14th known symphony.
'Hyperboles'	String Quartet No 4 (1960)	Pepin	
Hypochondriaca	Symphony in C, with trumpet solo (*c* 1780)	Schmidtbauer	Possibly adapted from music for a stage presentation.
Ilya Murometz	Symphony No 3, Op 42 (1911)	Glière	Ilya Murometz was a hero of Russian folk-legend.
'Incantation'	Piano Concerto No 4 (1956)	Martinů	
'Inextinguishable'	Symphony No 4, Op 29 (1916)	Nielsen	Written during the First World War, this work expresses the indomitability of the human spirit.
'In Memoriam Dylan Thomas'	Symphony No 4 (1954)	Jones, D	
'In Memory of Fauré'	String Quartet No 12 (1945)	Milhaud	Written to mark the Fauré centenary.
'In Praise of the Violin'	Violin Sonata in D, Op 19 (1928)	Vycpalek	
Inquietudine	Concerto in D for violin and strings, RV 234	Vivaldi	Possesses a restless mood.
'Intimate Pages'	String Quartet No 2 (1928)	Janáček	An autobiographical work dealing with the 74-year-old composer's feelings for a much younger woman, Kamila Stösslová.
Intimité L'	Étude, Op 10/3 (1833)	Chopin	
Irdisches und Göttliches in Menschenleben	Symphony No 7 in C for double orchestra, Op 121 (1841)	Spohr	'Mundane and Godly in the Lives of Men'. The work comprises a contest between childish innocence and worldly sophistication, the former overcoming the latter.
Irresolu, L'	Symphony in B flat, Post 11 (1780–90?)	Koželuh, L	
'Italian'	Concerto in F for harpsichord solo, BWV 971 (1735)	Bach	A rare example of a concerto without orchestra; *Italian* refers to the fact that the work is in the traditional three movements of Italian invention: fast–slow–fast.
'Italian'	Symphony No 4 (16) in A, Op 90 (1833)	Mendelssohn	A musical picture of the composer's impressions of Italy.

Name or subtitle	*Work*	*Composer*	*Remarks*
Jaune	Symphony for tape	Boisselet	Based on the past and future history of the Chinese people.
'Jena'	Symphony in C (*c* 1797)	Witt	Published in Jena, and long thought to be an early work of Beethoven.
'Jeremiah'	Symphony No 2 (1943)	Bernstein	
'Jeunehomme'	Piano Concerto in E flat, K 271 (1777)	Mozart	Perhaps written for Mlle Jeunehomme, who possibly visited Salzburg in 1776.
'Jocund Dance, The'	String Quartet No 10 (1920)	McEwen	
'Joyous Peasant'	Song Without Words in A, Op 102/5 (1845)	Mendelssohn	
'Jupiter'	Symphony No 41 in C, K 551 (1788)	Mozart	The earliest known use of the name was in 1819.
Kaddisch	Symphony No 3 (1963)	Bernstein	
'Kaleidoscope'	String Quartet No 1 (1930)	Janssen	
Kegelstadt	Trio in E flat for piano, clarinet, and viola, K 498 (1786)	Mozart	'Skittle-alley Trio', said to have been planned out in the composer's head during a game of skittles.
'Keltic'	Piano Sonata No 4 (1900)	MacDowell	
'Kreutzer'	Sonata in A for violin and piano, Op 47 (1803)	Beethoven	Dedicated to the French composer/violinist Rodolphe Kreutzer.
'Kreutzer Sonata'	String Quartet No 1 (1923)	Janáček	An example of art begetting art begetting art. Beethoven's 'Kreutzer Sonata' led to the writing of Tolstoy's book of the same name. Janáček wrote a piano trio on the subject in 1908, and much later dealt with it again in his first string quartet.
Kullervo	Symphony, Op 7 (1891–92)	Sibelius	Kullervo is a hero of Finnish legend.
Lamentatione d'Ariana	Concerto in E flat for violin and strings, Op 7/6 (1741)	Locatelli	
'Leningrad'	Symphony No 7 in C, Op 60 (1941)	Shostakovich	Composed during the Siege of Leningrad, while the composer was in the city.
Leonore	Symphony No 5 in E (1873)	Raff	Inspired by a ballad written by G A Bürger.
Levantino	Guitar Concerto (1948)	Palau	
'Linz'	Symphony No 36 in C, K 425 (1783)	Mozart	Composed in Linz.
'Little'	Symphony No 6 in C, D 589 (1818)	Schubert	So called simply to distinguish the work from the 'Great' Symphony, No 9, in the same key.

Name or subtitle	*Work*	*Composer*	*Remarks*
'Little Russian'	Symphony No 2 in C minor, Op 17 (1872)	Tchaikovsky	The finale uses a folk-song, 'The Crane', from Little Russia (ie the Ukraine).
Liturgique	Symphony No 3 (1945–46)	Honegger	A work of religious character. The movement titles are: I: *Dies irae*; II: *De profundis clamavi*; III: *Dona nobis pacem*.
'Lost Happiness'	Song Without Words in C minor, Op 38/2 (1838)	Mendelssohn	
'Lost Illusions'	Song Without Words in F sharp minor, Op 67/2 (1845)	Mendelssohn	
Madrigalesco	Concerto in D minor for strings, RV 129	Vivaldi	
'Maggot, A'	Organ Concerto No 3: second movement	Arne	A 'Maggot' is an old English dance.
Magueyes	String Quartet No 2 (1931)	Revueltas	
'Malak Requiem'	String Quartet No 2 (1970)	Nikolov	
Maniatico, Il	Symphony No 33 in C minor (1786)	Brunetti	There is a prominent solo cello part which runs wild and has to be calmed by the orchestra. One of Brunetti's great rivals in Madrid was Boccherini, who was famous as a cello-player.
'Maria Antonia'	Concerto in G minor for harpsichord and strings, Denn 7 (1777)	Reichardt	Dedicated to Maria Antonia.
'Martin Pescatore'	Concerto for strings (1971)	Dalby	
Mattinata	Quintet for marimba, three flutes, and double bass (1968)	Noda	
'May Breezes'	Song Without Words in G, Op 62/1 (1844)	Mendelssohn	
'May Day'	Symphony No 3 in E flat, Op 20 (1930)	Shostakovich	Written to commemorate the national holiday of the working classes.
'MCMLVI' (1956)	Viola Concerto (1963)	Sifona	
'Metamorphoses'	Symphony No 4, Op 55 (1949)	Bentzon	
Metamorfosi Sinfoniche	Symphony No 4 (1960)	Hallnäs	
'Minute Waltz'	Waltz in D flat, Op 64/1 (1847)	Chopin	Supposed to take only one minute to perform. Also called 'Dog Waltz'.
Mondo al rovescio, Il	See *Proteo*		
'Montevideo'	Symphony No 2	Gottschalk	
'Moonlight'	Sonata in C sharp minor, Op 27/2 (1801)	Beethoven	Imaginative title without authority.
'Morning Song'	Song Without Words in G, Op 62/4 (1844)	Mendelssohn	

Name or subtitle	*Work*	*Composer*	*Remarks*
Musica Notturna delle strade di Madrid, La	String Quartet in C, Gér 324 (1780)	Boccherini	'Night music in the streets of Madrid.' This wildly descriptive piece of merriment includes impressions of a little prayer bell, street singers, blind beggars, and a military retreat.
Musikalischer Spass	Serenade in F, K 522 (1787)	Mozart	This musical joke is on everyone from Mozart's contemporaries to the modern listener.
Musique pour célébrer des grandes hommes ...	Symphony in D	Reicha, A	See p 93 for details and full title.
Mutabile	Concerto for piano and chamber orchestra (1962)	Kohn	
'Mysterious Mountain'	Symphony No 2, Op 132 (1955)	Hovhaness	
Nanga Parvat	Symphony No 7, Op 178 (1959)	Hovhaness	
'Napoléon'	Sonata No 1 on the G string, Op 31 (1805)	Paganini	
'New World'	See 'From the New World'		
'Nightwatchman'	Serenade in C for bass singer and strings	Biber	Also known as *Ronde de Nuit, La.*
'Nobody Knows de Trouble I See'	Trumpet Concerto (1954)	Zimmermann	
Noire	Symphony	Boisselet	A musico-political work discussing the future of the Blacks.
'Norse'	Piano Sonata No 3 (1902)	MacDowell	
Notte, La	Bassoon Concerto in B flat, RV 501	Vivaldi	Descriptive works. RV 439 was later published as Op 10/2 for flute and strings (*c* 1729–30).
Notte, La	Concerto in G minor for flute, bassoon and strings, RV 439	Vivaldi	
Nugae	String Quartet No 5 (1912)	McEwen	
Nullte	Symphony in D minor (1864, revised 1869)	Bruckner	Symphony No '0', an unnumbered early work.
'Ocean'	Symphony No 2 in C, Op 42 (1854)	Rubinstein	
'October'	Symphony No 2 in C, Op 14 (1927)	Shostakovich	Commemorates the October Revolution. See also *1917*.
Olimpica	Symphony No 2 (1948)	Turski	First prize winner of the International Competition held to mark the first post-war Olympic Games (London, 1948).
'Organ Symphony'	Symphony No 3 in C minor, Op 78 (1886)	Saint-Saëns	An organ is prominent in the scoring.
'Origins'	Symphony for percussion (1952)	Brant	

Name or subtitle	*Work*	*Composer*	*Remarks*
'Overture in the Italian Style'	Symphony No 32 in G, K 318 (1779)	Mozart	A one-movement work with a slow section in central position. (See *Italian*, above.)
'Overtures in the Italian Style'	Overture in C, D 591 (1817) Overture in D, D 590 (1817)	Schubert	Both works imitate the features of the typical Rossini overture popular at that time.
Padovana, La	Canzona à eight for two instrumental choirs	Viadana	
'Paris'	Overture in B flat, K 311A (1778?)	Mozart	Doubtful. Supposed to have been written as a second 'Paris' Symphony during Mozart's visit there in 1778.
'Paris'	Symphony No 31 in D, K 297 (1778)	Mozart	This is the symphony Mozart is known to have written for Paris (see above).
'Passages'	Piano Sonata No 4 (1962)	Dahl	
'Pastoral' or *Pastorale*			For the 150 years from 1700 fashion demanded that every composer should produce at least one instrumental pastorale. During the first half of this period the pastorale had religious connotations, it being used as background music, so to speak, to Nativity scenes. Later, however (and earlier in the case of Vivaldi), the shepherds and shepherdesses were felt to have their own intrinsic musical value, so that a connection with events at Bethlehem became rare. In addition to the list below, there are well-known movements by Corelli, Torelli, Pez, and Locatelli, etc, usually in so-called 'Christmas' concertos. More recent *Pastorale* works invariably reflect country moods and events.
	Symphony (1952)	Ahnell	
	Symphony in D (1787)	Beecke	
	Symphony No 6 in F, Op 68 (1806)	Beethoven	
	Piano Sonata in D, Op 28 (1801)	Beethoven	
	Symphony in F (*c* 1780)	Cannabich	
	Piano Sonata No 2 (1959)	Dahl	
	Pastoral Symphony (1742)	Handel	'Symphony' used here in the sense of 'Interlude for instruments'; this is No 13 in *Messiah*.
	Symphony No 2, Op 22 (1954)	Johnsen	
	Symphony No 4 (1965)	Jones, C W	

Name or subtitle	*Work*	*Composer*	*Remarks*
	Symphony No 5 (1969)	Josephs	
	Symphony No 2	McPhee	
	Symphony No 2 (1918)	Milhaud	
	Woodwind Quintet (1943)	Persichetti	
	Flute Concerto (1978)	Rodrigo	Written for James Galway.
	Sonatas for harpsichord in D minor, L 413, Kk 9 in F, L 433, Kk 446 in C, L Supp 3, Kk 513	Scarlatti, D	Of the named sonatas which are, or could be, so called, we have chosen three of the best known.
	Symphony in D, DTB III i: D4	Stamic, J	
	Symphony in D minor	Tartini	
	Symphony No 3 (1922)	Vaughan Williams	
	Symphony in D (*c* 1750)	Werner	
Pastorella	Symphony in D, Op 5/3, BSB 27 (1761/62)	Gossec	
	Concerto in D for flute, oboe, violin, bassoon, and bass (or for two violins, bassoon, and bass), RV 95	Vivaldi	
Pastor Fido, Il	See 'Faithful Shepherd', above		
Pathétique	Piano Sonata in C minor, Op 13 (1798)	Beethoven	
	Symphony No 6 in B minor, Op 74 (1893)	Tchaikovsky	
Pauern Kirchfahrt genandt	Sonata in B flat for two violins, two violas, violone, and bass (late 17th century)	Biber	A country church-going, with imitations of the sounds of the Sabbath, ending up in the local tavern.
'Pedantic'	String Quartet No 1 (1916)	Cowell	
Piacere	Concerto in C for violin and strings, RV 180, Op 8/6 (*c*1725)	Vivaldi	
Piacevolezza	String Quartet No 4 in F, Op 44 (originally Op 19) (1906)	Nielsen	Title discarded by the composer when the work was published.
Podla Odkazu Drahého Otca	Symphony No 5 in F, Op 39 (1948)	Moyzes	The title means 'After the heritage of my dear father'. The work includes his father's sketches.
Poème	Piano Concerto (1939)	Landowski	
Poème Mystique	Violin Sonata No 2 (1924)	Bloch	
Poème Secret, Le	Piano Trio No 2 (1948)	Fumet	
'Polish'	Symphony No 3 in D, Op 29 (1875)	Tchaikovsky	The main theme of the finale is in the rhythm of a polacca.
'Post-horn'	Serenade in D, K 320 (1778)	Mozart	A solo post-horn figures in the second trio of the sixth movement.
'Prague'	Symphony No 38 in D, K 504 (1786)	Mozart	Written for performance in that city.
Preghiera	Violin Sonata, Op 24 (1828)	Paganini	
'Prodigal Son, The'	Symphony No 4 in C, Op 47 (1930, revised 1947: Op 112)	Prokofiev	Based partly on music used in the ballet of that name.

Name or subtitle	*Work*	*Composer*	*Remarks*
Proteo, Il	Concerto in F for violin, cello, and strings, RV 544	Vivaldi	In full: 'Proteus, or the World Turned upside-down'. An 'Echo' concerto in which the composer indulges in fantasies suggested by the title.
'Prussian'	String Quartets, K 575, 589, 590	Mozart	
'Prussian Sonatas'	Six keyboard Sonatas, W 48 (pub 1742)	Bach, C P E	The first works produced under the patronage of Frederick the Great, King of Prussia.
'Prussian Sonatas'	Six Sonatas for harpsichord, Denn 35 (pub 1775)	Reichardt	Dedicated to Frederike Luise von Pruessen.
Putain, La	Suite in G, Hoff Anhang G1	Telemann(?)	*The Prostitute.* This introduces themes and ideas drawn from 'low life' in Hamburg. Movement titles include: *Die Schneckenpost* (Tavern song); *Die Bauren Kirchweyh* (The Peasants' Church Dance)—compare *Pauern Kirchfahrt*, above—*Der Hexen-Tantz* (Seductress's Dance); *Die Baas Lisabeth* ('Cousin' Lizzie): and *Der Vetter Michel Ziehbart* (Playboy cousin Goatbeard).
'Rage over a Lost Penny'	Rondo a Capriccio in G for piano, Op 129 (1803)	Beethoven	An early 19th-century nickname perhaps indicating that the work seemed to be a storm in a teacup.
'Rain'	Violin Sonata No 1 in G, Op 78 (1879)	Brahms	
'Raindrop'	Prelude in D flat, Op 28/15 (1839)	Chopin	The insistent patter of rain outside his study window is supposed to have given Chopin the idea for the repeated notes to be heard in this Prelude.
'Razumovsky'	Three String Quartets, Op 59 (1806)	Beethoven	Dedicated to Count Razumovsky.
'Reformation'	Symphony No 5 (17) in D minor, Op 107 (1830)	Mendelssohn	Written to commemorate the 300th Anniversary of the Augsburg Confession.
'Regrets'	Song Without Words, Op 19b/2 in A minor (1830)	Mendelssohn	
Reliquie	Sonata in C, D 840 (1825)	Schubert	Refers to the fact that only the first two movements of this Sonata were completed. They were published in 1861 as *Last* [sic] *Sonata—Unfinished.*
Representatio Avium	Sonata in A for violin and bass	Biber	The 'birds' of the title include: bat, cuckoo, frog, hen, cock, quail, cat, and a 'March of the Gnats'.

Name or subtitle	*Work*	*Composer*	*Remarks*
'Restlessness'	Song Without Words in F sharp minor, Op 19b/5 (1830)	Mendelssohn	
'Resurrection'	Symphony No 3, Op 27 (1927)	Karel	
Résurrection, La	Symphony (1876)	Salvayre	Earlier called *Le Jugement dernier* and later *La Vallée de Josephat.*
'Revolutionary'	Étude in C minor, Op 10/12 (1833)	Chopin	
Rhenish	Symphony No 3 in E flat, Op 97	Schumann	Evokes the composer's feelings of life in the Rheinland.
Riposo, Il	Concerto in E for violin and strings, RV 234	Vivaldi	A relaxed and reposeful work.
Ritiro, Il	Concerto in E flat for violin and strings, RV 256	Vivaldi	
	Concerto in F for violin and strings, RV 294	Vivaldi	
'Romantic'	Symphony No 4 in E flat (1874, revised 1878 and 1880)	Bruckner	This work originally possessed a 'programme' in the Romantic manner which was later suppressed by the composer.
'Romantic Elegy'	Piano Trio No 2 (1926?)	Molnár	
'Romeo and Juliet'	Symphony, Op 17 (1839)	Berlioz	A programmatic 'Dramatic' symphony based on Shakespeare's play.
'Rosary Sonatas'	Sixteen Sonatas for violin and bass	Biber	Based on the 'Mysteries of Joy' (Nos 1–5), 'of Sorrow' (6–10), and 'of Glory' (11–16).
Rouge	Symphony	Boisselet	A politico-musical composition.
Ruck-Ruck	Clarinet Sonata (1947)	Eckhardt-Gramatté	
'Rumba'	Symphony No 2 (1935)	McDonald	Uses rumba rhythms in the third movement.
Rustica	Symphony No 1 (1949)	Panufnik	
'Rustic Wedding'	Symphony, Op 26 (1876)	Goldmark	(originally 'Ländliche Hochzeit').
Sacra	Symphony No 3 (1963)	Panufnik	
'Sadness of Soul'	Song Without Words in F, Op 53/4 (1841)	Mendelssohn	Also known as 'Berceuse'.
'Saga of a Prairie School'	Symphony No 7	Gillis	Programmatic work.
'Saint Anne's Fugue'	Fugue in E flat for organ, BWV 552	Bach	The theme is similar to the first line of the hymn 'Saint Anne' by Croft.
'Saint Vartan'	Symphony No 9, Op 180 (1950)	Hovhaness	Written to commemorate the 1500th anniversary of the death of Saint Vartan Marmikonian, the Armenian warrior, in 451.
Santa Lingua di Sant'Antonio	Concerto in D for violin, two oboes, and strings, RV 212	Vivaldi	An occasional work.
Santo Sepolcro, Al	Sonata in E flat for strings, RV 130	Vivaldi	Written for religious occasions.

Name or subtitle	*Work*	*Composer*	*Remarks*
	Symphony in B minor for strings, RV 169	Vivaldi	
S.A.R. di Sassonia	Concerto in G minor for three oboes, three violins, two flutes, two bassoons, two harpsichords, violas, and bass, RV 576	Vivaldi	Written for the Elector of Saxony in Dresden: 'Per la Sua Altezza Reale di Sassonia'.
'Scottish'	Symphony No 3 (15) in A minor, Op 56 (1829–42)	Mendelssohn	Like the 'Fingal's Cave' Overture, this work reflects the impressions the composer gained during his visit to Scotland.
'Seasons, The'	Symphony No 9 in B flat, Op 143 (1849)	Spohr	A descriptive work which treats the seasons. Like Glazunov's ballet, the cycle starts with 'Winter'.
'Seasons, The'	Four Violin Concertos, Op 8/1–4 (*c* 1725)	Vivaldi	
'Sea'	Symphony No 1 in C for soprano, baritone, chorus, and orchestra (1912)	Vaughan Williams	Based on Walt Whitman's poems. The movement titles are: I: 'A Song for All Seas, All Ships'; II: 'On the Beach at Night, Alone'; III: 'The Waves'; IV: 'The Explorers'.
Semplice	Symphony No 6 (1924–26)	Nielsen	
Semplice	Symphony No 6 (1951)	Rosenberg	
Senza Cantin	Concerto in D minor for violin and strings, RV 243	Vivaldi	The E string ('Cantin') is to be removed from the solo violin, thus rendering the concerto extremely difficult to play.
'Serenade'	Song Without Words in E, Op 67/6 (1845)	Mendelssohn	
Sérieuse	Symphony No 2 in G minor (1842)	Berwald	
'Shakespearian'	Symphony No 4 (1952)	Nystroem	
'Shepherd Boy'	Étude in A flat, Op 25/1 (1837)	Chopin	
'Shepherd's Complaint'	Song Without Words in B minor, Op 67/5 (1845)	Mendelssohn	Also known as 'Song of the Heather'.
Siegeslied	Symphony No 4 (1932–33) for soprano, chorus, and orchestra	Brian	'The Psalm of Victory', based on Luther's German text for Psalm 68.
'Silly'	Symphony, Op 2 (1949)	Moortel	
'Silly'	Symphony in E flat (1946)	Moross	
'Silver Pilgrimage'	Symphony No 15, Op 199 (1962)	Hovhaness	
'Simple'	Symphony, Op 4 (1934)	Britten	Written for the young. The movement titles are: I: 'Boisterous Bourée'; II: 'Playful pizzicato'; III: 'Sentimental Sarabande'; IV: 'Frolicsome Finale'.

Name or subtitle	*Work*	*Composer*	*Remarks*
Sinfonia da Requiem	Symphony, Op 20 (1940)	Britten	Written to the memory of the composer's parents.
Singulière	Symphony No 4 in C (1845)	Berwald	
Solennità di S. Lorenzo	See 'Feast of Saint Lawrence'		
'Song of the Heather'	Song Without Words in B minor, Op 67/5 (1845)	Mendelssohn	Also known as 'Shepherd's Complaint'.
'Song of the Night'	Symphony No 3	Szymanowsky	
'Song of Triumph'	Song Without Words in A minor, Op 53/5 (1841)	Mendelssohn	Also known as 'Folk Song'.
Sordino, Con	Concerto in F for flute, muted strings, and muted harpsichord, RV 434, Op 10/5 (*c* 1729–30)	Vivaldi	
Sospetto, Il	Concerto in C minor for violin and strings, RV 199	Vivaldi	
'Sound of Heaven, The'	Piano Sonata No 2, Op 38 (1941)	Valén	
'Spinning Song'	Song Without Words in C, Op 67/4 (1845)	Mendelssohn	Also known as 'Bee's Wedding.
SS Assunzione di Maria Vergine	See 'Assunzione', above		
'Storm at Sea'	Concerto in E flat for violin and strings, RV 253, Op 8/5 (*c* 1725)	Vivaldi	Both of Vivaldi's works depict the chaotic drama of a sea storm in their first movements; that of Zavateri does so in its last. However, it should be stated that such chaos, as depicted in the musical language of the early 18th century, is very mild indeed.
	Concerto in F for flute, oboe, violin, bassoon, and strings, RV 433 (Op 10/1 for flute and strings, *c* 1729–30)	Vivaldi	
	Concerto for violin and strings, Op 1/12 (1735)	Zavateri	
Stravaganza, La	Twelve Concertos for violin and strings, Op 4 (*c* 1712/13)	Vivaldi	
'Study'	Symphony in F minor (1863)	Bruckner	Originally meant by the composer to be an exercise in orchestration and composition, this work has established itself recently as a work in its own right.
'Sweet Remembrances'	Song Without Words in E, Op 19b/1 (1830)	Mendelssohn	
Symphonie Fantastique	See *Fantastique*, above		
'Symphony for Fun'	Symphony No $5\frac{1}{2}$	Gillis	The movement titles are: I: 'Perpetual Emotion'; II: 'Spiritual?'; III: 'Scherzofrenia'; IV: 'Conclusion!'.
'Symphony of a Thousand'	Symphony No 8 in E flat (1907)	Mahler	See Section V.
Szenen	Piano Sonata No 2 (1960)	Dahl	
Tarantella	Song Without Words in C, Op 102/3 (1845)	Mendelssohn	

Name or subtitle	*Work*	*Composer*	*Remarks*
'Tempest'	Sonata in D Minor, Op 31/2 (1802)	Beethoven	
Tempesta di Mare	See 'Storm at sea'		
Ten Days That Shook The World	Symphony No 1	Korchmarev	A vocal symphony based on the composer's opera of the same title (*c* 1925).
'Threnody'	String Quartet No 7 in E flat (1916)	McEwen	
'Titan, The'	Symphony No 1 in D (1888)	Mahler	Thus named by the composer, after the novel by Jean Paul.
'Torrent, The'	Étude in C sharp minor, Op 10/4 (1833)	Chopin	
'To the Memory of an Angel'	Violin Concerto (1935)	Berg	The 'Angel' was Manon Gropius, the daughter of Mahler's widow.
'To the Memory of My Mother'	String Quintet in B flat, Op 15 (1926)	Krejči	
'To the New-Born and Rediscovered Native Country'	Symphony No 4, Op 21 (1924)	Maliszewski	
'Tragic'	Symphony No 4 in C minor, D 417 (1816)	Schubert	Title added later by Schubert himself.
Tragica	Symphony No 6 in D minor (1948)	Brian	Originally written as the Overture (or Prelude) to a projected opera based on Synge's tragedy *Deirdre of the Sorrows*.
Tristesse	Étude in E, Op 10/3 (1833)	Chopin	
'Trout, The'	Quintet in A for piano and strings, D 667 (1819)	Schubert	The fourth movement is a set of theme and variations on the composer's song 'Die Forelle' ('The Trout'), D 550.
'Under Northern Skies'	Quintet for flute, oboe, clarinet, bassoon, and horn (1939)	McEwen	
'Unfinished'	Symphony No 8 in B minor, D 759 (1822)	Schubert	Long thought to consist of only two movements, attempts have been made recently to complete the work from the remaining sketches and from some of the *Rosamunde* music.
'Universe'	Symphony	Ives	A planned but only partially sketched work first considered in 1915, but not complete at the composer's death in 1951. (See Section V: Biggest?)
'Venetian Gondola Song'	Songs Without Words: in G minor, Op 19b/6 (1830); in F sharp minor, Op 30/6 (1834); in A minor, Op 62/5 (1844)	Mendelssohn	

Name or subtitle	*Work*	*Composer*	*Remarks*
Villanelle	Étude in G flat, Op 25/9 (1837)	Chopin	
Virtuosi Irgi	String Quartet No 1 (1965)	Nikolov	
Visions Choréographiques	Piano Concerto, Op 71 (1968)	Schibler	
Voces Intimae	String Quartet in D minor, Op 56 (1909)	Sibelius	An authentic title, suggested by the character of the slow (third) movement.
'Wagner'	Symphony No 3 in D minor (1873, revised 1878, 1889, and 1890)	Bruckner	Dedicated to that composer.
Wahrheit der Natur	Symphony in F, Perger 46 (1769?)	Haydn, J M	Taken from the music to a 'mythological operetta' of this title. The full title is: *Die Wahrheit der Natur in den drey irdischen Grazien, nämlich in der Dichtkunst, Musik, und Malerey.* ('The Truth of Nature, in the Three Earthly Graces, namely, Poetry, Music, and Painting'.)
Waldmaedchen	Partita in C for wind instruments (1800)	Beecke	
'Waldstein'	Piano Sonata in C, Op 53 (1803–4)	Beethoven	Dedicated to Count Waldstein.
Wanderer, Der	Fantasia in C for piano, D 760 (1822)	Schubert	The second movement is based on the song of this name, D 493.
'Wedge'	Fugue in E minor, BWV 548	Bach, J S	So called from the ever-widening intervals of the theme.
'Wellington's Victory'	See 'Battle of Vittoria', above		
'White Mass'	Sonata No 7 in F, Op 64 (1911)	Scriabin	
'William Tell'	Symphony No 1, Op 63 (1882)	Huber	
'Wine of Summer, The'	Symphony No 5 (1937)	Brian	Based on the poem by Lord Alfred Douglas.
'Winter'	Concerto in F minor for violin and strings, RV 297, Op 8/4 (*c* 1725)	Vivaldi	No 4 of four concertos descriptive of the four seasons.
'Winter Daydreams'	Symphony No 1 in G minor, Op 13 (1866)	Tchaikovsky	Taken from the title of the first movement: 'Daydreams on a Wintry Road'.
'Winter Wind'	Étude in A minor, Op 25/11 (1837)	Chopin	
'Within the Mirror of Time'	Piano Concerto (1974)	Suderburg	
'Württemburg'	Six Sonatas for keyboard, W 49 (pub 1744)	Bach, C P E	
Zartik Parkim	Concerto for piano and chamber orchestra, Op 77 (1948)	Hovhaness	

Name or subtitle	*Work*	*Composer*	*Remarks*
'1905'	Symphony No 11 in G minor, Op 103 (1957)	Shostakovich	Written to commemorate the abortive revolution of that year.
'1917'	Symphony No 12 in D minor, Op 112 (1961)	Shostakovich	Celebrates the successful Bolshevik Revolution of 1917. See also 'October'.

The composer of the most works to which nicknames have been appended is Franz Joseph Haydn. As the author of many hundreds of works, he was not averse to the occasional nickname to assist his audiences' memories, but most of the titles which have become attached to his compositions are not authentic, often stemming from publishers' sales efforts after the composer's death. The names in the following list, therefore, may be regarded as unauthentic unless otherwise stated.

It is believed that pp 130–134 of the first edition of this book was the first publication of a complete list of Haydn's musical nicknames together with explanations of their origins and meanings. For this second edition the explanations have been omitted: interested readers are requested to refer to the earlier edition.

NICKNAMES AND SUBTITLES OF WORKS BY HAYDN

Work and Title	*Date*
Symphonies	
No 1 in D, 'Lukaveč'	1759?
No 6 in D, *Le Matin*	1761
No 7 in C, *Le Midi*	1761
No 8 in G, *Le Soir*	1761
No 13 in D, '*Jupiter*'	1763
No 22 in E flat, 'The Philosopher'	1764
No 26 in D minor 'Lamentatione'	*c* 1768
No 27 in G, 'Brukenthal' or 'Hermannstädter'	*c* 1760
No 30 in C, *Alleluja*	1765
No 31 in D, 'Hornsignal'; also 'Auf dem Anstand'	1765
No 38 in C, 'Echo'	*c* 1766/68
No 39 in G minor, 'The Fist'	*c* 1768
No 43 in E flat, 'Mercury'	*c* 1771
No 44 in E minor, *Trauer*	*c* 1771
No 45 in F sharp minor, 'Farewell'	1772
No 48 in C, 'Maria Theresia'; also 'Sancta Theresia'	1769?
No 49 in F minor, *La Passione*	1768
No 53 in D, 'Imperial'	*c* 1777
No 55 in E flat, 'Schoolmaster'	1774
No 59 in A, 'Fire'	*c* 1766/68
No 60 in C, *Il Distratto*	1774
No 63 in C, *La Roxelane*	1777?
No 64 in A, *Tempora mutantur*	*c* 1775
No 69 in C, *Laudon*	*c* 1778
No 73 in D, *La Chasse*	1781
No 82 in C, 'The Bear'	1786
No 83 in G minor, 'The Hen'	1785
No 85 in B flat, *La Reine de France*	1785/86
No 88 in G, 'Letter V'	*c* 1787
No 92 in G, 'Oxford'	1789
No 94 in G, 'Surprise'	1791
No 96 in D, 'Miracle'	1791
No 100 in G, 'Military'	1794
No 101 in D, 'Clock'	1794
No 102 in B flat, 'Miracle'	1794/95
No 103 in E flat, 'Drum Roll'	1795
No 104 in D, 'London'	1795
Toy Symphony in C (Attrib.)	*c* 1788?
String Quartets	
Op 1, No 1 in B flat, *La Chasse*	1755–60?
Op 3, No 5 in F, 'Serenade' (Attrib.)	*c* 1760
Op 17, No 5 in G, 'Recitative'	1771
Op 20, Nos 1–6, 'Sun Quartets' also 'Great Quartets'	1772
Op 33, Nos 1–6, 'Russian Quartets', also *Gli Scherzi*	1781
Op 33, No 2 in E flat, 'Joke'	
Op 33, No 3 in C, 'Bird'	
Op 33, No 5 in G, 'How do you do?'	
Op 50, No 5 in F, 'Dream'	1787
Op 50, No 6 in D, 'Frog'	1787
Op 55, No 2 in F minor, 'Razor'	1788
Op 64, No 5 in D, 'Lark'; also 'Hornpipe'	1790

Work and Title	*Date*
Op 74, No 3 in G minor, 'Rider' or 'Horseman'	1793
Op 76, No 2 in D minor, 'Fifths'	1799
Op 76, No 3 in C, 'Emperor'	1799
Op 76, No 4 in B flat, 'Sunrise'	1799
Op 76, No 6 in E flat, 'Fantasia'	1799
Masses	
No 2 in E flat, 'Great Organ Mass'	*c* 1766
No 4 in G, 'Six-four-time Mass'	1772
No 5 in B flat, 'Little Organ Mass'	*c* 1775
No 6 in C, *Mariazellermesse*	1782
No 7 in C, 'Drum Mass', also 'Mass in Time of War'	1796
No 8 in B flat, *Heiligmesse*	1796
No 9 in D minor, 'Nelson Mass'	1798
No 10 in B flat, 'Theresia Mass'	1799
No 11 in B flat, 'Creation Mass'	1801
No 12 in B flat, 'Harmonie Mass'	1802
Other works with nicknames	
Divertimento in C, Hob II:11, 'Man and Wife', also 'The Birthday'	*c* 1761
Divertimento in E flat, Hob II:39, 'Echo'	*c* 1761
Divertimento in B flat, Hob II:46. 'St Anthony' (Attrib.)	pub 1780
Marches in E flat and C, Hob VIII: 1: 'Two Derbyshire Marches'	1795
March 'For the Prince of Wales', in E flat, Hob VIII:3; also 'For the Royal Society of Musicians'	1792
March in E flat, Hob VIII:4 Hungarian National March	1802
'Ox Minuet' in C, Hob IX:27 (Attrib.)	
Capriccio in G, Hob XVII:1 *Acht Sauschneider müssen seyn*	1765
Sonata in F, Hob XVII:F3: (Attrib.) *La Bataille de Rossbach*	
Divertimento in F, Hob XVIIa:1 *Il Maestro e lo Scolare*	*c* 1765?
Pieces for flute-clock, Hob XIX:	
No 4 in C, *Der Dudelsack*	1772
No 6 in F, *Kaffeeklatsch*	1772
No 8 in C, *Wachtelschlag*	1772

The work with the longest title is arguably a symphony in C by Pavel Vraničky, a Czech composer who wrote a number of works in Hungary. In the original Hungarian the title is:

A' Magyar Nemzet Örōme Midőn annak Tōrvényei, s' Sdabadságai II. Jósef Tsászár és Király alatt, kis Karátson havának (Januárius) 28dik napján 1790-ik Esztendőben, vissza állittattak vala. Egy Nagy Szimfónia Három darabból álland. I. A' Nemzet' első vigassága, s' ennek el terjesztése. II. A' Rendek' kellemetes érzékenysége, és azok közt vissza tértt Egyvesség. III. A' Koszég Orōme a' Szent Korona' vissza érkezése alkalmatosságával. Op 2.

An English translation of this name may be said to run: 'Joy of the Hungarian nation when her laws and freedoms were restored under Emperor and King Joseph II on the 28th day of the month of Circumcision (January) of the year 1790. A great symphony consisting of three pieces. I. The nation's first jollifications and its dissemination. II. The pleasant sensibilities of the states of the realm and the unity restored among them. III. The joy of the community on the occasion of the holy crown.' Op 2.

The symphony is scored for two flutes, two oboes, two bassoons, two horns, two clarini (trumpets), timpani, and strings, and was published by the firm of Imbault in Paris in 1791.

The most frequently used titles or nicknames are those which indicate that the works bearing them are 'short' or 'little'. It is not necessary to burden the reader with a detailed list, but during research a staggering 183 such works have emerged, disposed as follows:

Bref (1); *Brève* (41); *Brevis* (27); *Brevissima* (2, including a symphony of a duration of four minutes); 'Concise' (1); *De Poche* (1); *Di Miniatura* (1); *En Miniature* (1); 'In Miniature' (1); *Kleine* (8); 'Little' (29); 'A Little Symphony for the New Year'; a *Microsonata*; a *Microsinfonie*; 'Miniature' (11); a *Mini-Symphony*; *Petite* (4); a *Petite Sinfonie Concertante*; a *Petite Sinfonie Joyeuse*; *Piccola* (14); *Piccola Musica Concertata* (1); a *Piccola Sinfonia Giocosa*; *Piccolo* (6); 'A Quite Small Symphony'; 'Short' (23); 'A Short Concert'; 'Small' (2).

Familiar titles to unfamiliar music

Certain titles are inseparably associated with certain composers. 'New World', for instance, always brings to mind Dvořák, *La Traviata* suggests Verdi, and *Elijah* Mendelssohn. It is only slightly disconcerting to find the uniqueness of title of Vaughan Williams's *A Sea Symphony* threatened by the *Ocean Symphony* of Anton Rubinstein, Beethoven's Ninth Symphony having to share its name with a work by Holst, and 'Emperor' identifying a string quartet by Haydn, a piano concerto by Beethoven, and a waltz by Strauss. Other connections will doubtless spring from a study of the lists in this section.

A dig in the basement of the musical archives produces a handful of forgotten works the titles of which are extremely well known.

Barber of Seville, The: opera by Rossini (1816); also an opera by Paisiello (1782).

Belshazzar's Feast: oratorio by Walton (1931); also incidental music by Sibelius (1906).

Bohème, La: opera by Puccini (1896); also an opera by Leoncavallo (1897).

Christmas Oratorio, The: by Bach (1734); and also one by Johann Schelle (1648–1710), who composed at St Thomas's School, Leipzig, and whose oratorio was probably familiar to Bach.

Clemenza di Tito, La: opera by Mozart (1791); also a balletto by Caldara (*c* 1728).

Daphnis et Chloë: ballet by Ravel (1912); also ballet music by Boismortier (1747), and by Rousseau (*c* 1761).

Don Giovanni: opera by Mozart (1787); also an opera by Gazzaniga (1787).

Enigma Variations: orchestral work by Elgar (1899); also a solo piano work by Cipriani Potter (1858).

'Eroica': symphony (1803) and piano variations (1802) by Beethoven; also a solo violin sonata (in C, Op 29) by Tovey (1913).

Eugene Onegin: opera by Tchaikovsky (1879); also an opera by Prokofiev (1934, first performed in 1974).

Four Seasons, The (or *The Seasons*)*:* a series of four violin concertos by Vivaldi (*c* 1725); and a ballet by Glazunov (1913), an oratorio by Benedetto Marcello (1731), a lost cantata by Bach, a set of twelve piano pieces by Tchaikovsky (1876), Symphony No 2, Op 30 (1901) by H K Hadley, Symphony No 1 (1953) by V V de Lisa, a Symphony (1958) by Berger, and Symphony No 4 (1934) by Malipiero.

Job: 'A Masque for Dancing' by Vaughan Williams (1930); also a Symphony by E M Goldman (1963) and oratorios by Dittersdorf (1789) and by Parry, about which George Bernard Shaw, critic and executioner, said: 'I take *Job* to be, on the whole, the most utter failure ever achieved by a thoroughly respectworthy musician. There is not one bar in it that comes within fifty thousand miles of the tamest line in the poem.... This dreary ramble of Dr Parry's through the wastes of artistic error.... I hope he will burn the score, and throw *Judith* in when the blaze begins to flag.'

Masaniello: opera by Auber (1828); also an opera, *Masaniello furioso*, by Keiser (1706).

Mr Wu: song by George Formby (1933); also an opera by d'Albert (1932).

'Pathétique': sonata by Beethoven (1798); and a symphony by Tchaikovsky (1893); also an oratorio by Georgi Sviridov (20th century), and an overture by Kabalevsky.

Pelléas et Mélisande: opera by Debussy (1902); a Suite by Sibelius (1905) and Incidental Music by Fauré (1898).

Prometheus: ballet by Beethoven (*c* 1801); also an opera by Fauré (1900).

Ré Pastore, Il: opera by Mozart (1775); also an opera by Uttini (1755).

Ruy Blas: overture by Mendelssohn (1839); also an opera by Glover (1861).

Tempest, The: Fantasy overture by Tchaikovsky (1873) and a sonata by Beethoven (1802); also operas by Halévy (1850) and Gatty (1920), and Variations by Paganini (1828).

War Requiem: by Britten (1962); also *The Requiem for those who died in the war against Fascism* by Kabalevsky (1949).

Air and music

Music with an aerial connotation, from film, TV, and concert hall.

'Airplane Sonata' (1922)—Antheil
'Airborne Symphony' (1946)—Blitzstein
'Aspects of Flight', Op 48 (1974)—Stoker
The Battle of Britain (film): 'Aces High'—Ron Goodwin
The Dambusters March (film)—Eric Coates
'Lindbergh's Flight' (Cantata, 1929)—Weill
'Spitfire Prelude and Fugue' (film: *The First of the Few*, 1942)—Walton
Wings (BBC TV, 1978)—Alexander Faris
633 Squadron (film)—Ron Goodwin

In the following sections, new material has been added to supplement and partly replace that given in the first edition.

Animals and music

A collection of music with zoological connections. The more tenuous links with the animal kingdom such as operas entitled *Richard the Lionheart* or *Rip van Winkle* are omitted.

AMPHIBIANS

Frog

The Frog (galliard)—Morley
'The Marriage of the Frog and the Mouse' (part-song)—Ravenscroft
The Frogs (a comedy overture, 1935)—Bantock
The Frogs (after Aristophanes), Incidental Music—Kirby
The Frogs (after Aristophanes), Incidental Music—Leigh
The Frogs (after Aristophanes), Incidental Music—Commer
Frosch-Parthia (Frog Suite), for violin, cello, and bass (1755)—L Mozart
The Jumping Frog of Calavernas Country, for seven characters, chamber orchestra, and chorus (1949)—Foss
The Tadpoles, a Humoresque, Symphony No 9 in B flat, Op 108 (1939)—Williams
See also Nicknames and Subtitles: *Representatio Avium*
See also Haydn list

ARACHNIDS

Red Spider, opera—Drysdale
The Money Spider, opera (1897)—Lucas

BIRDS

Birds (General)

The Aviary (String Quintet in D, Gér 276, 1771)—Boccherini
'The Birds' (song, 1929)—Britten

Uccellatori (opera, 1759)—Gassmann
Deux Avares (opera, 1770)—Grétry
'Little Bird' (No 4 of *Lyric Pieces*, Op 43, 1884)—Grieg
'St Francis of Assisi Preaching to the Birds' (No 1 of *Two Legends* for piano, 1886)—Liszt
Oiseaux exotiques (1955)—Messiaen
Catalogues d'Oiseaux (1956–8)—Messiaen
The Cat and the Bird, song cycle (1872)—Mussorgsky
The Birds, suite (1927)—Respighi
Dance of the Birds, from opera *The Snow Maiden* (1882)—Rimsky-Korsakov
The Firebird, ballet (1910)—Stravinsky
As Wanton Birds, madrigal for five voices (1600)—Weelkes
The Birds, a one-act Extravaganza for six vocalists, two speakers, choir, orchestra, and off-stage recorder band (1968)—Maconchy
Fåglarna (The Birds), Op 56, for baritone, male chorus (with five soloists), percussion, and celesta (1962)—Bergman
The Birds (after Aristophanes), Incidental Music—Diepenbrock
The Birds, for soprano, chorus, and orchestra (1934)—Łabuński
See also Nicknames and Subtitles: *Representatio avium*
See also Haydn list

Birds (Specific)

The Blackbird, Symphony No 2 (1948)—Englund

Bluebird

Oiseau Bleu (opera, 1919)—Wolff
Bluebird (Pas de deux, after Tchaikovsky, 1941)—Stravinsky

Canary

Kanarienkantata—Telemann

Cocks and Hens

'Ballet of the Unhatched Chicks' (in *Pictures from an Exhibition*, 1874)—Mussorgsky
'When the Cock Begins to Crow' (catch)—Purcell
'Hens and Cocks' (in *Carnival of the Animals*)—Saint-Saëns
'Dance of the Cockerels' (from *Maskerade*, opera, 1906)—Nielsen
The Golden Cockerel (opera, 1909)—Rimsky-Korsakov
See also Haydn list

Cuckoo

'The Merry Cuckoo' (from *Spring Symphony*, Op 44, 1949)—Britten
Coucou (harpsichord piece)—Daquin
On Hearing the First Cuckoo in Spring (1912)—Delius
The Cuckoo and the Nightingale (Organ Concerto in F, Op 4 (set 2)/7)—Handel
'The Cuckoo in the Heart of the Wood' (in *Carnival of the Animals*)—Saint Saëns
'The Cuckoo Song'—Simpson

Cuckoo (Presto in C for harpsichord)—Gasparini
Cucu (capriccio, 1679)—Kerll
Sul Canto del Cucu (Toccata in A for harpsichord)—Pasquini
See also Nicknames and Subtitles

The song of the cuckoo is heard often in children's works such as Leopold Mozart's Cassation in G for orchestra and toy instruments.

Curlew

Curlew River (opera, 1964)—Britten
The Curlew (song cycle, 1922)—Warlock

Dove

The Wood Dove (symphonic poem, Op 110, 1896)—Dvořák
'The Dove' (Welsh part-song, 1931)—Holst

Duck

The Ugly Duckling (Op 18, 1914)—Prokofiev
Duo para pato y canario (Duet for Duck and Canary), for soprano and orchestra (1931)—Revueltas

Eagle

Eagle, Bird of the Air, for mezzo-soprano and orchestra (1956)—Marttinen

Falcon

'The Falcon Flew High' (chorus from opera *The Coachman at the Way-Station*)—Fomin

Finch

A Charm of Finches—Cowie

Goldfinch

See Nicknames and Subtitles

Goose

With the Wild Geese (1910)—Harty
The Golden Goose (choral ballet, 1926)—Holst
Mother Goose Suite (1908)—Ravel
The Wild Geese, Op 5, Tone Poem (1900)—Senilov

Lark

'Lo, Hear the Gentle Lark' (song)—Bishop
Horch, horch die Lerch (Lied, D 889, 1826)—Schubert
Horch, horch die Lerch (paraphrase after Schubert)—Liszt
The Lark Ascending (1914)—Vaughan Williams
See also Haydn list

Magpie

'Magpie' (song, 1867)—Mussorgsky
The Thieving Magpie (opera, 1817)—Rossini

Night Bird

El Ataja-Caminos (Night Bird), Symphony No 4 in B flat, Op 98 (1935)—Williams

Nightingale

Chinese Nightingale, Cantata (1928)—Engel
'The Nightingale' (*Satakieli*), song, Op 68/1 (1963)—Pylkkänen
The Nightingale, opera (1954)—Rogers
Nightingale, Violin Concerto in G minor (1955)—Perkins
'The Lover and the Nightingale' (No 4 of *Goyescas*, 1911)—Granados
The Cuckoo and the Nightingale (Organ Concerto in F, Op 4 (set 2)/7)—Handel
'Le Rossignol et la Rose' (song)—Saint-Saëns
'An die Nachtigal' (Lied, D 196, 1815)—Schubert
Song of the Nightingale (ballet, 1917)—Stravinsky
'The Nightingale, the Organ of Delight' (madrigal in three parts, 1603)—Weelkes
Nachtigal und Rabe (opera, 1818)—Weigl
Rosignol (opera, 1816)—Lebrun
'The Nightingale' (from *Sieben frühe Lieder*, 1908)—Berg
The nightingale plays a character in Ravel's *L'Enfant et les Sortilèges*, and supplies a voice as one of the toy instruments in Leopold Mozart's Cassation in G for orchestra and toys

Owl

The Owl and the Cuckoo, for soprano, guitar, and chamber ensemble (1964)—Salzman
'Owls–an Epitaph' (part-song, Op 53/4, 1907)—Elgar
'The Owl and the Pussycat' (song, 1966)—Stravinsky
'Sweet Suffolk Owl' (madrigal in five parts, 1619)—Vautor

Parrot

Funeral March for a Dead Parrot, for three oboes, bassoon, and mixed voices (the parrot's name was 'Jacko') (1859)—Alkan

Peacock

The Peacock Variations (1939)—Kodály

Phoenix

Phoenix Mass (1975, marking the renewal of the composer's creative energy after a fallow period)—Payne
Phoenix, symphony (1972)—Klatzon
The Phoenix, concerto for kettle-drums and orchestra (1969)—Parris
The Phoenix and the Turtle, opera (1962)—Musgrave
The Phoenix (Concerto in D for four bassoons, unaccompanied)—Corrette

Pigeon

Two Pigeons (ballet)—Messager

Quail

The quail is one of the toy musical instruments called for in Leopold Mozart's Cassation in G

Raven

'The Three Ravens' (part-song)—Ravenscroft
Nachtigal und Rabe (opera, 1818)—Weigl

Robin

Bonnie Sweet Robin (variations for harpsichord)—Bull

'Ah Robin' (madrigal)—Cornyshe
'Bonnie Sweet Robin'—Dowland
Bonny Sweet Robin (ricercare à four)—Simpson

Sparrow
Spatzenmesse in C (K 220, 1775)—Mozart
From the Book of Philip Sparrow (1971)—Orr

Stork
A Gólyā (The Stork), for chorus and piano (1827)—Mátray

Stormbird
Sturmvögel (opera, 1926)—Schjelderup

Swallow
'The Swallow Leaves Her Nest' (part-song, 1910)—Holst
Village Swallows (waltz)—Josef Strauss
'The Swallow' (part-song)—Morley

Swan
'The Silver Swan' (madrigal, 1614)—Gibbons
'A Swan' (song, Op 25/2, 1876)—Grieg
Schwannengesang (song cycle, D 957, 1828)—Schubert
'Swan of Tuonela' (No 3 of *Four Legends*, 1895)—Sibelius
Swan White (Op 54, 1908)—Sibelius
Swan Lake (ballet, Op 20, 1876)—Tchaikovsky

FISH

'Fish in the Unruffled Lakes' (song, 1937)—Britten

Goldfish
'Poissons d'or' No 6 of *Images*, 1905)—Debussy

Trout
'Die Forelle' (Lied, D 550, 1817)—Schubert
'The Trout' (Piano Quintet in A, D 667, the second movement of which is based on the melody of the above Lied, 1819)—Schubert
Die Forelle (paraphrase after Schubert, 1846)—Liszt

INSECTS

Life of the Insects, Incidental Music to Čapek's play (1947)—Hurník

Ant
The Ants, Comedy Overture, Op 7—Josephs

Bee
'Where the Bee Sucks' (song)—Arne
'Where the Bee Sucks' (song)—Johnson
'Where the Bee Sucks' (song, 1963)—Tippett
'The Flight of the Bumblebee' (from the opera *Tsar Sultan*, 1900)—Rimsky-Korsakov
'Sweet Honey-Sucking Bees' (madrigal in five parts, 1609)—Wilbye

See also Nicknames and Subtitles

Beetle
'The Beetle' (from *The Nursery* song cycle, 1872)—Mussorgsky

Butterfly
'Papillons' (song, Op 2)—Chausson
'Moths and Butterflies' (from *The Wand of Youth* Suite No 2, Op 1b, 1908)—Elgar
Papillons (for cello and violin, Op 77, 1898)—Fauré
'The Butterfly' (No 1 of *Lyric Pieces*, Op 43, 1884)—Grieg
Le Papillon (ballet, 1860)—Offenbach
Madame Butterfly (opera, 1904)—Puccini
Papillons (piano, Op 2, 1832)—Schumann
Les Papillons (ordre No 2)—Couperin
The Butterfly's Ball, cantata (1836)—Bishop
Black Butterfly, opera (1928)—Lavranga
See also Nicknames and Subtitles

Cricket
The Cricket on the Hearth (opera, 1914)—MacKenzie
Grillo del Focolare (opera, 1908)—Zandonai
Heimchen am Herd (opera, 1896)—Goldmark

Dragonfly
The Dragonflies, Fantasy for vocalist and orchestra (1879)—Blaramberg

Flea
'Song of the Flea' (1879)—Mussorgsky
'Herodiade's Flea' (discarded from *Façade*, 1923)—Walton

Fly
'The Fly' (song, 1966)—R R Bennett
'The Tale of the Small Fly' (from *Mikrokosmos*, vol 6)—Bartók

Gadfly
The Gadfly (suite of incidental music, Op 97, 1955)—Shostakovich

Gnat
See Nicknames and Subtitles: *Representatio avium*

Moth
'Moths and Butterflies' (from *The Wand of Youth* Suite No 2; Op 1b, 1908)—Elgar

Wasp
The Wasps (Aristophanic Suite, 1909)—Vaughan Williams
The Wasps (after Aristophanes) (1897)—Noble

MAMMALS

Ass
'Wild Asses' and 'Personages with Long Ears' (in *Carnival of the Animals*)—Saint-Saëns
Platero and I (1956) for solo guitar—Castelnuovo-Tedesco

Bat
Die Fledermaus (operetta, 1874)—J Strauss II
See also Nicknames and Subtitles: *Representatio Avium*

Bear
'The Tame Bear' and 'The Wild Bears' (from *The Wand of Youth* Suite No 2, Op 1b)—Elgar
The Bear (opera, 'Extravaganza', 1967)—Walton
Poem on the Tale of a Bear for soloists, chorus, and orchestra (1937)—Anatony Bogatirev
Bear Hunt (*Karhumpygnti*), symphonic poem for male chorus and orchestra (1948)—Tuukkanen
See also Haydn list, above

Cat
The Cat and the Bird (song cycle, 1872)—Mussorgsky
'The Owl and the Pussy Cat' (song, 1966)—Stravinsky
Cats, suite for clarinet and piano—Noble
La Chatte, ballet (1923)—Sauguet
My Cats, for voices and percussion (1968)—Pehkonen

Sir William Walton, composer of the opera 'Extravaganza' *The Bear*. (Royal College of Music)

The Cat's Duet, for two sopranos (*c* 1826)—attributed to Rossini, but probably by Robert Pearsall
L'Enfant et les Sortilèges (opera, 1925) includes a cat as one of its characters—Ravel
See also Nicknames and Subtitles

Cattle
Le Boeuf sur le toit (ballet, 1919)—Milhaud
The Wild Bull (electronic work)—Subotnik

Deer
The Enchanted Stag (cantata profana, 1930)—Bartók
Acteon Transformed into a Stag: Symphony No 75 in G (*c* 1784)—Dittersdorf
Prélude à l'apres-midi d'un faune (1894)—Debussy
'Like at the Hart' (anthem)—Howells
Der Steyrische Hirt (capriccio, 1679)—Kerll
La Chasse du Cerf (suite, 1708)—Morin

Dog
Variation XI: 'GRS' of the *Enigma Variations*, Op 36

Erik Satie, composer of *Limp Preludes for a Dog*. (Popperfoto)

(1899) begins with a musical picture of a dog leaping into a river—Elgar
Shaggy Dog, for flute, clarinet, trumpet, trombone, two saxophones, and piano (1947)—Imbrie
A Dog's Love, opera (1971)—McDonell
Limp Preludes for a Dog—Satie

Donkey
Little White Donkey, song—Ibert

Elephant
Waltzing Elephant, for narrator and orchestra (1945)—North
Babar le petit éléphant (*Children's Tale*, 1940)—Poulenc
Circus Polka for a Young Elephant (1942)—Stravinsky

Fox
The Cunning Little Vixen (opera, 1924)—Janáček
Rénard, Burlesque (1922)—Stravinsky
'Verses and Cantos *or* Foxes and Hedgehogs', for four voices, chamber ensemble, and live electronics (1967)—Salzman

Giraffe
Le Caméléopard, Symphonie de Ballet—Sauguet

Goat
Goat Paths, song—Howells
The Goat, operetta for children—Lissenko
Dance of the Goat, for flute—Honegger

Horse
The Bronze Horse (opera, 1835)—Auber
Ritterballett (1790)—Beethoven
Rodeo (1942)—Copland
En Habit de Cheval (two chorales and two fugues, 1911)—Satie
The Horses (three songs, Op 10, 1967)—Hugh Wood
My Horses (variations, *c* 1823)—Archduke Rudolf

Kangaroo
Kangaroo, for organ (1968)—Davies
Kangaroo Hunt, for piano and percussion (1971)—Lumsdaine

Leviathan
Leviathan, for double bassoon and orchestra—Gipps
Leviathan, symphonic poem (1974)—Cowie

Lion
Lions, for orchestra (1963)—Rorem
The Lion's Heart, oratorio (1931)—Kvapil
The Awakening of the Lion, for piano—Kontski

Mouse
Marriage of the Frog and the Mouse, The, part-song—Ravenscroft
Three Blind Mice, used in the first movement (Variations) of Havergal Brian's *Fantastic Symphony* (1907)
Variations on Three Blind Mice (1973)—Tavener
L'Enfant et les Sortilèges (opera, 1925) includes a mouse as one of its characters—Ravel

Ox
'I Have Twelve Oxen' (song, 1918)—Ireland
See also Haydn list: 'Ox Minuet'

Pig
See Haydn list: *Capriccio*

Seal
The Seal-Woman (opera, 1924)—Bantock

Sheep
'Sheep May Safely Graze' (from Cantata No 208, 1716)—J S Bach
Lie Strewn the White Flocks (pastoral)—Bliss
The Black Ram, opera (1952)—Parrott

Squirrel
L'Enfant et les Sortilèges (opera, 1925) includes a squirrel as one of its characters—Ravel

Tiger
The Tigers (opera)—Havergal Brian

Unicorn
The Unicorn in the Garden, opera (1956)—Russell Smith

Whale
Moby Dick, cantata—Herrmann
Moby Dick—Moore
Vox Balaenae (Voices of Whales) for three masked players, to be performed under a deep-blue light to give the impression of a prehistoric seascape in which the ancestors of the whale rejoiced. The instrumental-

Vox Balaenae **by the American George Crumb.**

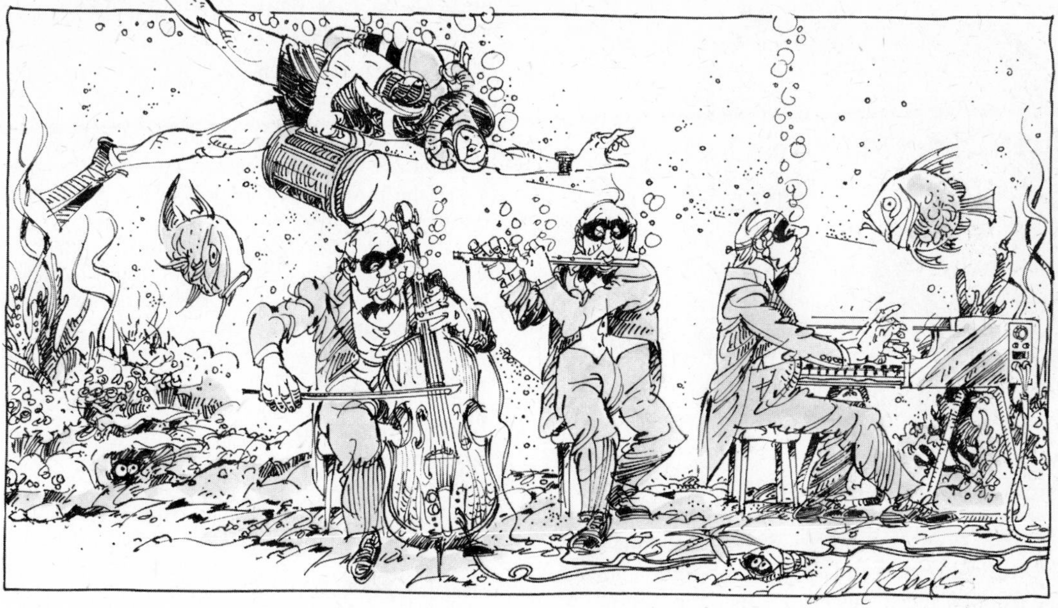

ists, playing respectively electric flute, electric cello, and electric piano, wear black masks—Crumb

The Whale (cantata, 1966)—Tavener

REPTILES

Dinosaur

Dinosaurus, for accordion and tape—Nordheim

Serpent

Serpent Dance (in ballet *The Truth About Russian Dancers*, 1920)—Bax

The Serpent, song (1970)—Ley

Snake

'Ye Spotted Snakes' (song in incidental music for *A Midsummer Night's Dream*, Op 61, 1842)—Mendelssohn

'*You Spotted Snakes*' (song, 1755)—J C Smith

WORMS

'The Worm' (song)—Dargomizhky

Animals in general are dealt with in several compositions:

Banchieri: *Contrapunto bestiale* (*c* 1600) in which the 'words' take the form of animal imitations.

J Bennett: *All Creatures Now* (1700).

Rudolph Ganz: *Animal Pictures*, Symphonic Poem (1901).

F J Haydn: *The Creation* (oratorio, 1797/98) mentions eagle, lark, dove, nightingale, whale, leviathan, lion, tiger, stag, horse, cattle, sheep, insects, and worm.

F J Haydn: *The Seasons* (oratorio, 1798/99) mentions lambs, fish, bees, and birds.

Janáček: *The Cunning Little Vixen* (opera, 1924) includes the characters of Owl, Gnat, Woodpecker, Badger, Cricket, Jay, Frog, Grasshopper, Hens, Dog, Fox, and of course the Vixen herself.

Poulenc: *Les Animaux Modèles* is an orchestral suite containing movements entitled 'The Amorous Lion', and 'The Two Cockerels'.

Prokofiev: *Peter and the Wolf*, a musical fairy-tale (1936) features the Bird, the Duck, the Cat, and the Wolf.

Saint-Saëns: *Carnival of the Animals*, a Grand Zoological Fantasy for two pianos and orchestra (1886), originally conceived for chamber group, mainly for the composer's own amusement. The suite has the following movements: 'Introduction and Royal March of the Lions'; 'Cocks and Hens'; 'Asses'; 'The Tortoise'; 'Elephant'; 'Kangaroos'; 'The Aquarium'; 'Personages With Long Ears'; 'The Cuckoo in the Heart of the Wood'; 'The Aviary'; 'Pianists'; 'Fossils'; 'The Swan'; 'Finale'.

Ruth Crawford Seeger: *Animal Folk-Songs for Children* (1950).

Sullivan and Stevenson wrote an opera entitled *The Zoo* (1875).

The Devil and music

The Devil and things diabolical have inspired composers for hundreds of years. The Orpheus legend of Greek mythology provided the material for many librettists and opera-composers: some of the fruits of these liaisons are listed in Section V under The Most Popular Opera Stories. In the ballet theatre, Orpheus has been dealt with by:

Deller: *Orpheus und Eurydike* (1763)
Killmayer: *La Tragedia di Orfeo* (1961)
Stravinsky: *Orpheus* (1947);

and in the concert hall by:

Dalby: *Orpheus*, for chorus and chamber orchestra (1972)
Liszt: *Orpheus* (tone poem, 1854)
Musgrave: *Orfeo II*, for flute and strings, written for James Galway (1976)

The Faust story, which first appeared in Germany in 1587, has also produced many operas based on the original story or a derivation thereof, together with a number of stage works:

J Berg: *Johannes Doctor Faust* (1966)
Berlioz: *The Damnation of Faust* (cantata, 1846)
Bertin: *Fausto* (opera, 1831)
Boïto: *Mefistofele* (opera, 1868)
Brian: *Faust* (1956)
Brüggemann: *Margherita* (opera, 1910)
Busoni: *Doktor Faust* (opera, 1925)
Gounod: *Faust* (opera, 1859)
Hervé: *Le Petit Faust* (opera, 1869)
Liszt: *A Faust Symphony* (1854)
Liszt: *Mephisto Waltz* (1881)
Moore: *The Devil and Daniel Webster* (opera, 1938)
Schumann: *Scenes from Goethe's 'Faust'* (1853)
Spohr: *Faust* (opera, 1816)
Wagner: *A Faust Overture* (1840, revised 1855)
Walter: *Doktor Faust* (opera, 1797)
Zöllner: *Faust* (opera, 1887)

Also concerned with the Devil and his works are the following pieces:

Arnić: piano concerto—*The Devil's Serenade* (1951)
Boccherini: *La Casa del Diavolo* (symphony, Gér 506, 1771): the finale is based on the 'Dance of the Furies' from Gluck's *Orfeo*
Dvořák: *The Devil and Kate* (opera, 1899)
Hiller: *Der Teufel ist los* (Singspiel, 1771) (usually translated as 'The Devil to Pay', this being the title of Coffey's original ballad opera)
Mussorgsky: *A Night on a Bare Mountain* (symphonic poem, 1867)
Paganini: *Le Streghe* (Witch's Dance), Op 8, for violin and orchestra (1813)
Saint-Saëns: *Danse Macabre* (symphonic poem, 1874)
Schubert: *Der Erlkönig* (Lied, D 325, 1815)
Scriabin: *The Black Mass*: Sonata No 9, Op 68 (1913)
Shipley's *The Seventh Enschian Key* is centred on the Satanic Mass
Stravinsky: *The Rake's Progress* (opera, 1951) and *The Soldier's Tale* (play with music, 1923) in which the Devil purchases the soldier's soul in the form of a violin
Tartini: *The Devil's Trill* (Sonata in G minor, *c* 1735): Tartini is said to have dreamed of hearing the Devil playing a sonata and, upon waking, the composer tried to recall the music and set it down in a sonata of his own
Weber: *Der Freischütz* (opera, 1821), in which the Devil has a speaking part
Weinberger: *Schwanda the Bagpiper* (opera, 1927)

In the Saint-Saëns, Stravinsky, and Tartini works the Devil is identified with a fiddle. Both Tartini and Paganini, supreme violinists in their respective ages, did nothing to discourage the rumour that their phenomenal techniques were in some way due to diabolical bargaining. A violin actually called 'Le violon du Diable' was made in 1734 by Giuseppe Guarneri del Gesú of Cremona.

Geography and music

A geographical tour in music, supplementing that in the first edition:

Africa
Symphony No 5, 'Africa' (1959)—Rogers
'Africa', Colonial Rhapsody—Lualdi

Argentina
Symphony 'Argentina' (1934)—Castro

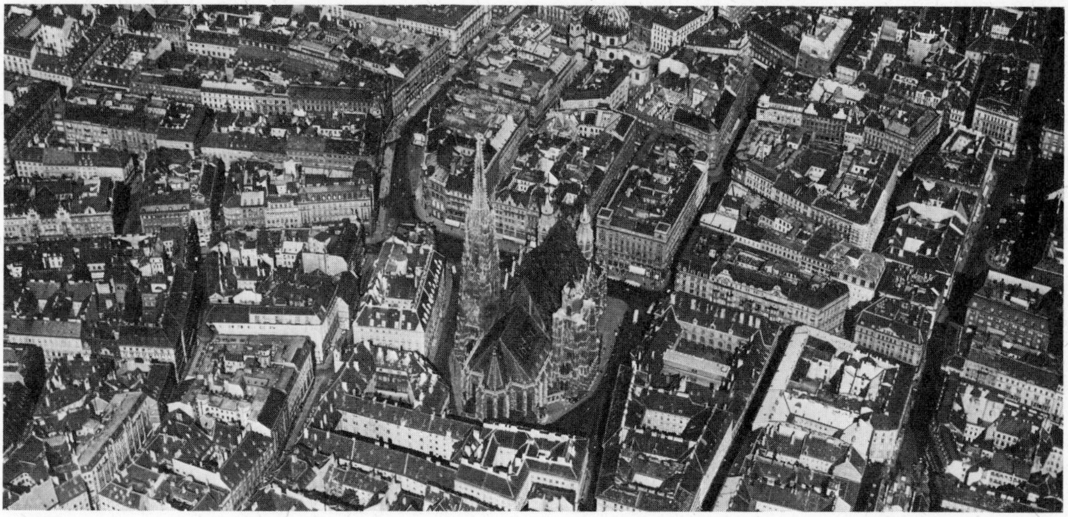

Vienna (showing St Stephen's Cathedral), commemorated in a Symphony by Graener. (Popperfoto)

Australia
An Australian Symphony—Evans
Van Diemen's Land, for speakers and chorus—Bauld

Austria
Symphony No 2, Op 110, 'Vienna'—Graener

Brazil
Symphony, 'Brazil'—Frank
Symphony No 4, 'Brasília' (1963)—Guarneri
Symphony No 2, 'Brasilia' (1960)—Guerra-Peixe
Symphony No 1 in C, Op 101, 'Brazilian'—Kreuder
String Quartet No 3 in D Minor, 'Brazil'—Nepomuceno

Canada
Symphony No 2, 'Ottawa' (1939)—Farnon

China
Symphony No 1, Op 11 (1914), 'China'—Dieren
Chinese Overture, 'The Willow Pattern'—Kirby

Cuba
Symphony, 'Cubana' (1965)—Rizo

Czechoslovakia
Symphony No 2, Op 65, 'Brno' (1946)—Chlubna

Denmark
Danish Festival Overture (1866)—Tchaikovsky

Egypt
Mârouf, The Cobbler of Cairo (opera, 1914)—Rabaud

England
Symphony No 1, 'Berkshire'—Andriessen
Symphony, Op 8, 'Cotswolds' (1900)—Holst
Hampstead Heath Bank Holiday Scherzo (1930)—Klenau
Symphony No 2 in A minor, 'Norwich' (1893)—German
Symphony No 2, Op 33, 'Nottingham' (1949)—Bush
Symphony No 3 in B flat, 'Westmorland' (1944)—Gibbs
Windsor Castle (opera, 1794)—Salomon
Cinque Port, a Suite in five movements—Blyton

Finland
Symphony in F minor, 'Finnish' (1897)—Mielck

France
Symphony No 10, 'France' (1944)—Lévy
Symphony, 'Normandie'—Thierac
Parisana, Tone Poem—Sterndale Bennett
Piano Concerto in E, *Les Adieux de Paris* (1814)—Hummel
Symphony No 4, 'The Siege of Paris'—Holmes
Symphony No 3, 'Parisienne' (1941)—Petrides
Le Gay Paris, for trumpet and wind nonet (1974)—Françaix
String Quartet No 16 in G, 'Provençale' (1936)—McEwen
Symphony No 8, 'Rhodanienne' (celebrating the river Rhodan) (1957)—Milhaud

Germany
Symphony No 3, 'Deutschland'—Mojsisovics
Symphony, 'Bremen' (1943)—Genzmer
Symphony, 'Dresden'—Matthus
Symphony No 8, 'Hanover' (1956)—Badings
Symphony No 1, 'Leipzig' (1945)—Laderman
Symphony No 3, 'Rostocker' (*c* 1975)—Gabichvadze

Greece
Symphony No 1, 'Greek' (1928)—Petrides

Holland
Symphony No 2, 'Holland' (1932)—Korchmarev
Symphony No 6, 'Amsterdamsche'—Dopper
'The Maid of Amsterdam', for orchestra—Kirby

Hungary
Symphony No 2 in B minor, Op 17, 'Hungarian' (1890?)—Major

Iceland
Symphony No 16, 'Icelandic' (1962)—Cowell

India
Symphony No 13 for orchestra and Indian instruments, 'Madras' (1958)—Cowell

Ireland
'Irish' Symphonies by Cunningham (Op 48); Esposito (1902); Harty (revised 1924); Leidzen; Martinon (No 3, 1948); and Stanford (No 3 in F minor, Op 28, 1882)

Israel
Cello Sonata, 'Israel' (1950)—Weinzweg
'Israel' Symphonies by Bloch (No 2, 1916); and Tortelier (1955)
Symphony, 'Jerusalem'—Seter
Jerusalem, for voices and orchestra—Steel

Italy
'Italian' Symphonies by Alaleona; Ghisi (1939); Salviucci (No 1, 1932); Vasilenko (No 3 for domras and balalaikas)
Symphony No 4, 'Bologna'—Perosi
Symphony No 2, 'Florentine'—Lunssens
Symphony No 1, 'Florence'—Perosi
Symphony No 2, 'Rome'—Perosi
Sinfonia di Roma—Lipkin
Symphony No 2 in F, 'Urbs Roma' (1856)—Saint-Saëns
Siena (Symphonic Poem, 1907)—Dyson
Symphony No 3, 'Venice'—Perosi
Il Carnivale di Venezia, Op 10, for violin and strings (1829)—Paganini

Japan
Symphony 'Japonaise'—Gallois-Montbrun
Symphony No 2, 'Hiroshima' (1949)—Aaltonen
Nagasaki, Oratorio for mezzo-soprano, chorus, and orchestra (1958)—Schnittke

Korea
Symphony No 2, 'Korean'—Polin

Lapland
Symphony No 3 in F minor, 'Lapland' (1915)—Peterson-Berger

Mexico
Mexico Overture—Hall

Poland
Symphony, 'Poland'—Hollander
Piano Sonata, 'Polonia' (1939)—Migot
Symphony in B minor, Op 24, 'Polonia' (1907)—Paderewski
Symphony No 2, 'Warsaw' (1945)—Woytowicz
Sonata for violin and piano, 'Warsaw' (1838?)—Paganini

Romania
Violin Concerto, 'Romanian'—Golestan

Russia
'Azerbaidzhan' (Symphonic Suite, 1950)—Amirov
Symphony No 2, 'Moscow' (1931)—Polovinkin
Symphony for accordion and orchestra, 'North Russian' (1931)—Schillinger
Symphony, 'Ukrainian'—Kalachevsky
Piano Concertino, 'Ukrainian'—Klebanov

Scandinavia
'Scandinavian' Symphonies by Casadesus; and Cowen (No 3 in C minor, 1880)

Scotland
Symphony in F sharp minor, 'Isle of Arran'—Foster

Spain
Violin Sonata No 2, Op 82, 'Española' (1934)—Turina
Symphony No 4, 'Spanish' (1937)—Schulhoff
Cello Concerto, 'Andaluso' (1937)—Zandonai
Guitar Concerto No 4, 'Andaluz' (1967)—Rodrigo
Symphony, 'Madrid' (1961)—Custer
Symphony No 2 in D, 'Murcia'—Palau Boix
Symphony, Op 23, 'Sevillana' (1920)—Turina

Switzerland
Symphony, 'Switzerland'—Darke

Tunisia
Symphony No 12, Op 166, 'Tunis'—Bentzon

United States of America
'American' Symphonies by Antheil (No 2, 1937); Gillis (No 1, 1940); Shure
Violin Concerto, 'American'—Gusikoff
'American Folk Symphony' in D—Spencer
Symphony No 2, 'Bostoniani' (1955)—Ibert
Piano Concerto, 'Broadway' (1964)—Rizo
Symphony, 'Chicago'—Mopper
Symphony, 'Louisiana' (1929)—Janssen
Symphony No 7, 'Louisville' (1954)—Badings
Symphony, 'Minneapolitana'—Veress
Symphony No 8, Op 40, 'Minnesota' (1959)—Saeverud
Symphony, 'Montana' (1953)—Baur
'New England' Symphonies by Kelley (No 1, 1922), and Orowan (No 1, 1967)
Violin Concerto, 'New England' (1941)—Wigglesworth
Symphony No 4, 'New York' (1967)—Gerhard
Symphony, 'Niagara'—Fry
Symphony, 'Oregon'—Avshalamov
Symphony, 'Pennsylvania'—Cadman

Symphony, 'Philadelphia'—Einem
Symphony No 3, Op 59, 'Philadelphia'—Josephs
'Pittsburg' Concerto for wind, percussion, and tape—Badings
Symphony No 8, 'San Francisco'—Harris
Symphony No 1 in F minor, 'San Francisco'—Willson
Symphony No 1, 'The Santa Fe Trail' (1934)—McDonald
Concerto for harpsichord, guitar, harp, and strings, 'Saratoga' (1972)—Josephs

Uruguay

Symphony No 2, 'Montevideo'—Gottschalk

Wales

Symphony No 4 in B flat, 'Welsh' (1884)—Cowen

Terrestrial

Piano Concerto No 2, 'The Continents' (1972)—Stevenson
Symphony No 1, Op 20, 'Earth'—Bringuer
Symphony No 2, 'Round the World' (1960)—Parrott
Symphony No 4, Op 64, 'North, East, South, West' (1911)—Hadley

SEAS AND MUSIC

'Arctic' Symphony No 4—Vasilenko
'Biscay' String Quartet No 6 in A (1913)—McEwen
'Caribbean' Concerto for harmonica and orchestra (1955)—Berger
'Mediterranean' Symphony (1948)—Montsalvatge
'North Sea Journey' Symphony (1880)—Swert

Early in the 19th century the American James Hewitt wrote a 12-movement overture describing his journey from England to America, and in 1960 Armin Schibler wrote his String Quartet No 4, Op 66 (with soprano), entitled *Meerfahrt* ('Sea Journey').

Del Mare symphonies exist by Malipiero (No 2, 1906) and Nystroem (No 4, 1948); there is a *Marine* Symphony (No 1, 1931) by Ibert and a *Maritime* Symphony by Le Grand.

Antarctica—See Nicknames and Subtitles

SPACE AND MUSIC

Moon

Der Mond, opera (1939)—Orff
Silver Apples of the Moon (electronic composition, 1967)—Subotnik
The Excursions of Mr Brouček to the Moon (opera, 1920)—Janáček
The World of the Moon (opera, 1750)—Galuppi
The World of the Moon (opera, 1777)—Haydn

Sun

Sun Music in five parts (I–IV for orchestra; V for chorus and percussion)—Sculthorpe
See also Haydn list

Planets

Urania, for orchestra (1965)—Garcia
Symphony No 3, Op 40, 'Uranus' (1956)—Penberthy

Beyond the Solar System

Symphony No 2, 'Ad Astra' (1943)—Isacsson
Aniara, space opera (1959)—Blomdahl
Atlas Eclipticalis, for string trio, harp, piano, clarinet, and percussion (in which the patterns of heavenly constellations are transcribed into musical shapes)—Cage
Symphony No 2, Op 19, 'Nebula in Andromeda' (1963)—Pospíšil
Sirius (The Dog Star, 8·7 Light Years from Earth), for tape, bass, soprano, bass clarinet, and trumpet, spacially arranged (1976)—Stockhausen
The Space Dragon of Galatar, an opera workshop project for voices, sound effects and piano—Paynter
Beyond the Universe, nine symphonic poems, Opp 140–148 (1973)—Penberthy

Medicine and music

The therapeutic power of music was discovered in 1942 by Mrs Cassandra Franklin, wife of Walter S Franklin, a retired President of the Pennsylvania Railroad. Mrs Franklin was a member of the 'Grey Ladies', an unpaid volunteer Red Cross organisation. During her work with patients at Tilton Army Hospital, near Fort Dix, New Jersey, she encouraged many of the war-wounded to remarkably quick and complete recoveries. Her methods are now widespread in America and are gradually gaining ground in Europe.

At times composers have taken illness or injury as inspiration. The most famous example is that of the String Quintet No 15, entitled *Le Quintette de la balle*, by George Onslow of Anglo-French descent. In 1829, whilst in a boar-hunting party, he paused to jot down a musical theme; a bullet struck his ear, partially deafening him. During his convalescence he completed his Quintet, using the theme that had brought his misfortune, and incorporated in the work pictures of his pain, fever, uneven pulse, and eventual recovery.

The Canadian doctor and part-time composer Forde McLoughlin wrote a tone poem entitled *Influenza* (1932); and the American Dr Hermann Parris composed a multi-movement suite, *The*

Hospital (1948), describing scenes and events leading up to an operation for appendicitis: 'A Nurse'; 'A Prayer Before the Operation'; 'The Operating Theatre'; and the operation itself: 'Anæsthesia'.

The Swedish composer Per-Gunnar Alldahl wrote a preventative piece, *Three Swedish Charms* (1971) for choir and drums, the purposes of which are (1) To Stem the Flow of Blood, (2) To Ease Pains, and (3) To Cure Warts and Corns.

An operation for the removal of a gallstone is depicted harrowingly in a piece for viol and continuo by Marin Marais, published in 1725; and earlier that century Johan Kuhnau in his Biblical Sonata No 4 in C minor describes *The Illness and Recovery of King Hezekiah.* There is also a *Hypochondriaca* Symphony in C for trumpet and orchestra (*c* 1780) by Joseph Schmidtbauer.

A doctor of the mind is commemorated in Richard Stoker's String Quartet No 3, called 'Adlerian', and inspired by the writings of Alfred Adler, the Viennese psychiatrist.

Months and seasons and music

January

'January Piece' (1967) for tape—Cary

April

Piano Concerto No 4, Op 85, 'April'—Palmgren

May

'May' symphonies by Bedřich (1960); Ivanov; Novák (Op 73, 1943); and Vacek (1974) 'The May Queen', tone poem—Bennett

July

Symphony, 'The Fourth of July'—Kurtz

'July 1968', for four-track tape (1968)—Englert

November

'November', for double bass and pre-recorded double bass (1967)—Budd

Music of the Seasons (*Evszakok zenéje*) for female chorus (1967)—Petrovics

Symphony, *Jahreszeiten* (1958)—Berger

Symphony No 2, Op 30, 'The Four Seasons' (1901)—Hadley

Symphony No 4 (called '*I*'), *Le Quattro Stagioni* (1934)—Malipiero

'The Four Seasons', Op 37 (words by Blake), for voice and string trio (1947)—Wordsworth

Spring

Symphony No 2, 'Break of Spring' (1913)—Langgaard

String Quartet No 3, Op 101, *Frühling* (1939)—Herrmann

Violin Sonata No 2, *Frühling* (1946)—Marx

Frühling symphonies by Abert (No 3, 1894); Huber (No 8, 1920); Mojsisovics (No 4)

Symphony No 3 in F, Op 61, *Im Frühling*—Rosenhain

Symphony No 8, Op 205, *Frühlingsklänge* (1878)—Raff

'Songs of Springtime', a cycle of seven choral songs (1934)—Moeran

'Springtime', for baritone and chorus, Op 60 (1966)—Bergman

'All in the Spring Wind' for orchestra (1952–3)—Chou Wen-Chung

'Spring' symphonies by Alpaerts (1907), Axman (No 3, 1928); Cikker (No 2, Op 15, 1937); Ehlert; Hovland (No 1, Op 20, 1953); Karel (No 4, 1938); Konvalinka (No 1, 1941–43); Krein; Křička (in D minor, Op 3, 1907, revised 1942; also called 'Youth'); Liukko (No 3, 1958); Paine (No 2 in A, 1880); Parchman (No 4, 1968); Winkler (No 2 in D, also called *Maiensymphonie*)

Printemps symphonies by Lajtha (No 4, Op 52, 1951); Milhaud (No 1, 1917)

Piano Trio, Op 25, 'Spring 1938' (1938)—Vačkář

La Primavera Violin Sonata (1838–9)—Paganini

Choral Symphony 'Springtime' (*Wiosna*)—Kazuro

Quartet No 2 for four guitars, *Primavera* (1973)—Biberian

Symphony *Primavera*—Benavente

'Spring', Symphonic Study—Cannon

Summer

Symphony No 2, 'Bitter Summer' (1969)—Bárta

'Summer' symphonies by Knight (No 4, 1966) and Melartin (No 4 in E, 1913)

Symphony No 1, *Dell' Estate*—Stockly

Oboe Concerto, 'Summer'—Straesser

Violin Concerto, 'Summer' (1944)—Rodrigo

Symphony No 9, Op 208, *Im Sommer* (1880)—Raff

'Summer and Smoke', opera—Hoiby

Concerto for orchestra, 'Summer' (1928)—Pizzetti

'A Summer Night', opera (1923)—Młynarski

'Summer's Last Will and Testament' for chorus and orchestra (1936)—Lambert

Autumn

'Autumn' symphonies by Marx (No 1, 1922); Moore (No 1, 1930); and Novák (Op 63, 1934)

Symphony No 3, 'Autumn Song' (1965)—Eckerberg

Symphony No 6, Op 33, 'English Autumn' (1964)—Morgan

'Eleven Echoes of Autumn 1965', for alto flute, clarinet, piano, and violin (1965)—Crumb

'Autumn '60', for orchestra (1960)—Cardew

Winter

'Winter Song' (1969)—Cary

'Winter' symphonies by Josephs (No 7, 1978); Nordoff (No 1, 1954); Raff (No 11, Op 214, 1882)

'Winter's Tale', Suite (1960)—Berkeley

'Winter Music'—Cage
'Winter Afternoons', Cantata for AATTBB and contrabass (1975, text by Emily Dickinson)—P Dickinson

Epiphany
String Quartet No 5, *Epiphanie* (1957)—Herrmann
String Quartet No 2, *de l'Epiphanie* (1959)—Poniridy

Easter
Symphony No 4 in C minor, Op 54, 'Easter Eve' (1905)—Foerster
Symphony No 4, Op 47, 'On an Easter Theme', (*Uppståndelse*) (1949)—Paulson
'Russian Easter Festival Overture' (1888)—Rimsky-Korsakov

Christmas
'The Christmas Tree', opera—Rebikov
Symphony for strings, Op 30, 'Christmas' (1941)—Pícha
'The Christmas Rose', opera for children (1932)—Bridge
'Christmas Eve Revels', opera—Lissenko
'A Song for Christmas' (1958)—Musgrave

Politics and music

In the widest sense, politics have often entered into music. Much war music is at base politically motivated: it is written to stir the people and/or to appease tough political masters, but it is evident from some of the works thus produced that the composers concerned would rather ignore the doings of the politicians and get on with the more benign occupation of composing music.

An exception is Luigi Nono. In 1970 he wrote *Y Entonses comprendio*, a homage to Che Guevara. It employs electronic sounds, three sopranos, and three comediennes. Part of the electronic soundtrack is of the voice of Fidel Castro reading his last letter from Guevara; elsewhere the performers, reading from passages by the revolutionary poet Carlos Franqui, shout their message at the audience. At the first performance in Brussels in 1970 the composer was to be found handing out political leaflets to the audience.

Others among the many 'message' works include 'Hands off Korea' (1950), an opera by the Czech political composer Miroslav Barvík; 'Ernesto Che Guevara (Revolutionary)—Symphonic Image' (1969), a homage by Svatopluk Havelka; Henze's bright red opera 'We Come to the River', premièred at the Royal Opera House, London, on 12 July 1976; and the opera 'Every Good Boy Deserves Favour' (1976) by André Previn, the action of which takes place inside a Soviet psychiatric hospital.

The Russian composer Nikolai Roslavets, for writing music considered 'modernist and unemotional', was sent to his death in Siberia and all references to him erased from textbooks.

Even a musical instrument has been used as a political object (see Section II, Unique Instruments: the 'Siena Piano').

A composer who combined his interest with politics and virtuoso pianism, reaching high in all three spheres, was Ignacy Jan Paderewski (1860–1941). He studied the piano with Leschetizky, wrote concertos, chamber and instrumental works and a symphony, and was the first Prime Minister of Poland (1919–21). He was incidentally the highest-paid serious pianist, accumulating a fortune of some $5 000 000, of which $500 000 was earned in the 1920–21 season.

Nearer our own time is Edward Heath, British Prime Minister 1970–74, who is an enthusiastic organist and choir conductor, and who has recorded with the London Symphony Orchestra as conductor.

Elsewhere we have discussed composers who have written very many works. Eastern politics seem to have dictated a strange opposite phenomenon: a work written by many composers, the *Yellow River Concerto*. It was apparently designed by a committee of six musicians, one of whom, Hsien Hsing-Hai, was chosen as the work's 'composer'. The concerto itself is a banal agglomeration of late 19th-century romanticism, shy acknowledgements of 'modern' style, and a tub-thumping vessel for the message of triumphant Chinese Communism.

Wars and music

The splendour of the uniforms, the excitement of the bugle calls, the thrill of the charge, and the rattle and boom of the guns have frequently inspired composers to write music depicting wars. Often the colourful stories of heroic deeds have drawn imaginative music from a composer who wished his audience to visualise the scene in lurid and harrowing detail: some even went as far as imitating the moans and cries of the wounded and dying at the end of the battle. Generally, however, the noble and exhilarating aspects were stressed,

and the victories were occasions for jubilant music and the firing of yet more cannon.

Since 1945 it has been realised by composers that there is no honour or pride in battle: an atomic war is a war in which no one wins, and composers have often turned to the ultimate in pessimism, drawing the picture of a silent, dead, and futureless planet. The Sixth Symphony of Vaughan Williams, for example, leaves one with a feeling of post-atomic desolation. He had accurately foretold the future in the mood of his Fourth Symphony (1935) in which the appalling years of the Second World War were implied. In Symphony No 5, written at the height of that war (1943), a scene of sunny post-war peace seems to be conveyed, but the last movement of the grim, disturbing Sixth Symphony (1947) is a long section of barely mobile music, never rising above pianissimo. The composer was reluctant to specify any programme for these three symphonies, but seen in the context of world events, their message is unmistakable.

The first composer to write war music appears to have been William Byrd, whose 'The Battell' for solo virginals dates from 1591.

A new selection of other war music (replacing the list given in the first edition) follows:

Bentzon: Symphony No 13, Op 181, 'Military'
Colicchio: 'D-Day: June 6th, 1944', for large orchestra
Collins: 'Threnody for a Soldier Killed in Action' (based on fragments left by Michael Heming, killed at El Alamein)
Damrosch: 'Dunkirk', for baritone, men's chorus, and small orchestra (1943)
Hervé: Symphony with voices, 'The Ashantee War' (1874)
Hewitt: 'Battle' Overture (1792)
Hewitt: Sonata, 'Battle of Trenton' (1797)
Kabalevsky: 'Before Moscow' (1942), an opera about the battle for that city in 1941
Kaprálová: Sinfonietta, 'Military'
Karaev: Symphony 'In Memory of the Heroes of the Great Fatherland War' (1943)
Knipper: Symphony No 3, Op 32, 'Far Eastern Army' (1933)
Kočzwara: 'The Battle of Prague' (*c* 1787) for piano (with violin, cello, and drum *ad lib*)
Lipińsky: Violin Concertos No 2 in D, Op 21, and No 3 in E minor, Op 24, both called 'Military'
Muradeli: Symphony No 2, 'The War of Liberation' (1947)
Paganini: Violin Sonata, Op 22, *Militaire* (*c* 1825)
Parrott: 'El Alamein', Symphonic Prelude (1944)
Piston: 'Fanfare for the Fighting French' (1943)
Polovinkin: Symphony No 4 in A, 'The Red Army' (1933)
Raimondi: Symphony in D, 'The Battle' (1785)
Riotte: 'The Battle of Leipzig' for piano
Smetana: 'Wallenstein's Camp', Symphonic Poem (1859)
Stanislav: Symphony, 'The Red Army' (1942)
Vaňhal: *Die Schlacht bei Würzburg*, for piano (1790)
Vaňhal: *Le Combat naval de Trafalgar et la morte de Nelson*, for piano (1805)
Vignerie: 'Battle of Marengo' for piano (1802)
Winter: *Schlacht Sinfonie* (1814), **the first symphony to include parts for human voice.**

On a more hopeful note, 'Victory' symphonies have been written by Kvapil (No 4, 1945) and Morris (No 2, 1936), and symphonies celebrating peace have been composed by Goleminov (No 3, 1970); Jurovský (No 1, 1950); Kálik; Midgley (No 1 in C); Neumann (for orchestra and chorus, 1954); and Vačkář (No 4 with chorus, 1949).

The most famous rhythmic pattern is the group of three short notes and one long one with

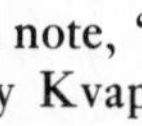

which Beethoven opened his Fifth Symphony. Speculation surrounds Beethoven's 'meaning': two popular theories are circulated, first the explanation attributed to Beethoven himself: 'Thus Fate comes knocking at the door', and secondly the notion that Beethoven, the nature-lover, was immortalising a bird call. The grim force with which the motif is projected in the first, third, and fourth movements of the symphony point more convincingly to fate than to a defence-

Beethoven, composer of the most famous musical rhythm. Sketches by J P Lyser, 1833. (Royal College of Music)

less yellowhammer as being the true inspiration; that is, if any extra-musical explanation at all is required.

The symphony, and particularly the first four notes, was chosen to act as a rallying-call for the peoples of Nazi-occupied Europe during the Second World War. The 'dit dit dit dah' rhythm is identical to the international Morse signal for the letter 'V', which came to be regarded as the symbol of ultimate victory. The letter was chalked on walls and doors, and the 'V-sign', immortalised by the Prime Minister, Mr (later Sir) Winston Spencer Churchill in his salute (palm outward) of the two raised fingers, was surreptitiously practised throughout the war-darkened Continent, to the serious detriment of Nazi morale. Transferred to sound, the signal was utilised in knocking on doors and windows or anywhere else to attract attention, and even during idle rail- or window-tapping while waiting in food queues.

Music notation		Morse		letter		Roman numeral		number	
	=	···–	=	V	=	V	=	5	=

Beethoven's Fifth Symphony, the start of which may be set to the words 'Vic-tor-y V'

The most potent factor in the propagation of this rhythm was its use by the BBC as a time signal between news broadcasts to occupied territories. Heard at intervals as a dull, insistent drum-tap to assist the tuning to home-made radios, it seemed to typify the dark, ominous will of the underground movements eventually to arise and over come the Nazi oppressors.

The signal was carefully chosen by the London planners. Once the rhythm itself had been chosen, it was essential for the actual sound to fulfil a number of requirements. It had to be absolutely distinctive; simple and easily remembered, and acoustically satisfactory. In short, the notes had to be heard clearly in poor receiving conditions, sometimes against atmospherics; it had to be of a tone quality to facilitate tuning, and above all it had to be audible at low-volume level, but not carry outside the cramped hide-outs in which it was listened to by news-hungry groups.

In 1942 the German SS General Reinhard Heydrich was killed by patriots in Czechoslovakia. As a reprisal, the German authorities ordered the entire destruction of the mining village of Lidice.

'The Hangman of Prague', SS Obergruppenführer Reinhard Heydrich.
(*Mayfair* magazine, Vol 13/7, p 40)

Every man was shot, along with 56 women; the rest of the women and children were removed to concentration camps and every building in the village was levelled. The Nazis attempted to wipe out entirely the very existence and memory of the village. As a mark of protest a number of towns elsewhere took the name of Lidice (among them San Geronimo, Mexico, and a completely new village near Joliet, Illinois), and the tragic village is commemorated in music in a moving tone poem by Bohuslav Martinů entitled *Memorial to Lidice*, completed the following year. At the climax of this work the 'Victory V' motif from Beethoven's Fifth Symphony dominates the music like a grim warning of revenge.

Lidice is also remembered in a work for double male chorus (1945) by Slavický and in Theodor Schaefer's 'Love Ballads'; and in 'The Immortal Village' (1949), Josef Plavec commemorated Ležáky, another village wiped out by the Nazis in 1942.

At the collapse of the Nazi forces in Europe on 8 May 1945, the call-sign of the Overseas Service of the BBC underwent a dramatic transformation. James Blades, who had recorded the wartime rhythm on an African slit-drum, re-recorded it using modern orchestral timpani which thundered out the call in a thrilling affirmation of victory.

Section 5
OPERA, CHORAL & VOCAL

Opera

'An *Opera* is a Poetical Tale, or fiction, represented by Vocal and Instrumental Musick, adorn'd with Scenes, Machines and Dancing. The suppos'd Persons of this Musical *Drama*, are generally Supernatural, as Gods and Goddesses, and Heroes, which at least are descended from them, and in due time are to be adopted into their number.' John Dryden

A chronological introduction

Dryden's 17th-century view of opera goes on in its snobbish way grudgingly to admit 'meaner persons' such as shepherds only if they are essential to the action, but the common person was strictly excluded for most of the time. Opera's subjects were later to include all manners and classes of people, and we may assume that the earliest ancestors of opera were also a little less high-class conscious, as has been hinted in Setting the Scene. In that Section, the earliest roots of opera were guessed at; now it is time to give a more definite presentation of the known facts concerning the components which may have led to the establishment of opera as a form.

400 BC
Greek tragedy of this period seems to have included singing as part of the drama. For instance, Euripides's play *Orestes* was performed with accompanying music, some of which may have been sung.

***c* 1283 AD**
Adam de la Hale (*c* 1240–88), a French trouvère known as the 'Hunchback of Arras', wrote *Le Jeu de Robin et de Marion*, which was performed in Naples at about this time. It is a kind of proto-opera in which a story is told in music. The title of this piece has led to the belief that the composer had some connection with the Sherwood Forest area of Nottinghamshire (Robin Hood; Maid Marian) and that he might even be identified with

the Sherwood minstrel Alan-a-Dale, since a similarity of name is apparent. However, there is no evidence that Hale ever came to England (his connections with Italy are stronger: he accompanied his employer, the Count of Artois, to Naples and Sicily, and he died in Italy), or that any part of the Robin Hood legend originated abroad. Neither does the story of *La Jeu de Robin et de Marion* bear a resemblance to any of the Robin Hood tales.[1] Regretfully, we must conclude that the approximate similarities in dates and names are coincidental.

1472
Angelo Poliziano's play *Orfeo* was produced in Mantua. Edward J Dent suggests that its structure indicates that many of the poems were sung.

16th century
The Italian composer Vincenzo Galilei, the father of the astronomer Galileo Galilei, produced songs and lute solos which may have assisted in the development of opera as a distinct art form. During the century, the setting of sacred texts and miracle plays to music gradually took three separate ways. These resulted in the following concepts which, despite elements from each which could be found in the others, had crystallised by about 1600 into:

MASQUE—a usually mythological play with poetry, music, and dancing, and other stage presentations, in which the actors wore masks.

ORATORIO—a presentation of a liturgical story with music, so called because it would be performed in an oratory rather than in a church or theatre.

OPERA—the Italian word for 'work' (compare *opus*; the Italian word for opera is *Melodramma*='melody'+'drama'). Its concern with stories of gods and heroes has already been described.

Another contributory stream was the *Commedia harmonica* productions of Orazio Vecchi around 1590. These comprised a series of madrigals arranged to form a dramatic continuity, but they were for chamber use and do not appear to have been produced on stage with 'props'. However, they may well have led to the series of steps that produced the widening popularity of opera in later decades.

[1] However, the famous English outlaw has not been overlooked by opera-writers: William Shield dealt with the story in 1784, and Sir Henry Rowley Bishop wrote an opera entitled *Maid Marion* in 1822. In America, Reginald de Koven composed an opera *Robin Hood* in 1890.

1597
The earliest true opera: *Daphne* by Jacopo Peri—lost. Although the music is lost, the libretto by Rinuccini survives together with some of the directions for the production. A big, terrifying serpent is required which is controlled by a man on all fours within. The creature is made to sway and undulate, to flap its wings and to breathe fire.

1600
The earliest surviving opera: *Eurydice* by Peri and Giulio Caccini (1546–1618). Caccini later that same year reset the same Eurydice story without assistance from any other composer. These works were performed at the house of Giovanni Bardi, Count of Vernio, in Florence.

1607
The earliest opera of which performances are still occasionally to be seen: Monteverdi's *Orfeo*. The instrumentation for this work was: two violini piccoli, first and second violins, violas, two viole da gamba, contrabass gamba, four recorders, two cornets, five trombones (alto, three tenor, bass), three trumpets. In addition a large complement of continuo instruments would have been required, including harpsichord, positive organ, lutes (harps?), viola da gamba, and bass gamba.

1627
The first German opera was *Daphne* by Heinrich Schütz. It was produced at Torgau but it has since entirely disappeared.

1629
The first Spanish opera (or 'pastoral eclogue') was *La Selva Sin Amor* ('The Forest Without Love'), sung in honour of King Philip IV. The composer's name and his music are lost, but it is known that the text of this one-act piece was by Lope de Vega. It was a predecessor of the *Zarzuela*, but this name did not come into use until *El Golfo de las Sirenas* (music anonymous; text by Calderón de la Barca) was given at the Palace of La Zarzuela on 17 January 1657. Calderón's piece is **the earliest surviving zarzuela.**

1637
The first public opera-house at which an admittance fee was charged was the San Cassiano Theatre in Venice. The first performance there was of *Andromeda* by Manelli, with a libretto by Ferrari.

1656
The first English opera, and the first opera ever heard in England. Sir William Davenant, who later became Poet Laureate, wrote a libretto for an entertainment he described as *The First Dayes Entertainment at Rutland House by Declamation and Musick: After the Manner of the Ancients.* This was a series of speeches between which vocal and instrumental music was performed. The music is lost. Later the same year Davenant's libretto *The Siege of Rhodes* was set to music by Henry Lawes, Henry Cooke, Matthew Locke, Charles Coleman, and George Hudson. The famous diarist John Evelyn entered the following comment after seeing the opera (5 May 1659): '... a new opera after the Italian way, in recitative music and scenes much inferior to the Italian composure and magnificence.'

1671
The first French opera was *Pomone* by Robert Cambert.

1674
The first occasion in England upon which the opera orchestra was brought to its present position in the theatre was for a performance of Locke's *Tempest* at Dorset Gardens Theatre, London. Hitherto the band had played on a concealed platform above the stage; now it was brought down to a position just below the line of sight of the audience, immediately in front of the stage.

1674
The first foreign opera heard in England was *Ariane* by Louis Grabu (?–*c* 1694) with a libretto by Cambert. It was in fact given in an English translation, and was performed on the occasion of the wedding of the Duke of York and Mary of Modena.

c 1675
The beginnings of a breakaway form—Pantomime—are to be found in the stage parodies of Thomas Duffett, whose operatic caricatures probably contained the origins of the conventions of the 'Principal Boy' being taken by a young actress, and the 'Dame' by a male comedian.

1692
The first opera to be based on a Shakespeare story was Purcell's *The Fairy Queen* adapted (by E Settle?) from *A Midsummer Night's Dream* and given at the Dorset Gardens Theatre, London, in April of that year.

1704
The first opera to be heard in Prague was Sartori's *La Rete di Vulcano.*

1710
The first opera in England to be performed entirely in Italian was *Almahide*, a pastiche by a group of composers led by Giovanni Bononcini. It was Italian opera in London which prompted Dr Johnson's famous description of 'an exotick and irrational entertainment'.

1711
The first opera by a Mexican composer and the first to be performed in South America was *La Parténope* by Zumaya, given on 1 May at the Viceregal Palace, Mexico City.

1732
Covent Garden Theatre, London, opened. It was modelled on the famous King's Theatre in the Haymarket, site of most of Handel's premières. Fire destroyed the Covent Garden Theatre in 1808, but it was subsequently rebuilt.

1733
The first opera by a Portuguese composer was *La Pazienza di Socrate* (written in Italian) by Francisco Antonio d'Almeida. The same year, Antonio José da Silva wrote the first Portuguese language opera: *Vida do grande D. Quixotte de la Mancha.*

1733
The first *opera buffa* was Pergolesi's *La Serva Padrona*, designed to be performed between the acts of his *opera seria Il Prigioneri Superbo.*

1735
The first opera heard in America was *Flora, or Hob in the Well* (a popular English ballad opera, composer unknown), produced at Charles Town (later Charleston), South Carolina.

1743
The birth of *Singspiel*, the German form of the English ballad opera, took place in Berlin with a translation of Coffey's *The Devil to Pay.* The style became more popular in 1764 when J A Hiller set the same story for performance at Leipzig.

Hiller, therefore, became known as 'the father of *Singspiel*'.

1755
The first Russian language opera was *Cephal i Prokris* (libretto by Sumarokov) by the Italian Araia, produced in St Petersburg on 10 March. **The first opera composed by a Russian** (but in Italian) was *Demofonte* (*c* 1770) by Berezowski; this was the **first opera by a Russian to be performed abroad**: in Bologna and Livorno in 1773. **The first Russian language opera by a Russian** appears to have been *Miller, Wizard, Cheat and Marriage-broker* (1779) by Sokolovsky.

1756
The first Danish language opera was *Gram og Signe* (libretto by Bredal) by Sarti and Kleen.

1767
The first ballad opera composed in America was *The Disappointment: or the Force of Credulity* (composer unknown), which included the song 'Yankee Doodle', also known as 'The Lexington March', adopted as America's unofficial anthem in 1782.

1778
The first Polish language opera was *Nedza Uszczęśliwiona* (Misery Contented) by Kamieński.

1786
The first opera to be performed in Turkey was by Heidenstam (name of opera unknown) given at Pera on 22 February.

1788
The first opera to be written by a Canadian was *Colas et Colinette* by Joseph Quesnel.

1794
The first American opera was *Tammanny* by James Hewitt.

1818
The first Norwegian language opera was *Fjeldeventyret* by Thrane.

1845
The first grand opera by a native American was *Leonora* by William Henry Fry.

1866
The first true Czech opera was *The Bartered Bride* by Smetana, one of eight operas by this composer.

1866
The first musical comedy was *The Black Crook*, words by Charles Barras, the music assembled from popular tunes of the day by Giuseppe Operti, which opened on Broadway, New York, in this year and ran for 474 performances in that production before persisting in popularity for a further quarter of a century in New York and the provinces.

1874
The first musical comedy with original music was *Evangeline*, an 'American Extravaganza' by Edward E Rice.

1883
The Metropolitan Opera House, New York, opened with the first American production of Gounod's *Faust*.

1888
The first Greek language opera was *The Parliamentary Candidate* (libretto by Makris) by the blind composer Xyndas.

1898
The first Finnish language opera was *Pohjan neito* (The Maid of Bothnia) by Frans Oskar Merikanto, with a libretto by Antti Rytkönen (produced at Viborg, 18 June 1908).

1953
The first 'wordless opera' (but also described as 'a tone poem for orchestra') was *Baldr* by the Icelandic composer Jon Leifs.

By the early 19th century a convention had grown up concerning terminology. **Grand opera** was defined as that in which all the words are set to music, from recitative, through aria, duet, trio, and other ensembles, to chorus.

The alternative term, **comic opera,** was reserved for opera in which some of the words were spoken.

If any differentiation is still necessary, it is time these old-fashioned terms were replaced. As it stands, works such as Beethoven's *Fidelio* and many other serious operas are deprived of the description 'grand' and are lumped together with 'comic' operas.

Operatic proliferation

As in all other art forms, once opera had become an established practice with its own rules and ingredients, and the public was used to the form and clamoured for more, the creators answered the demand with what seems like over-production. It has been estimated that at least 25 000 operatic libretti were written before the year 1800, and many of these libretti were set to music more than once—some a great many times. This profusion began early in the history of opera and did not cease until the end of the last century, as the following table shows. Of course, it is not possible always to be accurate as to the numbers of operas written by a given composer (Albinoni claimed to have written over 200 operas, never spending more than a week on any one, but only about 35 are known to us): often it is found that two or more composers share in the production of a single work, and sometimes it is difficult to draw a definite line between an opera and, say, an oratorio or a cantata. The totals below, therefore, are somewhat provisional, but there seems little doubt that the first (ie earliest) composer in the list has a clear lead over his rivals in operatic proliferation, judging by extant works.

Composer	*Number of operas*
Draghi, Antonio (1635–1700)	*c* 175
Scarlatti, Alessandro (1660–1725)	115
Keiser, Reinhard (1674–1739)	*c* 100
Hasse, Johann Adolf (1699–1783)	102, including 14 intermezzi and 23 pastiches
Galuppi, Baldassare (1706–85)	96, plus many pastiches
Gluck, Christoph Willibald von (1714–87)	107
Guglielmi, Pietro (1727–1804)	*c* 100
Piccinni, Nicolò (1728–1800)	139
Paisiello, Giovanni (1740–1816)	83, plus 16 cantatas, serenatas, etc
Müller, Wenzel (1767–1835)	100+
Bishop, Sir Henry Rowley (1786–1855)	69, plus arrangements and adaptations of other composers' operas; masques, ballets, etc
Offenbach, Jacques (1819–80)	104 operas and operettas

Operas set in unusual or exotic surroundings

The majority of operatic stories are set in a fairly narrow range of areas and periods. In the early days of operatic growth, the favourite settings were mythological, but gradually, as the popularity of opera required more and more works, and these in turn demanded further stories, writers of libretti widened their range to include ancient Rome, ancient Gaul, Spain, ancient and contemporary Russia, Switzerland, etc. The time span stretched from the old world of heroes and satyrs, through the Middle Ages, and right up to the then present day. Subjects, always somewhat lurid and improbable, included witchcraft and magic; in fact, magic is still a prime ingredient of opera. Political occurrences were also dealt with in operas from the 18th century onwards and were given an enormous boost in popularity by the French Revolution, during which composers in that torn country competed to prove their patriotism and loyalty to whichever side happened to be nearest—and heaven help them if they declared their allegiance to one side and then fell into the hands of the authorities on the other! Political operas were frequently taken seriously by audiences and authorities alike, the extreme example being the occasion in 1830 at which Auber's *Masaniello* was performed in Brussels. It is entirely due to the performance of this opera on 25 August of that year that patriotic feeling crystallised into revolution and Belgium won independence from Holland, a state which was finally ratified on 20 January 1831. Operas are meant to stir the emotions, but it is doubtful that even Auber expected such a violent and far-reaching reaction, and since he never attended performances of his own works, the news of it must have come as a considerable shock to him. *Masaniello*, then, is **the only opera so far to have sparked off a revolution.**

The first operatic treatment of domestic

tragedy, as opposed to comedy, was in Verdi's *Luisa Miller* (Naples, 1849), based on Schiller's play *Kabale und Liebe*. This was followed in Trieste the next year by the same composer's *Stiffelio* (later to provide much of the music for *Aroldo*, Rimini, 1857). *La Traviata* (Venice, 1853) and Charpentier's *Louise*, the latter set in the Paris slums (1900), also followed this trend.

However, the real purpose of this Section is to list operas which are set in other than the usual mid and south European locales. The usual disclaimer is necessary: such a list cannot—and need not—ever be complete, but the writer has so far been unable to trace any operas set in the Antipodes, a somewhat unjust state of affairs if true, now that Sydney has a spectacular opera-house.

Unusual setting	*Opera*	*Composer*
Baghdad	*The Barber of Baghdad* (1858)	Cornelius
Boston, Massachusetts	*A Masked Ball* (1859)	Verdi
Cairo and the Sahara Desert	*Marouf* (1914)	Rabaud
Californian Gold-rush	*The Girl of the Golden West* (1910)	Puccini
Ceylon	*The Pearl Fishers* (1863)	Bizet
China	*Turandot* (1926)	Puccini
	Turandot (1917)	Busoni
	The Nightingale (1914)	Stravinsky
	L'Eroe Cinese (1752)	Bonno
Egypt	*Aïda* (1871)	Verdi
	Djamileh (1872)	Bizet
	Thaïs (1894)	Massenet
	Zauberflöte (1791)	Mozart
Finland	*L'Etoile du Nord* (1854)	Meyerbeer
Gaza, Palestine	*Samson and Delilah* (1877)	Saint-Saëns
Heaven	*Mefistofele Prologue* (1868)	Boïto
Hell	*Francesca da Rimini* (1906)	Rakhmaninoff
Hell (part of the action)	*Orfeo* (1606)	Monteverdi
	Orfeo ed Euridice (1762)	Gluck
India	*Lakmé* (1883)	Delibes
	Savitri (1916)	Holst
Japan	*Iris* (1898)	Mascagni
	Madame Butterfly (1904)	Puccini
Lahore	*Le Roi de Lahore* (1877)	Massenet
Lima, Peru	*Le Carrosse du Saint-Sacrement* (1924)	Berners
Lisbon, on an ocean-going liner, and India	*L'Africaine* (1865)	Meyerbeer
Northern Norway	*Greysteel* (*The Bearsarks Come to Sirnadale*) (1906)	Gatty
Peru at the time of the Aztecs	*Opferung des Gefengenen* ('Sacrifice of the Prisoner') (1926)	Wellesz
Peru at the time of the Incas	*The Royal Hunt of the Sun* (1966–75)	Hamilton
Rhine, bed of the	*Das Rheingold* (1869)	Wagner
	Lurline (1860)	Wallace
	Lorelei (1863)	Bruch
	Elda (1880)	Catalani
Scotland: Northern Isles	*The Seal-Woman* (1924)	Bantock
On board HMS *Indomitable*	*Billy Budd* (1951)	Britten
On the moon (part of the action)	*Il Mondo della Luna* (1777)	Haydn
On a spaceship	*Aniara* (1959)	Blomdahl

Papageno, the bird-catcher, as depicted in the *Magic Flute*. (Mary Evans Picture Library)

Gilbert and Sullivan

The most successful musical partnership of all time is also the most famous. When the composer Arthur Seymour **Sullivan** (1842–1900) formed an association with William Schwenk **Gilbert** (1836–1911) in 1871 they founded a style of opera (or operetta) production in which their respective talents were complemented to such a degree that the resulting series of stage works inhabit a special branch of genius: a sublime blend of melody, wit, and high spirits.

A selection of scenes from Gilbert and Sullivan's popular works for the stage. Below left: *The Sorcerer*, **Below right:** *Trial by Jury*, **Bottom:** *The Mikado*, **Opposite top:** *The Pirates of Penzance*, **Opposite centre (left):** *Ruddigore*, **Opposite centre (right):** *HMS Pinafore*, **Opposite bottom:** *Princess Ida*. **(All courtesy The D'Oyly Carte Opera Co)**

Their first opera was *Thespis*, produced at the Gaiety Theatre on 23 December 1871, and it was followed by a succession of operas which continued for a quarter of a century.

1875 *Trial by Jury*
1877 *The Sorcerer*
1878 *HMS Pinafore*
1879 *The Pirates of Penzance*
1881 *Patience*

It was in 1881 that the Savoy Theatre, built specially for the presentation of Gilbert and Sullivan operas, was opened. The players who had been so successful, and who were to continue and increase this success for the next two decades at the theatre, were known as 'the Savoyards'. The famous series of stage works continued:

1882 *Iolanthe*
1884 *Princess Ida*
1885 *The Mikado*
1887 *Ruddigore*
1888 *The Yeoman of the Guard*
1889 *The Gondoliers*
1893 *Utopia Limited*
1896 *The Grand Duke*

SUBTITLES OF GILBERT AND SULLIVAN OPERAS
All of the operas carry subtitles, as follows:

Bunthorne's Bride, *Patience*, *or* (1881)
Castle Adamant, *Princess Ida*, *or* (1884)
Elixir of Love, *The Sorcerer*, *or the* (1877)
Flowers of Progress, *Utopia Ltd*, *or the* (1893)
Gods Grown Old, *Thespis*, *or the* (1871)
King of Barataria, *The Gondoliers*, *or the* (1889)
Lass that Loved a Sailor, *HMS Pinafore*, *or the* (1878)
Merryman and his Maid, *The Yeoman of the Guard*, *or the* (1888)
Novel and Original Cantata, *A—Trial by Jury* (1875)
Peer and the Peri, *Iolanthe*, *or the* (1882)
Slave of Duty, *The Pirates of Penzance*, *or the* (1879)
Statutory Duel, *The Grand Duke*, *or the* (1896)
Town of Titipu, *The Mikado*, *or the* (1885)
Witch's Curse, *Ruddigore*, *or the* (1887)

Although the success of the Savoy operas is unique in stage history because of the quality of the productions, and the delightful if uneven partnership between the providers of words and music, the concept itself was by no means new. Roots for the style can be traced in countless 'ballad' operas of the mid- and late 18th-century London theatres, and in comic opera from abroad.

A story circulates that, in a fit of spleen, and in an apparent attempt to belittle the mellow Sullivan and his music, Gilbert said: 'I know nothing about music. I merely know that there is composition and decomposition. That is what your song is—rot!' Perhaps because of such explosions, the famous partnership split up over a relatively trivial matter: the choice of a carpet for the Savoy Theatre.

Sullivan had by no means limited his associations with literary men to Gilbert; he tried hard to establish other connections both before and during his 'Gilbert days', but alas none had the popularity of the G and S productions. Here is a list of his other stage works, together with the names of the librettists:

BURNAND (Francis Cowley) AND SULLIVAN: *Cox and Box* (1867); *The Contrabandista, or The Lord of the Ladrones* (1867); *The Chieftain* (1894).
CARR AND SULLIVAN—see Pinero and Sullivan.
CHORLEY (Henry Fothergill) AND SULLIVAN: *The Sapphire Necklace* (1863–64, but never staged).
GRUNDY (Sidney) AND SULLIVAN: *Haddon Hall* (1892).
HOOD (Basil) AND SULLIVAN: *The Rose of Persia* (1899); *The Emerald Isle* (1901, the music completed by Edward German after Sullivan's death).
PINERO (Arthur), CARR (Comyns), AND SULLIVAN: *The Beauty Stone* (1898).
STEVENSON (BC) AND SULLIVAN: *The Zoo* (1875).

Sullivan's one excursion into grand opera was *Ivanhoe* (1891), with a libretto by Julian Sturgis after Walter Scott. In addition, Sullivan was a prolific hymn- and song-writer, the producer of incidental music for a number of plays including several by Shakespeare (*Henry VIII*, *Macbeth*, *The Merchant of Venice*, *The Merry Wives of Windsor*, and *The Tempest*), choral music, overtures, a Cello Concerto, and an 'Irish' Symphony in E major. There are also a few chamber and piano works.

The libretto

One component of an opera which is sometimes overlooked, often disregarded, and frequently libelled, but without which there would be no opera, is the libretto. It is not generally realised that usually the great majority of the words are completed before the composer sets to work on the music. No matter how much it may seem that the reverse is true, it is rarely possible to set the words of a drama to music which already exists.

Whether the stories always make sense is another matter. In an attempt to clarify the situation reached in Act 1 of Haydn's *La fedeltà premiata* (1780) the programme writer for a recent Glyndebourne production wrote:

> 'Lindoro has rejected Nerina and is courting Celia. Nerina is forgetting Lindoro and prefers Fileno. Melibeo desires Amaranta, but to win her must unite Lindoro and Celia. Amaranta vacillates between Melibeo and Perrucchetto. Perrucchetto alternates between Amaranta, Nerina, and Celia. Celia loves only Fileno, but must pretend not to. Fileno loves only Celia, and doesn't understand what is happening.'

One should remember Lord Chesterfield's charitable *bon mot*: 'Opera is a magic scene contrived to please the eye and the ear at the expense of the understanding.'

The word 'libretto'='little book' and comes from the time, near the beginning of operatic history, when the story and the music were bound separately. The earliest operatic singers were primarily actors who learnt their vocal parts by ear: to have the music *and* the words bound together would have made the book unnecessarily cumbersome.

Many famous writers have provided stories upon which operas have been based, while other writers have even made a speciality of the operatic libretto.

The casual attitude towards plot and the sense of the story is typified by an experience related by Dr Burney during a visit to an opera in Milan in 1771. Unfortunately he does not give the title of the opera, so we are unable to see just how much or little damage was done to the plot in this instance, but it is evident from this story that the last thing to be considered at an 18th-century Italian opera was the sense of the libretto. 'After this I went to the opera, where the audience was very much disappointed: Garibaldi, the first tenor, and the only good singer in it, among the men, being ill. All his part was cut out, and the baritone, in the character of a blustering old father, who was to abuse his son violently in the first scene, finding he had no son there, gave a turn to the misfortune, which diverted the audience very much, and made them submit to their disappointment with a better grace than they would have done in England; for, instead of his son, he fell upon the prompter, who here, as at the opera in England, pops his head out of a little trap door on the stage. The audience were so delighted with this attack upon the prompter, who is ever regarded as an enemy to their pleasures, that they encored the song in which it was made.'

The most successful librettist was Pietro Antonio Domenico Bonaventura Trepassi (1698–1782), the Italian poet who is better known by the name given to him by his adoptive father Vincento Gravina: Metastasio. The texts which he wrote, over 70 in number, were so popular during his lifetime that a list of his stories and the composers who set them would take on the appearance of a history of 18th-century opera. It is doubtful whether such a list could ever be completed (Grove says that some of his stories were set 60 or 70 times). His most popular libretti appeared between 1724 and 1734:

Didone Abbandonata (1724)
Siroe (*rè di Persia*) (1726)
Catone in Utica (1727)
Ezio (1728)
Alessandro nell'Indie (1729)
Semiramide riconosciuta (1729)
Artaserse (1730)
Adriano in Siria (1731)
Demetrio (1732)
Démophon (1733)
Olimpiade (1733)
Il Clemenza di Tito (1734)

After 26 stories which met with less acclaim came *Il Rè Pastore* in 1751, and a further series of less successful libretti terminated with his last, *Lucio Silla*, set by Mozart in 1772 and by J C Bach two years later.

COMPOSERS WHO WROTE THEIR OWN LIBRETTI

From early on in the history of opera, libretto-writing was an art distinct from the musical side of opera production. The librettist built up for himself a reputation for producing stories mainly in poetic form—the more musical the words, the more successful the opera was likely to be. Unfortunately, the result of putting music and poetry first was often that the story had to go last: as we have seen, nowhere are there such ludicrous, involved, fatuous stories as those in operatic libretti.

Some composers have tried to avoid the complications inherent in the task of setting another's words to music by producing their own libretti. Wagner is the best-known example: not once did he trust the story of another man, and he thereby evaded the deep philosophical questing for 'the right story' which Beethoven suffered. In the list below are to be found:

1. Composers who always produced their own libretti;
2. Composers who sometimes produced their own libretti; and
3. Composers who also produced stories for others to set to music.

Dimitri Shostakovich, author of libretti to his own operas. (Popperfoto)

This list is, of course, only a selection of the best-known composer/librettists.

1. Composers who always produced their own libretti

Berg, Alban (1885–1935), Austrian.
Boïto, Arrigo (originally Enrico) (1842–1918), Italian.
Borodin, Alexander Porphyrievich (1833–87), Russian.
Busoni, Ferruccio (1866–1944), Italian/Austrian.
Charpentier, Gustave (1860–1956), French. Although the libretto of *Louise* (1900) is credited to the composer, it was apparently contributed to by about a dozen writers, including Charpentier.
Chausson, Ernest (1855–99), French.
Delius, Frederick (1862–1934), English.
Hamilton, Iain (b 1922), Scottish.
Hervé (Florimond Ronger) (1825–92), French.
Indy, Vincent, d' (1851–1931), French.
Lortzing, Gustav Albert (1801–51), German.
Magnard, Albéric (1865–1914), French.
Schumann, Robert (1810–56), German.
Shostakovich, Dimitri Dimitrievich (1906–75), Russian.
Wagner, Richard (1813–83), German.

2. Composers who sometimes produced their own libretti

Abert, Johann Joseph (1832–1915), Bohemian.
Albert, Eugen d' (1864–1932), German (of French descent, born in Scotland).
Antheil, George (1900–59), American.
Arne, Thomas Augustin (1710–78), English.
Atterberg, Kurt (1887–1974), Swedish.
Bantock, Sir Granville (1868–1946), English.
Berlioz, Hector (1803–69), French.
Dittersdorf, Karl Ditters von (1739–99), Austrian.
Donizetti, Gaetano (1797–1848), Italian.
Glinka, Mikhail Ivanovich (1804–57), Russian.
Gounod, Charles François (1818–93), French.
Hindemith, Paul (1895–1963), German.
Holst, Gustav (1874–1934), English.
Janáček, Leoš (1854–1928), Czech.
Kienzl, Wilhelm (1857–1941), Austrian.
Křenek, Ernst (b 1900), Czech/German.
Lalo, Edouard (1823–92), French.
Leoncavallo, Ruggiero (1858–1919), Italian.
Malipiero, Gian Francesco (1882–1973), Italian.
Menotti, Gian Carlo (b 1911), Italian/American.
Mussorgsky, Modest Petrovich (1839–81), Russian.
Nono, Luigi (b 1924), Italian.
Pfitzner, Hans (1869–1949), German.
Pizzetti, Ildebrando (1880–1968), Italian.
Prokofiev, Sergei Sergeivich (1891–1953), Russian.
Rabaud, Henri (1873–1949), French.
Rezniček, Emil Nikolaus von (1860–1945), Austrian.
Rimsky-Korsakov, Nikolai Andreyevich (1844–1908), Russian.

Saint-Saëns, Charles Camille (1835–1921), French.
Schmidt, Franz (1874–1939), Austrian.
Schoeck, Othmar (1886–1957), Swiss.
Schoenberg, Arnold (1874–1951), Austrian.
Smyth, Dame Ethel Mary (1858–1944), English.
Spohr, Ludwig (1784–1859), German.
Strauss, Richard (1864–1949), German.
Stravinsky, Igor (1882–1971), Russian/French/American.
Tchaikovsky, Pyotr Ilyich (1840–93), Russian.
Telemann, Georg Philipp (1681–1767), German.
Tippett, Michael (b 1905), English.
Vaughan Williams, Ralph (1872–1958), English.
Weinberger, Jaromir (1896–1967), Czech.
Wieniawski, Adam Tadeusz (1879–1950), Polish.

3. Composers who also produced stories for others to set to music

Boïto, Arrigo (see above).
Menotti, Gian Carlo (see above).
Rousseau, Jean-Jacques (1712–78), French.

A number of writers have concentrated largely or exclusively on opera libretti. A list of the most prominent is given below, together with some of their most important successes and other remarks.

Barbier, Jules (1822–1901), worked with Carré on *Les Noces de Jeanette* (Masse, 1853); *Faust* (Gounod, 1859); *Philemon et Baucis* (Gounod, 1860); *Mignon* (Thomas, 1866); *Roméo et Juliette* (Gounod, 1867); *Hamlet* (Thomas, 1868), *Tales of Hoffmann* (Offenbach, 1881).

Calzabigi (or Calsabigi), Raniero da (1714–95) was friendly with Gluck, with whom he worked to bring about various operatic reforms. He provided Gluck with a number of libretti including *Orfeo ed Euridice* (1762), *Alceste* (1767), and *Paride ed Elena* (1770). He also wrote libretti for other composers (eg *Opera Seria* by Gassmann, 1769).

Cammarano, Salvatore (1801–52), author and theatre manager. His stories include: *Lucia di Lammermoor* (Donizetti, 1835); *Don Pasquale* (Donizetti, 1843); *Il Trovatore* (Verdi, 1853).

Carré, Michel (1819–72)—see Barbier.

Forzano, Gioachino (or Giovacchino) (1883–1958), provided the libretto for two-thirds of Puccini's *Il Trittico* (1819), ie *Suor Angelica*, and *Gianni Schicchi*. The story for the first part of the triptych, *Il Tabarro*, was written by Giuseppe Adami.

Ghislanzoni, Antonio (1824–93). His most famous story is *Aïda* (Verdi, 1870).

Gilbert, William Schwenk (1836–1911). The only librettist to be billed consistently above the composer. See above.

Goldoni, Carlo (1707–93), known as the 'Father of Opera Buffa', Goldoni wrote some 70 libretti, often using his pastoral name (Polisseno Feglio) or humorous anagrams (sometimes inexact) of his own name: Aldimiro Clog; Loran Glodici; Calindo Grolo; Sogol Cardoni. Galuppi was the best customer for Goldoni's libretti, setting about 20 stories, but as will be seen from the selection which follows, he was by no means the only composer to show an interest in these charming comedies: *La Generosità politica* (Marchi, 1736); *Il Negligente* (Ciampi, 1749; Paisiello, 1765); *La Contessina* (Maccari, 1743; Gassmann, 1770); *Il Mondo della Luna* (Galuppi, 1750; Haydn, 1777; Paisiello, 1783); *Arcifanfano* (Galuppi, 1750; Dittersdorf, 1777); *La Buona figliuola* (Duni, 1757; Piccinni, 1760); *La Pescatrice* (Paisiello, 1766; Piccinni, 1766; Haydn, 1770); *Lo Speziale* (Pallavicini, Act I, and Fischietti, Acts II and III, 1759; Haydn, 1768); *Il Ciarlatano* (Scolari, 1759).

Halévy, Ludovic (1834–1908), nephew of the composer Fromenthal Halévy. His collaboration with Henri Meilhac produced several Offenbach operettas, including *La Belle Hélène* (1864), *Barbe-Bleue* (1866), *La Vie Parisienne* (1866), and *La Périchole* (1868), and Bizet's opera *Carmen* (1875), and in association with H Crémieux, Offenbach's *Orphée aux enfers* (1858).

Illica, Luigi (1857–1919), best known for his partnership with Giuseppe Giacosa for Puccini's *La Bohème* (1896), *Tosca* (1900), and *Madame Butterfly* (1904). Illica was also responsible for many other less successful libretti: *Cristoforo Colombo* (Franchetti, 1892); *Andrea Chenier* (Giordano, 1896); *Iris* (Mascagni, 1898); *Germania* (Franchetti, 1902); *Siberia* (Giordano, 1903); *Tess* (Erlanger, 1909); *Isobeau* (Mascagni, 1911).

Piave, Francesco Maria (1810–76) wrote the libretti for Verdi's operas *Ernani* (1844), *Macbeth* (1847), *Rigoletto* (1851), and *La Traviata* (1853). He also collaborated with Boïto for Verdi's *Simon Boccanegra* (1857) but this was revised by Boïto in 1881.

Planché, James Robinson (1796–1880), best known for his *Oberon* (Weber, 1826).

Ponte, Lorenzo da (1749–1838), born Emanuele Conegliano, he worked as a writer in Dresden and Vienna until 1791, when he moved to London and opened a publishing house. From 1805 to his death he lived in Columbia, USA, and became an American citizen. As Mozart's best-known librettist, he produced *Le Nozze di Figaro* (1786), *Don Giovanni* (1787), *Così fan Tutte* (1790), as well as books for Bianchi (*Antigona*, 1796; *Merope*, 1797), Martín y Soler (*Una cosa Rara*, 1786; *L'Arbore di Diana*, 1787; *La Scola de'maritati*, 1795), and Salieri (*Il Ricco d'un giorno*, 1784; *Axur, Ré d'Ormus*, 1788).

Romani, Felice (1788–1865), the author of some 80 libretti, ten of which were set by Donizetti and sixteen by Mercadante. Bellini also chose a number of stories:

Il Pirata (1827); *Zaira* (1829); *La Straniera* (1829); *I Capuleti e i Montecchi* (1830); *Norma* (1831); *La Sonnambula* (1833) and *Beatrice di Tenda* (1833).

Romani's stories were also set by Carlo Conti, Carlo Coccia, Mayr, and Verdi (*Un Giorno di regno*, 1840).

Schikaneder, Emanuel (1751–1812), born Johann Schikeneder, he is best known for *Die Zauberflöte* (Mozart, 1791).

Scribe, Augustin Eugène (1791–1861), the so-called 'creator' of grand opera. He wrote the following stories set to music by Auber: *La Muette de Portici* (also called *Masaniello*), 1828; *Fra Diavolo*, 1830; *Le Dieu et la bayadère*, 1830; *Le Philtre*, 1831; *Gustav III*, 1833; *Le Domino Noir*, 1837; *Le Lac des Fées*, 1839; *Crown Diamonds*, 1841; and *L'Enfante prodigu*, 1837.

He achieved considerable success with Boieldieu—*La Dame Blanche* (1825); with Halévy—*La Juive* (1835); *Guido et Ginevra* (1838); *Le Juif errant* (1852); with Meyerbeer—*Robert le Diable* (1831); *Les Huguenots* (1836); *Le Prophète* (1849); *L'Etoile du Nord* (1854); *L'Africaine* (1865).

Zeno, Apostolo (1669–1750) wrote a number of stories which were set to music by various Venetian composers. Among these libretti were: *Faramondo* (1699); *Temistocle* (1700); *Antioco* (1705); *Lucio Papiro* (1719); *Ormisda* (1721); *Alessandro in Sidone* (1721); *Ornospade* (1727).

The world's first librettist was Ottavio Rinuccini (1562–1621). He provided the stories for the first operas; *Dafne* and *Euridice* (both 1600, with music by Peri) and *Arriana* (1608) with music by Monteverdi.

The most popular operatic stories are those based on ***Armida*, *Orpheus*, and *Alceste*.**

Armida is based on the poem *Gerusalemme liberata*, completed in 1575 by Torquato Tasso (1544–95), and has undoubtedly inspired more opera-composers and librettists than any other story. The following composers set the tale to music in greater or lesser accuracy, under different names:

Cherubini	1782	Persuis	1812
Dvořák	1904	Petri	1782
Ferrari	1639	Piccinni	1778
Gluck	1772	Pirasti	1785
Graun K H	1751	Righini	1803
Häffner	1801	Rossini	1817
Handel	1711	Sacchini	1772
Haydn F J	1784	Salieri	1771
Lully	1686	Traetta	1761
Mortellari	c 1782	Vivaldi	1718
Mysliveček	1779	Wesström	c 1770
Naumann	1773		

Orpheus, the legendary son of Apollo and the Muse Calliope, was written about by a number of classical writers, among them Ovid, Aristophanes, and Boëthius. His story has been set to music by numerous composers. Titles vary, but the basic story is the same:

Orfeo or *Orpheus*

Rossi	1647	J C Bach	1770
Sartori	1672	F H W Benda	1787
Keiser	1698	Roger-Ducasse	1913
K H Graun	1752	Rieti	1952
Barthélémon	1767		

Orfeo ed Euridice or *Orpheus und Euridike*,

Gluck	1762	Naumann	1786
Tozzi	1775	F J Haydn	1791
Bertoni	1776	Křenek	1926

Euridice

Peri	1600	Caccini	1602

Miscellaneous

Favola d'Orfeo	Monteverdi	1607
Pianto d'Orfeo	Belli	1616
Morte d'Orfeo	Landi	1619
Orphée aux enfers	Offenbach	1858
L'Orfeide	Malipiero	1922
Malheure d'Orphée	Milhaud	1926
Favola d'Orfeo	Casella	1932

For non-operatic musical settings of the legend of Orpheus, and for works dealing with other diabolical subjects, see The Devil and Music in Section IV.

The tragedy *Alceste* was written in 432 BC

Orpheus (*c* 450 BC) accompanying himself on the lyra. His story has served as the basis for countless operas. (Mary Evans Picture Library)

by Euripides (*c* 485–407 BC), and, although apparently not as popular as *Armida* and *Orpheus*, has nevertheless attracted much attention for stage presentation under varying names such as *Admetus* and *Getreute Alceste*, etc:

Boughton	1922	Handel (*Alceste*)	1750
Edelmann	*c* 1778	Lully	1674
Gluck	1767	Schürmann	1719
Gresnick	*c* 1781	Schweitzer	1773
Handel (*Admeto*)	1727	Strungk	1693
		Wellesz	1924

Beethoven chose his opera libretto with the greatest care. When he wrote *Fidelio* in 1805 he felt that it alone reflected his own socialistic idea of the survival of the lowly in the face of authoritarianism, at the same time as representing Beethoven's ideal situation of love between a man and his wife. The same story had been set before by Pierre Gaveaux in 1798, and by Ferdinando Paer in 1804. Later composers also set the story:

Anselm Hüttenbrenner in 1835
Saverio Mercadante in 1844
William Henry Fry in 1845.

The most frequent character to appear in English opera was Harlequin. English opera of the 18th century was a cross between continental comic opera, pantomime, and musical burlesque. It had its standard characters, such as the sailor home from the sea, the pompous gentleman who is almost invariably taken down a few pegs before the end of the evening's entertainment, and the young girl, often from the country, who usually manages to get her man. But the character who held most audiences was, ironically for an opera-player, the mute actor Harlequin himself, taken from the Arlecchino of the old Italian comedies.

The operas and pantomimes mentioned below are only those in which Harlequin, in various guises, figures in the title. Countless others exist in which the character appears for a greater or lesser part of the time, disporting himself most prominently in the section of the entertainment which came to be known as 'the Harlequinade'.

HARLEQUIN OPERAS

Title	*Date*	*Composer*
Chaos, or *Harlequin Phaeton*	*c* 1800	Russell
Choice of Harlequin, The, or the Indian Chief	1782	M Arne
Friar Bacon, or Harlequin Rambler	1784	Shield
Harlequin and Faustus, or the Devil will have his own	1793	Shield
Harlequin and Oberon	1798	Reeve
Harlequin and Quixotte	1797	Reeve
Harlequin Free mason	*c* 1780	Dibdin
Harlequin Junior, or the Magic Cestus	1784	Shield
Harlequin Marriner, or the Witch of the Oaks (from which comes the popular imitation Scottish song 'Comin' Thru' the Rye')	1796	Sanderson
Harlequin Rambler, or the Convent in an Uproar	1784	Shield
Harlequin's Almanack	1801	Reeve
Harlequin's Invasion (from which comes 'Heart of Oak')	1759	Boyce
Harlequin's Museum, or Mother Shipton Triumphant	1792	Shield
Harlequin Sorcerer, with the Loves of Proserpine (later to be known as ... *the Rape of Proserpine*)	1725	Galliard
Harlequin's Return	1798	Reeve
Harlequin Teague, or the Giant's Causeway, Op 19	1782	Arnold
Hermit, The, or Harlequin at Rhodes	*c* 1770	Collett
Magic Oak, The, or Harlequin Woodcutter	1799	Attwood
Merry Sherwood, or Harlequin Forester	1795	Reeve
Mirror, The, or Harlequin Everywhere	1779	Dibdin
Necromancer, The, or Harlequin Dr Faustus	1723	Galliard
Triumph of Mirth, The, or Harlequin's Wedding	1782	Linley, Jr
Wizard's Wake, The, or Harlequin's Regeneration	1805	Russell

Renowned opera singers of different generations: Dame Nellie Melba (left) and Elisabeth Schwarzkopf (right). (Courtesy EMI and Royal College of Music)

Unusual names

Many operas have unusual names in that they seem to have less weight than the operas themselves, or have mundane connotations which appear to be out of character with the concept of 'grand opera'. One such is Mozart's *Cosí fan tutte*, which may be translated as 'They all do it', or 'So do they all'. The names listed below go even further, in that they present odd combinations of syllables, or include strange words, or tell a whimsical tale in themselves. One opera, by Hubert Bath, not only has an odd name but was written by *just* the right composer!

Ali Hitsch Hatsch (1844), by Simon Sechter
Allamistakeo, by the Italian composer Giulio Viozzi
Bee-Bee-Bei, Op 36 (1933), by Edmund Rubbra
Bubbles (1923), by Hubert Bath
Buz-Gloak Child, The, a children's opera (1970), by Tim Higgs
Emelia di Liverpool (1824), by Donizetti
Genius of Nonsense, An Original, Whimsical, Operatical, Pantomimical, Farcical, Electrical, Naval, and Military Extravaganza, Op 27 (1784), by Samuel Arnold
Heironymus Knicker (1789), by Karl Ditters von Dittersdorf
Infidelio (1954), by Elizabeth Lutyens
Inkle and Yarico (1787), by Samuel Arnold
La Glu (1910), by Gabriel Dupont
Love Laughs at Locksmiths (1803), by Henry Condell
No Song, No Supper (1790), by Stephen Storace
Obi, or Three Finger'd Jack, Op 48, by Samuel Arnold
Ol-Ol (1928), by Alexander Nikolaevich Tcherepnin
Time off? Not a Ghost of a Chance (1971), by Elizabeth Lutyens
What a Blunder (1800), by John Davy

Operas about composers

A small group of works for which inspiration was drawn from the lives of earlier composers. The opera by Paul Graener takes a fact and exaggerates it; this, and the novel on the same subject by A E Brachvogel, has given posterity the completely wrong impression of Friedemann, the much-slandered son of J S Bach. Likewise, the opera by Rimsky-Korsakov takes a thread of supposition and turns it into a drama which might easily be believed by the gullible.

A scale model of the New Metropolitan Opera House, New York. Completed in 1966, the building replaced the earlier 'Met', opened in 1883. (Popperfoto)

Adam de La Hale (1880), by Ernst Frank
Chopin (1901), by Giacomo Orefice
The Damask Rose (1929) about, and with music based on that of, Chopin, by George Clutsam
Friedemann Bach (1931), by Paul Graener
Lavotta szerelme ('Lavotta's Love'). János de Izsépfalva et Kevelháza Lavotta (1764–1820) was a Hungarian composer whose exploits inspired operas of that name by Hubay and Barna, and another piece, *Lavotta elsö szerelme* ('Lavotta's First Love'), once attributed to Lavotta but actually by József Kossovits.
Lilac Time (1922), about, and using the music of, Franz Schubert. This is an English version by Clutsam of the operetta *Das Dreimädelhaus* (1915) by Heinrich Berté
Lully et Quinault (about a composer and his principle librettist), by Isouard (1812) and Berens (1859)
Mozart and Salieri (1898), by Rimsky-Korsakov
Paganini, by Franz Lehár
Palestrina (1917), by Hans Erich Pfitzner
Pergolesi (1868), by Serrao
Rossini in Neapel (1936), by Bernard Paumgartner
Franz Schubert, by Suppé
Alessandro Stradella (1844), by Friedrich von Flotow
Alessandro Stradella (1846), by Abraham Louis Niedermeyer
Taverner (1970), by Peter Maxwell Davies
Trillo del Diavolo (1899) by Falchi, based on a supposed incident in the life of Tartini
Ochsenmenuette (1823) by Seyfried, based on an incident in the life of Joseph Haydn. See nicknames in Section IV
Eduard Lassen wrote a 'Beethoven' Overture, not as an operatic prelude but as an independent concert piece.

OPERA ABOUT AN OPERA-SINGER

Maria Malibran (1925), by Robert Russell Bennett

Gioacchino Rossini, prolific composer of operas, amongst which is his setting of *Armida*. (Royal College of Music)

'Numbers'

The successive items (arias, choruses, ensembles, etc) in an opera are often referred to as 'numbers'. This practice dates back to the days when the first operas were emerging, yet it originated in a musical drama which is more in the nature of an oratorio than an opera: *La Rappresentazione di anima e di corpo*, by the Roman composer Emilio de' Cavalieri in 1600. The convention continued until the 19th century, when there was a move away from quartering the drama into parcels. The culmination, of course, came when Wagner conceived his music dramas as a whole, the music being virtually continuous from the first bars of the overture to the final curtain. This is one reason why it is artistically suspect to perform parts of a Wagner music drama out of context, a practice which gave rise to the expressive and accurate description of such excerpts as 'bleeding chunks'.

Since Wagner, several other composers have adopted the 'all-through' technique in opera, but a reaction has set in: Hindemith, in his opera *Cardillac* (1926), reverted to numbering the set pieces in the score, thus bringing the wheel full circle.

Operas employing unusual effects or 'props'

Massenet's *Esclarmonde* (1889) called for a magic lantern for the projection of certain magic scenes.

Giordano's *Fedora* (1898) requires the use of bicycles on stage.

Křenek's *Jonny Spielt Auf* (1927) calls for a car on the stage.

Sousa's *The American Maid* (1909) was the first operetta to call for a film projector: the film that is shown is of scenes from the Battle of San Juan Hill.

Sylvio Lazzari's *La Tour de feu* (produced at the Paris Opéra on 16 January 1928) is the **first opera to use cinematographic effects.**

Boughton's *The Birth of Arthur* (1908/9) opens with 'human scenery'. As the curtain rises a castle comes into view, at the foot of which is the sea. Tenors and basses, grouped structurally, in fact comprise the castle while the waves of the sea are suggested by undulating movements of the women of the chorus.

J H McDowell's 'theatre piece' *Tumescent Lingam* (1971) requires the services of oboe, chorus, tape, rock group, 101 people, one dog, film, and lights.

The opera to which the greatest number of composers contributed is *The Maid of the Mill* (1765), assembled by Samuel Arnold from music by J C Bach, Galuppi, Jommelli, and about 15 others, including Arnold himself.

The first opera to call for a church organ was Hérold's *Zampa*, given at the Paris Opéra-Comique on 3 May 1831. Just over six months later the same feature was required by Meyerbeer's *Robert le Diable*, at the Paris Académie on 21 November.

Hindemith's *Hin und Zurück* is an operatic palindrome. It progresses normally from begin-

George Antheil's *Transatlantic* (1929) calls for a bath-tub, from the depths of which the heroine sings an aria.

ning to middle, then the music and action reverse, the opera ending when the beginning is once more reached.

Pietro Raimondi, an Italian composer who became Musical Director of St Peter's, Rome, shortly before his death in 1853, wrote a number of serious and comic operas which, if performed simultaneously, make as much sense as when performed separately. This experimental design was extended also to three of the composer's oratorios. Percy Scholes remarked that it is 'presumably a kindly time-saving device in the interests of over-worked musical critics'.

The Swedish composer L J Werle's opera *Dreaming about Thérèse* is mounted in such a way that the audience becomes a kind of circular sandwich between the singers carrying the action in the centre, and the orchestra positioned round about the edges of the hall.

The first opera to make use of the leitmotif principle was not, as may be thought, by Wagner, who nevertheless made the technique his own, but appears as early as 1781 in Mozart's *Idomeneo.* It was also employed by Méhul in *Ariodant* (1799).

The longest opera ever written is the seven-act *The Life and Times of Joseph Stalin* by the American composer and architect Robert Wilson. When given at the Brooklyn Academy of Music on 14–15 December 1973 the performance took nearly 13 hours 25 minutes, making Rosenberg's 8-hour *Joseph and His Brethren* (1948) seem of quite modest length.

The world's shortest opera is Milhaud's *The Deliverance of Theseus*, first performed in 1928 and lasting a mere 7 minutes 27 seconds.

Stephen Oliver has written three 'instant operas' for children, each lasting from 9 to 10 minutes: *Old Haunts*, *Paid Off*, and *Time Flies*. All appeared in 1976.

The first Western opera to be staged with the revolving-stage facility was Mozart's *Don Giovanni* at the Munich Residenz Theatre in 1896; the stage-builder was Karl Lautenschläger.

The idea of the revolving stage, upon which three sets were built and scene changes were effected quickly by a one-third revolution of a turntable, originated in Japan in the 18th century. Therefore, it is not unlikely that performances of Oriental operas were performed on such stages many years before the Munich occasion.

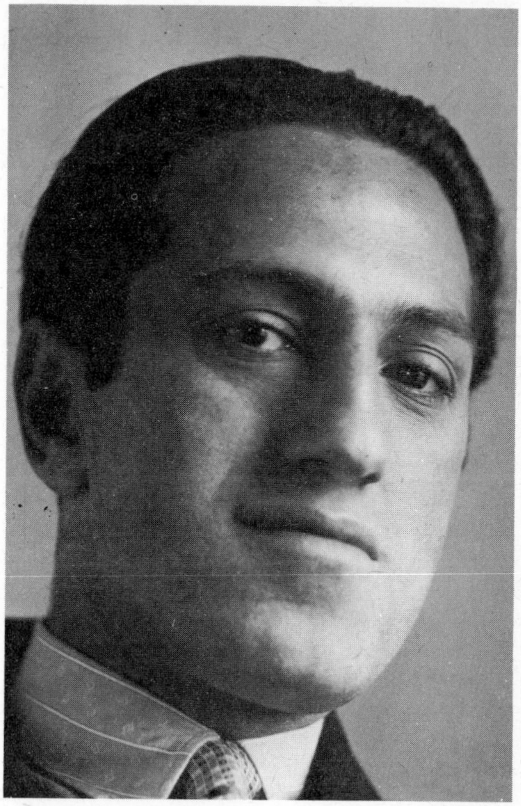

George Gershwin. (Radio Times Hulton Picture Library)

The first injunction taken out against an opera alleging damage of business potential was in respect of Hindemith's *Neues vom Tage* (1929). It was originated by the gas-heating company of Breslau in 1930 because of a scene in which the heroine takes a bath in water heated by electricity. She sings, in part:

Constant hot water,
No horrid smell,
No danger of explosion.

The first Black opera is *Treemonisha* by Scott Joplin, first performed in Harlem in 1915 and revived in 1972 by Atlanta University and recorded by DG in 1975.

The first 'jazz opera' was Porgy and Bess (1935) with music by George Gershwin and libretto by his brother Ira and D Heyward.

A purer jazz opera is *Sweeney Agonistes* by John Dankworth.

The highest vocal note called for by a composer is G‴

which occurs twice in Mozart's Concert Aria *Popoli di Tessacaglia*, KE 300B (K 316) (1778–9), and in an optional cadenza in Massenet's opera *Esclarmonde* of 1889. However, the soprano Lucrezia Aguiari (or Agujari) is reported by Mozart to have attained C‴ (ie:

in the 18th century, but pitch has since then risen by approximately a semitone, so this note would equate with today's B‴. Cleo Laine attains B‴ on the recording of 'Being Alive' by Stephen Sondheim of the RCA album 'Cleo's Greatest Show Hits', this being **the highest recorded note reached by human voice.**

Non-operatic vocal music

The earliest origins of vocal music were outlined in conjectural form in Section I. A Mesopotamian bas relief of the 7th century BC, preserved in the British Museum, London, throws light on early singing techniques. It shows a choir of six women and nine children with a group of instrumentalists nearby. One woman, presumably the leader, is squeezing her larynx in order to obtain the piercing, pinched tone still to be heard in music of the Middle- and Far-East.

A chronological survey

The two distinct styles—sacred and secular—often cross and overlap but, in order to clarify the lines, it has been necessary in the chart which follows to trace their development separately. The dates given are the earliest for which we have evidence.

Century	*Technical developments*	*Sacred music*	*Secular developments*
4th	Plainsong (four scales codified by Bishop Ambrose of Milan (*c* 333–397))	Ambrosian chant; Hymns	Accompanied and unaccompanied song in Latin. Folk-song
6th	Four further scales added by Pope Gregory 'The Great' (ruled 590–604). Chants always sung in unison. Pope Gregory established music schools in Roman religious establishments	Gregorian chant	
9th	Organum: doubling of the unison parts by another part a fourth lower. Beginnings of polyphony		
10th		Liturgical drama	
11th	Appearance of three-part harmony		Troubadours of south France; songs sung in the vernacular
12th	The rise of polyphony dictates that rhythms be indicated in conjunction with words. Plainsong with upper parts reinforced above	Conductus	Trouvères of northern France; Minnesingers of Germany Pastoral plays with music (developed later to opera)

Century	*Technical developments*	*Sacred music*	*Secular developments*
13th	Canon. Ten-part polyphony	Motets	Madrigals; Rondeaus; Part-songs
14th		Anthems	
15th		Passions	French chansons; Italian frottole in four parts
16th	Antiphonal polyphony; Homophony	Sacred concerti; Sacred symphonies	
17th	Voices with instruments	Oratorios	Masque (to opera)
18th		Symphonic Masses; National anthems	National songs; *Lieder* (German)
19th	General development of oratorio, Mass, song, *Lieder*, etc, without formal innovations		
20th	Atonalism		

The trouvères and Minnesänger of the 12th and 13th centuries were the first to secularise formal music. Important names among these artists are:

TROUVÈRES: Adam de la Hale, Guirant d'Espanha de Toloza, Guillaume d'Amiens.
MINNESÄNGER: Walter von der Vogelweide, Neidhart von Reventa1, Heinrich 'Frauenlob' (the last of the Minnesänger).

The earliest composers to write non-polyphonic (ie homophonic) music were Giovanni Bardi (1534–1612). Giulio Caccini (*c* 1545–1618), and Jacopo Peri (1561–1633), all based in Florence.

The earliest antiphonal instrumental music probably dates from the early 16th century. Adriaan Willaert (*c* 1480–1562), the Flemish composer, was appointed to the position of Music Director at St Mark's Cathedral in Venice. It is known that he experimented with antiphonal choruses in the cathedral, and it is impossible not to include that he made similar experiments with instrumental groups. One of his pupils, Andrea Gabrieli, also worked at St Mark's, and both he and his nephew Giovanni exploited antiphonal effects in their instrumental as well as their choral music.

Mass

The High Mass (or *Missa Solemnis*) is a large-scale choral work, often with orchestra since the 17th century, divided into a number of sections, or movements. Vocal soloists usually take a prominent part in the presentation of the words, which are always the same. The sections of the Latin text of the Ordinary are as follows:

Kyrie eleison	Lord have mercy on us	Greek, from pagan
Christe eleison	Christ have mercy on us	Gregorian addition
Gloria in excelsis Deo	Glory to God on High	Latinized from the Greek, *c* 600
Credo in unum Deum	I believe in one God	Added *c* 1000
Sanctus Dominus Deus Sabaoth	Holy Lord God of Hosts	Jewish
Benedictus qui venit in nomine Domini	Blessed is he that cometh in the name of the Lord	Subsection of the Sanctus
Agnus Dei	Lamb of God	Added in the 8th century

Composers of Masses are very numerous, the post-plainsong main line descending from Palestrina, through J S Bach, Haydn, Mozart, and Beethoven, and on into the 19th century with Schubert, Weber, Liszt, Gounod, and Bruckner. A restrictive Papal Bull, issued in 1903 by Pius X, prevented the continuation of this line, forcing composers to put the meaning of the words on a higher priority than the musical treatment of them. This has had the effect of diversifying the forms that choral music has taken during the present century and a number of important works have appeared which fit awkwardly or not at all into the established forms and principles.

Among these will be found Masses in national tongues, cantatas called symphonies, and some works which even the composer hesitated to label too definitely. A selection only is given:

Samuel Coleridge Taylor: *Hiawatha's Wedding Feast* (Op 30/1, 1898).
Frederick Delius: *Mass of Life* (1905) and *Requiem* (1904–5) both to secular words. The Mass is a German setting of Nietzsche's *Zarathustra.*
Ralph Vaughan Williams: Symphony No 1, *A Sea Symphony* (1910).
Arnold Schoenberg: *Die Glückliche Hand* (1913).
Zoltan Kodály: *Psalmus Hungaricus* (1923).
Leoš Janáček: *Mša Glagolskaya* ('Glagolitic Mass') (1926).
Igor Stravinsky: *Symphony of Psalms* (1930).
Carl Orff: *Carmina Burana* (1936).
Dmitri Shostakovich: Symphony No 13, *Babi Yar* (1962) and Symphony No 14 (1969).

The composer of the most Masses is Giovanni Pierluigi da Palestrina (*c* 1525–94), an Italian remembered as one of the greatest composers of the contrapuntal era. He set the Mass 93 times.

Dr Charles Burney, on his visit to Italy, described Battista San Martini (whom we now call Giovanni Battista Sammartini), as 'maestro di capella to half the churches in Milan, and the number of masses he has composed is almost infinite'.

On the continent of Europe *secular* Masses had a vogue in the late 15th and 16th centuries. They were usually based on words of a traditional nature, or on music from folk-sources.

The only English secular Masses of early days were written by John Taverner, Christopher Tye, and John Shepherd (or Shepheard). Each of these composers wrote a Mass with the title *Westron Wynde*.

Attempts to bring the principles of 'pop' music into the Church have been made by the Reverend Geoffrey Beaumont, whose *Twentieth Century Folk Mass* (1957) follows the Proper and Ordinary of the Mass, but introduces most of the current elements of 'Tin Pan Alley': pop-jazz rhythms, rock 'n' roll, song-hymns in the modern idiom, etc. The Reverend Beaumont was also known for composing hymns in the 'straight' style for use on television.

In 1970, John Dankworth also wrote a *Folk Mass*.

Missa Brevis

This is an important sub-category of the mass. The *Missa Brevis* (='Short Mass') is a setting of all the words of the Latin text in compressed form, usually running to less than half an hour. In order to obtain the maximum of contrast of tempi and texture, Mozart would deal with some parts of the text in a relaxed speed, compensating for the time thus 'lost' by running through other parts at high speed, often setting two or more vocal phrases in such a way that they were sung simultaneously. The reason for the rush, in Mozart's case, was that his employer, the Archbishop of Salzburg, demanded Masses to be over and done with in 30 minutes or less. He also stipulated that at the same time they had to feature the martial instruments of festivity: trumpets and drums. Perhaps he felt that what the music lacked in length and profundity would be made up in sheer concentrated noise. Of the several short Masses Mozart wrote, the best known is the so-called 'Coronation Mass' in C, K 317, of 1779.

Another definition of *Missa Brevis* is as a shortened version of the High Mass in which only the first two sections are performed.

Requiem

The Requiem, or *Missa pro Defunctis* (='Mass for the Dead') is a composition of mourning, once again set always to the same words. The sections of the text, which is a modified version of the High Mass, are as follows:

Requiem aeternam dona eis	Eternal rest given unto them
Kyrie eleison,	Lord have mercy on us,
Christe eleison	Christ have mercy on us
Dies irae	Day of wrath
Tuba mirum	Wondrous trumpet
Rex tremendae majestatis	King of majesty tremendous

Recordare, Jesu pie	Think, kind Jesus
Confutatis maledictus	When the wicked are confounded
Lacrimose dies illa	Day of mourning
Domine Jesu Christe	Lord Jesus Christ
Hostias et preces tibi, Domine	We offer Thee, Lord
Sanctus	Holy
Benedictus qui venit in nomine Domini	Blessed is he that cometh in the name of the Lord
Agnus Dei	Lamb of God

Prominent in the line of settings of the Requiem text are those by Michael Haydn (1771); Mozart (1791), whose setting was left unfinished at his death and was completed by Franz Xaver Süssmayr, his pupil; Berlioz (Paris, 1837); Bruckner (1849, revised in 1854 and again in 1894); Verdi (St Mark's, Milan, 1874); Fauré (1887); and Benjamin Britten (*War Requiem*, 1962). Brahms's *German Requiem*, first heard in Bremen Cathedral in 1868, is not a true Requiem in the accepted sense since it is based on German words from the Bible. It should more correctly be called an oratorio.

Oratorio

Oratorio had crystallised into a form distinct from masque and opera by about the year 1600, but in its treatment of a religious story in a semi-dramatic manner it ran alongside, and often almost collided with, opera itself.

Established in Rome in 1600, the oratorio has received the attention of many distinguished composers, from Cavalieri, through Schütz (*The Resurrection*, 1623; *Christmas Oratorio*, 1664), Pergolesi, J S Bach (*Christmas Oratorio*, 1734, in fact a collection of cantatas), Handel (*Messiah*, 1742, among many others), C P E Bach, Haydn (*The Seven Last Words*, 1785; *The Creation*, 1800; *The Seasons*, 1803), Beethoven (*Christ on the Mount of Olives*, Op 85, 1802), Rossini (*Moses in Egypt*, opera-oratorio, 1818), Spohr (*The Last Judgement*, 1825), Mendelssohn (*St Paul*, 1836; *Elijah*, 1847), Berlioz (*The Childhood of Christ*, 1854), Brahms (*German Requiem*, 1867, see above), Gounod (*Mors et Vita*, 1885), Elgar (*The Dream of Gerontius*, 1900; *The Apostles*, 1903), Honegger (*Le Roi David*, 1921), Vaughan Williams (*Sancta Civitas*, 1926), Walton (*Belshazzar's Feast*, 1931), and Tippett (*A Child of our Time*, 1940).

It will be seen that the type of text chosen for oratorio is most likely to be religious, but secular oratorios appear from time to time.

It should be noted that the usual method of distinguishing between opera and oratorio—that one has stage action and the other has not—is fallacious. In its earliest days, the oratorio was often accompanied by stage action; and even during the 19th century some of the more dramatic oratorios were sometimes presented as dramas. Perhaps the safest way to tell the two forms apart is to decide whether a performance of a given work will be less effective *without* stage presentation. If so, the work is an opera.

The composer of the first oratorio was Emilio di Cavalieri, whose oratorio *La Rappresentazione dell' anima e del corpo* ('The Representation of Soul and Body') was given in the oratory (hence oratorio) of the Church of Santa Maria in Vallicella, Rome, in 1600.

The spread of oratorio, after its appearance in Italy, came about in the following way:

FIRST GERMAN ORATORIO: *Historia der Auferstehung Jesu Christi* (1623) by Heinrich Schütz. This work, however, is an adaptation of a work by Antonius Scandellus (or Antonio Scandello): his *Resurrection*, of about 1573.

FIRST FRENCH ORATORIO: *Le Reniement de St Pierre* by Marc-Antoine Charpentier, composed about 1690.

FIRST ORATORIO HEARD IN ENGLAND: Handel's *Esther*, of 1720. The original title of the work was *Haman and Mordecai*.

FIRST ORATORIO WRITTEN IN RUSSIA: Giuseppe Sarti's *Oratorio for Catherine the Great* of about 1800.

FIRST ORATORIO HEARD IN AMERICA: an incomplete performance of Haydn's *Creation* was given in Bethlehem, Pennsylvania, in 1811. However, **the first oratorio to be composed by an American** was the *Hora Novissima* of 1893 by Horatio Parker.

The composer of the most oratorios was Antonio Draghi (1635–1700) who worked in Vienna. Between 1683 and 1700 he wrote 37 oratorios. (See also above: Operatic Proliferation.)

The best known of all oratorios is *Messiah* by George Frideric Handel. *Messiah* is known and loved the world over by musicians and, inexplicably, by those with neither musical nor religious interest in the work and who would admit to listening to no other example of serious music. The reason for this may be the vast exposure which has been given to the work, hardly a year passing without it being given at Christmas-time, and also often again at Easter, in most of the English-speaking musical centres of the world.

Its first performance took place on 13 April 1742, at the Music Room, Fishamble Street, Dublin. From there, the work came to London, where it was given at Covent Garden Theatre on 23 March 1743, after which it spread throughout the country: Oxford, 1749, arranged by William Hayes; Salisbury, 1750, under the organist and conductor John Stephens; Bath, 1755, organised by Passerini; Bristol, 1756; Gloucester, 1757, arranged by William Hayes; Worcester, 1758; Hereford, 1759, under the organist Richard Clack.

A performance in London's Westminster Abbey on 26 May 1784, held to commemorate the 25th Anniversary of Handel's burial there, was planned on a mammoth scale: 95 violins, 26 violas, 21 cellos, 15 double basses, 26 oboes, 26 bassoons, 6 flutes, 12 trumpets, 4 sets of kettle-drums and, to enrich the lower line, a double bassoon, and specially made 'double-base [*sic*] kettle drums'. The chorus numbered 257 voices in addition to the soloists. Joah Bates directed the performance from a harpsichord specially designed with levers connecting it to the organ, 19 ft (5·8 m) away.

But it was not only in the British Isles that *Messiah* became popular. Translations into German were made by Friedrich Klopstok (1774), Johann Herder (1781), and Johann Adam Hiller (1786). The work was earlier performed in Hamburg in English on 15 April 1772 under the direction of Michael Arne, its first performance in that country; it is reported that Gluck was present in the audience. Other German performances took place at Mannheim (1777), Schwerin (1780), Weimar (1780), Berlin (1786), and Leipzig (1786), these last two conducted by J A Hiller who controlled 200 performers.

Meanwhile, the tradition of excessively large performances of the work had not died in England. At the Handel Festivals at the Crystal Palace in 1857, and then annually from 1859 to 1926, the size of the choir frequently reached 4000.

An unusual secular oratorio appeared in 1935. Its title is *Wagadu Destroyed* by Vladimir Vogel, and it is scored for solo voices and chorus (sometimes using *Sprechgesang*—'speech-singing') and just five saxophones.

Pietro Raimondi composed three oratorios to be performed separately or simultaneously as one work. *Putifar*, *Giuseppe*, and *Giacobbe* (1845–48) were first performed separately and then together on 7 August 1852, to such success that the composer fainted with pleasure.

Passions

Although akin to the oratorio, the passion is of much greater antiquity. Its purpose is specifically to enact the Passion of Jesus Christ during Holy Week, and its roots lie in the old miracle and passion plays and in the very ancient Church convention of a semi-dramatic presentation of the Passion story in which the words of Christ (only) were chanted.

The earliest passions date from before 1440 and are by unknown English authors. They were designed for performance at Mass on Palm Sunday and other holy days. These examples approximately coincide with *Passions in a New Style* by the Belgian composer Gilles de Binchois (*c* 1400–60).

The earliest known polyphonic Passion settings are a *Luke Passion* and a *Matthew Passion* (the latter incomplete), both in Latin, dating from about 1450. The anonymous English composer(s?) set the choir parts only in polyphony: the solos are in plainsong.

By the beginning of the 17th century passions were being written in both Latin and the local language of the composer, the first break having come about during the 1520s, when Johann Walther (1496–1570) wished to bring the Passion story to a wider audience.

Important among composers of Easter Passion music are the following composers: Lassus, Victoria, Byrd, Schütz, Keiser, Bach, Handel, C P E Bach (who composed 21 cantatas on Passion subjects), Stainer (*The Crucifixion*, 1887), and Penderecki (*St Luke Passion*, 1966).

Te Deum

In full: *Te Deum Laudamus* ('To God we give Praise'). Just as a requiem is appropriate to a period of mourning, so is a *Te Deum* to a joyful occasion, such as a great victory. The *Te Deum* hymn is of extreme antiquity, as are most of the other sacred texts discussed in this Section, but the best-known settings date from the last 300 years or so. Famous examples have been composed by Purcell, Handel, Haydn, Berlioz, Bruckner, Verdi, Kodály, and Britten.

The joyful expression in the *Te Deum* of 1789 by Giuseppe Sarti (1729–1802), written to commemorate the victory of Prince Potemkin at Ochakov, extends to the use in the orchestra of bells, fireworks, and cannon.

Cantatas

The word 'cantata', usually considered to represent the vocal equivalent of 'sonata', nevertheless has a much wider application, so wide, in fact, that the word is merely one of convenience rather than, as with 'sonata', a fairly precise indication of the form and intention of the work concerned. The only certain feature to be expected of a cantata is that it will include at least one voice. Some cantatas are given above in the list of 20th-century choral works; these are among the largest and longest cantatas, but other examples might be much shorter, in several movements or in one continuous section, built along chamber lines or designed for pompous church ceremonies, with or without instrumental accompaniment; and the text chosen by the composer may range from deeply devotional to permissive.

The earliest cantatas appeared near the start of the 17th century and were for a time considered to fulfil a function similar to that of early opera. In the late 18th and early 19th centuries an alternative name for cantata, again revealing operatic connections, was 'scena', often built along the lines of an operatic recitative and aria.

The composer of the most cantatas is Allessandro Scarlatti, who wrote over 700 examples ranging from chamber works for one voice and continuo to elaborate 'Serenatas' for several voices, chorus, and orchestra. A M Bononcini wrote some 375 cantatas, and J S Bach also produced a great many. His normally quoted total of 212 may be reduced to allow for some spurious works, but is likely to be increased by the appearance of cantatas which are at present lost.

The oddest cantata was *Era la notte*, by an anonymous composer. It is in the Fitzwilliam Museum in Cambridge and was discussed in detail

Alessandro Scarlatti. (Mary Evans Picture Library)

by Thurston Dart in an article in *The Musical Times*, April 1971. Written in about 1700, the cantata seems to present performance difficulties just for the sake of it. For instance, the work is in B major (five sharps) but there is no key signature at the start of the piece. This necessitates a bewildering display of accidentals. In addition, the time signature varies constantly: 9/6, 5/9, 7/8, 6/7, 5/6, 3/5, 8/3, and use is made of the duple diminution symbol signifying that all notes and rests are to be given half their written value.

Ↄ

Dr Thurston Dart suggests that this is the work written in 1698 by Bononcini as a test for the young Handel during the latter's visit to Berlin.

Sacred concerto and Sacred symphony

Developed from the motet, the sacred concerto, or 'concerto ecclesiastico', has nothing to do with concerto in its later meaning of a soloist (or soloists) playing to orchestral support. Originally the word concerto meant a 'concerted' effort of several singers, players, etc, playing together. The old word 'symphony' (*sym*='together'; *phonia*='sound') has an identical meaning. A *concerto ecclesiastico*, therefore, merely meant a group of singers singing together in church.

This was, however, a richer form than the motet. Dramatic contrasts of mood and tone were introduced, and instruments were sometimes included. It will be seen that, with the use of instruments and contrasting timbres, the later meaning of concerto was already being heralded.

The earliest sacred concertos were written by the Gabrielis, Andrae and Giovanni, in about 1585. These were for voices unaccompanied. **The first accompanied concertos** were contained in *Kleine geistliche Concerten*, for voices and organ, written in 1636 by Heinrich Schütz. Before the style died out, other sacred concertos were written by Samuel Scheidt (1587–1654), etc.

Conductus, motet and madrigal

The conductus was an ecclesiastical devotional melody, the poetic text of which was sung simultaneously in several parts. Sometimes suitably secular tunes might be used in addition to the plainsong-based church melodies. Its name may be taken from the fact that it was usually in processional march rhythm and was sung as the choir was 'conducted' to its place. The style began in the 12th century and gradually evolved during the next 100 years into the freer motet form until, by the middle of the 15th century, the conductus as such became obsolete. The motet developed into a contrapuntal work, sometimes with as many as ten independent parts, and strictly speaking is by definition an unaccompanied piece, the word 'motet' being a diminutive of the Old French *mot*='given word' (compare 'motto') or 'Scriptural saying'.

About the same time as the appearance of the motet, ie the mid-13th century, similarly contrapuntal unaccompanied pieces were being written for secular use, worldly affairs borrowing back from the Church the melodies which had been appropriated from folk-music for the sacred conductus. These secular compositions originated in Italy as *madrigale*, the word losing its *e* as the form gained popularity and spread throughout Europe, becoming particularly well established in the Netherlands and England.

The basic origins of motet and madrigal were, then, sacred and secular respectively, but as the popularity of the works grew the terms became confused with each other (and with alternative local descriptions) until, by the 16th century, not one of the above definitions was inviolable. There were sacred madrigals, secular motets, instrumental accompaniment might be attached to either, and the contrapuntal nature might disappear altogether in compositions for accompanied or unaccompanied solo voice. In some isolated instances, the term 'madrigal' might even be attached to an instrumental piece without voices at all.

The oldest canon, and the oldest six-part polyphonic work is the famous 'Sumer is icumen in', of 13th-century England. The date often given as the origin of this 'round' or 'rota' is 1240, but argument is permissible among musicologists, the latest (firm) date found by the present writer being 1310. The text of this infinite round runs as follows:

Original	*Translation*
Sumer is icumen in,	Summer has arrived,
Lhude sing cuccu.	Loud sing the cuckoo.
Groweth sed and bloweth med	The seed is growing, the meadow flowering
And springeth the wde nu;	And the wood springs to life now;
Sing cuccu;	Sing cuckoo;
Awe bleteth after lomb,	Ewe bleats after the lamb,
Lhouth after calve cu;	The cow lows after the calf;
Bulloc sterteth, bucke verteth,	The bullock leaps, the buck stands high,
Murie sing cuccu.	Merry sings the cuckoo.
Cuccu, cuccu,	Cuckoo, cuckoo,
Wel singes thu cuccu.	Well sing you, cuckoo.
Ne swik thu naver nu.	Never stop now.

Evidence of earlier polyphony comes from a manuscript entitled *Musica Enchiriadis*, dating from the second half of the 9th century. This document is a treatise originally thought to have been written by the Monk Hucbald (*c* 849–930) in Belgium but now tentatively ascribed to one

Otger, about whom little is known except that he probably died early in the 10th century.

The earliest motet *Ex semine Abrahæ* is by an unknown English composer. It was found in Worcester Cathedral and dates from the 12th century. This is, however, an isolated example, and for the first major flowering of the motet it is necessary to turn to the Flemish and Dutch composers who worked in Italy during the late 13th to mid-14th centuries: Heinrich Isaac, Jacob Obrecht, and Adriaan Willaert.

The composer of the greatest number of motets was Luigi Palestrina, who in the 16th century wrote some 600 examples.

The earliest madrigals were published in Rome in 1533 by a group of unknown composers. It is possible, but not certain, that among them were madrigals by Constanzo Festa, and perhaps some by the Flemish composer Philippe Verdelot (who worked early in the 16th century), both of whom lived in Rome. **The first madrigal composers,** therefore, are given tentatively as Festa and Verdelot, but another Flemish composer of madrigals was working in Venice at that time: Adriaan Willaert (see motets above). It was round Willaert and his followers, such as the Flemish Jacob Arcadelt, that the madrigal achieved wide popularity.

The composer of the greatest number of madrigals was Filippo di Monte (1521–1603) who wrote in excess of 1000.

After the establishment of the madrigal style numerous composers took up the form in Italy in the second half of the 16th century, among them: Cyprien van Rore (another Flemish artist at Venice), Roland de Lassus, Orazio Vecchi, Luca Marenzio, Giovanni Croce, Carlo Gesualdo, Giovanni Gastoldi, Claudio Monteverdi.

The first madrigals published in England (which country could be called the madrigal's second home) was a collection entitled *Musica Transalpina*, thus neatly and memorably indicating its indebtedness to Italian originals, in 1588. This was a group collected by Nicholas Yonge, a singer at St Paul's Cathedral, but the works therein were not actually called by the name 'madrigal'.

The first English publication of madrigals, called thus, was in 1595, when Thomas Morley, an organist at St Paul's Cathedral and, therefore, probably acquainted with Yonge, published *Madrigalls to Four Voyces* of his own composition. Just as the madrigal had become popular in Italy, so too did the English take to the new style, and many composers followed Morley's example in the early 17th century: John Milton (*c* 1563–1647) (not to be confused with the author of the same name, whose dates are 1608–74), Michael Cavendish, Robert Jones, John Bennett, John Wilbye, Thomas Weelkes, John Farmer, Michael East.

The popularity of madrigals extended well into 18th-century England. In 1741 the Madrigal Society was formed in London by John Immyns, who practised law in the City. It proved so popular that there were not enough printed parts of the old madrigals to go round the gatherings; Immyns spent much time in copying out additional parts for these meetings. Existence of this and other societies has extended into the present century, and there is a ready market for gramophone records of madrigals. It is possible, therefore, to state that **the madrigal is the oldest form of music to have retained its popularity.**

Hymns

There are over 950 000 hymns in existence. **The earliest** is Hymn 91 in the Methodist School Hymnal, attributed to Clement of Alexandria (AD 170–220).

The earliest exactly datable hymn is the *Heyr Rimna Smiour* ('Hear, the Maker of Heaven') from 1208 by the Icelandic chieftain Kolbeinn Tumason.

The longest hymn is 'Hora novissima tempora pessima sunt; vigilemus', of 2966 lines, by Bernard de Cluny (12th century).

The longest English hymn is 'The sands of time are sinking', of 152 lines, by Mrs Anne Ross Cousins, *née* Cundell (1824–1906).

The shortest hymn is the anonymous (attributed to 'J Leland') one-verse 'Be present at our table, Lord'.

The most prolific hymn-writer is Mrs Frances Jane van Alstyne (1850–1915), known by her maiden name Fanny Crosby, who was blinded at the age of six weeks. Despite this disability she

Fanny Crosby, blind writer of over 8500 hymns. (Bettman Archive)

Charles Wesley, the most prolific male hymn writer. (Radio Times Hulton Picture Library)

wrote over 8500 hymns, 2500 more than the next most prolific: Charles Wesley (1707–88).

Song

The oldest song in the world is also **the oldest performable piece of music of any sort** to have come down to us. It dates from about 1400 BC and is apparently a semi-sacred song relating the loves and activities of the gods. The story of the discovery of the song is worth relating in some detail.

In March 1928 a peasant was tilling the soil on the site of the ancient city of Râs Shamra on the Mediterranean coast of Syria at a point due east from Cape Andreas, the northernmost tip of Cyprus. He accidentally came across a cave containing evidence of an early civilisation—fragments of earthenware vases and the like—dating back to the 13th century BC. Further excavations by C A F Schaeffer and G Chenet were commenced in 1929. They revealed clay tablets upon which was inscribed a hitherto unknown cuneiform writing which was laboriously deciphered by Hans Bauer, Charles Virolleaud, and Edouard Dhorme, the alphabet being established by 1931. However, new finds at the Râs Shamra site were to produce many more linguistic problems, one in particular being a tablet containing ten lines of cuneiform characters which defied translation.

It was not until 1959 that this problem was tackled by Dr Anne D Kilmer, Professor of Assyriology at the Columbia University College of Letters and Science at Berkeley, California. Dr Kilmer was eventually able to determine that the upper four lines of script were the lyrics of a song, and that the rest of the tablet contained instructions for its performance. Unfortunately, further work is required to complete the translation of these instructions, some of which have been partly obliterated by time and the action of ancient fires on the site, but enough can be gleaned to enable musicologists to decide that the musical scale used at that time by the Ugaritic tribe is similar in form to that familiar to us today.

Due to the position of Râs Shamra on the trade routes from the north and south areas of the Mediterranean to the East, the Ugarit peoples, a member of the Hebrew ethnic group, were subjected to a great many foreign influences from Egypt, Crete, and the Aegean countries. The Hurrian language, however, produced a cuneiform writing which is only vaguely related to other Near East scripts and seems to have maintained its individuality despite outside influences. Because of these factors it is at present impossible to decide whether the song, which begins 'Hamutu niyasa ziwe sinute', is a specifically Syrian (Ugaritic) creation, or an importation. At the present state of our knowledge, either possibility is equally likely.

Once Dr Kilmer had rendered the script into singable form in 1972, she arranged for Professor Robert Brown to construct an eleven-string lyre from birch and spruce, using as a pattern drawings preserved in the British Museum and made in the 1920s by Sir Leonard Woolley at an excavation site in Iraq.

The final step in the reconstruction was to bring the song to performance. On 6 March 1974, before an audience at Berkeley University, Richard L Crocker sang the song, accompanying himself on Professor Brown's reconstructed lyre. The performance was given in even crotchets, because the clay tablets have not yet revealed the rhythm to which the words should be sung.

The first known French song was a translation into that language from the Latin text 'Cantica Virginis Eulalie Concine Suavissona Cithara'. Its subject was the martyrdom of St Eulalia and it was sung to the accompaniment of a cithara. The date is AD 882.

The earliest composers of English art songs were Thomas Ravenscroft, whose first songs were published in 1609, and John Hilton. Ravenscroft's spirit, if not his name, lives on today in one of the most popular of all nursery songs: 'Three Blind Mice.'

The first song composed by an American was 'My Days Have Been So Wondrous Free' (1759) by the Philadelphian Francis Hopkinson.

The only known example of a song sung in a court of law was when the Attorney John Brett sang 'Home Sweet Home' (from Bishop's opera *Clari*) to the jury in an attempt to get an acquittal on sentimental grounds for his client Lloyd Grable, a bank robber, in October 1935. The jury gave Mr Grable 'life', but Mr Brett was evidently allowed to go free.

The most frequently played and sung song is 'Happy Birthday to You', written by Mildred

Mildred Hill, joint author of the most frequently sung song: 'Happy Birthday to You'.

and Patty Hill in 1893. Despite its popularity, the song did not achieve its first publication with the familiar words until 1935, it being sung previously to 'Good Morning to All'.

The most monotonous song is 'Ein Ton' (1859) by Peter Cornelius. The note B (the middle line of the treble clef) is repeated 80 times in 30 bars.

The composer of the most songs was James

Hook (1746–1827), who composed over 2000, among them 'The Lass of Richmond Hill'.

The first sea-shanty to be included in an opera occurs in *Omai* (1785) by William Shield.

Lieder

Lieder is often thought of simply as the German word for 'songs', but in truth the form has rather more to it than that. The idea grew from the desire of serious-minded composers, such as C P E Bach, C G Krause and Gluck, to set poetry of high artistic distinction to a keyboard accompaniment. These composers wrote 'Odes' and songs which are direct ancestors of the *Lied*.

The composer of the first true ***Lieder*** was Johann Rudolf Zumsteeg who worked for most of his life at Stuttgart. Claims for the distinction of the first *Lieder*-composer have been put forward also on behalf of Karl Friedrich Zelter and Johann Friedrich Reichardt both of whom worked in Berlin, but Zumsteeg seems to have prior claim and is generally regarded as the composer who originated the style from Bach's and Gluck's models. Schubert is said to have regarded Zumsteeg very highly and he produced about 600 *Lieder* of his own.

Other prominent composers of *Lied* were Loewe (about 350); Schumann (about 250); Brahms (about 200); and Wolf (about 300).

Works of massive proportions

At the start of the 19th century there was a general impulse towards giganticism in music. Huge gatherings of instrumentalists and singers were assembled for the performance of existing works (see Section VI: Concerts), but alongside these appeared new compositions actually written for colossal forces, among them the *Grande Messe des Morts* ('Great Mass for The Dead', ie Requiem), Op 5 by Hector Berlioz (1803–69), which was composed in 1837 and first performed in Paris on 5 December of that year. The composer conceived the work on an enormous scale: to the large orchestra were added four brass bands (one at each corner of the group of performers) and a choir of 700 or 800, but Berlioz insisted that proportions between singers and orchestra should be maintained. In the event, the first performance was given by a mere 500 singers.

Other ambitious works were composed during the 1800s, but a further series of records was set early in the new century, culminating in **the largest work of all time** in 1927.

In 1907 Gustav Mahler completed his Symphony No 8, and when it was performed for the first time three years later it came to be known by the exaggerated title 'Symphony of a Thousand'. A representative performance might be regarded as that given in Liverpool Cathedral in 1964 when 700 performers took part: 180 instrumental players and 520 singers. However, Mahler's forces were exceeded by those required for *Gurre-Lieder* of Arnold Schoenberg (1874–1951), which was completed in 1911: this calls for an extra choir and even more instruments. Then, after eight years of gestation in the composer's mind, came Havergal Brian's *Gothic Symphony* (at first known as Symphony No 2, but later renumbered as No 1) which was completed in 1927. In a radio interview, Brian admitted: 'It was never intended for performance: I expanded myself on something which might be regarded as impossible.' The 'impossibility' was removed in 1961, when Bryan Fairfax conducted a partly amateur first performance in the Westminster Hall, London. The first fully professional performance took place on 30 October 1966 under Sir Adrian Boult.

In this work 126 instruments are actually specified (Mahler: 62; Schoenberg: 69) *not including* the string band, which of course must be constituted in proportion with the rest of the forces.

In the chart which follows, the composers' requirements for these works are listed. Also shown for comparison are the instrumentation of the most ambitious of Bach's Brandenburg Concertos, of Beethoven's last and biggest symphony, and of Holst's most popular concert work.

Biggest?

As a supplement to the above, it should be mentioned that a potentially much larger work was conceived, but has never been performed, nor is it likely to be.

In 1915 the American Charles Ives, sketched out ideas for a work which was to be a musical equivalent of a scenic picture. It was to be in two

THE MOST MASSIVE WORK—A COMPARISON WITH EARLIER EXAMPLES	MAHLER: Symphony No 8 (1907)	SCHOENBERG: Gurre-Lieder (1901)	BRIAN: 'Gothic' Symphony (1919–27)	BACH: Brandenburg Concerto No 1 (1723)	BEETHOVEN: Choral Symphony No 9 (1823)	HOLST: The Planets (1916)
Vocalists						
Vocal soloists	8	5	4	–	4	–
Choruses	2 large mixed choirs; 1 choir of 400 children	3 four-part male choirs; 1 eight-part mixed choir	2 large double choirs; 1 children's choir	–	1 mixed choir	1 six-part female choir (hidden)
Woodwind						
Piccolos	1	4	2	–	1	2
Flutes	4	4	6	–	2	4
Alto flutes	–	–	1	–	–	1
Oboes	4	3	6	3	2	3
Oboe d'amore	–	–	1	–	–	–
Bass oboe	–	–	1	–	–	1
Cor anglais	1	2	2	–	–	1
Clarinets	3	3	5	–	2	3
High clarinets (E flat)	2	2	2	–	–	–
Bass clarinet	1	2 (A or B flat)	2	–	–	1
Bassett-horns	–	–	2	–	–	–
Bassoons	4	3	3	(1)	2	3
Contra Bassoons	1	2	2	–	1	1
Brass						
Horns	8	10	8 (+8*)	2	4	6
Trumpets	8	6	8 (+8*)	–	2	4
Bass trumpet	–	1	1	–	–	–
Cornets (E flat)	–	–	2	–	–	–
Alto Trombones	5	1	–	–	1	–
Tenor Trombones	2	4	3 (+8*)	–	1	2
Bass Trombone	–	1	1	–	1	1
Contrabass Trombone	–	1	2	–	–	–
Tenor Tuba	–	–	–	–	–	1
Tubas	1	1	2 (+8*)	–	–	1
Euphoniums	–	–	2	–	–	–
Keyboard						
Piano	1	–	–	–	–	–
Organ	1	–	1	–	–	1
Celesta	1	1	1	–	–	1
Glockenspiel	1	1	1	–	–	1
Harmonium	1	–	–	–	–	–
Harpsichord	–	–	–	1	–	–
Percussion						
Timpani	3 sets	6 sets	2 sets (+4 sets*)	–	1 set	2 sets
Side drums	–	1	2	–	–	1
Bass drums	1	1	2	–	1	1
Tenor drum	–	1	–	–	–	–
African long drum	–	–	1	–	–	–
Tambourines	–	–	2	–	–	1
Cymbals	1 pair	1 pair	6 large pairs	–	1 pair	1 pair

*4 Bands each of 2 horns, 2 trumpets, 2 trombones, 2 tubas, and timpani.

continued

	MAHLER: Symphony No 8 (1907)	SCHOENBERG: Gurre-Lieder (1901)	BRIAN: 'Gothic' Symphony (1919–27)	BACH: Brandenburg Concerto No 1 (1723)	BEETHOVEN: Choral Symphony No 9 (1823)	HOLST: The Planets (1916)
Percussion, cont'd						
Triangles	1	1	2	–	1	1
Gong	1	1	1	–	–	1
Xylophone	–	1	1	–	–	1
Tubular bells	1 set	–	1 set	–	–	–
Thunder Machine	–	–	1	–	–	–
Chimes	1	–	1	–	–	–
Bird scare	–	–	1	–	–	–
Chains	–	large	small	–	–	–
Strings						
Harps	2	4	–	–	–	2
Mandolin	1	–	–	–	–	–
Violins I	√	√	√	1	√	√
Violins II	√	√	√	1	√	√
Violas	√	√	√	1	√	√
Cellos	√	√	√	1	√	√
Double Bass	√	√	√	(1)	√	√

halves, played simultaneously, the listener being meant to concentrate on the 'upper' half only, as if he were gazing at the sky and the tree-tops. Meanwhile, the 'lower' half of the music would be perceived subconsciously, as if it were the foreground of the scene. The work is then played through again, the listener focusing on the 'lower' music (the foreground) while the 'upper' (sky) music is taken in subconsciously. It appears that Ives's original conception involved enormous vocal and instrumental armies, and that it then grew in his mind until, in 1936/37, he put down a crystallised formula:

Plan for a Universe Symphony
1. Formation of the countries and mountains.
2. Evolution in nature and humanity.
3. The rise of all to the spiritual.

For this work there were to be crowds of people scattered in huge groups in valleys and on mountain-tops, forming multi-part choirs. These were to be supported by various orchestras, also spatially arranged, so that the physical aspect of the scenic picture is paralleled in music. The composer gave no limit to the number of performers to be employed; neither did he give a limit to the length of the *Universe Symphony*: he considered that the idea was beyond the scope of any individual to carry out. He invited other composers to contribute to the work, also on a posterity basis, therefore turning the work, which was meant never to be finished, into **the longest piece of music ever written and unwritten,** since its length and contents are infinite.

National anthems

The concept of the national anthem, or national hymn, is not as old as is generally thought. Two hundred years ago there existed a bare handful of anthems praising national sovereignty. The popularity of anthems, started by that of England in the middle of the 18th century, was not fully launched until the patriotic fervour of the French Revolution gave the opportunity for the widespread acclaim of 'La Marseillaise' in 1795.

The first national anthem was 'Wilhelmus van Nassouwe' of the Netherlands, the music of which first appeared about 1572. The hymn was adopted as the Royal Anthem later in the 16th century. The words (only) of the Japanese anthem, however, are much older, dating from folklore of the 9th century.

The most widely known anthem melody is that to which are sung the words 'God Save our Gracious Queen'. This tune, the origin of which is buried in the volumes of keyboard dance music of the 16th century and may derive from vocal pieces of even earlier date (there are those who see its origin in the 16th-century Portuguese dance *La Folia*), was chosen or, more correctly, seemed to choose itself, to crystallise patriotic sentiment among the London theatre-goers of the mid-18th century. Three almost simultaneous occurrences combined to rocket the tune to the heights of popular acclaim: it was published as a national song in the *Thesaurus Musicus* of 1744 **(its first appearance in print)**; it was arranged in grand fashion by Dr Thomas Arne and received performances in London's Drury Lane Theatre in 1745, while another arrangement was used similarly in the Covent Garden Theatre during the same year; and, also in 1745, the *Gentleman's Magazine* published words to fit the tune—words which are basically the same as those familiar today.

Soon, the tune, if not the words, became known abroad. As early as 1761 the hymn 'Whitfield's' by George Whitfield was published by James Lyons in a collection called *Urania*, and once the grandeur and memorability of the melody was recognised by foreign authorities, it came to be adapted by them for local languages and requirements. **The first State to appropriate the tune** was Vienna in 1782 (subsequently to abandon it in favour of an even more striking melody—see below); Prussia followed in 1795, then Switzerland in 1811. Many German States took it up during the late 18th and 19th centuries (Baden; Bavaria; Mecklenberg; Schwerin, etc) and Liechtenstein followed about 1850. Meanwhile, America was using the tune for numerous word settings from 1832, the one most enduring being 'My Country, 'tis of Thee'. Sweden and Eire have taken the tune as a basis for unofficial national hymns in addition to their more thoroughly home-bred melodies.

The tune of 'God Save the King', therefore, has been the vehicle for words sung by England, her Commonwealth and Empire, America's millions, and many parts of Germany during the ages, in addition to Austria, Switzerland, and Sweden, among others. **No other national hymn is, and has been, so widely known.**

Composers have paid close attention to the tune since its earliest days. The following is a selection in chronological order of the most famous works in which it appears.

1746	Handel: *Occasional Oratorio.*
1763	J C Bach: Keyboard Concerto in D, Op 1/6.
1804	Beethoven: *Seven Variations on God Save the King.*
1812	Beethoven: 'Battle of Vittoria' Symphony.
1815	Weber: Cantata: *Kampf und Sieg*, J 190.
1818	Mayer: *Concert Variations on God Save the King.*
1818	Weber: *Jubel* Overture, J 245.
1829	Paganini: Variations for violin and orchestra, Op 9.
1831	Heinrich: Orchestral Fantasy *Pushmataha.*
1870/1	Brahms: *Triumphlied*, for chorus and orchestra, Op 55.
1891	Ives: *Variations, etc, on a National Hymn* for organ.
1892	Dvořák: Cantata: *The American Flag.*
1912	Ives: *Lincoln, The Great Commoner*, for chorus, orchestra, and piano.
1960	Boisselet: *Symphonie rouge*

Beethoven and Weber also made vocal arrangements of the melody. Both Ives and Dvořák based their works on 'God Save America'.

The most influential national anthem: the simple nobility of 'God Save the King' immediately aroused the envy of other countries. First came the claims as to authorship of the tune, from Scotland, Germany, France, and even Moravia. Such claims are still made today—and listened to—in some quarters, but the fact is that the true composer of the melody is not known and will probably never be known. The nearest we can get to the truth is that several tunes bear a resemblance to it, and it may have been arranged by any one of the contenders (Purcell and John Bull being among them) from a number of dance tunes of a folk-character. It would be delightfully tidy if one day evidence were to be unearthed to prove beyond doubt that the melody was written by the appropriately named John Bull (1562–1628), but history and musicology are unlikely to be as kind as that.

After the authorship claims came the 'borrowings': other territories using the tune for their own words—see above. Following that came the imitations, the greatest being that by Haydn for Austria. If it had not been for the introduction of 'La Marseillaise' in 1795, showing prospective national-anthem writers that an aggressive march would do to arouse national feeling just as well as would a hymn tune, the British anthem would have had even more imitations than it has.

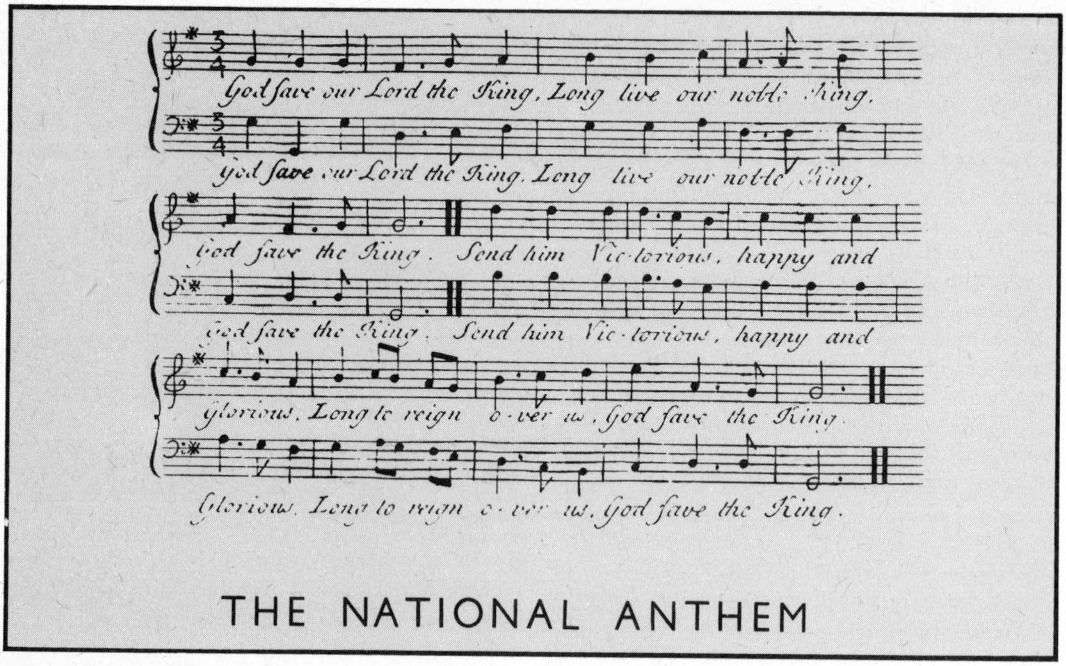

The first publication of the English National Anthem: in *Thesaurus Musicus*, 1744. (*The Queen*, May 1935/John Frost Historical Newspaper Service)

The national anthem with the most number of verses is that belonging to Greece. In 1823, Dionysios Solomós, the Greek poet, provided 158 four-line stanzas. For general use, however, the anthem is considerably shortened.

The longest anthem in the world is Argentina's 'Marcha de la Patria', composed by Blas Parera in 1813. It has an extended two-part Prelude, and a short instrumental link leading to a verse of 33 bars and a final chorus of 17 bars.

The only national hymn to have been written by a ruling monarch is 'Himno da Carta' of Portugal, composed and written by Pedro I of Brazil in 1822 to commemorate that country's independence from Portugal. Four years later he followed his father John VI as King of Portugal, and he brought home with him the anthem, leaving Brazil to replace it with its own hymn nearly 100 years later.

The 'Himno da Carta' is probably **the fastest composed in the world.** Legend has it that King Pedro I of Brazil commenced writing it at 5.30 pm on 7 September 1822, and completed it, words and music, by 9 pm. It was sung in São Paulo that same night by the King himself (an accomplished musician with an opera to his credit) and a full chorus.

The most travelled national hymn tune is that known as the 'Polish Prayer', which migrated across Europe as follows: Composed by the French singer Jean-Pierre Solié as an aria 'Qu'on soit Jalouse' in his opera *Le Secret* (1796), which was performed in 1810, in Poland. Arranged by the Polish composer Karol Kurpiński in 1815 as the Polish national hymn with the text beginning 'Bože coš Polske przez tak liezne wieki'. This anthem was forbidden in 1866 and replaced by the 'Hymn Polski' with words and music by J Wybicki. The descendant of the original Solié melody is heard today in Upper Silesia, and in Olomuč, Czechoslovakia, with a variant of the Polish words: 'Bože coš račil před tisice lety'. In Germany it is sung in public schools to more robust words, and was sung in the German Army as 'Zehntausend Mann, die zogen ins Manöver'. Finally, Italy has made of it a song beginning 'Vien qua, Dorina bella'.

Above left: Pope Pius IX (1846–1878—longest pontificate in history) for whose coronation Charles François Gounod (above) wrote *Marcia Pontificale*. (Mary Evans and Radio Times Hulton)

The only anthem to have been composed by a woman was 'Kent gij dat volk vol heldenmoed' ('Know Ye This Race of Bravery'), written as the Transvaal anthem in 1875 by Cathrine Felicie van Rees, who also composed operettas. This anthem has fallen out of use today, having been superseded by that for South Africa.

Anthems composed by famous composers. By far the best known, and also probably the greatest of all, is the 'Emperor's Hymn', by Franz Joseph Haydn. While he was in London, the ageing Austrian composer was repeatedly struck by the dignity of the British national anthem, 'God Save the King', which was played on every occasion of even the most modest importance. Back in Vienna, he composed a melody of similar nobility, incorporating it as the second movement of his String Quartet in C, Op 76, No 3. In this form it is given a set of four variations. The melody quickly became adopted in Austria and Germany as the national anthem or hymn, and it still survives as the national tune of the German Federal Republic (West Germany).

Paganini wrote Variations on Haydn's tune in his *Maestosa Sonata sentimentale* for violin (G string only) and orchestra (1828); and the peroration of Smetana's *Festival* Symphony in E (1854) is based on it.

Charles Gounod, the French composer, wrote his *Marcia Pontificale* in 1846 for the coronation of Pope Pius IX. This wordless march was adopted in 1949 as the official 'anthem' of the Vatican City. The tune used as a national hymn by Egypt (United Arab Republic) was reputedly written by Giuseppe Verdi (1813–1901), but there is no evidence that this attribution is correct. Probably the word was put about by Egyptian officials that the Italian composer was responsible, since the opera *Aïda*, written to commemorate the opening of the Cairo Opera House in 1871, had made him the most popular composer in that rather musicless nation.

Austria's present national anthem is an arrangement by V Kelerdorfer of Mozart's 'Brüder, reicht die Hand zum Bunde' from his *Masonic Cantata*,

K 623, written in 1791. Appropriate words were written by Paula Preradović.

The country with the most national songs is, and was, Germany. Some of the anthems were unofficial, the dates given referring only to the time when they first became widely known.

1. *Heil dir im Siegerkranz* (1794)
   Words: H Harries (1790) and B Schumacher (1793);
   Music='God Save the King'
2. 'Prussian People's Song' (*c* 1816)
   Words: J F L Duncker
   Music: G L P Spontini
3. *Ich bin ein Preusse* (1834)
   Words: B Thiersch
   Music: A H Neithardt
4. *Was ist des Deutschen Vaterland?* (*c* 1845)
   Words: E M Arndt (1813)
   Music: J Cotta (1813)
   (Alternative tune: G Reichardt (1826))
5. *Die Wacht am Rhein* (1854)
   Words: M Schneckenburger (1840)
   Music: K Wilhelm
6. *Deutschland, Deutschland über Alles* (adopted 11 August 1922)
   Words: A H H von Fallersleben (1841)
   Music: F J Haydn (1797)

Although this anthem has been replaced by the entries below, it still endures as the Anthem of West Germany with the words 'Einigkeit und Recht und Freiheit' (adopted 1950). The melody is still as powerfully evocative as ever, but the original opening words lost a deal of credibility during the Second World War when cartoonists, depicting the American and English 1000-bomber raids on German cities, had their crews singing 'Allies, Allies über Deutschland').

7. *Horst Wessel-Lied* (adopted by the Nazi Party in 1933)
   Words and Music: H Wessel
8. *Land des Glanens, Deutsches Land* (adopted in 1950 by West Germany, but almost immediately replaced with 6, with its new words)
   Words: R A Schröder
   Music: M H Reutter
9. *Auferstanden aus Ruinen* ('From the Ruins') (adopted by the East German authorities in 1949)
   Words: J R Becher
   Music: H Eisler

In former days, some of the German *Länder* or States had their own anthems, many of them based on the music of 'God Save the King', with words adapted to local rulers.

BAVARIA

1. *Heil unserm König, Heil!* (*c* 1805)
   Words: ?
   Music:='God Save the King'
2. *Bayern, O Heimatland* (1848)
   Words: F Beck
   Music: F Lachner
3. *Gott mit Dir, Du Land der Bayern* (*c* 1856)
   Words: M Öchsner
   Music: K M Kunz

HESSE

Heil, unserm Fürsten Heil (*c* 1800)
Words: ?
Music:='God Save the King'

MECKLENBURG-SCHWERIN

1. *Gott segne Friedrich Franz* (*c* 1795)
   Words: ?
   Music:='God Save the King'
2. *Heil Dir Paul Friedrich* (*c* 1825)
   Words: ?
   Music: ='God Save the King'

SAXONY

1. *Den König segne Gott*
   Words: G C A von Richter
   Music: ='God Save the King'
2. *Gott segne Sachsenland*
   Words: A Mahlmann
   Music:='God Save the King'

SCHLESWIG-HOLSTEIN

Schleswig-Holstein meerumschlungen
Words: M F Chemnitz
Music: C G Bellmann

WESTPHALIA

Ihr mögt den Rhein den stolzen preisen (1868)
Words: E Ritterhans
Music: P J Peters

WÜRTTEMBERG

1. *Heil unserm König, Heil* (*c* 1800)
   Words: ?
   Music:='God Save the King'
2. *Preisend mit viel Schönen Reden* (1826)
   Words: J Kerner
   Music: trad

The world's national hymns, anthems, and marches

The following list includes also songs which have assumed the importance of national tunes without being officially accepted as such. Among these are some songs which are certainly prominent in the folk-cultures of their respective countries without necessarily having the solemnity or decorum which would be required at important national events: Australia's 'Waltzing Matilda', for instance, or America's 'Yankee Doodle Dandy'. However, these tunes are included because they have proved their value in times of war in rousing the spirits, and sometimes the patriotic zeal, of soldiers of their nations.

The dates of adoption will be seen to differ considerably in some cases from the dates of composition, but where there is only a short delay between the dates it has been felt unnecessary to include the earlier date.

In some cases where a country has more than one anthem or national song, whether official or unofficial, chronological order has been adopted.

With the politics of the world in a fluid state it is not possible to prevent a list of this sort going out of date before it reaches the printers. However, it is felt that the list will be of use historically, which is the reason that many anthems (for instance, those of eastern European countries and Afghanistan and Iran), are included even though they have been submerged by political events.

Country	*Title*	*Date of adoption* * *unofficial*	*Words*	*Music*	*National/ Independence/ Saint day(s)*
Afghanistan	'Our Brave and Much-loved Ruler'	1930	M Makhtar	M Faruk	27 May
Africa (the whole continent)	'Nkosi Sikelel'i Africa'	?	E Sontonga (in Zulu)	E Sontonga (arr from trad)	
Albania	'Hymni i Flamurit'	1912	A Barseanu and A S Drenova	C Porumbescu	11 Jan 19 Nov
Algeria	'Par les foudres qui anéantissent'	?	M Zakaria	M Fawzi	
America	1. Yankee Doodle (The Lexington March)	1782*	Trad (*c* 1758) (new words by J Hewitt, 1797/98?)	Anon English or Dutch	4 July 27 Nov
	2. 'Hail Columbia'	1798*	J Hopkinson	P Phile	
	3. 'My Country, ' Tis of Thee'[1]	1832*	S F Smith	='God Save the King'	
	4. 'The Star-Spangled Banner'	1931 (3 Mar)	T Paine (1798); new words by F S Key (1814)	J S Smith	
Andorra	'Himne Andorrà'	?	D J Benlloch i Vivó	E Marfany	8 Sept
Argentina	'Marcha de la Patria: Oid, mortales, el grito sa grado Libertad'[2]	1813	V Lopez y Planes	J B Parera	25 May 7 July
Australia	1. 'Waltzing Matilda'	*c* 1900*	A B Paterson	Marie Cowan (after a Scottish melody)	26 Jan 25 Apr
	2. 'Advance, Australia Fair'	?	P D McCormick	P D McCormick	
	3. 'Australia Will be There'[3]	?	W W Francis	W W Francis	
Austria	1. 'Kaiserlied: Gott erhalte, Gott beschütze, unser Kaiser, unser Land' (see p 187)	1797 (12 Feb)	L L Haschka	F J Haydn	17 Apr 15 May
	2. 'Deutsch-Österreich, du herrliches Land'	1920	K Renner	W Kienzl	
	3. Österreichische Bundeshymne: Sei gesegnet ohne Ende'	1929 (13 Dec)	O Kernstock	F J Haydn (=1)	
	4. Austria was incorporated into Germany during the Nazi régime and was forced to adopt the words and music of Germany's anthem 6—see p 187				
	5. 'Land der Berge, Land am Strome'	1946 (22 Oct)	P Preradović	W A Mozart? (arr V Keldorfer) (see p 187)	

[1] See p 185.
[2] Longest national anthem.
[3] In 1973 the Australian National Anthem Quest Committee mounted a competition to find an anthem to replace 'God Save the Queen' as the official anthem. Some 1300 entries were received from amateur and professional composers—all were rejected.

Country	*Title*	*Date of adoption *unofficial*	*Words*	*Music*	*National/ Independence Saint day(s)*
Belgium	'La Brabançonne: Après des siècles d'esclavage'[4]	1830	H L A Dechet (known as 'Jenneval') and C Rogier	F van Campenhout (revised in Committee in 1951)	4 July
Bolivia	Himno Nacional: 'Bolivianos, el hado propicio'	1842	J I de Sanjinés	B Vincenti	9 Apr 6 Aug
Brazil	1. =Portugal's Anthem, qv				
	2. Himno Nacional: 'Ouviram do Ypiranga as margens plácidas'	1922	J O D Estrada	F M da Silva	7 Sept 11 Nov
Britain	'God Save the Queen'[5]	1745	?	?	23 Apr
Bulgaria	1. 'Shumi Maritza okarwawena' ('Foaming Maritza')	1885	N Živkov	G Šebek	
	2. 'Bulgaria mila, zemya na gheroi'	1950 (30 Dec)	N Furnadziev; M Issaew; E Bagrjana	G Dimitrov; G Zlatev-Tscherkin; S Obretenov	
Burma	'Gba majay Bma pyay' ('Give Burma a Place in your Hearts')	1948	Trad	T K B Thoung	4 Jan 12 Feb
Burundi	'Cher Burundi, ô doux pays'	1961	J-B Ntabokaja	M Barengayabo	
Cambodia	'Nokoreach'	1941	Chuon-Nat	Trad (arr F Perruchot and J Jekyll)	11 Nov
Cameroon	'Chant de Ralliement'	1957	R J Afame	S M Bamba and M Nyate	1 Jan
Canada	1. 'The Maple Leaf Forever'	1867	A Muir	A Muir	1 July
	2. 'O, Canada!' 'Terre de vos aïeux'	*c* 1880	French: A B Routhier English: R S Weir (1908)	C Lavalée	
Central African Republic	'National Hymn'	1958	B Boganda (President)	H Peppert	
Chad	'Peuple Tschadien'	1958	P Villard	L Jidrolle	
Chile	Himno Nacional: 'Dulce patria, recibe los votos'	*c* 1847	B de V y Pinato and E Lillo	R Carnicer	18 Sept
China Republic (Taiwan)	1. 'Tsung Kuoh hiung'	*c* 1912	Anon	Anon	10 Oct
	2. 'San min chu l'wu'	1929	Sun Yat-Sen	Ch'eng Mao-Yün	
People's Republic	3. 'Arise! We are Slaves No Longer'	1949	T'ien Han	Nie Eel	
Columbia	Himno Nacional: 'Oh! Gloria inmarcesible'	*c* 1905	R Núñez	O Sindici	20 July
Congo (formerly French Middle Congo)	'La Congolaise'	?	J Royer; J Spadilière; J Tandra	Trad	
Congo (formerly Belgian Congo)	'National Hymn'	?	S Boka	J Lutumba	
Costa Rica	Himno Nacional: 'Noble patria, tu hermosa bandera'	1853	J M Zeledón (1903, replacing anonymous words)	M M Gutiérrez	15 Sept

[4] In 1951 this anthem replaced the original Flemish 'De Vlaamsche Leeuw' of 1845, which had words by H v Peene and music by K Miry.
[5] See p 184 f.

Country	*Title*	*Date of adoption *unofficial*	*Words*	*Music*	*National/ Independence/ Saint day(s)*
Cuba	'La Bayamesa: Al combate corred Bayameses'	1868	P Figueredo	P Figueredo	20 May
Czecho-slovakia	'Kdi Domov Můj?[6]	1919	J K Tyl	F Škroup (1834)	
Dahomey	'Enfants du Dahomey, debout'	1960	Committee	G Dagnon	
Denmark	1. Royal Anthem: 'Kong Kristian'	c 1780*	J Ewald	D L Rogert	11 Mar 5 June
	2. National Anthem: 'Der er et yndigt Land' ('There is a winsome land')	1844*	A Ohlenschläger	H E Krøyer	
	3. 'Den gang jeg drog afsted'	19th cent	F Faber	J O E Horneman	
Dominican Republic	1. 'Himno de Capotillo'	c 1865	I M Calderón	I M Calderón	17 July
	2. Himno Nacional de la République Dominicana: 'Quisqueyanos valientes, alcemas'	1900	E Prud'homme	J Reyes (1883)	
Ecuador	'Salve! O Patria!'	1866	J L Mera	A Neumann (1866)	11 Aug
Eire	Amhrón na bhFiann ('The Soldier's Song') ('We'll sing a song a soldier's song')	1926 (July).	P Kearney	P Kearney and P Heaney (c 1917)	17 Mar
El Salvador	Himno Nacional: 'Saludemos la patria orgullosos'	1953	J J Cañas	J Aberle (c 1855)	15 Sept
Estonia	Eesti Hümn: 'Mu isamaa' ('My Country')	c 1917	J W Jannsen (1865)	F Pacius (1848) (The same tune as that of the Finnish anthem)	
Ethiopia (Abyssinia)	Hymne National: 'Etiopia hoy, des yibalish'	1930	Trad (selected by Committee)	K Nalbandian (1925)	5 May 23 July
Faroe Islands	'Tú alfagra land mílt,	1907	S av Skardi	P Alberg	19 July
Finland	'Maamme laulu' ('Our Land')	1848	J L Runeberg	F Pacius (=The Estonian anthem)	6 Dec
France	1. 'La Marseillaise'	1795 (15 July)	R de L'Isle	R de L'Isle (1792)	
	2. 'Partent pour la Syrie'[7]	1852	A de la Borde	L Drouet	
Gabon	'La Concorde'	1960	G Damas	G Damas	
Germany[8]					
Ghana	'Lift High the Flag of Ghana'	1957	P Gbeho	P Gbeho	6 Mar
Greece	Hymn to Freedom: 'Se gnorizo apo tin Kopsi'	1863	D Solomós (1823–24) (158 stanzas, see p 186	N Manzaros	25 Mar
Greenland	'Nangminek Erinalik' (The Danish Anthem is also used)	?	H Lund	J Petersen	
Guatemala	Himne Nacional: 'Guatemala feliz'	1887/1934	J J Palma	R A Oraile	15 Sept
Guinea	'Liberté'	?	–	A' Yaya	2 Oct
Haiti	'La Dessalinienne'	1903	J Lhérisson	N Geffrard	1 Jan
Honduras	Himno Nacional: 'Compatriotas, de Honduras los fueros'	1915	A C Coello	C Hartling	15 Mar 15 Sept

[6] This and the Slovak anthem were combined in 1919.
[7] La Marseillaise returned as the National Anthem in 1873.
[8] See above: **the country with the most National Songs, and the entry for Austria.**

Country	Title	Date of adoption *unofficial	Words	Music	National/ Independence Saint day(s)
Hungary	1. *Rákóczy March*	18th cent*	–	Trad (arr V Ružička (1810) and J Bihari)	
	2. 'Szózat' ('The Appeal'): 'Hazádnak rendűletlenűl hégy hive óh magyar!'	1836	M Vörösmarty	B Egressy	
	3. Himnusz: 'Isten áldd még a magyart'	1842	F Kölczey (1823)	F Erkel	
Iceland	Lofsöngur: 'O Gud vors land'	1874*	M Jochumsson	S Sveinbjörnsson	17 June
India	1. 'Vande Mataram'	*c* 1896	B C Chatergee	R Tagore	16 Jan
	2. 'Janâ-Ganâ-Manâ'	1950 (24 Jan)	R Tagore	R Tagore (arr H Murrill; N Richardson)	15 Aug
Indonesia	'Indonesia Raya' ('Indonesia, Fatherland')	1949	W R Supratman	W R Supratman	17 July
Iran	1. 'Salamati, Schah'	*c* 1873	Anon	P Lemaire	5 Aug
	2. Imperial Salute: 'Shahanshah i ma Zandah bada' A new anthem is yet to be announced	*c* 1934	H Afsar	D Nadjmi Moghaddam	26 Oct
Iraq	1. Iraq Royal Salute	1923	–	A Chaffon; A R Murray;	
	2. National Salute	1959	–	L Zambaka	
Isle of Man	Manx National Anthem	1907	W H Gill	Trad (arr W H Gill)	
Israel	'Hatikvah' ('Hope')				
	Zionist movement:	1897	N H Imber (Hebrew)	Trad	13 May
	Israel State:	1948	N Salaman (English)	(arr S Cohen)	
Italy	1. *Marcia Reale*	1834*	–	A Gabelli	6 June
	2. 'Inno di Garibaldi' (previously: 'Inno di guerra dei cacciatore delle Alpi'—'Battle Hymn of the Alpine Hunters')	1860*	L Mercantini	A Olivieri	
	3. Giovinezza	1922	M Manni	G Blanc, arr G Castoldo	
	4. 'Inno di Mameli:' 'Fratelli d'Italia, l'Italia s' è desta'	1946 (2 June)	G Mameli	M Novaro (1847)	
Ivory Coast	'Abidjanaise'	1960	Committee	P M Pango	
Japan	'Kimigayo' ('The Peaceful Reign')	1880*	Trad (9th cent)	H Hirokami (Revised F Eckert)	19 Apr 3 May 3 Nov
Johore	'Lago Bangsa Jahore'	1879	H M S B H Sulieman	M Galistan	
Jordan	''A shaal Maleek'	1946	A I Ar-Rifaa'i	A At-Tauuir	22 Mar 15 Mar
Kenya	'Land of the Lion'	1963	C Ryan	C Ryan	
Korea (South)	'Tonghai Moolkura Paiktu Sani''	1945	Trad	An Ik Tae	15 Aug
Korea (North)	'Morning Sun, shine over the Rivers and Mountains'	1949	Pak se Jen	Kim won Gûn	
Kuwait	National Salute	?	–	Trad	

Country	Title	Date of adoption *unofficial	Words	Music	National/ Independence/ Saint day(s)
Latvia	Nacionata Himna: 'Dievs, sveti Latviju'	1873*	K Baumanis	K Baumanis	
Lebanon	Humne Nationale: 'Kullu na lil watan lil 'ula lil'alam'	1926	R Nakhlé	W Sabra; M El-Murr	
Liberia	L'Inno Nazionale: 'Salve, Libera, Salve!'	c 1864	D B Warner	O Luca	16 July
Libya	'Ya Biladi'	1952	A B a Arebi	A Wahab	24 Dec
Liechten-stein	'Oberst am Jungen Rhein'	c 1850	H H Jauch	= 'God Save the King'	16 Aug
Lithuania	Lietuvos Himnas: 'Lietuva tévyné músu' ('Lithuania, my Country')	1918	V Kudirka	V Kudirka	
Luxemburg	'Ons Hémécht' ('Our Motherland')	1859	M Lentz	A Zinnen	23 Jan
Malagasi	'O bien-aimée terre de nos ancêtres'	1960	K Rabajaso	N Rabarsoa	
Malawi	'O God, bless our land Malawi'	1964	M F P Sanka	M F P Sanka	
Malaysia Malaya	'Negara Ku' ('My Country')	1957	M I A A Aziz	Trad	1 Feb 31 Aug
Mali	'A Ton Appel, Mali'	?	E Gambetta	E Gambetta	
Malta	1. 'Tifhira lil Mâlta' ('Mâlta's Song of Praise')	c 1910*	G A Vassallo (1870)	Trad	
	2. Innu Malti: 'Lil din l'art Helwa'	?	D K Psaila	R Samut	
Mauritania	Anthem	1958	–	Nikiprovetzki	
Mexico	Himno Nacional: 'Mexicanos, al grito de guerra'	1854 (16 Sept)	F G Bocanegra	J D Nunó, arr B Beltrán	16 Sept
Monaco	'Hymne Monegasque'	1867	L Canis	B de Castro	19 Nov
Morocco	'Hymne Cherifien'	1956	–	L Morgan	7 Mar
Nepal	'Shri màn gumbhira Nèpâli'	?	Trad	Trad	18 Feb
Nether-lands	1. 'Wilhelmus van Nassouwe'[9]	16th cent	P M van St Aldegonde (c 1590)	Trad (c 1572, first pub 1616)	30 Apr
	2. 'Wien Neerlandsch bloed' ('When Netherland Blood')	c 1830*	H Tollens	J W Wilms (1815)	
Newfound-land	'When Sunrays Crown the Pineclad Hills'	1901	C C Boyle	C H Parry	
New Zealand	'God Defend New Zealand'	1940	T Bracken	J J Woods (1876); R A Horne	6 Feb 25 Apr
Nicaragua	Himo Nacional: 'Salve a ti Nicaragua'	1939 (words)	S I Mayorga (1917)	A Castinove? (before 1821)	15 Sept
	'Hermosa Soberana'[10]	–	B Villatas	A Cousin	
Niger	'La Nigérienne'	1961	?	?	
Nigeria	'Nigeria, We hail Thee'	1960	L J Williams	Francis Benda	
Norway	1. 'Sønner av Norge' ('Children of Norway')	c 1850*	H Bjerregaard (1820) B Bjørnsson (1859)	C Blom (1820)	7 May
	2. 'Ja, vi elsker dette landet' ('Truly do we love this country')	1864	(1859)	R Nordraak	
	3. Gud signe vàrt dyre Fedreland		E Blix	C E F Weyse	
	4. Gud signé Noregs land		A Garborg	J Halvorsen	
Pakistan	'Pak sarzamin shabad' ('Pakistan, sacred country')	1953	A A H Jullunduri	A G Chagla	23 Mar 14 Aug

The first national Anthem.
[10] This song is sometimes mistaken for the Nicaraguan anthem.

Country	*Title*	*Date of adoption *unofficial*	*Words*	*Music*	*National/ Independence Saint day(s)*
Panama	Himno Istmeño: Alcanzamos por fin la victoria'	1903 (4 Nov)	D J de la Ossa	D S Jorgea	3 Nov
Paraguay	Himno Nacional: 'Paraguayos, República ó muerte!'	1846	F A de Figueroa	E Dupuy, or L Cavedagni	14 May 15 Nov
Peru	Himno Nacional: 'Samos libres, seámos lo siempre'	1821 (rev 1869)	J de la T Ugarte	J B Alzedo (rewritten 1912, by C Rebagliati)	28 July
Philippines	*Marcha Nacional Filipina*	1898	J Palma	J Felipe	4 July
Poland	1. Hymn Polski: 'Bože, coš Polske przez tak liezne wieki'[11]	1815	A Felinski	K Kurpinski (after J P Solié)	
	2. 'Z dyman pažarów z kurzem krwi bratniej'	*c* 1863	H Ujeski	J Nikorowicz	
	3. 'Jeszcze Polska nie zgineta'	1927	J Wybicki	?M K Oginski (*c* 1800)	
Portugal	1. Himno da Carta: 'O Patria, O Rei, o Povo'[12]	1822	King Pedro IV	King Pedro IV	10 June
	2. Hino Nacional a Portuguesa: 'Herois do mar'	1910	H L de Mendonça (1890)	A Keil (1890)	
Prussia	'Heil dir im Siegerkranz'[13]	1795	B Schuhmacher	='God Save the King'	
Romania	1. 'Trăiască Regele' ('Long Live the King')	1861 (22 Jan)	V Alexandri	E A Huebsch	
	2. 'Zarobite čatuse im uromă vămăn'	?	A Baranga	M Socor	
	3. 'Te Slavim, Români'	1953 (23 Aug)	E Frunza and D Desliu	M Socor	
Ruanda-Urindi (Rwanda)	'Rwanda, oh ma Patrie'	1962	M Habarurema	M Harbarurema	
Russia	1. 'Bože, Czarya khrani' ('God Save the Tsar')[14]	1833 (11 Dec)	V A Shukovski and A S Pushkin	A F Lvov (1833) (to replace the tune of 'God Save the King')	7 Nov
	2. 'The Internationale'[15]	1917	E Pottier (1871) (translated to Russian by A Y Kots, and again (1932) by A Gapov)	A or P Degeyter	
	3. 'Sóyus neroúshimyi respoublik svobodnyh'[16]	1944 (15 Mar)	S Mikhalkov and E Registan	A V Alexandrov	
	Byelorussia: 'A chto tam idzie?'[17]	1910	J Kupala	L M Rogowski	
San Marino	'Onore a te'	?	G Carducci	F Consolo	9 Sept
Saudi Arabia	National Hymn	1947	–	A R Al-Latib	22 Mar 20 May
Senegal	Fibres do mon cœur vert	1960	L S Senghor (President)	H Peppert	
Sierre Leone	High we Exalt Thee	1961	C N Fyle	J Akar	
Slavia[18]					
Slovakia	'Nad Tatru sa blyska'[19]	?	J Matůska (1844)	Trad	
Somalia	National Salute	1960	–	G Blanc	

11 The most migratory tune, see p 186. 12 The only Anthem to have been composed by a reigning monarch, see p 186.
13 See also Germany. 14 Forbidden in 1917. 15 Superseded in 1917, but still sung as the song of the Communist Party.
16 Once called 'The Song of Stalin, the words were revised in 1977 deleting all reference to that leader.
17 Armenia has its own anthem, with words by Sarmen and music by Khachaturian; it was approved in 1945.
18 See Yugoslavia. 19 See also Czechoslovakia.

Country	*Title*	*Date of adoption *unofficial*	*Words*	*Music*	*National/ Independence/ Saint day(s)*
South Africa	'Die Stem van Suid-Afrika' ('The Voice of South Africa')	1938	C J Langenhoven (1918)	M L de Villiers	31 May
Spain	*Marcha Real*	1770 (3 Sept); 1942	–	Anon (18th cent)	2 May 18 July
Sri Lanka	'Namō, Namō Mathā	1952	A Samarakoon	A Samarakoon	4 Feb
Sudan	'Nahnu djundul' lâh'	1956	A M Salih	A Murgan	1 Jan
Surinam	'Het Surinaamse Volkslied'	*c* 1893; 1954	C A Hoekstra	C de Puy (1876)	
Sweden	1. 'Bevare Gud vår Kung'	? *	?	= God Save the King	6 June
	2. 'Du Gamla, Du Frie'	1844*	R Dybeck	Trad (*c* 1810)	
	3. 'Ur Svenska hjertans djup en gang'	1844*	KWA Strandberg	J O Lindblad	
	4. 'Sverige, Sverige, Fosterland' ('Sweden, Sweden, My Fatherland')	1905	V v Heidenstam	W Stenhammar	
Switzerland	1. 'Rufst du, Mein Vaterland?' (Callest thou, Fatherland?')[20]	1811	J R Wyss (German)	= 'God Save the King'	1 Aug
	'O Monts indépendants'		H Röhrich (French)		
	'Ci chiami, o Patria'		Trad (Italian)		
	2. Swiss Psalm: 'Trittst im Morgenrot daher'	1841	L Widmar (German) C Chatelanet (French) Trad (Italian)	A Zwyssig	
Syria	'Humát al-diyári 'alaikum salám'	1939	K Mardam Bey	Fulayfel brothers	22 Mar 17 Apr
Tanzania (formerly Tanganyika)	'God Bless Tanzania' (The old Tanganyikan anthem)	1961	E Sontonga	E Sontonga	
Thailand	'Sanrasoen Phra Barami'	1934	Prince Narisar-anufadtivongs and King Rama VI	P C Duriyanga	24 June
Togo (French)	'Salut à loi de nos aïeux'	1960	A C Dosseh	A C Dosseh	
Trinidad/ Tobago	'Forged from the Love of Liberty'	1962	P S Castagne	P S Castagne	
Tunisia	1. March beylicale	*c* 1883*	–	Anon	25 July
	2. 'Âlâ khâllidî Yâ'	1958	J E Ennakache	S al Mahdi	
Turkey	'Istiklâl Marsi' ('March of Independence'): 'Korkma! Sönmez bu safak larda yüzen al sancak'[21]	1921(12 Mar)	M Akif Ersoy	M Zeki Ungor	29 Oct
Uganda	'O Uganda, May God Uphold Thee!'	1962	G Kakoma and P Wingard	G Kakoma	
United Arab Republic	1. Egyptian Royal Hymn (Served for the original UAR until Syria broke away in 1961)	1958	Committee (1940)	attrib G Verdi (*c* 1872) (see p 187)	1 Feb 22 Mar 18 June 23 July
	2. 'O Thou, my weapon' (Egypt only)	1960	S Shahien	K el Tawiel	
Upper Volta	'Fière Volta de mes aïeux'	1958	R Quedraogo	R Quedraogo	

[20] See p 185.
[21] Before 1921, a different anthem was composed for each ruler.

Country	Title	Date of adoption *unofficial	Words	Music	National/ Independence Saint day(s
Uruguay	Himno Nacional	1848(27 July)	F A de Figueroa	F Quijano and F J Deballi	25 Aug
Vatican	*Marcia Pontificale*	1949	–	C Gounod (see p 187 (1846)	
Venezuela	'Gloria al bravo pueblo'	1881(25 May)	V Salias (*c* 1810)	J J Landaeta (*c* 1810)	5 July
Vietnam (North)	The Vietnam Army Marches	1956	Van Cao	?	2 Sept
Vietnam (South)	'Quôc Thiêù Viêtnam' ('Youth of Vietnam')[22]	1948	L H Phuoc	L H Phuoc	
Wales	'Mae hen wlad fy nhadau' ('Land of My Fathers'	1858*	E James (English words by J Owen)	J James (Also used for the 'National Anthem' of Brittany with words by J Taldir)	1 Mar
Yemen	'Salimta Imaman Li' ar shilbi'	?	Trad	Trad	22 Mar
Yugoslavia	Serbs: 'Bože pravde' ('God of Justice')	1872	J Djordjewič	D Jenko	29 Nov
	Croats: 'Lijepa naša domovino' ('Our Fair Country')	1846	A Mihanovič	J Runjamin	
	Slavs: 'Naprey zastava Slave' ('Forward, Arise, Slav')	?	S Jenko	D Jenko	
	1. (In 1919 the three hymns were combined to form 'The King's Anthem')				
	2. 'Hej Slavni' ('Ho, You Slavs!') (The so-called Pan-Slav anthem)[23]	1945	Anon	=Polish anthem	

[22] Now presumably forbidden.
[23] In 1975 it was proposed by the Union of Yugoslav Composers that a new national anthem be adopted. That nominated was 'Sole Song' by Taki Hrisik.

Section 6
ORCHESTRAS & CONCERTS

These two vital factors in music-making are treated separately, but it should be borne in mind that their histories are so closely dovetailed that any division must be arbitrary. Orchestras, in the loosest possible sense, gave rise to concerts; and in turn concerts have given rise to more orchestras. Time and again throughout musical history, a series of concerts has led to the establishment of a permanent orchestra to play them, the orchestra then taking the name of the series. A good example is to be found in the series of Philharmonic Society concerts, begun in London in 1813. These led to the establishment of the Philharmonic Orchestra, later to be the Royal Philharmonic Orchestra which eventually led an autonomous existence. The name of the orchestra was revived when Sir Thomas Beecham founded a new organisation in 1946; therefore the present Royal Philharmonic Society and the Royal Philharmonic Orchestra have no connection with each other, the one existing as a concert-*promoting*, the other as a concert-*giving*, organisation.

Definitions

A few generally accepted words have unexpected origins:

ORCHESTRA: A Greek word referring to the space (and not to those occupying it) between the auditorium and the stage in a playhouse, a space in which dancing sometimes took place, accompanied by instruments (Gk: *orkheomai*='dance').

PHILHARMONIC: Gk: 'a lover of harmony' (therefore PHILOMUSICA='a lover of music').

SYMPHONY: As part of the name of an orchestra: taken from the primary concert work, perhaps to impute a seriousness of intention to the organisation. In America, SYMPHONY has taken the place of ORCHESTRA in popular usage. Therefore, for instance, Chicago Symphony is the complete and self-sufficient title for that concert-giving organisation.

Modern orchestras

The oldest orchestra still in existence is the Leipzig Gewandhaus Orchestra. It emerged from the Grosses Conzert, which began in 1743 and later became 'Liebhaber-Concerte' (1763) under Johann Adam Hiller. The name 'Gewandhaus Orchestra' dates from 1780, when a new room, specially built for the activities of this group of players, was built in the Gewandhaus ('Cloth-Merchants' House'). The Orchestra's most famous conductor was Mendelssohn, who took over in 1835. Until 1905 it was the convention that the orchestra should stand throughout the entire performance.

Since that time the conception of a permanently constituted body of players, whether municipally, corporately, or privately run, has given rise to a large number of orchestras. Among those still active are the following, listed in chronological order of their foundation.

1828

SOCIÉTÉ DES CONCERTS DU CONSERVATOIRE, Paris, founded by François Antoine Habeneck, the composer and violinist who gave French audiences their first opportunity to hear Beethoven's symphonies. The Orchestra gave its first concert on 9 March 1828 in the Conservatoire Théâtre, Habeneck conducting from the leader's position.

1840

LIVERPOOL PHILHARMONIC. The first concert was given on 12 March 1840 under the direction of John Russell. Philharmonic Hall was built for the Orchestra in 1849, but this was destroyed by fire in 1933.

1842

VIENNA PHILHARMONIC. Its first concert was on 28 March, conducted by Karl Otto Nicolai, the composer of *Merry Wives of Windsor.*

1842

NEW YORK PHILHARMONIC. At its first concert at the Apollo Rooms on 7 December, the conductor was Ureli Corelli Hill, co-founder with William Scharfenberg and Henry Christian Timm. The Orchestra joined with the New York Symphony in 1928, being known thereafter as the 'New York Philharmonic Symphony'.

1858

HALLÉ ORCHESTRA, Manchester, grew out of the Gentlemen's Concerts, Sir Charles Hallé taking them over on 1 January 1850. The first Hallé concerts were a subscription series started on 30 January 1858 at the Free Trade Hall, Manchester.

1864

MOSCOW PHILHARMONIC, launched under the directorship of Nikolai Rubinstein.

1878

NEW YORK SYMPHONY, founded by Walter Damrosch. It merged with the New York Philharmonic in 1928 to form the New York Philharmonic Symphony.

1881

BOSTON SYMPHONY, founded by Henry L Higginson. Symphony Hall was built in 1900.

1881

LAMOUREUX ORCHESTRA, Paris, founded by Charles Lamoureux.

1882

AMSTERDAM CONCERTGEBOUW. The first concert in the newly built Concertgebouw ('Concert House') was held on 11 April 1888, at which the conductor was Henri Viotta. The last item in the programme was Beethoven's 'Choral' Symphony.

1882

BERLIN PHILHARMONIC, a corporate body formed out of an orchestra led by Benjamin Bilse. The first concert given by the new Orchestra was conducted by one von Brenner on 17 October 1882: a long programme in three parts, each beginning with an overture. Hans von Bülow was conductor of the Orchestra from 21 October 1887 to 13 March 1893, and he gave the Orchestra's first concert in Philharmonic Hall on 5 October 1888, at which he played the piano solo part of Beethoven's *Choral Fantasia.*

1891

CHICAGO SYMPHONY founded by Theodor Thomas. The first concert in Orchestra Hall was held on 14 December 1904.

1893

CINCINNATI SYMPHONY. First principal conductor was Frank van der Stucken.

1893

MUNICH PHILHARMONIC. Established by Franz Kaim.

1894

CZECH PHILHARMONIC, formed as a society. The first concert was given on 4 January 1896: a programme of music by Dvořák, conducted by the composer.

1895

SAN FRANCISCO SYMPHONY.

1896

LOS ANGELES SYMPHONY.

1899

PITTSBURG SYMPHONY.

1900

PHILADELPHIA ORCHESTRA, established by Fritz Scheel.

1901

WARSAW PHILHARMONIC, founded under the protection of Prince Lubomirski and Count Zamoyski. The first principal conductor was Alexander Rajchman.

1903
MINNEAPOLIS SYMPHONY.

1904
LONDON SYMPHONY, formed as a co-operative organisation.

1907
ST LOUIS SYMPHONY.

1913
HAGUE RESIDENTIE, founded by Henri Viotta.

1916
CITY OF BIRMINGHAM SYMPHONY.

1918
CLEVELAND SYMPHONY. Principal conductor Nikolai Sokolov, the Russian composer and pupil of Rimsky-Korsakov.

1918
ORCHESTRA DE LA SUISSE ROMANDE, founded by Ernest Ansermet, who remained its principal conductor until his death in 1968.

1919
LOS ANGELES PHILHARMONIC.

1930
BBC SYMPHONY, founded by its principal conductor Sir Adrian Boult.

1932
LONDON PHILHARMONIC, founded by Sir Thomas Beecham; the orchestra became autonomous in 1939.

1945
PHILHARMONIA ORCHESTRA, founded by Walter Legge.

1964
NEW PHILHARMONIA, formed as a company out of the members of the Philharmonia Orchestra, which was wound up only a few days previously in March 1964. The component 'New' was discarded in 1977.

1967
ORCHESTRA DE PARIS, founded by its principal conductor Charles Munch.

In the foregoing list it will be noticed that a high proportion of the orchestras are American. The list is, however, by no means exhaustive for that country; in August 1970 it was estimated that there were 1436 orchestras active in that country, including 'community' orchestras. Among these were 30 major and 66 metropolitan orchestras. In addition there were 918 opera groups. In West Germany there are no fewer than 94 full-time professional orchestras.

Concerts

The earliest concerts, by which we mean music played together by a group of musicians and witnessed by passive listeners, must have taken place in the prehistory of music. Inevitably, music was listened to, as this has been part of its purpose from the start, so it follows that 'concerts' have existed ever since the day that two or three people grouped together to play their instruments simultaneously. In short, concerts have existed since the early days of humanity; it is merely references to them that have been lacking.

The earliest concert for which direct evidence exists took place in the 6th century BC. According to Daniel 3: 5, 7, 10, and 15, Nebuchadnezzar's orchestra in Babylon consisted of 'horn, pipe, lyre, trigon, harp, bagpipe, and every kind of music' (RV). The first reference to this court orchestra was set down in Aramaic in the 2nd century BC, and the standard translation given above appears to be only partly correct. Curt Sachs in his *The History of Musical Instruments* (1942) has returned to the original and retranslated the names:

Dr Sachs draws from this translation that the Biblical text describes not an ancient orchestra, but nothing less than a musical performance of 2600 years ago, since it would not make sense to enumerate a series of instruments (trumpet or horn, pipe, lyre, harps) and then say that they

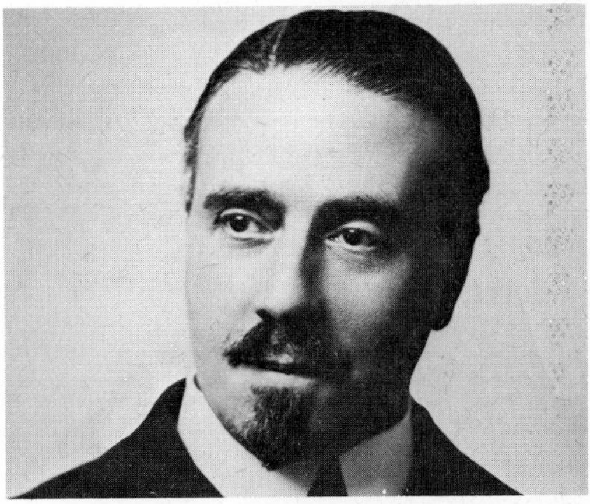

Sir Thomas Beecham, founder of the London Philharmonic Orchestra. (Radio Times Hulton Picture Library)

ORIGINAL (*in phonetic transliteration*)	ACCEPTED TRANSLATION (*in* RV)	CURT SACHS'S RETRANSLATION
Quarnā	horn	trumpet or horn (compare Lat: *cornu*='horn')
Mašroquītâ	pipe	pipe (from the verb *šriqâ*='whistling'; compare Middle English *scritch*, whence 'screech', 'shriek')
Qatros	lyre	lyre (from Gk: *kithara*)
Sabka	trigon	horizontal angular harp (an instrument similar in outline to a war machine of the time called *sabka*, which consisted of a boat with a vertical ladder at one end. The string pegs on the upright 'mast' of the instrument would have resembled the rungs of a ladder. The strings stretching from 'mast' to belly would account for the triangle suggested in 'trigon')
Psantrîn	harp	vertical angular harp (=Gk: *psalterion*)
Sūmponiah̄	bagpipe	a sounding together (=Gk: *symphonia*; 'the bagpipe', for which *symphonia* can be an alternative name, came much later)
Zmārâ	and every kind of music	rhythm and percussion group

sounded together (which is implied already), following this with the fact that they were accompanied by a rhythm group. He takes the final step by suggesting a new reading of the text: 'thus, a literal translation of the Aramaic text suggests the picture of a horn signal, followed by solos of oboe, lyre and harp [*sic*], and a full ensemble of these and some rhythmical instruments. It does not describe an orchestra, but an orchestral performance in the ancient Near East.'

The modern conception of 'concert' implies the kind of organisational control suggested by this Biblical text. There is another early reference to a concert in which the usual presence of such organisation is implied by a report of its exceptional absence: an instrumentalist in ancient Rome, a Greek by the name of Aristos, brought his players out on strike in about 309 BC over a dispute connected with meal-breaks. This is not only **the first musical stoppage due to strike action,** but it is also the earliest of all labour disputes.

The subsequent history of concerts (originally given as 'consorts' in England) is unrecorded until the 8th century.

The earliest known touring orchestra was a group of 40 Arabian females in the 8th century AD. This band made frequent pilgrimage journeys to Mecca under their leader Jarmila.

Some 15th-century manuscripts of instrumental pieces to be performed as accompaniment to dances are held in libraries at Berlin and Munich.

1482
The first Accademia, set up primarily for musical instruction, discussion, *and* performance, were held in Bologna.

1484
A similar Accademia was set up in Milan.

1570
First French concerts: Académie Baïf set up by Jean Antoine de Baïf at the court of Charles IX. Although clearly based on the Italian examples, these French meetings were less formal, consisting mainly of musical settings of poems written by members of the Académie.

1571
25 March. Waits sang and played shawms, recorders, sackbuts, violins, viols, and lutes from the turret of the Royal Exchange in London for the sole object of bringing pleasure to people living near by. This friendly practice was continued every Sunday (until stopped by Charles I in 1642) and holiday evenings from Lady Day to Michaelmas (until Pentecost in 1572).

*c*1576
Orchestras of organs, lutes, viols, recorders, and pandoras, together with voices, would entertain the audience for an hour before and half an hour after a play at theatres such as that at Blackfriars, London. The practice had become widespread by the early 17th century.

1580–*c*90
Nicholas Yonge gave private musical parties at his home in the City of London every day. Mostly these consisted of Italian (and English imitation) madrigals.

1672
30 September. Enter the demon finance for the first time: the musical performances at playhouses were not strictly what the audience had paid to see and hear; therefore, all musical performances up to that date had been free. **The first musical impresario** in the world was John Bannister or Banister. He was one of the 24 violinists of King Charles II's 'Musick', who saw a way to supplement his income. At Bannister's Music School, near the George Tavern, Whitefriars, every day at 4 pm were held concerts at which the performers, both instrumental and vocal, were placed out of sight behind a curtain. The public was allowed in to listen upon payment of 1s (5p) per head. These were **the world's first paid concerts.** In 1675 the organisation moved to Covent Garden, and later to Lincoln's Inn Fields, and finally to Essex Street, off the Strand.

1678
Thomas Britton, a coal-dealer, converted his Clerkenwell coal cellar into a concert-house and there, until his death, gave a series of concerts which started as diversions for his friends, but quickly grew famous among the gentry. Visitors are said to have included Handel and other famous musicians. At first, entrance was free, but as numbers increased, Britton was compelled to limit them by imposing a fee of 1s (5p) per concert or 10s (50p) per year.

Having established itself squarely in the environs of London, the habit of concert-giving, both for fun and for reward, became common:

1710
Jean Loeillet gave concerts of Italian and other music mainly for the flute at his London home.

1714
Hickford, the Dancing Master, gave over his room to concert-giving, first at James Street, Piccadilly, and, from about 1738, in Brewer Street, Soho, until 1779.

1720
The Academy of Ancient Music was formed to give concerts at the Crown and Anchor Tavern in the Strand. These continued until 1792.

1724
The Castle Society, another organisation centred upon a local inn, did likewise at the Castle Tavern in Paternoster Row, and later elsewhere.

While these and many other organisations flourished in the English capital, the practice of concerts was developing in the courts and residences of Germany and other European countries, growing out of the schools of music, the Collegia Musica, which themselves had evolved from the Italian Accademie, while in France another development of lasting importance was about to take place:

1725
Anne Philidor (Danican) founded the Concert Spirituels in Paris. These, the first true public concerts in France, were held in the Salle des Cent Suisses in the Château des Tuileries until 1784 and were extremely popular and influential, attracting the attention of composers from many other countries. For instance, to take the best-known example, Haydn wrote for the Concert Spirituels a fine set of six symphonies (Nos 82–87 in 1783–85, known as 'Paris' Symphonies), and even after the series of concerts ceased in 1791 there were attempts to revive the name (1805; 1830).

1731
The earliest known American secular concert was given on 16 December in Boston, Massachusetts. Announced as a 'Concert of Music on sundry instruments at Mr Pelham's Great Room', it began at 6 pm and tickets were 5s (25p) each. In the same year concerts began in Charles Town (later Charleston), South Carolina.

1736
Earliest concerts in New York.

1743
The first modern symphony orchestra was

established at the Court of the Elector Palatine, Duke Karl Theodor, at Mannheim. The orchestra was led by Jan Václav Antonín Stamic under whom it quickly became the finest band in the world. After a visit to Mannheim, Charles Burney was lost in admiration: 'An army of generals' was his description. After the death of Stamic the orchestra continued under a second generation of composer/player/conductors until 1778. (See Groups of Composers in Section III.)

Mannheim set an example for many royal households throughout Europe, among them the magnificent Esterházy Castle in rural Hungary at which Franz Joseph Haydn, who has fairly been called 'Father of the Modern Symphony Orchestra', composed for most of his working life until 1790.

A feature of 18th-century London which Haydn would have known during his visits (see below) was the gardens at which music was played. **The first** was at Marylebone (*c* 1650–1776) but **the most famous and longest established** (191 years) was at Vauxhall (1660–1859); another, at Ranelagh (1742–1803), should not be overlooked. These ornamental gardens supplemented the lively musical activities of the capital, which were mainly centred on the most famous concert-halls:

1760
Carlisle House in Soho Square (1760–80), run by Mrs Cornelys; **The Pantheon,** Oxford Street (1772–1814); **Hannover Square Rooms** (1775–1874), to which Johann Peter Salomon brought Haydn in 1791 for the start of his two highly successful London visits.

1776
The Concerts of Ancient Music commenced. They became known as the 'King's Concerts' from 1785 because of the regular attendance of King George III, and they continued until 1848.

1783
The professional concerts started, running until 1793.

The beginnings of the modern concert

By the end of the 18th century the concert principle was established throughout the musical world, but with the new century came new ideas, larger works of music and larger orchestras. Hitherto, the orchestra had been held together aurally by the leader sitting at a keyboard instrument and playing 'continuo', a device which had the dual purpose of giving the other players the tempo and beat, and filling in the missing middle harmonies of the work. As the 18th century progressed, however, this latter function became unnecessary, since the Mannheim composers had completed the harmonic structure with their imaginative use of wind and brass instruments, a technique which had been copied everywhere else.

The process of conducting with a stick seems to have grown out of three roots, and seeds of the practice appear to have been described as far back as the 13th century. In early 18th-century France it was the custom in the opera-house to beat out the rhythm loudly on the floor or a desk with a stick, a practice found as recently as 1895 in Pisa; in Mannheim Franz Xaver Richter would beat time inaudibly by waving a rolled-up music part in the air; and as the keyboard-conductor became less vital musically, the role of conductor devolved on to the leading violinist in some centres, and his lead with the bow would be followed by the other players. It was common for the conductor to face the audience until the mid-19th century.

Among the first to use a baton with any regularity was Johann Friedrich Reichardt, himself a violinist, harpsichordist, and composer in north Germany. It is known also that Mozart beat time soundlessly in Vienna, probably with expressive hand movements. Modern conducting, however, began with Berlioz, Spohr, and Wagner, and rapidly developed into an art form within itself.

With the larger music came the necessity for larger concert-halls:

1812
The Argyll Rooms, Regent Street, were opened in London, but were destroyed by fire in 1830.

1831
Exeter Hall, in use until 1880, replaced the Argyll Rooms.

1842
Crosby Hall, Bishopsgate Street, was built, to continue as a concert-hall until 1891.

1855
The first Crystal Palace season opened. There were winter seasons for the first five years, but in

Above: Handel Festival at Crystal Palace 1859. (Mary Evans Picture Library)

Below: Opening of the Royal Albert Hall of Arts and Sciences by Her Majesty, Queen Victoria, 29 March 1871. (Mary Evans Picture Library)

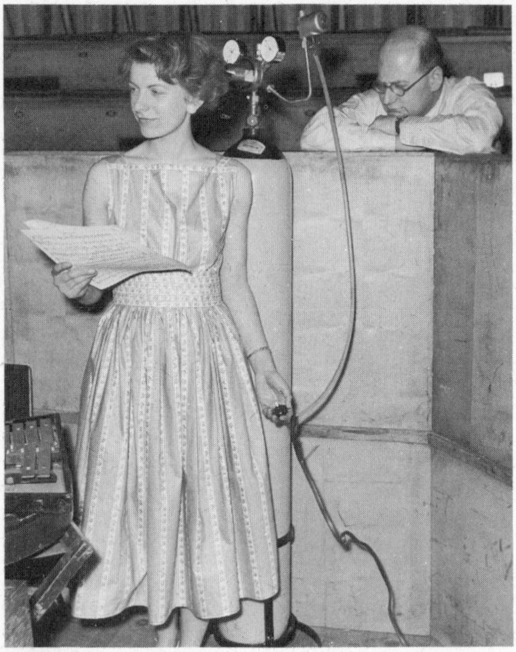

Symphony No 3 by Ernst Toch calls for the sound of escaping steam. At a concert at London's Royal Festival Hall in June 1958 Miss Margaret Cotton operates a 'hisser' while the inventor of the instrument, Gerard Hoffnung, relishes 'all the venom and threat of a wild jungle creature spitting at its enemy' (his own words). (Popperfoto)

1860 a summer season was inaugurated and the series continued until 1901, mainly under the direction of August Manns.

At the opening of the first summer season of the Crystal Palace concerts on 4 May 1860 an orchestra of about 3000 was led by Michael Andrew Angus Costa. The concert was given in memory of Mendelssohn and consisted of a performance of *Elijah* (for which the number of singers is not recorded) and the Overture and Wedding March from *A Midsummer Night's Dream*. The Band of the Coldstream Guards also 'assisted', and a torchlight exhibition followed the concert.

1871
Royal Albert Hall opened. The first concert, on 29 March, presented the following programme:
Prince Albert: *L'Invocazione all 'Armonia*.
Handel: 'Lascia ch'io piango'.
Curschmann: 'Ti Prego'.
Gounod: 'Salve dimora'.
Auber: 'Prayer' (from *Masaniello*).
Rossini: Overture: *The Thieving Magpie*.
The capacity of the Albert Hall is 7000–8000.

1893
Queen's Hall opened; it was destroyed in an air raid in 1941.

1901
Wigmore Hall opened.

1904
Aeolian Hall opened: it continued in use as a public concert-hall until 1941, when it was taken over by the BBC for use as a studio.

1951
Royal Festival Hall opened as part of the festivities surrounding the Festival of Britain. Its two smaller halls, in the same building complex: Elizabeth Hall for chamber performances and Purcell Room for recitals, were opened in March 1967.

For the future in London, the City authorities have an ambitious plan for an arts centre in The Barbican. This is to house a concert-hall (see seating plan) and is to be the permanent home of the London Symphony Orchestra, the Guildhall School of Music and Drama, a theatre, an art gallery, and a public library. In the same complex will be a students' hostel, restaurants and inns, shops,

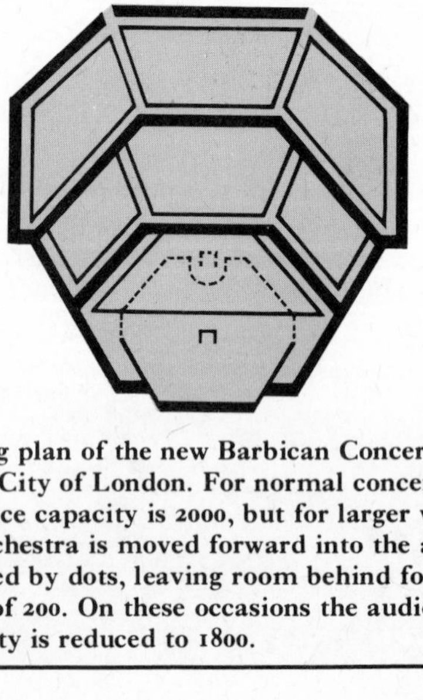

Seating plan of the new Barbican Concert Hall in the City of London. For normal concerts the audience capacity is 2000, but for larger works the orchestra is moved forward into the area outlined by dots, leaving room behind for a choir of 200. On these occasions the audience capacity is reduced to 1800.

The Sydney Opera House under construction; a photograph taken in 1965. (Popperfoto)

2000 flats and maisonettes, and ample parking accommodation. Pedestrians will be confined to elevated walkways. The concert hall is due to be completed during 1981.

Similar plans have been carried out, or are in the active planning stage, for many of the world's art centres, illustrating that accommodation for musical performance is now a matter of course in urban planning. This has not always been the case: music has too often been regarded as a pastime for the rich and therefore outside the reach and understanding of the masses (see below).

The most recent major musical building complex is the so-called 'Sydney Opera House', built on a point of land, Bennelong Point, projecting into Sydney Harbour. It may also hold the record for the slowest gestation of a concert building, since the period from inception of the idea to opening of the building was 18 years.

1955 It was announced that a concert/opera-giving edifice was to be built at Bennelong Point and designs were invited in a competition.
1957 The Danish architect Joern Utzon won the competition for his startling and boldly revolutionary design.
1958 Foundations commenced.
1963 Foundations completed.
1967 Exterior completed.
1973 Interior completed.

Total cost of the project was $A 102 000 000 which was obtained mainly through public lotteries.

Although called the 'Sydney Opera House', opera takes only a small part of the available space and is, indeed, rather poorly catered for in the design: the stage is too shallow to allow ambitious presentations, and wing area is severely restricted. Nevertheless, the name 'Opera House' is now established and is unlikely to be changed.

In all, there are some 900 rooms in the building, the major of which are:

Concert Hall, with seating for 2700.
Opera Theatre, with seating for 1550.
Drama Theatre, with seating for 550.
Recital Room/Cinema, with seating for 420.
Fully equipped recording hall.
Rehearsal Rooms.
Exhibition Hall.

The first opera to be staged in the Opera Theatre was Prokofiev's *War and Peace*, by the Australian Opera conducted by Edward Downes in September 1973.

Three weeks later, on 20 October 1973, the official opening was made by Queen Elizabeth II, and this was followed by a concert which concluded with a performance of Beethoven's Choral Symphony (No 9 in D minor, Op 125) conducted by Willem van Otterloo.

The largest opera-house in the world is the Metropolitan Opera House, Lincoln Center, New York, finished in 1966. Its capacity is 3800 seats in an auditorium 451 ft (137 m) deep and a stage measuring 234 ft (71 m) wide by 146 ft (44·5 m) deep.

The oldest European concert-hall still in use for musical performances is Holywell, in Oxford, England, opened in 1748.

Music for the masses

Early attempts were made to popularise so-called 'serious' music, among them the concerts of open-air music in the Champs-Élysées, Paris, under Philippe Musard in the late 1830s. These led directly to the famous Promenade Concerts:

1837
Henri Justin Valentine conducted a series of promenade concerts in Paris, but they were not well attended and ceased after one short season.

1839
Promenade Concerts à la Valentine opened at the Crown and Anchor Tavern in the Strand, London. In the same year began the **Original Promenade Concerts à la Musard** at the English Opera House.

1840–1
During the winter season there were three separate promenade concert series running in London, all well attended, but after many years this splitting of effort became channelled by the appearance of a single driving force:

1895
8 August, **the first of the Henry Wood Promenade Concerts** opened with Wagner's *Rienzi* Overture. Sir Henry Wood was the manager and principal conductor of the concerts from that date until his death in 1944. His services to music were recognised by a knighthood in 1911. The Promenade Concerts, which still continue with unabated popularity, were held at the Queen's Hall until its destruction in 1941, after which they transferred to the Royal Albert Hall. During post-war years the name most closely associated with 'the Proms' was that of Sir Malcolm Sargent.

Another successful operation in bringing music to a wider audience began in 1855 with the Crystal Palace Concerts which extended into the new century (see above). They were conducted throughout by August Manns in that spacious hall in spacious grounds, and furthered the 19th-century need for musical proletarianism in surroundings reminiscent of the 18th-century leisure and pleasure gardens.

In 1858 the optimistically titled 'Popular Concerts' began, being held every Monday and Saturday at St James's Hall. Being centred mainly on chamber music, their appeal was relatively limited, but they survived for 40 years, until 1898. Seventy years later (1968/69) the English Chamber Orchestra scored the distinction of being **the first chamber orchestra to make a world tour** (USA, Australia, New Zealand, Israel, Cyprus, Italy), giving a total of 28 concerts.

Popularity has always been the aim of those dedicated men and women who make music, of course, but the enthusiasm of the public can sometimes be carried to extremes:

The most encored work at one concert was the waltz *Sinngedicht* by Johann Strauss II: at the composer's first concert at Dommayer's Garden Restaurant in Vienna on Tuesday, 15 October 1844, this item, which had been designed to close the programme, did so with a vengeance, being encored 19 times.

The popularity of certain items is paralleled by the popularity of music in general.

The largest 'hall' used for regular performances of serious music is Hollywood Bowl,

First Night of the Proms, 1966, with two favourite 'Prom' personalities: Sir Malcolm Sargent conducts; Moura Lympany is the soloist. (Popperfoto)

opened in 1919 on a 20-hectare (50-acre) site in a natural depression, Beechwood Canyon, Hollywood. The summer series of 'Symphonies under the Stars' is held every year, and the seating capacity of 25 000 is not excessive.

The first British orchestra to play at the Hollywood Bowl was the London Symphony Orchestra in September 1974.

The greatest attendance at any 'classical' concert was 400 000 for the Boston Pops Orchestra under Arthur Fiedler on 4 July 1977, at the Hatch Memorial Shell, Boston, Massachusetts, USA.

Musical gatherings of gigantic proportions

The conception of large forces in the performance of organised music-making came early in the history of music. The **40-part** motet *Spem in alium* (for eight choirs of five separate voices each) of Thomas Tallis is an early example, and it is this kind of composition which led the Germans to accuse the English of being 'vastly fond of great noises that fill the ear'.

Arthur Fiedler, the conductor who attracted the largest classical audience of all time. (Decca Record Company Ltd)

However, the practice was not unknown on the Continent; the great *Festival Mass* originally thought to have been written by Orazio Benevoli for the consecration of Salzburg Cathedral in 1628, but now considered to be the work of an unknown composer working in Salzburg perhaps as late as 1682, was written for 16 vocal soloists, four four-part choirs, six orchestras, and two organs; **53 parts** in all. (This work, incidentally, one of the grandest in the history of church music, only narrowly escaped destruction and total oblivion when it was discovered behind the counter of a grocer's shop in Salzburg. But for the rapid, and probably rather startling, action of Innozenz Achleitner, once a Director of Music in Salzburg, a few hours would have seen the score distributed over a large part of the city it had been written to honour in the form of wrapping-paper.)

Later in England, Handel was responsible for another mammoth musical gathering when he wrote his *Musick for the Royal Fireworks* in 1749. The original idea was for the work to be played in the open air, and for this a massive assembly of woodwind, brass, and percussion was required: nine trumpets, three timpanists, nine horns, 24 oboes (ie three parts of respectively twelve, eight, and four per part), and twelve bassoons, a **total of 57**. For later performances indoors the wind/brass complement was reduced and a string band added.

Early in the 19th century the Czech composer Antonín Reicha conducted experiments with unusual positioning of orchestral forces, and with non-musical adjuncts (see Section IV); he also proposed an 'ideal' orchestra of twelve flutes, twelve oboes, twelve clarinets, twelve bassoons, twelve horns, six trumpets, six trombones, six pairs of timpani (tuned to accommodate all possible key combinations—an early move towards twelve-tone thinking), 60 violins, 18 violas, 18 cellos, and 18 double basses: **Total 192.**

With the revival in popularity of Bach's oratorios under the guiding hand of Mendelssohn, and the increase in choral societies in England and on the Continent, concerts involving **300 performers** became commonplace. In 1833, for instance, a performance of *St Matthew Passion* was given in Leipzig by **230 singers** and an orchestra enlarged to over **100 players**, including eight each of oboes and clarinets, 46 violins, and ten double basses. Considerations of authenticity were put last (viz the clarinets).

Performances of Handel's *Messiah* at the Crystal Palace Handel Festivals (1857, then every year from 1859 to 1926 with the exceptions of war years) regularly attracted choirs of **between 3000 and 4000**, but here again the degree of fidelity to Handel's intentions was in inverse proportion to the size of the forces.

The largest orchestra ever assembled was one of 20 100, on 28 June 1964, at the Ullevaal Stadium, Oslo, of Norges Musikkorp Forbund bands from all Norway.

The largest amateur choir numbered 40 000 in the Vasco da Gama Stadium in Rio de Janeiro in 1940. Leading the singers was the Brazilian composer Heitor Villa-Lobos who for many years had been interested in mammoth-sized groups. In 1931 he had amassed a **choir of 12 000 voices** in São Paulo, four years later he led a **choir of 30 000, plus 1000 instrumentalists** and thereafter increased the numbers for each successive annual patriotic display until the 1940 record.

In this connection should be mentioned also the experiments of Patrick Sarsfield Gilmore, a bandmaster of Irish origin, who assembled an orchestra of **2000 instrumentalists and a choir of 20 000** for the World Peace Jubilee at Boston, Massachusetts, on 17 June 1872, the conductor being Johann Strauss II. The violinists numbered more than 350 on this occasion. This assembly followed a previous gathering in 1869, when the forces were merely 1000 instrumentalists and 10 000 voices.

The most massive musical gathering of all time occurred in 1971 in Bethlehem, Pennsylvania. Both amateur and professional performers took part in a performance of *Alleluja* by the American composer Robert Moran. It involved rock groups, marching bands, gospel singing groups, church bells, firework displays, light shows, and the entire population of the town of Bethlehem which, in 1960, numbered 75 408. With an assumed population increase during the intervening eleven years, plus the numerous artists imported for the occasion, a conservative estimate would put the number of 'performers' involved in the performance in excess of **76 000.**

The first concert to attempt to popularise the Negro spiritual among white people took place in June 1872 at the Coliseum, Boston, Massachusetts. The concert was given by the Fisk Jubilee Singers, conducted by Johann Strauss II.

Section 7 MUSIC LITERATURE

Without the facility of rendering on to the written or printed page a precise indication of what music sounds like, the entire art would rely for its continuity on improvisation and memory. Performances of large-scale works would be impossible, and instrumental groups would have to invent anew each time they performed. There would be no such thing as a 'standard classic' because nothing would be standard for more than a few performances, and no single piece of music would be given the opportunity to become a classic; its spread would be restricted to a local audience, temporally and geographically.

This is one aspect of 'written music'. The literature of music goes much wider than this, however, into the realms of musical dictionaries, encyclopaedias, biographies, periodicals, criticism, and musicology—all, be it noted, impossible if precise indications of the sound of music were not able to be transferred to paper.

The oldest surviving musical notation. In Section V we discussed the oldest song in the world, dating from 1400 BC. Some 400 years earlier there existed a heptatonic scale which was deciphered from a clay tablet by Dr Duchesne Guillemin in 1966–67. The tablet was discovered at Nippur Sumer, now Iraq.

The beginnings of the present notation system were created about the year 1020 by the Italian monk Guido d'Arezzo (*c* 990–1050). He saw the need for a method by which to teach his singing pupils to sing unfamiliar songs at sight, and the system he invented has the genius of simplicity. He realised that his singers knew many hymns extremely well from memory (indeed, there was no other way of performing the tunes at that time). By taking various prominent syllables from a well-known hymn, the relative pitches of which were well implanted in the minds of his pupils, he devised a scale based on the vocal sounds 'ut–re–mi–fa–sol–la(te–ut)'. The notes in parenthesis were added later to complete the scale. This method is still used to indicate the octave C–C, sometimes the syllable 'doh' replacing 'ut'.

The text of the hymn which d'Arezzo used runs: 'UTqueant laxis REsonare fibris MIra gestorum FAmuli tuorum, SOLve polluti LAbii reatum, Sancte Iohannes'.

His next step was to establish a bass line in red ink to indicate the note 'fa' (F), another above it in yellow for 'ut' (C), and between them a scratched line made with a needle for 'la' (A). Using the lines, and all the spaces below, between, and above them, d'Arezzo was able to indicate positions for all the notes in the range from E to D. Rather later another line was added, clefs were invented to establish registers, and the other conventions were introduced to lead, by the mid-17th century, to the musical notation we know now.

Modern notation

Explanations of some familiar symbols:

Clef = **key**, ie indication of the register

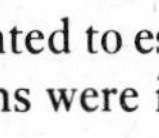

= **G clef.** A representation of a medieval letter G, the focal point of which indicates the line G.

= **F clef.** A relic of the medieval letter F, centred on the F line.

=**C clef.** Its centre point, which may be fixed on any line, indicates the position of middle C.

♭ =**Flat.** This sign flattens all the notes of the pitch indicated which follows it in the bar.

♯ =**Sharp.** This sign sharpens all the notes of the pitch indicated which follow it in the bar.

♮ =**Natural.** Indicating that a previously flattened or sharpened note is to return to its natural pitch.

=**Repeat** (or da capo). This sign instructs the player(s) to return to the beginning of the movement or piece, or to the sign: 𝄋

=Repeat the section shown between the signs.

Note lengths and their equivalent rests

In the early days of musical notation there were four note lengths: the double long (a black rectangle with a tail), the long (a black square with a tail), the breve, ie 'short' (a black square without a tail), and the semibreve, ie 'half-short' (a black diamond). A diminution of values has occurred since then so that we have today reached a situation in which the very longest note ever to be encountered is called 'short', and the longest generally used note is called 'half-short'.

Note	*Rest*	*Names*	*Meaning*
		breve (double whole note)	short
		semibreve (whole note)	half-short
		minim (half-note)	shortest (ie minimum)
		crotchet (quarter-note)	hook or crook from its old appearance
		quaver (eighth-note)	to trill, or quaver (quiver) in very short notes
		semiquaver (sixteenth-note)	half-quaver
		demisemiquaver (thirty-second-note)	half of half a quaver
		hemidemisemi-quaver (sixty-fourth-note)	half of half of half a quaver
		semihemidemi-semiquaver (hundred-and-twenty-eighth-note)	half of half of half of half a quaver

Time signatures

3/4 =three quarter-notes (crotchets) to the bar

4/4 or C =four quarter-notes to the bar

3/8 =three eighth-notes to the bar.

Other time signature meanings may be inferred from these examples.

During the present century composers have felt the need to extend all the above symbols and meanings in order to bring ever-more strict specifications of their requirements to the notice of their performers. One of the simplest extensions was made by the Romanian-born Greek composer Xenakis who, in order to reduce the difficulty in reading many leger lines (additional lines above or below the staves to carry higher or lower notes), adopted the practice where necessary of adding a continuous line to represent the note B above the B above the treble clef, and another line to represent the D below the D below the bass clef, thus:

Bar lines

Known more accurately in America as 'measures', bars divide the music into given periods to assist rhythmic stability, but in the 18th century C P E Bach sometimes encouraged expressive rhythmic freedom by dispensing with bar lines, a device taken up later by Beethoven, Stravinsky, and Satie. Federico Mompou developed a technique, *Primitivista*, in the second decade of the present century in which both bar lines and key signatures are dispensed with.

Music in print

The earliest printed music is a book of plainsong issued in Esslingen, near Stuttgart, Germany, in 1473. It is Johannes Gerson's *Collectorium super Magnificat*, printed by Conrad Fyner. **The earliest English printed music** was in Ranulf Higden's book *Policronicon*, which appeared in 1482, printed by Caxton, but the musical example itself had to be impressed on each copy by hand and some copies escaped the process. For the reprint in 1495 Wynken de Worde ingeniously contrived to incorporate the example in the printing process by using the square bottoms of ordinary type to represent notes.

The earliest publishing house devoted almost entirely to music-printing was established in Venice in 1501 by Ottaviano dei Petrucci (1466–1539).

The oldest American printed music appeared in the ninth edition of *The Bay Psalm Book* in 1698 (its earlier editions, the first in 1640, were without music; its last edition of more than 70 was published in 1773). A direct-to-print song, bypassing the usual manuscript stage, was 'Marching Through Georgia' by the composer and music compositor Henry Clay Work. He commemorated General Sherman's famous march of 1864 by setting the song directly into print.

Musical dictionaries

One of the most useful branches of musical literature is the section which contains works which explain and clarify the terms, often obscure and usually foreign, for the benefit of the non-specialist reader. While usually fulfilling this function admirably, it should not be overlooked that, except for the most basic, these volumes are of prime value to the professional musician as a depository of facts necessary to his work. Such works of reference have a long and noble history.

The first musical dictionary is the *Terminorum Musicae Diffinitorium*, compiled by Johannes Tinctoris and published at Treviso about 1498. It defines 291 terms related to Renaissance musical practice and theory, and has been considered so vital to the correct understanding of this period that it has been translated into German (1863), French (1951), English (1963), and Italian (1965).

The first combined musical dictionary and collection of musical biographies was Johann Gottfried Walther's *Musikalisches Lexicon, oder musikalische Bibliothek*, first published in Berlin in 1732 and reprinted by Bärenreiter in 1953.

The first biographical music dictionary was *Grundlage einer Ehren-Pforte* ..., by Johann Mattheson who also published the first music criticism (see below) in 1740. The majority of the biographies were first-hand contributions by the subjects themselves.

Modern music encyclopaedias

The latest, and the largest, in the succession of musical cyclopaedias come from Germany and England.

Die Musik in Geschichte und Gegenwart. Allgemeine Enzyklopädie der Musik, edited by Friedrich Blume and published by Bärenreiter. Volume I appeared in 1949. Written throughout in German but giving a world-wide coverage, it seeks to incorporate the very latest in musical research in its composer biographies and comprehensive lists of works, but since the first volume was issued so many years ago it is clear that musicology has outrun the entries in the early part of the alphabet. Nevertheless, it is an unrivalled source-book of information containing often greatly extended articles of intricate detail.

Grove's Dictionary of Music and Musicians, founded by Sir George Grove. Multi-volume reference work in English, covering much the same ground as *Die Musik* ... above, but with less attention paid to lesser composers, particularly in the matter of their composition lists. Five editions have appeared to date, each one greater and more extensive than the last:

I Edited by Sir George Grove: 4 volumes, 1878–89.
II Edited by J A Fuller-Maitland: 5 volumes, 1904–10.
III Edited by H C Colles: 5 volumes, 1927–28.
IV Edited by H C Colles: 5 volumes, plus supplement to the third edition, 1940.
V Edited by Eric Blom: 9 volumes, 1954 plus Supplement 1961.

The sixth edition is in preparation and is promised for 'about 1981'. It will be in 20 volumes, and the editor is Stanley Sadie.

Mention should also be made of the American *Harvard Dictionary of Music*, edited by Willi Apel with A T Davison.

In addition to these long-lasting reference works there is a healthy business in musical magazines in all the musically aware countries of the world. Essentially journalistic, these publications nevertheless carry a vast amount of information which fails to find a place between hard covers: many of the articles, particularly those dealing with musicological subjects by some of the most eminent writers in the field, should achieve a more secure permanency. Fortunately, Detroit Information Service Inc publishes its own periodical which is devoted to indexing the material in others, thereby preventing this valuable material from being buried unknown in library basements.

Journals

The first musical journal was *Musica Critica*, edited by Johann Mattheson. The first number was published in Hamburg in 1722; it contained **the first published music criticisms.**

After this date the useful if not always responsible practice of musical criticism was slow to spread.

The first French musical journal, *Journal de Musique Française et Italienne*, appeared in 1764.

The first British musical journal, *The New Musical and Universal Magazine*, appeared in 1774.

The first American musical journal, *American Musical Magazine*, appeared in 1786.

But by the end of the 18th century the art of criticism was well established, particularly in Germany, where the really serious business of discussing the art of music in scientific detail was begun by the *Allgemeine Musikalische Zeitung*, first published in Leipzig in 1798.

The oldest still-existing British musical magazine is *The Musical Times*, which first appeared in 1844, as *The Musical Times and Singing Class Circular*. It was based on *Mainzer's Musical Times and Singing Circular*, founded by the German musician Joseph Mainzer in 1842.

The first Czech language music periodical was *Cecilia*, founded by Josef Krejčí in 1848.

Musical criticism

We have already noted, above, the first printed musical criticisms (in Mattheson's *Musica Critica*) in 1722.

The first English music criticism of any consequence appeared in 1752, when Charles Avison published his *Essay on Musical Expression.*

The first French music criticism appeared in a pamphlet *Letter on French Music*, written by Jean-Jacques Rousseau and published in 1753. It was written specifically to attack the French operatic school and to praise the Italian. A sharp divide had been caused in Parisian taste by the performance the previous year of an old opera by Destouches, very much in the old-fashioned French style, and the rival appearance of Italian artists in Pergolesi's *La Serva Padrona* (1733). This led to **one of the first musical hoaxes**: the performance of an opera said to be by an Italian composer living in Vienna but actually, as was later revealed, by the Frenchman Dauvergne. After this opera, *Les Trocqueurs* (1753) written in imitation of the Italian style, Dauvergne reverted to the French method, feeling perhaps that he had won the day by having an Italian-style French opera acclaimed and that he could now return to the serious matter of making real French operas.

The first American music criticism did not appear until *Dwight's Journal of Music*, published in Boston in 1852.

Programme notes

The earliest programme notes appear to have been prepared by the French Prime Minister

Cardinal Mazarin to apprise the audience of events in a performance of Rossi's Italian opera *Orfeo*, given in Paris in 1647.

The composer as author

A selection of books, both autobiographical and otherwise, written by composers, giving insight into the backgrounds, philosophies, intentions, and aspirations of the composers concerned. Dates are those of publication unless otherwise stated. English translations of foreign works are listed where known. Predominantly didactic books (eg: Aaron Copland's *What to Listen for in Music*) are excluded.

Antheil, G: *Bad Boy of Music* (1945)
Arditi, L: *My Reminiscences* (1896)
Bax, A: *Farewell My Youth* (1944)
Berlioz, H: *Mémoires de Berlioz* (1870; Eng trans 1912: *Memoirs*; 1932: *Memoirs from 1803 to 1865*)
Berners, A: *First Childhood* (1934)
A Distant Prospect (1945)
Cage, J: *Silence* (1961)
A Year from Monday (1969)
Empty Words: Writings '73–'78 (1980)
Copland, A: *Copland on Music* (1960)
Cornelius, P: *Autobiographie* (1874)
Czerny, K: *Erinnerungen aus meinem Leben* (*c* 1860, reprinted 1968)
Dittersdorf, K: *Lebensbeschreibung* (completed 1799, two days before his death; Eng trans 1896)
Doráti, A: *Notes of Seven Decades* (1979)
Foote, A: *An Autobiography* (1946)
Gyrowetz, A: *Biographie* (1847; new edition edited by Alfred Einstein, 1915)
Hindemith, P: *A Composer's World* (1952)
Honegger, A: *Je suis compositeur* (1951; Eng trans: *I Am a Composer*, 1966)
Ives, C: *Essays Before a Sonata, The Majority, and other Writings by Charles Ives* (Ed Boatwright, 1970)
Autobiographical Memos (Ed Kirkpatrick, 1971)
Jackson, W of Exeter: *Observations on the Present State of Music in London* (1791)
Kelly, M: *Reminiscences* (2 vols, actually written by Theodore Hook, 1826)
Mackenzie, A: *A Musician's Narrative* (1927)
Martin, F: *Un compositeur médite sur son art* (*Écrits et pensées recueillis par sa femme*) (1978)
Mason, D G: *Music in My Time and other Reminiscences* (1938)
Mason, W: *Memories of a Musical Life* (1901)
Milhaud, D: *Notes sans musique* (1949; Eng trans: *Notes Without Music*, 1952)
Nielsen, C: *My Childhood in Funen* (1927; Eng trans 1953)
Living Music (1929; Eng trans 1953)
Partch, H: *Genesis of a Music* (1949)
Prokofiev, S: *Autobiography, Articles, Reminiscences* (a collection published in English in Moscow, 1954?)
Notes from Childhood (Eng trans: *Prokofiev by Prokofiev: a Composer's Memoir*, 1979)
Quantz, J J: Autobiography in *Selbstbiographien deutscher Musiker*, 1948; extracts in Eng trans in Paul Nettl's *Forgotten Musicians*, 1951
Rimsky-Korsakov, N: *My Musical Life* (1876–1906; Eng trans 1942)
Rubinstein, A: *Autobiography* (1889; Eng trans 1890)
Recollections of 50 Years (1892; Ger trans 1895)
Satie, E: *Mémoires d'un Amnésique* (1953)
Scott, C: *My Years of Indiscretion* (1924)
Bone of Contention (1969)
Sessions, R: *The Musical Experience of Composer, Performer, Listener* (1951)
Shostakovich, D: *Testimony: The Memoirs of Shostakovich* as related to and edited by Solomon Volkov (1979)
Smetana, B: *Smetana ve vzpomínkách a dopisech* (1939; Eng trans: *Smetana—Letters and Reminiscences* 1953)
Smythe, E: *Impressions that Remained* (2 vols, 1919)
Streaks of Life (1921)
As Time Went On (1935)
What Happened Next (1940)
Sousa, J P: *Marching Along: Recollections of Men, Women and Music* (1928)
Spohr, L: *Selbstbiographie* (1861; Eng trans 1865; 1878)
Stanford, C V: *Pages from an Unwritten Diary* (1914)
Strauss, R: *Betrachtungen und Erinnerungen* (Ed Schuh, 1949; Eng trans: *Recollections and Reflections*, 1953)
Stravinsky, I: *Chroniques de ma vie* (2 vols 1935; Eng trans: *Chronicles of My Life*, 1936; 1975)
Also to be noted are:
The Poetics of Music (1947)
Themes and Conclusions (1972)
and a series of volumes by Stravinsky and Robert Craft:
Conversations With Stravinsky (1959)
Memories and Commentaries (1960)
Expositions and Developments (1962)
Dialogues and a Diary (1968)
Telemann, G P: Autobiography included in a collection of biographies published by Johann Mattheson in 1740: *Grundlage einer Ehrenpforte* (modern ed, Berlin 1910)
Thomson, V: *The State of Music* (1939)
The Musical Scene (1945)
Virgil Thomson (1966)
Tippett, M: *Moving into Aquarius* (1959)
Tomášek, J V: Autobiography in periodical *Libuše* (1845 *et seq*; Eng trans: *Excerpts from the Memoirs of J V Tomášek*, in *Musical Quarterly*, 1946)

Vaughan Williams, R: *Some Thoughts on Beethoven's Choral Symphony, with writings on other musical subjects* (1953)
Wagner, R: *Mein Leben* (1911; Eng trans: *My Life*, 1911)
Weingartner, P: *Lebenserinnerungen* (2nd ed, 1928; Eng trans: *Buffets and Rewards*, 1937)

Musicology

This activity may be described as the study in depth of subjects peripheral to the practice and performance of music; alternatively, the pursuit of information on all aspects of music and musicians except that of actual performance. The value of such study is not always evident at first, but the gradual building up of a large body of facts surrounding music is useful in establishing other facts directly concerning the music, even though the usefulness of this peripheral information might not become apparent for many years after its publication. To take an example, it is well known that Brahms liked to smoke strong cigars. The actual make of these cigars can be of little interest to future generations since the cigars themselves no longer exist and Brahms was foremost a composer, not a cigar-smoker. However, if it can be proved that, in order to obtain his favourite make of cigar, Brahms travelled to another town on a given date, that much more is known about his life, and his appearance in that town on a certain date may assist in establishing the date of a piece of music. This imaginary example can be paralleled by real ones. For instance, the records of doctors who attended Schumann prove that his hand injury was not caused by his invention and use of a mechanical device to strengthen the third finger: there was already a deterioration in his hand action brought about by mercury poisoning (due to the then accepted treatment for syphilis) which led him to try to strengthen the hand mechanically (see Eric Sams's closely reasoned article in *The Musical Times*, December 1971).

The most obviously useful musicological study is into the background of the actual music of a composer, and one of the most obvious benefits to come from this kind of study is the thematic catalogue (see below).

The first stirrings of musicology were published in 1798 in the Leipzig magazine *Allgemeine Musikalische Zeitung*. The magazine *Cäcilia*, printed in Mainz by Schott from 1824 to 1850, went into musicological subjects even more deeply, and the contemporary *Neue Zeitschrift für Musik*, edited by Schumann, appeared in Leipzig from 1835. It dealt almost exclusively with the then modern movements in music.

The first use of the term 'musicology', or the German equivalent *Musikwissenschaft*, was in 1863, when Friedrich Chrysander published his periodical *Jahrbuch für musikalische Wissenschaft*.

The ultimate in musicology may be said to have been reached with the private publication of volume I of the *Life of Wagner* in 1898. It was assembled from a huge collection of manuscripts, letters, and other paraphernalia, by Mary Burrell, a life-long admirer of the composer's music, and was engraved in script, with countless reproductions and photographs included. This first volume was 3 in (7·5 cm) thick, 30 in (76 cm) tall, and 21 in (53 cm) wide, and covered merely the first 21 years of Wagner's life. (A copy sold for £209 at Sotheby's, London, on 9 February 1976.) The planned succeeding volumes did not appear, due no doubt to the removal of the driving force with the death of Miss Burrell in 1898, but much of the material she so assiduously collected was made available to the public in *Letters of Richard Wagner*, published in America in 1950.

Italian musical indications

A few words might be said in explanation of those Italian musical terms which, because of their frequent appearance on concert programmes and record sleeves, have become part of the English language.

That Italian is by tradition the language of music is understandable since virtually all the important forms of music (the only notable exceptions being the symphonic, or tone, poem, and serial music) had their origins in that country. The convention is so well established world-wide that even Russian programme notes printed in Cyrillic revert to the Roman type when words such as 'andante' appear in the text. During concert intervals in England it is not uncommon for these directions to merge into the conversation, to the complete understanding of all parties no doubt, in criticisms such as 'I don't think his finale was as cantabile as it might have been.'

It is entertaining to compare the musical meanings, as accepted for centuries, with the common Italian usage. Where there is no significant difference between the two, the latter has been omitted, and only the most common terms are included. The less common directions will be found in reference books of a more specialist nature than the present volume. Abbreviations, where commonly recognised, are given in brackets.

Direction	*Musical use*	*Common Italian use*
A Capella	in the style of church music (ie voices without instruments)	at chapel
Accelerando	increasing the tempo gradually	making haste
Acciaccatura	a short grace-note	something crushed
Adagietto	a short (small) adagio	–
Adagio (Ad^{o})	slow; faster than largo and grave	slowly; at leisure
Affettuoso	tender, affectionate, pathetic	–
Allegretto (All^{tto})	light, cheerful; in tempo between allegro and andante	diminutive of allegro
Allegro (All^{o})	lively, briskly	gay, cheerful, merry
Amoroso	tenderly, gently, affectionately	lover; loving
Andante (And^{te})	moving easily; flowing; at a walking pace	going, current, flowing; (a) fair (price)
Andantino (And^{tino})	slightly slower than andante	diminutive of andante
Appassionato	passionate, intense	eager, enthusiastic
Appoggiatura	long grace-note	something which leans
Aria	tune, song, usually for a single voice	air, wind, song
Assai	very, more, extremely	much, copiously
Attacca	commence the next movement immediately	attack
Brillante	bright, sparkling, brilliant	–
Brio	fire, vigour	fire, vivacity
Cadenza	a solo showpiece usually near the end of a piece	–
Cantabile	in the singing style	–
Canzona	a graceful and elaborate song	ballad, song
Capriccio(so)	a capricious or fanciful composition	caprice, whim
Coda	an ending piece	end, queue, tail
Col	with the	–
Comodo	with ease, comfortably	convenience, ease, leisure
Con	with	by, with
Crescendo	with a gradually increasing tone	growing
Decrescendo	opposite of crescendo	–
Diminuendo	decrease of power	abatement
Dolce	sweetly, softly, gently	dessert, sweet, soft
Dolente	sorrowful, pathetic	–
Energ(et)ico	energetic, emphatic	energetic, powerful
Espressivo	expressively	–
Fantasia	fancy, caprice	–
Finale	final section or movement	–
Forte (*f*)	loud	forcible, heavy, high, loud, strong
Fortissimo (*ff*)	very loud	augmentative of forte
Fuga	a strict contrapuntal work	escape, flight
Fugato	in fugal style	–
Fuoco	fire, energy, passion	fire
Garbo	simplicity, grace, elegance	courtesy, grace, politeness
Gentile	noble, pleasing, graceful	courteous, kind, polite
Giocoso	humorous, merry	facetious, jocose
Grave	majestical, serious, slow	heavy, serious

Direction	Musical use	Common Italian use
Grazia	grace, elegance	favour, grace, mercy
Grazioso	graceful, smooth, elegant	dainty, gracious, pretty
Intermezzo	an interlude	–
Lamentoso	lamenting, mournful	–
Larghetto	slow, but not as slow as largo	
Largo	slow, broad, solemn	breadth, width, room
Legato	smooth, slurred	tied, connected
Lento	slow	loose, slow, sluggish
Maestoso	majestically, dignified	–
Marcato	strongly marked, emphasised	–
Mesto	melancholy	–
Mezzo	middle (mezzo *f*=half loud)	–
Moderato (Mod*to*)	moderately quick	–
Molto	much	–
Moto	movement	agitation, exercise, impulse, motion
Obbligato	necessary, obligatory	–
Pesante	weighty, heavy, ponderous	–
Pianissimo (*pp*)	very quiet	augmentative of piano
Piano (*p*)	quiet	–
Più	more (più forte=louder)	–
Pizzicato (pizz)	the strings are to be plucked instead of bowed	pinched
Poco	little	–
Pomposo	stately, grand	pompous
Prestissimo	very quickly	augmentative of presto
Presto (P*o*)	quickly, rapidly	soon, quick
Quasi	like, as it were	–
Ralentando (ral)	a gradual slowing of the tempo	–
Ricercare	any musical work employing novelty in design	to enquire into; seek, research into
Risoluto	resolutely, boldly	–
Ritardando (rit; ritard)	a gradual slowing of the tempo	–
Ritenuto (rit)[1]	a sudden slowing of the tempo	–
Scherzo	jest, a lively piece	freak, jest, trick
Sempre	always	–
Senza	without	–
Sforzando	forced, greatly stressed	–
Sordino	a mute, muted	–
Sostenuto	sustained, sonorous	–
Sotto voce	with half the voice	in an undertone
Spiccato	very detached, bouncing the bow	to stand out, be prominent
Spirito	energy, spirit	courage, ghost, spirit, wit
Spiritoso	energy, spirit	alcoholic, witty
Staccato	pointed, distinctly separated	–
Tanto	so much, as much	
Tosto	quick, swift	hard
Tranquillo	tranquilly, quiet	–
Tutti	all, the entire group	–
Vivace	lively, briskly	bright, sprightly

[1] Because of the common abbreviation of 'rit' for both 'ritardando' and 'ritenuto' it is better to use 'ralentando' instead of the former to avoid error.

SOME EXTREMES

The slowest tempo indication is 'Adagio molto assai'. This is rarely used, 'Adagio assai' usually sufficing.

The fastest would be some such combination as 'Prestissimo assai possibile' (literally, 'as extremely very fast as possible').

The quietest indication was *pppppp* (literally *piú piú piú piú piú piano* or 'more more more more more quiet') in the first movement of Tchaikovsky's Symphony No 6 (1893), and in bar 37 of the duet for Otello and Desdemona in Act 1 of Verdi's *Otello* (1887), but it is assumed that this direction has been surpassed in more recent music, in which no extreme seems too extraordinary.

The ultimate in quiet music must be silence itself. Silence has been used as an integral part of music from the earliest days: one thinks of the effective use of pauses towards the ends of certain Bach fugues, and the dramatic silences in many of Haydn's works (the first movements of Sym-

Fingal's Cave, on the Isle of Staffa, the inspiration for Mendelssohn's evocative *Hebrides* Overture. (Scottish Tourist Board)

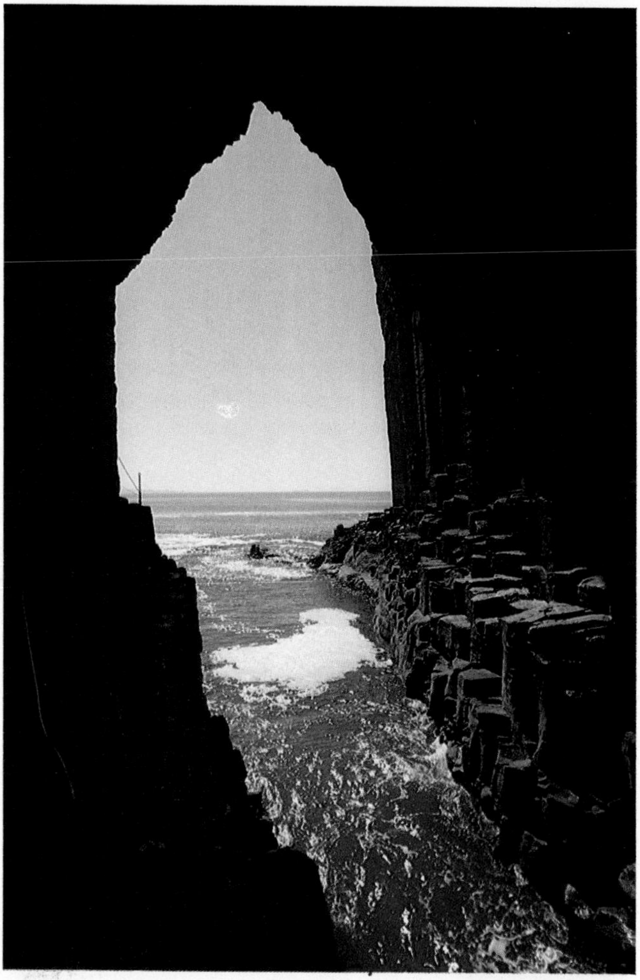

Holywell Music Room, Oxford, where Handel played. The oldest concert hall still in use, the interior was arranged by James Wyatt in 1780. (Angelo Hornak/ Vision International)

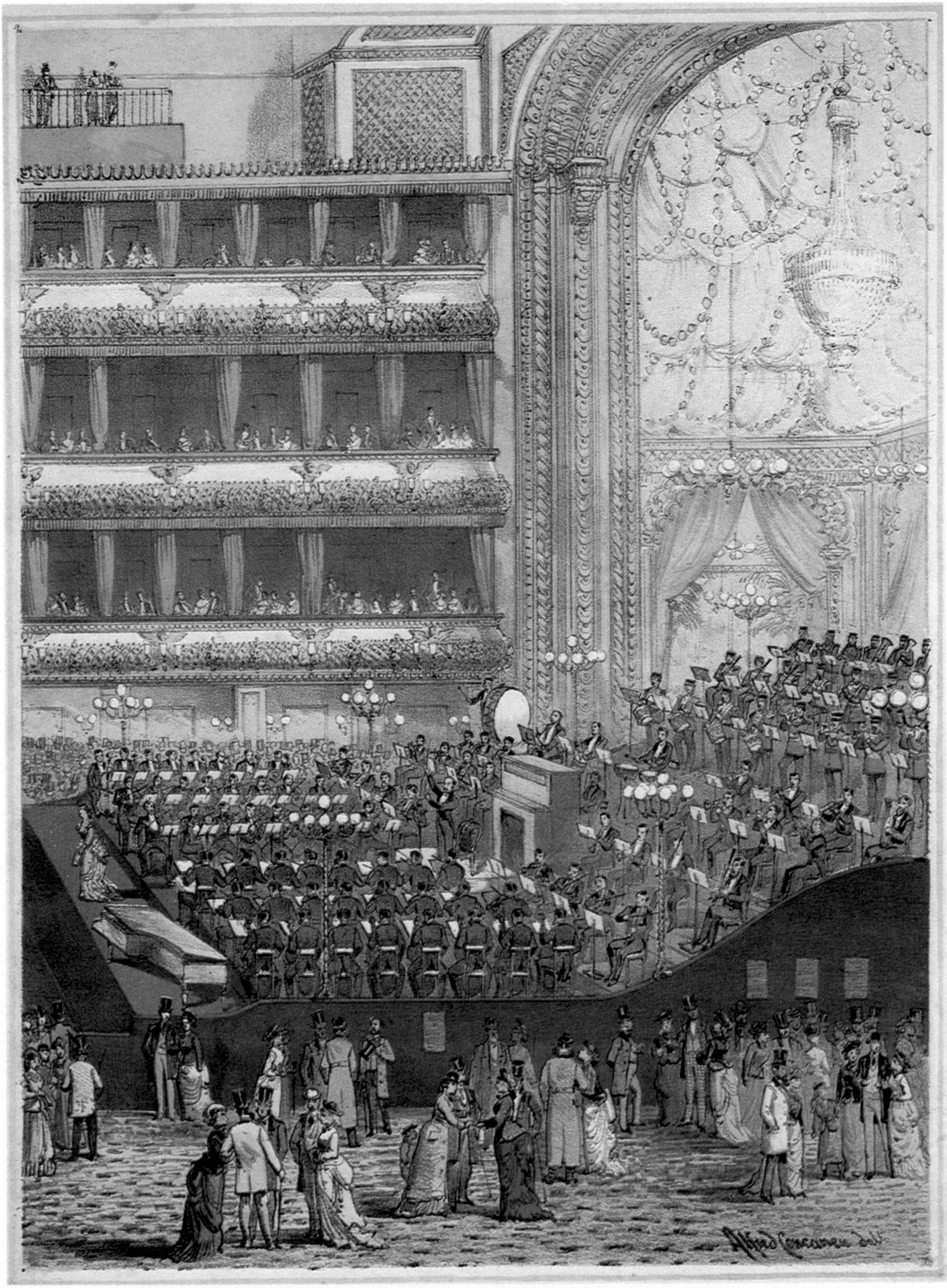

An early Promenade Concert at Covent Garden Theatre. (Spellman Collection)

An exotic title-page for one of Puccini's most popular operas. (Scala/Vision International)

Walter von der Vogelweide, German Minnesinger. (Mary Evans Picture Library)

Every morning
a concert grand,
Giv'n by our famous
Nursery Band.

An impromptu concert with an appreciative audience. Nister's Holiday Annual, 1895. (Mary Evans Picture Library)

Above: The late Elvis Presley, 'The King of Rock 'n' Roll', award-winner supreme.

Left: A Black-and-White Minstrel, banjo under arm, in a London street in 1881. (Mary Evans Picture Library)

Right: Frank Sinatra, whose appearance at the Maracaña Stadium, Rio de Janeiro, on 26 January 1980 drew the largest-ever audience to a solo artist's performance (estimated to be 175 000).

A 19th-century flute musical box. (Siegfrieds Mechanisches Musikkabinett, Rüdesheim)

A flute-clock, made by Kleemeyer about 1800. It was for such an instrument that Joseph Haydn produced 32 short compositions. (Siegfrieds Mechanisches Musikkabinett, Rüdesheim)

Hupfeld Jazz Orchestrion (1926). (Siegfrieds Mechanisches Musikkabinett, Rüdesheim)

Musical puppet merry-go-round (c 1900). (Siegfrieds Mechanisches Musikkabinett, Rüdesheim)

phonies 39 in G minor (*c* 1768), and 80 in D minor (*c* 1783/84), are particularly effective examples).

The present century has seen many extensions of this use of silence. György Ligeti's Chamber Concerto (1969) ends with two whole bars of silence, carefully conducted, presumably to avoid the destruction of the effect of the close by the sudden, and aurally shattering, intrusion of applause.

It is when silence is used, not as an adjunct to music, but instead of it, that one must question the validity of certain pieces of so-called 'music'. John Cage, in 1952, 'wrote' a work entitled *4′ 33″*, this being the length of, to quote the composer, 'a piece in three movements during which no sounds are intentionally produced'. Any group of instruments, and presumably singers, may join in provided only that they make no musical sound for the duration of the three 'movements'. Cage's contention is that there is always something to hear so long as one is alive and has ears to hear it. He has a valid point there, but as far as the writer is aware he has not explained why, in order to hear this silence, one has to pay to sit watching motionless artists; nor does it explain the presence of those artists. Cage has written also works entitled *26′ 1.1499* for string player (1955) and *34′ 46.776* for piano (1954) and similarly named pieces.

The loudest indication will coincide with the occasion on which a composer tires of writing the letter *f*. Indications such as *ffff* are quite common in modern music, sometimes with the addition of *fz* to add force to the power: *fffffz*. The addition or subtraction of one *f* in such indications makes no difference in actual performance because, by the time the players reach *fff* they are playing as loud as they know how anyway. It becomes a matter of degree, and of judgement by the conductor: if he sees a piece of music with *fff*, building up to a final *fffz*, it is up to him to ensure that the players are not stretched to the utmost for the *fff*, and that something is in reserve for the additional *z*.

The longest indication (and perhaps the most ambivalent) is that for the *Kyrie* of Beethoven's Mass in C, Op 86 (1808): *Andante con moto assai vivace, quasi Allegretto, ma non Troppo.*

The first dynamic indications are possibly those (*forte*, *piano*) used in 1639 by Domenico Mazzochi.

The first accelerando in music occurs in Haydn's Symphony No 60 in C, *Il Distratto* (1774). At the end of the fifth movement (Adagio) a repeated phrase occurs four times, over the third of which Haydn writes 'Allegro'. It is evident from the nature of the music and the character of the symphony as a whole that Haydn intended some bizarre effect here, and although he did not specify 'accelerando' it is safe to assume that that is what he meant. However, as early as 1591 William Byrd indicated by the use of progressively shorter note lengths that he intended an accelerando at the end of his descriptive keyboard work *The Battell.*

The first crescendo. As with accelerando, we may conjecture that the first crescendo in music was not marked as such but its existence is indicated unmistakably in the music.

Rossini earned the nickname 'Signor Crescendo' because of his striking use of the effect (known irreverently as 'the Rossini steamroller'), not least in his popular overtures. However, the invention of the device is credited to Johann Simon Mayr (1763–1845), who constructed greatly extended crescendi lasting over a number of bars and built up by successive entries of instruments. The true origin of the crescendo dates back much further than this in fact. The Mannheim orchestra under Jan Vačlav Stamic (1717–57) employed the effect frequently as part of its internationally famous virtuosity while the operas of Nicolo Jommelli (1714–74) also incorporated it as a structural entity. Many passages of repeated figuration in the earlier Italians such as Vivaldi (1678–1741) and Albinoni (1671–1745) invite this swelling treatment without actually calling for it in the music. It may be assumed that performances would include the effect as a matter of course (it is difficult to imagine a completely deadpan rendering of some of Vivaldi's symphonies, for instance) so the composers saw little point in stating the obvious in the scores. The dynamic succession *f*, *più f*, *ff* (literally 'loud', 'more loud', 'very loud') appears occasionally in Vivaldi's music, but the concept of a gradual tonal increase was doubtless well known before then in choral music, in which graded dynamics were required for expressive purposes.

The first 'hairpins' < > indicating minute crescendi and diminuendi are found in the violin sonatas of Giovanni Antonio Piani (*c* 1690–1760+), published in 1712.

Opus

Opus is an Italian noun meaning 'work' or 'piece' and is related to *opera* in that an opera is a 'work' with music for the stage. (Italian for 'opera' is *dramma per musica*.) An opus number should identify the approximate chronology of a composer's works, but it is a far from infallible guide. For instance, in the cases of Beethoven and Schubert the highest numbers are often attached to early works because they were published posthumously.

The highest opus number, 798, appears to have been achieved by Karl Czerny who, nonetheless, composed over 1000 works, some of them large collections.

Thematic catalogues

In appearance there are few less musical of music publications than a thematic catalogue. For the most part it consists of a series of musical staves, each giving the beginning of a piece of music (the *incipit*, or 'beginning') interspersed with virtually unreadable lines of abbreviations indicating sources. Careful reading of the introduction and foreword, and a valiant effort to memorise the list of abbreviations will help to unravel some of the meanings of these supposedly elucidatory lines of letters and numbers, but the production as a whole is likely to remain daunting in the extreme to the ordinary music-lover.

In fact, the thematic catalogue is one of the most vitally useful tools the musicologist has in his perpetual struggle to classify and codify the formidable quantity of music since the first pieces were written down (see the beginning of this Section). It lists, in some kind of logical order, the contents of a group of works by one composer or a group of composers, and it identifies each work in a way as near foolproof as possible: by actually quoting the start of each piece of music. The opening theme or incipit of a piece of music is almost as unique to that work as is a person's fingerprint—it is extremely rare to find two pieces of music in which the opening two or three bars are alike in every particular, and the longer the quoted *incipit* the less likely even that remote circumstance becomes. To illustrate this point, let us take the example of Haydn's Symphony No 70, which was used as model for a Symphony in D by the Polish composer Karol Pietrowsky. A listener knowing one of these works and then coming afresh to the other would be struck by the extraordinary resemblances between the music of the works' respective first and last movements, but an examination of the incipits of each, although indicating a resemblance, unfailingly identifies the two pieces of music as absolutely distinct. The incipits quoted are of the first violin part only, and the examples are limited to the first three bars of each movement.

Haydn: Symphony 70: first movement:

Pietrowsky: Symphony in D: first movement:

Haydn: Symphony 70: last movement:

Pietrowsky: Symphony in D: last movement:

Once the uniqueness of each piece of music is recognised it will be seen how useful a thematic catalogue can be.

As another example, let us take Beethoven's symphonies. In referring to the Symphony in A, we can mean only Symphony No 7 since that is the only symphony he wrote in that key; similarly, all the other symphonies may be identified explicitly by key only, except Nos 6 and 8, which are both in F major. In this case, however, No 6 is known as the 'Pastoral' Symphony whereas No 8 has no subtitle, thus confusion is again avoided.

When we turn to Vivaldi's concertos we are faced with a completely different and inherently defeating situation in which there are more than 20 Violin Concertos in C, only two of them with subtitles. Of the remainder, 16 are in the standard three-movement form of fast–slow–fast, and eight of these have the identical movement markings of Allegro; Largo; Allegro. Of these, several are without even the notoriously misleading opus numbers. Clearly, some method of visual identification is required to distinguish between these works, and between the similar potential confusions among Vivaldi's concertos in G, D, A, etc. The thematic catalogue rescues us from this confusion, and by referring to the numerical position of the work in the standard thematic catalogue of Vivaldi's concertos it is possible to pinpoint which work is meant with unmistakable accuracy.

It is only during the present century that the value of the thematic catalogue has been widely appreciated, but it is so well established as a research implement today that any deep research into a composer of the past loses much of its usefulness without one. The following examination of the field will illustrate just how widely accepted is the thematic catalogue, not only in the dusty corridors of music research, but also in the general identification requirements of concert programmes and the catalogues of music-publishers and record companies.

The first thematic catalogue is a single-page list giving 22 Psalm themes, published as part of *The Book of Psalms in Metre* in London in 1645.

The largest thematic catalogue is that issued in parts and supplements over a quarter of a century from 1762 to 1787 by the Leipzig music-publisher Johann Gottlob Immanuel Breitkopf (1719–94). In total, the catalogue contains some 14 000 incipits of music ranging in form from song to symphony, and its 888 pages include the identification of music by over 1000 composers. Breitkopf's catalogue was intended to advertise the manuscript and printed music for sale at his Leipzig premises; he was not to know that it was to prove an almost priceless source of information for researchers into the musical scene of the 18th century, and that its value is considered to be so great today that the entire catalogue and supplements were republished in fascimile by Dover in New York in 1966, under the guiding influence of Professor Barry S Brook of the City University of New York.

A much larger thematic catalogue is in preparation in New York by Professor Jan la Rue, who has been collecting material for a Union Thematic Catalogue of 18th-Century Symphonies and Concertos for more than 20 years. Some 25 000 incipits are listed so far; in order to cross-reference these incipits efficiently, assistance is being sought of electronic data-processing techniques. The future holds promise of a thematic catalogue of potentially infinite proportions: see RISM below.

The best-known thematic catalogue is the *Chronologisch-thematisches Verzeichniss sämmtlicher Tonwerke W A Mozart's* by Ludwig Ritter von Köchel, the first edition of which was published by Breitkopf and Härtel in Leipzig in 1862 (just 100 years after the beginning of Breitkopf's own thematic house catalogue, see above). The latest edition of more than 1000 pages (nearly double the page-count of the original) incorporates the work put in on the catalogue in 1937 by Alfred Einstein and was published in 1964 under the editorship of Franz Geigling, Alexander Weinmann, and Gerd Sievers, but it is still referred to as 'The Köchel Catalogue', or just 'K'. For years it has been known by the concert-going public that, whereas most composers' music is identified by 'opus', Mozart's are known by the letter 'K' and a number. These numbers have become so identified with the works to which they attach that it is common in musical circles to hear comments such as 'What do you think of Klemperer's K 550?'

The thematic catalogue with the most beautiful title-page is the first of the two catalogues prepared in about 1785 for the music collection of the Comte d'Ogny (1757–90). This first catalogue lists orchestral and instrumental music (the second is devoted to vocal works) and it was written anonymously by someone who had a better eye for calligraphic excellence than for musicological detail. The hand-painted title-page is a production of extreme beauty. (See first edition).

A LIST OF THEMATIC CATALOGUES

In the following chart are listed the most important published thematic catalogues which give all or a major part of the works of their chosen composers. The numbers in these publications are generally more reliable than opus identifications, which are usually only publishers' references. It is relevant to note that the opus numbers originally appended to Mozart's works are nowadays never encountered, and those by which Schubert's music is identified have almost entirely given way to 'D' numbers.

There are four basic types of catalogue:

1. Chronological, in which the composer's works are arranged in their proved or surmised order of composition (often by reference only to the opus numbers), regardless of genre.
2. Genre, in which the works are grouped according to type and regardless of chronology.
3. Chronological within genre.
4. Tonality within genre.

The following thematic catalogues each dealing with the works of more than one composer should also be mentioned as being of particular value to the music-researcher. It should be noted, however, that once again it has proved necessary to be arbitrarily selective since there is now such an enormous literature of thematic catalogues available to the specialist that nothing less than a separate book would do justice to the subject. Such a book exists (see the Bibliography under Brook, Barry S); it may come as a surprise to those with an awareness in this field only of Köchel's Mozart catalogue that Professor Brook's bibliography contains no less than 1444 annotated entries.

Composer	*Symbol*	*Compiler*	*Type*
Abel*	Kn	Walter Knape, 1971	2
Albinoni*†	Gia	Remo Giazotto, 1945	2
Albrechtsberger	Som	László Somfai, 1961–67	3
C P E Bach	Wq	Alfred Wotquenne, 1905 (reprint, 1964)	3
J C Bach*	Terry	Charles Sanford Terry, 1929 (reprint, 1967)	3
J S Bach	BWV or S	Wolfgang Schmieder, 1950 (BWV=*Bach-Werke-Verzeichnis*)	2
W F Bach	F	Martin Falck, 1913	4
Beethoven*†	Kinsky	Georg Kinsky and Hans Halm, 1955	1
Boccherini*	Gér	Yves Gérard, 1969	3
Camerloher	Z	Benno Ziegler, 1919	2
Chopin*†	Fr	E W Fritsch, 1870	2
	Brown	Maurice J E Brown, 1960	1
Clementi*	Allorto	Riccardo Allorto, 1959	1
	Tyson	Alan Tyson, 1967	1
F Couperin	Cauchie	Maurice Cauchie, 1949	1
Dittersdorf	Kr	Carl Krebs, 1900	3
F X Dušek	Sýkora	Václav Jan Sýkora, 1958	2
Dvořák*	Sourek	Otakar Sourek, 1917	1
Field	Hop	Cecil Hopkinson, 1961	1
Franck	Mohr	Wilhelm Mohr, 1969	2
Fux	Köchel	Ludwig Ritter von Köchel, 1872	2
G Gabrieli	Kenton	Egon Kenton, 1967	1
Gluck	Wq	Alfred Wotquenne, 1904	1
J G Graun	M	Carl H Mennicke, 1906	4
K H Graun	M	Carl H Mennicke, 1906	4
Handel	B	Berend Baselt, 1974	3
Hasse	M	Carl H Mennicke, 1906	4

Composer	*Symbol*	*Compiler*	*Type*
F J Haydn*	Hob	Anthony van Hoboken, Vol I: Instrumental music, 1957 Vol II: Vocal music, 1971	3
J M Haydn	Perger	Lothar Perger, 1907 (instrumental)	2
	Klafsky	Anton Klafsky, 1925 (church)	2
Hoffstetter* (J U A and R)	Gottron	Adam Gottron, Alan Tyson, and Hubert Unvericht, 1968	2
L Koželuh	Post	Milan Poštolka, 1964	3
Locatelli*†	Koole	Arend Koole, 1949	1
J-B Loeillet*	Priestman	Brian Priestman, 1952	1
J Loeillet*	Priestman	Brian Priestman, 1952	1
Mahler	Martner	Knud Martner, in preparation	1
Martinů	Saf	Miloš Safranek, 1961	1
Monteverdi	Zimm	Franklin B Zimmerman, in preparation	2
L Mozart	DTBIX/2	Max Seiffert, 1908 (included in a volume of *Denkmäler der Tonkunst in Bayern*)	2
W A Mozart	K, or KV	Ludwig Ritter von Köchel, 1862 (reprinted and revised 1964, see p. 227)	1
Offenbach	Al	Antonio de Almeida, 1974	1
Pugnani	Zsch	Elsa M Zschinsky-Troxler, 1939	2
Purcell	Zimm	Franklin B Zimmerman, 1963	2
Roman	Bengtsson	Ingmar Bengtsson, 1955	2
Rosetti	Kaul	Oskar Kaul, 1912	2
	Schmid	Hans Schmid, 1968	2
D Scarlatti	Longo	Alessandro Longo, 1937	4
	Kk	Ralph Kirkpatrick, 1970	1
Schubert*	D	Otto Erich Deutsch, 1951, 2nd Ed, 1978	1
Sibelius*†	T	Ernst Tanzberger, 1962	2
Soler	M	Frederick Marvin, 1963–?	4
	R	Father Samuel Rubio, 1960–?	2
J Strauss I	S/R	Max Schönherr and Karl Reinöhl, 1954	3
R Strauss	MvA	Erich H Müller von Asow, 1955–68	1
Tartini	Dounias	Minos Dounias, 1935	4
Tchaikovsky*†	J	Boris Jurgenson, 1897	2
Telemann‡	SS	Käthe Schaefer-Schmuck, 1932 (keyboard works)	2
	Hörner	Hans Hörner, 1933 (Passion music)	2/3
	Hoff	Adolf Hoffmann, 1969 (orchestral suites)	4
	Kross	Siegfried Kross, 1969 (concertos)	2
Torelli*	Gie	Franz Giegling, 1949	2
Viotti*	Pou	Arthur Pougin, 1888	2
	Gia	Remo Giazotto, 1956	1
Vivaldi*	RV	Peter Ryom, 1974	2/4
	Fanna	Antonio Fanna, 1968	2
Wagenseil	Mich	Helga Michelitsch, 1966 (keyboard works) 1973 (Orchestral and Chamber works)	2
Wagner	Kast	Emerich Kastner, 1878	1
Weber*	J	Friedrich Wilhelm Jähns, 1871	1+2
Zach	Komma	Karl Michael Komma, 1938	2

*The established opus numbers are misleading and should be disregarded in favour of information given in the thematic listing.
† The established opus numbers give a good idea of chronology.
‡ A complete catalogue of Telemann's music, incorporating the above catalogues in revised form and to be known as TWV—*Telemann-Werke-Verzeichnis*—is in preparation by Bärenreiter Verlag of Kassel.

Basel University Library: list of manuscript music of the 18th century (1957).

Breitkopf: see above.

Brook, Barry S: *Catalogue of French Symphonies* (and associated works; also of some foreign symphonies published in France) *of the second half of the 18th century* (1962).

Duckles and Elmer: *Thematic catalogue of a manuscript collection of 18th-century Italian instrumental music in the University of California, Berkeley Music Library* (1963). Although mainly of Italian music, other countries' composers are not entirely excluded.

Dunwalt: a manuscript catalogue compiled by, or under the direction of, Gottfried Dunwalt in 1770. It lists over 500 orchestral and instrumental works in Dunwalt's possession at that time. The catalogue is preserved in the British Museum.

Hummel: a publisher's catalogue with six supplements (a seventh was announced but apparently not issued) of music published between 1754 and 1774. The catalogue and the known supplements were published in facsimile with an introduction by Cari Johansson in 1973.

Ludwig Ritter von Köchel, author of the best-known thematic catalogue, an exhaustive listing of the works of W A Mozart.

Kade, Otto: a catalogue with supplements of the music libraries of Duke Friedrich Franz III and the Mecklenburg-Schwerin Collections (1893–1908).

Karlsruhe: four manuscript catalogues of the collections of early music in the Badische Landesbibliothek at Karlsruhe.

Mannheim: a list of the symphonies written in the 18th century by composers of the Mannheim School. See Section III.

d'Ogny: two manuscript catalogues of instrumental and vocal music in the collection of Comte d'Ogny (1757–90). The catalogues were prepared about 1785 with the utmost attention to beauty of presentation, and the first catalogue (of orchestral and instrumental music) was graced with a finely executed title-page (see above).

RISM: the initials stand for 'Répertoire International des Sources Musicales'. This organisation's ambition is to collect for international availability a thematic listing of nothing less than the entire musical printed and manuscript holdings of all the sources (libraries, museums, etc) of the world. An international project of this magnitude, requiring the goodwill and funds of many separate institutions, will require very many years of patience and tenacity before beginning to approach useful completion, and the number of incipits to be included will run into millions. The Czechoslovakian affiliate has reported that cataloguing has been completed for 186 000 works, and the holdings of other collections still awaiting thematic cataloguing is formidable: East Germany: 53 000; West Germany: 88 000; Hungary: 20 000, etc.

Music appreciation

The first step towards the establishment of music appreciation as a regular subject in school curriculae could be said to be an article written by Agnes Mary Langdale in 1908, published that year in *The Crucible*.

The first broadcast music appreciation courses were begun by Walter Damrosch over the American NBC Network in 1928.

The most powerful forces in the widening of musical appreciation were the writings of Sir Donald Francis Tovey, whose carefully argued and imaginative writings on music were originally used as programme notes mostly for the Reid Concerts Orchestra in Edinburgh earlier this century.

As *Essays in Musical Analysis*, they were first published in hardback form by the Oxford University Press in 1935 and have achieved enormous and totally justified popularity, serving as an unattainable standard for later writers.

Section 8

THE 20th CENTURY SCENE

While the main stream of serious music continued into the 20th century from roots established and precepts suggested during the 19th (and even, in some instances, before that, for example, the Neo-classicism of the 1920s), the field of musical art in this century has been extended and enriched by new and vital forces: popular music and jazz.

Notable firsts in jazz and popular music

The first use of the word jazz in print seems to have been in the *San Francisco Bulletin*, 6 March 1913, by Peter Tamony, referring to an enthusiastic baseball-player. **The first use in connection with any kind of dance music** goes back to a song used in the Deep South during the 1880s, part of which ran thus:

> Ol' man Johnson's jazzin' around,
> Don't stop him, don't stop him or
> he'll fall to the ground.

It appears to have had an obscene sexual connotation in Chicago, where anyone causing irritation or annoyance could be told to 'jazz off', but D J 'Nick' LaRocca, leader and cornetist of the Original Dixieland Jazz Band, explained that he never heard the word in his home city of New Orleans, nor anywhere else until he reached Chicago with what was then (1916) called simply the Original Dixieland Band. One night, while the band was playing a slow number for dancing, an excited (?inebriated) member of the audience got up from his seat and yelled, 'Jazz it up, boys! Jazz it up!' meaning, presumably, play faster and/or louder. The name was at once adopted to describe the improvised, rhythmically stimulating music

The Worlds Greatest Entertainers
ORIGINAL DIXIELAND JAZZ BAND
Direct from the La Marne, Atlantic City
ORIGINAL DIXIELAND JAZZ BAND
ORIGINAL DIXIELAND JAZZ BAND
CREATORS OF JAZZ
AT HAMPTON HALL
WILKES-BARRE, PA.
THURSDAY, SEPTEMBER 29th
Dancing 8 to 1
Balcony Reserved for Spectators
POSITIVELY THE FIRST TIME IN THIS CITY
HEAR THEIR FOLLOWING VICTOR RECORDS
At the Jazz Bows Ball, Ostrich Walk—18457
Bluin the Blues, Sensation Rag—18483
Dixieland Jazz Band, Livery Stable Blues—18255
Skeleton Jangle, Tiger Rag—18472
Crazy Blues, Home Again Blues—18729
Margie. Palesteena—18747
Sweet Mama, Busy Rose—18722
ADMISSION - - $1.10

The first jazz band to record, and the first to bring jazz music to the notice of the world.

the band played, which was quite unlike any other heard up to that time. The music of the New Orleans street parades, as remembered and re-created decades later by survivors of the early years of the century, was much more loosely syncopated in the manner of ragtime, and the improvisation seems to have been limited to the clarinettist, who wove an impromptu obbligato to the melody played by the cornet(s) and on the harmonies supplied by the trombones, horns and, sometimes, saxophones.

The story of the Black drummer named Charles (abbreviated to 'Chas'—or in a different account, James, abbreviated to 'Jas') who could produce a propulsive rhythm on his assorted kitchenware, as well as his regular drums, is probably apocryphal; he is further alleged to have been addressed by his Italian (or was he French?) leader when required to perform this diverting act, 'Chas! Chas! I want Chas! Play it, Chas!' and so on. The likelihood of a white European leading a dance band including a member of the Black race in the Deep South seems remote, to say the least, even in those days.

Greatest influences in jazz

Nick LaRocca (cornet)—leader and manager of the Original Dixieland Jazz Band. By his attack, phrasing, and tone he greatly influenced the teenage Bix Beiderbecke who later influenced many younger musicians, among them Red Nichols from Utah, Andy Secrest from Indiana, and Bobby Hackett from Massachusetts.

Louis Armstrong (cornet and trumpet) virtuoso, bandleader, and comedian, regarded by most as *the* outstanding influence over all jazzmen, at least subsequent to the mid-1920s, even some who did not play cornet or trumpet.

Miff Mole (trombone)—a superb technician who could make a straight and commonplace arrangement interesting by just a short, brilliantly constructed 'break' or a four-bar solo. He influenced many trombonists such as Tommy Dorsey, Jimmy Harrison, Abe Lincoln, and Don McIlvaine (the last of whom played with Warner's Seven Aces in Atlanta in the mid-1920s).

Hard times experienced by jazz musicians

Most jazz musicians underwent varying degrees of privation during the Depression years as the kind of music that had made them prosperous a decade earlier went out of fashion generally, at least in America. Those who were technically able to adapt to the more orthodox methods of playing dance music from prepared scores did so, and began a new era of prosperity for themselves (notably the bandleaders Benny Goodman, Glenn Miller, Jimmy and Tommy Dorsey, Artie Shaw, Jack Teagarden, etc). Those who were not, usually took up other employment or joined the bands of other leaders whose penchant was for the occasional 'hot' solo (eg Ted Lewis used Muggsy Spanier, cornet, and Don Murray, clarinets and saxophones; Paul Whiteman employed Bunny Berigan, trumpet, and Jack Teagarden, trombone; and Leo Reisman even used the services of Duke Ellington's ex-trumpet soloist, James 'Bubber' Miley).

Chronological chart illustrating the effects of outside influences on the development of twentieth century popular music (one or two representative examples of each trend are given)

1900

Original ragtime 1901 (reaction against fashionable decorum)
'There's a Girl in the Heart of Maryland'
'The Trail of the Lonesome Pine' (Ballard MacDonald–Harry Carroll)

1910

Commercial ragtime 1911–12
'Alexander's Ragtime Band' (Irving Berlin)
'Everybody's Doing It'
'Hitchy Koo' (L. Wolfe Gilbert–Lewis F. Muir–Maurice Abrahams)

Syncopated popular and romantic songs
'When it's Apple-Blossom Time in Normandy' (Mellor–Gifford–Trevor)

FIRST WORLD WAR 1914–18

Patriotic songs (comic, optimistic, confident)
'When the Moon Shines Bright on Charlie Chaplin' (Chatterway–Stanning–Mills)
'Pack Up Your Troubles' (Felix Powell)
'Goodbye-ee' (R. P. Weston–Bert Lee)
'Over There' (George M. Cohan)
'Long Boy' (Barclay Walker)
'When You Come Back' (George M. Cohan)

1920

Commercial blues (cynical, disillusioned)
'Love Ain't Nothin' But the Blues' (Lou Alter)
'If I Can't Get the Sweetie I Want, I Pity the Sweetie I Get' (Jean Schwartz)

Jazz (1919+)
(Abandoning of existing conventions)

USA Prohibition (Gangsters, 'Beer Barons', high living on credit. Reckless expansion of the economy)

WALL STREET CRASH 1929
WORLD DEPRESSION

1930

Sentimental and nostalgic songs mainly American
'Little White Lies' (Walter Donaldson)
'Home' (Peter van Steeden)

Crooning
'Learn to Croon' (Sam Coslow)

Pseudo-Hill-Billy songs
'The Last Round-Up' (Billy Hill)
'Wagon Wheels' (Peter de Rose)
'Roll Along, Covered Wagon' (Jimmy Kennedy)

Latin-American numbers
'The Peanut Vendor' (Marion Sunshine–Moises Simons)
'Mama Inez' (Eliseo Grenet)

Rumbustious optimistic numbers, mostly in 6/8 time and mainly British
'Jolly Good Company'
'There's a Good Time Coming'
'Give Yourself a Pat on the Back' (Butler Wallace)

Better times (1934+)
Vocalists more in evidence in dance bands, sharing credits with bandleaders (romantic style) 'Swing' music: orchestrated jazz: jitterbugs defying (or escaping from) international tensions

SECOND WORLD WAR 1939–45

1940

Patriotic and confident
'The White Cliffs of Dover' (Burton-Kent)
'Lords of the Air' (Davy Burnaby–Michael North)
'When the Lights Go On Again All Over the World' (Seiler–Marcus–Benjamin)
'This is Worth Fighting For' (Sam Stept–Eddie de Lange)
'This is the Army, Mr Jones' (Irving Berlin)

Defiant
Adolf (Annette Mills)
'Der Fuehrer's Face' (Oliver Wallace)

Nonsense and escapist songs
'Mairzy Doats and Dozy Doats' (Milton Darke–Al Hoffman–Jerry Livingston)
'Rose O'Day' (Charles Tobias–Al Lewis)

Parting songs Nostalgia
'We'll Meet Again' (Ross Parker)
'The Lovely Weekend' (Ted Heath)
'Ma! I Miss Your Apple Pie' (Carmen Lombardo–John Loeb)
'Don't Sit Under the Apple Tree' (Lew Brown–Charlie Tobias–Sam Stept)

AFTERMATH OF WAR 1945–50

Luxurious orchestral work (film themes, etc)
1950
'Limelight' (Charles Chaplin)
'The Glass Mountain' (Nino Rota)
'The Days of Wine and Roses' (Henry Mancini)

Nostalgia for the 1920s and 1930s
'Let's Do it Again' (O'Connor–Hartley)
'Music! Music! Music!' (Weiss-Baum)

Reaction against the establishment

HIGHER LIVING STANDARDS 1955–65

Enormous growth of Record industry: the 'Top Twenty'
TV

Country Music Rock 'n' Roll
'Rock Around the Clock' (Bill Haley)
Lawlessness–Soul music

The trends of the last thirty years or so are discussed more fully in the text.

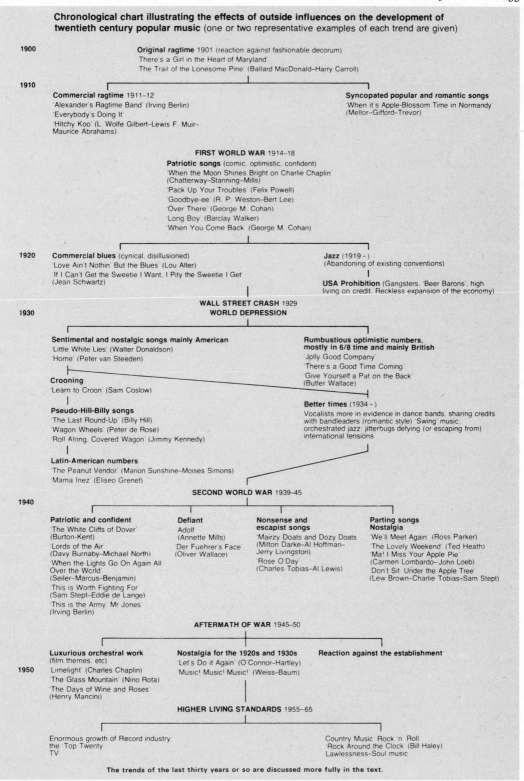

Despite the rather precarious, somewhat hand-to-mouth existence ('scufflin' as it was known) these musicians led at that time particularly, there are very few cases of anyone straining beyond endurance and committing suicide as a result. It is thought that Jack Purvis, a trumpet-player much influenced by Louis Armstrong, who played with the Hal Kemp Orchestra and the California Ramblers in 1929–31, may have committed suicide in 1962; Sterling Bose did so in 1952 (he was a New Orleans trumpet-player who worked with the Arcadian Serenaders in St Louis in the mid-1920s, and Ray Noble in New York a decade later); Ben Pollack hanged himself in 1971 while apparently prosperous as a *restaurateur* and occasional musician, aged 68. The most outlandish example of a suicide among dance musicians was the British clarinettist and saxophonist Arthur Lally, who had worked with Bert Ambrose in the 1920s and 1930s. He was a licensed pilot, and had a bitter hatred of Adolf Hitler and his works. After failing his medical examination for the Royal Air Force in 1940, he volunteered to fly a bomber, solo if need be, over Berchtesgaden, Hitler's 'retreat', and destroy it utterly by aerial bombardment. When this was refused by the War Office, the disconsolate but hate-filled Arthur Lally, convinced he was useless, returned home and gassed himself. Harry Berly, a brilliant violist and tenor saxophonist, who had recorded string quartets for the National Gramophonic Society label in the mid-1920s and hundreds of sides of dance music with Ray Noble, Lew Stone, and others, in the 1930s, became likewise obsessed with the idea that he could do better, and better, but that he was an inferior musician and no one wanted to know about him. He threw himself under a London Underground train in 1937. Similarly, under the strains of bills he could not meet, Tommy Smith, trumpet-player first with Jack Hylton's Kit-Kat Band (1925 and later) and latterly with Jack Payne and the BBC Dance Orchestra, threw himself under a train entering Victoria Station on 21 June 1931.

Instruments used predominantly or exclusively in jazz and dance music

BANJO

The most popular instrument in the 19th-century 'black and white minstrel' troupes became one of the most customary soloists in the very earliest days of sound recording, due to its plangent tone that made a lifelike impression in the crude wax blocks and cylinders then in use. Coincident with the invention of sound recording (see Section IX) came the development of ragtime from Black dances, revivalist meetings, and white American folk-song, in the accompaniment to which the easily portable, easily learned, widely audible banjo figured very largely. When jazz superseded ragtime as a national dance fashion, the banjo continued to provide the basic rhythm for many years, partly because it could be heard above the 'front line' of brass and saxophones, and partly because of its established superiority as a recording voice under pre-electric conditions. As dance music and, to some extent, jazz became more sophisticated towards the end of the 1920s, and as electric recording became the accepted method, the banjo quite rapidly lost favour to the guitar, until by the mid-1930s, it was practically never used except when a band was playing a 'country-style' number, or deliberately trying to sound old-fashioned. With the revival of interest in original jazz and ragtime that arose after the Second World War and culminated in the 'trad boom' of the late 1950s and early 1960s, the banjo became a *sine qua non* of the 'traditional jazz' bands, the first of which (Lu Watters's Yerba Buena Jazz Band of San Francisco) used two.

BOTTLE

Ordinary glass bottles have been used in jazz of the more basic kind in two ways: certain cornettists have been known to mute their instruments with 'Coke' bottles in the absence of a more conventional device, and recordings exist of empty bottles being used as percussion instruments. An outstanding example of this is a record made in 1929 in New York for OKeh under the name of 'Blind Willie Dunn's Gin Bottle Four,' on which the bottle is 'played' by no less a celebrity than song-writer Hoagy Carmichael, in company with Joe 'King' Oliver on cornet, Eddie Lang (who was in fact Blind Willie Dunn) and Lonnie Johnson on guitars, and J C Johnson, composer of many popular successes of the time, on piano. Tuned bottles were blown in a performance of the Andante of Haydn's 'Surprise' Symphony (No 94 in G) in the Hoffnung Music Festival Concert in London on 13 November 1956, perhaps the first 'serious' use of the instrument. Since then, bottles have been used in *Arcana 19* (1962) by the Japanese composer Kuniharu Akiyama.

GLASS

Glass drinking-tumblers have been used in jazz in the following contexts: Herman 'Woodie' Walder, clarinettist of Bennie Moten's Kansas City Orchestra, during the mid-1920s, was often featured as soloist playing—if that is the word—his mouthpiece into a glass, with rather bizarre effect. Also on at least one recording session (for Victor in 1929) the great trombonist Jack Teagarden substituted a glass for the bell of his horn, thereby giving the sound a rather restricted, muted character, but very acceptable within the context of the rest of the band that consisted of paper-and-comb, banjo, string bass (played pizzicato), and drums. Instruments made of glass, other than the bottle referred to above, are not known to have been used in popular music, other than what the recording files describe as 'glass xylophone', recorded experimentally in 1908 by Chris Chapman playing the ragtime classic 'Dill Pickles Rag', with such astonishing tonal realism that it could pass for electric recording.

GOOFUS

A strange hybrid instrument, made to resemble a saxophone by sight, but sounding like a harmonica. It was built on similar lines to the former instrument, and the reeds were arranged in such a way that the keys of the 'saxophone' operated them and produced a rather thin, wheezy mouth-organ sound, wind pressure being supplied by either the player's lungs or a pair of bellows. Also known as the 'couesnophone' (after the French musical instrument-makers Couesnod) or 'queenophone', it became fashionable in some dance bands from 1924 to the end of the decade. The principal exponents were Don Redman, one of the saxophonists in the Fletcher Henderson orchestra, and the white bass saxophonist Adrian Rollini, who used it on many of the casual recording sessions in which he took part, and in Fred Elizalde's Orchestra in the Savoy Hotel, London, where he played during 1928 (see also Section II).

HARMONICA

The humble 'mouth-organ', although comparatively recently elevated to concert-platform status by the American Larry Adler, has always featured prominently in small country-style dance and jazz bands, but rarely in urban groups. One of the few city-based harmonica-players to achieve any sort of recognition through recordings is Robert Cooksey, who made a remarkable series of delightful records for Victor in 1926 and 1927 accompanied by guitarist Bobby Leecan, or by the latter's Need-More Band. Cooksey (from Philadelphia) also recorded in 1927 for Pathé as a member of the Dixie Jazzers Washboard Band, and in 1926 for Victor as one of the South Street Trio (one of these was also Bobby Leecan). 'Field recordings' made on location by the major American companies during the 1920s often used harmonica-players, mostly Blacks such as the leader of the Memphis Jug Band, Will Shade, and the soloist of Cannon's Jug Stompers, Noah Lewis. But this also included the white New Orleansian Alvin Gautreaux, who took part in one Victor recording in that city in 1927 under the leadership of John Hyman, cornetist of an otherwise conventional Dixieland unit. Among the country blues artists who made many records as harmonica-players, the best known is 'Sonny' Terry, who has made frequent visits to Great Britain in the company of his guitar-playing partner Brownie McGhee; Terry's surrealistic, almost nightmarish 'Hootin' Blues' became a best-seller in England during the mid-1950s. The harmonica virtuoso Borrah Minevitch, American based, but formerly a frequent visitor to Britain also, began his recording career as the soloist of a group called the 'Dizzy Trio', on Victor in 1924, playing a number called 'Hayseed Rag'. The country-style singer Carson Robinson, known as a guitarist and whistler, was also often used as a harmonica-player on dance records during the 1920s, but the instrument's voice lacks the carrying power to enable it to match successfully the combined efforts of a brass team or saxophone section so that, in former times, it was used only sparingly in such small groups as mentioned above. However, modern amplification has enabled harmonica-players to compete with more conventional wind instruments on equal terms.

HOT FOUNTAIN PEN

A miniature clarinet, with a range of one octave, devised by Adrian Rollini as a 'stunt' for use in small jazz bands; it was not a generally accepted instrument, hardly surprisingly, as like the harmonica its tone was soft and its carrying power very limited. Rollini is the only well-known exponent of it, usually on records by Joe Venuti's Blue Four and sometimes with Fred Elizalde's Orchestra.

JEW'S HARP

Most often found in country-style dance bands or in conventional urban orchestras when playing commercial numbers with a rural flavour; very rarely used at all in jazz. Records by city-based professional recording artists such as Carson Robinson, Vernon Dalhart, and Frank Luther sometimes use a jew's harp, as its curiously nasal, restricted tonal range and limited carrying power make it acceptable when the other instruments present are two or three strings, but there is obviously no point in attempting its use in even a small jazz or dance band using several brass and woodwind instruments.

JUG

The widely used substitute for expensive conventional brass or string bass instruments among the less affluent members of Black dance bands throughout the Southern States during the first half of the century was a stone or metal jug, with narrow neck and wide capacity. By blowing across the opening with varying degrees of wind-pressure, it was found possible to reproduce accurately and effectively the sound of both the more conventional types of bass. Some jug-blowers blew or hummed into beer- or even oil-cans, and could thus assume the role of trombonist in addition. Records by the Dixieland Jug Blowers, imade in Chicago for Victor in 1926, have two jug-players, Earl MacDonald and Henry Clifford, who produce the trombone and tuba parts with remarkable fidelity. Victor and OKeh records between 1927 and 1934 often featured an outstanding unit known as the Memphis Jug Band; this varied instrumentally from session to session and often from one title to the next, and included, besides the one jug and the usual banjo and/or guitar, other unusual instruments such as harmonica and kazoo. Clarence Williams, the pianist from Louisiana who directed hundreds of recordings in New York between 1921 and 1941, was also something of a jug-blower, though he confined his activities in this direction principally to marking the off-beat on a limited number of notes. One of the best of the Memphis jug men was Gus Cannon, whose Jug Stompers (a trio of jug, harmonica, and guitar) made many Victor recordings between 1928 and 1930. The leader also played banjo simultaneously with the jug, having the latter attached by a metal rod to the neck of the banjo. It may be a point of sociological significance that there are virtually no white jug-blowers in the history of American popular music.

The 20th-century jazz use of bottle and jug has a forerunner in the shape of this earthenware water jug, through the spout of which the player hums, modifying the sound with rhythmic movements of his left hand over the mouth of the vessel. The engraving dates from the early 18th century.

KAZOO

A 'toy' instrument well known to most children, consisting basically of a metal lozenge-shaped device, with an orifice covered by a membrane, into which the performer hums or imitates the approximate sound of a muted trumpet or cornet, the body of the instrument acting as an acoustic amplifier. Although principally (and more effectively) used by Black country-based bands, and by some units recording in New York under the direction of such as Clarence Williams, some white musicians have developed the art of kazoo-playing to a degree of accuracy enabling the instrument to participate in full-sized jazz bands. Among these is the clarinet- and saxophone-player Larry Abbott, who made hundreds of records with Harry Reser, the banjoist, and his various bands (such as the Clicquot Club Eskimos, the Jazz Pilots, the Six Jumping Jacks, and others); his playing is not at all strident, but it fits the context of the band perfectly. The drummer of the California Ramblers in the 1920s was usually Stan King, who was also an occasional kazoo-player.

The most outstanding performer was also a drummer—Tony Sbarbaro, latterly known as 'Tony Spargo', formerly of the Original Dixieland Jazz Band, and, until not long before his death in 1969 at the age of 72, drummer with Phil Napoleon's Original Memphis Five. He had constructed a kazoo shaped like a small bugle, from which he could produce the most amazing impressions of a first-class cornetist. On records by the Napoleon Band on Victor and Columbia in 1956 and thereafter, as well as on records made under the name of the Original Dixieland Jazz Band for Vocalion in 1935, and for Commodore in 1946, among others, he does so without losing the rhythm he maintains as drummer in the normal way. The pioneer kazoo man was Dick Slevin, of the Mound City Blue Blowers, consisting of paper-and-comb, banjo, and guitar besides kazoo, which played in London at the Piccadilly Grill in the spring of 1925; he too was more of the muted variety.

Mention should be made of an Englishman named John Gunn, whose kazoo-playing with the Original Barnstormers Spasm Band between 1957 and 1960 rivalled Tony Sbarbaro's for its realistic impressionism. He too constructed a sophisticated piece of equipment from a large biscuit-tin, from which a substitute trombone effect could be produced, acoustically amplified; but his usual method was to use a kazoo with a small horn attached for amplification of the 'trumpet' sound (see also Section II).

MELLOPHONE

A member of the French horn family occasionally used in jazz and dance music and usually played by Dudley Fosdick. He was a member of Ted Weems's Orchestra during the late 1920s and early 1930s, and afterwards played with Guy Lombardo's Royal Canadians, as well as recording groups under such names as the All Star Orchestra (Victor, 1927–28), Miff Mole's Molers, and Red Nichols's Five Pennies (1928); his broad, rich tone and wide range added an interesting sound to the ensemble passages, and he was a capable soloist. Bill Trone, trombonist with Don Voorhees and his Orchestra in 1927, also sometimes used a mellophone, and a decade later, Eddie Sauter, doubled on this and trumpet with various bands before joining Benny Goodman as arranger. One other performer on the mellophone who can be judged from his records was the bandleader and trombonist Blue Steele (whose band played in Memphis) on Victor records in the late 1920s.

OCARINA

The 'sweet potato' is rarely used in conventional jazz or dance music; though, perhaps rather oddly, one of the foremost exponents was the late Harry Berly, violist with Roy Fox's Band at the Monseigneur Restaurant, Piccadilly, London, late of a chamber music group and tenor saxophonist with Roy Fox and Lew Stone, also at the Monseigneur. The ocarina is more often found in country-and-western groups, although dance bands wishing to produce a rural effect have sometimes employed it, and the famous quartet of ocarinas used on stage in 'Bidin' My Time' (from the show *Girl Crazy*, New York, 1930) was reproduced on various danc-band recordings of the number.

PAPER-AND-COMB

The most primitive of all 'melody' instruments has one outstanding performer in jazz: the late William 'Red' McKenzie, leader of the Mound City Blue Blowers, who recorded with his comb on many sessions, producing a pleasantly cloudy effect, suggesting a distant muted cornet.

SUITCASE

The substitute for a bass drum used by Josh Billings on some of the later records of the Mound City Blue Blowers.

SWANEE- (or SLIDE) WHISTLE

Another instrument whose normally dulcet tones are incompatible with a brass or saxophone section in a jazz or dance band, but which has been used to good effect as a solo voice to give an extra and distinctive sound to a performance. The first recording session undertaken by Paul Whiteman and his orchestra (Camden, New Jersey, 9 August 1920) featured a swanee-whistle on the best-seller *Whispering*, and the player (Warren Luce) was used by Whiteman on several subsequent recordings. Other performers, but much better known for their work on conventional instruments, are Louis Armstrong, cornet and trumpet master, who appeared as swanee-whistle soloist on a record made in 1926 of his Hot Five (*Who 'sit*), and his colleague in Joe 'King' Oliver's Jazz Band three years before, Warren 'Baby' Dodds, the drummer, who plays swanee-whistle on Oliver's records of *Sobbin' Blues* and *Buddy's Habit*.

WASHBOARD

The old-fashioned metal or wooden board with ridges became a useful substitute for a drum when it was discovered that a sound similar to a drumroll could be produced by running the fingers, each wearing a thimble, up and down the ridges. It was not long before 'refinements' such as small cymbals and tap-boxes were screwed or clamped to the board which turned it into a miniature drum kit for those not in a financial position to buy a real full-sized one. Such artists as Floyd Casey (with Clarence Williams), Eddie Edinborough (with Bobby Leecan), Bruce Johnson (with the Washboard Serenaders), Jimmy Bertrand and Jasper Taylor (with many bands in Chicago) could give as good a rhythmic backing to a full-scale band as many of their more conventionally equipped colleagues. The British comedian-actor Deryck Guyler, a life-long connoisseur of jazz, is Britain's most proficient washboard performer.

Partnerships

In the popular music world of the 20th century, the composition of words and music has been generally a matter of *ad hoc* arrangement between lyric-writer and composer, rather than of teams of writers working almost indissolubly. The following exceptions, however, produced some remarkable results over the years.

DE SYLVA–BROWN–HENDERSON

'Bud' de Sylva, Lew Brown, and Ray Henderson composed a large number of extremely popular songs in the years of their partnership from 1926 to 1931. All had written successful numbers individually prior to this period (de Sylva wrote ''N' Everything' in 1918 with Al Jolson and Gus Kahn; Lew Brown produced 'Chili Bean' in 1919 with Albert von Tilzer, and 'Why Did I Kiss That Girl?' in 1923 with Ray Henderson, who in turn had written 'Humming' in 1920 with Louis Breau and 'Georgette' in 1922 also with Lew Brown). Their best-known numbers, many of them composed for Broadway shows and the early talking pictures, are as follows:

1926 'Black Bottom' (*George White's Scandals*)
'Lucky Day' (*George White's Scandals*)
'The Birth of the Blues' (*George White's Scandals*)
'It All Depends on You'

1927 'So Blue'
'Just a Memory'
'Broken Hearted'
'(Here Am I,) Broken Hearted'

Bruce Johnson with his *ad hoc* drum kit based on an ordinary domestic washboard. (Max Jones, Music Books)

'Magnolia' ('Mix the Lot—What Have You Got?')
'The Best Things in Life are Free' (*Good News*)
'The 'Varsity Drag' (*Good News*)
'Good News' (*Good News*)
'Lucky in Love' (*Good News*)

1928 'Together'
'I'm on the Crest of a Wave'
'That's Just My Way of Forgetting You'
'The Song I Love'
'Sonny Boy' (Film *The Singing Fool*)
'You're the Cream in my Coffee' (*Hold Everything*)
'For Old Times' Sake'

1929 'Turn On the Heat (Film *Sunny Side Up*)
'If I Had a Talking Picture of You' (Film *Sunny Side Up*)
'I'm a Dreamer—Aren't We All?' (Film *Sunny Side Up*)
'You've Got Me Pickin' Petals Off o' Daisies' (Film *Sunny Side Up*)
'I'm in Seventh Heaven' (Film *Song of Songs*)
'Little Pal' (Film *Song of Songs*)
'Why Can't You?' (Film *Song of Songs*)
'Used to You' (Film *Song of Songs*)

1930 'Thank Your Father'

1931 'Come to Me' (Film *Indiscreet*)
'One More Time'
'You Try Somebody Else'

DUBIN–WARREN

Al Dubin and Harry Warren worked as a team for many years during the 1930s; Harry Warren had already written big successes such as 'Pasadena' (1924), and during the late 1930s he composed a wordless number for the trumpet-band-leader 'Red' Nichols to use as a signature tune (*Wail of the Winds*). Dubin–Warren successes include:

1932 'Shuffle Off to Buffalo' (Film *42nd Street*)
'42nd Street' (Film *42nd Street*)
'Young and Healthy' (Film *42nd Street*)
'You're Getting to be a Habit with Me' (Film *42nd Street*)

1933 'The Boulevard of Broken Dreams' (Film *Moulin Rouge*)
'Shadow Waltz' (Film *Gold Diggers of 1933*)
'We're in the Money' (Film *Gold Diggers of 1933*)
'Keep Young and Beautiful' (Film *Roman Scandals*)
'Build a Little Home' (Film *Roman Scandals*)
'Shanghai Lil' (Film *Footlight Parade*)
'By a Waterfall' (Film *Footlight Parade*)

1934 'I'll String Along With You' (Film *Twenty Million Sweethearts*)
'Wonder Bar' (Film *Wonder Bar*)

1935 'She's a Latin from Manhattan' (Film *Go Into Your Dance*)
'About a Quarter to Nine' (Film *Go Into Your Dance*)
'Lulu's Back in Town' (Film *Broadway Gondolier*)
'The Rose in Her Hair' (Film *Broadway Gondolier*)
'The Words Are in My Heart' (Film *Gold Diggers of 1935*)
'Lullaby of Broadway' (Film *Gold Diggers of 1935*)

1936 'I'll Sing You a Thousand Love Songs' (Film *Cain and Mabel*)
'With Plenty of Money and You' (Film *Gold Diggers of 1937*)

1937 'September in the Rain' (Film *Melody for Two*)

GEORGE AND IRA GERSHWIN

Although George Gershwin composed the music for many songs *without* lyrics by his brother Ira, and though Ira survived him to supply words to the music of other composers, as a team they provided the words and music to the following well-remembered and often-revived musical productions and films:

1924 *Lady, Be Good* (including 'Fascinating Rhythm'; 'I'd Rather Charleston'; 'The Half of it Dearie Blues'; and the title-song; also originally 'The Man I Love').

1925 *Tell Me More* (including 'Why Do I Love You?' and the title-song); *Tip-Toes* (including 'Looking for a Boy'; 'When Do We Dance?'; 'That Certain Feeling'; 'Sweet and Low Down').

1926 *Oh, Kay!* (including 'Someone to Watch Over Me'; 'Maybe'; 'Clap Yo' Hands'; 'Do Do Do')

1927 *Funny Face* (including ''S Wonderful'; 'My One and Only'; 'He Loves and She Loves'; 'High Hat')

1930 *Strike Up the Band* (including 'The Man I Love'; and the title-song); *Girl Crazy* (including 'I Got Rhythm' and 'Embraceable You')

1931 *Delicious* (film including the title-song).

1936 *Shall We Dance?* (film including 'They Can't

Take that Away from Me'; 'I've Got Beginner's Luck'; 'Let's Call the Whole Thing Off'; 'Slap that Bass'; 'They All Laughed').

1937 *The Goldwyn Follies* (film including 'Love Walked In'; 'Our Love is Here to Stay').

RICHARD RODGERS–LORENZ HART

American team who contributed words and music to the following musical productions between 1925 and 1942, when the partnership split up (Hart died the following year):

1925 *Garrick Gaieties* (first edition—'Manhattan'; 'Sentimental Me').

1926 *The Girl Friend* (including 'The Blue Room' and the title-number); *Garrick Gaieties* (second edition—'Mountain Greenery'); *Peggy Ann* (including 'A Tree in the Park').

1927 *A Connecticut Yankee* (produced in London as *A Yankee at the Court of King Arthur*) (including 'Thou Swell'; 'My Heart Stood Still', the latter not in the London production, but used instead in *One Dam Thing after Another*).

1928 *Present Arms* (including 'You Took Advantage of Me'; 'Do I Hear You Saying "I Love You"?').

1929 *Spring is Here* (including 'With a Song in My Heart'; 'Yours Sincerely'); *Heads Up!* (including 'A Ship Without a Sail').

1930 *Simple Simon* (including 'Ten Cents a Dance'; 'Dancing on the Ceiling').

1931 *America's Sweetheart* (including 'I've Got Five Dollars').

1932 *Love Me Tonight* (film, including 'Mimi').

1933 'Lover' (independent waltz song).

1934 'Blue Moon' (independent slow fox-trot ballad).

1935 *Jumbo* (including 'My Romance').

1936 *On Your Toes* (including 'There's a Small Hotel'; 'Slaughter on Tenth Avenue'; and the title-song).

1937 *Babes in Arms* (including 'Where or When'; 'Johnny One Note'; 'The Lady is a Tramp'; *I'd Rather be Right* (including 'Have You Met Miss Jones?').

1938 *I Married an Angel* (including title-song); *The Boys from Syracuse* (including 'This Can't Be Love'; 'Sing for Your Supper').

1940 *Pal Joey* (including 'I Could Write a Book'; 'Bewitched (Bothered and Bewildered)').

1942 *By Jupiter* (including 'Wait Till You See Her'; 'Nobody's Heart').

RICHARD RODGERS–OSCAR HAMMERSTEIN II

Upon the death of Lorenz Hart, Richard Rodgers teamed up for another successful partnership with Oscar Hammerstein II.

1943 *Oklahoma* (including 'Oh! What a Beautiful Morning'; 'People will say We're in Love'; 'The Surrey With the Fringe on Top').

Andrew Lloyd Webber (left) and Tim Rice, composer and lyricist of *Jesus Christ Superstar*, which closed on 23 August 1980 after an eight-year run of 3357 performances. (Heartaches Ltd: Robert Duncan)

1945 *Carousel* (including 'June is Bustin' Out all Over'; 'If I Loved You'; 'You'll Never Walk Alone').
1945 *State Fair* (20th Century Fox film; including 'It Might as Well be Spring'; 'It's a Grand Night for Singing').
1947 *Allegro* (including 'Money isn't Everything'; 'The Gentleman is a Dope').
1949 *South Pacific* (including 'Some Enchanted Evening'; 'Younger than Springtime'; 'This Nearly Was Mine').
1951 *The King and I* (including 'Hello Young Lovers'; 'Getting to Know You'; 'Shall We Dance?').
1953 *Me and Juliet* (including 'No Other Love'; 'I'm Your Girl').
1955 *Pipe Dream* (including 'All Kinds of People'; 'All at Once You Have Her').
1957 *Cinderella* (CBS Television show, including 'Ten Minuets Ago'; 'Do I Love You Because You're Beautiful?'). This show was watched in all by between 75 000 000 and 100 000 000 people.
1958 *Flower Drum Song* (including 'I Enjoy Being a Girl'; 'Don't Marry Me').
1959 *The Sound of Music* (including 'My Favourite Things'; 'Climb Ev'ry Mountain'; 'Edelweiss').

ANDREW LLOYD WEBBER–TIM RICE

1968 *Joseph and the Amazing Technicolour Dreamcoat* (including 'Any Dream Will Do').
1970 *Jesus Christ Superstar* (title-song).
1976 (first stage performance: London, June 1978) *Evita* ('Don't Cry for Me Argentina').

Jazz and dance musicians who died in unusual circumstances

Barnes, Walter. Burned to death with eight members of his band when the club where they were playing in Natchez, Mississippi, caught fire on 23 April 1940; aged 33.

Bowlly, Al. Popular British vocalist who was killed by a land-mine during an air raid on London in the early hours of 17 April 1941, aged (probably) 43.

Green, Charlie. Trombonist who found himself locked out of his house in New York on 29 February 1936, and froze to death while sleeping on the doorstep, aged about 36.

Hicks, Edna. Blues singer who was burned to death when the flat-iron she was using set the material alight (1925).

Johnson, Ken. Trinidadian bandleader who was killed with several members of his band, as well as many patrons, when the Café de Paris, London, was hit during an air raid on 8 March 1941.

Martin, Carroll. Trombonist with Isham Jones's Orchestra in Chicago for many years. He was killed when the car in which he was being driven with his instrument pulled up suddenly, throwing him forward on to his trombone with such force that it buckled under the impact, penetrating his chest and lungs. Date unknown, but about 1940.

McMurray, Loring. Prominent New York alto saxophonist with Sam Lanin's Orchestra during the early 1920s. He made his nose bleed by blowing it, contracted septicaemia and died, while still around 30 years old. Date unknown, but believed to be about 1925.

Melrose, Frank. Chicago pianist of great ability whose mutilated body was found by a road side out of Hammond, Indiana, on 1 September 1941, aged 33. Cause of death still uncertain (murder or road accident?).

Miller, Glenn. Trombonist and bandleader who, as Major Glenn Miller, left an English airfield to fly to newly liberated Paris on the Morning of 15 December 1944, to direct the American Expeditionary Force Band which had preceded him there. Neither he nor his plane was ever seen again.

Moten, Bennie. Black ragtime pianist and bandleader from Kansas City. He died there aged 40 on 3 April 1935, following complications and loss of blood as a result of a tonsillectomy.

Smith, Bessie. 'The Empress of the Blues', who died from loss of blood and severe arm, head, and chest injuries after a road accident on 26 September 1937. She was found in the road by a local surgeon who took her to hospital, where she died the next morning, aged 42.

Smith, Clarence. 'Pine Top' the pianist who pioneered the boogie-woogie style of playing, was killed by a gunman's bullet not intended for him as he played in a Chicago night-club on 14 March 1929, aged 24.

Thomas, Hersal. Teenage pianist whose death

on 3 July 1926 at the age of 17 may have been due to food poisoning. But whether this was due to the unfit condition of the food, or to poison having been introduced into it by a jealous girl-friend, has never been finally settled.

Vincent, Eddie. Trombonist pioneer who was working in Chicago in 1927. Going down a rickety wooden staircase one night after playing, his trombone fell from his grasp. While trying to save it, the balustrade collapsed and he was killed in the fall.

Waller, Thomas 'Fats'. World-famous Black pianist who contracted pneumonia while returning home after a tiring tour, and died aboard the train the *Santa Fé Chief*, aged 39, on 15 December 1943. Twelve years earlier, he had recorded 'Dallas Blues' and sung the lyrics as follows: 'Gonna put myself on the Santa Fé and go, go, go ...'.

Women jazz and dance music artists

Benson, Ivy. British bandleader during the Second World War who achieved considerable popularity with her all-girls' band, with which she played alto saxophone.

Donegan, Dorothy. Pianist of the boogie-woogie persuasion who worked in Chicago in the late 1930s and early 1940s; an artist of considerable talent, but very little recorded.

Dreiwitz, Barbara. American tuba-player of considerable ability, frequently plays with Black veteran jazz musicians, the only white member of the band and the only girl in it.

Hardin, Lil. Second wife of Louis Armstrong, whom she met when they both played in Joe 'King' Oliver's famous Creole Jazz Band in Chicago in 1922 (married 5 February 1924, divorced 1932). Trained at Fisk University, piano abilities not restricted to the jazz idiom. Died on stage in St Louis while taking part in a memorial concert to her ex-husband, August 1971.

Hutton, Ina Ray. Blonde bandleader of all-girls' band that was very popular in America during the mid-1930s, but which recorded strangely little; she appeared in several films.

Ivy Benson playing the saxophone with her All Girl Orchestra, 1945. (Radio Times Hulton Picture Library)

Ronell, Ann. American composer of such great successes as 'Willow, Weep for Me'; 'Rain on the Roof' (both 1932); 'Who's Afraid of the Big, Bad Wolf?' (1933).

Snow, Valaida. Trumpet-player in the virtuoso style who became very popular in Europe during the five years prior to the outbreak of the Second World War. She was interned by the Nazis in Denmark in 1940, repatriated in 1943, and resumed her musical career in America, where she died in 1956, aged 56.

Stobart, Kathleen. British tenor saxophonist in the modern idiom who achieved great popularity during the 1940s and 1950s.

Suesse, Dana. American composer of many light pieces, not all in the dance idiom, but best known for 'Ho Hum!' and 'Whistling in the Dark' (1931), and 'My Silent Love' (1932) (strangely subtitled 'A Jazz Nocturne').

Terry, Thelma. Diminutive American string bass player of an outstanding ability that rivalled her male colleagues; led a band known as her 'Play Boys' in Chicago in the late 1920s, all of them being men.

Wayne, Mabel. American composer of many colossal hits, such as 'In a Little Spanish Town' (1926), 'Ramona' (1927), 'Chiquita' (1928), 'It Happened in Monterey' (1929), 'Alone on the Range' (1933), 'Little Man, You've Had a Busy Day' (1934), and 'Home Again' (1935).

Williams, Mary Lou. One of the most versatile of all American jazz pianists, a Black girl with a gift for playing ragtime, swing, or 'modern' jazz. She also composed a piano suite *The Zodiac*, arranged for many outstanding bands, Black and white, including Andy Kirk's, Benny Goodman's, Earl Hines's, Tommy Dorsey's, Glen Gray's, and Gus Arnheim's. She lived in England from 1952 until 1954 and has devoted much of her life to religious study and the Bel Canto Charity Organisation.

Early starters and long-lived musicians

Adler, Larry. Born Baltimore, 1914; began playing harmonica while still at school, and made his first record with Bob Haring's Colonial Club Orchestra in July 1930 ('Hittin' the Bottle'); thereafter in much demand, leading to London début in C B Cochran's revue *Streamline* (Palace, 28 September 1934), and subsequent world fame as the premier virtuoso harmonica-player, for whom Ralph Vaughan Williams composed a rhapsody for harmonica, piano, and orchestra (1952).

Anka, Paul. Canadian-born (1941) song-writer and singer who, at the age of twelve, showed talent as an impersonator. Three years later he made his first record as a singer, and his first best-seller, *Diana*, was made in 1957 when he was 16.

Blake, Eubie. Born Baltimore, 1883. He was playing ragtime during its formative years and composed 'Charleston Rag' (published 1899); subsequently wrote many first-class rags, and the score of the long-running all-Black revue *Shuffle Along* (opened at 63rd Street Theatre, New York, 23 May 1921, and ran for 504 performances); also composed 'Memories of You' (1930), a permanent best-seller; toured England with (then) partner Noble Sissle, popular singer, 1925–26. During his 80s he made LP albums of his own and other composers' works, and at 92 appeared on BBC Television demonstrating an amazingly flexible piano style and a dance routine he had been using for over 70 years.

Goodman, Benny. Born Chicago, 1909; played first professional job (and recorded) with Ben Pollack's Californians there in 1926; left Pollack in 1929 and has since become identified as the most widely and generously gifted clarinettist in jazz, for whom Bela Bartók wrote a trio for clarinet, violin, and piano, who has recorded and frequently broadcast works such as Mozart's Concerto for clarinet and orchestra and works by Weber, J S Bach, and others; may be said to have launched the 'Swing era' in 1935 when his band, after a very shaky start, became a national, then an international favourite; many films, including *Hollywood Hotel* (1938), *Stage Door Canteen* (1943), and *Sweet and Low Down* (1945); provided part of the sound-track of the Walt Disney cartoon *Make Mine Music* (1945).

Hampton, Lionel. Born Louisville, Kentucky, 1909; first records and first work with important band in 1929 as drummer with Paul Howard's Quality Serenaders in Culver City, California; joined Benny Goodman's Trio to make it a Quartet, on vibraphone, 1936, later formed a big band and embraced the 'modern' idiom.

Hanshaw, Annette. Born New York, 1910; self-taught as singer of current popular songs, discovered by recording executive at the age of 15 and for the next eight years recorded, filmed and was 'The Personality Girl of Radio'. Enormously popular for her musicianly, shy style; played piano and ukulele and composed extra words for many of her songs.

Johnson, Bill. Born New Orleans, Louisiana, 1872; played bass with the Original Creole Orchestra that toured the country about 1911, and bass and banjo with 'King' Oliver's Jazz Band in Chicago in 1923; still playing occasionally until his 90s; died 1969 aged 97.

Kaufman, Irving. Born New York, 1890; began singing as a boy. His keen sense of pitch, prodigious memory of lyrics, and the ability to sing them with expression made him ideal for dance band and other vocal recording work; perfect diction and mellow tenor can be heard on (he estimates) some 6000 recordings made between 1913 and 1974; at 84 he contributed some contemporary singing to two albums of his earlier work, sounding very little different despite his advanced age.

Osmond, Jimmy. Born 1963; at nine, one of the principal attractions of the Osmond family group that made sensational success with American and British children of about the same age.

Robinson, Sugar Chile. Born 1942; young Black pianist who made a great success in 1951 in London at the age of nine, but little has been heard of him since.

Rose Marie. Born 1925; recording and doing radio work at seven, continued this through her teens and still makes occasional night-club, radio, and television appearances.

Selvin, Ben (1898–1980); a bandleader at 17, made first records with his Novelty Orchestra at 19, and between then and 1934 recorded thousands of sides with many front-rank musicians on all labels, great and small; became an executive for RCA Victor.

Shapiro, Helen. Born London, 1946, a star at 14, with a strangely deep, almost masculine voice. Her popularity began to fade as 'rock' music took over in the mid-1960s.

Tormé, Mel. Born Chicago, 1924; appeared as child prodigy vocalist at three with the Coon-Sanders Orchestra; as teenager sang with Artie Shaw's Orchestra and during the 1950s made many very useful tours on both sides of the Atlantic as soloist (nicknamed 'The Velvet Fog' from the huskiness of his voice).

Van Eps, Fred, Sr. Began recording in 1897 as banjo soloist on Edison wax cylinders, made hundreds of records of all kinds during the next 30 to 40 years, then crowned his career in 1950 by making a long-playing record at 80.

Waller, Thomas, 'Fats'. Born New York, 1904; wrote first song 'Squeeze Me' at 15 in 1919, began recording career on discs and piano rolls at 18 in 1922. Made hundreds more during 39 years of life, many as pipe-organ solos of popular songs, blues, and arrangements of Negro spirituals.

Wonder, Stevie. Blind rock singer who burst into popularity at the age of twelve during the late 1960s, offering the raw material of the idiom with little refinement but with considerable success, especially among connoisseurs of the style.

Versatile musicians

Avalon, Frankie. A singer and, later, film star, who began as a brilliant trumpeter during his earliest years.

Bechet, Sidney. One of the greatest jazz soloists of all, born in New Orleans, 14 May 1897, died in Paris, 14 May 1959. Sidney Bechet played with musicians of all persuasions in the jazz spectrum, white and Black, pioneer and modern. As one of the principal soloists of the Southern Syncopated Orchestra that played in England between the summer of 1919 and the autumn of 1921, he attracted the attention of Ernest Ansermet, the Swiss conductor, who almost alone among his colleagues, recognised the artistic merit of Bechet's music. Sidney Bechet usually played clarinet and soprano saxophone, but recorded using tenor saxophone, piano, string bass, and drums on a multi-recording date for Victor in 1941, and on one session in 1924 with Clarence Williams's Blue Five on OKeh, he played sarrusophone; legend has it he noticed the instrument in a second-hand shop on his way to the studio, impulsively bought it and insisted on trying it out on the record ('Mandy, Make Up Your Mind'), much to the amusement of his colleagues.

Beiderbecke, Bix. One of the best-known and most-respected white jazz musicians, Bix Beiderbecke was a cornet-player from Davenport, Iowa, who received his inspiration from records of the Original Dixieland Jazz Band while still a schoolboy. Although only 28 when he died (in New York on 6 August 1931), he had played with two of the finest dance organisations in the USA, those of Jean Goldkette and Paul Whiteman. He had expanded his love of jazz to include the impressionist work of Maurice Ravel, Claude Debussy, Eastwood Lane, Igor Stravinsky, and others. He loved to play piano, and does so on four records—one made with his first professional band, the Wolverine Orchestra (*Big Boy*, 1924), two informal trio records with his friends, saxophonist Frank Trumbauer and guitarist Eddie Lang (*For No Reason At All in C* and *Wringin' and Twistin'*, 1927) and one entirely solo (*In a Mist* or *Bixology*, 1927). In all his other records he played cornet, despite the trend among his colleagues to using trumpet, preferring the broader tone.

Brilhart, Arnold. An outstandingly versatile and

talented musician who played all the members of the saxophone family, in addition to flute and oboe; able to sight-read and thus very much in demand for work on all kinds of recording sessions, radio and theatre work. He recorded principally with Yerkes's SS Flotilla Orchestra, the California Ramblers, Ben Selvin's Orchestra, Roger Wolfe Kahn's Orchestra, and the Dorsey Brothers' Orchestra. He has long been a manufacturer of instruments and accessories.

Buckley, Neil. Vocalist with Don Bestor and his Orchestra during the 1930s. Neil Buckley later forsook the music world and became Mayor of a town in New Jersey.

Carter, Benny. Plays trumpet, clarinet, soprano, alto and tenor sax, piano. Played with Clarence Williams, Charlie Johnson, McKinney's Cotton Pickers and Fletcher Henderson. Also arranger (for Henry Hall's Band in *c* 1936) and led his own band from 1939.

Colonna, Jerry. The hoarse-voiced mustachioed eccentric comedian of American films was once a 'hot jazz' trombonist with Joe Herlihy's Orchestra in New York during the late 1920s; he recorded thus on Edison Diamond Discs.

Dankworth, John. As the leading alto-sax player, Johnny (as he then was) Dankworth for many years held his band at or near the top of the profession. His interest in serious music has increased over the years: in 1958 he collaborated with Matyás Seiber on the *Improvisations for Jazz Band and Symphony Orchestra.* More recently (1971) a string quartet by John Dankworth was performed in London, and the previous year he composed a *Folk Mass.* He has also written a Jazz opera: *Sweeney Agonistes*, a piano concerto, and several works for orchestra, including Theme and Variations (1980) for the Royal Philharmonic Orchestra.

Day, Doris. Born Doris Cappelhoff in 1924, Doris Day became vocalist with Barney Rapp's Orchestra in 1940, then joined Les Brown's Orchestra for a year. She branched out as a vocal soloist, as many dance-band singers have done, but after making several successful musical films, she discovered her talent as a non-singing light comedienne, and the majority of her subsequent films (made during the late 1950s and after) show her in this capacity.

Top: Stephane Grappelli, the best-known jazz violinist. Above: Humphrey Lyttelton, versatile British jazz musician, now also a popular broadcaster. (Both pictures: Black Lion Records)

Dorsey, Jimmy. The elder of the famous Dorsey brothers, born in Shenandoah, Pennsylvania, 29 February 1904. Jimmy Dorsey was regarded during the late 1920s and 1930s as the greatest saxophonist in the world, but he could also give an excellent performance on trumpet, as Joe Venuti's Blue Six playing *Pink Elephants* (Columbia) attests. Jimmy Dorsey also played clarinet and baritone saxophone, and does so on many records, switching from one to the other easily, sometimes via his usual alto saxophone; he died on 12 June 1957.

Downing, Rex. Trombonist with the Coon-Sanders Orchestra during the latter half of the 1920s and until the end of the band's life, Rex Downing subsequently gave up music and became a magistrate.

Durante, Jimmy 'Schnozzle'. A favourite American comedian with a guttural Bronx accent and a large nose. Jimmy Durante was originally a ragtime pianist who quickly absorbed the 'new' jazz idiom (1918), formed the Original New Orleans Jazz Band (afterwards giving his own name to it) and recorded on Gennett and OKeh with this quintet, in the closest approximation to the pioneer Original Dixieland Jazz Band known at that time. He later recorded with Bailey's Lucky Seven on Gennett (1921), under the direction of Sam Lanin.

Elman, Ziggy. Benny Goodman's high-note trumpet-player of the late 1930s began his career on trombone with Alex Bartha's Hotel Traymore Orchestra in Atlantic City. His style is quite unlike the rather brash trumpet work of the Swing era.

Hughes, David. A successful pop singer in the 1950s, he turned his attention to opera in the mid-1960s. He has sung at Glyndebourne and the Welsh National Opera as a tenor, and has made a number of records. He is best remembered, perhaps, for his portrayal of Don José in Bizet's *Carmen*.

Johnson, Bob. One of the alto saxophonists in the Harry Yerkes entourage in the early 1920s, later gave up music and became a stockbroker in New York. From the Yerkes records of the time, he appears to have been an excellent musician.

Lindsay, Joe. The trombonist with Armand J Piron's New Orleans Orchestra who in 1925 or 1926 switched to playing string bass. The sturdy, melodic trombone of the Piron records for Victor, OKeh, and Columbia in 1923 and 1924 gave way to the athletic, powerful string bass heard on the first three Victor dates in 1926 by Jelly-Roll Morton's Red Hot Peppers.

Nunez, Alcide. New Orleans-born clarinetist with the Original Dixeland Jazz Band (1916), the Louisiana Five (1918–20), and Harry Yerkes's bands (1920). He abandoned the music world in later years and joined the police force.

Ormandy, Dr Eugene. World-famous symphony-orchestra conductor who began his professional career as violinist (Cameo records, 1923–24) and bandleader (OKeh records, 1928–30), also directing accompaniments to OKeh popular vocalists (eg Annette Hanshaw).

Previn, André. German-born conductor, American citizen. Recognised as a great authority on all kinds of concert music and a very popular British television personality, albeit sometimes in the role of a comedian, at which he is as expert as he is a conductor. André Previn made many fine records for Victor and other labels in America as a jazz pianist during the late 1940s and early 1950s, and has since embarked on a series of successful classical recordings for RCA, CBS, EMI, and Polygram.

Rignold, Hugo. For many years conductor of the Liverpool Philharmonic Orchestra, Hugo Rignold was principal violinist and 'hot' jazz soloist on that instrument with Jack Hylton's Orchestra between 1925 and 1930. He was rightly regarded as Britain's foremost exponent of what was then a daringly experimental new style of playing in the jazz idiom. He led his own orchestra during the 1930s, recording dance music for Columbia.

Rollini, Adrian. Born in New York in 1904, Adrian Rollini was the absolute master of the bass saxophone, a seemingly unwieldy instrument for a dance band, but after learning to play piano and xylophone, he added the largest of the saxophone family to his repertoire along with other instruments (goofus, hot fountain pen—see above—drums, and vibraphone). On Joe Venuti's Blue Five record of *Pink Elephants*, made for Columbia in 1933, he plays bass saxophone, vibraphone, piano, and goofus in that order.

The golden age of big bands

The first British big band was formed by Archibald Joyce in London in 1911.

The first American big band was Art Hickman's (San Francisco, 1915).

The most successful band of the 1920s–30s was Paul Whiteman's (see below).

The longest-lasting band was Guy Lombardo's Royal Canadians, an American band formed in 1923 and dissolved 54 years later in 1977. The British bandleader Joe Loss founded his band in 1930. It is still active today.

The most imitated band is that of Glenn Miller, whose style was copied by the following bands:

1940 Bob Chester and his Orchestra
1946 First Official Glenn Miller Orchestra, led by

	Tex Beneke (directed by Ray McKinley)
Early 1950s	Ralph Flanagan, also Jerry Gray and his Orchestra
1956	Ray McKinley
1966	Buddy de Franco
1970s	Sid Lawrence

The first American band to use a vocalist of its own, not recruited solely for making records: Ted Lewis (New York, 1920)—himself.

The first British band to use a vocalist of its own was the Savoy Havana Band (London, 1922)—Ramon Newton

BANDS WITH WHICH FAMOUS VOCALISTS, ACTORS AND ACTRESSES FIRST SANG

Artist	*Band*	*Date*
The Andrews Sisters	Leon Belasco	1937
Fred Astaire	Leo Reisman	1931
Mildred Bailey	with a section of Paul Whiteman's Orchestra	1929
Lucille Ball	Desi Arnaz	1941
The Boswell Sisters	Jackie Taylor	1930
Perry Como	Ted Weems	1936
Bing Crosby	Don Clark	1926
Doris Day	Les Brown	1940
Gloria de Haven	Jan Savitt	1942
Alice Faye	Rudy Vallée	1933
Ella Fitzgerald	Chick Webb	1935
Betty Grable	in her real name, Ruth Haag, with husband Harry James	1947
Billie Holiday	Benny Goodman	1933
Stanley Holloway	Jack Hylton	1926
Betty Hutton	Vincent Lopez	1939
Peggy Lee	Benny Goodman	1941
Vera Lynn	Howard Baker	1935
Fred MacMurray	George Olsen	1929
Tony Martin	Tom Gerun	1934
Dick Powell	Charlie Davis	1928
Anne Shelton	Ambrose	1940
Dinah Shore	Xavier Cugat	1939
Frank Sinatra	Harry James	1939
Arthur Tracy	Manolo Castro	1931
Clifton Webb	Leo Reisman	1933

BANDS FEATURING COMPOSERS SINGING THEIR OWN NUMBERS

Harold Arlen (with Leo Reisman, 1933, 1934, 1937)
Hoagy Carmichael (with Paul Whiteman, 1927; with Sunny Clapp, 1931)
Noel Coward (with Leo Reisman, 1933)
Johnny Mercer (with Paul Whiteman, 1934; with Benny Goodman, 1939)
Frank Sinatra (with Tommy Dorsey, 1941)

Paul Whiteman, 'The King of Jazz'. (Popperfoto)

BANDLEADERS AS UNEXPECTED VOCALISTS

Stan Kenton singing a duet with Benny Goodman with the Hollywood Hucksters, 1947.
Glenn Miller singing with the Dorsey Brothers' Orchestra, 1934.
Leo Reisman singing with his own orchestra, 1931.
Benny Goodman singing with his own orchestra, 1936.

FIFTY BEST-SELLING BANDS AND THEIR RECORDS

The original issue is shown first where two makes are given; the second is the British equivalent of an American original, and *vice versa*.

Ambrose: Trees; Let's Put Out the Lights and Go to Sleep (both HMV, 1932)
Charlie Barnet: Skyliner (American Decca/Brunswick, 1945)
Count Basie: Doggin' Around (American Decca/Brunswick 1937)
The Benson Orchestra of Chicago: Ain't We Got Fun?; Wabash Blues (Victor/HMV, 1921)
Bunny Berigan: I Can't Get Started with You (Victor/HMV, 1937)
Bertini: Samum—A Classical Foxtrot (!) (Sterno and Zonophone, 1932)
Les Brown: Sentimental Journey (Columbia, 1945)
California Ramblers: The Sheik (Vocalion, 1921); California, Here I Come (Columbia, 1924); The Blue Room (Columbia, 1926)
Coon-Sanders' Original Nighthawk Orchestra: Deep Henderson (Victor/HMV, 1926)
Billy Cotton: Somebody Stole My Gal (Regal Zonophone, 1933); Lambeth Walk (Rex, 1938); In a Golden Coach (Decca, 1953); I Saw Mummy Kissing Santa Claus (Decca, 1953); Friends and Neighbours (Decca, 1954)
Bob Crosby: South Rampart Street Parade (American

Decca, 1937); Big Noise from Winnetka (American Decca, 1938)

Jimmy Dorsey: Green Eyes; Tangerine (both American Decca/Brunswick, 1941)

Tommy Dorsey: Song of India (Victor/HMV, 1937); On the Sunny Side of the Street (Victor/HMV, 1944); Tea for Two Cha Cha (American Decca/Brunswick, 1958)

Duke Ellington: Mood Indigo (Brunswick, 1930); Take the 'A' Train (Victor/HMV, 1941); Skin Deep (Philips, 1954)

Roy Fox: Oh Mo'nah! (Decca, 1931); Lullaby of the Leaves (Decca, 1932)

Jan Garber: What Do I Care What Somebody Said? (Victor/HMV, 1927); Was it a Dream? (Columbia, 1928)

Geraldo: Jealousy (Columbia, 1932); Poinciana (Parlophone, 1945)

Carroll Gibbons: I Won't Dance (Columbia, 1935)

Benny Goodman: King Porter Stomp (Victor/HMV, 1935); Bach Goes to Town (Victor/HMV, 1938); Why Don't You Do Right? (Columbia/Parlophone, 1942)

Henry Hall: The Teddy Bears' Picnic (Columbia, 1932)

Woody Herman: At the Woodchoppers' Ball (American Decca/Brunswick, 1939)

Art Hickman: Sweet and Low (Columbia, 1919); The Japanese Sandman/Avalon (Columbia, 1920)

Jack Hylton: Coal Black Mammy (HMV, 1921); Babette (HMV, 1925); I'm Looking Over a Four-leaf Clover (HMV, 1927); My Sin (HMV, 1929); Rhymes (Zonophone; Decca, 1931)

Harry James: The Flight of the Bumble Bee; Trumpet Rhapsody; You Made Me Love You; Strictly Instrumental (all Columbia/Parlophone, 1941); By the Sleepy Lagoon (Columbia/Parlophone, 1942)

Isham Jones: Ma!; Wabash Blues (Brunswick, 1921); Stardust (Brunswick, 1930)

Harry James, American band-leader and virtuoso trumpeter. (Verve Records)

Roger Wolfe Kahn: Sometimes I'm Happy (Victor/HMV, 1927); Crazy Rhythm (composer's version) (Victor/HMV, 1928)

Hal Kemp: F D R Jones (Victor/HMV, 1938)

Stan Kenton: The Peanut Vendor; Artistry in Rhythm (both Capitol, 1947)

Gene Krupa: Drummin' Man (Columbia/Parlophone, 1939); Tuxedo Junction (Columbia/Parlophone, 1940)

Sam Lanin: Who? (Columbia, 1925); Hallelujah! (Banner/Imperial, 1927); Exactly Like You (Perfect/Imperial, 1930)

Ted Lewis: When My Baby Smiles at Me (Columbia, 1920); Good Night (Columbia, 1927); She's Funny That Way (Columbia, 1928)

Guy Lombardo: Charmaine (Columbia, 1927); Where the Shy Little Violets Grow (Columbia, 1928); A Cottage For Sale (Columbia, 1930)

Vincent Lopez: Nola (OKeh/Parlophone, 1922); What'll I Do (OKeh/Parlophone, 1924)

Joe Loss: In the Mood (Regal Zonophone and HMV, 1940); Wheels Cha Cha (HMV, 1961); The Maigret Theme; Must be Madison (both HMV, 1962)

Glenn Miller; Moonlight Serenade; In the Mood (both Bluebird/HMV, 1939); Chattanooga Choo-choo (Bluebird/HMV, 1941); American Patrol (Victor/HMV, 1942)

Ray Noble: Good Night, Sweetheart (HMV/Victor, 1931); Love is the Sweetest Thing (HMV/Victor, 1932); Isle of Capri (HMV/Victor, 1934)

George Olsen: Who? (Victor, 1925); Hi-diddle-diddle (Victor/HMV, 1926); The Best Things in Life are Free (Victor/HMV, 1927); Sonny Boy (Victor/HMV, 1928)

Jack Payne: Stein Song (Columbia, 1930); The Clouds Will Soon Roll By (Imperial, 1932); Smoke Gets in Your Eyes (Rex, 1934)

Leo Reisman: I Bring a Love Song (Victor/HMV, 1930)

Harry Roy: Bugle Call Rag; Canadian Capers (both Parlophone, 1933)

Savoy Havana Band: Three O'Clock in the Morning (Columbia, 1922); Gigolette; After the Storm/Dream Daddy (both Columbia, 1924); Side by Side (HMV, 1927)

Savoy Orpheans: What'll I Do? (Columbia, and on HMV as 'The Romaine Orchestra', 1924); Valencia (HMV, as 'Savoy Havana Band', 1926); Charmaine (HMV, 1927)

Ben Selvin: Dardanella (Victor/HMV, 1919); Broadway Melody (Columbia, 1929)

Artie Shaw; Begin the Beguine (Bluebird/HMV, 1938)

Nat Shilkret: Broadway Melody (Victor/HMV, 1929)

Joseph C Smith: Yellow Dog Blues (Victor/HMV, 1919)

Lew Stone: The Continental/Smoke Gets in your Eyes (Regal Zonophone, 1934)

Waring's Pennsylvanians: Any Ice Today, Lady? (Victor/HMV, 1926); Jericho (Victor/HMV, 1929)

Ted Weems: Heartaches (American Decca/Brunswick, 1938)

Paul Whiteman: The Japanese Sandman/Whispering (Victor/HMV, 1920); The Parade of the Wooden Soldiers (Victor/HMV, 1922, re-made 1928); Rhapsody in Blue (with George Gershwin, the composer, at the piano) (Victor/HMV, re-make 1927: the original was a very poor seller in 1924/25); Side by Side (Victor/HMV, 1927); Ramona (Victor/HMV, 1928); all six titles from Whiteman's film 'King of Jazz' (Columbia, 1930); Slaughter on Tenth Avenue (Victor/HMV, 1936)

Country Music

Country Music reflects the living, breathing influences of the day-to-day life of the ordinary working man, his wife and family. Its identity evolved from the ambiance of the pioneer environment, gathering rich influences as the early settlers from the Eastern states and migrants from Europe and the British Isles moved westward across America with their guitars, banjos, and zithers singing about their exploits, hopes, hardships, religions, loves, and booze. A localised, individual art, its audiences were strictly limited until the gramophone began to widen its appeal.

The first commercial recording of Country Music was made on 14 June 1923 by Fiddlin' John Carson. It was a coupling of 'The Little Old Log Cabin in the Lane' and 'The Old Hen Cackled and the Rooster's Going to Crow'.

The Father of Country Music is generally recognised to be Jimmie Rodgers (1897–1933), who made his recording *début* on 4 August 1927, with 'Soldier's Sweetheart'. He is unique in that during his recording life (1927–33) it is estimated that he sold in excess of five million 78 rpm records, a remarkable feat at the time of the 'Depression'. He was elected the **first member of the Country Music Hall of Fame** in 1961, and his recordings are still selling in vast numbers all around the world. Album tributes to him have been made by such 'Kings of Country Music' as Ernest Tubb, Merle Haggard, Lefty Frizzell (who, according to *Billboard* magazine dated 27 October 1951, had four songs in its first ten top-selling Country records), and Hank Snow (whose first recording for RCA Victor called 'Lonesome Blue Yodel' and 'Prisoned Cowboy' was made in

Johnny Cash, envoy of America's Country Music. (CBS Records)

1936; he had **at least one record on the Country best-selling charts for 22 consecutive years—1949–70**).

One of the most significant recording sessions in Country Music history was the million-seller triple album called 'Will the Circle be Unbroken', recorded in 1973 with the Nitty Gritty Dirt Band and guest appearances by such famous people as Earl Scruggs, Roy Acuff (elected as the **first living member of the Country Music Hall of Fame in 1962**), Mother Maybelle Carter ('Queen of Country Music'), Doc Watson, Merle Travis, and many others.

The biggest-selling single by a female artist in the history of Country Music is 'Stand by Your Man' by Tammy Wynette, recorded in 1968 and selling well over two million copies. It reached No 1 on the British charts when re-released in 1975.

The first Country Music singer to reach international stardom was Jim Reeves, who died in a plane crash in Tennessee on 13 July 1964, aged 44. His first successful record was 'Mexican Joe', recorded in 1952. From 1955 to 1968 in America he had one or more records in the Top Ten every year and even though his tragic death occurred many years ago he still counts amongst the top ten artists with the most charted records both there and in England. **He was elected to the Country Music Hall of Fame in 1967.**

One of the most successful female singer/song writers of Country Music in the 1970s is Dolly Parton. She has become a Country Super Star. Her first hit was 'Dumb Blonde' in 1967. Since then she has had many hits, 'Jolene' reaching No 7 in the British Hit Parade in May 1976.

The 1950s

ENTER ROCK 'N' ROLL

A blend of Gospel, Jazz, Rhythm and Blues, Country, Boogie, and the music of the Southern Blacks, which seized the imagination of American youngsters and for a time swept away all competition, invading the rest of the world's markets irresistibly.

The first use of the term 'rock 'n' roll' was by American broadcaster Alan Freed, who in 1951 hosted an R&B record show entitled 'Moondog's Rock 'n' Roll Party' while working at WJW in Cleveland. He probably adapted the title of the old blues song 'My Baby Rocks Me with a Steady Roll'.

The first American rock 'n' roll hit was 'Sh-boom' which was originally sung by an unknown Black group in the spring of 1954, and which soon entered the pop charts the following year in a version by the group known as The Crewcuts.

The first world-wide rock 'n' roll hit was 'Rock Around the Clock' by Bill Haley and his Comets in 1955, when it was played behind the credits of the disturbing but successful film 'Blackboard Jungle'. (This number was originally recorded in April 1954.) Bill Haley and his Comets first reached the charts in both America and England in 1954 with their number 'Shake, Rattle and Roll'.

The individual artist with the most Gold Record Awards (38) is Elvis Presley ('The King of Rock 'n' Roll') spanning 1958 to January 1979. His first single, 'That's All Right Mama', was recorded in June 1954, and his first TV appearance was in the autumn of 1955 on the Tommy Dorsey Show in America. 'Heartbreak Hotel', his first Gold Disc, was recorded on 10 February 1956, and he first hit the No 1 spot in the British Hit Parade in June 1957 with 'All Shook Up'; the earlier numbers 'Heartbreak Hotel' and 'Hound Dog' both reached No 2 in the British charts. His total No 1 chart-toppers in Britain now number 17, a total shared only by The Beatles.

One of the greatest singer/song-writers is Chuck Berry, who made his first recording, 'Maybellene' in 1955 (disc-jockey Alan Freed being named as co-writer). It sold over a million copies.

One of the first British hits to reach the American charts was 'Rock Island Line' by Lonnie Donegan in 1956. This number was originally issued in 1954 as part of an LP.

Britain's first rock 'n' roll band was Tony Crombie and his Rockets who, in 1956, entered the British charts with 'Teach You to Rock'.

Britain's first rock 'n' roll star was Tommy Steele who, in October 1956, entered the charts with 'Rock With the Caveman'. His first No 1 was 'Singing the Blues' later the same year.

The most successful American female rock 'n' roll artist is Connie Francis. Her first hit record was 'Who's Sorry Now' in 1958, and over the next five years she scored 25 hit numbers.

The British artist who has spent most weeks in the charts (774) from 1958 to 1974 is Cliff Richard. His first entry was with 'Move It' (1958) and then between July 1959 and March 1968 he had nine 'No 1s' in the British charts.

Voted Best New Artist in America in 1959 and winning the Grammy Award for **Best Vocal Performance (Male)** was the late Bobby Darin. His recordings of 'Dream Lover' and 'Mack the Knife' both became British chart-toppers, in May and September 1959 respectively.

The major Rock 'n' Soul artist is James Brown, whose first hit called 'Please, Please, Please' was recorded in 1956. He reached No 1 on the 'Soul Board' in 1959 with 'Try Me'.

The 1960s

The first Twist record, called 'The Twist' by Chubby Checker, was recorded originally in 1959 as a 'B' side to 'Teardrops on Your Letter', sung by Hank Ballard. It entered the British Top Fifty in 1960 and again in 1962, reaching No 14.

Paul McCartney (left) showing his unique rhodium disc to another record-holder, Wayne Sleep, the ballet dancer who himself set a record with an *entrechat douze*. Centre is Paul's American wife Linda and Norris McWhirter, editor of the *Guinness Book of Records*, which states that Paul is the most successful songwriter of all time. The televised presentation took place in London on 24 October 1979. (Photo Reportage Ltd)

One of the most successful 'Trad Bands' of the early 1960s was Kenny Ball and his Jazz Men. During 1960–62 he regularly entered both the British and the American hit parades, his best-seller being 'Midnight in Moscow', released in the Autumn of 1961.

One of the most commercially successful Modern Jazz instrumental groups of the early 1960s was Dave Brubeck and his Quintet. His single of 'Take Five' entered the Top Ten in October 1961 and soon became a million-seller.

The first British rock group to reach No 1 on the American Billboard chart were The Tornados in 1962 with their version of 'Telstar'.

The best-known writer of 'Protest Songs' is Bob Dylan. Between 1961 and 1964 his songs protesting on behalf of civil rights and anti-war movements such as 'Blowin' in the Wind', 'Masters of War', and 'Hard Rain' were a great stimulus to those caught up in anti-nuclear marches and protests. His change from acoustic to electric guitar in 1965, in line with current 'rock' trends, gave him increased commercial appeal abroad, but his first entry in the British charts in that year was with 'Times They Are a-Changin'', made earlier with acoustic guitar.

The most successful American pop-folk group of the decade were Peter, Paul and Mary; it was through them that the songs of Bob Dylan were first introduced to a mass audience. One of the their biggest hits was 'Blowin' in the Wind', released in 1963.

The most notable American female folk-protest movement singer is Joan Baez. She made her *début* at the Newport Folk Festival in 1959; her first entry into the British Top Ten came in 1965 with 'There but for Fortune'.

The only British female soloist to have three 'No 1s' in the British Hit Parade is Sandie Shaw: 'There's Always Something There To Remind Me' (October 1964), 'Long Live Love (May 1965), 'Puppet on a String' (March 1967). This last won the Eurovision Song Contest later that year.

The most successful group of singers of all time are The Beatles: George Harrison, MBE, John Winston (later John Ono) Lennon, MBE, James Paul McCartney, MBE, and Richard Starkey (Ringo Starr), MBE. The history of The Beatles began in 1956 when Paul McCartney, John Lennon, and George Harrison formed a skiffle group known as 'The Quarrymen'. Their first recording was made under the name The Beat Brothers in Hamburg for Polydor in 1961 with vocalist Tony Sheridan ('My Bonnie'/'When The Saints Go Marching In') by which time the original trio (Harrison, Lennon, and McCartney) had been supplemented by Stuart Sutcliffe (guitar) and Pete Best (drums). This Polydor disc sold 100 000 copies in Germany on its own merits before going on to over one million in 1964 on the impetus of the success of the reconstituted group from 1962. After the death of Stuart Sutcliffe and the replacement of drummer Pete Best by Ringo Starr, The Beatles signed a contract with EMI. **Their first entry into the British Hit Parade** was in October 1962 with 'Love Me Do' (which reached No 17). Their second entry reached No 2 in January 1963 ('Please Please Me'). **Their first No 1** was 'From Me to You' (Spring 1963) and their **last** was 'Ballad of John and Yoko' in the summer of 1969. They managed, during their phenomenally successful years together, to have 17 British No 1 hits, this total being equalled only by Elvis Presley. **Their first Gold Disc** (one million sales) was 'She Loves You', recorded in April 1963, and their recording of 'Can't Buy Me Love' became the **first British disc ever to achieve one million sales** (ie: firm orders) before its issue (on 20 March, 1964).

The greatest advance sale of all time was the 2 100 000 achieved in America by the same disc.

The top-selling British record of all time is 'I Want to Hold Your Hand', released in late 1963 with sales of over 13 million. **The fastest selling double-album,** called simply 'The Beatles', sold almost two million in its first week of release in 1968.

The second top group in the British Top Ten charts in the 1960s with 8 'No 1s' between 1964 and 1969 was The Rolling Stones. Their first disc was 'Come On', recorded in 1963, and their first No 1 in the British Hit Parade was 'It's All Over Now', in July 1964. In America 'Satisfaction' reached No 1 in 1965.

The 1970s

The most successful British group of the early 1970s was The Slade, having six 'No 1s' in the British Top Ten during 1970–73. Their first disc was 'Get Down and Get With It', recorded in 1971, and later that same year they had their first No 1 called 'Coz I Luv You'.

The most popular American family group of the early and mid-1970s was The Osmonds: Alan (b 1949), Wayne (b 1951), Merrill (b 1953), Jay (b 1955), Donny (b 1957), Marie (b 1959), and Jimmy (b 1963). Their first chart hit in America was 'One Bad Apple', released in 1971. In 1972 Donny's solo number called 'Puppy Love' reached No 1 in the British Top Ten. This was followed later the same year by little Jimmy making No 1 with 'Long Haired Lover from Liverpool'. In 1973 Marie reached No 2 in Britain with 'Paper Roses', and 1974 saw Donny and Marie singing duets, their first success being 'I'm Leaving it Up to You' followed by 'Morning Side of the Mountain' (1975).

The first female to win the Ivor Novello Award for Best Ballad is the British singer/song writer Lynsey de Paul in 1974 with 'Won't Somebody Dance with Me?', a feat she repeated in 1975 with the theme music from the TV series 'No Honestly'. Her first recording, 'Sugar Me', reached No 5 in the British charts in August 1972. Since then she has written a great many Top Twenty hits, sometimes in conjunction with Barry Blue.

The top Swedish singing group of the decade is ABBA, formed in 1973 (the name ABBA being made up from the artists' Christian names: Agnetha Fältskog, Bjorn Ulvaeus, Benny Andersson, and Anni-Frid Lyngstad). They have so far had seven 'No 1s' in the British Hit Parade (spring 1974–spring 1978), a total topped only by Elvis Presley, The Beatles, Cliff Richard, and The Rolling Stones.

The world No 1 concert attraction during the decade was the rock super group Led Zeppelin, who managed, without releasing a UK single, to have eight top LP albums in the British charts during 1970–76.

The best-known of all English Punk groups is The Sex Pistols headed by John Lydon alias Johnny Rotten. Their first Top Fifty entry was 'Anarchy in the UK' in December 1976, and their most popular number was 'God Save the Queen' (June 1977) which reached No 2. Within a matter of months during 1976–77 the group signed with three record companies, two of which cancelled their contracts, The Sex Pistols being awarded around £100 000 in settlements.

The most successful composer and performer in the world is James Paul McCartney. After The Beatles disbanded, Paul McCartney and his wife Linda formed the instrumental group

ABBA (from *l* to *r*) Anni-Frid Lyngstad, Bjorn Ulvaeus, Benny Andersson and Agnetha Fältskog. Sweden's 'super-group' who won the 1974 Eurovision Song Contest with 'Waterloo', which sold 5 000 000 copies worldwide and became Abba's first number one single in the UK.

Wings. Their first success, 'Another Day', reached No 2 in the British charts in February 1971 (although credited to Paul McCartney). Their first No 1, 'Mull of Kintyre' (1977), became **the first single to sell over two million copies in the UK.**

FACTS AND FEATS

US singles charts were first published by *Billboard* on 20 July 1940, when No 1 was 'I'll Never Smile Again', by Tommy Dorsey. The Beatles have had most No 1 records (20) and Elvis Presley has had the most hit singles on *Billboard's* 'Hot 100'— 97 from 1956 to May 1979.

UK singles charts were first published in *New Musical Express*, dated 14 November 1952, when No 1 was 'Here in My Heart' sung by Al Martino.

The longest total chart-presence was the 122 weeks achieved by 'My Way', sung by Frank Sinatra, in nine separate runs from 2 April 1969 into 1972. **The record for an uninterrupted stay** is 56 weeks for Engelbert Humperdinck's 'Release Me' from 26 January 1967.

The highest paid musician. Liberace earns more than $2 million each 26-week season, with a peak of $138 000 (£49 285) for a single night's performance at Madison Square Gardens, New York City, USA, in 1954.

The most successful solo recording artist is Bing Crosby who, on 9 June 1960, was presented with a platinum disc to commemorate the claimed sale of 200 million records from the 2600 singles and 125 albums he has recorded. On 15 September 1970 he received a second platinum disc when Decca announced a sale of 300 650 000 discs. His global sales on 179 labels, according to royalty reports to July 1975, have totalled 400 000 000. His first commercial recording was 'I've Got the Girl' recorded on 18 October 1926 (master No W 142785—take 3) issued on the Columbia label, and his first million seller was 'Sweet Leilani' in 1937.

BRITISH WINNERS OF THE EUROVISION SONG CONTEST

1967 Sandie Shaw: 'Puppet on a String'
1969 Lulu: 'Boom Bang-a-Bang' (joint first with The Netherlands, Spain, and France)
1976 Brotherhood of Man: 'Save Your Kisses for Me'

The first pop group ever to appear at the London 'Proms' was The Soft Machine, at the Royal Albert Hall on 23 August 1970.

The greatest claimed attendance at a Pop Festival has been 600 000 for the 'Summer Jam' at Watkin's Glen, New York, USA, on 29 January 1970, of whom about 150 000 actually paid.

The highest recorded paid attendance for a single pop group is 76 229 at the concert by the British group Led Zeppelin at The Silver Dome, Pontiac, Michigan, USA, on 30 April 1977. The gross takings were $792 361 (£446 094).

The biggest selling double album world wide at the time of publication is the Bee Gees' soundtrack for the Paramount film 'Saturday Night Fever', recorded in 1977. This album, which includes contributions by many other artists, has sold 25–30 million copies.

The largest selling British album recorded in Britain is 'Jesus Christ Superstar' by Andrew Lloyd Webber and Tim Rice with sales of nearly six million double-album sets by the end of 1978.

The most successful song-writer in terms of sales of single records is Paul McCartney, formerly of The Beatles, later of Wings. Between 1962 and 1 January 1978 he wrote jointly or solo 43 songs which sold one million or more.

DANCE TUNES AND POPULAR SONGS BASED PARTIALLY OR WHOLLY ON THEMES FROM 'SERIOUS' MUSIC

Popular song	*Based on*
'Avalon' (Al Jolson–Vincent Rose, 1920)	First eight bars correspond to 'O dolce bacio, languide carezze' in 'E Lucevan Le Stelle' from *Tosca* (Puccini)
'Castle of Dreams' (Joseph McCarthy–Harry Tierney, 1919)	Waltz No 6 in D flat major, Op 64/1 ('Minute Waltz') (Chopin)
Catherine (Musical comedy by Reginald Arkell and Fred de Crésac, 1923)	Entire score based on melodies by Tchaikovsky
'Concerto for Two' (Bob Haring–Jack Lawrence, 1941)	Piano Concerto No 1 in B flat minor, Op 23, first movement (Tchaikovsky)
'The Echo Told Me a Lie' (Barnes–Fields–John, 1949)	Theme from *Capriccio Italien* (Tchaikovsky) (also known as 'Bella ragazza dalle trecce bionde')
'Full Moon and Empty arms' (Buddy Kaye–Ted Mossman, 1945)	Piano Concerto No 2 in C minor, Op 18 (Rakhmaninoff)
'Gypsy Moon' (Igor Borganoff, 1932)	'Zigeunerweisen' (Sarasate)
'Horses' (Byron Gay, 1926)	'Troika' (Tchaikovsky)
'I'd Climb the Highest Mountain (If I Knew I'd Find You)' (Lew Brown–Sidney Clare, 1926)	*Humoresque* (Dvořák)
'If I Should Lose You' (Earl Burtnett–Robert Stowell, 1927)	Symphony No 5 in E minor, Op 64, second movement (Tchaikovsky)
'If You Are but a Dream' (Jaffe–Fulton–Bonx, 1945)	*Romance* (Rubinstein)
'I'm Always Chasing Rainbows' (Harry Carroll, 1918)	Fantaisie-Impromptu in C sharp minor, Op 66 (posth) (Chopin)
'In an 18th-century Drawing Room' (Raymond Scott, 1939)	Keyboard Sonata in C, K 545, first movement (Mozart)
'Intermezzo' (Bob Haring–Heinz Provost, 1940)	Theme from *Tristan und Isolde* (Wagner)
Kismet (Musical comedy by Robert Wright and George Forrest, 1953)	Entire score based on melodies by Borodin
'The Lamp is Low' (Peter DeRose–Bert Shefter–Mitchell Parrish, 1939)	*Pavane pour une Infante Défunte* (Ravel)
Lilac Time (Musical comedy by Adrian Ross, 1923)	Entire score based on melodies by Schubert
'Mignonette' (Horatio Nicholls, 1926)	Minuet in G (Beethoven)
'Moon Love' (André Kostelanetz, 1939)	Symphony No 5 in E minor, Op 64, second movement (Tchaikovsky)
'My Moonlight Madonna' (William Scotti–Paul Francis Webster, 1933)	*Poème* (Fibich)
'Night' (Seymour Simons, 1922)	'Dance of the Little Swans', from *Swan Lake Ballet* (Tchaikovsky)
'One Night in June' (Ted Snyder–Henry Lange, 1922)	Verse taken from the melody of *Barcarolle* (Tchaikovsky)
'One Summer Night' (Sam Coslow–Larry Spier, 1927)	*Songs My Mother Taught Me* (Dvořák)

Popular song	*Based on*
'On the Isle of May' (Mack David–André Kostelanetz, 1939)	Quartet No 1 in D major, Op 11, Andante cantabile (Tchaikovsky)
'Our Love' (Larry Clinton–Buddy Bernier–Bob Emmerich, 1939)	*Romeo and Juliet* Fantasy Overture (Tchaikovsky)
'Peter Gink' (George L Cobb)	'Anitra's Dance' from *Peer Gynt* Suite No 1 (Grieg)
'Play that Song of India Again' (Irving Bibo–Leo Wood–Paul Whiteman)	'Chanson Hindoue' from *Sadko* (Rimsky-Korsakov)
'Russian Rag' (George L Cobb, 1918)	Prelude in C sharp minor, Op 3/2 (Rakhmaninoff)
Song of Norway (Musical comedy by Robert Wright and George Forrest, 1944)	Entire score based on melodies by Grieg
Summer Song (Musical comedy by Eric Maschwitz, 1956)	Entire score based on melodies by Dvořak
'The Things I Love' (Harold Barlow–Lew Harris, 1941)	Melody in A flat major, Op 42/3 (Tchaikovsky)
'Till the End of Time' (Buddy Kaye–Ted Mossman, 1945)	Polonaise in A flat major, Op 53 (Chopin)
'Tonight We Love' (Bobby Worth–Freddy Martin, 1939)	Piano Concerto No 1 in B flat minor, Op 23, first movement (Tchaikovsky)
'Two Lovely Black Eyes' (Charles Coborn, 1892)	'Vieni sul mar!' (Neapolitan folk-song)
'Wagon Wheels' (Billy Hill–Peter DeRose, 1933)	Symphony No 9 in E minor, Op 95, second movement (Dvořák)
'Wild Horses' (K C Rogan, 1952)	'Die wilde Jagd' (Schumann)

Modern 'serious' developments

The intention behind jazz and popular music was initially to free the art from the stuffy rules and conventions of the late 19th century, but in so doing it established its own strict formulae. Nevertheless, it led the way to freedom in serious music, a freedom which was seized gratefully by many composers as a licence to compose music which went totally against the conventions of the musical establishment. It is, however, not always evident that audiences seized this new-found freedom with equal gratitude: the 20th century has seen the creation of a wide gulf between the composer and his public, and it is into this gulf that pop, dance, and jazz musicians stepped, bringing music to a public which could not be bothered to follow the intellectual convolutions of 'serious' composers.

The cult of 'anything goes' in modern serious music began early in the century, firstly with a strong move away from the binding restrictions of traditional tonality. This led to the experiments in atonalism of the so-called 'Second Viennese School' (see Section III: Groups of Composers), led by Arnold Schoenberg.

The first composer to write music in the twelve-tone discipline was Josef Matthias Hauer (1882–1959), who postulated the technique in 1912.

Side by side came the predominantly tonality orientated *avant-gardism* of Stravinsky and Bartók, the latter relying greatly upon the untamed musical language of the folk-people of his native Hungary.

The elemental power and the cacophonic effect of some of the music of these and other composers inevitably led to audience reaction. An oft-quoted account of the first performance, in Paris under Pierre Monteux, of Stravinsky's *Rite of Spring* on 29 May 1913 gives an early example of this reaction. This also indicates that the 'new' music had its adherents, this in turn indicating that the future for such music, although subject to vicissitudes, was assured. We are told by Carl van Vechen, who attended the first performance of the ballet, that the start of the music was greeted with polite smiles, then a few laughs, but as the music got properly under way the audience divided itself into sharply opposed camps. There were those for whom the noise was intolerable and who left in bewilderment, and others who were angered by the tasteless joke being played on them (the Comtesse de Pourtalès rose to her feet and complained loudly that she had not been so insulted in 60 years). On the other hand there were those for whom the music released feelings of exultant physical emotion, like the man who beat out the rhythm with his fists on top of van Vechen's head. Afterwards, the composer, the conductor, the impresario (Diaghilev), and the leading dancer (Nijinsky) went to a restaurant to discuss the historic event. They were, in Stravinsky's words, 'excited, angry, disgusted, and ... happy'.

A large number of excellent recordings of *Rite of Spring* exist. The music's powerful rhythmic impetus, the jagged, mesmeric power of its melodies, and the uncompromising use of severe harmonies illustrate better than thousands of words the new and disturbing musical influences at work before the First World War, influences which spread dynamically through the music of the next 50 years, affecting branches of the art as diverse as chamber music and big band jazz.

That these influences were indeed disturbing is proved by the events of the early 1920s; concert-halls in Italy and France were transformed into war areas as modernists and traditionalists clashed. Marinetti's concerts, for instance, were frequently accompanied by flying vegetables and crockery, brought in presumably by fanatics expecting trouble. In Germany, modern music also experienced growing pains: Kurt Weill's opera *The Rise and Fall of the City of Mahagony* was met with stink-bombs at first, but as feelings rose the event turned to tragedy. A man was struck with a beer-mug (in an opera-house?) and killed outright.

American composer Aaron Copland, who helped to bring the sounds of traditional and modern American life into the concert hall. (CBS Records/Clive Barda)

Of course, in an era of musical anarchy, there are always musicians for whom the established forms of the past provide all the material they need to compose their greatest thoughts. In their way, these 'traditionalist' composers exercise an expanding influence on music. Travelling by a less violent and radical road, taking shorter steps and producing music which is less initially disagreeable, they gradually bring the art of music to a pitch at which the experimentation of the *avant-gardistes*, although obviously retaining their positions, are not impossibly separated from the traditional pulse of musical development.

Among the important composers of the 20th century are:

Avant-gardistes/ Experimenters	*Traditionalists*
Schoenberg (1874–1951)	Elgar (1857–1934)
Ives (1874–1954)	R Strauss (1864–1949)
Bartók (1881–1945)	Nielsen (1865–1931)
Stravinsky (1882–1971)	Sibelius (1865–1957)
Dallapiccola (1904–75)	Vaughan Williams (1872–1958)
Messiaen (b 1908)	Rakhmaninoff (1873–1943)
Cage (b 1912)	Prokofiev (1891–1953)
Xenakis (b 1922)	Shostakovich (1903–75)
Nono (b 1924)	Barber (b 1910)
Stockhausen (b 1928)	Britten (1913–76)

(Some composers in the above list could be regarded as having a foot in each camp.)

This list purposely has not been brought too close to the present. It is simply not possible to perceive today which of the composers who have come to prominence during the last decade or so will prove to be influential forces tomorrow.

For the sake of interest rather than to infer importance, a selection of extravagances of the so-called 'serious' modern composers are noted here.

Henri Pousseur, the Belgian composer born in 1929, has written a piano work, *Caractères I*, in which a piece of paper with holes cut in it is placed over the music. The pianist plays only the portions of music he can read through the holes.

This idea is symptomatic of the modern attitude whereby the composer puts the responsibility of much of the composing on to the creative artist. Other composers who allow, or insist on, the artists' imagination, co-operation, or luck to create the music they, the composers, have ostensibly composed include John Cage, Morton Feldman, Toshi Ichiyanagi, Terry Riley, Christian Wolff, LaMonte Young, and Cornelius Cardew.

An extreme among extremes of non-composition is reached in Wolfgang Fortner's *Marginalien* for orchestra. It consists of a few basic ideas—little more than motific fragments—upon which the performers have to improvise. The score has a great many completely empty staves to allow for this improvisation. A visual equivalent of the work would be a jigsaw puzzle with no ultimate solution in terms of a recognisable picture, in which the puzzler is free to create his own patterns.

A rather more imaginative idea on the part of the composer occurs in Pierre Boulez's *Domaines* of 1968. The leading player is a solo clarinettist; distributed round the stage are small groups of instrumentalists ready to be brought into musical life as the clarinettist, roving freely among them, approaches each in turn at random, playing his instrument and inviting them to join in with impromptu playing of their own based on what the leader is playing.

Of course, many of these works result in music emerging in different keys simultaneously. This effect, bitonality or polytonality, is a regular ingredient of modern music, but it is not generally realised that it is not new. As long ago as the late 17th century H I F Biber included in his Suite in D, *Battalia*, a descriptive movement in which the strings each play a different melody in a different key to imitate a wild gathering in an inn: the soldiers, more than a little merry, sing folk-tunes against each other on the night before the battle. Much later, early in the 19th century, further bitonal experiments were carried out by Antonín Reicha. It was Reicha, too, who explored possibilities of microtones in music, experimenting with intervals of less than a semitone. This idea has been taken up during the 20th century by a number of composers, among them the Russian Vishnegradsky, the Moravian Hába brothers Alois and Karel, and the Englishman John Herbert Foulds.

The use of microtones and bitonality were raised to the status of high art by Charles Ives early this century. His *Three Pieces* (1923–24) calls for two pianos to be tuned a quarter-tone apart, and his sextet *Hallowe'en* (1907) is scored for first violin played in C major, a second violin played in B major, a viola played in D flat, a cello played in D major, and an atonal piano. The sixth member (*ad lib*) is a drummer who joins in the last repetition, which is to be played 'as fast as possible without disabling any player or instrument'.

The first opera to use microtones was written in 1910 (but not performed until 1927) by the Italian Vittorio Gnecchi: *La Rosiera*.

John Cage, the American experimental composer, has been responsible for a great many innovations in a century of novelties, some of which approach the magnitude of hoaxes. On 7 February 1943, at the Museum of Modern Art in New York, he mounted a programme of purely percussion music of works by Lou Harrison, Henry Cowell, José Ardevol, Amadeo Roldan, and himself. The instruments included a bewildering mass of objects both expected and unexpected on a concert platform: orchestral bells, temple gongs, cymbals, tamtams, marimba, thundersheets, oxen bells, cowbells, car brake drums (when suspended and struck, these give off a resounding bell-like note), anvils, dragons' mouths, woodblocks, rice-bowls, claves, buzzer, wind glass, flower-pots, tin cans, Niger drum, button gongs, and an audio-frequency oscillator. A note was inserted at the foot of the programme: 'Sound equipment furnished by the Sound Effects Department of the Columbia Broadcasting System.'

It may be wondered what artistic value is to be gained from some of John Cage's extravagancies, as in his *4′ 33″* (see Section VII) and perhaps even more particularly in his Piano Concert of 1963. During a performance of this work turkeys were released from a coffin. Much earlier, in 1942, Cage wrote a piece for voice and piano entitled *The Wonderful Widow of Eighteen Springs*. For the performance, the pianist is instructed to keep the keyboard lid closed and to hit various parts of the outside and inside of the instrument in accordance with directions in the score.

John Cage is a mycologist. If he had been able to exchange certain of his skills with Schobert (see Unfortunate Composers in Section III) the musical world might have been the better off.

Other strange occurrences in the age of 'anything

goes', chosen at random: In *Terretektorh* by Xenakis, the 60 instrumentalists are distributed among the audience.

Stockhausen's *Momente* (1962–72) calls for instrumentalists and singers, but the singers are expected to play various percussion instruments, to scrape their feet on the floor, to tongue-click, stamp, shuffle, finger-click, hand-clap, and knee-slap, in addition to making a variety of vocalisations from unvoiced ssssh-ings and prrrr-ings to screaming.

La Monte Young's *Composition 1960#7* must have **the shortest written score.** It consists of the two notes B–F′ sharp with the direction 'To be held for a very long time'. At a New York performance by a string trio this 'long time' was 45 minutes, during which a whole series of subsidiary sounds was produced, mostly by the audience. Those content to enjoy the 'composition' without objection were rewarded by a mesmeric experience induced by 'a whole inner world of fluctuating overtones in the open fifth as sustained by the players' (H W Hitchcock).

The Canadian composer Udo Kasemets wrote in 1966 a piece entitled *Variations* (*on Variations* [*on Variations*]). A few words and syllables varied into a poetic text are then varied by Kasemets. Further variation is encouraged when the work is performed, the responsibility for this final variational step once again devolving on to the performers.

Having relied upon the performer to create his work for him, the composer then treats him badly: for a performance of 'Goldstaub', from *Aus den Sieben Tagen* by Stockhausen, the four performers are required to live in isolation without food for four days before the concert. This calls for a dedication altogether beyond the call of duty.

There are reports of rock groups smashing their instruments after their performances, but **the only work during which an 'instrument' is smashed for a purely musical effect** at the climax is *Home Made*, written in 1967 by the American Alvin Curran, a pupil of Elliott Carter. *Home Made* is full of bizarre effects, among them fragments of texts taken from Shakespeare, Clark Coolidge, Chaucer, and Lewis Carroll: at one point there is a coloratura rendering of the first line only of 'In Your Easter Bonnet'. The instruments are flute, alto flute, piccolo, double bass, and percussion, to which are added whistles, piano and organ played by the soprano, squeaky rubber toys, and a pane of glass. At the height of the piece the pane of glass is smashed.

Children's toys have figured in Hiller's *Machine Music* (1964), police whistles in Kagel's *Match* (1964), a referee's whistle in Ibert's *Divertissement* (1930), and a roulette wheel and office machines in Satie's *Parade* (1917).

The use of unconventional materials for musical effects is widely practised by both 'serious' and 'popular' artists and composers. One of the strangest combinations was invented in 1974 by Tristram Cary in his soundtrack for Richard Williams's animated feature film *I Vor Pittfalks*. A condom was stretched over a microphone and then scratched with the fingernails. The resulting sound would defy accurate identification by even the most acute listener.

(See also Unconventional Playing Methods in Section II, at the end of Orchestral Instruments Today.)

Each one of these odd methods of producing new music breaks some kind of record, which is why this section has departed from the presentation used elsewhere in this book. The reader is invited to decide for himself whether, for instance, Alvin Curran's *Home Made* is the first piece to include a soprano playing keyboard instruments, set Lewis Carroll to music, make use of the timbre of squeaky rubber toys, or incorporate the sound of smashing glass. Perhaps it breaks all these records; or none of them. The modern composer in his quest for new sounds, or notoriety, or money, often takes literally the rule-breaking techniques of Beethoven, Wagner, Stravinsky, and Stockhausen, believing, perhaps rightly, that posterity will acclaim his latest gimmick, and that he will be instrumental, as were those great men before him, in altering the course of musical development. We should hesitate to blame him for trying, reserving our strictures for the works which do not 'come off'. If enough works in a particular style, or employing a particular technique or philosophy, are met with silence or hostility, that track of development will die out no matter how strong the impulse and publicity which set it off. The public is the deciding factor. If the listener wants to hear more of a certain style, that style will flourish. If not, it will join the many thousands of defunct notions with which musical history is littered.

Section 9

MECHANICAL MUSIC MAKING

In Section I: Setting the Scene, we discussed the probable way in which the mind of emerging man was fascinated from the start with music-making. There, we assumed without evidence, simply because evidence is not available, that the drive to make music was so strong that it might almost be equated with the urge to communicate verbally; in fact, music is generally regarded as an extension of speech and, therefore, a more sophisticated way of making contact with other humans.

As the gregarious nature of man, and later his artistic nature, drove him to make music, so his ingenious mind impelled him to find ways of making it without direct contact with instruments. In this sphere, however, we do not have to resort to guesswork since mechanical music-making, being more recent than 'natural' music-making, is fairly well documented.

For our purposes we have cast the net wide to include, even if only as a passing mention, all forms of making music mechanically—therefore we have drawn up the following definition:

An itinerant organ-grinder with a barrel-organ, as depicted in Bonanni's *Gabinetto Armonico* of 1716.

mechanical music-making covers any process in which, or by which, music may be made at will by an individual without his direct contact with a musical instrument.

Within this concept, surprisingly, falls one of the earliest and most primitive of all instruments—although it cannot really be regarded as 'mechanical'—upon which the player did not play, and over which he had little control. **The earliest mechanical musical instrument** within our terms of reference, then, is the aeolian harp (see Section II).

The earliest concept of mechanical music, as such, dates from the 4th century BC. The great philosopher Plato reasoned that the only means of knowing the time at night would be by a mechanism which made a noise at each hour. Borrowing his ideas from the Egyptians and the Romans, Plato designed a water-organ which would produce a little tune from its pipes when the flow of water reached a certain weight, this timed to take one hour. It remains a mystery whether this musical clock was ever built since no example has been preserved, but water-organs of about the same period have been discovered, none so far apparently having any connection with time-telling.

The first barrel-and-pin mechanism for producing music was invented shortly after, and perhaps concomitant with, the appearance of clockwork in about 1000. This mechanism served as the heart of most types of mechanical intrument for many years, including organs, carillons, snuff-boxes, jewel-cases, sewing-boxes, and the like, until the appearance of the pneumatic drive. It may be taken that the majority of the following inventions use the barrel-and-pin principle or a variation of it.

The oldest water-powered organ still in playing condition is the so-called 'Salzburg Hornwerk', also called 'Stier' (or 'bull') because of its characteristic loud chord of F–A–C included in each piece of music. Built in 1502, it was owned by Archbishop L von Kreutschach. Its 350 pipes were used for only one tune, an old chorale, until the instrument aroused the interest of Leopold Mozart, father of the great Wolfgang Amadeus, in 1759. Leopold wrote a set of variations on the chorale, called the resulting piece *March*, composed further pieces, *February*, *May*, *June*, *July*, *September*, and *October*, and invited his friend Johann Ernst Eberlin to contribute tunes for the rest of the months. The pieces are still to be heard on the same instrument in Salzburg today.

The water-powered barrel-organ was invented at the latest in 1615 by Solomon de Caus. In 1618, Robert Fludd (known as 'Fluctibus') published designs in *De Naturae Simia* for mechanical music-makers, but no practical models are known to have been built as a result.

The first metronome was invented in the late 17th century by Étienne Loulié (*c* 1640–*c* 1701), a Parisian theorist and music teacher. It stood nearly 6 ft (2 m) tall, but no example has survived. Perhaps this is the device described as a 'pendulum' that Michel d'Affilard called for to indicate tempo in his sight-singing manual *Principes très faciles pour bien apprendre la musique*, published in Paris in 1691. Maelzel's famous metronome dates from 1816.

György Ligeti composed his *Poème Symphonique* (1962) for 100 metronomes which are lined up on stage before an audience, set off, and simply left to run down.

The first chiming watch was invented in 1686 by either Daniel Quare or Charles Clay, the court case of 1717 apparently not deciding the issue. These early chiming watches were rather bulky: a much slimmer design was possible with the invention of the helical spring gong by Julien le Roy of Paris in about 1780.

The first mechanical bird-song was invented in 1765 in France. The idea soon became popular and different styles were built into small square boxes which stood beside, or inside, canaries' cages to teach the birds to sing. The name of the device, 'Serinette', comes from the French word for canary: *serin*, but models were designed also for blackbirds, and even curlews. A later development was the imitation singing-bird made by the firm of Jaquet-Droz (father and son) in the late 18th century, in which the little birds had not only a lifelike song but also realistic movements of head and tail.

The first musical-box was made by the Swiss watch-maker Antoine Favre, who registered his invention on 15 February 1796 in Geneva. The barrel-and-pin arrangement was developed to a high degree of sophistication, but the resulting cylinder-and-tongue principle was the same.

The earliest mechanical page-turner was a pedal-operated device invented by the American composer John Antes in 1800.

The first manufactory specifically founded for making musical watches, snuff-boxes, etc, was opened in Geneva in about 1810 by Henri Capt, the Longchamps Brothers, Moise Aubert, and Pierre Rochat, following on from a cottage industry started there a few years earlier by Philippe Mayland and Isaac Piquet. It was Philippe Mayland who invented **the radial-tooth disc**, as a variation on the pinned barrel, in about 1810.

The first mechanical orchestra was the Panharmonicon, which Maelzel invented in Vienna about 1804. It was designed to produce a very wide range of sounds to approach the then modern symphony orchestra of two each of flutes, oboes, clarinets, bassoons, trumpets, horns, trombones, drums, and the usual complement of strings. In 1813 Beethoven wrote for Maelzel's instrument his 'Battle of Vittoria' Symphony, Op 91, later rescoring it for live orchestra.

The 'barrel-organ' which used to be such a familiar sight and sound on the streets of London was invented by Mr Hicks of that city about 1820. It was in fact not a barrel-organ of the accepted type: basically a barrel-and-pin design, no organ pipes are involved. Leather-covered hammers strike the strings much in the manner of a pianoforte, but the player has much less control over volume and 'touch' than with a conventional piano. A better name for the instrument, which ironically is the best-known barrel-organ of all, was the street-piano. Prints and period films of the 19th-century London scene are rarely complete without the

Queen Victoria's musical bustle (see below).

organ-grinder (usually apparently of Italian origin), his monkey and his cup.

The first paper-roll organs were made in 1827. These replaced the usual mechanical tracker actions with pneumatic levers, and it was found that a paper roll of indefinite length could replace the barrel and pins. Although experiments were successful and patents were secured in the 1840s in both England and France, the idea was slow to catch on, and it was not until the appearance of the Organette in 1878 that the paper-roll model became commercially viable. The most famous makers were Mignon, Celestina, and Seraphone, all from the late 19th century.

The first musical omnibus followed the invention of that method of transport very quickly, in 1827. The presence of the vehicle was announced by an automatic coach-horn fanfare triggered off by the driver's foot. This mobile musical-box was invented by Davrainville in Paris.

Musical clothing, as opposed to artefacts worn on the person such as watches, seems to have been invented in 1875. Queen Victoria was presented with a musical bustle which played the National Anthem when she sat down. Fortunately, the monarch is excused from the convention which dictates that all should rise in the presence of the royal tune; otherwise a certain amount of oscillation might have resulted.

The first pinned disc with pins affixed to one of its flat surfaces (and therefore not to be confused with the radial-tooth disc of about 1810) was invented in 1886. The inventors Ellis Pan and Paul Lochmann, working independently in London and Leipzig respectively, seem to have hit upon the idea virtually simultaneously. The English version was called the 'Symphonion', and the German 'Polyphon'. The inventors decided to pool resources and produce the Symphonion from about 1890.

The automatic piano-player was invented by the American E S Votey in 1897. It was an eerie machine with felt-covered fingers, and it had to be pushed up to the piano so that these fingers might play upon the keys. A later development was to incorporate the mechanism inside the piano, and this invention was called the 'Pianola'. This in turn led to the reproducing piano on which, instead of the paper roll activating the keys, a live pianist punched holes in a blank roll as he played. Grieg, Paderewski, Busoni, and other famous players of the period made paper rolls in this way which still survive.

The first player-pianos and organs, operated

by paper rolls and pneumatic action, were invented in Freiburg-im-Breisgau by Emil Welte in 1887. Known at first as the 'Orchestrion', they sometimes were equipped with Turkish military instruments: triangle, cymbals, and bass drum.

A 'recital' of piano rolls made by Friedmann, Hofmann, Paderewski, and others was given by the Player Piano Group in November 1975 at London's Purcell Room.

The first electronic musical instrument was the 'Telharmonium' of 1906, the work of the Canadian scientist Thaddeus Cahill.

The Æolian Orchestrelle was invented about 1900. Basically a paper-roll organ, this had many additional facilities for varying the performance at the will of the operator. It was marketed by the Æolian Company of London.

The Etherophone was invented in 1920 by the Russian Leo Theremin. As the player's hand approaches the antenna a pitch sounds and rises as the hand gets nearer. The other hand operates a cut-out device to separate the successive notes if required, and a pedal controls volume. Descendants of this instrument are the Ondes Martenot (invented by Maurice Martenot in 1928, and first used in a symphony in Koechlin's No 2); N Langer's and J Halmagyi's Emicon of about 1930, Friedrich Trautwein's Trautonium (1930), and others. Trautonium Concertos and Concertinos were composed by Hindemith (1931); Genzmer (1939), and Baur (for mixture Trautonium and string quartet, 1955); and there is a Theremin Concerto (1947) by Berezowsky.

A Welte Orchestrion. (Mary Evans Picture Library)

A Polyphon pinned-disc player dating from the 1880s. (Popperfoto)

The Superpiano of 1927, invented by E Spielmann. Depression of a key operates a lamp the light of which is turned into electrical vibrations via a photocell.

The Neo-Bechstein, marketed by Bechstein of Berlin from 1931, is an electronic piano which will delay the decay of a note and even increase its intensity in a crescendo by the means of a system of eighteen microphones and an amplifier.

From this stage, and with the rise in popularity of the gramophone, the reign of mechanical musical instruments subsided until the end of the 1950s, when various mechanical organs appeared. They use the more recent invention of tape in their construction and are really sophisticated versions of the electronic organ, requiring a certain amount of skill from the performer. Recent examples are almost unbelievably complicated, with keys offering a variety of dance or march rhythms merely upon their depression, switches modifying the tones to produce imitations of orchestral instruments, further keys to give slow or rapid vibrato, and many other refinements. Such instruments have found their way into 'pop' recording studios on many occasions, and it is nowadays difficult to decide whether, for instance, a bossa nova beat is the work of a sweating rhythm group or a depressed key.

The longest electronic organ marathon was set up in February 1973 by Vincent Bull of Scunthorpe, Lincs, who established a record of 122 hours continuous playing. Some kind of sartorial record may have been set up at the same time since the musical feat was achieved in 'drag', Mr Bull being known locally as 'Vanessa'.

The most elaborate barrel-organ ever to be constructed was called the 'Apollonicon' and it was on exhibition in Regent's Park, London, between 1817 and 1840. It possessed three barrels, but could also be played manually from six consoles.

We have omitted very many inventions of merit (and otherwise) which flooded the music-shops between the wars and since. Many of these instruments have passed into history, but one still has a wide use, particularly in the lighter music fields: the Hammond Organ. Invented during the early 1930s by Laurens Hammond and marketed by his company in Chicago for the first time in 1935, it is cleverly designed so that an extremely wide variety of sounds may be obtained from a relatively small console instrument. Like the Neo-Bechstein, for instance, the Hammond Organ is not a mechanical instrument in the true sense since it requires to be played by a musician before it will make music. It is included here simply because its method of sound production (rotating wheels inducing currents which are amplified and modified electronically) differs from the acoustic mechanics of conventional instruments.

Before concluding this survey of mechanical instruments, it should be mentioned that the mechanical carillon was extremely popular in the 18th century. Handel composed for one belonging to Queen Caroline, but one of the most famous was installed in the Cathedral Tower overlooking the Market Square in Bruges, Belgium, in 1743.

Composers who wrote for mechanical instruments

When considering this, one must remember that many of the actual makers of the instruments concerned produced their own music while others took popular airs of their period. In this way, many operatic transcriptions have issued from piano rolls, musical-boxes, and jewel-cases without the composers being aware that their music was being put to such use.

The earliest composer specifically to write for a mechanical instrument was Peter Philips (*c* 1565–*c* 1630), the English composer who spent much of his working life on the European continent. He wrote and arranged music for the water-powered barrel-organ of Solomon de Caus. Other prominent composers who have turned their attention to mechanical instruments include:

C P E Bach: Pieces for musical clock, Wq 193/5–10.

Beethoven: The 'Battle of Vittoria' Symphony mentioned above; also a Scherzo and other pieces for mechanical organ.

Eberlin: The music for the Salzburg Hornwerk mentioned above; also pieces for a hydraulic organ at Heilbrunn.

Handel: Pieces for Clay's Musical Clock owned by Queen Caroline.

Haydn: His 32 Pieces for Flötenuhr ('flute-clock') were written for clocks made in 1772, 1792, and 1793 by Father Primitivus Niemecz, Prince Esterházy's librarian. Haydn called the instrument Laufwerk ('barrel-work').

Hindemith: His Op 42 is incidental music for mechanical organ for the film *Felix the Cat* (1927). His works also include pieces for mechanical piano, gramophone, pianola, and 'electric ether-wave apparatus' (Trautonium).

L Mozart: The Salzburg Hornwerk pieces mentioned above.

W A Mozart: Including Fantasias in F minor, K 594 and 608 (1790/1) for Flötenuhr.

Pieces for mechanical instruments also exist by W F Bach, H L Hassler, J M Haydn, Kirnberger, and Quantz. The modern English composer John White has shown an imaginative interest in mechanical instruments, mounting a Concert of Automata at the New Arts Laboratory, London, on 11 October 1970. The audience was encouraged to wander round the instruments, or exhibits, which included a steam kettle blowing a chord, an electric mandolin, bells being dragged along the floor, and water dripping on to a cymbal. The same composer's *C major Machine* is a work in which a steam-operated machine plays a toy piano (ignoring the black notes) in an endless series of permutations.

Composers who wrote for the player-piano

Casella, Goossens, Hiller, Hindemith, Howells, Stravinsky, plus *Music for Player Piano* (1964), a computer-organised piece on a player-piano roll by J C Tenney.

Composers who imitated mechanical instruments in conventional music

Bartók: in his String Quartet No 3.
Kodály: Háry János: *Spielwerk*.
Liadov: *The Musical Snuff-box*.
Mahler: street organ imitations often play a dramatic role in his symphonies.
Shostakovich: Film Music: *The Gadfly*, Op 97 (1955).

Mechanical imitations of musical instruments

The inventions discussed so far, although sometimes superficially similar to conventional instruments, were all conceived primarily as independent creations. A completely different category takes the real thing as a starting-point and mechanises it:

MECHANICAL VIRGINALS, operated by barrel-and-pin mechanism and owned by King Henry VIII in the 1540s.

MECHANICAL ORGAN combined with a carillon was sent by Queen Elizabeth I to the Turkish Sultan in 1599.

MECHANICAL TRUMPETER invented by Maelzel of Austria in about 1810.

MECHANICAL ACCORDION, called Tanzbär ('dancing bear'), made in Germany about 1892.

MECHANICAL BANJOS AND MANDOLINS made in America about 1894 by the Wurlitzer Company. They were partly automatic, partly manual.

MECHANICAL VIOLIN produced about 1908 by the American Mills Novelty Company. The strings were vibrated by a circular bow which ran round the body of the instrument. Shortly afterwards the Hupfeld Company in Germany constructed an entirely mechanical **string quartet**: two violins, viola, and cello.

In this connection reference must be made to probably one of the most ingenious inventors of all time who happened to turn his brilliant mind to mechanical musical instruments. He was Jacques de Vaucanson who was born in 1709 in southern France and who moved to Paris in 1735. In 1738 he astonished the French capital with a model of a man which actually played a flute by expelling air across the mouthpiece through the lips and playing a tune by stopping the holes with minute fingers. A little later Vaucanson produced an even more complicated model of a fife-drummer which blew on a pipe and beat a drum simultaneously.

Recorded sounds

Today the best-known type of mechanical music-making is the gramophone record, alongside which, and gradually growing in prominence, is the pre-recorded tape. The record began humbly in the late 19th century as an aid to office dictation, but its usefulness as a home-entertainment commodity was quickly realised while its business use faded out, ironically to be brought back in the mid-20th century as an offshoot of the domestic product.

For 120 years the record has undergone an almost continuous process of gradual improvement, the progress of which may best be illustrated by the following chronology, which details other important events surrounding this amazing growth.

1857
The French scientist, Leon Scott built a device which he called 'phonautograph'. It registered movements made by a vibrating body on to a smoked cylinder.

1877
The phonograph invented by Thomas Edison. A foil coating stretched round a cylinder was engraved with a stylus. In June of that year, Lillie Moulton (*née* Greenough and later Hagermann-Lindencrone), the singer born in Cambridge, Massachusetts, wrote: 'There is also another in-

Edison with his phonograph. (Mary Evans Picture Library)

vention called phonograph, where the human voice is reproduced, and can go on forever being reproduced. I sung in one through a horn and they transposed this on a platina roll and wound it off.... The intonation—the pronunciation—I could recognise as my own, but the *voice*—dear me!'

Edison's historic 'Mary Had a Little Lamb' was the **first piece of poetry ever to be recorded**; Mrs Moulton's was **the first song.** Edison's invention was patented on 19 February 1878 (patent No 200 521).

Charles Cros, working independently in Paris, proposed a very similar invention utilising a disc instead of a cylinder, but Cros's gadget was probably never built.

1884
The German-born Emile Berliner recorded 'The Lord's Prayer' on a cylinder now preserved in the BBC Record Library. This is **the oldest surviving gramophone record.**

1886
Patent (No 341 214) taken out for a cylinder in which a wax coating replaced the foil.

1887
The gramophone invented by Berliner. Patent taken out for **the first disc**: glass, coated with lamp-black.

The first record company founded: North American Phonograph Company, on 14 July.

1890
First recording studios set up on Fifth Avenue, New York, by the New York Phonograph Company.

1891
First record catalogue produced by Columbia Phonograph Company. It was ten pages in length.

1897
First operatic arias recorded in Milan.

1898
First UK record company, The Gramophone Company, was established in Maiden Lane in London, with its branch, Deutsche Grammophon Gesellschaft, in Hanover.

The telegraphone, forerunner of the tape recorder, invented by Valdemar Poulsen of Denmark using steel wire and tape.

1899
First factory devoted exclusively to the production of gramophone records was set up in Hanover. It had 14 presses and produced discs of 5 in (12·7 cm) and 7 in (17·8 cm) diameter.

First French record company established in May: Compagnie Française du Gramophone, in Paris.

Painting by Francis Barraud, **His Master's Voice,** was modified by the artist (replacing its cylinder with a disc) and bought by The Gramophone Company. In time it became **the most famous trade-mark in the world.** The painting was taken from life: the dog's name was Nipper, and a memorial plaque was placed over his grave in Eden Street, Kingston-upon-Thames, by The Gramophone Company in 1949.

1900
A catalogue of 5000 recordings published by The Gramophone Company. **Paper labels introduced** (hitherto, the record contents were scratched into the centre wax by hand), with black print on a red background.

The first 10 in (25·4 cm) discs made in America. The Gramophone and Typewriter Company founded in London.

1901
International Zonophone Company and the Victor Talking Machine Company founded.

1902
18 March: first Caruso recordings made in a hotel room in Milan. **First Melba records issued,** with a specially designed 'Melba' label. **First Gramophone Company Red Label catalogue issued,** consisting entirely of operatic artists with one exception: Jan Kubelik, the Czech violinist and father of composer and conductor, Rafael.

It is worth mentioning at this point a curious development in instrument-building: in order to amplify the tone to assist recording, the Stroh-violin (and other stringed instruments) was developed in London. In this design, the soundbox of the instrument is replaced by a diaphragm and trumpet. Later designs used a microphone and loudspeaker, with a pedal to control the volume.

1903
First complete opera recording: Verdi's *Ernani* by Italian HMV, issued on 40 single-sided discs.

1904
First record company to be devoted entirely to serious music: Società Italiana di Fonotipia.

1905
First recordings of chamber music (isolated movements by Mendelssohn and Schumann). **First double-sided discs** issued by German Odeon.

1906
First console gramophone, made in America, the Victrola, 4 ft (1·22 m) high and with a downward-pointing horn.

1907
Dame Nellie Melba laid the foundation-stone of HMV factory at Hayes, Middlesex.

1909
First commercial recording of a complete symphony: Beethoven's No 5 in C minor, with the Berlin Philharmonic Orchestra conducted by Arthur Nikitsch.

1913
The Decca portable gramophone introduced.

1917
First jazz recordings: 'Canary Cottage', by the Frisco Jazz Band, featuring saxophonist Rudy Wiedoeft, recorded 10 May and issued on cylinder: Edison Blue Amberol 3241; 'Darktown Strutters' Ball'/'Indiana', by the Original Dixieland Jazz Band, recorded 30 January, and issued 31 May on Columbia A-2297.

1918
First vocal refrain on a dance record: 'Mary', sung by Harry Macdonough, Charles Hart, and Lewis James, with Joseph C Smith's Orchestra, recorded in New York on 29 July and issued in November on Victor 18500 (USA), and in October 1920 in the UK on HMV B-1100.

1919
The first jazz record to be released in the UK: 'At the Jazz Band Ball'/'Barnyard Blues', by the Original Dixieland Jazz Band, recorded on 16 April and released on Columbia 735.

1920
First experiments with electrical recording were made on Armistice Day, 11 November, by Messrs Guest and Merriman in London.

The first million-seller was Paul Whiteman and his Ambassador Orchestra playing 'The Japanese Sandman' and 'Whispering', issued in November on Victor 18690 and in UK in January 1921 on HMV B-1160.

First English recording of a dance band with vocal refrain was 'Puck-a-Pu', sung by Eric Courtland (pseudonym of Ernest Pike), with the Mayfair Dance Orchestra conducted by George W Byng, recorded at Hayes, Middlesex, on 9 November and issued the following February. (There were various other records made with vocal chorus effects prior to the above, especially in England by the Savoy Quartet on HMV, but these were more in the nature of 'novelty' groups where the star performer was a vocalist who also played one of the two banjos used.)

1923
First magazine devoted to gramophone records: *The Gramophone*, founded by Sir Compton Mackenzie. **First royal recording** made by King George V and Queen Mary at Buckingham Palace.

1924
The smallest functional gramophone record, of which 250 copies were pressed, was made by HMV. It was $1\frac{3}{8}$ in (3·5 cm) diameter and contained a performance of 'God Save the King'.

The first musical score to include a gramophone recording was Respighi's *Pines of Rome*, in which a disc of a nightingale's song is heard.

1925
First electrical recordings issued: 'Adeste Fideles' by a 4850-strong choir at the Metropolitan Opera House, New York; Tchaikovsky: Symphony No 4 in F minor, by the Royal Albert Hall Orchestra conducted by Sir Landon Ronald. *Joan of Arkansaw*, by the Mask and Wig Club Orchestra and Double Male Quartet, recorded in New York on 16 March (issued on Victor 19626); 'Feelin' Kind o' Blue' by Jack Hylton and his Orchestra with vocal refrain by Jack Hylton, recorded in Hayes on 24 June (issued on HMV B-2072). (One title made electrically immediately prior to this, on the same session, was never issued; it was called 'Ah-Ha!'). **First location recording** was made in the Arcadia Ballroom, Detroit, on the night of 29 January, in the presence of some 5000 dancers, by Finzel's Arcadia Orchestra of Detroit, and issued on OKeh 40298. The title was 'Laff it Off', and the vocalist was Charlotte Meyers.

1927
First British disc-jockey: Christopher Stone. Ernest Lough recorded 'Oh, For the Wings of a Dove'/'Hear My Prayer', one of the most popular classical discs of all time.

1928
First serious piece of music to be issued on disc before being heard in live performance was Kurt Atterburg's Symphony No 6. It was written to commemorate Schubert's centenary, and with it the composer won a £2000 prize offered for the occasion by the Columbia Gramophone Company.

1929
Decca Gramophone Company launched in London in February. It grew out of the musical instrument makers Barnett Samuel and Sons Ltd, and took its name from the Decca portable gramophone of 1913.

The last cylinder records were produced.

1931
HMV and Columbia joined forces in March to produce Electrical and Musical Industries (EMI). HMV issued **the first Society issues** (dependent upon prior subscription: the first was the Hugo Wolf Song Society). **First experiments in long-playing records.** The first recording sessions made at $33\frac{1}{3}$ rpm specifically for LP were: Classical and semi-classical: Victor L 24000, recorded 21 May and issued later that year, made by the Victor Concert Orchestra. The titles included:

MacDowell: 'To a Wild Rose'
Brahms: 'Lullaby'
Beethoven: Minuet in G
Léhar: 'Vilja', from *The Merry Widow*
Gossec: Gavotte.

1932
LP experiments continued with a jazz record: Victor L 16007, recorded New York 9 February by Duke Ellington and his Orchestra. The titles were: 'East St Louis Toodle-Oo'; 'Lots o' Fingers;' 'Black and Tan Fantasy'.

(Other jazz LPs appeared at the same time but were composed of dubbings of existing 78s. The first jazz LPs in UK were entirely of dubbings from 78s of various ages and no jazz made specifically for LP seems to have been issued until some considerable time had elapsed after Decca's launch of LP in the UK in June 1950.) The 1931–32 LPs were close-grooved shellac pressings.

1933
First stereo discs made experimentally by EMI after a process designed by A D Blumlein of that company. The method used was that finally chosen in refined form for the first commercial release of stereo discs 25 years later.

1938
Cellulose acetate tape developed for recording music.

1939
Decca enters the field of navigational aids (radar).

1940
The first purchase tax levied on gramophone records: $33\frac{1}{3}$ per cent. Decca introduced "ffrr' records made after a new process designed by Arthur Haddy (ffrr = 'full frequency range recording').

1941
First public jam session recording took place in the EMI studios, Abbey Road, St John's Wood, London, on the afternoon of Sunday, 16 November, organised by *The Melody Maker*. Four items from the considerable number played were issued in January 1942 as follows:

10 in (25·4 cm) HMV B-9249 'Tea For Two'.
10 in (25·4 cm) HMV B-9250 'St Louis Blues'.
12 in (30·5 cm) HMV C-3269 'Honeysuckle Rose'/ 'I've Found a New Baby'.

1942
First golden disc was one sprayed by RCA Victor for presentation to bandleader and trombonist Glenn Miller on 10 February to commemorate the success of his 'Chattanooga Choo-Choo'.

1948
First vinyl records released in America on 21 June. The research which led to their release was headed by Dr Peter Goldmark of the Columbia Broadcasting System Research Laboratories, at which he was in charge of the development of colour television. The gestation of LP took three years (building upon the principles of the early experiments of 1932) and cost $250 000. Disc sizes were 10 in (25·4 cm) and 12 in (30·5 cm); speed $33\frac{1}{3}$ rpm.

1949
First 7 in (17·8 cm) 45 rpm discs issued in January by RCA in America.

1950
First LPs issued in the UK in June by Decca.

1951
First public demonstration of 'stereosonic' (later stereophonic) **tapes** by EMI in London.

1952
First UK release of 45 rpm 7 in (17·8 cm) discs by HMV in October; EMI also announced their first $33\frac{1}{3}$ long-playing discs in the same month.

1953
Philips Electrical Industries of Holland entered the record-producing market.

1954
First releases of Deutsche Grammophon records (Archive Series) in UK.

1958
First stereo records introduced in the UK by Pye Group Records in June. Decca and EMI followed later the same year. First LP of any kind to reach 1 000 000 sales was the original cast recording of *My Fair Lady*, issued by Philips in May. First classical record to reach 1 000 000 sales was issued by RCA in America and the UK: Tchaikovsky's Piano Concerto No 1 in B flat minor, played by the winner of the first International Tchaikovsky Competition held in Moscow in April of that year: Van Cliburn, with an orchestra conducted by Kirill Kondrashin.

1959
First magazine tape cassettes issued by the Garrard Enginering and Mechanical Co, Ltd, in September. These magazines, using standard $\frac{1}{4}$ in (6·3 mm) tape at a playing speed of $3\frac{3}{4}$ ips were the ancestors of the modern cassette.

1963
First tape cassette with $\frac{1}{8}$ in (3.2 mm) recording at $1\frac{7}{8}$ ips announced by Philips Electrical at the Berlin Audio Show.

1965
First pre-recorded cassettes announced at Eindhoven, Holland, by Philips in November. Launch of the tape cartridge, primarily for in-car entertainment.

1966
Invention of the Dolby noise-reduction system, developed by Dr R Dolby of Dolby Laboratories Ltd in Great Britain. This 'stretching' process, whereby the background surface 'mush' of the tape is lowered electronically to below audible range, revolutionised the quality available from tape. When applied to the cassette format for the first time in 1970 it brought the quality of the 'compact cassette' up to a level at which it could compete with the stereo disc.

1966/67
American disc sales during this winter season for the first time exceeded $1 000 000 000.

1971
First quadraphonic discs issued in America in October; the first UK issues took place the following April.

1976
New tape cassette formulations. Philips announced the 'Mini Cassette' for office use. Size and tape speed are reduced, and the playing time totals 30 minutes. National Panasonic announced a similar, but incompatible, cassette. The 'Unisette' by BASF and the 'Elcaset' by Matsushita and other Japanese makers, offer, uncompatibly, $\frac{1}{4}$-inch tape and $3\frac{3}{4}$ ips tape speed.

1979
First digital recording (on conventional vinyl

discs) announced for public release in February by Decca in the UK.

LONGEST PLAYING

In the foregoing chronology it was noted that the first experiments with long-playing discs occurred in 1931, but the first commercially successful vinyl discs appeared in 1948. The average side-length in 1948, and still regarded as standard, is about 25 minutes, but owing to sophisticated cutting techniques this time-limit has been increased on many records.

The longest long-playing records are included in the American Mercury set 940477 containing, complete on eleven discs, Furtwängler's 1950 La Scala performance of Wagner's *Ring*. A note on the album front claims playing times of 'up to 43 minutes per side'. In the late 1950s, the American Vox Company issued some discs to revolve at $16\frac{2}{3}$ rpm, theoretically giving double the playing time of the standard $33\frac{1}{3}$ rpm disc, but these met with little success due to the reduction of quality brought about by the slow linear speed; spoken-word discs had rather more success. On the Japanese market are to be found $33\frac{1}{3}$ rpm discs with up to 45 min *per side*, and coupling works of the length of Beethoven's 7th Symphony and Tchaikovsky's 'Pathétique' Symphony, but they have not so far been made available in the West.

OTHER FACTS OF THE RECORD INDUSTRY

The earliest recorded work to sell 1 000 000 copies was 'Vesti la giubba' ('On With the Motley') from Leoncavallo's *I Pagliacci*, performed by Enrico Caruso and first recorded by him on 12 November 1902.

The most recorded song: two songs have each been recorded over 1000 times: 'Yesterday' (Lennon and McCartney) with 1186 versions between 1965 and 1 January 1973; and 'Tie a Yellow Ribbon Round the Old Oak Tree' (Irwin Levine and L Russell Brown) with more than 1000 from 1973 to 1 January 1979. W C Handy's 'St Louis Blues' (1914) and Hoagy Carmichael's 'Stardust' (1927) have each been recorded between 900 and 1000 times.

The busiest recording artist is the Indian Miss Lata Mangeshker who, between 1948 and 1974, has recorded at least 25 000 solo, duet, and chorus-backed songs in 20 Indian languages. She frequently has five recording sessions per day and has 'backed' 1800 films.

The greatest seller of any gramophone record to date is 'White Christmas' by Irving Berlin with 25 000 000 for the Crosby single recorded 29 May 1942, and more than 100 million in other versions.

The fastest-selling long-playing disc of all time is *John Fitzgerald Kennedy—A Memorial Album*, recorded on 22 November 1963, the day of Mr Kennedy's assassination, which sold four million copies at 99¢ (then 35p) in six days (7–12 December 1963).

The top-selling classical LP is Van Cliburn's recording of Tchaikovsky's Piano Concerto No 1, totalling 2 500 000 sales up to January 1970.

MASSIVE RECORDING PROJECTS

The longest LP set is the Argo recording of the *Complete Works of William Shakespeare* on 137 double-sided discs, made in 1957–64. The next largest recording project was the complete symphonies of Haydn. This task has been carried out twice, by the Musical Heritage Society (USA) and by Decca (UK). The Musical Heritage Society series, made by the Vienna Chamber Orchestra under Ernst Maerzendorfer, was completed on 49 discs early in 1972, and offered on subscription in the USA; the Decca issues with the Philharmonia Hungarica under Antal Dorati on 48 discs were completed in September 1974. The Dorati is the 'bigger' project (despite its two fewer LP sides) because it includes complete recordings of alternative versions of two symphonies, whereas the Musical Heritage series incorporates these alternatives as 'conflations'.

THE QUEST FOR HIGH FIDELITY

High Fidelity ('Hi-Fi' for short) has been the aim of technicians involved in sound reproduction almost from the start, but the term itself has gained prominence only since the Second World War. Hi-Fi may be defined as an attempt to reproduce from the speaker(s) a sound as near as possible in quality to that reaching the microphone(s) in the recording studio. The fact that it cannot be measured, and cannot, therefore, be defined other than subjectively, has meant that unscrupulous manufacturers may emblazon their electronic products with the legend 'High Fidelity' without fear of prosecution under the British Trades Descriptions Act (1968), and other controls elsewhere, no matter how far from the original sound the results from their products may be.

In the following chart the authors' own subjective impressions have been brought to bear on a graph giving the successive steps attained by manufacturers in the ascent to 'the closest approach to the original sound'. The graph should be used in conjunction with the foregoing chronological chart.

It is possible that the gradual rise in software quality will increase during the coming years: there are, furthermore, strong rumours that a 'breakthrough' in Hi-Fi, and in particular in the manufacture and permanence of software, is imminent, and this will be paralleled by a similar revolution in the design and manufacture of playing equipment. The demise of the record-playing stylus in favour of the laser beam, and the banishment of signal-carrying wires in favour of radio waves are signalled; also the days of the loudspeaker, as we know it, are numbered in hundreds rather than thousands. In short, it is foreseen that audio equipment in the 1980s will be totally different in design and appearance from what we have been used to.

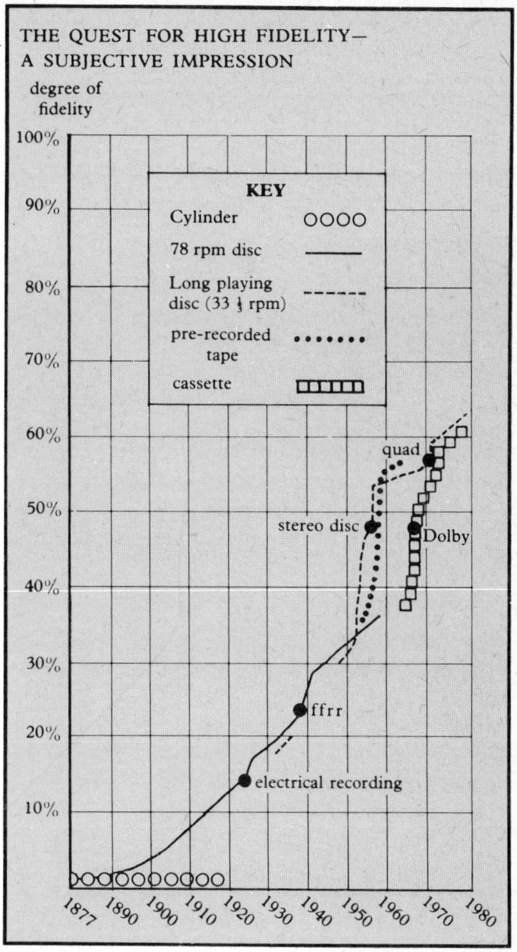

Radio

In addition to records and tape, radio has played an important role in the broadcasting of music.

The earliest form of mechanical music broadcasting was devised in 1873. In that year a contrivance in the form of a tent with pipes was invented by L J Lefèbre in Holland. Called the 'Kiosk Hollandia', it was designed to convey the sound of the orchestra, via a subterranean pipeline, acoustically 'to great distances'. The music, performed in the tent, was in some manner thrown downwards into the mouth(s) of the pipe(s). Reports at the time promulgated by the manufacturers F J Weygard were in favour of the contraption, some even going so far as to say that the quality of the musical sound issuing from the far end of the tube was an improvement on the original.

The following brief chronological list gives important events in the history of music broadcasting.

1920

February: **first public broadcasting station** opened by the Marconi Company near Chelmsford, England.

Spring: **The first disc-jockey** was Dr Frank Conrad, a technician employed by the Westinghouse Company in Pittsburgh, Pennsylvania. He was making experimental broadcasts from a workshop over his garage, playing records loaned from a local shop. Fellow experimenters who picked up his broadcasts got in touch with him and asked him to play their favourite records. His was **the first request programme**, although an involuntary one.

15 June: Dame Nellie Melba became **the first radio artist** when she broadcast from the Marconi Company studios in Chelmsford, Essex. This was **the first music broadcast in and from England.**

15 September: **the first American broadcast by a dance band** was given by Paul Spech and his Orchestra from Detroit.

1922
The British Broadcasting Company formed (British Broadcasting Corporation from 1927). **The first British dance band** (unnamed; with singer Harold Mann) **to broadcast** was heard in December.

1923
8 January: **the first opera to be broadcast** was Mozart's *Die Zauberflöte*, given by the British National Opera Company from Covent Garden.

26 February: **the first British broadcast by a named dance band** was given by Marius B Winter and his Orchestra.

1927
July: **the first British disc-jockey**, Christopher Stone, began a series of programmes of one hour every Friday lunchtime on 2LO from Savoy Hill, London.

1946
29 September: **the BBC opened the Third Programme** designed specifically for the performance of serious music, drama, and 'educational' programmes.

1949
Geoffrey Bush wrote an Overture entitled *Yorick* in memory of one of the most popular radio comedians, Tommy Handley.

A RADIO HOAX

The chaotic aspect of much modern music led to an interesting experiment, and the perpetration of a triple musical hoax by Dr Hans Keller of the BBC. On 5 June 1961 a concert was broadcast in which one of the works was *Mobile* for percussion and tape by Pyotr Zak. Later in the same programme the work was given again, as is sometimes done with new works with which it is anticipated that the audience will have difficulties of comprehension. Criticisms of Mr Zak's work were written by the noted critics Donald Mitchell and Jeremy Noble: each found the *Mobile* to be a poor work.

It was later announced that the broadcast had been a hoax. Hans Keller, whose idea it was, explained that the work came about when he and Susan Bradshaw (another member of the BBC Music Department) had wandered round a studio hitting various percussion instruments at random. One microphone was set aside in a corner and attached to an echo chamber for the production of mock electronic sounds. The second performance, later in the same programme, was carried out in the same way, without any reference to the effects produced in the earlier one, and neither was rehearsed in any way. The work was, therefore, a three-way hoax: there was no Pyotr Zak; there were no percussion-players (although perhaps Dr Keller is here underestimating his colleague and himself); and there was no tape. Furthermore, the 'repeat' was merely another impromptu performance.

For a broadcast on Sunday, 13 August 1961, more than two months after the original programme, the critics were invited to discuss this odd hoax with its creator, and it was during this discussion that the reason for the experiment emerged. Apparently, Dr Keller viewed current musical events less than enthusiastically and set out quite deliberately to fool the audience and critics into thinking that they were hearing a new work. The critics were not trapped into believing the work to be good, but they were fooled into taking it seriously. Dr Keller's point was that it was only in the musical climate of that time that such a hoax could be possible, and 'to enquire how far a non-work could be taken for a work'. In the time of Mozart, he explained, any attempt to pass off random noise as music would have been discovered immediately; it could never have been taken seriously, as had the *Mobile*. It might be considered that Dr Keller went to extreme lengths to prove the self-evident fact that music of Mozart's time was organised along stricter lines than music of the mid-20th century.

Television

Television has proved less successful for serious music broadcasts, but has nevertheless been active in the field.

The first opera ever televised was Act III (only) of Gounod's *Faust* by the BBC in June 1937.

The first TV opera was Menotti's *Amahl and the Night Visitors* (1952); since then there have been several operas designed primarily for the small screen, among them Britten's *Owen Wingrave* (1971) and R Murray-Schafer's *Loving/Toi* (1965) which incorporates advanced production and musical techniques.

The longest-serving TV musical director is Bert Hayes of Margate, Kent. He has been in charge of music on TV since the early post-war days of the medium, acting as musical director for series such as 'Crackerjack', 'Lennie the Lion', 'Whistle Stop', and 'Hopscotch', and has been associated with series starring Michael Bentine, Basil Brush, David Nixon, and Shani Wallis.

Electronic music and musique concrète

It may be necessary for the benefit of some readers to begin by defining these terms, especially now that the origins are obscured by time and the two separate streams have merged.

MUSIQUE CONCRÈTE: THE TECHNIQUES

Literally, this is music composed of concrete, or natural, as opposed to manufactured, sounds. The real sounds which form its basis are modified electronically, sometimes to the point at which they cease to bear any relation whatever to the original. For instance (see diagram p 275) a single note played forte on a piano (A) might be recorded and then the tape containing that note manipulated. The initial attack of the note might be removed (B); the reverberation might be extended enormously beyond its natural length, perhaps with alterations to the volume intensity during its length (C); or the natural fall of the volume might be copied and recopied endlessly and segments of the decay placed end to end to form a series of recurring fades, like a shallow saw-tooth edge (D); certain frequencies among the harmonics might be filtered out or exaggerated (E), or the basic sound itself removed to leave only the upper partials (F); pitch might be varied upwards or downwards, or both (G); the initial attack of the note (which we may have removed, remember) might be copied and repeated without its decay (H); any one of these possibilities might be played backwards (J) and/or combined with any others (K), and so on.

These examples by no means exhaust the possibilities of manipulation from just one piano note: imagine the world of sound available to a musique concrète composer with a whole keyboard at his disposal. But these composers need not stop at the piano, or at musical instruments in general. Any natural sound whatsoever, whether man-produced (factory whistle; car engine; spinning top, etc) or natural (animal noises, thunder, sea waves, etc) might be taken and manipulated at the composer's discretion, the only limit being his imagination. The greatest skill seems to be in obtaining the widest spectrum of sounds from the least varied sound sources.

ELECTRONIC MUSIC: THE TECHNIQUES

This music is likely to appeal more to the purist. No natural sounds are used at all in pure electronic music; every sound is produced electronically from sine waves generated by oscillators. Once recorded on to tape these sine waves may be subjected to manipulation similar to that in musique concrète, but modification of the waves themselves is often inflicted via the controls of the oscillator before recording takes place. Once again extremely wide spectrums of sound are at the disposal of the composer, and as in the case of the composer of musique concrète the results are often of a complexity and dramatic variety not obtainable from conventional instruments.

Shortly after the Second World War, when these two types of music experimentation were still forming into distinct lines of development, the composers collaborated to a certain extent (Stockhausen worked in Paris with Pierre Schaeffer, for instance). By the early 1950s, however, the lines were fully separated, only to come together again later to their mutual advantage. The techniques of electronic composition have progressed so far today that they have outstripped those of the more laborious-to-make musique concrète, and the latter term, apart from certain small cliques which regard the technique as a hobby rather than a viable musical form of expression of future significance, has dropped out of use. Electronic composers may, and do, employ 'concrete' sounds in their quest for sources, but the moulding of these sources is carried out strictly according to electronic music principles. An example is *Relativity*, produced in the BBC Radiophonic Workshop by Lily Greenham (realised by Richard Yeoman-Clark and Peter Howell), and first broadcast on 18 April 1975, in which the basic sound sources are words spoken by actors and then manipulated and juxtaposed electronically.

MUSIQUE CONCRÈTE: THE HISTORY

The origins of musique concrète may be said to have begun many years before the introduction of the term itself. The Futurist movement led by Luigi Russolo (Italian) was working towards the principles of musique concrète and electronic music, ie *away* from the production of music by traditional instruments, but Russolo and his followers still 'played' their instruments according to a score, even though the skills required in playing them seemed to be restricted to those of handle-turning and button-pressing. A few words of explanation are called for.

Balilla Pratella (Italian) wrote an orchestral work entitled *Musica Futuristica* in 1912. In this piece, Pratella incorporated naïve and banal ideas in an attempt, apparently, to get away from the ever-more complex musical designs of the late Romantics. This work caught the attention of Russolo, who felt that standard orchestral instruments were unsuitable for the kind of machine-like effects at which Pratella was aiming. Russolo invented an entirely new type of orchestra in 1913, which he called the 'Futurist Orchestra'. Its 'instruments' were machines which generated whistles, hisses, buzzes, and explosions: some were electrically driven, others produced their noise by the turn of a handle. Russolo tried out the first of his noise machines, or 'intonarumori', on 2 June 1913. It was called 'scoppiatore' ('exploder'). In less than a year he had invented and built 18 more instruments, and in Milan on 21 March 1914 he gave **the first Noise Concert.** The instruments which appeared included *crepitatori* ('cracklers'), *gorgogliatori* ('bubblers' or 'gurglers'), *rombatori* ('roarers'), *ronzatori* ('buzzers'), *sibilatori* ('hissers'), *stropicciatori* ('rubbers' or 'scrapers'), *ululatori* ('howlers'), and of course the *scoppiatori*. The titles of the works performed, all by Russolo, included *Dawn in the City*, *Gathering of Aircraft and Automobiles*, and *Battle at the Oasis*. Reports suggest that the weird noises of the machines produced a scene similar to that created at the Paris première of Stravinsky's *Rite of Spring*: the audience made more noise than the performers. Nevertheless, further Noise Concerts were given in many different countries, and the noise-making movement received attention and a certain amount of verbal support from Stravinsky, Milhaud, Honegger, Varèse, and Ravel, but the only composer outside Russolo's immediate circle to write music to include *intonarumori* was Pratella, whose opera *L'Aviatore Dro* (1915) placed them alongside conventional instruments in the orchestra pit.

Russolo was heartened by the interest, if not by any measure of public acclaim, with which his concerts were received, and he went on to build his most ambitious machine in 1920, a noise-organ called 'Russolofono'.

Unfortunately, the movement passed all too completely into history. Russolo himself seems to have lost interest after a few years, the instruments he took so much trouble to make have disappeared completely, and only one record of *intonarumori* was made: *Chorale* and *Serenata* (HMV R 6919) by Luigi Russolo and his brother Arturo in 1921. Furthermore, virtually all the music, which was written in an easily understood modification of standard score-writing, has vanished, only seven bars of the opening of *Dawn in the City* surviving.

The next step towards musique concrète was an uncanny mixture of that technique and electronic music: in 1939 John Cage wrote *Imaginary Landscape I* which is a blend of sine waves recorded onto 78 rpm discs, plus muted piano and cymbal tones.

The first use of the term 'musique concrète' was by Pierre Schaeffer in 1948, when he founded the Groupe de Recherches Musicales at the ORTF studios in Paris. Out of the numerous experiments, **the first work to appear in the new**

form was his *Étude aux chemins de fer*, made without the aid of a tape recorder and using the sound from a whistling top, recorded on to 78 rpm discs using the 'closed groove', or repeating groove, method. Sound-mixing was carried out with the use of multiple pick-ups and turntables. Many works were created in this way, but it will be realised that, without the permanence offered by a tape recorder, every performance would be subject to variations and the successful realisation of planned effects would often be a matter of luck.

The Phonogène was invented by Pierre Henry in 1950. This device, based on a complicated principle utilising revolving tape *record* and *playback* heads, enabled composers to alter the speed at which a sound source is recorded.

Pierre Schaeffer's associates who also produced their own works in the early days of musique concrète were Pierre Henry, Philippe Arthuys, and Michel Philippot.

A VISUAL REPRESENTATION OF THE SOUND POSSIBILITIES AVAILABLE FROM A SINGLE PIANOFORTE NOTE USING MUSIQUE CONCRÈTE TECHNIQUES

A A pianoforte note. Vertical measurement approximates to range; thickness of line to sound amplitude.

B The same note deprived of its initial attack.

C The same note, minus attack, but with its decay extended in duration and modified in amplitude and range.

D The natural fall of the note copied and repeated.

E The original note with segments of sound filtered out or amplified.

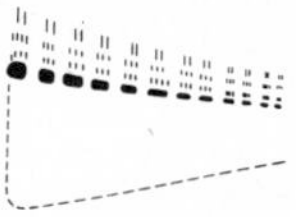

F The original note filtered out altogether, leaving only the upper partials and harmonics.

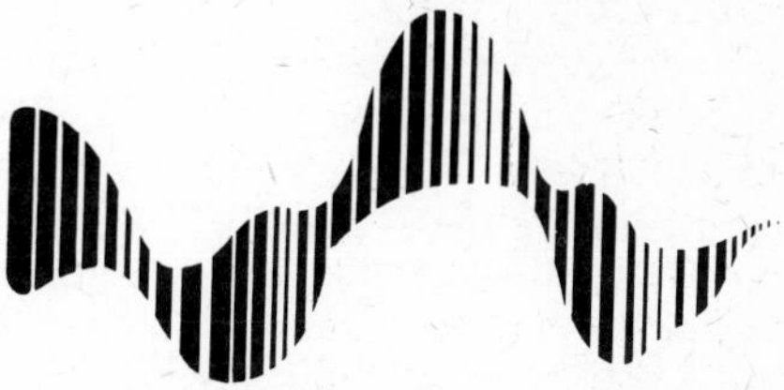

G The original note with pitch variations added to the extended decay.

etc.

H The modified attack of the note repeated in quick succession.

J A manipulated example (in this case D) played backwards.

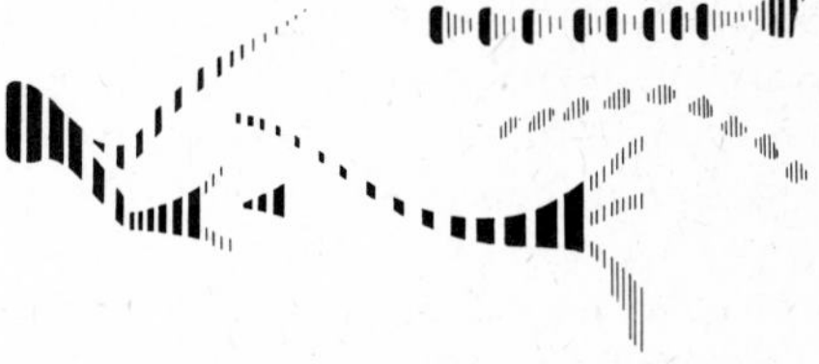

K An imaginative combination of the above manipulations.

The first recordings of musique concrète were issued by Ducretet Thompson in France in 1955 (DUC 6; DUC 9) and in England the following year (DTL 93090; DTL 93121); they contained pieces by all the composers mentioned above.

ELECTRONIC MUSIC: THE HISTORY

It might be claimed that all musique concrète is electronic music since it depends upon electronic apparatus to bring it to performance. As explained above, pure electronic music is that in which the sound sources are made entirely by oscillators, but the earliest steps towards this state were taken in the musique concrète studios of the ORTF in Paris by various assistants and associates of Pierre Schaeffer. Gradually the two movements split apart.

The first studio for the production of electronic music was founded in Cologne by Dr Herbert Eimert in 1951 with the assistance of Cologne Radio. Among those who experimented with the primitive equipment then available were Friedrich Trautwein, Robert Beyer, Meyer-Eppler, Gottfried Michael Koenig, Ernst Křenek, Karlheinz Stockhausen, and Herbert Eimert himself.

The first broadcast of electronic music, in which many of these composers took part, was transmitted on 15 October 1951 by Cologne Radio, but there had been one or two broadcast talks concerning the subject prior to this. **The first record of electronic music** to be issued was a transcript of this broadcast, made available to a limited circle shortly afterwards.

The first commercially issued discs of electronic music were made at the Cologne Studios and issued by Deutsche Grammophon Gesellschaft: they were 10 in (25·4 cm) discs (LP 16132, 16133, and 16134, later to be renumbered as LPE 17242, 17243, and 17244) and appeared in Germany in 1954 and in Britain in 1959. They included music by Křenek, Eimert, Koenig, and Stockhausen. The last-named composer has made the claim that his *Electronic Study I* (on LP 16132) was the first work to make use entirely of sounds generated from sine waves, but its date (1953) seems to put it slightly later than other experiments in the field. That work was, however, undeniably **the earliest electronic work to be issued in a commercial recording.**

Recent developments include the use of electronic music, both taped and live (see below) in conjunction with traditional musicians and instruments.

The longest tape composition is the confusingly titled *Memories of the Future*, Op 79 (1972), by Geoffrey Sentinella, which lasts twelve hours.

In *Sequenza III*, written by the Italian composer Berio in 1963 for the American singer Cathy Berberian, the artist is required to modify her voice as if it were being subjected to electronic manipulation.

COMPUTER MUSIC

The recent history of electronic music has seen a widening of its scope, not only by the admission of 'concrète' sound sources as a legitimate adjunct to composing, but also into the apparently ubiquitous sphere of EDP: electronic data processing by computer, and even further into a technique known as 'live electronics' (inferring, perhaps, that studio-produced electronic music is moribund).

The first computer music to come before the public was issued by American Decca on a disc (DL 79103; English Brunswick STA 8523) in late 1962. It presented music by Dr J R Pierce of the Bell Telephone Laboratories, and his associates Dr M V Mathews, David Lewin, and others, played by an IBM 7090 computer and converted to music by a digital-to-sound transducer. Possibly the two most remarkable items in this recording are a computerised rendering of a *Fantasia* by Orlando Gibbons in which the sounds of a consort of recorders are imitated so closely as to be almost indistinguishable from the real thing, and 'A Bicycle Built for Two', arranged by Dr Mathews, for which the computer was programmed to sound like a human voice (with a strong American accent) singing one of the verses and accompanying itself on an imitation bar-room piano.

In January 1975 it was announced that a computer had been developed which would, as the operator played upon its keyboard, picture the music on a screen in conventional music type. The machine has been developed by Dr Brian Sykes of the Computer Laboratory of Cambridge University, England. Not only would it project the played notes on its screen; it would also punch holes in a tape so that the instrument could play the music back later—*just* like the reproducing player-piano of the turn of the century.

LIVE ELECTRONICS

Live electronics first appeared in 1960 in the USA: John Cage's *Cartridge Music* employs record pick-up cartridges and contact microphones to collect inaudible sounds for amplification. Since then the discipline has spread to Europe, live performers' voices and the sounds from their instruments being distorted and manipulated electronically in public performance. A good example from 1968 is *Pendulum Music* by Steve Reich. Three pendulum microphones are swung from their leads above loudspeakers which are at the other end of the reproducing chain. The amplifiers are then turned up to induce feedback howl which varies and pulses in time to the swings of the microphones. As the movements of the microphones reduce, the variations in feedback are correspondingly lessened until at a stationary position the howl is steady. A fade-out brings the work to an end.

SYNTHESISERS

Mention should be made of the commercial success of the synthesiser pioneered by Dr Robert Moog in America in 1964. Both Walter (now Wendy—see Female Composers) Carlos and Hans Wurman have produced transcriptions of classical and popular music on a Moog (pronounced *Moge*) Synthesiser, starting in 1969, and despite the groans of the critics there can be no denying that some of these arrangements have artistic merit and high entertainment value. Don Banks wrote original music for the synthesiser in his *Meeting Place* (1970) for chamber players, jazz group, and live electronics, and synthesisers are part of the standard equipment of 'progressive pop' groups.

Bibliography

See also Section VII: Music Literature. In addition to those books mentioned specifically below, acknowledgement is made to countless indispensable books and scores which have contributed to the collection of facts in this volume, either directly or indirectly, over the years.

Apel, Willi, *Harvard Dictionary of Music* (1970)

Bonanni's Gabinetto Armonico, reprinted by Dover, New York, 1964

British Phonographic Committee, The, *The British Record*, London, 1959

Brook, Barry S, *Thematic Catalogues in Music—An Annotated Bibliography*, Pendragon Press, New York, 1972

Charroux, Robert, *The Mysterious Past*, Futura, London, 1974

Clemencic, René, *Old Musical Instruments* (translated by David Hermges), Weidenfeld & Nicolson, London, 1968

Cowell, Henry and Sidney, *Charles Ives and His Music*, OUP, London, 1955

Davidson, Gladys, *Standard Stories from the Operas*, T Werner Laurie, London, 1944

Dent, Edward J, *Alessandro Scarlatti*, Edward Arnold, London, 1905 (2nd Ed, 1950)

Dent, Edward J, *Opera*, Penguin, Middlesex, 1940

Ewen, David, *The Complete Book of Classical Music*, Robert Hale, London, 1966

Fétis, F J, *Biographie Universelle des Musiciens*, Didot, Paris, 1862

Geiringer, Karl, *Musical Instruments, Their History in Western Culture from the Stone Age to the Present Day* (translated by Bernard Miall), George Allen & Unwin, London, 1943

Gillett and Frith (editors), *Rock File 4*, Panther, London, 1977–8

Goodkind, Herbert K, *Violin Iconography of Antonio Stradivari, 1644–1737*, Author, Larchmont, New York, 1972

Green, Stanley, *The Rodgers and Hammerstein Story*, W H Allen, London, 1963

Grove's Dictionary of Music and Musicians, 5th Edition, Ed Eric Blom, Macmillan, London, 1954

Hardy and Laing, *Encyclopaedia of Rock*, Aquarius, London, 1977

Headington, Christopher, *The Bodley Head History of Western Music*, Bodley Head, London, 1974

Hitchcock, H Wiley, *Music in the United States: A Historical Introduction*, Prentice-Hall, New Jersey, 1969

Hughes, Gervase, and Thal, Herbert van, *The Music Lover's Companion*, Eyre & Spottiswoode, London, 1971

International Music Guide, Tantivy Press, London (annually)

International Who's Who in Music, Ed Ernest Kay (7th Ed), Cambridge, 1975

Jacobs, Arthur, *A New Dictionary of Music* (4th Ed), Penguin, Middlesex, 1978

Jacobs, Arthur, and Sadie, Stanley, *Opera—A Modern Guide*, Pan, London, 1964

Jenkins, Jean L, BA, *Eighteenth Century Musical Instruments: France and Britain*, Victoria and Albert Museum, London, 1973

Jenkins, Jean L, BA, *Musical Instruments (preserved in) The Horniman Museum*, London (2nd Ed), ILEA, London, 1970

Kostelanetz, Richard (Ed), *John Cage—Documentary Monographs in Modern Art*, Allen Lane/Penguin, London, 1971

Kühn, Herbert, *On the Track of Prehistoric Man* (translated by Alan Houghton Broderick), Arrow, London, 1958

Loewenberg, Alfred, *Annals of Opera 1597–1940*, Societas Bibliographica, Geneva, 1942; 1955

Mellers, Wilfrid, *Music in a New Found Land*, Barrie & Rockliffe, London, 1964

Nettl, Paul, *National Anthems* (translated by Alexander Gode), Ungar, New York, 1952

Nyman, Michael, *Experimental Music, Cage and Beyond*, Cassel and Collier Macmillan, London, 1974

Ord-Hume, Arthur W J G, *Clockwork Music*, George Allen & Unwin, London, 1972

Palmer, King, *Teach Yourself Orchestration*, English University Press, London, 1964

Pincherle, Marc, *Vivaldi, Genius of the Baroque* (translated by Christopher Hatch), Gollancz, London, 1958

Pincherle, Marc, *The World of the Virtuoso* (translated from the French by Lucile H Brockway), Gollancz, London, 1964

Pleasants, Henry, *The Great Singers*, Gollancz, London, 1967

Rice, Jo and Tim, Gambaccini, Paul, Read, Mike, *The Guinness Book of British Hit Singles* (2nd Ed), Guinness Superlatives, London, 1979

Robbins Landon, Howard Chandler, and Chapman, Roger E, *Studies in 18th Century Music—A Tribute to Karl Geiringer on his 70th Birthday*, George Allen & Unwin, London, 1970

Robbins Landon, Howard Chandler, *The Symphonies of Joseph Haydn*, Universal Edition and Rockliff, London, 1955

Rushmore, Robert, *The Singing Voice*, Hamish Hamilton, London, 1971

Rust, Brian, *American Dance Bands Discography*, Arlington House, New York, 1976

Rust, Brian, and Walker, Edward, *British Dance Bands Discography, 1912–1939*, Storyville, Essex, 1973

Rust, Brian, and Debus, Allen G, PhD, *The Complete Entertainment Discography*, Arlington House, New York, 1973

Rust, Brian, *The Dance Bands*, Ian Allen, London, 1972

Rust, Brian, *Jazz Records, 1897–1942*, Storyville, Essex, 1961; 1962; 1964; 1970

Rust, Brian, and Allen, Walter C, *King Joe Oliver*, Sidgwick & Jackson, London, 1958

Rust, Brian, *London Musical Theatre, 1894–1954*, BIRS, London, 1958

Rust, Brian, and Harris, Max, *Recorded Jazz: A Critical Guide*, Pelican, London, 1960

Sachs, Curt, *The History of Musical Instruments*, Dent, London, 1942

Scholes, Percy A, *The Oxford Companion to Music* (9th Ed), OUP, London, 1956

Shaw, Arnold, *The Rock Revolution*, Collier-Macmillan, London, 1969

Shaw, Martin, and Coleman, Henry, *National Anthems of the World*, Blandford, London, 1963

Shestack, Melvin, *The Country Music Encyclopaedia*, Omnibus, New York, 1977

Tallis, David, *Musical Boxes*, Muller, London, 1971

Vinton, John (Ed), *Dictionary of 20th Century Music*, Thames & Hudson, London, 1974

Warwick, Alan R, *A Noise of Music*, Queen Anne Press, London, 1968

Young, Percy M, *Choral Music of the World*, Abelard-Schuman, London, 1969

Young, Percy M, *The Concert Tradition*, Routledge & Kegan Paul, London, 1965

Index of names

See also chart of pseudonyms in Section 3. Asterisks denote illustrations.

Aaltonen, Erkki (b. 1910), 146
ABBA, 252, 253*
Abbott, Larry (b. 1900), 237
Abel, Carl Friedrich (1723-87), 67, 96, 228
Abert, Johann Joseph (1832-1915), 164
Abrams, Daniel (20th C), 32
Achleitner, Innozenz (20th C), 208
Ackermann, Alexander (1446-1506), 71
Acuff, Roy (b. 1903), 249
Adam de la Hale (c1230/40-c87), 70, 153, 173
Adam, Johann Ludwig (1758-1848), 56
Adami, Giuseppe (1878-1946), 165
Adélaïde de France (1732-1800), 114
Adler, Alfred (1870-1937), 148
Adler, Larry (b. 1914), 235, 243
Affilard, Michel d' (15th C), 261
Agricola, A—*see* Ackermann, A
Aguiari, Lucrezia (1743-83), 172
Ahnell, Emil (20th C), 127
Akiyama, Kuniharu (b. 1929), 235
Akutagawa, Yasushi (b. 1925), 93
Alabiev, Alexander Alexandrovich (1787-1851), 62
Alaleona, Domenico (1881-1928), 146
Albert, Eugene Francis Charles d' (1864-1932), 78, 137, 164
Albert, Prince (of Saxe-Coburg-Gotha) (1819-61), 54, 204
Alberti, Giuseppe Battista (or Matteo) (1685-1751), 66
Albinoni, Tommaso (1671-1745), 86, 95, 157, 225, 228
Albrechtsberger, Johann Georg (1736-1809), 65, 69, 96f, 108, 228
Alcock, John (1715-1806), 56
Alcott family, 117
Aldana, Mario Kuri (b. 1932), 36
Aldrovandini, Giuseppe (1672-1707), 66
Aleotti, Raffaela (c1570-1638+), 63
Aleotti, Vittoria (c1575-?), 63
Alfonso X (King of Castile) (1221-84), 55
Alfvén, Hugo (1872-1960), 109
Alkan, Charles-Valentin (1813-88), 107, 139
Alldahl, Per-Gunnar (b. 1943), 148
Allison, Horace (20th C), 46
Allorto, Riccardo (b. 1920), 228
Alma-Tadema, (Sir) Lawrence (1836-1912), 47
Almeida, Antonio de (b. 1928), 229
Almeida, Francisco Antonio d' (?-1755), 155
Alpaerts, Flor (1876-1954), 148
Alstyne, Frances Jane Van—*see* Crosby, F.
Amati, Nicolò (1596-1684), 32, 49
Ambros, Vladimir (1891-1956), 114
Ambrose, Bert (20th C), 234, 247
Ambrose (Bishop of Milan) (c333-397), 172
Amirov, Fikret (b. 1922), 146
Anderson, George Frederick (c1801-76), 57
Andrew Sisters, 247
Andriessen, Jurriaan (b. 1925), 96, 145
Anka, Paul (b. 1941), 243
Anna Amalia (Princess of Prussia) (1723-87), 55
Anne (Queen of England) (1665-1714), 57
Ansermet, Ernest (1883-1968), 199, 244
Antar (7th C), 114
Antes, John (1740-1811), 261
Antheil, George (1900-59), 96, 137, 146, 164, 170, 213
Antill, John (b. 1904), 14
Apel, Willi (b. 1893), 212
Apergis, Georges A (b. 1945), 33
Araújo, João Gomes de (1846-1942), 58
Arcadelt, Jacob (c1514-c67), 179
Archer, Violet (*née* Balestreri) (b. 1913), 63
Ardévol, José (b. 1911), 122, 257
Arditi, Luigi (1822-1903), 213
Arensky, Antonii (1861-1906), 107
Arezzo, Guido d' (c990-1050), 209
Argento, Domenick Joseph (b. 1927), 116
Aristophanes (c1450-c1388 BC), 166
Aristos (3rd C, BC), 200
Arlen, Harold (b. 1905), 247
Arma, Paul—*see* Weisshans
Armstrong, Louis (1900-71), 232, 234, 238, 242
Arnault, Henri, of Zwolle (?-1466), 46
Arnaz, Desi (20th C), 247
Arne, Michael (1740-86), 167, 176
Arne, Thomas Augustine (1710-78), 37, 125, 140, 164, 185
Arnheim, Gus (20th C), 243
Arnić, Blaž (b. 1901), 62, 144
Arnold, Malcolm (b. 1921), 46
Arnold, Samuel (1740-1802), 167, 168, 170
Arthuys, Philippe (20th C), 275
Artois, Count of (13th C), 154
Arutyunyan, Alexander (b. 1920), 31
Astaire, Fred (b. 1899), 247
Aston, Hugh (?-1522), 112
Atterberg, Kurt (1887-1974), 164, 268
Attey, John (15?-c1640), 67
Attwood, Thomas (1765-1838), 167
Auber, Daniel (1782-1871), 137, 142, 157, 166, 204
Aubert, Moise (19th C), 261
Auden, Wystan Hugh (b. 1907), 114
Auric, Georges (b. 1899), 66
Avalon, Frankie (b. 1939), 244
Avison, Charles (1709-70), 95, 212
Avshalamov, Jacob (b. 1919), 146
Axman, Emil (1887-1949), 148

Bacewicz, Grazyna (1913-69), 63
Bach family, 67
Bach, Carl Philipp Emanuel (1714-88), 37, 66, 67, 70, 80, 111, 119, 121, 129, 134, 175, 176, 182, 211, 228, 264
Bach, Johann Christian (1735-82), 37, 63, 67, 70, 80, 95, 107, 109, 163, 166, 170, 185, 228
Bach, Johann Christoph Friedrich (1732-93), 67, 70
Bach, Johann Sebastian (1685-1750), 18, 21, 22, 31, 37, 44, 58, 59, 64, 67, 72, 84-87 *passim*, 94, 104*, 107, 110, 111, 116, 123, 130, 134, 137, 142, 168, 174, 175, 176, 177, 182f, 208, 216, 228, 243
Bach, Wilhelm Friedmann (1710-84), 66, 67, 168, 228, 264
Bachschmidt, Anton Adam (1705/9-c80), 31
Badarzewska-Baranowska, Tekla (1838-61), 63
Badings, Henk (b. 1907), 30, 145, 146, 147
Baez, Joan (b. 1941), 251
Baffo, Giovanni (16th C), 99
Baïf, Jean Antoine de (1532-89), 200
Bailey, Mildred (1907-51), 247
Baker, Howard (b. 1902), 247
Balakirev, Mily Alexeyevich (1837-1910), 65, 77
Ball, Kenny (b. 1931), 251
Ball, Lucille (b. 1911), 247
Ballard, Hank (b. 1936), 250
Banchieri, Adriano (c1565-1634), 95, 143
Banks, Don (1923-80), 277
Bannister, John (1630-79), 201
Bantock, (Sir) Granville (1868-1946), 64, 138, 142, 158, 164
Barber, Samuel (1910-81), 108, 256
Barbier, Jules (1822-1901), 165
Barbirolli, (Sir) John (1899-1970), 32
Barchunov, ? (20th C), 24
Bardi, (Count) Giovanni (1534-1612), 66, 154, 173
Barna, ?, 169
Barnes, Walter (1917-40), 241
Barnet, Charlie (b. 1913), 247
Barras, Charles (19th C), 156
Barraud, Francis (1856-1924), 266
Barraud, Henry (b. 1900), 95
Bárta, Lubor (1928-72), 148
Barth, Hans (1897-1956), 96
Bartha, Alex (20th C), 246
Barthélémon, François-Hippolyte (1741-1808), 166
Bartók, Béla (1881-1945), 39, 95, 108, 110, 140, 141, 243, 255f, 265
Bartoš, Josef (b. 1902), 121
Barvík, Miroslav (b. 1919), 149
Baselt, Berend (b. 1939), 228
Basie, 'Count' William (b. 1904), 247
Bas(s)evi, Giacomo (1682-1738) (Cervetto), 70
Bates, Joah (1741-99), 176
Bath, Hubert (1883-1945), 168
Baton, Charles (?-1758), 42
Baudrier, Yves (b. 1906), 66
Bauer, Hans (1878-1937), 180
Bauld, Alison (b. 1944), 145
Baur, Jürg (b. 1918), 146, 263
Bax, Arnold Edward Trevor (1883-1953), 57, 64, 72, 95, 118, 143, 213
Beach, Amy Marcy (*née* Chaney) (1867-1944), 63, 92
Beat Brothers, The, 251
Beatles, The, 250f
Beaumont, Geoffrey (1903-70), 174
Bechet, Sidney (1897-1959), 244
Beck, František (1723-1809), 65
Becker, John Joseph (1886-1961), 115, 122
Bedford, David (b. 1937), 19, 39, 96
Bedford, Steuart (20th C), 63*, 64
Bedřich, Jan (b. 1932), 148
Bedyngham, John (15th C), 70
Beecham, (Sir) Thomas (1879-1961), 197, 199*
Beecke, Ignaz von (1733-1805), 127, 134
Bee Gees, The, 253
Beer, Johann (1655?-1700?), 35, 96
Beer, Joseph A (1744-1811), 30
Beethoven, Ludwig van (1770-1827), 15, 26, 30, 31, 36, 39, 55, 60, 65, 74, 82, 83-87 *passim*, 88f, 92, 93, 94, 95, 96, 108, 109, 110, 111, 112, 113, 114-134 *passim*, 136, 137, 142, 150f, 151*, 156, 164, 167, 169, 174, 175, 182f, 185, 198, 211, 214, 225, 226, 228, 254, 258, 261, 264, 267, 268, 270
Beiderbecke, Bix (1903-31), 232, 244
Belasco, Leon (20th C), 247
Belcher, Supply (1751-1836), 77
Belli, Domenico (c1550-1618+), 166
Bellini, Vincenzo (1801-35), 165
Benavente, Regina (20th C), 148
Benda family, 67f
Benda, František (1709-86), 66, 67
Benda, Friedrich Heinrich Wilhelm (1742-1812/14), 67, 166
Benda, Jiří Antonín (1722-95), 66
Bendinelli, Cesare (17th C), 31
Benedict, (Sir) Julius (1804-85), 74
Beneke, Tex (b. 1914), 247
Benevoli, Orazio (1602-72), 35, 208
Bengtsson, Lars Ingmar Olof (b. 1929), 229
Ben Haim, Paul (b. 1897), 71
Benjamin, Arthur (1893-1960), 46
Bennett, John (c1570-c1620), 143, 179
Bennett, Robert Russell (1894-1979), 140, 169
Benson, Ivy (b. 1910), 242*
Bentine, Michael (b. 1924), 273
Bentzon, Nils Viggo (b. 1919), 95, 107, 125, 146, 150
Berberian, Cathy (b. 1933), 63, 276
Berens, Johan Herman (1826-80), 169
Berezovsky, Nicolai (b. 1900), 263
Berezowsky, Maxim Sosonowisch (1745-77), 92, 156
Berg, Alban (1885-1935), 66, 133, 139, 164
Berg, Josef (b. 1927), 144
Berger, Francesco (1834-1933), 58
Berger, Theodor (b. 1905), 137, 147, 148
Bergman, Erik Valdemar (b. 1911), 138, 148
Bergonzi, Giuseppe (?-before 1750), 32
Berigan, Roland Bernard 'Bunny' (1909-42), 232, 247
Berio, Luciano (b. 1925), 18, 276
Bériot, Charles Auguste de (1802-70), 59
Berkeley, Lennox Randal (b. 1903), 148
Berlin, Irving (b. 1888), 71, 270
Berliner, Émile (1851-1929), 266
Berlioz, Louis Hector (1803-69), 16, 32, 34, 35, 39, 43, 47, 78, 83, 93, 94, 112, 119, 120, 122, 130, 144, 164, 175, 177, 182, 202, 213
Berly, Harry (?-1937), 234, 237
Berners, (Lord) Gerald (1883-1950), 77, 158, 213
Bernier, René (b. 1905), 67
Bernstein, Leonard (b. 1918), 114, 124
Berry, 'Chuck' Charles Edward (b. 1931), 250
Berté, Heinrich (1858-1924), 169
Bertin, Louise Angélique (1805-77), 144
Bertini, Giuseppe (c1756-1847+), 56
Bertini, ? (20th C), 247
Bertoni, Ferdinando Giuseppe (1732-1813), 166
Bertrand, Jimmy (1900-60), 238
Berwald, Franz Adolf (1796-1868), 116, 131, 132
Best, Pete (20th C), 251f
Bestor, Don (1888-1969), 245
Beyer, Robert (20th C), 276
Bianchi, Giovanni Baptista (18th C), 165
Biber, Heinrich Ignaz Franz von (1644-1704), 38f, 126, 128, 129, 130, 257
Biberian, ? (20th C), 148
Bickler, Miss (18th C), 37
Billings, Josh (20th C), 237
Billings, William (1746-1800), 77
Billington, Elizabeth (1765?-1818), 63
Bilse, Benjamin (1816-1902), 198
Binchois, Gilles de (c1400-60), 176
Binder, Christlieb Siegmund (1723-89), 20
Bishop, Henry Rowley (1786-1855), 78, 139, 140, 154, 157
Bittner, Julius (1874-1939), 62, 77
Bizet, Georges Alexander César Léopold (1838-75), 19, 36, 49, 72, 158, 165, 246
Blacher, Boris (1903-75), 95
Blades, James (20th C), 152
Blake, Eubie (b. 1883), 243
Blake, William (1757-1827), 148
Blaremberg, Pavel Ivanovich (1841-1907), 140
Blažek, Zdenek (b. 1905), 121
Bliss, (Sir) Arthur (1891-1975), 57, 96, 142
Bliss, Philipp Paul (1872-1933), 74
Blitzstein, Marc (1905-64), 137
Bloch, Ernest (1880-1959), 95, 109, 128, 146
Blodek, Vilém (1834-74), 60
Blom, Eric Walter (1888-1959), 212
Blomdahl, Karl Birger (1916-68), 147, 158
Blue, Barry (20th C), 252
Blume, Friedrich (1893-1975), 211
Blumlein, A D (19th C), 268
Blyton, Carey (b. 1932), 145
Bocaccini, ? (20th C), 96
Boccherini, Luigi (1743-1805), 71, 74, 80, 109, 110, 125, 126, 138, 144, 228
Boëthius, Anicus Manlius Severinus (470-525), 81, 166
Bogatirev, Anatoly (b. 1913), 141
Bogusławski, Edward (b. 1940), 96
Bohrer, Caspar (1744-1809), 33
Boieldieu, François Adrien (1775-1834), 166
Boismortier, Joseph Bodin de (c1691-1755), 30, 137
Boisselet, Paul (b. 1917), 124, 126, 130, 185
Boïto, Arrigo (1842-1918), 144, 158, 164, 165
Boleyn (Bullen) (Queen) Anne (1507?-36), 54
Bomtempo, João Domingos (1775-1842), 92
Boni, Carlo (18th C), 110
Bonno, Giuseppe (1710-88), 158
Bononcini, Antonio Maria (1675-1726), 177
Bononcini, Giovanni (1670-1755), 66, 155
Bonporti, Francesco Antonio (1672/8-1740/9), 65, 95, 110
Borde, Jean Benjamin de la (1734-94), 61
Borodin, Alexander Porphyrievich (1833-87), 65, 77, 87, 164, 254
Borup-Jørgenssen, Axel (b. 1924), 108
Bose, Sterling (?-1952), 234
Boswell Sisters, 247

Boughton, Rutland (1878-1960), 167, 170
Boulanger, Lili (Juliette Marie Olga) (1893-1918), 63
Boulanger, Nadia (Juliette) (1887-1979), 56, 63, 64
Boulez, Pierre (b. 1926), 19, 257
Boult, (Sir) Adrian Cedric (b. 1889), 182, 199
Bourgeois, Derek (b. 1942), 32, 93
Bourges, Clémentine de (?-1561), 63
Bourguignon, Francis de (b. 1890), 67
Bow, Clara (20th C), 93
Bowles, Paul Frederick (b. 1910), 77
Bowlly, Al (*c*1898-1941), 241
Boyce, William (1710-79), 57, 60, 94, 167
Brachvogel, Albert Emil (1824-76), 168
Bradshaw, Susan (b. 1931), 272
Brahms, Johannes (1833-97), 64, 83, 84-87 *passim*, 94, 95, 107, 108, 110, 111, 118, 120, 129, 175, 182, 185, 214, 268
Brain, Dennis (1921-57), 15
Brandenburg, Christian Ludwig (Markgrave of) (18th C), 116
Brant, Henry Dreyfus (b. 1913), 27, 34, 126
Breau, Louis (20th C), 238
Bredal, Niels Krog (1733-78), 156
Breitkopf, Johann Gottlob Immanuel (1719-94), 227, 230
Brenner, von (19th C), 198
Brenta, Gaston (b. 1902), 67
Brian, William Havergal (1876-1972), 58, 92, 121, 131, 133, 134, 142, 144, 182f
Bridge, Frank (1879-1941), 149
Bright, Dora (1863-1952), 63
Brilhart, Arnold (20th C), 244
Bringuer, Estela (20th C), 147
Britten, Edward Benjamin (1913-76), 29, 76, 107, 108*, 131, 132, 137, 138, 139, 140, 158, 175, 177, 256, 273
Britton, Dorothy Guyver (b. 1922), 63
Britton, Thomas (1644-1714), 201
Bronsart, Ingeborg von (*née* Starck) (1840-1913), 63
Brook, Barry S (b. 1924), 227, 229, 230
Brotherhood of Man, The, 253
Brown, James (b. 1928), 250
Brown, Les (b. 1912), 245, 247
Brown, Lew (20th C), 238
Brown, Maurice John Edwin (1906-75), 228
Brown, Robert (20th C), 181
Brubeck, David Warren (b. 1920), 251
Bruch, Max (1838-1920), 158
Bruckner, Anton (1824-96), 35, 84-87 *passim*, 126, 130, 132, 134, 174, 175, 177
Brüggemann, Alfred (1873-1959), 144
Bruhns, Nicholaus (1665-97), 111
Brunetti, Gaetano (1745?-1808), 125
Buckley, Neil (20th C), 245
Budashkin, Nikolay Pavlovich (b. 1910), 20
Budd, Harold (b. 1936), 148
Bull, John (*c*1562-1628), 111, 139, 185
Bülow, Hans Guido von (1830-94), 198
Bürger, Gottfried August (1747-94), 124
Burnand, Anton (=Strelezki, A; Esipoff, S) (1859-1907), 71
Burnand, Francis Cowley (1836-1917), 162
Burney, (Sir) Charles (1726-1814), 80, 163, 174, 202
Burrell, Mary (1850-98), 214
Burri, Karl (20th C), 48
Burton, John (1730-82), 37, 112
Buschmann, Friedrich (19th C), 38
Bush, Alan Dudley (b. 1900), 145
Bush, Geoffrey (b. 1920), 272
Busoni, Ferruccio (1866-1924), 95, 107, 144, 158, 164, 262
Büsser, Paul Henri (1872-1973), 58
Butterworth, George Sainton Kaye (1885-1916), 61, 108
Buxtehude, Dietrich (1637-1707), 111
Byng, George W (20th C), 267
Byrd, William (1543-1623), 150, 176, 225
Byron, (Lord) George Gordon Noel (1788-1824), 122

Caamaño, Roberto (b. 1923), 96
Cabezón, Antonia de (*c*1510-*c*66), 59
Caccini, Francesca (18th C), 63
Caccini, Giulio (*c*1546-1618), 63, 66, 154, 173
Cadman, Charles Wakefield (1881-1946), 146
Caesar—*see* Smegergill
Caffi, Francesco (1778-1874), 58
Cage, John (b. 1912), 26, 40, 77, 113, 147, 149, 213, 225, 256, 257, 274, 277
Cahill, Thaddeus (19th-20th C), 263
Caldara, Antonio (*c*1678-1736), 137
Calderón de la Barca (1600-81), 154
Calegori, Maria Caterina (1644-?), 63
Calzabigi (Calsabigi), Raniero da (1714-95), 165
Cambert, Robert (1628-77), 60, 155
Cambini, Giovanni Giuseppe (1746-1825), 80, 110
Camerloher, Placidus von (1718-82), 228
Cammarano, Salvatore (1801-52), 165
Campian, Thomas (1567-1620), 67, 77
Candeille, Amélie Julie (1767-1834), 63
Cannabich, Christian (1731-89), 65, 127
Cannabich, Karl Konrad (1764-1806), 65
Cannon, Gus (b. 1883), 236
Cannon, Philip (b. 1929), 148
Čapek, Karel (1890-1938), 140
Capt, Henri (19th C), 261
Cardew, Cornelius (b. 1936), 148, 257
Carey, Henry (1690-1743), 61
Carlos, Walter (Wendy) (b. 1939), 64, 277
Carmi, Avner (b. 1900), 48
Carmichael, Hoagland 'Hoagy' (b. 1899), 234, 247, 270
Caroline Amelia (of Augustenberg) (1792-1866), 55
Caroline (Queen) (1683-1737), 264
Carr, Comyns J (19th C), 162
Carré, Michel (1819-72), 165
Carrillo, Julián (1875-1965), 56
Carrol, Lewis (=Dodgson, C L) (1832-98), 258
Carson, Fiddlin' John (?-1935), 249
Čart—*see* Zarth
Carter, Benny (Bennett Lester) (b. 1907), 245
Carter, Elliott (b. 1908), 258
Carter, Mother Maybelle (b. 1909), 249
Caruso, Enrico (1873-1921), 267, 270
Cary, Tristram Ogilvie (b. 1925), 148, 258
Casadesus, Henri (1879-1947), 80, 146
Casals, Pablo (1876-1973), 58
Casella, Alfredo (1883-1947), 166, 265
Casey, Floyd (1900-67), 238
Cash, Johnny (b. 1932), 249*
Cassadó, Joaquín (1867-1926), 118
Castelnuovo Tedesco, Maria (1895-1968), 35, 141
Castro, Juan José (1895-1968), 144
Castro, Manolo (20th C), 247
Castro, Ricardo (1864-1907), 92
Castro, Ruz Fidel (b. 1927), 149
Catalani, Alfredo (1854-93), 158
Catelinet, Philip (20th C), 32
Catherine the Great (1729-96), 92
Cauchie, Maurice (1882-1968), 228
Caus, Solomon de (17th C), 261, 264
Cavalieri, Emilio de' (1550-1602), 66, 169, 175
Cavalli, Pietro Francesco (1602-76), 31
Cavendish, Michael (1565-1628), 67, 179
Cazzati, Maurizio (*c*1620-77), 31
Ceremuga, Josef (b. 1930), 117
Cervetto—*see* Bas(s)evi, G
Chabrier, Alexis Emmanuel (1841-94), 60, 109
Chadwick, George Whitefield (1854-1931), 58
Chamfrey, Richard (?-?), 59
Chaminade, Cécile (1857-1944), 63
Chaplin, Charles Spencer (1889-1977), 93
Chapman, Chris (20th C), 235
Charles I (King of England) (1600-49), 55, 57, 61, 200
Charles II (King of England) (1630-85), 55, 57, 201
Charles IX (King of France) (1550-74), 200
Charpentier, Gustave (1860-1956), 58, 158, 164
Charpentier, Marc-Antoine (1634-1704), 175
Charrière, Isabelle de (1740-1805), 63
Chaucer, Geoffrey (*c*1340-1400), 258
Chausson, Ernest (1855-99), 62, 140, 164
Chavez, Carlos (b. 1899), 96
Checker, 'Chubby' Ernest Evans (b. 1941), 250
Chenet, G (20th C), 180
Cherubini, Luigi (1760-1842), 94, 166
Chester, Bob (b. 1908), 246
Chiabrera, Gabriello (1552-1638), 66
Chlubna, Osvald (b. 1893), 118, 145
Chok Yin Tai (20th C), 96
Chopin, Fryderyk Franciszek (1810-49), 32, 78, 85-87 *passim*, 95, 111, 112, 113, 114-134 *passim*, 169, 228, 254f
Chorley, Henry Fothergill (1808-72), 162
Chou Wen-Chung (b. 1923), 148
Christian VIII (King of Denmark) (1786-1848), 55
Christofori, Bartolomeo (1655-1731), 37, 47
Chrysander, Friedrich (1826-1901), 214
Churchill, Winston Leonard Spencer (1874-1965), 92, 152
Ciampi, Legrenzio Vincenzo (*c*1719-62), 165
Cianchettini, Veronica Rosalie (*née* Dušek) (1779-1833), 63
Cikker, Ján (b. 1911), 148
Cimarosa, Domenico (1749-1801), 65
Clack, Richard (18th C), 176
Clapp, Sunny (20th C), 247
Clark, Don (20th C), 247
Clarke, Jeremiah (*c*1659/63?-1703/7), 61
Clay, Charles (18th C), 261
Clemens, Jacobus (non Papa) (*c*1510-*c*56), 70
Clement of Alexandria (170-220), 179
Clementi, Muzio (1752-1832), 36, 111, 116, 118, 228
Cliburn, Van (Harvey Lavan) (b. 1934), 269, 270
Clifford, Henry (20th C), 236
Cluny, Bernard de (1090-1153), 179
Clutsam, George H (1866-1951), 169
Coates, Eric (1886-1957), 108, 137
Coccia, Carlo (1782-1873), 166
Cochran, (Sir) Charles Blake (1872-1951), 243
Coffey, Charles (?-1745), 144, 155
Coleman, Charles (17th C), 155
Coleridge Taylor, Avril Gwendolen (b. 1903), 63
Coleridge Taylor, Samuel (1875-1912), 174
Colicchio, ? (20th C), 150
Colles, Henry Cope (1879-1943), 212
Collet, Henri (1885-1951), 66
Collett, John (18th C), 167
Collins, Anthony Vincent Benedictus (1893-1970), 150
Colloredo (Archbishop of Salzburg) (1732-1812), 117, 174
Colonna, Jerry (b. 1904), 245
Commer, Franz (1813-87), 138
Como, Perry (Pierino) (b. 1912), 247
Condell, Henry (1757-1824), 168
Conrad, Frank (20th C), 271
Conti, Carlo (1796-1868), 166
Cooke, Henry (*c*1616-72), 155
Cooksey, Robert (*c*1900-?), 235
Coolidge, Clark (20th C), 258
Coolidge, Elizabeth Sprague (1864-1953), 115
Coperario, Giovanni (=Cooper, J) (*c*1570-1627), 71
Copland, Aaron (b. 1900), 20, 71, 117, 142, 213, 256*
Corbusier, Le (20th C), 78
Corelli, Arcangelo (1653-1713), 32, 71, 86, 95, 127
Corkine, William (17th C), 67
Cornelius, Peter (1824-74), 158, 181, 213
Cornelys, Teresa (Cornelis de Rigerboos) (1723-?), 202
Cornyshe, William (?-*c*1523), 140
Corrette, Michel (1709-95), 139
Costa, Michael Andrew Angus (1808-94), 204
Cotton, Billy (1899-1969), 247
Cotton, Margaret (20th C), 204*
Couperin, François (1668-1733), 140, 228
Courtland, Eric—*see* Pike, E
Cousins, Anne Ross (1824-1906), 179
Coward, (Sir) Noël (1899-1973), 247
Cowell, Henry (1897-1965), 14, 39, 93, 117, 128, 146, 257
Cowen, (Sir) Frederic Hymen (1852-1935), 146, 147
Cowie, Edward (b. 1943), 139, 142
Craft, Robert Lawson (b. 1923), 213
Cramer, François (1772-1848), 57
Crawford, Marion (19th C), 61
Crawford (Seeger), Ruth (1901-53), 57, 63, 64, 143
Crémieux, Hector (19th C), 165
Creston, Paul (=Guttoveggio, J) (b. 1906), 36, 38
Crevier, Philip L (20th C), 113
Crewcuts, The, 250
Crispi, Giovanni Pietro Maria (1737-97), 80
Croce, Giovanni (*c*1558-1609), 179
Crocker, Richard L (20th C), 181
Croft, William Philip (1678-1727), 130
Crombie, Tony (20th C), 250
Cros, Charles (1842-88), 266
Crosby, Bing (Harris Lillis) (1904-77), 247, 253, 270
Crosby, Bob (b. 1913), 247
Crosby, Fanny (=Alstyne, F J van) (1850-1915), 179, 180*
Crumb, George (b. 1929), 14, 39, 143, 148
Cugat, Xaver (b. 1900), 247
Cui, César Antonivich (1835-1918), 65, 77
Cunningham, Michael G (20th C), 146
Curran, Alvin (b. 1938), 258
Curschmann, Karl Friedrich (1805-41), 204
Cusins, William George (1833-93), 57
Custer, Arthur (b. 1923), 146
Czerny, Karl (1791-1857), 34, 213, 226

Daetwyler, Jean (b. 1907), 15
Dahl, Ingolf (1912-70), 77, 127, 132
Dahmen, Wilhelm Jr (1769-99), 61
Dai-Keong Lee (20th C), 93
Dalayrac, Nicholas (1753-1809), 35
Dalby, Martin (b. 1942), 125, 144
Dale, Benjamin James (1885-1943), 32
Dale, Kathleen (*née* Richards) (b. 1895), 63
Dalhart, Vernon (20th C), 236
Dallapiccola, Luigi (1904-75), 78, 256
Damrosch, Walter Johannes (1862-1950), 150, 198, 230
Dankworth, John (b. 1927), 49, 171, 174, 245
Danzi, Franz (1763-1826), 65
Daquin, Louis Claude (1694-1772), 138
Dargomizhky, Alexander (1813-69), 143
Darin, Bobby (Walden Robert Cassotto) (1936-73), 250
Darke, Harold Edwin (b. 1888), 146
Dart, Robert Thurston (1921-71), 177
Dauvergne, Antoine (1713-97), 212
Davenant, William (1606-68), 155
David (King) (*c*1025-*c*960 BC), 21, 40, 97*
Davies, Dotie (=Temple, H) (1859-1938), 63
Davies, Henry Walford (1869-1941), 57
Davies, Hugh (b. 1943), 142
Davis, Charlie (b. 1900), 247
Davison, Archibald Thompson (b. 1883), 212
Davrainville, ? (1784-*c*1852), 262
Davy, John (1763-1824), 14, 168
Dawson, Peter (=McColl, J P) (1882-1961), 72
Day, Doris (=Cappelhoff, D) (b. 1924), 245, 247
Debain, Alexandre François (1809-77), 38
Debussy, Claude Achille (1862-1918), 30, 94, 137, 140, 141, 244
Deiro, Pietro (20th C), 38
Dejancker, Theo (20th C), 67
Delibes, Leo (1836-91), 158
Delius, Frederick Fritz Albert Theodor (1862-1934), 59, 108, 138, 164, 174
Deller, Johann Florian (1729?-73), 144
Delvincourt, Claude (1888-1954), 62
Denner, Johann Christopher (1655-1707), 27
Dent, Edward Joseph (1876-1957), 154
Destouches, André Cardinal (1672-1749), 212
Deutsch, Otto Erich (1883-1968), 229
Dhorme, Edouard (1881-?), 180
Diaghilev, Serge (1872-1929), 256
Dianda, Hilda (b. 1925), 63
Dibdin, Charles (1745-1814), 37, 77, 167
Dickinson, Emily (1830-86), 149
Diepenbrock, Alphonse (1862-1921), 138
Dieren, Bernard van (1884-1936), 110, 145
Dietrich, Albert Hermann (1829-1908), 120
Dietrich, Marlene (Losch, M M von) (b. 1902), 93

Disney, Walt(er Elias) (1901–66), 243
Distler, Hugo (1908–42), 61
Dittersdorf, Karl Ditters von (1739–99), 33, 65, 80, 92, 137, 141, 164, 165, 168, 213, 228
Dlugoszewski, Lucia (b. 1931), 63
Dodds, Warren 'Baby' (1898–1959), 238
Dodgson, Stephen (b. 1924), 35
Dolby, (Dr) Raymond (b. 1933), 269
Dolmetsch, Arnold (1858–1940), 18
Donegan, Dorothy (20th C), 242
Donegan, Lonnie (b. 1931), 250
Donizetti, Gaetano (1797–1848), 30, 60, 164, 165, 168
Dopper, Cornelius (1870–1939), 146
Doráti, Antal (b. 1906), 213, 270
Dorsey, Jimmy (1904–57), 232, 245, 247f
Dorsey, Tommy (1905–56), 232, 243, 245, 247f, 250, 253
Douglas, (Lord) Alfred (1870–?), 134
Douglas, Richard Roy (b. 1907), 78
Dounias, Minos (b. 1913), 229
Dowland, John (1563–1626), 67, 140
Downes, Edward Thomas (b. 1924), 206
Downing, Rex (20th C), 245
Draeseke, Felix (1835–1913), 35
Draghi, Antonio (1635–1700), 157, 175
Dragonetti, Domenico (1763–1846), 33
Dreiwitz, Barbara (b. 1952), 242
Drinker, Sophie Hutchinson (b. 1888), 63
Druzecký, Jiří (1745–1819), 35
Dryden, John (1631–1700), 153
Drysdale, G J Learmont (1866–1909), 138
Dubensky, Arcady (1890–1959), 26, 33
Dubin, Al (20th C), 239
Du Bois, ? (20th C), 116
Duckles, Vincent (20th C), 230
Ducré, Pierre, 78
Duffett, Thomas (17th C), 155
Dukas, Paul (1865–1935), 66, 109
Duke, Vernon (=Dukelsky, V) (1903–69), 71
Duncan, Trevor (20th C), 71
Duni, Egidio Romoaldo (1709–75), 165
Dunwalt, Gottfried (18th C), 230
Dupin, Paul (1865–1949), 60, 72
Dupont, Gabriel (1878–1914), 168
Dupré, Marcel (1886–1971), 66
Durante, Jimmy 'Schnozzle' (1893–1980), 245
Dürer, Albert (1471–1528), 41
Durey, Louis (1888–1978), 66
Durkó, Zsolt (b. 1934), 27, 96
Dussek, Jan Ladislav (1760–1812), 63, 228
Dvořák, Antonín (1841–1904), 38, 85, 86, 88, 94, 95, 107, 108, 109, 114, 115, 118, 120, 136, 139, 144, 166, 185, 198, 228, 254f
Dvorkin, Judith (b. 1930), 63
Dylan, Bob (=Zimmerman, R A) (b. 1941), 251
Dyson, (Sir) George (1883–?), 146

East, Michael (c1580–1648), 179
Eberlin, Johann Ernst (1702–62), 261, 264
Eccles, John (1668–1735), 57
Eckerberg, Axel Sixten Lennard (b. 1909), 148
Eckhardt-Gramatté, Sophie-Carmen (b. c1902), 122, 130
Edelmann, Johann Friedrich (1749–94), 62, 167
Eder, Helmut (b. 1916), 30, 32
Edinborough, Eddie (20th C), 238
Edison, Thomas Alva (1847–1931), 265, 266*
Edward VII (King of England) (1841–1910), 57
Edward VIII (King of England) (1894–1974), 57
Edwards, 'Professor' Jimmy (b. 1920), 49
Ehlert, Ludwig (1825–84), 148
Eichner, Ernst (1740–77), 65
Eimert, Herbert (1903–72), 276
Einem, Gottfried von (b. 1918), 108, 147
Einstein, Alfred (1880–1952), 59, 213, 227
Elgar, (Sir) Edward William (1857–1934), 56*, 57, 84–86 *passim*, 107, 137, 139–142 *passim*, 175, 256
Elizabeth I (Queen of England) (1533–1603), 25, 265
Elizabeth II (Queen of England) (b. 1926), 57, 206
Elizalde, Fred (1907–74), 235, 236
Ellington, Edward Kennedy 'Duke' (1899–1974), 232, 248, 268
Elman, Ziggy (1914–68), 246
Elmer, Minnie (20th C), 230
Emerson, Ralph Waldo (1803–82), 117
Enescu, Georges (1881–1955), 109
Engel, Lehman (b. 1910), 139
Englert, Giuseppe Giorgio (b. 1927), 148
Englund, Einar (b. 1916), 138
Erlanger, Frédéric d' (1868–1943), 72, 165
Ernst, Ludwig (Landgrave of Hessen) (1667–1739), 55
Erskine, Thomas Alexander (Earl of Kelly) (1732–87), 65
Esplá, Oscar (1886–1976), 56
Esposito, Michael (1855–1929), 146
Esterházy, (Prince) Nikolaus (1714–90), 42
Esterházy, (Prince) Paul Anton (1635–1713), 55
Eugenie (Princess) (1830–89), 55
Euripides (c485–407 BC), 153, 167
Evans, Lindley (20th C), 145
Evelyn, John (1620–1706), 155

Fairbanks, Douglas (Sr) (1883–1939), 93
Fairfax, Bryan (b. 1925), 182
Falchi, Stanislao (1851–1922), 169
Falck, Martin (1880–1953), 228
Falla, Manuel de (1876–1946), 21, 112, 122
Fanna, Antonio (20th C), 106, 229
Fantini, Girolamo (c1600–?), 31
Faris, Alexander (b. 1921), 137
Farkas, Ferenc (b. 1905), 33
Farmer, John (16th–17th C), 179
Farnon, Robert (b. 1917), 84, 93, 145
Farrar, Ernest Bristow (1885–1918), 61
Fasch, Johann Friedrich (1688–1758), 94, 116
Fauré, Gabriel (1845–1924), 123, 137, 140, 175
Favre, Antoine (18th–19th C), 261
Faye, Alice (b. 1911), 247
Fayrfax, Robert (1464–1521), 78
Fel, Antoine (1694–1771), 60
Feld, Jindrich (b. 1925), 38
Feldman, Morton (b. 1926), 257
Fenby, Eric William (b. 1906), 59, 76
Ferdinand II (King of Naples) (1751–1825), 42
Ferdinand III (Emperor of Austria) (1608–57), 54
Fernstrøm, John (b. 1897), 96
Ferrari, Benedetto (1597–1681), 154, 166
Ferrari, Luc (b. 1929), 39
Ferri, Antonio (19th C), 48
Ferris, Arthur K (20th C), 44
Festa, Constanzo (c1490–1545), 179
Fibich, Zdenek (1850–1900), 56, 109, 254
Fiedler, Arthur (1894–1979), 207*
Field, John (1782–1837), 112, 228
Fils, Antonín (Filtz, Anton) (c1730–60), 27, 65
Fischer, Wilhelm (1886–1959), 91
Fischietti, Domenico (1720/9?–c1810), 165
Fiske, Roger Elwyn (b. 1910), 108
Fitzgerald, Ella (b. 1918), 247
Flanagan, Ralph (b. 1919), 247
Fleischman, Veniamin (1922–41), 61
Fleites, Virginia (b. 1916), 63
Flosman, Oldřich (b. 1925), 118
Flotow, Friedrich von (1812–82), 61, 169
Flower, Eliza (1803–46), 63
Floyd, Alfred Ernest (1877–1974), 58
Fludd, Robert (Fluctibus) (1574–1637), 261
Foerster, Josef Bohuslav (1859–1951), 56, 64, 118, 149
Fomin, Evstignei Ipatovich (1761–1800), 139
Foote, Arthur William (1853–1937), 213
Ford, Thomas (1580–1648), 67
Fordell, Erik Fritiof (b. 1917), 92
Formby, George (1905–61), 137
Fortner, Wolfgang (b. 1907), 257
Forzano, Gioachino (1883–1958), 165
Fosdick, Dudley (1902–57), 237
Foss, Lukas (=Fuchs, L) (b. 1922), 71, 138
Foster, Myles Birket (1851–1922), 146
Fouldes, John Herbert (1880–1939), 257
Fox, Malcolm (20th C), 113
Fox, Roy (b. 1901), 237, 248
Françaix, Jean (b. 1912), 145
Franchetti, Alberto (1860–1942), 165
Francis, Connie (b. 1938), 250
Franck, César (1822–90), 38, 93, 94, 95, 111, 228
Franco, Buddy de (b. 1923), 247
Frank, Ernst (1847–89), 60, 169
Frank, Marcel G (20th C), 145
Frankel, Benjamin (1906–73), 26, 96
Franklin, Benjamin (1706–90), 26
Franklin, Cassandra (20th C), 147
Franklin, Walter S (20th C), 147
Franqui, Carlos (20th C), 149
Fränzl, Ignaz (1736–1803), 65
'Frauenlob'—*see* Meissen, H von
Frederick the Great—*see* Friedrich II
Frederike Luise (of Prussia) (18th C), 129
Freed, Alan (1922–65), 250
Frescobaldi, Girolamo (1583–1643), 111
Freudenfeld, August (18th C), 27
Frichot, André Louis Alexandre (1760–1825), 15
Friederici, Christian Ernst (1712–79), 38
Friedmann, Ignacy (1882–1948), 263
Friedrich II, der Grosse (King of Prussia) (1712–86), 18, 54, 55, 67, 107, 111, 129
Friedrich Wilhelm II (1744–97), 55
Friedrich Wilhelm III (1770–1840), 55
Friml, Rudolf (1880–1972), 56
Fritsch, E W (19th C), 228
Frizzell, 'Lefty' (b. 1928), 249
Fry, William Henry (1815–64), 146, 156, 167
Fuller-Maitland, John Alexander (1856–1936), 212
Fumet, Dynam-Victor (1867–1949), 128
Furtwängler, Wilhelm (1886–1954), 270
Fux, Johann Joseph (1660–1741), 228

Gabashvili, Nana (b. 1962), 63
Gabichvadze, Revaz (b. 1913), 145
Gabrieli, Andrea (1520–86), 95, 110, 173, 178
Gabrieli, Giovanni (1557–1612), 95, 108, 173, 178, 228
Gadomski, Henryk (1907–41), 61
Gaigerova, Varvana (b. 1903), 63
Galilei, Galileo (1564–1642), 154
Galilei, Vincenco (1520–91), 154
Galliard, Johann Ernst (1678–1749), 30, 167
Gallo, Alberto (18th C), 91
Gallois-Montbrun, Raymond (20th C), 146
Galuppi, Baldassare (1706–85), 70, 93, 147, 157, 165, 170
Galway, James (b. 1939), 128, 144
Ganz, Rudolf (1877–1972), 58, 143
Garber, Jan (1897–1978), 248
Garbo, Greta (Gustafson, G) (b. 1905), 93
Garcia, Fernando (b. 1930), 147
Garibaldi, ? (18th C), 163
Gasparini, Don Quirino (1721?–78), 139
Gassmann, Florian Leopold (1729–74), 138, 165
Gastoldi, Giovanni Giacomo (?–1622), 179
Gatty, Nicholas Comyn (1874–1946), 137, 158
Gautier, Pierre (c1642–97), 62
Gautreaux, Alvin (20th C), 235
Gaveaux, Pierre (1761–1825), 167
Gazzaniga, Giuseppe (1743–1818), 137
Geiringer, Karl (b. 1899), 47
Geissler, Fritz (b. 1921), 77
Geminiani, Francesco (1687–1762), 33*
Genzmer, Harald (b. 1909), 145, 263
George I (King of England) (1660–1727), 57
George II (King of England) (1683–1760), 54, 57
George III (King of England) (1738–1820), 57, 60, 202
George IV (King of England) (1762–1830), 57
George V (King of England) (1865–1936), 57, 76, 267
George VI (King of England) (1895–1952), 57
Geraldo (Bright, G) (?–1975), 248
Gérard, Yves (20th C), 228
Gerhard, Roberto (1896–1970), 38, 123, 146
German, Edward (Jones) (1862–1936), 71, 109, 145
Gersch, Stephen (b. 1948), 112
Gershwin, George (1898–1937), 36, 171*, 239f, 249
Gershwin, Ira (20th C), 171, 239f
Gerson, Johannes (15th C), 211
Gerun, Tom (20th C), 247
Gesualdo, Carlo (c1560–1613), 61, 179
Ghisi, Federico (b. 1901), 146
Ghislanzoni, Antonio (1824–93), 165
Giacosa, Giuseppe (1847–1906), 165
Giazotto, Remo (b. 1910), 86, 228f
Gibbons, Carroll (1903–54), 248
Gibbons, Orlando (1583–1625), 140, 276
Giegling, Franz (20th C), 91, 227, 229
Gilbert, William Schwenk (1836–1911), 160f, 165
Gillis, Don (b. 1912), 130, 132, 146
Gilmore, Patrick Scarsfield (1829–92), 208
Gilson, Paul (1865–1942), 67
Giordano, Umberto (1867–1948), 165, 170
Gipps, Ruth (b. 1921), 30, 63, 142, 145
Giuliani, Mauro (1781–1828), 77
Giustini, Lodovico (18th C), 37
Glantz, Georg (c1740–?), 34, 35, 93
Glanville-Hicks, Peggy (b. 1912), 63
Glazunov, Alexander Konstantinovich (1865–1936), 64, 131, 137
Glière, Reinhold (1875–1956), 96, 123
Glinka, Mikhail Ivanovich (1804–57), 164
Glover, William Howard (1819–75), 137
Gluck, Christoph Willibald von (1714–87), 16, 25, 94, 144, 157, 158, 165f, 176, 182, 228
Gnecchi, Vittorio (1876–1954), 257
Godard, Benjamin Louis Paul (1849–95), 63
Godowsky, Leopold (1870–1938), 78
Goldkette, Jean (1899–1961), 244
Goldman, Edward M (20th C), 137
Goldmark, Karl (1830–1915), 130, 140
Goldmark, Peter (1906–77), 269
Goldoni, Carlo (1707–93), 165
Goleminov, Marin (b. 1908), 150
Golestan, Stan (1875–1956), 146
Goodman, Benny (b. 1909), 232, 237, 243, 246, 247, 248
Goodwin, Ronald Alfred (b. 1925), 137
Goossens, Eugene (1893–1962), 265
Gordigiani, Luigi (1806–60), 71
Gossec, François-Joseph (1734–1829), 36, 58, 128, 268
Gottlieb, Mark (20th C), 52
Gottron, Adam (20th C), 228
Gottschalk, Louis Moreau (1829–69), 92, 125, 147
Goudimel, Claude (c1510–72), 62
Gounod, Charles François (1818–93), 58, 64, 73, 93, 144, 156, 164, 165, 174, 175, 187, 204, 273
Goyers, John (19th C), 47
Grable, Betty (Haag, R) (1916–73), 247
Grabowska, (Countess) Klementyna (1771–1831), 63
Grabu, Louis (c1638–94?), 57, 155
Graener, Paul (1872–1944), 145, 168f
Granados, Enrico (1867–1916), 61, 139
Grandis, Renato de (b. 1927), 77
Grappelli, Stephane (20th C), 245*
Grassi, Francesco (17th–18th C), 70
Graun, Johann Gottlieb (1703–71), 66, 92, 228
Graun, Karl Heinrich (1701–59), 44, 66, 166, 228
Graupner, Johann Christoph (1683–1760), 92
Gravina, Gian Vincento (17th–18th C), 163
Gray, Glen (1906–63), 243
Gray, Jerry (20th C), 247
Green, Charlie (c1900–36), 241
Greene, Maurice (1695–1755), 57
Greenham, Lily (20th C), 274
Gregory the Great (Pope) (c540–604), 172
Grenié, G J (1756–1837), 38
Gresnick, Antoine Fréderick (1752/5–99), 167
Gretchaninov, Alexander Tikhonovich (1864–1956), 56
Grétry, André Ernest Modeste (1742–1813), 34, 94, 138
Grieg, Edvard Hagerup (1843–1907), 87, 95, 138, 140, 255, 262
Gropius, Manon (1917–35), 133
Grossi, Andrea (17th–18th C), 66
Grossi, Lodovico Viadana (1564–1645), 127
Grove, (Sir) George (1820–1900), 211
Groven, Eivind (b. 1901), 42
Grundy, Sidney (19th C), 162

Guarneri, Andrea (?-1698), 49
Guarneri, Mozart Camargo (b. 1907), 145
Guarneri del Gesú, Giuseppe (1698-1744), 32, 144
Guerra-Peixe, Cesar (b. 1914), 145
Guevara, Ernesta Che (1928-67), 149
Guglielmi, Pietro (1727-1804), 157
Gui, Vittorio (1885-1975), 56
Guida (of Naples) (19th C), 42
Guillaume d'Amiens (13th C), 173
Guillemin, Duchesne (20th C), 209
Guirant, d'Espanha de Toloza (12th C), 173
Gunn, John (b. 1932), 237
Gurney, Ivor Bertie (1890-1937), 60
Gusikoff, ? (20th C), 146
Guyler, Deryck (b. 1908), 238
Gyrowetz, A—*see* Jirovec

Haas, Pavel (1899-1944), 61
Hába, Alois (1893-1972), 257
Hába, Karel (b. 1898), 257
Habeneck, François Antoine (1781-1849), 198
Hackett, Bobby (1916-76), 232
Haddy, Arthur (b. 1906), 268
Hadley, Henry Kimball (1871-1937), 137, 147, 148
Haffner family, 122
Haffner, Johann Christian Friedrich (1759-1833), 166
Haggard, Merle (b. 1937), 249
Haibl, Jakob (1762/5-1826), 93
Hainl, François (1807-73), 77
Hale, Adam de la—*see* Adam de la Hale
Halévy, Jacques François Fromental Élie (1799-1862), 31, 72, 137
Halévy, Ludovic (1834-1908), 165, 166
Haley, Bill (William John Clifton) (b. 1925), 250
Halffter, Eseriche Ernesto (b. 1905), 112
Hall, Henry (b. 1898), 245, 248
Hall Jahn (b. 1943), 146
Hallé, (Sir) Charles (1819-95), 198
Hallnäs, Johan Hilding (b. 1903), 125
Halm, Hans (20th C), 228
Halmagyi, J (20th C), 263
Hamilton, Catherine (*née* Barlow) (*c*1738-82), 63
Hamilton, Iain Ellis (b. 1922), 158, 164
Hammer, Franz Xaver (*c*1750-1813), 72
Hammerstein, Oscar II (1895-1960), 240f
Hammond, Laurens (1895-1973), 264
Hampton, Lionel (b. 1909), 243
Handel, George Frideric (1685-1759), 10, 18, 22, 26f, 30, 34, 36, 37, 43, 52, 59*, 69, 84-86 *passim*, 122, 123, 127, 138, 139, 155, 166, 167, 175f, 177, 185, 201, 203, 204, 208, 228, 264
Handley, Tommy (1895-1949), 272
Handy, William Christopher (1873-1958), 270
Hanshaw, Annette (b. 1910), 243, 246
Hanson, Raymond (1913-76), 31
Hanuš, Jan (b. 1915), 95, 96
Hardelot, Guy d' (1858-1936), 72
Hardin, Lil (1900-71), 242
Haring, Bob (20th C), 243
Harris, Clement Hugh Gilbert (1871-97), 61
Harris, Roy Ellsworth (1898-1979), 38, 78, 79*, 147
Harris, William (1883-1973), 56
Harrison, Jimmy (1900-31), 232
Harrison, Lou (b. 1917), 39, 257
Hart, Charles (20th C), 267
Hart, Lorenz (1895-1943), 240
Hartley, Walter Sinclair (b. 1927), 32
Hartwig, ? (18th C), 94
Harty, Herbert Hamilton (1879-1941), 139, 146
Harvey, Lillian (20th C), 93
Hasse, Johann Adolf (1699-1783), 31, 70, 157, 228
Hassler, Hans Leo (1564-1612), 264
Hauer, Josef Matthias (1883-1959), 66, 255
Havelka, Svatopluk (b. 1925), 149
Haven, Gloria de (b. 1925), 247
Hawkins, (Sir) John (1719-89), 69
Hawkins, ? (18th-19th C), 38
Hawthorne, Nathaniel (1804-64), 117
Haydn, Franz Joseph (1732-1809), 21, 30, 31, 38, 42, 47, 52, 55, 65, 68*, 70, 71, 83-87 *passim*, 92, 93, 95, 96, 105, 108, 109, 111, 112, 113, 120, 122, 135ff, 137, 143, 147, 158, 163, 166, 169, 174, 175, 177, 185f, 201, 202, 216, 224, 225, 226, 228, 234, 264, 270
Haydn, Johann Michael (1737-1806), 30, 34, 42, 68, 109, 134, 165, 175, 228
Hayes, Bert (20th C), 273
Hayes, William (1705-77), 176
Heath, Edward (b. 1916), 149
Hebenstreit, Pantaleon (1669-1750), 20, 44
Heckel, Wilhelm (1856-1909), 35
Heger, Robert (1886-1978), 56
Heidenstam, Gerard Johan Baltzar af (1746-1803), 156
Heiniö, Mikko (b. 1948), 117
Heinrich, Anthony Philipp (1781-1861), 185
Helene, Paulowna (Princess) (1824-73), 55
Helmbrecht, Christian Friedrich Franz (18th-19th C), 59
Heming, Michael Savage (1920-42), 150
Henderson, Fletcher (1898-1952), 235, 245
Henderson, Ray (1896-1969), 238
Henry IV (King of England) (1367-1413), 54
Henry V (King of England) (1387-1422), 54
Henry VIII (King of England) (1491-1547), 18, 54, 265
Henry, Pierre (b. 1927), 275
Henze, Hans Werner (b. 1926), 149
Herder, Johann Gottfried von (1744-1803), 176
Herlihy, Joe (20th C), 245
Herman, Woody (b. 1913), 118, 248
Hernandez, Gisela (b. 1910), 63
Hérold, Louis Joseph Ferdinand (1791-1833), 170
Herrmann, Bernard (1911-75), 142
Herrmann, Hugo (1896-1967), 148, 149
Herschel, Jacob (*c*1734-92), 60
Herschel, Wilhelm Friedrich (1738-1822), 60, 77
Hervé (Ronger, F) (1825-92), 72, 144, 150, 164
Hespos, Hans Joachim (b. 1938), 96
Heward, Leslie Hays (1897-1943), 92
Hewitt, James (1770-1827), 147, 150, 156
Heydrich, (General) Reinhard (1904-42), 152*
Heyward, Edwin Dubose (1885-1940), 171
Hickford, Thomas (17th C), 201
Hickman, Art (1886-1930), 246, 248
Hicks, Edna (?-1925), 241
Hieronymus (16th C), 21
Higden, Ranulf (13th C), 211
Higginson, Henry L (19th C), 198
Higgs, Tim (20th C), 168
Hill, Alfred (1870-1960), 56
Hill, Mildred (19th-20th C), 181*
Hill, Patty S (?-1946), 181
Hill, Susannah (18th C), 60
Hill, Ureli Corelli (1802-95), 198
Hiller, Johann Adam (1728-1804), 144, 155f, 176, 198
Hiller, ? (20th C), 258, 265
Hilton, John (1599-1657), 181
Hindemith, Paul (1895-1963), 18, 44, 61, 76, 108, 110, 120, 164, 170, 171, 213, 263, 264, 265
Hines, Earl (b. 1905), 243
Hirsch, Hans Ludwig (b. 1937), 77
Hitler, Adolf (1889-1945), 234
Hoboken, Anthony van (b. 1887), 228
Hodgson, Peter (b. 1928), 30
Hoesslin, Franz von (1885-1946), 62
Hoffmann, Adolf (20th C), 76, 229
Hoffman, Bruno (b. 1913), 25*
Hoffmann, Ernst Theodor Amadeus (1776-1822), 77
Hoffmeister, Franz Anton (1754-1812), 33, 122
Hoffnung, Gerard (1925-59), 15, 32, 49, 204*, 234
Hofmann, Josef Casimir (1876-1957), 71, 263
Hofstetter, Johann Urban Alois (1742-1818), 228
Hofstetter, Romanus (?-*c*1785), 228
Hofstetter, unspec., 15
Hoiby, Lee (b. 1926), 148
Holbein, Hans (1497?-1543), 36
Holbrooke, Josef Charles (1878-1958), 30, 64
Holiday, Billie (1918-59), 247
Hollander, Benoit (1853-1942), 146
Hollins, Alfred (1865-1942), 59
Holloway, Robin (b. 1943), 64
Holloway, Stanley (b. 1890), 247
Holmboe, Vagn (b. 1909), 36, 95, 116
Holmes, Alfred (1837-76), 145
Holoubek, Ladislav (b. 1913), 122
Holst, Gustav Theodore (1874-1934), 39, 52, 63, 108, 137, 139, 140, 145, 158, 164, 182f
Holst, Imogen Clare (b. 1907), 63*
Holzbauer, Ignaz Jacob (1711-83), 65, 74
Honegger, Arthur (1892-1955), 66, 118, 125, 142, 175, 213, 274
Hood, Basil (1864-1917), 162
Hood, Robin (13th C?), 153f
Hook, James (1746-1827), 182
Hook, Theodore Edward (1788-1841), 213
Hopekirk, Helen (1856-1945), 63
Hopkins, Antony (b. 1921), 72
Hopkinson, Cecil (b. 1910), 228
Hopkinson, Francis (1737-91), 181
Horn, unspec., 15
Hörner, Hans (b. 1911), 229
Horowitz, Joseph (b. 1926), 35
Hovhaness-Chakmajian, Alan (b. 1911), 92, 93, 96, 115-134 *passim*
Hovland, Egil (b. 1924), 148
Howard, Paul (20th C), 243
Howell, Peter (20th C), 274
Howells, Herbert (b. 1892), 141, 142, 265
Hrac(z)ek, Antonius Ireneus Ignać (1724-77), 116
Hsien Hsing-Hai (20th C), 149
Hubay, Jenö (1858-1937), 169
Huber, Hans (1852-1921), 134, 148
Hucbald (*c*849-930), 178
Hudson, George (17th C), 155
Huë, Georges Adolphe (1858-1948), 56
Hughes, David (1929-72), 246
Hugo, Victor Marie (1802-85), 94
Humes, Tobias (?-1645), 67
Hummel, Johann Nepomuk (1778-1837), 77, 145
Humperdinck, Engelbert (1854-1921), 58
Humperdinck, Engelbert (b. 1936), 253
Hurník, Ilja (b. 1922), 140
Huss, Henry Holden (1862-1953), 56
Huss, John (Jan) (1369-1415), 56
Hüttenbrenner, Anselm (1794-1868), 167
Hutton, Betty (b. 1921), 247
Hutton, Ina Ray (b. 1916), 242
Huygens, (Sir) Constantijn (1596-1687), 56
Hylton, Jack (1892-1965), 234, 246, 247, 248, 268
Hyman, John (b. 1899), 235

Iaccini—*see* Jacc(h)ini
Ibert, Jacques (1890-1962), 142, 146, 147, 258
Ichiyanagi, Toshi (b. 1933), 40, 257
Illica, Luigi (1857-1919), 165
Imbrie, Andrew (b. 1921), 142
Immyns, John (?-1764), 179
Indy, Vincent d' (1851-1931), 164
Ingelius, Axel Gabriel (1822-68), 92
Ireland, Francis (1721-80), 72, 77
Ireland, John (1879-1962), 142
Irvid, Richard (1829-1903), 72
Isaac, Heinrich (*c*1450-1517), 179
Isacsson, Fredrik Donatus (1883-1962), 147
Isouard, Nicoló (1775-1818), 168
Ivanov, Mikhail Mikhailovich (1849-1927), 148
Ives, Charles (1874-1954), 39, 77, 110, 117, 133, 182, 185, 213, 256, 257
Izbicki-Maklakiewicz, Franciszek (1915-39), 61

Jacc(h)ini, Giuseppe Maria (*c*1670-*c*1727), 32, 66, 107
Jackson, William (of Exeter) (1730-1804), 213
Jacob, Gordon (b. 1895), 77
Jacobina, Agnes Marie (1847-1925), 63
Jähns, Friedrich Wilhelm (1809-88), 229
James I (King of England) (1566-1625), 55, 57
James II (King of England) (1633-1701), 57
James, Harry (b. 1916), 247, 248*
James, Lewis (?-1956), 267
Janáček, Leoš (1854-1928), 108, 109, 123, 124, 142, 143, 147, 164, 174
Janigro, Antonio (20th C), 91
Jannings, Emil (20th C), 93
Janotha, Marie Cecilia Natalia (1856-1932), 64
Janssen, Werner (b. 1899), 124, 146
Jaquet-Droz, Henri Louis (1752-91), 261
Jaquet-Droz, Pierre (1721-90), 261
Jarmila (8th C), 200
Jaubert, Maurice (1900-40), 61
Jeunehomme, Mlle ? (18th C), 124
Jiránek, Alois (1858-1950), 56
Jírovec, Vojtech (=Gyrowetz, A) (1763-1850), 213
Johannson, Cari (b. 1921), 230
Johanson, Sven-Eric (20th C), 42
John IV (King of Portugal) (1604-56), 55, 186
Johnsen, Hallvard (b. 1916), 127
Johnson, Bill (1872-1969), 243
Johnson, Bob (20th C), 246
Johnson, Bruce (20th C), 238*
Johnson, Charlie (20th C), 245
Johnson, J C (20th C), 234
Johnson, Ken (?-1941), 241
Johnson, Lonnie (1889-1970), 234
Johnson, Robert (*c*1583-1633), 140
Johnson, Samuel (1709-84), 155
Jolivet, André (1905-74), 38, 66
Jolson, Al (1886-1950), 238
Jommelli, Niccolo (1714-74), 170, 225
Joncières, Victorin de (=Rossignol, F L; 'Jennius') (1839-1903), 72
Jones, Charles W (b. 1910), 127
Jones, Daniel (b. 1912), 123
Jones, Isham (*c*1894)-1952), 241, 248
Jones, Robert (*c*15?-*c*1617), 67, 179
Joplin, Scott (1868-1917), 171
Joseph Michael Xaver Francis John Poniatowski (Prince) (1816-73), 55
Joseph I (Emperor of Austria) (1678-1711), 55
Joseph II (Emperor of Hungary) (1741-90), 136
Josephine Clementine (Princess) (1764-1820), 55
Josephs, Wilfred (b. 1927), 128, 140, 147
Joyce, Archibald (20th C), 246
Jullien, Louis Antoine . . . (1812-60), 60, 74f
Jurgenson, Boris (1864-1921), 229
Jurovský, Šimon (1912-63), 150

Kabalevsky, Dmitri (b. 1904), 137, 150
Kabeláč, Miroslav (b. 1908), 118
Kade, Otto (1819-1900), 230
Kaempfer, Joseph (18th C), 47
Kagel, Mauricio (b. 1932), 39, 258
Kahn, Gus (20th C), 238
Kahn, Roger Wolfe (1908-57), 245, 248
Kaim, Franz (19th C), 198
Kalabis, Viktor (b. 1923), 122
Kalachevsky, Mikhail (1851-1910), 146
Kálik, Václav (1891-1951), 150
Kamieński, Lucjan (1885-?), 156
Kaminsky, Valter (20th C), 21
Kapr, Jan (b. 1914), 110
Kaprálová, Vítězslava (1915-40), 150
Karaev, Kara Abdul'faz Ogly (b. 1918), 150
Karas, Anton (20th C), 20
Kardos, István (20th C), 33
Karel, Rudolf (1880-1945), 130
Karg-Elert, Siegfried (1877-1933), 38
Karl Theodor (Elector of Mannheim) (1724-99), 65, 202
Kasemets, Udo (b. 1919), 258
Kastner, Emerich (1820-94), 229
Kastner, Jean Georges (1810-67), 30
Kaufman, Irving (b. 1890), 243
Kaul, Oskar (1885-1957), 229
Kazuro, Stanisław (1882-?), 148
Keiser, Reinhard (1674-1739), 137, 157, 166, 176
Keler-Béla, Adalbert von (1820-82), 72
Kelerdorfer, V (20th C), 187
Keller, Hans Heinrich (b. 1919), 272
Kelley, Edgar Stillman (1857-1944), 121, 146
Kelly, Michael (1762-1826), 213
Kemp, Hal (1905-40), 234, 248
Kennedy, John Fitzgerald (1917-63), 270
Kenton, Egon (20th C), 228

Kenton, Stanley Sydney Newcomb (1912-79), 247, 248
Kerll, Johann Caspar (1627-93), 139, 141
Khachaturian, Aram (1903-78), 64, 95, 115
Kienzl, Wilhelm (1857-1941), 44, 164
Killmayer, Wilhelm (b. 1927), 144
Kilmer, Anne D (20th C), 180f
King, Stan (1900-49), 237
Kinscella, Hazel Gertrude (b. 1893), 64
Kinsky, Georg (1882-1951), 228
Kirby, Percival Robson (1887-?), 138, 145, 146
Kirk, Andy (b. 1898), 243
Kirkpatrick, Ralph (b. 1911), 112, 229
Kirnberger, Johann Philipp (1721-83), 55, 66, 67, 264
Klafsky, Anton Maria (1877-1947), 228
Klatzon, Peter James Leonard (20th C), 139
Klebanov, Dmitri (b. 1907), 146
Kleen, Johann Christoph (18th C), 156
Klemperer, Otto (1885-1973), 227
Klenau, Paul August von (1883-1946), 145
Klinger, Friedrich Maximillian von (1752-1831), 82
Klopstock, Gottlieb Friedrich (1724-1803), 176
Knape, Walter (20th C), 228
Knipper, Lev (1898-1974), 150
Köchel, Ludwig Alois Ferdinand Ritter von (1800-77), 227f, 230*
Koczwara, František (c1750-91), 60, 150
Kodály, Zoltan (1882-1967), 20, 38, 139, 174, 177, 265
Koechlin, Charles (1867-1950), 93, 263
Koenig, Gottfried Michael (20th C), 276
Kohn, Karl (b. 1926), 126
Kolb, K (18th C), 110
Kolneder, Walter (b. 1910), 106
Komma, Karl Michael (b. 1903), 229
Kondrashin, Kiril Petrovich (b. 1914), 269
Kontski, Antoine de (1817-99), 142
Konvalinka, Miloš (b. 1919), 148
Koole, Arend Johannes Christian (b. 1908), 228
Korchmarev, Klementy Arkadievich (1899-1958), 133, 146
Kossovits, József (19th C), 169
Koven, Henry Louis Reginald de (1859-1920), 154
Koželuh, Leopold Antonín Tomas (1752-1818), 65, 123, 228
Kramer, Christian (c1788-1834), 57
Krause, Christian Gottfried (1719-70), 182
Krause, Johann Georg (17th-18th C), 42
Krebs, Carl (1862-1921), 228
Krein, Julian Grigorevich (b. 1913), 148
Kreisler, Fritz (1875-1962), 80
Krejčí, Josef (1821-81), 212
Krejčí, Miroslav (1891-1964), 133
Křenek, Ernst (b. 1900), 164, 166, 170, 276
Kreuder, Peter (20th C), 145
Kreutschach, (Archbishop) L von (17th C), 261
Kreutzer, Rodolphe (1766-1831), 124
Křička, Jaroslav (1882-1969), 115
Kross, Siegfried (b. 1930), 229
Krupa, Gene (1909-73), 248
Kryzhanovsky, Ivan Ivanovich (1867-1924), 77
Kubelik, Jan (1880-1940), 267
Kučera, Václav (b. 1929), 118
Kuhnau, Johann (1660-1722), 112, 148
Kurpiński, Karol (1785-1857), 186
Kurtz, Eugene (20th C), 148
Kvapil, Jaroslav (1892-1958), 142, 150

Labor, Josef (1842-1924), 59
Łabuński, Feliks Roderyk (b. 1892), 138
Lachenmann, Helmut Friedrich (b. 1935), 120
Laderman, Ezra (b. 1924), 145
Laine, Cleo (20th C), 172
Lajtha, László (1892-1963), 148
Laks, Szymon (b. 1901), 62
Lally, Arthur (?-1940), 234
Lalo, Victor Antoine Edouard (1823-92), 164
Lambert, Constant (1905-51), 148
Lambert, George Jackson (1794-1880), 60
Lamoureux, Charles (1834-99), 198
Landi, Stefano (c1590-c1655), 166
Landowski, Marcel (b. 1915), 128
Lane, Eastwood (1879-1951), 244
Lane, Elizabeth (b. 1964), 64
Lang, Eddie (1902-33), 234, 244
Lang, Margaret Ruthven (1867-1972), 58, 64
Langdale, Agnes Mary (19th-20th C), 230
Langer, N (20th C), 263
Langgaard, Rued (1893-1952), 148
Lanier, Nicholas (1588-1666), 55, 57
Lanin, Sam (b. 1888), 246, 248
Laparra, Raoul (1876-1943), 61
Lara, Adelina de (1872-?), 72
Lara, Isidore de (=Cohen, I) (1858-1935), 72
LaRocca, 'Nick' (1889-1961), 231, 232
Larsson, Lars-Erik (b. 1908), 108
LaRue, Jan (20th C), 227
Lassen, Eduard (1830-1904), 169
Lassus, Roland de (1532-94), 70, 176, 179
Lautenschläger, Karl (19th C), 171
Lavotta, Janós de Izsépfalva et Kevelháza (1764-1820), 169
Lavranga, Denis (1864-1941), 140
Lawes, Henry (1596-1662), 155
Lawes, William (1602-45), 61
Lawrence, Sid (b. 1925), 247
Layard, Austen Henry (1817-94), 50
Lazzari, Sylvio (1857-1944), 170
Lebrun, Louis Sébastien (1764-1829), 139
Leclair, Jean-Marie (1697-1764), 60
Led Zeppelin, 252, 253
Lee, Peggy (Egstrom, N D) (b. 1920), 247
Leecan, Bobby (c1900-?), 235, 238
Lefanu, Nicola (b. 1947), 64
Lefèbre, L J (19th C), 271
Lefèbre-Wély, Louis James Alfred (1817-69), 38
Legge, Walter (1904-79), 199
Le Grand, Robert (19th C), 147
Lehár, Franz (1870-1948), 169, 268
Lehmann, Elizabeth (Liza) Mary Frederika (1862-1918), 63, 64
Leidzen, Erik (20th C), 146
Leifs, Jón (1899-1968), 156
Leigh, Walter (1905-42), 61, 138
Leiviskä, Helvi Lemmikki (b. 1902), 64
Leland, J, 179
Lennon, John Winston (Ono) (1940-80), 270
Leo, Leonardo (1694-1744), 95
Leoncavallo, Ruggiero (1858-1919), 137, 164, 270
Leopold I (Emperor of Austria) (1640-1705), 55
Leopold II (Emperor of Austria) (1747-92), 117
Leschetizky, Theodor (1830-1915), 149
Lesueur, Jean-François (1760-1837), 35, 39
Lesur, Daniel (b. 1908), 66
Levidi, Dimitri (1886-1951), 38
Levine, Irwin (20th C), 270
Lévy, Ernst (b. 1895), 145
Lewin, David (20th C), 276
Lewin, Frank (20th C), 34
Lewis, Noah (20th C), 235
Lewis, Ted (1892-1971), 232, 247, 248
Ley, Salvador (b. 1907), 143
Liadov, Anatol (1855-1914), 265
Liberace (b. 1919), 253
Lichtenthal, Peter (1780-1853), 77
Ligeti, György (b. 1923), 225, 261
Lincoln, Abe (b. 1907), 232
Lindsay, Charles MacHenry (20th C), 47
Lindsay, Joe (1894-1950), 246
Linjauna, Jaakko Armas (Lindeman) (b. 1909), 72
Linko, Ernst Frederik (Lindroth) (b. 1889), 72
Linley, Francis (1771-1800), 59
Linley, Thomas Jr (1756-78), 62, 167
Linnala, Eino Mauno A (Bergman) (b. 1896), 72
Lipiński, Karol Jósef (1790-1861), 150
Lipkin, Malcolm (b. 1932), 146
Lisa, V V de (20th C), 137
Lissenko, Nikolay Vitalevich (1842-1912), 142, 149
Liszt, Ferencz (1811-86), 48, 57, 71, 85-87 *passim*, 93, 103*, 109, 111, 138, 139, 140, 144, 174
Liukko, Eino (b. 1906), 148
Lloyd, Albert Lancaster (1908-78), 10
Lloyd Webber, Andrew (b. 1948), 240*, 241, 253
Locatelli, Pietro Antonio (1695-1764), 95, 115, 120, 124, 127, 228
Lochmann, Paul (19th C), 262
Locke, Matthew (c1630-77), 155
Loder, Kate Fanny (1825-1904), 64
Loeillet family, 68, 228
Loeillet, Jean-Baptiste (1680-1730), 68, 201, 228
Loewe, Johann Carl Gottfried (1796-1869), 182
Lombardo, Guy (1902-77), 237, 246, 248
Longchamps brothers (19th C), 261
Longo, Alessandro (1864-1945), 229
Lopatnikov, Nikolay Lvovich (b. 1903), 34
Lopez, Vincent (1898-1975), 247, 248
LoPresti, Ronald (b. 1933), 96
Lortzing, Gustav Albert (1801-51), 164
Loss, Joe (b. 1909), 246, 248
Lough, Ernest (b. 1913), 268
Louis Ferdinand (Prince of Hohenzollern (1772-1806), 55
Louis XIV (King of France) (1638-1715), 62
Loulié, Étienne (c1640-c1701), 261
Lualdi, Adriano (1887-?), 144
Lubomirski (Prince) (20th C), 199
Lucas, Clarence (1866-1947), 138
Luce, Warren (20th C), 238
Lully, Jean-Baptiste (1632-87), 26f, 41, 62, 68, 94, 166, 167
Lulu (Laurie, M) (b. 1948), 253
Lumbye, Hans (1810-74), 36
Lumsdaine, David (20th C), 142
Lunssens, Martin (1871-1944), 146
Luther, Frank (20th C), 236
Luther, Martin (1483-1546), 131
Lutosławsky, Witold (b. 1913), 95
Lutyens, Elisabeth (b. 1906), 64, 168
Lvov, Alexei Feodorovich (1798-1870), 60
Lympany, Moura (b. 1916), 207*
Lynn, Vera (b. 1919), 247
Lyser, Johann Peter (19th C), 151
Lyttleton, Humphrey (b. 1921), 245*

McCabe, John (b. 1939), 107, 118
McCartney, James Paul (b. 1942), 250f, 251*, 252, 270
McCartney, Linda (b. 1942), 251*, 252
MacDonald, Earl (1890-1949), 236
McDonald, Harl (1899-1955), 116, 130, 147
Macdonough, Harry (20th C), 267
MacDowell, Edward (=Thorn, E) (1861-1908), 58, 73, 124, 126, 268
McDowell, John Herbert (b. 1926), 142, 170
McEwen, (Sir) John Blackwood (1868-1948), 124, 126, 133, 145, 147
MacFarren, George Vance (1813-87), 59
McGhee, Walter 'Brownie' (b. 1914), 235
McIlvaine, Don (20th C), 232
MacKenzie, Alexander Campbell (1847-1935), 80, 140, 213
Mackenzie, (Sir) Compton (1882-1972), 267
McKenzie, William 'Red' (1899-1948), 237
McKinley, Ray (b. 1910), 247
McLoughlin, Forde (20th C), 147
Macmahon, Desmond (b. 1898), 31
Macmillan, (Sir) Ernest Campbell (b. 1893), 62
MacMurray, Fred (b. 1908), 247
McMurray, Loring (c1895-c1925), 241
McPhee, Colin (1901-64), 128
McWhirter, Norris (b. 1925), 251*
Maccari, ? (18th C), 165
Maconchy, Elizabeth (b. 1907), 64, 138
Maelzel, Johann Nepomuk (1772-1838), 261, 265
Maerzendorfer, Ernst (20th C), 270
Magnard, Lucien Denis Gabriel Albéric (1865-1914), 61, 164
Mahler, Gustav (1860-1911), 35, 38, 84, 90, 109, 132, 133, 182f, 229, 265
Mainzer, Joseph (1801-51), 212
Major, Jakab Gyula (1858-1925), 146
Makarova, Nina Vladimirovna (b. 1908), 64
Makris, Niklos (19th C), 156
Malibran, Maria Felicita (1808-36), 169
Malipiero, Gian Francesco (1882-1973), 56, 118, 137, 147, 148, 164, 166
Maliszewski, Witold (1873-1939), 133
Malvezzi, Cristofano (1547-97), 66
Manelli, Francisco (1595-1667), 154
Manfredini, Francesco Maria (1673-1748?), 95
Mangeshker, Lata (b. 1928), 270
Mann, Harold (20th C), 272
Manns, August (1825-1907), 204, 206
Marais, Marin (1656-1728), 34, 148
Marcello, Alessandro (c1684-c1750), 73, 84, 116
Marcello, Benedetto (1686-1739), 137
Marcheselli, Domenico (=Accademico Formato) (18th C), 27
Marchesio, Rebecca (19th C), 48
Marchi, Antonio (18th C), 165
Marenzio, Luca (1553-99), 71, 179
Maria Antonia Walpurgis (Electress of Saxony) (=E T P A) (1724-80), 125
Maria Theresa Ahlefeldt (1755-1823), 55
Marić, Ljubica (b. 1909), 64, 116
Marie Antoinette (Queen of France) (1755-93), 55
Marín, José (1619-99), 80
Marin, Marie-Martin Marcel de (Vicomte) (1769-1861+), 57
Marinetti, Filippo Tommaso (1876-1944), 256
Marini, Biagio (1597-1665), 111
Marino, Gianbattista (1569-1625), 66
Marpurg, Friedrich Wilhelm (1718-95), 66
Marschner, Heinrich August (1795-1861), 112
Marsh, John (=Sharm) (1752-1828), 73
Martenot, Maurice (1898-1980), 38, 263
Martigni, Gianbattista (18th C), 68
Martin, Carroll (?-c1940), 241
Martin, François (1727-57), 68
Martin, Frank (1890-1974), 21, 95, 96, 108, 213
Martin, Philipp (18th C), 68
Martin, Tony (b. 1912), 247
Martín y Soler, Vincente (1754-1806), 68, 165
Martinelli, Antonio (18th C), 68
Martines (Martinez), Marianne von (1744/5-1812), 68
Martinetti (=Martinelli?), 68
Martinez de la Roca, Joaquin (17th-18th C), 68
Martini, Giovanni Battista ('Padre') (1706-84), 68, 92
Martini, Martino, various, 68 (*see* also Sammartini)
Martini, Ubaldo (16th C), 48
Martini il Tedesco—*see* Schwarzendorf, J P A
Martino, Al (b. 1927), 253
Martinon, Jean (1910-76), 146
Martinů, Bohuslav Jan (1890-1959), 77, 95, 108, 109, 123, 152, 229
Martirano, Salvatore (b. 1927), 78
Martner, Knud (20th C), 229
Marttinen, Tauno (b. 1912), 117, 139
Marvin, Frederick (20th C), 229
Marx, Joseph (1882-1964), 148
Mary (Queen of England) (1867-1953), 267
Mascagni, Pietro (1863-1945), 158, 165
Maschitti, Michele (c1664-1760), 58
Masefield, John (1878-1967), 96
Mason, Daniel Gregory (1873-1953), 213
Mason, William (1829-1908), 213
Masse, Felix Marie Victor (1822-84), 165
Massenet, Jules Emile Frédéric (1842-1912), 158, 170, 172
Matěj, Josef (b. 1922), 118
Mathews, Max V (b. 1926), 276
Mátray, Gábor (1797-1875), 140
Mattheson, Johann (1681-1764), 31, 83-87 *passim*, 211f, 213
Matthus, Siegfried (20th C), 145
Maxfield, Richard Vance (1927-69), 61
Maxwell Davies, Peter (b. 1934), 169
May, Frederick (b. 1911), 60
Maybrick, Michael (1844-1913), 71
Mayer, Charles (1799-1862), 185
Mayland, Philippe (19th C), 261
Mayr, Johann Simon (1763-1845), 166, 225
Mayuzumi, Toshiro (b. 1929), 36
Mazarin, Jules (1602-61), 213
Mazzochi, Domenico (1592-1665), 225

Mc ...—*see* Mac, above
Méhul, Etienne Nicolas (1763–1817), 94, 171
Meilhac, Henri (1831–97), 165
Meissen, Heinrich von ('Frauenlob') (?–1318), 173
Melartin, Erkki Erik Gustaf (1875–1937), 148
Melba, (Dame) Nellie (*née* Porter Mitchell, N) (1859–1931), 168*, 267, 272
Melrose, Frank (1908–41), 241
Mendelssohn-Bartholdy, Fanny Cacilie (1805–47), 64
Mendelssohn-Bartholdy, Jakob Ludwig Felix (1809–47), 15, 43, 64, 74, 76, 84–87 *passim*, 93, 94, 95, 109, 111, 113, 114–134 *passim*, 136, 137, 143, 175, 198, 204, 208, 267
Mennicke, Carl H (1867–1933), 228
Menotti, Gian Carlo (b. 1911), 79, 164, 165, 273
Menuhin, Yehudi (b. 1916), 56*
Mercadante, Giuseppe Saverio Raffaele (1795–1870), 165, 167
Mercer, Johnny (1909–77), 247
Mercure, Pierre (1927–66), 62
Merikanto, Frans Oskar (1868–1924), 156
Messager, André Charles Prosper (1853–1929), 63, 139
Messiaen, Oliver (b. 1908), 38, 62, 66, 111, 138, 256
Metastasio (=Trepassi, P) (1698–1782), 163
Meyer, Philippe-Jacques (1737–1819), 93
Meyerbeer, Giacomo (1791–1864), 35, 44, 72, 158, 166, 170
Meyer-Eppler (20th C), 276
Meyers, Charlotte (20th C), 268
Miaskovsky, Nikolai Yakovlevich (1881–1950), 92
Michelitsch, Helga (Scholz-) (b. 1945), 229
Midgley, Charles (20th C), 150
Mielck, Ernest Leopold Christian (1877–99), 145
Migot, Georges (b. 1891), 146
Mihalovici, Marcel (b. 1898), 121
Miley, James 'Bubber' (1903–32), 232
Milhaud, Darius (1892–1974), 46, 66, 93, 96, 110, 115, 117, 123, 128, 141, 145, 148, 166, 171, 213, 274
Miller, Alton 'Glenn' (1904–44), 232, 241, 246, 248, 269
Mills, Alvin (20th C), 115
Milton, John (*c*1563–1647), 179
Milton, John (1608–74), 179
Minevitch, Borrah (20th C), 235
Mitchell, Donald Charles Peter (b. 1925), 272
Miyoshi, Akira (b. 1933), 36
Mlynarski, Emil (1870–1935), 148
Moberg, Ida Georgina (1859–1947), 64
Moczyński, Zygmunt (1871–1941), 61
Moeran, Ernest John (1894–1950), 86, 109, 148
Moeschinger, Albert Jean (b. 1897), 117
Mohr, Wilhelm (b. 1904), 228
Mojsisovics, Roderich von (1877–1953), 145, 148
Mole, Miff (1898–1961), 232, 237
Molique, Wilhelm Bernhard (1802–69), 38
Molnár, Antal (b. 1890), 130
Molter, Johann Melchoir (*c*1695–1765), 92
Mompou, Federico (1893–?), 211
Monn, Georg Mathias (1717–50), 65, 91
Monte, Filippo di (=Philippe de Mons) (1521–1603), 179
Monteux, Pierre (1875–1964), 255
Monteverdi, Claudio (1567–1643), 35, 70, 154, 158, 166, 179, 229
Montsalvatge, Xavier Bassols (b. 1912), 147
Moog, Robert (b. 1934), 277
Moore, Douglas Stuart (1893–1969), 142, 144, 148
Moore, Patrick (b. 1923), 78
Moorehead, John (?–1804), 60, 61
Moorman, Charlotte (20th C), 113
Moortel, Arie van de (20th C), 131
Mopper, Irving (20th C), 146
Moran, Robert (b. 1937), 96, 208
More, Margaret Elizabeth (b. 1903), 64
Morgan, David Sydney (20th C), 148
Morgan, Justin (1747–98), 78
Morin, Jean-Baptiste (1677–1745), 141
Morley, Thomas (1557–1603), 138, 140, 179
Moross, Jerome (b. 1913), 131
Morris, Harold (b. 1890), 150
Morrison, Julia (20th C), 119
Mortellari, Michele (*c*1750–1807), 166
Mortimer, Philip (=Knight, J P) (1812–87), 72
Morton, 'Jelly-Roll' (1885–1941), 246
Moten, Bennie (1894–1934), 235, 241
Moulton, Lillie (19th C), 265
Mouret, Jean-Joseph (1682–1748), 108
Mouton, Charles (1626–1720+), 58
Moyses, Alexander (b. 1906), 114, 128
Mozart, Franz Xaver (1791–1844), 69
Mozart, Johann Georg Leopold (1719–87), 15, 41, 42, 69, 93, 116, 138, 139, 229, 261, 264
Mozart, Wolfgang Amadeus (1756–91), 14, 15, 30, 32, 39, 61, 65, 67–69 *passim*, 76, 77, 80, 83–87 *passim*, 93, 95, 96, 107, 109–114 *passim*, 137, 140, 158, 163, 165, 166, 168, 169, 171, 172, 174, 175, 187, 202, 227–230 *passim*, 243, 254, 264, 272
Müller, Wenzel (1767–1835), 157
Muller von Asow, Erich H (b. 1892), 229
Munch, Charles (1898–1968), 199
Muradeli, Vano (1908–70), 150
Murray, Don (20th C), 232
Murray-Schafer, R (20th C), 273
Musard, Philippe (1793–1859), 206
Musgrave, Thea (b. 1928), 64, 139, 144, 149
Mussorgsky, Modest Petrovich (1839–81), 64, 65, 78, 85, 138–141 *passim*, 144, 164
Mustel, August (19th C), 36
Müthel, Johann Gottfried (1728–88), 109
Mysliveček, Josef (1737–81), 70, 73, 78, 166

Napoleon III (1808–73), 47
Napoleon, Phil (b. 1900), 236
Nathan, Isaac (1792–1864), 62
Naumann, Johann Gottlieb (1741–1801), 166
Nazareth, Ernesto (1863–1934), 60
Nebuchadnezzar (King of Babylon) (5th C BC), 199
Nedbal, Oscar (1874–1930), 61
Nelson, Oliver (b. 1932), 36
Nepomuceno, Alberto (1864–1920), 145
Neruda, Josef (1804–76), 61
Nettl, Paul (1889–?), 213
Neumann, Věroslav (b. 1931), 150
Newman, Ernest (1868–1959), 110
Newton, Ramon (20th C), 247
Nichelmann, Christoph (1717–62), 66
Nichols, 'Red' (1905–65), 232, 237, 241
Nicolai, Karl Otto (1810–49), 198
Niedermeyer, Abraham Louis (1802–61), 61, 169
Nielsen, Carl August (1865–1931), 32, 34, 39, 90, 109, 111, 119, 120, 123, 128, 131, 138, 213, 256
Niemecz, (Father) Primitivus (18th C), 264
Nietzsche, Friedrich (1844–1900), 174
Nijinsky, Vaslav (1890–1950), 256
Nikitsch, Arthur (1855–1922), 267
Nikolov, Lazar Kostov (b. 1922), 125, 134
Nikolovski, Vlastimir (20th C), 42
Nipper (?–1895), 266
Nixon, David (1923–77), 273
Noble, Jeremy (b. 1930), 272
Noble, Ray (1903–77), 234, 248
Noble, Thomas Tertius (1867–1953), 141
Noda, Teruyuki (b. 1940), 125
Noel, George (18th C), 44
Nome, Siri (20th C), 113
Nono, Luigi (b. 1924), 149, 164, 256
Nordheim, Arne (b. 1931), 143
Nordoff, Paul (1909–77), 148
Nørgård, Per (b. 1932), 96
North, Alex (b. 1910), 142
Novák, Vitěslav (1870–1949), 148
Novello, Ivor (1893–1951), 72, 252
Novotný, Jaroslav (1886–1918), 61
Nunez, Alcide (1884–1934), 246
Nyman, Michael (20th C), 40
Nystroem, Gösta (1890–1966), 131, 147

Obousser, Robert (1900–57), 61
Obrecht, Jacob (1453–1505), 179
Oehlenschläger, Adam Gottlob (1779–1850), 107
Offenbach, Jacques (1819–80), 52, 72, 140, 157, 165, 166, 229
Ogny, (Le Comte de) (1757–90), 227, 230
Oliver, Joe 'King' (1885–1938), 234, 238, 242f
Oliver, Stephen (20th C), 171
Oliveros, Pauline (b. 1932), 64
Olsen, George (1893–1971), 247, 248
Onslow, André Georges Louis (1784–1853), 147
Operti, Giuseppe (19th C), 156
Orefice, Giacomo (1865–1922), 169
Orff, Carl (b. 1895), 49, 147, 174
Original Dixieland Jazz Band, 231, 232*, 237, 244, 246, 267
Ormandy, Eugene (b. 1899), 246
Orowan, Thomas F (20th C), 146
Orr, Robin (b. 1909), 140
Os, Albert van (12th C), 37
Oscar I (King of Portugal) (1799–1859), 55
Osmonds, The, 244, 252
Otger, ? (9th–10th C), 179
Otlet, Robert (20th C), 67
Ovid (43 BC–18 AD), 166

Paccagnini, Angelo (b. 1930), 96
Pachelbel, Johann (1653–1706), 111
Pade, Else Marie (b. 1924), 64
Paderewski, Ignacy Jan (1860–1941), 80, 146, 149, 262, 263
Padlewski, Roman (1915–44), 61
Paer, Ferdinando (1771–1839), 167
Paganini, Nicolo (1782–1840), 30, 34, 38, 75*, 76, 110, 112, 126, 128, 137, 144, 146, 148, 150, 169, 185, 187
Paine, John Knowles (1839–1906), 148
Paisiello, Giovanni (1740–1816), 93, 137, 157, 165
Palau Boix, Manuel (b. 1893), 124, 146
Palestrina, Giovanni Pierluigi da (*c*1525–97), 70, 72, 169, 174, 179
Pallavicini, Carlo (*c*1630–88), 165
Palmgren, Selim (1878–1951), 148
Pan, Ellis (19th C), 262
Panufnik, Andrezej (b. 1914), 130
Paradies (Paradisi), Maria Theresia (1759–1824), 60
Parchman, Gen Louis (20th C), 148
Parera, Blas (19th C), 186
Parker, Horatio (1863–1919), 175
Parratt, Walter (1841–1924), 57
Parris, Robert (b. 1924), 139, 147
Parrott, Horace Ian (b. 1916), 32, 142, 147, 150
Parry, John (?–1782), 60, 137
Parsons, Robert (?–1570), 62
Parsons, William (1746–1817), 57
Partch, Harry (1901–74), 42, 213
Parton, Dolly (b. 1946), 250
Pasquini, Bernardo (1637–1710), 66, 139
Passerini, ? (18th C), 176
Paul, Jean (20th C), 133
Paul, Lynsey de (b. 1951), 252
Paulson, Gustav (b. 1898), 149
Paumgartner, Bernhard (1887–1968), 169
Payne, Jack (1899–1969), 234, 248
Payne, Malcolm (20th C), 139
Paynter, J (20th C), 147
Pearsall, Robert Lucas (1795–1856), 141
Pedrini, Theodoric (1670–1745), 72
Pedro IV (King of Portugal) (?–1831), 55, 186
Pedrotti, Carlo (1817–92), 61
Pehkonen, Elis (b. 1947), 141
Pelham, ? (18th C), 201
Penberthy, James (20th C), 117, 147
Penderecki, Krzystof (b. 1933), 176
Pepin, Clermont (b. 1926), 123
Perger, Lothar Herbert (19th C), 228
Pergolesi, Giovanni Battista (1710–36), 155, 169, 175
Peri, Jacobo (1561–1633), 66, 154, 166, 173
Perkins, Horace James (20th C), 139
Perosi, Lorenzo (1872–1956), 146
Pérotin-le-Grand (*c*1160–*c*1220), 54
Persichetti, Vincent (b. 1915), 128
Persius, Louis Lue Loiseau de (1769–1819), 166
Pert, Morris (b. 1947), 115
Perti, Giacomo Antonio (1661–1756), 58, 66
Pesaro, Domenico da (16th C), 20, 44
Peter, Paul and Mary, 251
Petersen-Berger, Olof Wilhelm (1867–1942), 146
Petri, Christoph (18th C), 166
Petrides, Petro John (b. 1892), 145
Petrovics, Emil (b. 1930), 148
Petrucci, Ottaviano dei (1466–1539), 22, 211
Pez, Johann Christoph (1664–1716), 127
Pfitzner, Hans Erich (1869–1949), 35, 114, 164, 169
Philidor, Anne Danican (1681–1728), 201
Philip IV (King of Spain) (1605–65), 154
Philippot, Michel Paul (b. 1925), 275
Philips, Peter (*c*1565–*c*1635), 264
Phumiphon Adunet (King of Thailand) (b. 1927), 54, 55
Piani, Giovanni Antonio (*c*1690–1760+), 226
Piave, Francesco Maria (1810–76), 165
Piccinni, Nicolò (1728–1800), 157, 165, 166
Pícha, František (1893–1964), 149
Pierce, J R (20th C), 276
Pietrowsky, Karol (18th C), 226
Pike, Ernest (=Courtland, E) (20th C), 267
Pilkington, Francis (*c*1562–1638), 67
Pincherle, Marc (1888–1974), 106
Pinero, Arthur Wing (1855–1934), 162
Pinto, George Frederick (1786–1806), 72
Pinto, Tommaso (1714–83), 72
Piquet, Isaac (19th C), 261
Pirasti, ? (18th C), 166
Piron, Armand J (1888–1943), 246
Piston, Walter (1894–1976), 150
Pius IX (Pope) (1792–1878), 187*
Pius X (Pope) (1835–1914), 174
Pizzetti, Ildebrando (1880–1968), 148, 164
Placuzzi, Gioseffo (18th C), 91
Planché, James Robinson (1796–1880), 165
Plato (428/7–348/7 BC), 260
Plavec, Josef (b. 1905), 152
Pleyel, Ignaz Joseph (1757–1831), 95, 109, 110
Pockrich, Richard (*c*1690–1759), 25
Podešva, Jaromír (b. 1927), 96
Pokorný, Franz Xaver Thomas (1728–94), 74
Polin, Claire (b. 1926), 146
Poliziano, Angelo (1454–94), 154
Pollack, Ben (1903–71), 234, 243
Polovinkin, Leonid (1894–1949), 146, 150
Ponce, Manuel (1882–1948), 112
Poniridy, George (b. 1892), 118, 149
Ponte, Lorenzo da (1749–1838), 165
Poot, Marcel (b. 1901), 67
Popora, Nicolò Antonio (1685/6–1766/8), 65, 68
Pospíšil, Juraj (b. 1931), 147
Potter, Philip Cipriani Hambly (1792–1871), 137
Pougin, Arthur (1834–1921), 229
Poulenc, Francis (1899–1963), 37, 66, 116, 142, 143
Poulsen, Valdemar (19th C), 266
Pound, Ezra (1884–1972), 62
Pourtalès (Comtesse de) (19th–20th C), 256
Pousseur, Henri (b. 1929), 256
Powell, Dick (1904–63), 247
Powell, Felix (1878–1942), 61
Pratella, F Balilla (1880–1955), 274
Preradović, Paula (20th C), 188
Presley, Elvis Aaron (1935–77), 223*, 250, 252f
Previn, André George (b. 1930), 149, 246
Preyer, Gottfried (1807–1901), 58
Priestman, Brian (b. 1927), 228
Prieto, Maria Teresa (b. *c*1915), 64
Prokofiev, Sergei (1891–1953), 117, 120, 128, 137, 139, 143, 164, 206, 213, 256
Puccini, Giacomo (1858–1924), 137, 140, 158, 165, 219, 254
Pugnani, Giulio Gaetano (1731–98), 80, 229
Purcell, Henry (1659–95), 30, 61, 121, 138, 155, 177, 185, 229
Purkis, John (1781–1849), 60
Purvis, Jack (?–1962), 234
Pylkkänen, Tauno Kullervo (b. 1918), 139

Quantz, Johann Joachim (1697–1773), 62, 83, 85, 107, 213, 265
Quare, Daniel (17th C), 261

Quesnel, Joseph (1749–1809), 156
Quinault, Philippe (1635–88), 169

Rabaud, Henri (1873–1949), 145, 158, 164
Raff, Joachim (1822–82), 114, 124, 148
Raimondi, Pietro (1786–1853), 110, 150, 171, 176
Rajchman, Alexander (19th–20th C), 199
Rakhmaninoff, Sergei (1873–1943), 84, 95, 111, 158, 254f
Rameau, Jean-Philippe (1683–1764), 35, 58
Rapp, Barney (20th C), 245
Rasmussen, Mary (20th C), 105
Ravel, Maurice (1875–1937), 137, 139, 141, 142, 244, 254, 274
Ravenscroft, Thomas (*c*1590–*c*1633), 138, 139, 142, 181
Rawlings, Alfred William (1860–1924), 73f
Rawlings, Charles Arthur (1857–1919), 73f
Rawlings, Edward Ernest (1871–1919), 74
Rawlings, Emily (1851–1940), 74
Rawlings, Walter Thomas (1865–88), 74
Razumovsky (Count) Andrey Kyrillovich (1752–?), 129
Rebikov, Vladimir (1866–1920), 149
Rechberger, Herman (b. 1947), 40
Reda, Siegfried (1916–68), 37
Redman, Don (1900–64), 235
Reed, Carol (b. 1906), 20
Rees, Catherine Felice van (19th C), 64, 187
Reeve, William (1757–1815), 167
Reeves, Jim (1920?–64), 249
Reger, Max (1873–1916), 111
Regondi, Giulio (1822–72), 38
Reich, Steve (b. 1936), 277
Reicha, Antonín (1770–1836), 93, 126, 208, 257
Reichardt, Johann Friedrich (1752–1814), 125, 129, 182, 202
Reichardt, Juliane (1752–83), 68
Reilly, Tommy (b. 1919), 46
Rein(c)ken, Johann Adam (1623–1722), 58
Reinöhl, Karl (20th C), 229
Reisman, Leo (1897–1961), 232, 247, 248
Reisserová, Julie (1888–1938), 64
Rennes, Catharina van (1858–1940), 64
Reser, Harry (*c*1896–1966), 237
Respighi, Ottorino (1879–1936), 70, 77, 118, 138, 268
Reventál, Neidhart von (?–1240), 173
Revueltas, Silvestre (1899–1940), 125, 139
Rezniček, Emil Nikolaus von (1860–1945), 164
Rheinberger, Joseph G (1839–1901), 113
Riadis, Emil (1890–1935), 72
Rice, Edward E (19th C), 156
Rice, Tim (b. 1944), 240*, 241, 253
Richard, Cliff (b. 1940), 250, 252
Richard I, Cœur de Lion (King of England) (1151–99), 54*
Richter, František Xaver (1709–89), 65, 202
Ridout, Alan (b. 1934), 95
Riegel, Henri-Joseph (1741–99), 37
Rieger, Gottfried (1764–1855), 56
Riegger, Wallingford (1885–1961), 71
Rieti, Vittorio (b. 1898), 166
Righini, Vincenzo (1756–1812), 166
Rignold, Hugo Henry (1905–76), 246
Riley, Terry Mitchell (b. 1935), 113, 257
Rimsky-Korsakov, Nikolai (1844–1908), 21, 61, 64f, 78, 83–87 *passim*, 92, 114, 138, 140, 149, 164, 168, 169, 199, 213, 255
Rinuccini, Ottavio (1562–1621), 66, 154
Riotte, Philipp Jacob (1776–1856), 150
Rizo, Maro (20th C), 145, 146
Robinson, Carson (20th C), 235, 236
Robinson, Sugar Chile (b. 1942), 244
Rochat, Pierre (19th C), 261
Rockefeller, Laura Spelman (19th C), 50
Rodenwald, Carl Joseph (1735–1809), 66
Rodgers, Jimmie (1897–1933), 249
Rodgers, Richard (1901–80), 240f
Rodrigo, Joachin (b. 1902), 35, 60, 95, 121, 122, 128, 146, 148
Rodríguez, Esther (b. 1920), 64
Roger-Ducasse, Jean Jules Amabile (1873–1954), 166
Rogers, Bernard (1893–1968), 139, 144
Roldan, Amadeo (1900–39), 257
Rolla, Alessandro (1757–1841), 15
Rolle, Johann Heinrich (*c*1716–85), 66
Rolling Stones, The, 252
Rollini, Adrian (1904–56), 235, 246
Roman, Johan Helmich (1694–1758), 70, 229
Romani, Felicé (1788–1865), 165f
Ronald (-Russell), Landon (1873–1938), 268
Ronell, Ann (20th C), 242
Ropartz, Joseph Guy (Marie) (1864–1955), 56
Rore, Cyprien van (1516–65), 179
Rorem, Ned (b. 1923), 142
Rosenigrave, Thomas (1690–1766), 60
Rose Marie (b. 1925), 244
Rosenberg, Franz (18th C), 27
Rosenberg, Hilding Constantin (b. 1892), 131, 171
Rosenhain, Jacob (1813–94), 148
Rosetti, Franz Anton (1750–92), 96, 229
Roslavets, Nikolay Andreyevich (1881–1944), 149
Rosseter, Philip (*c*1575–1623), 67
Rossi, Luigi (1598–1653), 166, 213
Rossi-Ebreo, Salomone (*c*1570–*c*1630), 110
Rossini, Gioacchino Antonio (1792–1868), 15, 39, 43, 70, 75, 76f, 83–85 *passim*, 127, 137, 139, 166, 169*, 175, 204, 225
Rousseau, Jean-Jacques (1712–78), 78, 137, 165, 212
Roxburgh, Edwin (b. 1937), 96
Roy, Harry (1900–71), 248
Roy, Julien le (18th C), 261
Rubbra, Edmund (b. 1901), 168
Rubinstein, Anton (1829–94), 126, 136, 213, 254
Rubinstein, Nikolai (1835–81), 198
Rubio, Samuel (20th C), 229
Rudhyar, Dane (b. 1895), 72
Rudnev, Andrej (1878–1958), 76
Rudolf, Johannes Joseph Rainer (Archduke; Archbishop of Olmütz) (1788–1831), 55, 77, 114, 115, 142
Ruggles, Carl (1876–1971), 58
Russell, Bob (20th C), 232
Russell, John (19th C), 198
Russell, William (1777–1813), 167
Russell Brown, L (20th C), 270
Russolo, Arturo (20th C), 274
Russolo, Luigi (1885–1947), 274
Rutherlyn, Norman (b. 1931), 92
Rylek-Staňková, Blažena (b. 1888), 64
Ryom, Peter (20th C), 106, 229
Rytkönen, Antti (19th–20th C), 156

Sacchini, Antonio Maria Gasparo Gioacchino (1730–86), 166
Sachs, Curt (1881–1959), 13f, 25, 199
Sadat, Muhammad Anwar-as- (President) (b. 1918), 48
Sadie, Stanley John (b. 1930), 212
Saeverud, Harald Sigurd Johan (b. 1897), 146
Safranek, Miloš (20th C), 229
Sahl, Michael (20th C), 96
Saint George, Joseph Boulogne (Chevalier de) (1739–99), 80, 92
Saint Germain (Comte de) (?–?), 58, 71
Saint-Saëns, Camille Charles (1835–1921), 26, 36, 37, 76, 84, 111, 126, 138–146 *passim*, 158, 165
Salieri, Antonio (1750–1825), 61, 65, 69, 93, 165, 166, 169
Salomon, Johann Peter (1745–1815), 145, 202
Salvayre, Gaston Gervais Bernard (1847–1916), 130
Salviucci, Giovanni (1907–37), 146
Salzedo, Leonard (b. 1921), 96
Salzman, Eric (b. 1933), 139, 142
Sammartini, Giovanni Battista (1698/1701–75), 44, 69, 174
Sammartini, Giuseppe (*c*1693–*c*1750/1), 69
Sams, Eric (20th C), 214
Sanderson, James (1769–*c*1841), 167
San Martini—*see* Sammartini
San Martino—*see* Sammartini
Sarasate y Naascuez, Pablo Martín Melitón (1844–1908), 254
Sargent, (Sir) Harold Malcolm Watts (1895–1967), 206, 207*
Sarnecka, Jagwiga (1878–1913), 64
Sarti, Giuseppe (1729–1802), 95, 156, 175, 177
Sartori, Antonio (*c*1620–?), 155, 166
Satie, Erik Alfred Leslie (1866–1925), 113, 142*, 211, 213, 258
Sauguet, Henri (b. 1901), 141, 142
Sauter, Eddie (20th C), 237
Savitt, Jan (1913–48), 247
Sax, Adolphe Antoine Joseph (1814–94), 30
Sbarbaro, Tony (1897–1969), 237
Scandellus, Antonius (1517–80), 175
Scarlatti, Domenico (1687–1757), 21, 60, 85, 93, 111, 112, 116, 117, 128, 177, 229
Scarlatti, Giuseppe (1718/23–77), 93
Scarlatti, Pietro Alessandro Gasparo (*c*1660–1725), 26, 94, 112, 157, 177*
Schaale, Christian Friedrich (1713–1800), 66
Schaefer, Theodor (1904–69), 152
Schaefer-Schmuck, Käthe (b. 1908), 229
Schaeffer, C A F (20th C), 180
Schaeffer, Pierre (b. 1910), 273–276 *passim*
Schaffrath, Christoph (1709–63), 66
Scharfenberg, William (1819–95), 198
Scheel, Fritz (19th–20th C), 198
Scheidt, Samuel (1587–1654), 178
Schelle, Johann (1648–1710), 137
Schibler, Armin (b. 1920), 134, 147
Schikaneder, Emanuel (1751–1812), 166
Schiller, Günther (b. 1925), 64
Schiller, Johann Christoph Friedrich von (1759–1805), 158
Schillinger, Joseph (1895–1943), 38
Schjelderup, Gerhard (1859–1933), 140
Schmid, Hans (20th C), 229
Schmidt, Franz (1874–1939), 165
Schmid(t)/Schmitt (various), 69
Schmidtbauer, Joseph Alois (1718–1809), 74, 123, 148
Schmieder, Wolfgang (b. 1912), 228
Schmiedt, Siegfried (18th C), 69
Schneider, Johannes Leicham (18th C), 31
Schnell, ? (18th C), 38
Schnittke, Alfred (b. 1934), 146
Schoberlechner, Franz (1797–1843), 77
Schobert, Johann (*c*1720–67), 62, 257
Schoeck, Othmar (1886–1957), 165
Schoemaker, Maurice (b. 1890), 67
Schoenberg, Arnold (1874–1951), 35, 61, 65, 108, 165, 174, 182f, 255
Scholes, Percy (1877–1958), 171
Schönherr, Max (b. 1903), 229
Schubert, Franz Peter (1797–1828), 65, 75–77 *passim*, 83–87 *passim*, 110–112 *passim*, 117, 121, 122, 124, 127, 129, 133, 134, 139, 140, 144, 169, 174, 226, 228, 229, 254, 268
Schuh, Willi (b. 1900), 213
Schulhoff, Erwin (1894–1942), 146
Schuman, William Howard (b. 1910), 114
Schumann, Clara Josephine (1819–96), 64
Schumann, Robert Alexander (1810–56), 38, 60, 64, 83–87 *passim*, 107, 110–112 *passim*, 120, 122, 130, 140, 144, 164, 182, 214, 255, 267
Schürmann, Georg Caspar (*c*1672–1751), 167
Schütz, Heinrich (1585–1672), 154, 175, 176, 178
Schwarzendorf, Johann Paul Aegidius (1741–1816), 68
Schwarzkopf, Elisabeth (b. 1915), 168*
Schweitzer, Anton (1735/7–87), 167
Scolari, Giuseppe (1720–*c*69), 165
Scott, Cyril (1879–1970), 56, 213
Scott, (Lady) John Douglas (*née* Spottiswoode, AA), (1810–1900), 64
Scott, Leon (19th C), 265
Scott, (Sir) Walter (1771–1832), 162
Scriabin, Alexander Nikolayevich (1872–1915), 83–87 *passim*, 111, 115, 118, 134, 144
Scribe, Augustin Eugène (1791–1861), 166
Scruggs, Earl (b. 1924), 249
Scudo, Pierre (1806–64), 60
Sculthorpe, Peter Joshua (b. 1929), 147
Sechter, Simon (1788–1867), 168
Secrest, Andy (1907–77), 232
Seeger, Charles (1887–1979), 57
Seeger, Michael (20th C), 57
Seeger, Peggy (20th C), 57
Seeger, Pete (b. 1929), 57, 64
Seiber, Matyás (1905–60), 38, 72, 245
Seiffert, Max (1878–1959), 229
Seigel, Louis (20th C), 47
Selvin, Ben (1898–1980), 244, 245, 248
Senilov, Vladimir Alexandreyevich (1875–1918), 139
Sentinella, Geoffrey (20th C), 277
Sepúlveda, Maria Luisa (b. 1898), 64
Serrao, Paolo (1830–1907), 169
Sessions, Roger (1896–1976), 213
Seter, Mordecai (20th C), 146
Settle, Elkanah (1648–1724), 155
Sex Pistols, The, 252
Seyfried, Ignaz Xavier Ritter von (1776–1841), 169
Shade, Will (20th C), 235
Shakespeare, William (1564–1616), 155, 162, 258, 270
Shankar, Ravi (b. 1920), 24*, 96
Shapiro, Helen (b. 1946), 244
Shaw, Artie (b. 1910), 232, 244, 248
Shaw, George Bernard (1856–1950), 137
Shaw, Sandie (b. 1947), 251, 253
Shchedrin, Rodion (b. 1932), 39
Shelton, Anne (b. 1925), 247
Shepherd, John (*c*1520–*c*63), 174
Sheridan, Tony (b. 1941), 251
Sherman, General (1820–91), 211
Shield, William (1748–1829), 57, 154, 167, 182
Shilkret, Nat (b. 1889), 248
Shipley, ? (20th C), 144
Shore, Dinah (b. 1917), 247
Shostakovich, Dmitri (1906–75), 39, 61, 83–88 *passim*, 109, 115–135 *passim*, 141, 164*, 174, 213, 256, 265
Shure, R Deane (20th C), 146
Shushakov, Yuri (b. 1925), 20
Sibelius, Jan Julius Christian (1865–1957), 56, 57*, 83–87 *passim*, 90, 95, 109, 124, 134, 137, 140, 229, 256
Sievers, Gerd (b. 1915), 227
Sifona, ? (20th C), 125
Siklós, Albert (1878–1942), 73, 93
Silva, Antonio José de (18th C), 155
Simpson, Thomas (*c*1578–*c*1623), 138, 140
Sinatra, Francis Albert (b. 1915), 223*, 247, 253
Siret, Nicolas (1663–1754), 56
Sissle, Noble (b. 1889), 243
Slade, The, 252
Slatford, Rodney (20th C), 33
Slavický, Klement (b. 1910), 152
Sleep, Wayne (20th C), 251*
Slevin, Dick (20th C), 237
Smareglia, Antonio (1854–1929), 60
Smart, Henry Thomas (1813–79), 60
Smegergill, William (17th C), 71
Smetana, Bedřich (1824–84), 60, 120, 150, 156, 187, 213
Smith, Bessie (1898–1937), 241
Smith, Clarence 'Pinetop' (1905–29), 241
Smith, John Christopher (1712–95), 59, 143
Smith, John Stafford (1750–1836), 69
Smith, Joseph C (1896–1937), 248, 267
Smith, Russell (b. 1927), 142
Smith, Theodor (18th C), 69
Smith, Tommy (?–1931), 234
Smythe, (Dame) Ethel Mary (1858–1944), 64, 165, 213
Snow, Hank (b. 1914), 249
Snow, Valaida (1900–56), 242
Soft Machine, The, 253
Sokolov, Nikolai (1859–1922), 199
Sokolovsky, ? (18th C), 156
Soler, Antonio (1729–83), 68, 229
Solié, Jean-Pierre (1755–1812), 186
Solomon (King), (*c*937 BC–?), 48
Solomós, Dionysios (1798–1857), 186
Somfai, László (b. 1934), 96f, 228
Somis, Giovanni Battista (1686–1763), 117
Sommer, Hans (1837–1922), 73
Sommer, ? (19th C), 35
Sondheim, Stephen (20th C), 172
Sor, Ferdinando (1778–1839), 112
Šourek, Otakar (1886–1960), 228
Sousa, John Philip (1854–1932), 49, 170, 213
Spanier, 'Muggsy' (1906–67), 232
Specht, Paul (20th C), 272
Spencer, James H (20th C), 146
Spengel, Heinrich L (Ritter von), (*c*1775–1865), 56

Spielmann, E (20th C), 263
Spinaccino, Francesco (15th–16th C), 22
Spinetti, Giovanno (15th C?), 25
Spivakovsky, Michael (20th C), 46
Spohr, Louis (1784–1859), 109, 117, 121–123 *passim*, 131, 144, 165, 175, 202, 213
Stadler, Alfred (1889–1943), 61
Stadler, Jacob (17th C), 45
Staggins, Nicholas (?–1700), 57
Stainer, John (1840–1901), 176
Stamic, Jan Vačlav Antonín (1717–57), 27, 65, 128, 202, 225
Stamitz, Johann Anton Thaddäus (1753–1820), 65
Stamitz, Karl Philipp (1746–1801), 30, 65, 109
Stanford, Charles Villiers (1852–1924), 35, 146, 213
Stanislav, Josef (b. 1897), 150
Stanley, John (1713–86), 56, 57, 60, 80, 95
Starzer, Joseph (1726–87), 31
Stasov, Vladimir Vasilevich (1824–1906), 64
Stcherbatchev, Vladimir (1889–1952), 110
Steel, Christopher (b. 1939), 146
Steele, Blue (20th C), 237
Steele, Tommy (b. 1936), 250
Stephan, Rudi (1887–1915), 61
Stephens, John (*c*1727–80), 176
Sterndale Bennett, William (1816–75), 145
Stevenson, Benjamin Charles (19th C), 143, 162
Stevenson, Ronald (b. 1928), 147
Stewart, Barbara D (20th C), 47
Still, William Grant (1895–1978), 92
Stinson, Iain (20th C), 38
Stobart, Kathleen (20th C), 242
Stocker, ? (20th C), 46
Stockhausen, Karlheinz (b. 1928), 147, 256, 258, 274, 276
Stockly, Raymond (20th C), 148
Stoker, Richard (b. 1938), 137, 148
Stolz, Robert (1881–1975), 58
Stölzel, Gottfried Heinrich (1690–1749), 67
Stone, Christopher R (1882–1965), 268, 272
Stone, Lew (1897–1969), 234, 237, 248
Storace, Stephen (1763–96), 168
Stösslová, Kamila (20th C), 123
Stradella, Allessandro (*c*1642–82), 61, 91, 95, 169
Stradivarius, Antonio (*c*1644–1737), 10, 32, 44, 45, 49
Straesser, Ewald (20th C), 148
Straus/Strauss—various, 69f
Strauss, Johann I (1804–49), 69, 229
Strauss, Johann II (1825–99), 20, 69, 137, 141, 206, 208
Strauss, Josef (1827–70), 69, 140
Strauss, Richard Georg (1864–1949), 30, 35, 36, 39, 69, 94, 165, 213, 229, 256
Stravinsky, Igor (1882–1971), 39, 56, 109, 118, 122, 138–142 *passim*, 144, 158, 165, 174, 211, 213, 244, 255f, 258, 265, 274
Strong, George Templeton (1856–1948), 57
Strozzi, P (16th C), 66
Strungk, Nicolaus Adam (1640–1700), 34, 167
Stuart, Leslie (1866–1928), 73
Stucken, Frank van der (1858–1929), 198
Sturgis, Julian Russell (19th C), 162
Subotnik, Morton (b. 1933), 141, 147
Suda, Stanislav (1865–1931), 60
Suderburg, ? (20th C), 134
Suesse, Dana (20th C), 242
Sullivan, (Sir) Arthur Seymour (1842–1900), 35, 143, 160f
Sumarokov, Alexander Petrovich (1718–77), 156
Suolahti, Heikki Theodor (1920–36), 76
Suppé-Demelli, Franz von (1819–95), 73, 169
Susskind, Walter (1913–80), 109
Süssmayr, Franz Xaver (1766–1803), 175
Sutcliffe, Stuart (1939–61), 251f
Sutherland, Margaret (b. 1897), 64
Svendsen, Johan Severin (1840–1911), 108
Svento, Truvor (1910–39), 61
Sviridov, Georgi (b. 1915), 137
Sweelinck, Jan Pieterzoon (1562–1621), 111
Swert, Jules de (1843–91), 147
Sydeman, William (b. 1928), 33
Sykes, (Dr) Brian (20th C), 276
Sýkora, Václav Jan (b. 1918), 228
Sylva, 'Bud' de (20th C), 238
Synge, John Millington (1871–1909), 133
Szymanowski, Karol (1882–1937), 132

Tailleferre, Germaine (b. 1892), 64, 66
Tallis, Thomas (*c*1510–85), 207
Tamony, Peter (20th C), 231
Tanzberger, Ernst (20th C), 229
Tartini, Giuseppe (1692–1770), 95, 111, 118, 128, 144, 169, 229
Tasso, Torquato (1544–95), 166
Tate, Phyllis Margaret Duncan (b. 1911), 64
Tausch, Julius (1827–95), 35
Tavener, John (b. 1944), 64, 142, 143
Taverner, John (*c*1495–1545), 169, 174
Taylor, Jack(ie) (20th C), 247
Taylor, Jasper (1894–1964), 238
Tchaikovsky, Peter Il'ich (1840–93), 29, 35, 36, 38, 83, 85–87 *passim*, 95, 125, 128, 134, 137, 138, 140, 145, 165, 216, 229, 254f, 268, 269, 270
Tcherepnin, Alexander Nikolaevich (1899–1977), 168
Teagarden, Jack (1905–64), 232, 235
Telemann, Georg Philipp (1681–1767), 18, 31, 32, 75, 76, 94, 109, 110, 118, 129, 138, 165, 213, 228
Temple, Hope—*see* Davies, D
Templeton, Alec Andrew (1909–63), 60
Tenney, James C (b. 1934), 265
Teplov, Grigorii Nikolayevich (1719–89), 78
Terrell, Saunders—*see* Terry, S
Terry, Charles Sanford (1864–1936), 228
Terry, 'Sonny' (b. 1911), 235
Terry, Thelma (20th C), 242
Thalberg, Sigismund (1812–71), 77
Theremin, Leon (1896–*c*1938), 263
Therese (Princess) (1836–1914), 55
Thibault IV (King of Navarre) (1201–53), 55
Thierac, Jacques (20th C), 145
Thomas, Ambrose (1811–96), 165
Thomas, Dylan Marlais (1914–53), 123
Thomas, Hersal (1909–26), 241
Thomas, Theodor (1835–1905), 198
Thomson, Virgil Garnet (b. 1896), 213
Thompson, (Sir) Henry (19th C), 64
Thoreau, Henry David (1817–62), 117
Thrane, Valdemar (1790–1828), 156
Tilzer, Albert von (20th C), 238
Timm, Henry Christian (1811–92), 198
Tinctoris, Johannes (*c*1436–*c*1511), 211
Tippett, Michael Kemp (b. 1905), 140, 165, 175, 213
Toch, Ernst (1887–1964), 204
Toesca della Castellamonte—*see* Toeschi, K J
Toeschi, Karl Joseph (*c*1723/32–88), 65
Tolstoy, Leo Nikolayevich (1828–1910), 124
Tomášek, Václav Jaromir (1774–1850), 213
Tomasi, Henri (1901–71), 35, 107
Tomasini, Luigi Aloysius (1741–1808), 122
Toop, Richard (b. 1945), 113
Torelli, Giuseppe (1658–1709), 27, 31, 32, 35, 66, 90f, 95, 107, 127, 229
Torme, Mel (b. 1925), 244
Tornados, The, 251
Tortelier, Paul (b. 1914), 146
Tovey, (Sir) Donald Francis (1875–1940), 137
Tozzi, Antonio (18th C), 166
Tracy, Arthur (b. 1904), 247
Traetta, Tommaso Michele (1727–79), 166
Trautwein, Friedrich (1888–1957), 263, 276
Travis, Merle (b. 1917), 249
Tregian, Francis (*c*1574–1619), 62
Trepassi, P A D B—*see* Metastasio
Tritto, Giacomo (1733–1824), 56
Trone, Bill (20th C), 237
Trumbauer, Frank (1902–56), 244
Trutovsky, Vasilii Fiodorovich (*c*1740–*c*95), 21
Tubb, Ernest (b. 1944), 249
Tudor, David (b. 1926), 40
Tumason, Kolbeinn (1173–1208), 179
Turina, Josquin (1882–1949), 112, 146
Turski, Żbigniew (b. 1908), 126
Tuth-Ankh-Amon (14th C BC), 48
Tuukkanen, Kalervo (b. 1909), 141
Tveitt, Geirr (b. 1908), 42
Tye, Christopher (*c*1497–1572/3), 174
Tyson, Alan (20th C), 228
Tzarth, G - *see* Zart(h)

Uhl, Alfred (b. 1909), 121
Umberto (Crown Prince) (19th C), 48
Unverricht, Hubert (20th C), 228
Uttini, Francesco Antonio Baldassare (1723–95), 137
Utzon, Joern (20th C), 205

Vacek, Milos (b. 1928), 148
Vačkář, Dalibor (b. 1905), 148, 150
Valén, Olas Fartein (1887–1952), 132
Valentine, Henri Justin (1785–1865), 206
Vallée, Rudy (b. 1901), 247
Van Eps, Fred (Sr) (1870–1952), 244
Vaňhal, Jan Křtitel (1739–1813), 33, 150
Varèse, Edgard (1885–1965), 274
Vartan Marmikonian (Saint) (?–451), 93, 130
Vasilenko, Sergei Nikiforovich (1872–1956), 146, 147
Vaucanson, Jacques de (1709–*c*69), 265
Vaughan Williams, Ralph (1872–1958), 32, 35, 52, 56, 63, 64, 83–86 *passim*, 114, 128, 131, 136, 137, 139, 141, 150, 165, 174, 175, 214, 243, 256
Vautor, Thomas (17th C), 139
Vecchi, Orazio (1550–1605), 154, 179
Vechen, Carl van (20th C), 255
Vega, Lope de (1562–1635), 154
Venuti, Joe (1904–78), 236, 245, 246
Verdelot, Philippe (*c*1500–*c*67), 179
Verdi, Giuseppe (1813–1901), 35, 56, 136, 158, 165, 166, 175, 177, 187, 216, 267
Veress, Sándor (b. 1907), 146
Viadana, Lodovico—*see* Grossi, L
Vicentino, Nicola (*c*1511–72), 46
Victoria (Queen of England) (1819–1901), 47, 54, 57, 70, 78, 80, 203, 262
Victoria, Tomás Luis de (*c*1548–1611), 176
Vièrne, Louis Jules (1870–1937), 61, 111
Vièrne, René (1878–1918), 61
Vignerie, Bernard (1761–1819), 39, 150
Villa-Lobos, Heitor (1887–1959), 112, 208
Vinaccesi, Benedetto (1670–1719), 110
Vincent, Eddie (?–1927), 242
Vincent, Heinrich Joseph (1819–1901), 73
Vinci, Leonardo da (1452–1519), 38
Viotta, Henri (1848–1933), 198, 199
Viotti, Giovanni Battista (*c*1755–*c*1824), 95, 229
Viozzi, Giulio (b. 1912), 168
Virolleaud, Charles (1879–?), 180
Vishnegradsky, Ivan (1893–?), 257
Vivaldi, Antonio Lucio (1678–1741), 22, 26f, 31, 38, 44, 70, 75, 80, 83–87 *passim*, 91, 93, 95, 106f, 114–134 *passim*, 137, 166, 225, 227, 229
Vogel, Vladimir (1896–?), 176
Vogelweide, Walter von der (*c*1165–*c*1230), 173, 220*
Volkov, Solomon (b. 1944), 213
Vomáčka, Boleslav (1887–1965), 117
Voorhees, Don (20th C), 237
Voříšek, Jan Hugo (1791–1825), 112
Vorlová, Slávka (b. 1894), 64
Votey, E S (19th C), 262
Vraničky, Pavel (1756–1808), 65, 93, 136
Vuillaume, Jean-Baptiste (1798–1875), 47
Vycpálek, Ladislav (1882–1969), 123

Wagenseil, Georg Christoph (1715–77), 31, 65, 74, 92, 229
Wagner, Cosima (1837–1930), 103*
Wagner, Wilhelm Richard (1813–83), 35, 36, 38, 43, 74, 75*, 93, 103*, 108, 144, 158, 164, 169, 170, 171, 202, 206, 214, 229, 254, 258, 270
Walder, Herman 'Woodie' (20th C), 235
Waldstein, (Count) Ferdinand von (1762–1823), 134
Wallace, William (1860–1940), 94, 117
Wallace, William Vincent (1812–65), 158
Waller, Thomas 'Fats' (1904–43), 242, 244
Wallis, Shani (20th C), 273
Walpole, Horace (1717–97), 58
Walsh, Henry (18th C), 36
Walter, Bruno (1876–1962), 77, 144
Walther, Johann (1496–1570), 176
Walther, Johann Gottfried (1684–1748), 211
Walton, (Sir) William Turner (b. 1902), 36, 87, 95, 108, 137, 140, 141*, 175
Warlock, Peter (=Heseltine, P) (1894–1930), 61, 73, 139
Warren, Harry (20th C), 239
Wartensee, Franz Xaver Joseph Peter Schnyder von (1786–1868), 26
Watson, 'Doc' (b. 1923), 249
Watters, Lu (b. 1911), 234
Watts, Robert (20th C), 39
Wayditch von Verhovac, Gabriel (1888–1969), 73
Wayne, Mabel (20th C), 243
Webb, 'Chick' (1907–39), 247
Webb, Clifton (1891–1966), 247
Weber, Carl Maria Friedrich Ernst von (1786–1826), 39, 83–87 *passim*, 93, 94, 108, 112, 144, 174, 185, 229, 243
Webern, Anton (von) (1883–1945), 61, 66
Weelkes, Thomas (*c*1575–1623), 138, 139, 179
Weems, Ted (1901–58), 237, 247, 249
Weidinder, Anton (18th C), 105
Weigl, Joseph (1766–1846), 93, 139
Weill, Kurt (1900–50), 122, 137, 256
Weinberger, Jaromir (1896–1967), 144, 165
Weinert, Antoni (1751–1850), 58
Weingartner, Paul Felix von (1863–1942), 35, 214
Weinmann, Alexander (20th C), 227
Weinzeg, Johan (b. 1913), 146
Weir, Judith (b. 1954), 64
Weissberg, Julia Lazarevna (1878–1942), 64
Weisshans, Imre (b. 1905), 71
Weldon, Georgina (*née* Thomas) (1837–1914), 64
Wellesz, Egon (1885–1974), 64, 158, 167
Welte, Emil (19th C), 263
Wennerberg-Reuter, Sara Margareta (1875–?), 64
Werle, Lars Johan (b. 1926), 171
Werner, Gregor Joseph (1695–1766), 128
Wesley, Charles (1707–88), 180*
Wesley, Samuel (1766–1837), 60, 62
Wesström, Anders (*c*1720–81), 166
Wheatstone, (Sir) Charles (1802–75), 38
White, John (b. 1936), 32, 112, 265
Whiteley, John (20th C), 38
Whiteman, Paul (1890–1967), 232, 238, 244, 246, 247*, 249, 267
Whitfield, George (18th C), 185
Whitman, Walt(er) (1819–92), 131
Widor, Charles Marie Jean Albert (1845–1937), 36, 57, 60, 111, 121
Wiedoeft, Rudy (1894–1940), 267
Wieniawski, Adam Tadeusz (1879–1950), 165
Wigglesworth, Frank (b. 1918), 146
Wilbye, John (1574–1638), 140, 179
Wilde, Johann (18th C), 43
Wilhelmina Caroline (of Ansbach) (1683–1737), 54
Wilhelmina (Markgräfin von Bayreuth) (1709–58), 55
Willaert, Adriaan (*c*1480–1562), 173, 179
William III (1650–1702) and Mary (1662–94), 57
William IV (King of England) (1765–1837), 57
Williams, Alberto (1862–1952), 138, 139
Williams, Clarence (1893–1965), 236, 238, 244, 245
Williams, Grace (1906–77), 64
Williams, Mary Lou (b. 1910), 243
Williams, Richard (20th C), 258
Williamson, Malcolm (b. 1931), 57, 115
Willmers, Heinrich Rudolf (1821–78), 60
Willson, Meredith (20th C), 147
Wilson, Robert (20th C), 171
Wings, 253
Winkler, Karl (20th C), 148
Winter, Marius B (20th C), 272
Winter, Peter von (1754–1825), 92, 116, 150
Wise, Michael (*c*1648–87), 62
Witt, Jeremias Friedrich (1770–1837), 124
Witzthumb, Ignace (1720–1816), 58
Wolf, Aaron (1817–70), 71
Wolf, Hugo (1860–1903), 60, 182, 268
Wolf(f), Adolf Friedrich (?–1788), 68

Wolf(f), Maria Carolina (18th C), 68
Wolff, Albert Louis (1884–1970), 138
Wolff, Christian (b. 1934), 257
Wolzogen, Hans Paul (Freiherr von) (1848–1938), 103*
Wonder, Stevie (b. 1950), 244
Wood, Antony à (c1640–95), 62
Wood, (Sir) Henry Joseph (1869–1944), 72, 206
Wood, Hugh (b. 1932), 142
Woolley, (Sir) Charles Leonard (1880–1960), 181
Wordsworth, William (b. 1908), 148
Work, Henry Clay (1832–84), 211
Wotquenne, Alfred (1867–1939), 228
Woytowicz, Bolesław (b. 1899), 146
Wurman, Hans (20th C), 277
Wyatt, James (18th C), 217
Wybicki, J (19th C), 186
Wynette, Tammy (b. 1942), 249
Wynken de Worde (?–1534), 211
Wynne, David (b. 1900), 73

Xenakis, Iannis (b. 1922), 78, 210, 256, 258
Xyndas, Spyridon (1814–96), 60, 156

Yarmovsky, Mathis (19th C), 48
Yeoman-Clark, Richard (20th C), 274
Yerkes, Harry (20th C), 245, 246
Yonge, Nicholas (?–1619), 179, 201
Young, LaMonte (b. 1935), 40, 257, 258
Young, William (?–1671), 111
Yriarte, Tomás (1750–91), 72

Zach, Jan (1699–1773?), 229
Zamoyski, (Count) (19th–20th C), 199
Zandonai, Riccardo (1883–1944), 140, 146
Zart(h), Jiří (1708–74), 65
Zavateri, Lorenzo Gaetano (18th C), 132
Zavertal, Ladislas Joseph Philip Paul (1849–1942), 58
Zelter, Karl Friedrich (1758–1832), 182
Zeno, Apostolo (1669–1750), 166
Ziegler, Benno (1884–1945), 228
Zimmerman, Franklin B (b. 1923), 229
Zimmermann, Bernd Alois (1918–70), 61, 126
Zmeskall, Nicolaus von Domanovecz (?–c1828), 119
Zoeller, Karl (Carli) (1840–89), 62
Zöllner, Heinrich (1854–1941), 144
Zschinsky-Troxler, Elsa Margherita von (20th C), 229
Zulehner, Charles (1770–1830), 80
Zumaya, Manuel (1680–1740), 155
Zumsteeg, Johann Rudolf (1760–1802), 182
Zweers, Bernard (1854–1924), 60

Index of instruments

(For ranges of modern instruments, see pp 28–29)

accordion, 38, 72
aeolian harp, 40, 260
Alphorn, 15
alto—*see* viola
anvil, 257
Apollonicon—*see* orchestrion
Archicembalo, 46
Archiorgano, 46
arpa—*see* harp
aulos, 15

bagpipes, 16, 40f, 41*, 199f
balalaika, 20, 146
bandonion, 96
banjo, 222*, 234, 249
barrel-organ, 260*, 261f
Baryton, 42
basset-horn, 15
basson—*see* bassoon
bassoon, 30, 42
— double, 30
Becken—*see* cymbals
bells, 35, 49f, 51*, 257, 265
— cow, 257
— oxen, 257
— tubular, 35, 50
'black pudding'—*see* serpent
Blockflöte—*see* recorder
bohaiu, 19
bongos, 19
bottle, 234
brake drum, 257
Bratsche—*see* viola
buccina, 18, 31
bugle, 11
bull-roarer, 11, 14
busine, 18

caisse claire—*see* drum, side
carillon, 50*
— mechanical, 264
castanets, 14, 35
celesta, 36
cello, 32f, 38, 45*, 107, 111
Cembalo—*see* harpsichord
Chinese blocks—*see* wood blocks
chromomelodeon, 42
cinelli—*see* cymbals
clarinet, 15, 27*, 107
— bass, 35
— basset, 15, 96
clarino—*see* trumpet
clave, 257
clavecin—*see* harpsichord
clavicembalo—*see* harpsichord
clavichord, 20, 25, 44
clavicylindre—*see* glass harmonica
clavicytherium—*see* spinet
comb-and-paper, 19, 221*, 235, 237
concertina, 38
conch-shell, 9*
condom, 258
contrabasso—*see* double bass
contrafagotto—*see* bassoon, double
contrebasse—*see* double bass
contrebasson—*see* bassoon, double
cor—*see* horn
cor-anglais, 15, 30, 42, 96
cornamusa—see *bagpipe*
cornemusa—*see* crumhorn
cornemuse—*see* bagpipe
cornet, 15f
cornett, 15f, 16*
— bass—*see* serpent
corno—*see* horn
corno inglese—*see* cor-anglais
cornu, 13*, 200
couched harp—*see* spinet
couesnophone, 235
crembalum, 96f
cromorne—*see* crumhorn
crot, crowd, crowth, cruit—*see* crwth
crumhorn, 16
crwth, 20, 32
cymbalom, 20f, 24
cymbals, 14, 34, 39, 257

dactylomonocordo, 42
didjeridoo, 16f, 17*
domra—*see* balalaika
double bass, 33, 38, 39, 44, 96
dragons' mouths, 257
drum, 18, 45
— bass, 35, 39
— frame, 19
— friction, 19
— hourglass, 19
— kettle, 34, 39, 96
— Niger, 257
— non-membrane, 7
— pit, 8
— side, 34
— slit, 19
— snare, 34
— steel, 14
dulcimer, 10, 20, 21, 37*
— Appalachian, 20
dulzian—*see* bassoon

electric instruments, 143
electronic instruments, 273f
Englisches Horn—*see* cor-anglais
English horn—*see* cor-anglais
euphon—*see* glass harmonica
euphonium, 35

Fagott—*see* bassoon
fagotto—*see* bassoon
fiddle, 20
— *see also* violin
fidel—*see* Fiedel
fidla, 42
fidula—*see* Fiedel
Fiedel, 20, 21
flageolet, 18
flauto—*see* flute
flauto a becco—*see* recorder
flauto d'eco—*see* recorder
Flöte—*see* flute
flowerpot, 257
Flügelhorn, 35
flute, 8, 12, 15, 26f, 96, 111
— alto, 35
— beak, 18
— reindeer bone, 8*
flûte-à-bec—*see* recorder
flûte douce—*see* recorder
fortepiano, 21, 25

gamba, bass, 110
— descant, 110
Geige—*see* violin
gigja, 42
glass harmonica, 25f
glass, pane of, 258
glass xylophone, 235
glasses, 25*, 235
Glockenspiel, 36, 40, 50
gongs, 14, 26, 36, 257
— button, 257
goofus, 235
gran casa—*see* drum, bass
gravicembalo—*see* harpsichord
grosse caisse—*see* drum, bass
grosse Trommel—*see* drum, bass
guimbarde, 96
guitar, 20, 22, 35, 45*, 112, 249
gusla, 21
gusli, 21

Hackbrett—*see* dulcimer
Hammerklavier, 112
Handäoline, 38
Hardanger fiddle, 42
Harfe—*see* harp
harmonica, 46, 235
harmonium, 38, 44
harp, 7*, 20, 24, 34, 96, 97*, 98*
harpsichord, 21, 24, 25, 37, 46*, 96, 99*, 111
hautbois—*see* oboe
Heckelphone, 35
Hifthorn—*see* oliphant
hisser, 204*
horn, 10, 15, 31, 39, 46
— animal, 8
— bass, 15
— cow, 8
— hunting, 8, 46*, 96
— post, 8, 35, 96
horseshoes, 14
hot fountain pen, 235
huchet—*see* oliphant
hurdy-gurdy, 41, 42, 43*
hydraulis, 37
hydrodaktulopsychicharmonica, 44

ilpirra—*see* didjeridoo
intonarumori, 274

Jews harp, 105*, 236
jug, 236*

kaffir piano—*see* sansa
karnyx, 17
kazoo, 19, 47, 236f
kettle, 265
Kielflügel—*see* harpsichord
kithara, 7*
Klarinette—*see* clarinet
kleine Flöte—*see* piccolo
kleine Trommel—*see* drum, side
Kontrabass—*see* double bass
Kontrafagott—*see* bassoon, double
Kornett—*see* cornett
Krummhorn—*see* crumhorn

likembe—*see* sansa
lira—*see* lyra
lituus, 13*, 17
lur, 17
lute, 10, 20, 21f, 111
— varieties, 22f
lyra, 7*, 20, 24, 102*
lyra da braccio, 32
lyra-organizzata, 42
lyre, 22, 24, 32, 181, 199f

mandolin, 35, 107
mandora—*see* lute
marimba, 36, 125, 257
— *see also* sansa
mašroquītâ, 200
Maultrommel, 96f
mbira—*see* sansa
mechanical instruments, 224*, 261f
Mellophone, 237
mirliton, 19
monochord—*see* tromba marina
mouth organ—*see* harmonica
musical boxes, 14
— *see also* mechanical instruments
musette, 119
— *see also* bagpipe

nail violin, 42
New String Family, 33*, 34
Nonengeige—*see* tromba marina

oboe, 15, 27*, 96
— tenor, 30
oboe d'amore, 96
ocarina, 47, 237
octobass, 47
office machines, 258
oliphant, 43
Ondes Martenot, 38
ophicleide, 15, 32, 43
Orchestrion, 44, 263*
organ, 18, 36f, 51f, 96, 102*, 111
— bellows, 98*
— church, 51
— cinema, 51
— Hammond, 264
— mechanical, 264
— paper-roll, 262
— stalacpipe, 13
— travelling, 52
— water, 51, 260
— Wurlitzer, 52
organistrum—*see* hurdy-gurdy
orgue expressif, 38
oscillator, 257
ottavino—*see* piccolo

panpipes, 17, 110
Pantaleon, 20, 44
paper-and-comb—*see* comb-and-paper
Pauken—*see* drum, kettle
penny-whistle, 107
pentachord, 96
petite flûte—*see* piccolo
pianoforte, 10, 20, 21, 24, 37f, 39, 47, 111
— mechanical, 263
— quarter-tone, 96
— Siena, 47*, 48, 149
— toy, 265
piatti—*see* cymbals
piccolo, 26
pifferi—*see* bagpipe
pipe, reed, 8, 10
— and tabor, 19
Piston (Kornett)—*see* cornet
pistone—*see* cornet
Polyphon, 263*
Posaune—*see* trombone
psalterion, 200

psaltery, 10, 21, 24
psantrîn, 200

qatros, 200
quarnā, 200
queenophone, 235

rattle, 8, 36
rebec—*see* violin
recorder, 15, 18, 26
reindeer bone flute, 8*
rice-bowl, 257
roulette wheel, 258
Russolofono, 274

sabka, 200
sackbut, 15
— *see also* trombone
salmoè, 27, 107
salterio tedesca—*see* dulcimer
sansa, 14
sarrusophone, 244
sassofono—*see* saxophone
saxophone, 15, 30, 96
schalmey—*see* salmoè
Schlangenrohr—*see* serpent
Schnabelflöte—*see* recorder
Schreierpfeife—*see* crumhorn
schryari—*see* crumhorn
scraper, 9
serpent, 16, 43*
serpentcleide—*see* ophicleide
shawm, 18
sistrum, 14
sitar, 24*, 96
Sousaphone, 96
spinet, 25
squeaky rubber toys, 258
stamping-stick, 8
stone star, 14
suitcase, 237
sūmponiah, 200
swanee (slide) whistle, 237f
sweet potato—*see* ocarina
symphonia, 200
— *see also* hurdy-gurdy
syrinx—*see* panpipes

tabor, 19
tambour, 19
— militaire—*see* drum, side
tambourine, 18, 19, 36
tamburo militare—*see* drum, side
tamtam—*see* gong
temple blocks, 36
theorbo, 107
— *see also* lute
thumb piano—*see* sansa
thundersheet, 257
tibia, 15
timbales—*see* drum, kettle
timpani—*see* drum, kettle
tin can, 257
toum—*see* sansa
tournebout—*see* crumhorn
Trautonium, 263
triangle, 34
trigon, 199f
tromba—*see* trumpet
tromba marina, 44, 107
tromba de laquais, 105
trombe de béarn, 105
trombone, 8, 15, 31f, 105
trombula, 96f
tromp, 105
Trompete—*see* trumpet
trompette—*see* trumpet
Trummscheidt—*see* tromba marina
trump, 105
trumpet, 8, 11, 15, 27, 30, 48*, 96
— conch-shell, 9*
— early, 18
— slide, 105
'Turkish' instruments, 263
tympanon—*see* dulcimer
tuba, 15, 32, 49
— bass, 43
— Wagner, 8, 35

ukulele, 35

Ventilkornett—*see* cornet
vibraphone (vibra-harp), 36
viel—*see* violin
viele, 119
vielle, 20
viol, 20, 21, 22, 32
— bass, 39
viola, 32
viola d'amor, 22, 42, 44
viola pomposa, 44
violin, 32, 38, 49*, 111
— family, 10, 20, 21, 33
— Chinese, 96
— electric, 96
— Stroh, 267
violon—*see* violin
violoncello—*see* cello
violone—*see* double bass
virginals, 25

washboard, 238*
whistle, 258
wind glass, 257
wind machine, 36
wood blocks, 36, 257

xylophone, 36*

yamstick, 14

zampogna, 9*
zeze—*see* sansa
Zink(e)—*see* cornett
zither, 20, 249
zmārâ, 200